ABNORMAL PSYCHOLOGY

ABNORMAL PSYCHOLOGY

Clinical Perspectives on Psychological Disorders

SEVENTH EDITION, DSM-5 UPDATE

SUSAN KRAUSS WHITBOURNE

University of Massachusetts Amherst

RICHARD P. HALGIN

University of Massachusetts Amherst

Mc
Graw
Hill
Education

ABNORMAL PSYCHOLOGY: CLINICAL PERSPECTIVES ON PSYCHOLOGICAL DISORDERS, DSM-5 UPDATE, SEVENTH EDITION

Published by McGraw-Hill Education, 2 Penn Plaza, New York, NY 10121. Copyright © 2014 by McGraw-Hill Education. All rights reserved. Printed in the United States of America. Previous editions © 2013, 2010, and 2007. No part of this publication may be reproduced or distributed in any form or by any means, or stored in a database or retrieval system, without the prior written consent of McGraw-Hill Education, including, but not limited to, in any network or other electronic storage or transmission, or broadcast for distance learning.

Some ancillaries, including electronic and print components, may not be available to customers outside the United States.

This book is printed on acid-free paper.

3 4 5 6 7 8 9 0 DOW/DOW 1 0 9 8 7 6 5 4

ISBN   978–1–259–13338–1
MHID   1–259–13338–9

Senior Vice President, Products & Markets: *Kurt L. Strand*
Vice President, General Manager, Products & Markets: *Michael Ryan*
Vice President, Content Production & Technology Services: *Kimberly Meriwether David*
Managing Director: *William Glass*
Director: *Krista Bettino*
Senior Director of Development: *Dawn Groundwater*
Senior Development Editor: *Judith Kromm*
Editorial Coordinator: *Chantelle Walker*
Senior Digital Development Editor: *Sarah Colwell*
Marketing Managers: *AJ Laferrera/Ann Helgerson*
Director, Content Production: *Terri Schiesl*
Content Project Manager (Print): *Peggy J. Selle*
Content Project Manager (Media): *Katie Klochan*
Senior Buyer: *Carol Bielski*
Design: *Srdjan Savanovic*
Cover Image: © *JGI/Jamie Grill/Blend Images/Corbis*
Lead Content Licensing Specialist: *Keri Johnson*
Compositor: *Aptara®, Inc.*
Typeface: *10/12 Times LT*
Printer: *R. R. Donnelley Willard*

All credits appearing on page or at the end of the book are considered to be an extension of the copyright page.

Library of Congress Cataloging-in-Publication Data

Cataloging-in-Publication Data has been requested from the Library of Congress.

The Internet addresses listed in the text were accurate at the time of publication. The inclusion of a website does not indicate an endorsement by the authors or McGraw-Hill Education, and McGraw-Hill Education does not guarantee the accuracy of the information presented at these sites.

www.mhhe.com

To our families, with love and appreciation

Susan Krauss Whitbourne and Richard Halgin are Professors of Psychology at the University of Massachusetts Amherst. Both teach large undergraduate classes in addition to teaching and supervising doctoral students in developmental and clinical psychology. Their clinical experience has covered both inpatient and outpatient settings. Professors Whitbourne and Halgin are Fellows of the American Psychological Association. They co-edited *A Case Book in Abnormal Psychology: From the Files of Experts* (Oxford University Press), containing case studies written by leading international authorities in the field of psychopathology.

Professor Whitbourne received her PhD from Columbia University and has dual specializations in life-span developmental psychology and clinical psychology. She taught at the State University of New York at Geneseo and the University of Rochester. At the University of Massachusetts, she received the University's Distinguished Teaching Award, the Outstanding Advising Award, and the College of Arts and Sciences Outstanding Teacher Award. In 2001, she received the Psi Chi Eastern Region Faculty Advisor Award and in 2002, the Florence Denmark Psi Chi National Advisor Award. In 2003, she received both the APA Division 20 and Gerontological Society of America Mentoring Awards. She served as the Departmental Honors Coordinator from 1990–2010 and currently is the Psi Chi Faculty Advisor and the Director of the Office of National Scholarship Advisement in the Commonwealth Honors College. The author of sixteen books and over 160 journal articles and book chapters, Professor Whitbourne is regarded as an expert on personality development in mid- and late life. She is on the APA Board of Educational Affairs, was on the Membership Board and Committee for the Structure and Function of Council, and chaired the Policy and Planning Board. She is APA Council Representative to Division 20 (Adult Development and Aging), having also served as Division 20 President. She is a Fellow of APA's Divisions 20, 1 (General Psychology), 2 (Teaching of Psychology), 12 (Clinical Psychology), and 35 (Society for the Psychology of Women). A Fellow of the Gerontological Society of America, she serves on the Executive Board of the Behavioral and Social Sciences Section. In 2007, she was the Psi Chi Eastern Region Vice President and in 2009 was the Program Chair of the 2009 National Leadership Conference. Professor Whitbourne served as an item writer for the Educational Testing Service, was a member of APA's High School Curriculum National Standards Advisory Panel, wrote the APA High School Curriculum Guidelines for Life-Span Developmental Psychology, and serves as an item writer for the Examination for Professional Practice of Psychology and as Chair of the Council of Professional Geropsychology Training Programs. Her 2010 book, "The Search for Fulfillment" was nominated for an APA William James Award. In 2011, she was recognized with a Presidential Citation from APA. In addition to her academic writing, she edits a blog on *Psychology Today* entitled "Fulfillment at Any Age."

Professor Halgin received his PhD from Fordham University and completed a fellowship in the Department of Psychiatry at New York Hospital-Cornell Medical Center prior to joining the faculty of the University of Massachusetts in 1977. He is a Board-Certified Clinical Psychologist with over four decades of clinical, supervisory, and consulting experience. At the University of Massachusetts, he received the Distinguished Teaching Award, the Alumni Association's Distinguished Faculty Award, and was nominated for the Carnegie Foundation's U.S. Professor of the Year Award. His teaching was recognized by the Danforth Foundation and the Society for the Teaching of Psychology. Professor Halgin is the author of sixty journal articles and book chapters in the fields of psychotherapy, clinical supervision, and professional issues in psychology. He is also the editor of *Taking Sides: Controversial Issues in Abnormal Psychology*, Sixth Edition (McGraw-Hill). Professor Halgin served as Chair of the Committee of Examiners for the Psychology Graduate Record Examination, as an Associate Member of the Ethics Committee of the American Psychological Association, and currently serves on the Massachusetts Board of Registration of Psychologists.

BRIEF CONTENTS

CONTENTS

CHAPTER **3**
Assessment 46

CHAPTER **4**
Theoretical Perspectives 70

CHAPTER **8**

Anxiety, Obsessive-Compulsive, and Trauma- and Stressor-Related Disorders 184

Case Report: Barbara Wilder 185

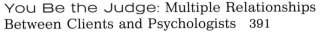

CHAPTER 15
Ethical and Legal Issues 378

Case Report:
Mark Chen 379

Reflecting the latest edition of the *Diagnostic and Statistical Manual (DSM-5)* and available as a print book and Smartbook (McGraw-Hill's adaptive reading experience), *Abnormal Psychology: Clinical Perspectives and Psychological Disorders,* provides a complete solution for your course.

McGraw-Hill Connect Abnormal Psychology

Abnormal Psychology is available to instructors and students in traditional print format as well as online within McGraw-Hill's Connect® **Abnormal Psychology,** an integrated assignment and assessment platform. Connect's online tools make managing assignments easier for instructors—and make learning and studying more motivating and efficient for students.

Experience Adaptive Reading with *SmartBook*

McGraw-Hill *SmartBook*™ is the first and only adaptive reading experience available for the higher education market. Powered by an intelligent diagnostic and adaptive engine, SmartBook facilitates and personalizes the reading process by identifying what content a student knows and doesn't know through adaptive assessments. As the student reads, SmartBook constantly adapts to ensure the student is focused on the content he or she needs the most to close any knowledge gaps.

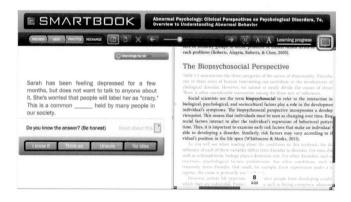

Experience a New Classroom Dynamic with *LearnSmart*

How many students *think* they know what they know but struggle on the first exam? McGraw-Hill's ***LearnSmart*™** adaptive learning system identifies students' metacognitive abilities and limitations, identifying what they know—and more importantly, what they don't know. Using Bloom's Taxonomy and a highly sophisticated "smart" algorithm, *LearnSmart* creates a customized study plan, unique to every student's demonstrated needs. With virtually no administrative overhead, instructors using *LearnSmart* are reporting an increase in student performance by one letter grade or more.

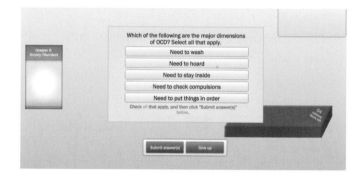

New *Faces: Interactive*

Faces: Interactive is an assignable and assessable learning environment that allows students to "interact" with real people living with psychological disorders. Through its unique interactive video program, *Faces* presents students with an opportunity to develop their critical thinking skills and gain a deeper understanding of psychological disorders. Twelve different disorders are presented, including ADHD, Borderline Personality Disorder, Schizophrenia, and Post-Traumatic Stress Disorder. *Faces: Interactive* is available exclusively through Connect.

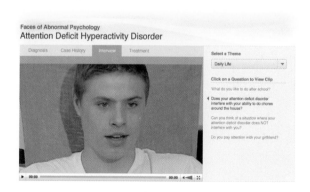

Real-Time Reports

These printable, exportable reports show how well each student (or section) is performing on each course segment. Instructors can use this feature to spot problem areas before they crop up on an exam.

Accessible Storytelling Approach and Empirically Supported Research

The seventh edition of *Abnormal Psychology* focuses on providing an accurate, understandable, concise, and up-to-date view of this rapidly evolving field. In particular, we have taken a thorough look at the literature and synthesized the information to provide the most relevant theories and research for you to study. We have added new features to give you an appreciation for the ethical issues that confront mental health professionals and the current controversies in the field around changes in the diagnostic system. **"You Be the Judge"** presents you with controversial ethical questions specific to the content of the chapter. **"What's New in the DSM-5"** feature summarizes the changes from *DSM-IV-TR* to *DSM-5*. We have also revised each chapter based on

principles of what is called "evidence-based treatment." These features will give you a contemporary view of the field as it is now and will also provide you with a solid basis for understanding how this ever-changing field continues to progress.

In writing the seventh edition, we have significantly sharpened the focus of each chapter to provide you with as vibrant a picture as possible of this remarkable field in psychology. If you've seen a previous edition, you will notice a distinct change that, while still focused on "talking to the student," does so in a way that reflects the learning style of today's students. We realize that students take many credit hours and that each course (particularly in psychology) seems to be getting increasingly demanding. Therefore, we want you to be able to grasp the material in the least amount of time, but with similar depth as students found in our previous editions.

You Be the Judge

Psychiatric Neurosurgery

As we discussed in Chapter 4, psychiatric neurosurgery is increasingly being used to give clinicians a tool for controlling the symptoms of obsessive-compulsive disorder. However, to what extent is surgical intervention justifiable to control the existence of psychological symptoms? Moreover, this surgery is not reversible. The debate over psychosurgery goes back to the mid-twentieth century when physician Walter Freeman traveled around the country performing approximately 18,000 leucotomies in which he severed the frontal lobes from the rest of the brain to control the unmanageable behaviors of psychiatric patients. The idea was that by severing the frontal lobes from the limbic system, the patients would no longer be controlled by their impulses.

As was true in the early twentieth century, when clinicians employed lobotomies to manage otherwise intractable symptoms of psychiatric patients, is it possible that future generations will look upon cingulotomies and similar interventions as excessively punitive and even barbaric? On the other hand, with symptoms that are so severe and disabling, is any method that can control them to be used even if imperfect?

Gillett (2011) raised these issues regarding the use of current psychosurgeries. By altering the individual's brain through such radical techniques, psychiatrists are tampering with a complex system of interactions that make up the individual's personality. Just because they "work," and because no other methods are currently available, does this justify making permanent changes to the individual's brain? The victims of the leucotomies performed by Freeman "improved" in that their behavior became more docile, but they were forever changed.

Q: *You be the judge:* Is it appropriate to transform the person using permanent methods whose basis for effectiveness cannot be scientifically established? As Gillett concludes, "burn, heat, poke, freeze, shock, cut, stimulate or otherwise shake (but not stir) the brain and you will affect the psyche" (p. 43).

What's New in the DSM-5

Schizophrenia Subtypes and Dimensional Ratings

The *DSM-5* authors implemented major changes in their approach to diagnosing schizophrenia. As we mentioned at the beginning of the chapter, they eliminated the subtypes of schizophrenia. Instead, using a scale that is in Section 3, clinicians assign a diagnosis of schizophrenia to which they can add a rating of the individual's symptoms along a set of dimensions, as Table 6.3 shows.

By eliminating the subtypes of schizophrenia, the *DSM-5* authors sought to improve both the diagnostic reliability and validity of the system. They also sought to have a more quantifiable basis for research on the disorder's causes as well as for treatment planning. For example, a clinician evaluating the results of cognitive-behavioral therapy could use the ratings of hallucination and delusion severity to determine whether the intervention is reducing the specific symptoms toward which they are targeting treatment.

The *DSM-5* authors also decided to include cognitive impairment as a dimension in the Section 3 severity ratings, given the importance of cognitive deficits in current understandings of the individual's ability to carry out social and occupational activities and to carry out the tasks involved in everyday living. In this regard, a neuropsychological assessment could inform the diagnostic process (Reichenberg, 2010).

The *DSM-5* authors considered, but decided not to, eliminate schizoaffective disorder as a separate entity.

Although not there yet, the *DSM-5* authors believe that clinicians will eventually diagnose schizophrenia as a "spectrum" disorder. This would mean, potentially, that even diagnoses long in use in psychiatry would disappear, including schizophreniform disorder, schizoaffective disorder, and the two personality disorders associated with schizophrenic-like symptoms.

The current system in the *DSM-5* represents a step in moving away from the old categorization system and toward the dimensional approach. By including severity ratings rather than subtypes in Section 3, they are making it possible for clinicians and researchers to track individuals over time in a quantifiable fashion.

How Will You Study "Abnormal" Human Behavior?

The field of abnormal psychology covers the full spectrum of human behavior throughout the life span. From infancy through later adulthood, the process of development propels us through a vast range of experiences. Some of these experiences, invariably, include encounters with distressing emotions, behaviors, inner experiences, and interactions with other people. There is no sharp dividing line between "normal" and "abnormal," as you will learn in this book, nor do people spend their entire lives in one or the other of these realms.

Abnormal psychology is particularly fascinating because it reflects so many possible variations in human behavior, particularly as these evolve over time in an individual's life. Learning about abnormal psychology can be a goal for you in and of itself, but you more than likely will find yourself drawn to its practical applications as a basis for learning how to help others. Whether or not you decide to enter a helping profession, however, you will find knowledge of this field useful in whatever profession you decide to pursue as well as your everyday life.

Clinical Perspectives on Psychological Disorders

The subtitle of this seventh edition, *Clinical Perspectives on Psychological Disorders*, reflects the emphasis in each of the prior editions on the experience of clients and clinicians in their efforts to facilitate each individual's maximum functioning. We present an actual case study at the beginning of each chapter that typifies the disorders in that chapter. At the end of the chapter, we return to the case study with the outcome of a prescribed treatment on the basis of the best available evidence. Throughout the chapter, we translate the symptoms of each disorder into terms that capture the core essence of the disorder. Our philosophy is that students should be able to appreciate the fundamental nature of each disorder without necessarily having to memorize diagnostic criteria. In that way, students can gain a basic understanding that will serve them well regardless of their ultimate professional goals.

The Biopsychosocial Approach

An understanding of psychological disorders requires an integrative approach, particularly as researchers begin to understand increasingly the connections among the multiple dimensions that influence people throughout life.

We are adopting the *biopsychosocial* approach—incorporating biological, psychological, and sociocultural contributions to psychological disorders. Neuroscience research is increasingly becoming relevant to the understanding of psychopathology, but at the same time, so are issues related to social context including diversity of social class, race, and ethnicity. These factors combine in complex ways, and throughout the book, we explain how they apply to particular psychological disorders.

The Life-Span Approach

Individuals grow and change throughout life, and we feel that it is essential to capture the developmental dimension in helping students understand the evolution of psychological disorders over time. Therefore, we have incorporated research and theories that provide relevant understandings of how the disorders that we cover emerge and modulate from childhood through adulthood. We also emphasize the interactive and reciprocal effects of "nature" (genetics) and "nurture" (the environment) as contributors to psychological disorders.

The Human Experience of Psychological Disorders

Above all, the study of abnormal psychology is the study of profoundly human experiences. To this end, we have developed a biographical feature entitled **"Real Stories."** You will read narratives from the actual experiences of celebrities, sports figures, politicians, authors, musicians and artists ranging from Beethoven to Herschel Walker. Each Real Story is written to provide insight into the particular disorder covered within the chapter. By reading these fascinating biographical pieces, you will come away with a more in-depth personal perspective to use in understanding the nature of the disorder.

The Scientist-Practitioner Framework

We have developed this text using a scientist-practitioner framework. In other words, you will read about research informed by clinical practice. We present research on theories and treatments for each of the disorders based on the principles of "evidence-based practice." This means that the approaches that we describe are tested through extensive research informed by clinical practice. Many researchers in the field of abnormal psychology also treat clients in their own private offices, hospitals, or group practices. As a result, they approach their work in the lab with the knowledge that their findings can ultimately provide real help to real people.

Chapter-by-Chapter Changes

The most significant change in this updated edition is the integration of the *DSM-5* in every chapter where it applies. Even the table of contents has been reorganized to reflect this important new edition of the *DSM*.

Another major change you will notice is in the order of authors. After many years of teaching, research, and writing, the new first author (Professor Whitbourne) is bringing her classroom style into the writing of this text. Professor Whitbourne also writes a popular *Psychology Today* blog called "Fulfillment at Any Age," and she has adapted the material in the previous editions to reflect the empirically informed but accessible reading style that has contributed to the success of this blog.

In addition, we added a research assistant to the team who brings a more youthful and contemporary perspective to particular features within the text. An advanced clinical psychology graduate student at American University at the time of this writing, Jennifer O'Brien wrote the "Real Stories" features and the case studies that begin and end each chapter. Changing any identifiable details, she brought her work into these cases from her practicums at a college counseling center, a Veterans Administration Hospital, a judicial court system, and a women's therapy clinic. In addition to her outstanding academic credentials, Jennifer happens to be Professor Whitbourne's younger daughter. She is a member of Psi Chi, APAGS (the APA Graduate Student association), and the recipient of an outstanding undergraduate teaching assistant award. Her dissertation research, on the therapeutic alliance, will provide new insights into understanding this fundamental component of effective psychotherapy. She currently works as a researcher at the Veterans Administration Medical Center in Jamaica Plain, Boston, MA.

We have added two particularly exciting features to the seventh edition found in most chapters:

- **"What's New in *DSM-5*"** This feature summarizes the changes from *DSM-IV-TR* to *DSM-5*. Not only does it highlight the new edition of the *DSM*, but it also demonstrates how the definition and categorization of psychological disorders changes over time.

- **"You Be the Judge"** The ethical issues that psychologists grapple with are an integral part of research and practice. In these boxed features, we highlight a specific aspect of one of the disorders that we discuss in the chapter and present a question for you to answer. You will be the judge in deciding which position you want to take, after we inform you of both sides of the issue at stake.

To make it easier for previous users of the text to see what's changed, a summary of the most important revisions to each chapter follows.

CHAPTER 1: Overview to Understanding Abnormal Behavior

- Reduced length of sections on history of abnormal psychology
- Clarified the biopsychosocial perspective section
- Added a section on Behavioral Genetics
- Expanded the discussion of the developmental perspective

CHAPTER 2: Diagnosis and Treatment

- Replaced the description of the *DSM-IV-TR* with a section on the *DSM-5*
- Added material on the *International Classification of Diseases (ICD)* system
- Provided greater focus on evidence-based practice

CHAPTER 3: Assessment

- Provided up-to-date information on the WAIS-IV and its use in assessment
- Greatly expanded the section on neuropsychological assessment, including computerized testing
- Updated and expanded treatment of brain imaging methods
- Retained projective testing but with less focus on detailed interpretation of projective test data

CHAPTER 4: Theoretical Perspectives

- Retained the classic psychodynamic theories, but with updates from current research
- Expanded greatly the discussion of biological theories, and moved these to the beginning of the chapter
- Provided more detail on the cognitive-behavioral perspective to use as a basis for subsequent chapters that rely heavily on treatment based on this perspective

CHAPTERS 5-14: Neurodevelopmental Disorders to Personality Disorders

- Where appropriate, incorporated information about how *DSM-5* changed conceptualization of these disorders, including changes in terminology

- Expanded the coverage of biological theories, including studies on genetics, epigenetics, and neuroimaging

- Completely updated treatment sections, giving emphasis to those approaches to treatment recommended through evidence-based practice.

- Included newer therapies including mindfulness/meditation, relaxation, and Acceptance and Commitment Therapy

- Revised tables and figures to provide more readily accessible pedagogy

CHAPTER 15: Ethical and Legal Issues

- Expanded the discussion of APA's Ethics Code, including a table that summarizes its most important features

- Updated the cases with newer information, including a section on Kendra's Law

- Revised the section on forensic psychology, including examples from relevant case law

Blackboard

Do More

Through McGraw-Hill's partnership with Blackboard, *Abnormal Psychology: Clinical Perspectives on Psychological Disorders* offers a seamless integration of content and tools:

- Seamless gradebook between Blackboard and Connect
- Single sign-on providing seamless integration between McGraw-Hill content and Blackboard
- Simplicity in assigning and engaging your students with course materials

 Craft your teaching resources to match the way you teach! With McGraw-Hill Create, **www.mcgrawhillcreate.com,** you can easily rearrange chapters, combine material from other content sources, and quickly upload content you have written, such as your course syllabus or teaching notes. Find the content you need in Create by searching through thousands of leading McGraw-Hill textbooks. Arrange your book to fit your teaching style. Create even allows you to personalize your book's appearance by selecting the cover and adding your name, school, and course information. Order a Create book and you'll receive a complimentary print review copy in 3–5 business days or a complimentary electronic review copy (eComp) via e-mail in about an hour. Go to **www.mcgrawhillcreate.com** today and register. Experience how McGraw-Hill Create empowers you to teach *your* students *your* way.

Tegrity Campus is a service that makes class time available all the time by automatically capturing every lecture in a searchable format for students to review when they study and complete assignments. With a simple one-click start and stop process, users capture all computer screens and corresponding audio. Students replay any part of any class with easy-to-use browser-based viewing on a PC or Mac. Educators know that the more students can see, hear, and experience class resources, the better they learn. With Tegrity Campus, students quickly recall key moments by using Tegrity Campus's unique search feature. This search helps students efficiently find what they need, when they need it, across an entire semester of class recordings. Help

turn all your students' study time into learning moments immediately supported by your lecture.

 CourseSmart e-Textbook This text is available as an eTextbook at **www.CourseSmart.com.** At CourseSmart your students can take advantage of significant savings off the cost of a print textbook, reduce their impact on the environment, and gain access to powerful Web tools for learning. CourseSmart eTextbooks can be viewed online or downloaded to a computer. The eTextbooks allow students to do full text searches, add highlighting and notes, and share notes with classmates. CourseSmart has the largest selection of eTextbooks available anywhere. Visit **www.CourseSmart.com** to learn more and to try a sample chapter.

Support Materials

The following ancillaries are available to accompany *Abnormal Psychology*, Seventh Edition. Please contact your McGraw-Hill sales representative for details concerning policies, prices, and availability, as some restrictions may apply.

For the Instructor

The password-protected instructor side of the Online Learning Center at www.mhhe.com/whitbourne7eupdate contains the Instructor's Manual, Test Bank files, PowerPoint Presentations, Image Gallery, and other valuable material to help you design and enhance your course. Ask your local McGraw-Hill representative for your password.

The **Instructor's Manual** provides many tools useful for teaching the seventh edition. For each chapter, the Instructor's Manual includes an overview of the chapter, teaching objectives, suggestions and resources for lecture topics, classroom activities, and essay questions designed to help students develop ideas for independent projects and papers.

The **Test Bank** contains over 2,000 testing items. All testing items are classified as conceptual or applied, and referenced to the appropriate learning objective. All test questions are compatible with EZTest, McGraw-Hill's Computerized Test Bank program, which runs on both Macintosh and Windows computers and includes an editing feature that enables instructors to import their own questions, scramble items, and modify questions to create their own tests.

The **PowerPoint Presentations** are the key points of each chapter and contain key illustrations, graphs, and tables for instructors to use during their lectures.

Acknowledgments

The following instructors were instrumental in the development of the text, offering their feedback and advice as reviewers:

David Alfano, *Community College of Rhode Island*

Bryan Cochran, *University of Montana*

Julie A. Deisinger, *Saint Xavier University*

Angela Fournier, *Bemidji State University*

Richard Helms, *Central Piedmont Community College*

Heather Jennings, *Mercer County Community College*

Joan Brandt Jensen, *Central Piedmont Community College*

Cynthia Kalodner, *Towson University*

Patricia Kemerer, *Ivy Tech Community College*

Barbara Kennedy, *Brevard Community College-Palm Bay*

Joseph Lowman, *University of North Carolina-Chapel Hill*

Don Lucas, *Northwest Vista College*

James A. Markusic, *Missouri State University*

Mark McKellop, *Juniata College*

Maura Mitrushina, *California State University-Northridge*

John Norland, *Blackhawk Technical College*

Karen Clay Rhines, *Northampton Community College*

Ty Schepis, *Texas State University*

William R. Scott, *Liberty University*

Dr. Wayne S. Stein, *Brevard Community College*

Marla Sturm, *Montgomery County Community College*

Terry S. Trepper, *Purdue University-Calumet*

Naomi Wagner, *San Jose State University*

Nevada Winrow, *Baltimore City Community College*

A great book can't come together without a great publishing team. We'd like to thank our editorial team, all of whom worked with us through various stages of the publishing process. Special gratitude goes to our editor, Krista Bettino, whose vision helped us present the material in a fresh and student-oriented manner. Barbara Heinssen, Development Manager, aided in development and redesign of this new edition. Anne Fuzellier, Managing Editor, and Chantelle Walker, Editorial Coordinator, assisted us through the complex publication process. Sarah Colwell, Digital Development Editor, and Neil Kahn, Digital Product Analyst, ensured that the material is translated into digital media, allowing greater access for students and instructors. Laura Byrnes, Marketing Coordinator, also deserves our special thanks.

A Letter from the Author

I am very glad that you are choosing to read my textbook. The topic of abnormal psychology has never been more fascinating or relevant. We constantly hear media reports of celebrities having meltdowns for which they receive quickie diagnoses that may or may not be accurate. Given all of this misinformation in the mind of the public, I feel that it's important for you to be educated in the science and practice of abnormal psychology. At the same time, psychological science grabs almost as many headlines in all forms of news media. It seems that everyone is eager to learn about the latest findings ranging from the neuroscience of behavior to the effectiveness of the newest treatment methods. These advances in brain-scanning methods and studies of psychotherapy effectiveness are greatly increasing our understanding of how to help people with psychological disorders.

Particularly fascinating are the *DSM-5* changes. Each revision of the *DSM* brings with it controversies and challenges and the *DSM-5* is no exception. Despite challenges to the new ways that the *DSM-5* defines and categorizes psychological disorders, it is perhaps based more than any earlier edition on a strong research base. Scientists and practitioners will continue to debate the best ways to interpret this research. We all will benefit from these dialogues.

The profession of clinical psychology is also undergoing rapid changes. With changes in health care policy, it is very likely that more and more professionals ranging from psychologists to mental health counselors will be employed in providing behavioral interventions. By taking this first step toward your education now, you will be preparing yourself for a career that is increasingly being recognized as vital to helping individuals of all ages and all walks of life to achieve their greatest fulfillment.

I hope you find this text as engaging to read as I found to write. Please feel free to e-mail me with your questions and reactions to the material. As a user of McGraw-Hill's Connect in my own introductory psychology class, I can also vouch for its effectiveness in helping you achieve mastery of the content of abnormal psychology. I am also available to answer any questions you have, from an instructor's point of view, about how best to incorporate this book's digital media into your own teaching.

Thank you again for choosing to read this book!

Best,
Susan Krauss Whitbourne, PhD
swhitbo@psych.umass.edu

Overview to Understanding Abnormal Behavior

OUTLINE

Learning Objectives

1.1 Distinguish between normal but unusual behavior and between unusual but abnormal behavior.

1.2 Understand how explanations of abnormal behavior have changed through time.

1.3 Articulate the strengths and weaknesses of research methods.

1.4 Describe types of research studies.

CHAPTER 1

Case Report: Rebecca Hasbrouck

Demographic information: 18-year-old Caucasian female.

Presenting problem: Rebecca self-referred to the university psychotherapy clinic. She is a college freshman, living away from home for the first time. After the first week of school, Rebecca reports that she is having trouble sleeping, is having difficulty concentrating in her classes, and often feels irritable. She is frustrated by the difficulties of her coursework and states she is worried that her grades are beginning to suffer. She also reports that she is having trouble making friends at school and that she has been feeling lonely because she has no close friends here with whom she can talk openly. Rebecca is very close to her boyfriend of three years, though they have both started attending college in different cities. She was tearful throughout our first session, stating that, for the first time in her life, she feels overwhelmed by feelings of hopelessness. She reports that although the first week at school felt like "torture," she is slowly growing accustomed to her new lifestyle, but she still struggles with missing her family and boyfriend, as well as her friends from high school.

Relevant past history: Rebecca has no family history of psychological disorders. She reported that sometimes her mother tends to get "really stressed out" though she has never received treatment for this.

Symptoms: Depressed mood, difficulty falling asleep (insomnia), difficulty concentrating on schoolwork. She reported no suicidal ideation.

Case formulation: Although it appeared at first as though Rebecca was suffering from a major depressive episode, she did not meet the diagnostic criteria. While the age of onset for depression tends to be around Rebecca's age, given her lack of a family history of depression and that her symptoms were occurring in response to a major stressor, the clinician determined that Rebecca was suffering from Adjustment Disorder with depressed mood.

Treatment plan: The counselor will refer Rebecca for psychotherapy. Therapy should focus on improving her mood, and also should allow her a space to discuss her feelings surrounding the major changes that have been occurring in her life.

Sarah Tobin, PhD
Clinician

Rebecca Hasbrouck's case report summarizes the pertinent features that a clinician would include when first seeing a client after an initial evaluation. Each chapter of this book begins with a case report for a client whose characteristics are related to the chapter's topic. A fictitious clinician, Dr. Sarah Tobin, who supervises a clinical setting that offers a variety of services, writes the case reports. In some instances, she provides the services, and in others, she supervises the work of another psychologist. For each case, she provides a diagnosis using the official manual adopted by the profession known as *The Diagnostic and Statistical Manual of Mental Disorders, Fifth Edition (DSM-5)* (American Psychiatric Association, 2013).

At the end of the chapter, after you have developed a better understanding of the client's disorder, we will return to Dr. Tobin's description of the treatment results and expected future outcomes for the client. We also include Dr. Tobin's personal reflections on the case so that you will gain insight into the clinician's experience in working with psychologically disordered individuals.

The field of abnormal psychology is filled with countless fascinating stories of people who suffer from psychological disorders. In this chapter, we will try to give you some sense of the reality that psychological disturbance is certain to touch everyone, to some extent, at some point in life. As you progress through this course, you will almost certainly develop a sense of the challenges people associate with psychological problems. You will find yourself drawn into the many ways that mental health problems affect the lives of individuals, their families, and society. In addition to becoming more personally exposed to the emotional aspects of abnormal psychology, you will learn about the scientific and theoretical basis for understanding and treating the people who suffer from psychological disorders.

This young woman's apparent despair may be the symptoms of a psychological disorder.

1.1 What Is Abnormal Behavior?

It's possible that you know someone very much like Rebecca, who is suffering from more than the average degree of adjustment difficulties in college. Would you consider that person psychologically disturbed? Would you consider giving this person a diagnosis? What if a person you knew was not only depressed, but also showed up on your floor seemingly ready to harm herself? At what point do you draw the line between someone who has a psychological disorder and someone who, like Rebecca, has an adjustment disorder? Is it even necessary to give Rebecca any diagnosis at all? Questions about normality and abnormality such as these are basic to our understanding of psychological disorders.

Conditions like Rebecca's are likely to affect you in a very personal way. Perhaps you have been unusually depressed, fearful, or anxious, or maybe the emotional distress has been a step removed from you: Your father struggles with alcoholism, your mother has been hospitalized for severe depression, a sister has an eating disorder, or your brother has an irrational fear. If you have not encountered a psychological disorder within your immediate family, you have very likely encountered one in your extended family and circle of friends. You may not have known the formal psychiatric diagnosis for the problem, and you may not have understood its nature or cause, but you knew that something was wrong and recognized the need for professional help.

Until they are forced to face such problems, most people believe that "bad things" happen only to other people. Other people have car accidents, succumb to cancer, or become severely depressed. We hope that reading this textbook will help you go beyond this "other people" syndrome. Psychological disorders are part of the human experience, touching the life—either directly or indirectly—of every person. As you read about these disorders and the people who suffer with them, you will find that most of these problems are treatable, and many are preventable.

1.2 The Social Impact of Psychological Disorders

Put yourself in the following situation. An urgent message awaits you from Jeremy's mother. Your best friend in high school, Jeremy has just been admitted to a psychiatric hospital and begs to see you, because only you can understand what he is going through. You are puzzled and distressed by this news. You had no idea that he had any psychological problems. What will you say to him? Can you ask him what's wrong? Can you ask him how he feels? Do you dare inquire about what his doctors have told him about his chances of getting better? What will it be like to see him in a psychiatric hospital? Do you think you could be friends with someone who has spent time in such a place?

Now imagine the same scenario, but instead you receive news that Jeremy was just admitted to the emergency room of a general hospital with an acute appendicitis. You know exactly how to respond when you go to see him. You will ask him how he feels, what exactly is wrong with him, and when he will be well again. Even though you might not like hospitals very much, at least you have a pretty good idea about what hospital patients are like. It does not seem peculiar to imagine Jeremy as a patient in this kind of hospital. It would probably be much easier for you to understand and accept your friend's physical illness than his psychological disorder, and you would probably not even consider whether you could be friends with him again after he is discharged.

People with psychological disorders often face situations like Jeremy's in which the people close to them aren't sure how to respond to their symptoms. Even worse, they experience profound and long-lasting emotional and social effects even after their symptoms are brought under control and they can resume their former lives. They also must cope with the personal pain associated with the disorder itself. Think about

The family of individuals with psychological disorders face significant stress when their relatives must be hospitalized.

Rebecca and her unhappiness. Rather than enjoying her newly found independence while at college like her classmates, she is experiencing extreme amounts of sadness and loneliness. She is unable to focus on her studies, make new friends, or even sleep.

Social attitudes toward people with psychological disorders range from discomfort to outright prejudice. Language, humor, and stereotypes all portray psychological disorders in a negative light and people often fear that people suffering from these disorders are violent and dangerous. There seems to be something about a psychological disorder that makes people want to distance themselves from it as much as possible. The result of these stereotypes is social discrimination, which only serves to complicate the lives of the afflicted even more.

In the chapters that follow, you will read about a wide range of disorders involving mood, anxiety, substance use, sexuality, and thought disturbance. The case descriptions will give you a glimpse into the feelings and experiences of people who have these disorders, and you may find that some of these individuals seem similar to you or to people you know. As you read about the disorders, put yourself in the place of the people who have these conditions. Consider how they feel and how they would like people to treat them. We hope that you will realize that our discussion is not about disorders, but about the people with these disorders.

1.3 Defining Abnormality

How would you define abnormal behavior? Read the following examples. Which of these behaviors do you regard as abnormal?

- Finding a "lucky" seat in an exam
- Inability to sleep, eat, study, or talk to anyone else for days after a lover says, "It's over between us"
- Breaking into a cold sweat at the thought of being trapped in an elevator
- Swearing, throwing pillows, and pounding fists on the wall in the middle of an argument with a roommate
- Refusing to eat solid food for days at a time in order to stay thin
- Engaging in a thorough hand-washing after coming home from a bus ride
- Believing that the government has agents who are eavesdropping on telephone conversations
- Drinking a six-pack of beer a day in order to be "sociable" with friends after work

If you're like most people, you probably found it difficult to decide between normal and abnormal. It is surprisingly difficult to make this distinction, but it is important to establish some criteria for abnormality.

The mental health community currently uses diagnostic procedures to decide on whether a given individual fits the criteria for abnormality. There are currently five criteria for a psychological disorder. The first is that of "clinical significance," meaning that the behavior involves a measurable degree of impairment. The behavior must also have diagnostic validity, meaning that the diagnoses predict future behavior or responses to treatment. Second, the behavior reflects a dysfunction in psychological, biological, or developmental processes. Third, the behavior usually is associated with significant distress or disability in important realms of life. Fourth, the individual's behavior cannot be socially "deviant" as defined in terms of religion, politics, or sexuality. Fifth, conflicts between the individual and society are not counted as psychological disorders unless they reflect a dysfunction within the individual. Thus, in some oppressive political symptoms, people were "diagnosed" as having a psychological disorder when in reality, the government sought to find a way to silence protestors. When making diagnoses, clinicians not only evaluate each of these criteria but also weigh the potential disadvantages of diagnosing behavior as "abnormal" versus providing a diagnosis that will permit the client to receive insurance coverage for the disturbance.

This young woman is distressed over her inability to fall asleep, but does this mean she has a psychological disorder?

1.4 What Causes Abnormal Behavior?

However defined, we can best conceptualize abnormal behavior from multiple perspectives that incorporate biological, psychological, and sociocultural factors.

Biological Causes

The biological domain includes genetic and environmental influences on physical functioning. People with psychological disorders may inherit a predisposition to developing behavioral disturbances. Of particular interest are inherited factors that alter the functioning of the nervous system. There are also physiological changes that affect behavior, which other conditions in the body cause, such as brain damage or exposure to harmful environmental stimuli. For example, a thyroid abnormality can cause a person's moods to fluctuate widely. Brain damage resulting from a head trauma can result in aberrant thought patterns. Toxic substances or allergens in the environment can also cause a person to experience disturbing emotional changes and behavior.

Psychological Causes

Psychological causes of abnormal behavior involve disturbances in thoughts and feelings. As you will learn in this book, there are a variety of alternative explanations of abnormal behavior that focus on factors such as past learning experiences, maladaptive thought patterns, and difficulties coping with stress. The varying theoretical perspectives within abnormal psychology reflect differences in assumptions about the underlying causes of human behavior. Treatment models based on these theoretical perspectives reflect these varying assumptions.

Sociocultural Causes

The term *sociocultural* refers to the various circles of influence on the individual ranging from close friends and family to the institutions and policies of a country or the world as a whole. Discrimination, whether based on social class, income, race and ethnicity, or

TABLE 1.1 Causes of Abnormal Behavior

Biological	Genetic inheritance
	Physiological changes
	Exposure to toxic substances
Psychological	Past learning experiences
	Maladaptive thought patterns
	Difficulties coping with stress
Sociocultural	Social policies
	Discrimination
	Stigma

stigma
A label that causes certain people to be regarded as different, defective, and set apart from mainstream members of society.

gender, can influence the development of abnormal behavior. For people who are diagnosed with a psychological disorder, social stigmas associated with being "mental patients" can further affect their symptoms. A **stigma** is a label that causes us to regard certain people as different, defective, and set apart from mainstream members of society. In addition to increasing the burden for them and for their loved ones, a stigma deters people from obtaining badly needed help, and thereby perpetuates a cycle in which many people in need become much worse. The stigma of psychological disorders affects people from ethnic and racial minorities more severely than those from mainstream society. For example, European-American adolescents and their caregivers are twice as likely as members of minority groups to define problems in mental health terms or to seek help for such problems (Roberts, Alegría, Roberts, & Chen, 2005).

The Biopsychosocial Perspective

Table 1.1 summarizes the three categories of the causes of abnormality. Disturbances in any of these areas of human functioning can contribute to the development of a psychological disorder. However, we cannot so neatly divide the causes of abnormality. There is often considerable interaction among the three sets of influences.

biopsychosocial
A model in which the interaction of biological, psychological, and sociocultural factors is seen as influencing the development of the individual.

Social scientists use the term **biopsychosocial** to refer to the interaction in which biological, psychological, and sociocultural factors play a role in the development of an individual's symptoms. The biopsychosocial perspective incorporates a developmental viewpoint. This means that individuals must be seen as changing over time. Biopsychosocial factors interact to alter the individual's expression of behavioral patterns over time. Thus, it is important to examine early risk factors that make an individual vulnerable to developing a disorder. Similarly, risk factors may vary according to the individual's position in the life span (Whitbourne & Meeks, 2011).

As you will see when reading about the conditions in this textbook, the degree of influence of each of these variables differs from disorder to disorder. For some disorders, such as schizophrenia, biology plays a dominant role. For other disorders, such as stress reactions, psychological factors predominate. For other conditions, such as post-traumatic stress disorder, that result, for example, from experiences under a terrorist regime, the cause is primarily sociocultural.

However, certain life experiences can protect people from developing conditions to which they are vulnerable. Protective factors, such as loving caregivers, adequate health care, and early life successes, reduce vulnerability considerably. In contrast, low vulnerability can heighten when people receive inadequate health care, engage in risky behaviors (such as using drugs), and get involved in dysfunctional relationships. The bottom line is that we can best conceptualize abnormal behavior as a complex interaction among multiple factors.

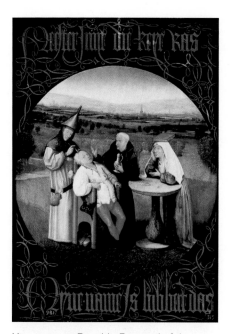

Hieronymous Bosch's *Removal of the Stone of Folly* depicted a medieval "doctor" cutting out the presumed source of madness from a patient's skull. The prevailing belief was that spiritual possession was the cause of psychological disorder.

The Greeks sought advice from oracles, wise advisors who made pronouncements from the gods.

1.5 Prominent Themes in Abnormal Psychology throughout History

The greatest thinkers of the world, from Plato to the present day, have attempted to explain the varieties of human behavior that constitute abnormality. Three prominent themes in explaining psychological disorders recur throughout history: the spiritual, the scientific, and the humanitarian. **Spiritual explanations** regard abnormal behavior as the product of possession by evil or demonic spirits. **Humanitarian explanations** view psychological disorders as the result of cruelty, stress, or poor living conditions. **Scientific explanations** look for causes that we can objectively measure, such as biological alterations, faulty learning processes, or emotional stressors.

spiritual explanations
Regard psychological disorders as the product of possession by evil or demonic spirits.

humanitarian explanations
Regard psychological disorders as the result of cruelty, stress, or poor living conditions.

scientific explanations
Regard psychological disorders as the result of causes that we can objectively measure, such as biological alterations, faulty learning processes, or emotional stressors.

Spiritual Approach

The earliest approach to understanding abnormal behavior is spiritual; the belief that people showing signs of behavioral disturbance were possessed by evil spirits. Archeological evidence dating back to 8000 B.C. suggests that the spiritual explanation was prevalent in prehistoric times. Skulls of the living had holes cut out of them, a process called "trephining," apparently in an effort to release the evil spirits from the person's head (Maher & Maher, 1985). Archeologists have found evidence of trephining from many countries and cultures, including the Far and Middle East, the Celtic tribes in Britain, ancient and recent China, India, and various peoples of North and South America, including the Mayans, Aztecs, Incas, and Brazilian Indians (Gross, 1999).

Another ancient practice was to drive away evil spirits through the ritual of exorcism, a physically and mentally painful form of torture carried out by a shaman, priest, or medicine man. Variants of shamanism have appeared throughout history. The Greeks sought advice from oracles who they believed were in contact with the gods. The Chinese practiced magic as a protection against demons. In India, shamanism flourished for centuries, and it still persists in Central Asia.

In this modern-day re-enactment of the Salem Witchcraft trials, a woman is tortured for her supposed crimes.

Dorothea Dix was a Massachusetts reformer who sought to improve the treatment of people with psychological disorders in the mid-1800s.

During the Middle Ages, people widely practiced magical rituals and exorcism, and administered folk medicines. Society considered people with psychological difficulties sinners, witches, or embodiments of the devil, and they were punished severely. Malleus Maleficarum, an indictment of witches written by two Dominican monks in Germany in 1486, became the Church's justification for denouncing witches as heretics and devils whom it had to destroy in the interest of preserving Christianity. The Church recommended "treatments" such as deportation, torture, and burning at the stake. Women were the main targets of persecution. Even in the late 1600s in colonial America, the Puritans sentenced women accused of witchcraft to death by hanging.

Humanitarian Approach

The humanitarian approach developed throughout history, in part as a reaction against the spiritual approach and its associated punishment of people with psychological disorders. Poorhouses and monasteries became shelters, and although they could not offer treatment, they provided some protective measures. Unfortunately, these often became overcrowded, and rather than provide protection themselves, they became places where abuses occurred. For example, society widely believed that psychologically disturbed people were insensitive to extremes of heat and cold, or to the cleanliness of their surroundings. Their "treatment" involved bleeding, forced vomiting, and purging. It took a few courageous people, who recognized the inhumanity of the existing practices, to bring about sweeping reforms. By the end of the eighteenth century, hospitals in France, Scotland, and England attempted to reverse these harsh practices. The idea of "moral treatment" took hold—the notion that people could develop self-control over their behaviors if they had a quiet and restful environment. Institutions used restraints only if absolutely necessary, and even in those cases the patient's comfort came first.

Conditions in asylums again began to worsen in the early 1800s as facilities suffered from overcrowding and staff resorted to physical punishment to control the patients. In 1841, a Boston schoolteacher named Dorothea Dix (1802–1887) took up the cause of reform. Horrified by the inhumane conditions in the asylums, Dix appealed to the Massachusetts Legislature for more state-funded public hospitals to provide humane treatment for mental patients. From Massachusetts, Dix spread her message throughout North America and Europe.

Although deinstitutionalization was designed to enhance the quality of life for people who had been held years in public psychiatric hospitals, many individuals left institutions only to find a life of poverty and neglect on the outside.

Over the next 100 years, governments built scores of state hospitals throughout the United States. Once again, however, it was only a matter of time before the hospitals became overcrowded and understaffed. It simply was not possible to cure people by providing them with the well-intentioned, but ineffective, interventions proposed by moral treatment. However, the humanitarian goals that Dix advocated had a lasting influence on the mental health system. Her work was carried forward into the twentieth century by advocates of what became known as the mental hygiene movement.

Until the 1970s, despite the growing body of knowledge about the causes of abnormal behavior, the actual practices in the day-to-day care of psychologically disturbed people were sometimes as barbaric as those in the Middle Ages. Even people suffering from the least severe psychological disorders were often housed in the "back wards" of large and impersonal state institutions, without adequate or appropriate care. Institutions restrained patients with powerful tranquilizing drugs and straitjackets, coats with sleeves long enough to wrap around the patient's torso. Even more radical was the indiscriminate use of behavior-altering brain surgery or the application of electrical shocks—so-called treatments that were punishments intended to control unruly patients (see more on these procedures in Chapter 2).

Public outrage over these abuses in mental hospitals finally led to a more widespread realization that mental health services required dramatic changes. The federal government took emphatic action in 1963 with the passage of groundbreaking legislation. The Mental Retardation Facilities and Community Mental Health Center Construction Act of that year initiated a series of changes that would affect mental health services for decades to come. Legislators began to promote policies designed to move people out of institutions and into less restrictive programs in the community, such as vocational rehabilitation facilities, day hospitals, and psychiatric clinics. After their discharge from the hospital, people entered halfway houses, which provided a supportive environment in which they could learn the necessary social skills to re-enter the community. By the mid-1970s, the state mental hospitals, once overflowing with patients, were practically deserted. These hospitals freed hundreds of thousands of institutionally confined people to begin living with greater dignity and autonomy. This process, known as the deinstitutionalization movement, promoted the release of psychiatric patients into community treatment sites.

Unfortunately, the deinstitutionalization movement did not completely fulfill the dreams of its originators. Rather than abolishing inhumane treatment, deinstitutionalization created another set of woes. Many of the promises and programs hailed as alternatives to institutionalization ultimately failed to come through because of inadequate

Table 1.2 Healthy People 2020 Goals

In late 2010, the U.S. government's Healthy People project released goals for the coming decade. These goals are intended both to improve the psychological functioning of individuals in the United States and to expand treatment services.

- Reduce the suicide rate.
- Reduce suicide attempts by adolescents.
- Reduce the proportion of adolescents who engage in disordered eating behaviors in an attempt to control their weight.
- Reduce the proportion of persons who experience major depressive episodes.
- Increase the proportion of primary care facilities that provide mental health treatment onsite or by paid referral.
- Increase the proportion of children with mental health problems who receive treatment.
- Increase the proportion of juvenile residential facilities that screen admissions for mental health problems.
- Increase the proportion of persons with serious mental illness (SMI) who are employed.
- Increase the proportion of adults with mental disorders who receive treatment.
- Increase the proportion of persons with co-occurring substance abuse and mental disorders who receive treatment for both disorders.
- Increase depression screening by primary care providers.
- Increase the proportion of homeless adults with mental health problems who receive mental health services.

SOURCE: http://www.healthypeople.gov/2020/topicsobjectives2020/pdfs/MentalHealth.pdf

planning and insufficient funds. Patients shuttled back and forth between hospitals, halfway houses, and shabby boarding homes, never having a sense of stability or respect. Although the intention of releasing patients from psychiatric hospitals was to free people who had been deprived of basic human rights, the result may not have been as liberating as many had hoped. In contemporary American society, people who would have been in psychiatric hospitals four decades ago are moving through a circuit of shelters, rehabilitation programs, jails, and prisons, with a disturbing number of these individuals spending long periods of time as homeless and marginalized members of society.

Contemporary advocates of the humanitarian approach suggest new forms of compassionate treatment for people who suffer from psychological disorders. These advocates encourage mental health consumers to take an active role in choosing their treatment. Various advocacy groups have worked tirelessly to change the way the public views mentally ill people and how society deals with them in all settings. These groups include the National Alliance for the Mentally Ill (NAMI), as well as the Mental Health Association, the Center to Address Discrimination and Stigma, and the Eliminate the Barriers Initiative. The U.S. federal government has also become involved in antistigma programs as part of efforts to improve the delivery of mental health services through the President's New Freedom Commission (Hogan, 2003). Looking forward into the next decade, the U.S. government has set the 2020 Healthy People initiative goals as focused on improving significantly the quality of treatment services (see Table 1.2).

Scientific Approach

Early Greek philosophers were the first to attempt a scientific approach to understanding psychological disorders. Hippocrates (ca. 460–377 B.C.), considered the founder of modern medicine, believed that there were four important bodily fluids that influenced physical and mental health, leading to four personality dispositions. To treat a psychological disorder would require ridding the body of the excess fluid. Several hundred years later, the Roman physician Claudius Galen (A.D. 130–200) developed a system of medical knowledge based on anatomical studies.

Dr. Benjamin Rush, founder of American psychiatry, was an ardent reformer who promoted the scientific study of psychological disorders.

Scientists made very few significant advances in the understanding of abnormality until the eighteenth century. Benjamin Rush (1745–1813), the founder of American psychiatry, rekindled interest in the scientific approach to psychological disorders. In 1783, Rush joined the medical staff of Pennsylvania Hospital. Appalled by the poor hospital conditions, he advocated for improvements such as placing psychologically disturbed patients in their own wards, giving them occupational therapy, and prohibiting visits from curiosity seekers who would visit the hospital for entertainment.

Reflecting the prevailing methods of the times, Rush also supported the use of bloodletting and purging in the treatment of psychological disorders as well as the "tranquilizer" chair, intended to reduce blood flow to the brain by binding the patient's head and limbs. Rush also recommended submerging patients in cold shower baths and frightening them with death threats. He thought that fright inducement would counteract the overexcitement that he believed was responsible for the patients' violent behavior (Deutsch, 1949).

In 1844, a group of 13 mental hospital administrators formed the Association of Medical Superintendents of American Institutions for the Insane. The organization eventually changed its name to the American Psychiatric Association. German psychiatrist Wilhelm Greisinger published *The Pathology and Therapy of Mental Disorders* in 1845, which proposed that "neuropathologies" were the cause of psychological disorders. Another German psychiatrist, Emil Kraepelin, promoted a classification system much like that applied to medical diagnoses. He proposed that disorders could be identified by their patterns of symptoms. Ultimately, this work provided the scientific basis for current diagnostic systems.

Positive psychology emphasizes personal growth through meditation and other alternate routes to self-discovery.

The scientific approach to psychological disorders also gained momentum as psychiatrists and psychologists proposed behavior models that included explanations of abnormality. In the early 1800s, European physicians experimented with hypnosis for therapeutic purposes. Eventually, these efforts led to the groundbreaking work of Viennese neurologist Sigmund Freud (1856–1939), who in the early 1900s developed psychoanalysis, a theory and system of practice that relied heavily on the concepts of the unconscious mind, inhibited sexual impulses, and early development.

Throughout the twentieth century, psychologists developed models of normal behavior, which eventually became incorporated into systems of therapy. The work of Russian physiologist Ivan Pavlov (1849–1936), known for his discovery of classical conditioning, became the basis for the behaviorist movement begun in the United States by John B. Watson (1878–1958). B. F. Skinner (1904–1990) formulated a systematic approach to operant conditioning, specifying the types and nature of reinforcement as a way to modify behavior. In the twentieth century, these models continued to evolve into the social learning theory of Albert Bandura (1925–), the cognitive model of Aaron Beck (1921–), and the rational-emotive therapy approach of Albert Ellis (1913–2007).

In the 1950s, scientists experimenting with pharmacological treatments invented medications that for the first time in history could successfully control the symptoms of psychological disorders. Now, patients could receive treatments that would allow them to live for extended periods of time on their own outside psychiatric hospitals. In 1963, the Mental Retardation Facilities and Community Mental Health Center Construction Act proposed patient treatment in clinics and treatment centers outside of mental hospitals. This legislation paved the way for the deinstitutionalization movement and subsequent efforts to continue to improve community treatment.

Most recently, the field of abnormal psychology is benefiting from the **positive psychology** movement, which emphasizes the potential for growth and change throughout life. The movement views psychological disorders as difficulties that inhibit the individual's ability to achieve highly subjective well-being and feelings of fulfillment. In addition, the positive psychology movement emphasizes prevention rather than intervention. Instead of fixing

positive psychology
Perspective that emphasizes the potential for growth and change throughout life.

problems after they occur, it would benefit people more if they could avoid developing symptoms in the first place. Although its goals are similar to those of the humanitarian approach, the positive psychology movement has a strong base in empirical research and as a result is gaining wide support in the field.

1.6 Research Methods in Abnormal Psychology

Non

As you've just learned, the scientific approach led to significant advances in the understanding and treatment of abnormal behavior. The essence of the scientific method is objectivity, the process of testing ideas about the nature of psychological phenomena without bias before accepting these ideas as adequate explanations.

The scientific method involves a progression of steps from posing questions of interest to sharing the results with the scientific community. Throughout the scientific method, researchers maintain the objectivity that is the hallmark of the scientific approach. This means that they do not let their personal biases interfere with the data collection or interpretation of findings. In addition, researchers must always be open to alternative explanations that could account for their findings.

Although the scientific method is based on objectivity, this does not mean that scientists have no personal interest in what they are studying. In fact, it is often quite the opposite. Many researchers become involved in the pursuit of knowledge in areas that relate to experiences in their own lives, particularly in the field of abnormal psychology. They may have relatives afflicted with certain disorders or they may have become puzzled by a client's symptoms. In conducting their research, however, they cannot let these personal biases get in the way.

Thus, in posing questions of interest, psychological researchers may wonder whether a particular kind of experience led to an individual's symptoms, or they may speculate about the role of particular biological factors. Clinical psychologists are also interested in finding out whether a certain treatment will effectively treat the symptoms of a disorder. In either case, the ideal approach to answering these questions involves a progression through a set of steps in which the psychologist proposes a hypothesis, conducts a study, and collects and analyzes the data. Eventually, they communicate results through publication in scientific journals.

1.7 Experimental Design

Non

When using experimental design in research, an investigator sets up a test of a hypothesis by constructing a manipulation of a key variable of interest. The variable that the investigator manipulates is called the **independent variable,** meaning that the investigator controls it. The investigator sets up at least two conditions that reflect different levels of the independent variable. In most cases, these conditions are the "experimental" or treatment group (the group that receives the treatment) and the "control" group (the group that receives no treatment or a different treatment). The researchers then compare the groups on the **dependent variable,** which is the variable that they observe. Key to the objectivity of experimental research is the requirement that the researchers always randomly assign participants to the different groups. A study would be flawed if all the men were in the experimental group, for example, and all the women were in the control group.

In research on the causes of abnormal behavior, it may be difficult to set up a true experimental study. Many of the variables that are of most interest to psychologists are ones that the investigator cannot control; hence, they are not truly "independent." For example, depression can never be an independent variable because the investigator cannot manipulate it. Similarly, investigators cannot randomly assign people to groups based on their biological sex. Studies that investigate differences among groups not determined by random assignment are known as "quasi-experimental."

independent variable
The variable whose level is adjusted or controlled by the experimenter.

dependent variable
The variable whose value is the outcome of the experimenter's manipulation of the independent variable.

The majority of true experimental studies in abnormal psychology, at least those on humans, test not the causes of abnormal behavior, but the effectiveness of particular treatments where it is possible to design randomly assigned control and experimental groups. Investigators evaluate a treatment's effectiveness by comparing the groups on dependent variables such as symptom alleviation. There may be more than one experimental group, depending on the nature of the particular study.

It is common practice in studies evaluating therapy effectiveness to have a **placebo condition** in which participants receive a treatment similar to the experimental treatment, but lacking the key feature of the treatment of interest. If the study is evaluating effectiveness of medication, the placebo has inert ingredients. In studies evaluating effectiveness of therapy, scientists must design the placebo in a way that mimics, but is not the same as the actual therapy. Ideally, the researchers would want the placebo participants to receive treatments of the same frequency and duration as the experimental group participants who are receiving psychotherapy.

Expectations about the experiment's outcome can affect both the investigator and the participant. These so-called "demand characteristics" can compromise the conclusions about the intervention's true effectiveness. Obviously, the investigator should be as unbiased as possible, but there still may be subtle ways that he or she communicates cues that affect the participant's response. The participant may also have a personal agenda in trying to prove or disprove the study's supposed true intent. The best way to eliminate demand characteristics is to use a **double-blind** method, which shields both investigator and participant from knowing either the study's purpose or the nature of the patient's treatment.

In studies involving medication, a completely inert placebo may not be sufficient to establish true experimental control. In an "active placebo" condition, researchers build the experimental medication's side effects into the placebo. If they know that a medication produces dry mouth, difficulty swallowing, or upset stomach, then the placebo must also mimic these side effects or participants will know they are receiving placebos.

> ## What's New in the DSM-5
>
> ### Definition of a Mental Disorder
>
> There are five criteria for a mental disorder in the *DSM-5*, the same number as was included in *DSM-IV*. The criteria still refer to "clinically significant" to establish the fact that the behaviors under consideration are not passing symptoms or minor difficulties. *DSM-5* refers to the behaviors as reflecting dysfunction in psychological, biological, or developmental processes, terms that *DSM-IV* did not use. Both the *DSM-IV* and *DSM-5* state that disorders must occur outside the norm of what is socially accepted and expected for people experiencing particular life stresses. *DSM-5* also specifies that the disorder must have "clinical utility," meaning that, for example, the diagnoses help guide clinicians in making decisions about treatment. During the process of writing the *DSM-5*, the authors cautioned against changing the lists of disorders (either adding to or subtracting) without taking into account potential benefits and risks. For example, they realized that adding a new diagnosis might lead to labeling as "abnormal" a behavior previously considered "normal." The advantage of having the new diagnosis must outweigh the harm of categorizing a "normal" person as having a "disorder." Similarly, deleting a diagnosis for a disorder that requires treatment (and hence insurance coverage) might leave individuals who still require that treatment vulnerable to withholding of care or excess payments for treatment. With these cautions in mind, the *DSM-5* authors also recommend that the criteria alone are not sufficient for making legal judgments or eligibility for insurance compensation. These judgments would require additional information beyond the scope of the diagnostic criteria alone.

placebo condition
Condition in an experiment in which participants receive a treatment similar to the experimental treatment, but lacking the key feature of the treatment of interest.

double-blind
An experimental procedure in which neither the person giving the treatment nor the person receiving the treatment knows whether the participant is in the experimental or control group.

1.8 *Non* Correlational Design

Studies based on a correlational design involve tests of relationships between variables that researchers cannot experimentally manipulate. We express the correlation statistic in terms of a number between +1 and −1. Positive numbers represent positive correlations, meaning that, as scores on one variable increase, scores on the second variable increase. For example, because one aspect of depression is that it causes a disturbance in normal sleep patterns, you would expect then that scores on a measure of depression would be positively correlated with scores on a measure of sleep disturbances. Conversely, negative correlations indicate that, as scores on one variable increase, scores on the second variable decrease. An example of a negative correlation is the relationship between depression and self-esteem. The more depressed people are, the lower their scores are on a measure of self-esteem. In many cases, there is no correlation between

Being Sane in Insane Places

In the early 1970s, psychologist David Rosenhan embarked upon a groundbreaking study that was to shatter people's assumptions about the difference between "sane" and "insane." Motivated by what he regarded as a psychiatric diagnostic system that led to the hospitalization of people inappropriately diagnosed as having schizophrenia, Rosenhan and his co-workers decided to conduct their own experiment to put the system to the test. See whether you think their experiment proved the point.

Eight people with no psychiatric history of symptoms of any kind, employed in a variety of professional occupations, checked themselves into psychiatric hospitals complaining about hearing voices that said, "Empty," "Hollow," and "Thud." These were symptoms that psychiatric literature never reported. In every other way, the "pseudopatients" provided factual information about themselves (except their names and places of employment). Each pseudopatient was admitted to his or her respective hospital; once admitted, they showed no further signs of experiencing these symptoms. However, the hospital staff never questioned their need to be hospitalized; quite the contrary, their behavior on the hospital wards, now completely "normal," was taken as further evidence of their need for continued hospitalization. Despite the efforts of the pseudopatients to convince the staff that there was nothing wrong with them, it took from 7 to 52 days for their discharge. Upon their release, they received the diagnosis of "schizophrenia in remission" (meaning that they, for the moment, no longer would have a diagnosis of schizophrenia).

There was profound reaction in the psychiatric community to the Rosenhan study. If it was so easy to institutionalize nonpatients, wasn't there something wrong with the diagnostic system? How about the tendency to label people as "schizophrenic" when there was nothing wrong with them, and to hang on to the label even when they no longer showed any symptoms? Additionally, the pseudopatients reported that they felt dehumanized by the staff and failed to receive any active treatment. Once on the outside, they could report to the world at large about the failings of psychiatric hospitals to provide appropriate treatment. True patients would not have received so much sympathetic press, and therefore, would not have paved the way for the deinstitutionalization movement that was to follow the study's widespread dissemination.

Now, you be the judge. Do you think that it was unethical for Rosenhan to devise such a study? The mental health professionals at the hospitals had no idea that they were the "subjects" of the study. They had responded to what seemed to them to be serious psychological symptoms by individuals voluntarily seeking admission. At the point of discharge, the fact that the doctors labeled the pseudopatients as being in remission implied that they were symptom-free, but there was no reason for the staff to doubt the truth of the symptoms. On the other hand, had the staff known they were in a study, they might have reacted very differently, and as a result, the study would not have had an impact.

How about the quality of this study from a scientific point of view? There was no control condition so it was not truly an experiment. Moreover, the study did not take objective measures of the staffs' behavior, nor were there direct outcome measures that the researchers could statistically analyze.

Q: *You be the judge:* Was Rosenhan's study, with its flaws, worthwhile? Did the ends justify the means?

two variables. In other words, two variables show no systematic relationship with each other. For example, depression is unrelated to height.

Just knowing that there is a correlation between two variables does not tell you whether one variable causes the other. The correlation simply tells you that the two variables are associated with each other in a particular way. Sleep disturbance might cause a higher score on a measure of depression, just as a high degree of depression might cause more disturbed sleep patterns. Or, a third variable that you have not measured could account for the correlation between the two variables that you have studied. Both depression and sleep disturbance could be due to an underlying physiological dysfunction.

Investigators who use correlational methods in their research must always be on guard for the potential existence of unmeasured variables influencing the observed results. However, beyond simply linking two variables to see if they are correlated, researchers can use advanced methods that take more complex relationships into account. For example, we can assess the relative contributions of sleep disturbances, self-esteem, gender, and social class with correlational methods that evaluate several related variables at the same time.

1.9 Types of Research Studies Non

How do investigators gather their data? There are several types of studies that psychologists use. The type of study depends in large part upon the question and the resources available to the investigator. Table 1.3 summarizes these methods.

Survey

Investigators use a **survey** to gather information from a sample of people representative of a particular population. They use surveys primarily in studies involving a correlational design when investigators seek to find out whether potentially related variables actually do relate to each other as hypothesized. In a survey, investigators design sets of questions to tap into these variables. They may conduct a survey to determine whether age is correlated with subjective well-being, controlling for the influence of health. In this case, the researcher may hypothesize that subjective well-being is higher in older adults, but only after taking into account the role of health.

Researchers also use surveys to gather statistics about the frequency of psychological symptoms. For example, the Substance Abuse and Mental Health Services Administration of the U.S. government (SAMHSA) conducts yearly surveys to establish the frequency of use of illegal substances within the population. The World Health Organization (WHO) conducts surveys comparing the frequency by country of psychological disorders. These surveys provide valuable epidemiological data that can assess the health of the population.

survey
A research tool used to gather information from a sample of people considered representative of a particular population, in which participants are asked to answer questions about the topic of concern.

Table 1.3 Research Methods in Abnormal Psychology

Type of Method	Purpose	Example
Survey	Obtain population data	Researchers working for a government agency attempt to determine disease prevalence through questionnaires administered over the telephone.
Laboratory study	Collect data under controlled conditions	An experiment is conducted to compare reaction times to neutral and fear-provoking stimuli.
Case study	An individual or a small group of individuals is studied intensively	A therapist describes the cases of members of a family who share the same unusual disorder.
Single case experimental design	The same person serves as subject in experimental and control conditions	Researchers report on the frequency of a client's behavior while the client is given attention (experimental treatment) and ignored (control condition) for aggressive outbursts in a psychiatric ward.
Behavioral genetics	Attempt to identify genetic patterns in inheritance of particular behaviors	Genetic researchers compare the DNA of people with and without symptoms of particular psychological disorders.

REAL STORIES

Vincent van Gogh: Psychosis

"There is safety in the midst of danger. What would life be if we had no courage to attempt anything? It will be a hard pull for me; the tide rises high, almost to the lips and perhaps higher still, how can I know? But I shall fight my battle . . . and try to win and get the best of it."
Vincent van Gogh, December, 1881.

Vincent van Gogh, a Dutch-born post-impressionist painter, lived most of his life in poverty and poor physical and mental health. After his death, his work grew immensely in recognition and popularity. His now instantly recognizable paintings sell for tens of millions of dollars, while during his lifetime his brother, Theo, mainly supported the painter, sending him art supplies and money for living expenses. Van Gogh struggled with mental illness for much of his life, spending one year in an asylum before the last year of his life, when he committed suicide in 1890 at the age of 37.

Though the specific nature of van Gogh's mental illness is unknown, his 600 or so letters to Theo offer some insight into his experiences. Published in 1937, *Dear Theo: The Autobiography of Vincent van Gogh* provides an unfiltered glimpse into all aspects of his life including art, love, and his psychological difficulties. Van Gogh never received a formal diagnosis in his lifetime, and to this day many psychologists argue over the disorder from which he may have been suffering. Psychologists have suggested as many as 30 possible diagnoses ranging from schizophrenia and bipolar disorder to syphilis and alcoholism. Van Gogh's constant poor nutrition, excessive consumption of absinthe, and a tendency to work to the point of exhaustion undoubtedly contributed to and worsened any psychological issues he experienced.

Van Gogh's romantic life was highlighted by a series of failed relationships, and he never had children. When he proposed marriage to Kee Vos-Stricker in 1881, she and her parents turned him down because he was having difficulty supporting himself financially at the time. Kee was a widow with a child and van Gogh would not have been able to support the family fully. In response to this rejection, van Gogh held his hand over a lamp flame, demanding her father that he be allowed see the woman he loved, an event he was later unable to recall entirely. Unfortunately for van Gogh, the affection was never reciprocated. His longest known romantic relationship lasted for one year, during which he lived with a prostitute and her two children.

Van Gogh first learned to draw in middle school, a hobby that he carried on throughout his failed attempt at becoming a religious missionary. He failed his entrance exam for theology school in Amsterdam, and later failed missionary school. In 1880 he decided to devote his life to painting. After attending art school in Brussels, van Gogh moved around the Netherlands and fine-tuned his craft, often living in poverty and squalid conditions. He spent some time living with his parents, but never stayed with them long due to his tumultuous relationship with his father. By 1885, he began to gain recognition as an artist and had completed his first major work, *The Potato Eaters*. The following year, he moved to Paris where he lived with his brother and began to immerse himself in the thriving art world of the city. Due to his poor living conditions, van Gogh's health began to deteriorate, and so he moved to the countryside in the south of France. There he spent two months living with and working alongside his good friend and fellow painter Paul Gauguin. Their artistic differences led to frequent disagreements that slowly eroded their amiable companionship. In *Dear Theo*, Johanna van Gogh, Vincent's sister-in-law, writes about

Vincent Van Gogh's *Starry Night over the Rhone*, painted in 1888, one year before his death.

the notorious incident that took place on December 23, 1888. Van Gogh, "in a state of terrible excitement and high fever, had cut off a piece of his own ear, and had brought it as a gift to a woman in a brothel. There had been a violent scene; Roulin, the postman, managed to get him home, but the police intervened, found Vincent bleeding and unconscious in bed, and sent him to the hospital."

After the incident, van Gogh was committed to an asylum in Saint-Remy de Provence, France, for about one year. While in the hospital, he often reflected on the state of his mental health in letters to his brother:

"These last three months do seem so strange to me. There have been moods of indescribable mental anguish, sometimes moments when the veil of time and of inevitable circumstance seemed for the twinkling of an eye to be parted. After all, you are certainly right, damn well right; even making allowance for hope, the thing is to accept the probably disastrous reality. I am hoping to throw myself once again wholly into my work, which has got behindhand."

While hospitalized and working on recovering from his "attacks," van Gogh spent most of his time working feverishly on painting, often finding inspiration in the scenery surrounding the asylum. For van Gogh, painting was a welcome relief that he hoped would cure his illness. Of his experiences with mental illness, he wrote ". . . I am beginning to consider madness as a disease like any other, and accept the thing as such; whereas during the crises themselves I thought that everything I imagined was real." It is clear from many of his letters that he had been experiencing hallucinations and perhaps delusions—two hallmark symptoms of psychological disorders involving psychosis, such as schizophrenia.

After his release from the asylum, van Gogh participated in art shows in Brussels and Paris. Though he remained artistically productive, his depression deepened until on July 29, 1890, he walked into a field and shot himself in the chest with a revolver, dying two days later. Van Gogh's last words, according to his brother who had rushed to be at his side at his deathbed, were "the sadness will last forever."

In his lifetime, Vincent van Gogh sold only one painting; in 1990 his *Portrait of Dr. Gachet* sold for $82.5 million, making it one of the most expensive paintings ever sold. His priceless work graces galleries around the globe and has an invaluable influence in the art world. Had his story taken place now, with many different options for psychological treatment of psychotic symptoms and depression, his life might not have been cut short so tragically.

Researchers report epidemiological data about the occurrence of psychological symptoms and disorders in terms of the time frame over which it occurs. The **incidence** of a disorder is the frequency of *new* cases of a disorder within a given time period. Respondents providing incidence data state whether they now have a disorder that they have never had before but now are experiencing. Incidence information can cover any time interval; people tend to report it in terms of one month, six months, and one year. Investigators use incidence data when they are interested in determining how quickly a disorder is spreading. For example, during an epidemic, health researchers need to know how to plan for controlling the disease, and so incidence data is most pertinent to this question.

incidence
The frequency of new cases within a given time period.

The **prevalence** of a disorder refers to the number of people who have *ever* had the disorder over a specified period of time. To collect prevalence data, investigators ask respondents to state whether, during this period of time, they experienced the symptoms of the disorder. The time period of reference can be the day of the survey, in which case we call it point prevalence. There is also one-month prevalence, which refers to the 30 days preceding the study, and lifetime prevalence, which refers to the entire life of the respondent. For example, researchers may ask respondents whether they smoked cigarettes at any time during the past month (one-month prevalence) or whether they ever, in their lifetimes, used cigarettes (lifetime prevalence). Typically, lifetime prevalence is higher than one-month or point prevalence because the question captures all past experience of a disorder or a symptom.

prevalence
The number of people who have ever had a disorder at a given time or over a specified period.

Laboratory Studies

Researchers carry out most experiments in psychological laboratories in which participants provide data under controlled conditions. Participants are exposed to conditions based upon the nature of the experimental manipulation. For example, investigators may show participants stimuli on computer screens and ask them to respond. The collected data might include speed of reaction time or memory for different types of stimuli.

Laboratory studies may also involve comparison of brain scan responses taken under differing conditions. Another type of laboratory study may involve observing people in small group settings in which the investigators study their interactions.

Although laboratories are ideal for conducting such experiments, they may also be appropriate settings for self-report data such as responses to questionnaires. Researchers can ask participants to complete their responses in a fixed period of time and under conditions involving a minimum of distractions. They may also provide them with self-report instruments to complete on a computer, allowing for the investigator to collect data in a systematic and uniform fashion across respondents.

The Case Study Method

case study
An intensive study of a single person described in detail.

Many of the researchers, from what the profession regards as classic studies in early abnormal psychology, based their findings on the **case study,** which is an intensive investigation of an individual or small group of individuals. For example, Freud based much of his theory on reports of his own patients—the development of their symptoms and their progress in therapy. In current research, investigators carry out case studies for a number of reasons. They afford the opportunity to report on rare cases, or the development of a disorder over time may be the focus of the study. For example, a clinical psychologist may write a report in a published journal about how she provided treatment to a client with a rare type of fear.

qualitative research
A method of analyzing data that provides research with methods of analyzing complex relationships that do not easily lend themselves to conventional statistical methods.

The advantage of an in-depth case study is also a potential disadvantage in that it does not involve enough experimental control to make a useful addition to the literature. Investigators using case studies, therefore, must be extremely precise in their methods and, as much as possible, take an objective and unbiased approach. There are standards for use in **qualitative research** that can ensure that researchers present case study data in a way that will be valuable to other investigators.

Single Case Experimental Design

single case experimental design
Design in which the same person serves as the subject in both the experimental and control conditions.

In a **single case experimental design (SCED)**, the same person serves as the subject in both the experimental and control conditions. Particularly useful for studies of treatment effectiveness, a single-subject design typically involves alternating off-on phases of the baseline condition ("A") and the intervention ("B"). The profession also refers to SCEDs as "ABAB" designs, reflecting the alternation between conditions A and B. Figure 1.1 shows an example of an SCED involving self-injurious behavior.

In cases where withholding the treatment in the "B" phase would present an ethical problem (because of an elimination of an effective treatment), researchers use a variation called the multiple baseline method. In a multiple baseline design, the researcher applies the treatment in an AB fashion so that it is never removed. The observation occurs across different subjects, for different behaviors, or in different settings. The researcher takes repeated measures of behavior in relation to introduction of the treatment. For example, in treating a suicidal client, an investigator may first target suicidal thoughts, and second, target suicidal behaviors. The power of the design is in showing that the behaviors change only when the researcher introduces specific treatments (Rizvi & Nock, 2008).

Investigations in Behavioral Genetics

concordance rate
Agreement ratios between people diagnosed as having a particular disorder and their relatives.

Researchers in the field of behavioral genetics and psychopathology attempt to determine the extent to which people inherit psychological disorders. Behavioral geneticists typically begin an investigation into a disorder's genetic inheritance after observing that the disorder shows a distinct pattern of family inheritance. This process requires obtaining complete family histories from people whom they can identify as having symptoms of the disorder. The investigators then calculate the **concordance rate,** or agreement ratios, between people diagnosed as having the disorder and their relatives. For example, a

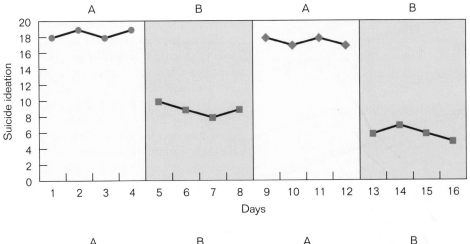

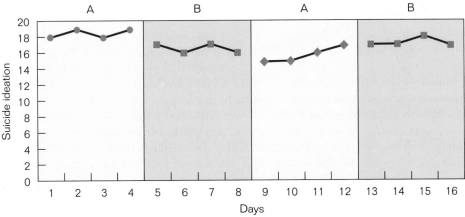

FIGURE 1.1 ABAB Design

In an ABAB design, researchers observe behaviors in the "A" phase, institute treatment in the "B" phase, and then repeat the process. In this hypothetical study, suicide ideation seems to improve with treatment in the top set of graphs but shows no effect of treatment in the bottom set of graphs (Rizvi & Nock, 2008).

researcher may observe that 6 out of a sample of 10 twin pairs have the same diagnosed psychological disorder. This would mean that, among this sample, there is a concordance rate of .60 (6 out of 10). We would expect an inherited disorder to have the highest concordance between monozygotic or identical twins (whose genes are the same), with somewhat lower rates between siblings and dizygotic or fraternal twins (who are no more alike genetically than siblings of different ages), and even lower rates among more distant relatives.

A second approach in behavioral genetics is to study families who have adopted. The most extensive evidence available from these studies comes from the Scandinavian countries, where the governments maintain complete birth and adoption records. The research studies two types of adoptions. The first is an adoption study in which researchers establish the rates of the disorder in children whose biological parents have diagnosed psychological disorders, but whose adoptive parents do not. If the children have the disorder, this suggests that genetic factors play a stronger role than the environment. In the second adoption study, referred to as "cross-fostering," researchers examine the frequency of the disorder in children whose biological parents had no disorder, but whose adoptive parents do.

Twin studies are a third method of behavioral genetics. In these studies, researchers compare monozygotic twins reared together to those reared apart. Theoretically, if twins reared apart share a particular disorder, this suggests that the environment played a relatively minor role in causing that behavior.

These kinds of studies enable researchers to draw inferences about the relative contributions of biology and family environment to the development of psychological disorders. However, they are imprecise and have several potential serious flaws. Adoption studies can be suggestive, but are hardly definitive. There may be unmeasured characteristics of the adoptive parents that influence the development of the disorder in the children. The most significant threat to the usefulness of twin studies is the fact that the majority of monozygotic twins do not share the same amniotic sac during prenatal development (Mukherjee et al., 2009). They may not even share 100 percent of the same DNA (Ollikainen et al., 2010).

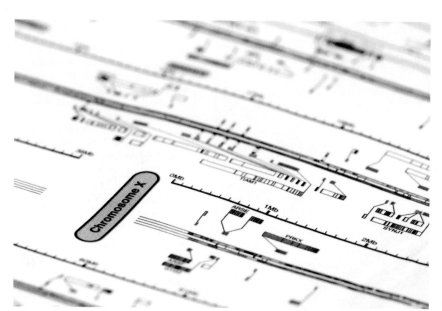

Gene mapping is revolutionizing the way that scientists understand and treat psychological disorders.

gene mapping
The attempt by biological researchers to identify the structure of a gene and the characteristics it controls.

molecular genetics
The study of how genes translate hereditary information.

In **gene mapping** researchers examine and connect variations in chromosomes to performance on psychological tests or diagnosis of specific disorders. **Molecular genetics** studies how genes translate hereditary information. We use these methods in the study of abnormal psychology to determine how hereditary information translates into behavior disorders. They have led to widespread advances in the understanding of such disorders as autism, schizophrenia, and various anxiety disorders (Hoffman & State, 2010).

Bringing It All Together: Clinical Perspectives

As you come to the close of this chapter, you now have an appreciation of the issues that are central to your understanding of abnormal psychology. We have tried to give you a sense of how complex it is to define abnormality, and you will find yourself returning to this issue as you read about many of the disorders in the chapters that follow. We will elaborate on the historical perspective in subsequent chapters as we look at theories of and treatments for specific disorders. Currently, developments are emerging in the field of abnormal psychology at an unbelievable pace due to the efforts of researchers applying the techniques described here. You will learn more about some of these research methods in the context of discussions regarding specific disorders. You will also develop an understanding of how clinicians, such as Dr. Sarah Tobin, look at the range of psychological disorders that affect people throughout the life span. We will give particular attention to explaining how disorders develop and how we can best treat them. Our discussion of the impact of psychological disorders forms a central theme for this book, as we return time and again to consideration of the human experience of psychological disorders.

Return to the Case: Rebecca Hasbrouck

An intern saw Rebecca at the counseling center once a week for 12 consecutive weeks. During the first few sessions she was often tearful, especially when talking about her boyfriend and how lonely she was feeling. In therapy, we worked on identifying her emotions and finding coping skills for dealing with stress. Eventually, Rebecca's feelings of sadness lifted as she became accustomed to her life on campus and was able to make a few close friends. Since she was feeling better, her sleeping also improved, which helped her to concentrate in class more easily, allowing her to perform better, and thus, feel more confident in herself as a student.

Dr. Tobin's reflections: It was clear to me in our initial session that Rebecca was a young woman who was having a particularly difficult time dealing with ordinary adjustment issues in adapting to college. She was overwhelmed by the many new experiences confronting her as well, and she seemed particularly unable to cope with being on her own and being separated from her support network including her family and boyfriend. Her high academic standards added to her stress and because she didn't have social support, she was unable to talk about the difficulties she was having, which surely perpetuated her problems. I am glad that she sought help early on before her difficulties became exacerbated and that she responded so well to treatment.

SUMMARY

- Questions about normality and abnormality are basic to our understanding of psychological disorders. They can affect us in very personal ways.

- Social impact can affect psychological disorders. Social attitudes toward people with psychological disorders range from discomfort to prejudice. Language, humor, and stereotypes all portray psychological disorders in a negative light. Stereotypes then result in social discrimination, which only serves to complicate the lives of the affected even more.

- The mental health community currently uses five diagnostic criteria to measure abnormality: 1) clinical significance, 2) psychological, biological, or developmental dysfunction, 3) significant distress or disability, 4) not defined as "deviant" in terms of religion, politics, or sexuality, and 5) socio-political conflicts must reflect dysfunction in the individual in order to be considered psychological disorders. While these five criteria can serve as the basis for defining abnormality, often there is an interaction.

- Causes of abnormality incorporate biological, psychological, and sociocultural factors. Scientists use the term biopsychosocial to refer to the interaction between these factors and their role in the development of an individual's symptoms.

- Three prominent themes in explaining psychological disorders that recur throughout history include 1) spiritual, 2) scientific, and 3) humanitarian. **Spiritual** explanations regard abnormal behavior as the product of possession by evil or demonic spirits. **Humanitarian** explanations view psychological disorders as the result of cruelty, stress, or poor living conditions. **Scientific** explanations look for causes that we can objectively measure, such as biological alterations, faulty learning processes, or emotional stressors.

- Researchers use various methods to study the causes and treatment of psychological disorders. These include 1) the scientific method, which involves a progression of steps from posing questions of interest to sharing the results with the scientific community, 2) experimental design, which tests a hypothesis by constructing a manipulation of a key variable interest, and 3) correlational design, which involves tests of relationships between variables that researchers cannot experimentally manipulate.

- Types of research studies include **surveys, lab studies,** and **case studies.** Surveys enable researchers to estimate the incidence and prevalence of psychological disorders. In a laboratory, participants are exposed to conditions based on the nature of the experimental manipulation. Case studies enable the researcher to intensively study one individual. This can also involve single-subject design, where the researcher studies one person at a time in both the experimental and control conditions, as he or she applies and removes treatment in alternating phases.

- Investigations in the field of behavioral genetics and psychotherapy attempt to determine the extent to which people inherit psychological disorders. Different studies enable researchers to draw inferences about the relative contributions of biology and family environment to the development of psychological disorders, but they are imprecise and have potential serious flaws.

KEY TERMS

Biopsychosocial 8
Case study 20
Concordance rate 20
Dependent variable 14
Double-blind 15
Gene mapping 22
Humanitarian 9

Incidence 19
Independent variable 14
Molecular genetics 22
Placebo condition 15
Positive psychology 13
Prevalence 19
Qualitative research 20

Scientific 9
Single case experimental
 design (SCED) 20
Spiritual 9
Stigma 8
Survey 17

Diagnosis and Treatment

OUTLINE

Learning Objectives

2.1 Describe the experiences of the client and the clinician

2.2 Assess the strengths and weaknesses of the *DSM* approach to psychological disorders

2.3 Identify the *International Classification of Diseases (ICD)*

2.4 Explain steps of the diagnostic process

2.5 Describe treatment planning and goals

2.6 Explain the course and outcome of treatment

CHAPTER 2

Case Report: Peter Dickinson

Demographic information: 28-year-old Caucasian male.

Presenting problem: Peter's girlfriend of one year, Ashley, referred him to an outpatient mental health clinic. He is in his second year of working as a defense attorney at a small law firm. Ashley reported that about six months ago, Peter's parents began divorce proceedings, at which point she noticed some changes in his behavior. Although his job had always been challenging, Peter was a hard worker who devoted himself to his studies throughout his academic career and had been just as motivated at his current job. Since the divorce, however, Ashley reported that Peter had only been sleeping a few hours a night and was having trouble keeping up with his caseload at work. It had gotten so bad that the firm considered firing him.

When he was seen at the psychotherapy clinic, Peter reported that the past six months had been very difficult for him. Although he stated he had always been a "worrier," he couldn't get his parents' divorce off his mind, and it was interfering with his ability to focus and perform well at his job. He described most of the worried thoughts as fears that his parents' divorce would destroy their lives as well as his. He stated that he would worry that somehow their divorce was his fault, and that once the thought entered his mind, it would play on repeatedly like a broken record. He also explained that Ashley had threatened to break up with him if he didn't "get it together," about which he was also spending a great deal of time worrying. He stated that he constantly worried that he had ruined her life and that this thought was also very repetitive.

Peter was noticeably anxious and irritable throughout the session, especially when talking about his parents or about Ashley. Early in the session, he expressed that he had been feeling very tense all day and that his stomach was "in knots." Throughout the session, his legs and hands were fidgety, and he stood up and sat down in his chair several times. He stated that since starting his new job, he had become very short-tempered with people, and often felt "wired" and tense, and as a result had a difficult time concentrating on his work and sleeping soundly. He explained that he couldn't remember the last time he felt calm or didn't worry about anything for an entire day. He also stated that he could barely think about anything other than his parents' divorce and his relationship problems with Ashley, even if he tried to get his mind off it. He reported that prior to learning of his parents' divorce, he was mainly "obsessive" about his work, which he noted was similar to how he was as an undergraduate and in law school. He stated that he was usually afraid that he would make an error, and would spend more time worrying about failing than actually doing his work. As a result, he said, he often had little time for friends or romantic relationships because he would feel guilty if he were engaging in pleasurable activities rather than focusing on his work. A serious relationship of four years ended after his ex-girlfriend grew tired of what she had called his "obsession" with working and his neglect of their relationship. Currently, faced with losing his job and another important relationship, Peter stated that he realizes for the first time that his anxiety might be interfering with his life.

Relevant history: Peter reported that his mother had a history of panic attacks and his father had taken anxiety medication, though he was unable to recall any further details of his family history. He stated that since he could remember he had "always" felt anxious and often worried about things more than other people. He remembered a particular instance in high school when he barely slept for two weeks because he was preparing for an argument for his school's debate team. Peter stated he has never had any psychotherapy or taken any psychiatric medication. He reported that although his worrying often makes him feel "down," he has never felt severely depressed and has no history of suicidal ideation.

Symptoms: Difficulty sleeping through the night, restlessness, difficulty concentrating, irritability. Peter stated that he found it difficult to control the worry and he spent most of his time worrying about either his parents' divorce, work, or his relationship with Ashley.

Case formulation: Peter meets all of the required *DSM-5* criteria for Generalized Anxiety Disorder (GAD). He had been displaying excessive worry for more days than not for at least the past six months, was unable to control his worry, and presented four of the six main

symptoms associated with GAD. Additionally, Peter's worry was not related to fears of having a panic attack (as in Panic Disorder), or about being in social or public situations (as in Social Anxiety Disorder). His anxiety was causing him significant problems at work and in his relationship with Ashley. Finally, Peter's anxiety was not the result of substance use.

Treatment plan: Peter's treatment plan will involve a combination of two approaches. First, he will be referred to a psychiatrist for antianxiety medication to ease the physical symptoms of his anxiety. Cognitive behavioral psychotherapy will also be recommended, as this has been shown to be the most effective current therapeutic modality for treating GAD.

Sarah Tobin, Ph.D.
Clinician

Peter's life was thrown into havoc by the worsening of his anxiety symptoms, putting him at risk of losing his job and his relationship. Dr. Tobin's treatment plan suggests a set of steps to address Peter's immediate symptoms and ultimately to bring him longer-term relief. In this chapter, you will learn about how clinicians proceed through the steps of diagnosis and treatment planning. In order to help you understand these steps, we will introduce you to the fundamental concepts that guide these key processes.

2.1 Psychological Disorder: Experiences of Client and Clinician

psychologist
Health care professional offering psychological services.

client
A person seeking psychological treatment.

Psychologists are health care professionals offering psychological services. Those working in the field of abnormal psychology examine not only the causes of abnormal behavior, but also the complex human issues involved in the therapeutic process. Throughout this text, you will read many cases of individual **clients** who seek treatment to alleviate their symptoms so they can lead more fulfilling lives. We begin this exploration by introducing you to the relevant players of "client" and "clinician."

The Client

patient
In the medical model, a person who receives treatment.

People working in the area of abnormal psychology refer to individuals seeking psychological intervention as **"client"** and **"patient."** In this book, our preference is to use the term *client,* reflecting the view that the people in treatment collaborate with those who treat them. We feel that the term *patient* carries with it the connotation of a passive rather than active participant. However, there are times when it is appropriate to use the term *patient* such as in the context of "outpatient treatment" and "patients' rights."

In this context, we wish to point out that you should definitely avoid some terminology and call people with psychological disorders by the name of their disorder. If you call someone a "schizophrenic" you are equating the person with the disorder. Instead, you will show greater sensitivity if you refer to the individual as "a person with schizophrenia." People are more than the sum of their disorders. By using your language carefully, you communicate greater respect for the total person.

The Clinician

In this book, we refer to the person providing treatment as the **clinician.** There are many types of clinicians who approach clinical work in a variety of ways, based on their training and orientation. **Psychiatrists** are people with degrees in medicine (MDs) who receive specialized advanced training in diagnosing and treating people with psychological disorders. **Clinical psychologists** have an advanced degree in the field of psychology and are trained in diagnosis and therapy. Clinical psychologists cannot administer medical treatments, but some U.S. states, such as Louisiana and New Mexico, as of 2011, grant them prescription privileges. Other states are also pushing to pass similar legislation.

There are two types of doctorates in psychology. The doctor of philosophy (PhD) is typically awarded for completing graduate training in research. In order to be able to practice, people who get their PhD's in clinical psychology also complete an internship. The doctor of psychology (PsyD) is the degree that professional schools of psychology award and typically involves less training in research. These individuals also must complete an internship in order to practice. Counseling psychologists, with either a doctorate in education (EdD) or (PhD) also serve as clinicians.

A trusting, positive relationship between therapist and client is crucial to a good therapeutic outcome.

Professionals with master's degrees also provide psychological services. These include social workers, master's-level counselors, marriage and family therapists, nurse clinicians, and school psychologists. The mental health field also includes a large group of individuals who do not have graduate-level training but serve a critical role in the functioning and administration of the mental health system. Included in this group are occupational therapists, recreational therapists, and counselors who work in institutions, agencies, schools, and homes.

clinician
The person providing treatment.

psychiatrists
People with degrees in medicine (MDs) who receive specialized advanced training in diagnosing and treating people with psychological disorders.

clinical psychologist
A mental health professional.

2.2 The Diagnostic Process

In order to treat psychological disorders, clinicians must first be able to diagnose them. The diagnostic process requires, in turn, that clinicians have a systematic approach to classifying the disorders they see in their clients. A diagnostic manual serves to provide consistent diagnoses across people based on the presence or absence of a set of specific symptoms. Without an accurate diagnostic manual, it is impossible for the clinician to decide on the best treatment path for a given client. Researchers also use diagnostic manuals to provide investigators with consistent terminologies to use when reporting their findings.

The profession uses two factors in evaluating a diagnostic manual's ability to do its job. The first is **reliability,** meaning that practitioners will apply the diagnoses consistently across individuals who have a particular set of symptoms. A manual would not be very useful if the symptom of sad mood led one clinician to assign a diagnosis of some sort of depressive disorder and another to assign a diagnosis of some type of anxiety disorder. The second factor is **validity,** meaning that the diagnoses represent real and distinct clinical phenomena.

Current diagnostic manuals are based on the medical model in that they focus on accurately labeling groups of symptoms with the intention of providing targeted treatments. Not everyone in the mental health system is comfortable with this model. Those who object note that the current diagnostic systems assume that there is a recognizable distinction between normality and abnormality. In addition, by labeling a collection of behaviors as constituting a "disease," manual use can heighten the tendency to stigmatize those whose behavior falls outside the norm.

reliability
When used with regard to diagnosis, the degree to which clinicians provide diagnoses consistently across individuals who have a particular set of symptoms.

validity
The extent to which a test, diagnosis, or rating accurately and distinctly characterizes a person's psychological status.

What's New in the DSM-5

Changes in the DSM-5 Structure

All editions of the *DSM* have generated considerable controversy, and the fifth edition seems to be no exception. The most significant changes concerned the multiaxial system—the categorization of disorders along five separate axes. The *DSM-5* task force decided to eliminate the *DSM-IV-TR* multiaxial system and instead follow the system in use by the World Health Organization's *International Classification of Diseases (ICD)*. Axis I of the *DSM-IV-TR* contained major "syndromes," or illness clusters. Axis II contained diagnoses of personality disorders and what was then called mental retardation. Axis III was used to note the client's medical conditions. Axis IV rated the client's psychosocial stresses, and Axis V rated the client's overall level of functioning. The task forces also considered using a dimensional model instead of the categorical model represented by *DSM-IV-TR*. However, in the end, they chose not to do so. The current organization begins with neurodevelopmental disorders and then proceeds through "internalizing" disorders (characterized by anxiety, depressive, and somatic symptoms) to "externalizing" disorders (characterized by impulsive, disruptive conduct and substance use symptoms). The hope is that eventually there will be new research allowing future diagnostic manuals to be based on underlying causes rather than symptoms alone.

Despite these criticisms, mental health professionals must rely on diagnostic systems if for no other reason than to allow their clients to receive treatment in hospitals and reimbursement from health care providers. Insurance companies utilize the diagnostic codes they provide to determine payment schedules for both in-hospital and outpatient care.

It is worthwhile to be alert to the criticisms of these diagnostic systems, particularly since they serve as a reminder that it is the person, and not the disease, that clinicians aim to help.

Clinicians use the standard terms and definitions contained in the ***Diagnostic and Statistical Manual of Mental Disorders (DSM)*** published by the American Psychiatric Association. We have organized this text according to the most recent version, which is the *DSM-5*, or fifth edition (American Psychiatric Association, 2013). The *DSM-IV* organized diagnoses using five separate axes. It defined an **axis** as a category of information regarding one dimension of an individual's functioning. The **multiaxial system** in the *DSM-IV-TR* was intended to allow professionals to characterize clients in a multidimensional way. In addition, *DSM-5* contains a "Section III," which includes assessment measures and diagnoses not considered well-established enough to be part of the main system. These diagnoses may become incorporated into the next edition of *DSM-5* or a "*DSM-5.1*," should clinical and research data support their inclusion.

Diagnostic and Statistical Manual of Mental Disorders (DSM)

A book published by the American Psychiatric Association that contains standard terms and definitions of psychological disorders.

axis

A class of information in *DSM-IV* regarding an aspect of the individual's functioning.

multiaxial system

A multidimensional classification and diagnostic system in the *DSM-IV-TR* summarizing relevant information about an individual's physical and psychological functioning.

International Classification of Diseases (ICD)

The diagnostic system of the World Health Organization (WHO)

The Diagnostic and Statistical Manual (DSM-5)

DSM-5 is divided into 22 chapters that include sets of related disorders. The chapters are organized so that related disorders appear closer to each other. Psychological and biological diseases often relate to each other. A number of diagnoses in *DSM-5* have embedded within them a medical diagnosis such as a neurological disease that produces cognitive symptoms. However, if an illness that is primarily medical is not specified in *DSM-5*, clinicians may specify such conditions using the standard *ICD* diagnoses for those conditions. You can read examples of disorders in each category in Table 2.1.

Most mental health professionals outside the United States and Canada use the World Health Organization's (WHO) diagnostic system, which is the ***International Classification of Diseases (ICD)***. WHO developed the *ICD* as an epidemiological tool. With a common diagnostic system, the 110 member nations can compare illness rates and have assurance that countries employ the same terminology for the sake of consistency. The tenth edition *(ICD-10)* is currently in use; it is undergoing a major revision, and WHO projects that *ICD-11* will be available no earlier than 2014. The *ICD* is available in WHO's six official languages (Arabic, Chinese, English, French, Russian, and Spanish), as well as in 36 other languages.

Additional Information

The *DSM-IV-TR* contained a separate "axis," or dimension for specifying the client's physical illnesses. By specifying the client's physical illnesses, the clinician transmits information that has important therapeutic implications. For example, a person with chronic

TABLE 2.1 Disorders in DSM-5

Category	Description	Examples of diagnoses
Neurodevelopmental disorders	Disorders that usually develop during the earlier years of life, primarily involving abnormal development and maturation	Autism spectrum disorder Specific learning disorder Attention-deficit hyperactivity disorder
Schizophrenia spectrum and other psychotic disorders	Disorders involving symptoms of distortion in perception of reality and impairment in thinking, behavior, affect, and motivation	Schizophrenia Brief psychotic disorder
Bipolar and related disorders	Disorders involving elevated mood	Bipolar disorder Cyclothymic disorder
Depressive disorders	Disorders involving sad mood	Major depressive disorder Persistent depressive disorder
Anxiety disorders	Disorders involving the experience of intense anxiety, worry, fear, or apprehension	Panic disorder Agoraphobia Specific phobia Social anxiety disorder
Obsessive-compulsive and related disorders	Disorders involving obsessions and compulsions	Obsessive-compulsive disorder Body dysmorphic disorder Hoarding disorder
Trauma and stressor-related disorders	Responses to traumatic events	Post-traumatic stress disorder Acute stress disorder Adjustment disorder
Dissociative disorders	Disorders in which the normal integration of consciousness, memory, sense of self, or perception is disrupted	Dissociative identity disorder Dissociative amnesia
Somatic symptom disorders	Disorders involving recurring complaints of physical symptoms that may or may not be associated with a medical condition	Illness anxiety disorder Functional neurological symptom disorder
Feeding and eating disorders	Disorders characterized by severe disturbances in eating behavior	Anorexia nervosa Bulimia nervosa Binge eating disorder
Elimination disorders	Disorders involving bladder and bowel disturbances	Enuresis (bladder) Encopresis (bowel)
Sleep-wake disorders	Disorders involving disturbed sleep patterns	Insomnia disorder Narcolepsy
Sexual dysfunctions	Disorders involving disturbance in the expression or experience of sexuality	Erectile disorder Female orgasmic disorder Premature ejaculation
Gender dysphoria	Mismatch between biological sex and gender identity	Gender dysphoria
Disruptive, impulse-control, and conduct disorders	Disorders characterized by repeated expression of impulsive or disruptive behaviors	Kleptomania Intermittent explosive disorder Conduct disorder
Substance-related and addictive disorders	Disorders related to the use of substances	Substance use disorders Substance-induced disorders

TABLE 2.1 (Continued)

Neurocognitive disorders	Disorders involving impairments in thought processes caused by substances or medical conditions	Mild neurocognitive disorder Major neurocognitive disorder
Personality disorders	Disorders in an individual's personality	Borderline personality disorder Antisocial personality disorder Narcissistic personality disorder
Paraphilic disorders	Disorder in which a paraphilia causes distress and impairment	Pedophilic disorder Fetishistic disorder Transvestic disorder
Other mental disorders	Conditions or problems for which a person may seek professional help	Other specified mental disorder due to another medical condition
Medication-induced movement disorders and other adverse effects of medication	Disturbances that can be traced to use of medication	Tardive dyskinesia Medication-induced postural tremor
Other conditions that may be a focus of clinical attention	Conditions or problems for which a person may seek medical help	Problems related to abuse or neglect Occupational problem

SOURCE: Reprinted with permission from the *Diagnostic and Statistical Manual of Mental Disorders*, Fifth Edition. Copyright © 2013 American Psychiatric Association.

heart disease should not receive certain psychiatric medications. In addition, knowing about a client's medical condition can provide important information about the mental disorder's etiology, which is its presumed cause. It would be useful to know that a middle-aged man appearing in treatment for a depressive disorder for the first time had a heart attack six months ago. The heart attack may have constituted a risk factor for the development of depression, particularly in a person with no previous psychiatric history.

In providing a total diagnostic picture of the client's psychological disorder, clinicians may also decide it is important to specify particular stressors that are affecting the individual's psychological status. In these cases, clinicians can use a set of codes in the *ICD* that indicate the presence of psychosocial and environmental problems known as "Z" codes. These may be important because they can affect the diagnosis, treatment, or outcome of a client's psychological disorder. A person first showing signs of an anxiety disorder shortly after becoming unemployed presents a very different diagnostic picture than someone whose current life circumstances have not changed at all in several years. For the most part, environmental stressors are negative. However, we might consider positive life events, such as a job promotion, as stressors. A person who receives a major job promotion may encounter psychological difficulties due to his or her increased responsibilities and demands with the new position. We have selected several examples of *ICD-10 Z* codes for Table 2.2.

Clinicians may want to include their overall judgment of a client's psychological, social, and occupational functioning. An instrument known as the WHO Disability Assessment Schedule (WHODAS) is included as a section of the *DSM-5* so clinicians can provide such a rating. We provide 12 of the questions from the WHODAS in Table 2.3.

Culture-Bound Syndromes

culture-bound syndromes
Recurrent patterns of abnormal behavior or experience that are limited to specific societies or cultural areas.

Within particular cultures, there are idiosyncratic patterns of symptoms, many of which have no direct counterpart to a specific *DSM-5* diagnosis. **Culture-bound syndromes** are behavior patterns that exist only within particular cultures. To qualify as a culture-

TABLE 2.2 Examples from Z Codes in *ICD-10*

Problem	Examples
Problems related to education and literacy	Underachievement in school
Problems related to employment and unemployment	Change of job Sexual harassment on the job Military deployment status
Problems related to housing and economic circumstances	Homelessness Extreme poverty Low income
Problems related to social environment	Acculturation difficulty
Other problems related to primary support group, including family circumstances	Problems in relationship with spouse Disappearance and death of family member Alcoholism and drug addiction in family
Problems related to certain psychosocial circumstances	Unwanted pregnancy

SOURCE: http://www.icd10data.com/ICD10CM/Codes/Z00-Z99/Z55-Z65

bound syndrome, the symptoms must not have any clear biochemical or physiological sources. Only that particular culture, and not others, recognizes the symptoms of a culture-bound syndrome. Table 2.4 describes examples of some of the best-studied culture-bound syndromes.

TABLE 2.3 Questions on the WHODAS

In the past 30 days, how much difficulty did you have in:		None	Mild	Moderate	Severe	Extreme or cannot do
S 1	Standing for long periods such as 30 minutes?	1	2	3	4	5
S 2	Taking care of your household responsibilities?	1	2	3	4	5
S 3	Learning a new task, for example, learning how to get to a new place?	1	2	3	4	5
S 4	How much of a problem did you have joining in community activities (for example, festivities, religious or other activities) in the same way as anyone else can?	1	2	3	4	5
S 5	How much have you been emotionally affected by your health problems?	1	2	3	4	5
S 6	Concentrating on doing something for ten minutes?	1	2	3	4	5
S 7	Walking a long distance such as a kilometre [or equivalent]?	1	2	3	4	5
S 8	Washing your whole body?	1	2	3	4	5
S 9	Getting dressed?	1	2	3	4	5
S 10	Dealing with people you do not know?	1	2	3	4	5
S 11	Maintaining a friendship?	1	2	3	4	5
S 12	Your day to day work/school?	1	2	3	4	5

SOURCE: http://www.who.int/classifications/icf/WHODAS2.0_12itemsINTERVIEW.pdf

TABLE 2.4 Examples of Culture-Bound Syndromes

Certain psychological disorders, such as depression and anxiety, are universally encountered. Within particular cultures, however, idiosyncratic patterns of symptoms are found, many of which have no direct counterpart to a specific diagnosis. These conditions, called culture-bound syndromes, are recurrent patterns of abnormal behavior or experience that are limited to specific societies or cultural areas.

This table describes some of the best-studied culture-bound syndromes and forms of distress that may be encountered in clinical practice in North America, as well as the *DSM-IV-TR* categories they most closely resemble.

Term	Location	Description
Amok	Malaysia	Dissociative episode consisting of brooding followed by violent, aggressive, and possibly homicidal outburst. Precipitated by insult; usually seen more in males. Return to premorbid state following the outburst.
Ataque de nervios	Latin America	Distress associated with uncontrollable shouting, crying, trembling, and verbal or physical aggression. Dissociation, seizure, and suicidal gestures possible. Often occurs as a result of a stressful family event. Rapid return to premorbid state.
Bilis and colera	Latin America	Condition caused by strong anger or rage. Marked by disturbed core body imbalances, including tension, trembling, screaming, and headache, stomach disturbance. Chronic fatigue and loss of consciousness possible.
Bouffée délirante	West Africa and Haiti	Sudden outburst of agitated and aggressive behavior, confusion, and psychomotor excitement. Paranoia and visual and auditory hallucinations possible.
Brain fag	West Africa	Difficulties in concentration, memory, and thought, usually experienced by students in response to stress. Other symptoms include neck and head pain, pressure, and blurred vision.
Dhat	India	Severe anxiety and hypochondriacal concern regarding semen discharge, whitish discoloration of urine, weakness, and extreme fatigue.
Falling out or blacking out	Southern United States and the Caribbean	A sudden collapse, usually preceded by dizziness. Temporary loss of vision and the ability to move.
Ghost sickness	American Indian tribes	A preoccupation with death and the deceased. Thought to be symbolized by bad dreams, weakness, fear, appetite loss, anxiety, hallucinations, loss of consciousness, and a feeling of suffocation.
Hwa-byung (wool-hwa-byung)	Korea	Acute feelings of anger resulting in symptoms including insomnia, fatigue, panic, fear of death, dysphoria, indigestion, loss of appetite, dyspnea, palpitations, aching, and the feeling of a mass in the abdomen.
Koro	Malaysia	An episode of sudden and intense anxiety that one's penis or vulva and nipples will recede into the body and cause death.
Latah	Malaysia	Hypersensitivity to sudden fright, usually accompanied by symptoms including echopraxia (imitating the movements and gestures of another person), echolalia (irreverent parroting of what another person has said), command obedience, and dissociation, all of which are characteristic of schizophrenia.

Term	Location	Description
Mal de ojo	Mediterranean cultures	Means "the evil eye" when translated from Spanish. Children are at much greater risk; adult females are at a higher risk than adult males. Manifested by fitful sleep, crying with no apparent cause, diarrhea, vomiting, and fever.
Pibloktog	Arctic and sub-Arctic Eskimo communities	Abrupt dissociative episode associated with extreme excitement, often followed by seizures and coma. During the attack, the person may break things, shout obscenities, eat feces, and behave dangerously. The victim may be temporarily withdrawn from the community and report amnesia regarding the attack.
Qi-gong psychotic reaction	China	Acute episode marked by dissociation and paranoia that may occur following participation in qi-gong, a Chinese folk health-enhancing practice.
Rootwork	Southern United States, African American and European populations, and Caribbean societies	Cultural interpretation that ascribes illness to hexing, witchcraft, or sorcery. Associated with anxiety, gastrointestinal problems, weakness, dizziness, and the fear of being poisoned or killed.
Shen-k'uei or *Shenkui*	Taiwan and China	Symptoms attributed to excessive semen loss due to frequent intercourse, masturbation, and nocturnal emission. Dizziness, backache, fatigue, weakness, insomnia, frequent dreams, and sexual dysfunction. Excessive loss of semen is feared, because it represents the loss of vital essence and therefore threatens one's life.
Shin-byung	Korea	Anxiety and somatic problems followed by dissociation and possession by ancestral spirits.
Spell	African American and European American communities in the southern United States	Trance state in which communication with deceased relatives or spirits takes place. Sometimes connected with a temporary personality change.
Susto	Latinos in the United States and Mexico, Central America, and South America	Illness caused by a frightening event that causes the soul to leave the body. Causes unhappiness, sickness (muscle aches, stress headache, and diarrhea), strain in social roles, appetite and sleep disturbances, lack of motivation, low self-esteem, and death. Healing methods include calling the soul back into the body and cleansing to restore bodily and spiritual balance.
Taijin kyofusho	Japan	Intense fear that one's body parts or functions displease, embarrass, or are offensive to others regarding appearance, odor, facial expressions, or movements.
Zar	Ethiopia, Somalia, Egypt, Sudan, Iran, and other North African and Middle Eastern societies	Possession by a spirit. May cause dissociative experiences characterized by shouting, laughing, hitting of one's head against a hard surface, singing, crying, apathy, withdrawal, and change in daily habits.

2.3 Steps in the Diagnostic Process

The diagnostic process involves using all relevant information to arrive at a label that characterizes the client's disorder. This information includes the results of any tests given to the client, material gathered from interviews, and knowledge about the client's personal history. Clinicians use the first phase of working with clients to gather this information prior to proceeding with the treatment itself.

Diagnostic Procedures

Key to diagnosis is gaining as clear a description as possible of a client's symptoms, both those that the client reports and those that the clinician observes. Dr. Tobin, when hearing Peter describe himself as "anxious," immediately assumes that he *may* have an anxiety disorder. However, clients do not always label their internal states accurately. Therefore, the clinician also must attend carefully to the client's behavior, emotional expression, and apparent state of mind. The client may express anxiety, but his behavior may suggest that instead he is experiencing a mood disorder.

Clinicians first listen to clients as they describe the experience of their symptoms, but they must next follow this up with a more systematic approach to diagnosis. As you will learn in Chapter 3, a variety of assessment tools give the clinician a framework for determining the extent to which these symptoms coincide with the diagnostic criteria of a given disorder. The clinician must determine the exact nature of a client's symptoms, the length of time the client has experienced these symptoms, and any associated symptoms. In the process, the clinician also obtains information about the client's personal and family history. By asking questions in this manner, the clinician begins to formulate the **principal diagnosis**—namely, the disorder most closely aligned with the primary reason the individual is seeking professional help.

For many clients, the symptoms they experience reflect the presence of more than one principal diagnosis. In these cases, we use the term **comorbid,** meaning literally two (or more) disorders. Comorbidity is remarkably common. A major investigation, known as the National Comorbidity Survey (NCS), showed that over half of respondents with one psychiatric disorder also had a second diagnosis at some point in their lives. The most common comorbidities involve drug and/or alcohol abuse with other psychiatric disorders.

Differential diagnosis, the ruling out of alternative diagnoses, is a crucial step in the diagnostic process. It is important for the clinician to eliminate the possibility that the client is experiencing a different disorder or perhaps an additional disorder. Peter states that he is anxious, and his symptoms suggest the disorder known as "general anxiety disorder," but Dr. Tobin needs to consider whether this diagnosis best suits his symptoms or not. It is possible that Peter suffers from panic disorder, another anxiety disorder involving the experience of panic attacks. His symptoms may also suggest social anxiety disorder. Alternatively, he might be suffering from adjustment difficulties following the divorce of his parents or the stress of his job. He may even have a substance use disorder, an undiagnosed medical condition, or even a third disorder. Dr. Tobin's initial diagnosis must be tested against these possibilities during the assessment period of treatment.

The diagnostic process can take anywhere from a few hours to weeks depending on the complexity of the client's presenting symptoms. The client and clinician may accomplish therapeutic work during this time, particularly if the client is in crisis. For example, Dr. Tobin will start Peter on antianxiety medications right away to help him feel better. However, her ultimate goal is to arrive at as thorough an understanding as possible of Peter's disorder. This paves the way for her to work with Peter throughout the treatment process.

principal diagnosis
The disorder that is considered to be the primary reason the individual seeks professional help.

comorbid
The situation that occurs when multiple diagnostic conditions occur simultaneously within the same individual.

differential diagnosis
The process of systematically ruling out alternative diagnoses.

Case Formulation

Once the clinician makes a formal diagnosis, he or she is still left with a formidable challenge—to piece together a picture of how the disorder evolved. With the diagnosis, the clinician can assign a label to the client's symptoms. Although informative, this label does not tell the client's full story. To gain a full appreciation of the client's disorder, the clinician develops a **case formulation**: an analysis of the client's development and the factors that might have influenced his or her current psychological status. The case formulation provides an analysis that transforms the diagnosis from a set of code numbers to a rich piece of descriptive information about the client's personal history. With this descriptive information, the clinician can design a treatment plan that is attentive to the client's symptoms, unique past experiences, and future potential for growth.

Understanding the client from a developmental perspective is crucial to provide a thorough case formulation. In Dr. Tobin's work with Peter, she will flesh out the details of her case formulation as she gets to know him better in the initial therapy phases. Her case formulation will expand to include Peter's family history, focusing on the divorce of his parents, as well as the possible causes of his perfectionism and concern over his academic performance. She will try to understand why he feels so overwhelmed at work and gain a perspective on why his relationship with Ashley has been so problematic. Finally, she will need to investigate the possible role of his mother's panic attacks and how they relate to Peter's experience of anxiety symptoms. To aid in differential diagnosis, Dr. Tobin will also evaluate Peter's pattern of substance use as well as any possible medical conditions that she did not detect during the initial assessment phase.

case formulation
A clinician's analysis of the factors that might have influenced the client's current psychological status.

Cultural Formulation

Clinicians need to account for the client's cultural background in making diagnoses. A **cultural formulation** includes the clinician's assessment of the client's degree of identification with the culture of origin, the culture's beliefs about psychological disorders, the ways in which the culture interprets particular events, and the cultural supports available to the client.

We might expect cultural norms and beliefs to have a stronger impact on clients who strongly identify with their culture of origin. The client's familiarity with and preference for using a certain language is one obvious indicator of cultural identification. A culture's approach to understanding the causes of behavior may influence clients who strongly identify with their culture. Exposure to these belief systems may influence the expression of a client's symptoms.

Even if a client's symptoms do not represent a culture-bound syndrome, clinicians must consider the individual's cultural framework as a backdrop. Members of a given culture attach significant meanings to particular events. For example, within certain Asian cultures, an insult may provoke the condition known as *amok*, where a person (usually male) enters an altered state of consciousness in which he becomes violent, aggressive, and even homicidal. In Peter's case, although he is a product of middle-class white background, it is possible that cultural factors are influencing his extreme preoccupation with his academic performance. Perhaps his family placed pressure on him to succeed due to their own incorporation of belief in the importance of upward mobility. They may have pressured him heavily to do well in school, and as a result, he felt that his self-worth as an individual depended on his grades. As an adult, he is unable to shake himself from this overly harsh set of values.

Clinicians should look within the client's cultural background as a way of determining available cultural supports. Clients from certain cultures, particularly Black,

cultural formulation
Includes the clinician's assessment of the client's degree of identification with the culture of origin, the culture's beliefs about psychological disorders, the ways in which the culture interprets particular events, and the cultural supports available to the client.

Symptoms of psychological disorders often vary based on the culture the individual belongs to.

Hispanic, Latino, and Asian, have extended family networks and religion, which provide emotional resources to help individuals cope with stressful life events.

Cultural formulations are important to understanding psychological disorders from a biopsychosocial perspective. The fact that psychological disorders vary from one society to another supports the claim of the sociocultural perspective that cultural factors play a role in influencing the expression of abnormal behavior.

Psychologists are increasingly gaining education in training in working within the multicultural framework to take into account not only a client's race and ethnicity, but also age, gender, sexual orientation, and disability status, among others (American Psychological Association, 2002). Through such education, clinicians can learn how to adapt not only their diagnostic methods more generally but to adopt a multicultural approach throughout treatment.

2.4 Planning the Treatment

treatment plan
The outline for how therapy should take place.

Clinicians typically follow up the diagnosis phase by setting up a **treatment plan,** the outline for how therapy should take place. In the treatment plan, the clinician describes the treatment goals, treatment site, modality of treatment, and theoretical approach. The decisions the clinician makes while putting the treatment plan together reflect what he or she knows at the time about the client's needs and the available resources. However, clinicians often revise the treatment plan once they see how the proposed intervention methods are actually working.

Goals of Treatment

The first step in treatment planning is for the clinician to establish treatment goals, ranging from immediate to long term. Ideally, treatment goals reflect what we know about both the disorder and the recommended therapy, and the particular needs and concerns of the individual client.

The immediate goal of treating clients in crisis is to ensure that their symptoms are managed, particularly if they are at risk to themselves or others. Peter, for example,

You Be the Judge

Psychologists as Prescribers

In 2002, New Mexico became the first state to approve prescription privileges for psychologists. Louisiana followed shortly thereafter, passing similar legislation in 2004. These landmark pieces of legislation are paving the way for other states to take similar action. However, the question remains controversial. In 2010, the Oregon legislature passed a bill (SB 1046) granting prescriptive authority to psychologists, but Governor Ted Kulongoski vetoed the bill, in response to pressure from various lobbying groups, including psychiatrists.

There are several arguments against the granting of prescription privileges to psychologists. Unlike psychiatrists, psychologists do not receive medical training and therefore do not have the undergraduate pre-medical training or the years of medical school, internship, and residency that physicians receive. Philosophically, research-oriented psychologists argue that the granting of prescription privileges takes away from the notion that psychologists are scientists as well as practitioners. Psychologists should not be in the business, they argue, of handing out medication. A second argument against prescription privileges concerns the role of medication in psychological treatment. From this perspective, psychologists should be focused on psychotherapy. The long-term benefits of psychotherapy, these critics argue, are equal to if not greater than the long-term benefits of medication for the majority of disorders including major depression, anxiety disorders, and other nonpsychotic disorders. In the exceptional cases of serious mental illness, such as schizophrenia and bipolar disorder, psychologists can work as a team with psychiatrists to maintain their clients on long-term medication regimens.

The arguments in favor of prescription privileges are also compelling. If psychologists have the power to prescribe medications, they can do a better job than psychiatrists do integrating medication into psychotherapy. From the client's point of view, there is greater continuity of care, in that the individual does not need to see more than one mental health practitioner. Psychologists in favor of prescription privileges also point to the fact that specialized training is required for a clinical psychologist to be able to prescribe medications aimed at psychological disorders. Therefore, the psychologists who do prescribe have an equal knowledge base as do physicians. A second argument in favor of prescription privileges is that there are other nondoctoral level health professionals with this legal power including psychiatric nurse practitioners and psychiatric nurse specialists, among others, although the exact nature of their privileges varies across states.

The American Psychological Association's Practice Directorate continues to lobby in favor of more widespread acceptance of prescription privileges across the United States. However, as the Oregon case demonstrates, this legislation is likely to face a rocky road in other states.

Q: *You be the judge:* Does having prescription privileges reduce the scientific status of psychology as a profession? Would you prefer that the psychologist you might see for treatment can also incorporate medications into your treatment?

---

needs psychiatric treatment in order to bring his anxiety symptoms under control. The clinician may need to hospitalize a client who is severely depressed and suicidal. The treatment plan may only include this immediate goal until the clinician gains a broader understanding of the client's situation.

Short-term goals are aimed at alleviating the client's symptoms by addressing problematic behavior, thinking, or emotions. The plan at this point might include establishing a working relationship between the clinician and client, as well as setting up specific

At this crisis center, telephone counselors are available 24 hours a day.

objectives for therapeutic change. Another short-term goal might be to stabilize a client taking medications, a process that might take as long as several weeks or longer if the first round of treatment is unsuccessful. In Peter's case, Dr. Tobin will need to ensure that the medications he is receiving are in fact helping to alleviate his anxiety. She will also need to work with the psychiatrist to monitor any adverse side effects. Her short-term goals with Peter will also include beginning to examine the nature of his anxiety and how he can start to manage his symptoms using psychological interventions.

Long-term goals include more fundamental and deeply rooted alterations in the client's personality and relationships. These are the ultimate aims of therapeutic change. Ideally, the long-term goals for any client are to cope with the symptoms of the disorder and to develop a strategy to manage them, if not achieve complete recovery. Depending on the nature of the client's disorder, available supports, and life stress, these long-term goals may take years to accomplish. Dr. Tobin's long-term goals with Peter are to take him off the medication. At the same time, she would plan to help him gain an understanding of the causes of his symptoms, and in the process, reduce their severity if not eliminate them altogether.

In many cases, clinicians carry out treatment goals in a sequential manner. First the clinician deals with the crisis, then handles problems in the near future, and finally addresses issues that require extensive work well into the future. However, many clients experience a cyclical unfolding of stages. New sets of immediate crises or short-term goals may arise in the course of treatment. Or there may be a redefinition of long-term goals as the course of treatment progresses. It is perhaps more helpful to think of the three stages not as consecutive stages per se, but as implying different levels of treatment focus.

Treatment Site

Clinicians juggle a number of issues when recommending which treatment site will best serve the client. Treatment sites vary in the degree to which they provide a controlled environment and in the nature of the services that clients will receive. Clients who are in crisis or are at risk of harming themselves or others need to be in controlled environments. However, there are many other considerations including cost and insurance coverage, the need for additional medical care, availability of community support, and the projected length of treatment. In some cases, clinicians recommend client treatment in outpatient settings, schools, or the workplace.

Psychiatric Hospitals In a psychiatric hospital, a client receives medical interventions and intensive forms of psychotherapy. These settings are most appropriate for clients at risk of harming themselves or others and who seem incapable of self-care. In some cases, clinicians may involuntarily hospitalize clients through a court order until they can bring the symptoms under control (we will discuss this in more detail in Chapter 15).

Specialized Inpatient Treatment Centers Clients may need intensive supervision, but not actual hospital care. For these individuals, specialized inpatient treatment centers provide both supportive services and round-the-clock monitoring. These sites include recovery treatment centers for adults seeking to overcome substance

Community treatment centers, like this one, provide much needed care to individuals with a wide range of psychological disorders.

addiction. Clinicians may also recommend this treatment site to children who need constant monitoring due to severe behavioral disturbances.

Outpatient Treatment By far, the most common treatment site is a private therapist's outpatient clinic or office. **Community mental health centers (CMHCs)** are outpatient clinics that provide psychological services on a sliding fee scale for individuals who live within a certain geographic area. Professionals in private practice offer individual or group sessions. Some prepaid health insurance plans cover the cost of such visits, either to a private practitioner or to a clinician working in a health maintenance organization (HMO). Agencies supported partially or completely by public funds may also offer outpatient treatment. Dr. Tobin will see Peter in outpatient treatment because his symptoms are not sufficiently severe to justify hospitalization.

Clients receiving outpatient services will, by necessity, receive more limited care than what they would encounter in a hospital, in terms of both the time involved and the nature of the contact between client and clinician. Consequently, clinicians may advise that their clients receive additional services, including vocational counseling, in-home services, or the support of a self-help organization, such as Alcoholics Anonymous.

Halfway Houses and Day Treatment Programs Clients with serious psychological disorders who are able to live in the community may need the additional support that they will receive in sites that are intended to serve the needs of this specific population. These facilities may be connected with a hospital, a public agency, or a private corporation. **Halfway houses** are designed for clients who have been discharged from psychiatric facilities, but who are not yet ready for independent living. A halfway house provides a living context with other deinstitutionalized people, and it is staffed by professionals who work with clients in developing the skills they need to become employed and to set up independent living situations. **Day treatment programs** are designed for formerly hospitalized clients as well as for clients who do not need hospitalization, but do need a structured program during the day, similar to what a hospital provides.

Other Treatment Sites Clinicians may recommend that their clients receive treatment in the places where they work or go to school. School psychologists are

community mental health center (CMHC)
Outpatient clinic that provides psychological services on a sliding fee scale to serve individuals who live within a certain geographic area.

halfway house
A community treatment facility designed for deinstitutionalized clients leaving a hospital who are not yet ready for independent living.

day treatment program
A structured program in a community treatment facility that provides activities similar to those provided in a psychiatric hospital.

Guidance counselors are often the first professionals to whom troubled students turn for professional assistance.

modality
Form in which the clinician offers psychotherapy.

individual psychotherapy
Psychological treatment in which the therapist works on a one-to-one basis with the client.

family therapy
Psychological treatment in which the therapist works with several or all members of the family.

group therapy
Psychological treatment in which the therapist facilitates discussion among several clients who talk together about their problems.

milieu therapy
A treatment approach, used in an inpatient psychiatric facility, in which all facets of the milieu, or environment, are components of the treatment.

trained to work with children and teenagers who require further assessment or behavioral interventions. In the workplace, Employee Assistance Programs (EAP) provide employees with a confidential setting in which they can seek individual treatment in the form of counseling, assistance with substance abuse, and family treatment. These resources may prove important for clinicians who wish to provide their clients with as many resources over the long term as possible.

Modality of Treatment

The **modality,** or form in which the clinician offers psychotherapy, is another crucial component of the treatment plan. Clinicians recommend one or more modalities depending on the nature of the client's symptoms and whether or not other people in the client's life should be involved.

Clients receive treatment on a one-to-one basis in **individual psychotherapy.** In couples therapy, both partners in a relationship, and in **family therapy,** several or all family members are involved in treatment. In family therapy, family members may identify one person as the "patient." The therapist, however, views the whole family system as the target of the treatment. **Group therapy** provides a modality in which clients who face similar issues can openly share their difficulties with others, receive feedback, develop trust, and improve their interpersonal skills.

A clinician may recommend any or all of these modalities in any setting. Specific to psychiatric hospitals is **milieu therapy,** which is based on the premise that the milieu, or environment, is a major component of the treatment. Ideally, the milieu is organized in a way that allows clients to receive consistently therapeutic and constructive reactions from all who live and work there. In addition to traditional psychotherapy, clients participate in other therapeutic endeavors through group or peer counseling, occupational therapy, and recreational therapy.

Milieu therapy involves many patients participating within a community setting.

Determining the Best Approach to Treatment

Whatever treatment modality a clinician recommends, it must be based on the choice of the most appropriate theoretical perspective or combination of perspectives. Many clinicians are trained according to a particular set of assumptions about the origins of psychological disorders and the best methods of treating these disorders. Often, this theoretical orientation forms the basis for the clinician's treatment decisions. However, just as frequently, clinicians adapt their theoretical orientation to fit the client's needs.

After decades of debate regarding which treatments are most effective, and for whom, psychologists adopted the principles of **evidence-based practice in psychology**—clinical decision making that integrates the best available research evidence and clinical expertise in the context of the cultural background, preferences, and characteristics of clients (American Psychological Association Presidential Task Force on Evidence-Based Practice, 2006). In other words, clinicians should base their treatments on state-of-the-art research findings that they adapt to the particular features of the client, taking into account the client's background, needs, and prior experiences. Clinicians currently use these criteria as the basis for curricula in graduate programs and postdoctoral continuing education (Collins, Leffingwell, & Belar, 2007).

As you read in this book about various disorders and the most effective treatments, it will be important to keep in mind the empirical basis for the treatment conclusions. Findings from efficacy studies shed light on appropriate interventions, but they are insufficient for conclusively determining what is most effective with real people with complex problems.

evidence-based practice in psychology
Clinical decision making that integrates the best available research evidence and clinical expertise in the context of the cultural background, preferences, and characteristics of clients.

2.5 The Course of Treatment

The way treatment proceeds is a function of the clinician's and client's contributions. Each has a part to play in determining the outcome of the case, as does the unique interaction of their personalities, abilities, and expectations.

The Clinician's Role in Treatment

Above and beyond whatever techniques a clinician uses to treat a client's problems, the quality of the relationship between the client and clinician is a crucial determinant of whether therapy will succeed or not. A good clinician does more than objectively administer treatment to a client. The best clinicians infuse a deep personal interest, concern, and respect for the client into the therapeutic relationship. Dr. Tobin will work with Peter in the initial weeks of therapy to establish this solid basis for their further work together.

The Client's Role in Treatment

In optimal situations, psychotherapy is a joint enterprise in which the client plays an active role. It is largely up to the client to describe and identify the nature of his or her disorder, to describe personal reactions as treatment progresses, and to initiate and follow through on changes.

The client's attitudes toward therapy and the therapist are an important part of the contribution the client makes to the therapeutic relationship. There is a special quality to the help that the client is requesting; it involves potentially painful, embarrassing, and personally revealing material that the client is not accustomed to disclosing to someone else. Most people are much more comfortable discussing their medical, legal, financial, and other problems outside the realm of emotions. Social attitudes toward psychological disorders also play a role. People may feel that they should be able to handle their emotional problems without seeking help. They may believe that, if they can't solve their

REAL STORIES

Daniel Johnston: Bipolar Disorder

"Wherever I am, I have music in my heart."

Daniel Johnston, born on January 22, 1961, is an American singer-songwriter well known for his unique musical talent as well as his lifelong struggle with bipolar disorder. The 2005 documentary, *The Devil and Daniel Johnston*, depicts his incredible story from childhood in West Virginia to the present day. Though Daniel has had an extraordinary musical career, his tumultuous journey with mental illness is not unlike that of many other individuals who suffer from severely debilitating psychological disorders. Through his music, Daniel expresses both the soaring, sometimes delusional manias and the dark, unbearable depths of depression he has faced throughout his life.

The youngest of five children, Daniel's mother, Mabel, recalls that ". . . he was different . . . I noticed that from the start." As a teenager, inspired mostly by comic books, he took on countless artistic endeavors including drawing and making playful movies about his life at home. His creativity helped him gain attention from friends and classmates, but also endlessly frustrated his highly religious and traditional parents, who would rather he spend his time attending church, working, and helping out around the house. Daniel's passion for creating has remained with him his entire life. In the words of Daniel's best friend, David Thornberry, "He exudes art . . . he can't stop making art."

As with many individuals with severe mood disorders, Daniel's behavior began to change for the worse after leaving home for college. His family was used to him acting differently than his peers, but in college Daniel started to become confused and disoriented. A visit to the family physician resulted in a diagnosis of manic-depression (bipolar disorder). Unable to continue with the challenges he faced at school, he returned home and enrolled in a small arts college in nearby Ohio. In art school, Daniel met and subsequently fell in love with his classmate Laurie. Though they never had a romantic relationship and she went on to marry another man, Daniel's unrequited love for her has been one of his most powerful creative muses and also caused his first major depressive episode. It was at this point, his mother recalls, that he began to play the piano and write songs.

Daniel was having trouble in his courses at art school, and so his family once again took him out of school. This time they sent him to live with his older brother in Houston, in hopes that he could start building a productive life. Daniel worked part-time at a local amusement park and began recording music in his brother's garage. After his brother grew frustrated that Daniel was not finding stable work, he sent him to live with his sister, Margie. One morning, Margie noticed that Daniel had never returned home the night before. His family did not hear from Daniel for months; when they did, they learned that he had spontaneously purchased a moped and joined a traveling carnival. When the carnival stopped in Austin, Texas, Daniel was assaulted on the fair grounds and fled to a local church for help. He was able to find housing in Austin and began taking his homemade tape-recorded albums to local musicians and newspapers. One of the local musicians he met was Kathy McCarthy. The two briefly dated, and after meeting him, Kathy remembers, "It was undeniable after one or two weeks that something was dreadfully wrong with him."

In one scene of *The Devil and Daniel Johnston*, he reads a detailed account of the characteristics of an individual with his condition, stating, "There you have it. I'm a manic depressive with grand delusions." The majority of his delusions were paranoid and religious in nature, perhaps the result of his highly religious upbringing. Although Daniel was well aware of his illness, at the time he was doing little to assuage it. In Austin, Daniel began to smoke marijuana and regularly experimented with LSD, causing several bizarre and sometimes violent episodes. Simultaneously, Daniel's music career began to blossom as he gained recognition as well as notoriety for his music and his often bizarre live performances.

In 1986, a Christmas gathering with his siblings soon turned into a horrifying event. Daniel began preaching about Satan to his family, and began attacking his brother,

Daniel Johnston's songs provide a glimpse into his struggles with mental illness.

breaking his rib. Frightened by his behavior, and unsure of what to do, his siblings drove him to a nearby bus station. Soon after, the police discovered Daniel at the University of Austin, splashing in the middle of a pond and again preaching about Satan. It was at this point that his friends and family began to realize that, as one friend put it, "he was a really sick person." While his music had been a way for him to filter the demons in his mind, Daniel's illness was beginning to wreak havoc on his life, and drastic measures were necessary to ensure he did no further harm to others or to himself. Doctors prescribed Daniel the antipsychotic medication, Haldol, and he spent the entire year of 1987 in bed (what he called his "lost year"). Although he was stabilized, Daniel found himself unable to write any music during this period. Indeed, throughout his life and like many individuals with bipolar disorder, Daniel often struggled with

medication compliance. He felt that he was better at creating and performing when his mind was allowed to run free rather than be confined to the numbness he felt while on medication.

Because he often went off his medication, Daniel experienced a five-year whirlwind of breakdowns that cycled between delusional mania and clinical depression, resulting in numerous hospitalizations that lasted months at a time. When first going off his medication, Daniel's behavior and mood were normal for up to a few days until he would quickly and unexpectedly take a turn for the bizarre. In one particular instance, Daniel had stopped taking his medication before playing to a large auditorium for a music festival in Austin, Texas. The appearance was one of the most acclaimed performances of his career. Shortly afterwards however, when he and his father boarded the two-person plane to take them home

to West Virginia, Daniel seized the controls from his father, sending their plane crashing toward the ground. Luckily, Daniel's father was able to regain control of the plane in time, and they survived after landing on a treetop. Daniel's father now recalls that at the time Daniel believed he was Casper (from the children's cartoon about Casper the friendly ghost), and that taking over the plane was a heroic act.

Since that dark period of his life, Daniel has been stable in large part because of his supportive network of family and friends. He lives with his parents in Waller, Texas, and continues to write music and tour around the world. Many regard Daniel Johnston as one of the most brilliant singer-songwriters in American history. His heartbreaking battle with mental illness has been a destructive yet inspiring force in his work that blurs the line between artistic creativity and mental illness.

---

own emotional problems, it means they are immature or incompetent. Moreover, having to see a clinician may make a person believe that he or she is "crazy." Although attitudes toward therapy are becoming more accepting in current Western culture, there is still a degree of potential shame or embarrassment that clients must confront.

Most people would, though, feel less inclined to mention to acquaintances that they are in psychotherapy for personal problems. The pressure to keep therapy secret usually adds to a client's anxiety about seeking professional help. To someone who is already troubled by severe problems in living, this added anxiety can be further inhibiting. With so many potential forces driving the individual away from seeking therapy, the initial step is sometimes the hardest to take. Thus, the therapeutic relationship requires the client to be willing to work with the clinician in a partnership and to be prepared to endure the pain and embarrassment involved in making personal revelations. Moreover, it also requires a willingness to break old patterns and to try new ways of viewing the self and relating to others.

2.6 The Outcome of Treatment

In the best of all possible worlds, the treatment works. The client remains in treatment until the treatment runs its course, shows improvement, and maintains this improved level of functioning. Many times, though, the road is not so smooth, and either the client does not attain the treatment plan goals or unanticipated problems arise.

Clinicians find it particularly frustrating when their clients do not seem willing to follow through on their desire to change. Change is very difficult, and many clients have become so accustomed to living with their symptoms that the necessary effort to solve the problem seems overwhelming. At times, clinicians also face frustration over financial constraints. They may recommend a treatment that they are confident can succeed, but that is financially infeasible. In other cases, people in the client's life refuse to participate in the treatment, even though they play central roles. Other pragmatic issues can disrupt therapy: Clients may move, lose jobs, or lack consistent transportation to the clinic. Over time, those in the mental health field learn that they are limited in how effective they can be in changing the lives of people who go to them for help. However, as you will learn in this book, therapy is usually effective and the majority of treatments do result in significant improvement.

Return to the Case: Peter Dickinson

Peter was prescribed antianxiety medication through the psychiatrist at the mental health clinic. Within four weeks, he reported that he was able to sleep through the night and was feeling less restless. His psychotherapy focused on relaxation techniques such as deep breathing as well as cognitive techniques such as labeling and challenging his worrying, and coming up with various ways to cope with stress rather than worrying excessively. Therapy was also helpful for Peter to discuss and sort through his feelings about his parents' divorce, and to understand how his anxiety affected his romantic relationships.

Dr. Tobin's reflections: Typical of many individuals with GAD, Peter has always felt like a constant "worrier," but this anxiety was recently aggravated by a stressful event: his parents' divorce. Additionally, his lack of sleep was likely contributing to his difficulty with the concentration that is necessary for keeping up with the standards of work required by his career. Since he had been doing well at work up until this point, he may not have felt that his anxiety was a problem. His anxiety may have also gone unnoticed due to the intense pressure and sacrifice that face all individuals who work in Peter's career area. It was clear however, that Peter worried about many issues to a greater degree than do others in his situation. At the time he presented for treatment, however, it was clear that his inability to control his worry over his parents and his girlfriend were causing major problems in his work and social life. Not only that, but his past anxiety had caused problems that he did not recognize at that time. For many people who suffer from GAD, the longer it goes untreated the worse it may get. Fortunately for Peter, his girlfriend recognized that he was struggling and was able to obtain help for his overwhelming anxiety. I am pleased with the progress of therapy so far, and am hopeful that given his many strengths, Peter will be able to manage his symptoms through the psychological methods over which he is gaining mastery. Peter has the potential to be a successful lawyer, and given the strength of his relationship with Ashley, I am hopeful that he will be able to turn his life around with only a slight chance of re-experiencing these symptoms.

SUMMARY

- The field of abnormal psychology goes beyond the academic concern of studying behavior. It encompasses the large range of human issues involved when a client and a clinician work together to help the client resolve psychological difficulties.

- People working in the area of abnormal psychology use both "**client**" and "**patient**" to refer to those who use psychological services. Our preference is to use the term "client," reflecting the view that clinical interventions are a collaborative endeavor.

- The person providing the treatment is the **clinician.** There are many types of clinicians who approach clinical work in a variety of ways based on training and orientation. These include psychiatrists, clinical psychologists, social workers, counselors, therapists, and nurses. The field also includes those who do not have graduate-level training. These include occupational therapists, recreational therapists, and counselors who work in institutions, agencies, schools, and homes.

- Clinicians and researchers use the *Diagnostic and Statistical Manual of Mental Disorders,* fifth edition (*DSM-5*) which contains descriptions of all psychological disorders. In recent editions, the authors of the *DSM* have strived to meet the criterion of reliability so that a clinician can consistently apply a diagnosis to anyone showing a particular set of symptoms. At the same time, researchers have worked to ensure the validity of the classification system so that the various diagnoses represent real and distinct clinical phenomena.

- The *DSM-5* presents diagnoses organized into 22 chapters. The classification system is descriptive rather than explanatory, and it is categorical rather than dimensional.

- The diagnostic process involves using all relevant information to arrive at a label that characterizes a client's disorder. Key to diagnosis is gaining as clear a description as possible of a client's symptoms, both those that the client reports and those that the clinician observes. **Differential diagnosis,** the ruling out of alternative diagnoses, is a crucial step in the diagnostic process.

- To gain full appreciation of the client's disorder, the clinician develops a **case formulation:** analysis of the client's development and the factors that might have influenced his or her current psychological status.

- A **cultural formulation** accounts for the client's cultural background in making diagnoses.

- **Culture-bound syndromes** are behavior patterns that we find only within particular cultures.

- Clinicians typically follow up the diagnosis phase by setting up a **treatment plan,** the outline for how therapy should take place. The first step in a treatment plan is for the clinician to establish treatment goals, ranging from immediate to long-term.

- Treatment sites vary in the degree to which they provide a controlled environment and in the nature of the services that clients receive. These include psychiatric hospitals, specialized inpatient treatment centers, outpatient treatment ranging from a private therapist's outpatient clinic or office, or a community-based mental health center. Other treatment sites include halfway houses, day treatment programs, or places of work or school.

- **Modality,** or the form in which one offers psychotherapy, is also a crucial component of the treatment plan. It can be **individual, family, group,** or **milieu** therapy. Whatever treatment of modality a clinician recommends, it must be based on the choice of the most appropriate theoretical or combination of perspectives.

- In optimal situations, psychotherapy is a joint enterprise in which clients play an active role. In the best of all possible worlds, the client remains in treatment until the treatment runs its course, and the client shows improvement and maintains the improved level of functioning. While not always successful, therapy is usually effective, and the majority of treatments do result in significant improvement.

KEY TERMS

Assessment

Learning Objectives

3.1   Define key concepts of assessment

3.2   Describe clinical interviews

3.3   Identify mental status examination

3.4   Explain intelligence testing

3.5   Describe personality testing

3.6   Recognize behavioral assessment

3.7   Identify multicultural assessment

3.8   Explain neuropsychological assessment

3.9   Describe neuroimaging

CHAPTER 3

Case Report: Ben Robsham

Reason for referral: Ben is a 22-year-old Caucasian male with 12 years of formal education who was referred to the clinic by his supervisor following an incident in which he hit his head while operating a subway train. While driving above ground, Ben reported that the brakes had jammed while he was coming to an intersection where pedestrians were crossing. Using the emergency brake, Ben was able to stop the train, but the abrupt halt caused him to hit his head on the glass window and temporarily lose consciousness. He is unable to recall what happened directly after hitting his head. Ben took a two-week leave of absence after the incident, and continued to avoid going to work for the two following weeks. When the supervisor called him, Ben stated, "I can't leave my house. They'll come and get me."

Relevant history: Ben has no history of psychiatric treatment. He stated that he has never experienced depression or anxiety, and that he typically feels "just fine," which has made the recent changes in his psychological state all the more disturbing to him. Ben reported that he has never used drugs and only occasionally drinks when he is in a social environment. Additionally, Ben reported that his maternal grandfather and uncle had both been diagnosed with schizophrenia. Finally, Ben reported having no remarkable past or current medical history.

Case formulation: Because Ben's symptoms emerged following the incident, Ben will be referred for neuropsychological testing to rule out possible traumatic brain injury.

Diagnosis: Rule out mild neurocognitive disorder due to traumatic brain injury with behavioral disturbance.

Treatment plan: After an initial intake interview at the university, Ben was referred for further psychological evaluation and psychiatric consultation to Dr. Martin Washington, a neuropsychologist. The tests administered by Dr. Washington are in Table 3.1.

Sarah Tobin, PhD
Referring Clinician

TABLE 3.1 Tests Administered to Ben

Clinical Interview
Wechsler Adult Intelligence Scale, Fourth Edition (WAIS-IV)
Trail-Making Test, Parts A and B
Clock Drawing Test
Paced Auditory Serial Addition Test (PASAT)
Boston Naming Test, Second Edition (BNT)
Wechsler Memory Scale (WMS)
Minnesota Multiphasic Personality Inventory-2 (MMPI-2)

3.1 Characteristics of Psychological Assessments

psychological assessment

A broad range of measurement techniques, all of which involve having people provide scorable information about their psychological functioning.

A **psychological assessment** is a procedure in which a clinician provides a formal evaluation of an individual's cognitive, personality, and psychosocial functioning. As you will see in Ben's case, a comprehensive assessment proved valuable in helping to understand the nature of his symptoms and potential directions for treatment.

Clinicians conduct assessments under a variety of conditions. In many cases, clinicians use the assessment process to provide a diagnosis, or at least a tentative diagnosis, of an individual's psychological disorder. However, clinicians may also use assessments for a variety of other reasons. For example, in forensic assessments, clinicians determine whether a suspect meets the criteria of being competent to stand trial. Clinicians might also provide information that employers can use to evaluate an individual's appropriateness for a particular job. Assessments are also useful when clinicians consult about an individual's level of functioning in a specific area. An older woman experiencing memory problems may seek neuropsychological assessment to determine whether she has a cognitive impairment that will require further intervention.

For Ben, the assessment process is critical to understanding the nature of his current symptoms. The clinician must evaluate the potential roles of both brain injury and what may have been the appearance of symptoms unrelated to the train incident. His immediate treatment plan and his long-term psychological development will depend on the outcome of the evaluation. Dr. Tobin provided an initial evaluation, and as a result of this assessment, she decided to refer Ben to a neuropsychologist.

To be useful, clinicians must hold assessments to standards that ensure that they provide the most reproducible and accurate results. The reliability of a test indicates the consistency of the scores it produces. In other words, it should produce the same results regardless of when it is given, and the individual should answer test items in similar fashion. The test's validity reflects the extent to which a test measures what it is designed to measure. An intelligence test should measure intelligence, not personality. Before using a given test, clinicians should be aware of its reliability and validity, information that is readily available in the published literature about the instrument.

standardization

A psychometric criterion that clearly specifies a test's instructions for administration and scoring.

The profession strives to design tests so that the results they produce don't vary from clinician to clinician. The criterion of **standardization** clearly specifies a test's instructions for administration and scoring. Each individual receiving the test should have the same amount of time, and each person scoring the test should do so in the same manner according to the same, predefined criteria. Furthermore, a given score on the test that one person obtains should have a clear meaning. Ideally, the test's designers have a substantial enough database against which to compare each test-taker's scores.

A patient completes a visual-spatial task as part of a neuropsychological assessment.

In addition to determining a test's reliability and validity, it is important to take into account its applicability to test-takers from a diversity of backgrounds. Increasingly, test publishers are designing their measures for usage with a variety of individuals in terms of ability level, first language, cultural background, and age. For example, clinicians may need to adapt assessment instruments for use with older adults, who may require larger print, slower timing, or special writing instruments for use with those who have arthritis (Edelstein, Martin, & McKee, 2000). Even so, clinicians need to ensure that they are using the most appropriate instrument for a given client.

When interpreting test results, clinicians need to ensure that they don't fall into the trap of the so-called "Barnum Effect." Named after legendary circus owner P. T. Barnum, this is the tendency for clinicians unintentionally to make generic and vague statements about their clients that do not specifically characterize the client. Here's an example of a Barnum Effect statement: "Julia is often shy around other people, but at times she can be very outgoing. When presented with a challenge, she can often perform very well, but she occasionally becomes nervous and intimidated." These two sentences *could* apply to Julia, but they could also apply to most other people. Therefore, they don't say anything special about Julia. Furthermore, most people would find it difficult to disagree with this feedback. You are most likely to encounter the Barnum Effect in situations such as reading your horoscope or a fortune cookie, which are written so generally that they could apply to anyone. These are relatively harmless situations, unless you decide to invest a great deal of money on the basis of such an unreliable prognosticator. In a clinical situation, the problem is that such statements are not particularly insightful or revealing and do not help inform the assessment process.

Clinicians should keep up with the literature to ensure that they are using the best assessment methods possible. Evidence-based assessment includes (1) relying on research findings and scientifically viable theories; (2) using psychometrically strong measures; and (3) empirically evaluating the assessment process (Hunsley & Mash, 2007). By following these guidelines, clinicians ensure that they will evaluate their clients using the most current and appropriate materials available. For example, a seasoned clinician may have a preference for using the assessment methods she learned about in graduate school, but she should be constantly alert for newer procedures that rely on newer technology or research. According to criterion (3), she should also develop evaluation methods to assess whether her assessments are providing useful information about her clients.

For example, consider the case of an assessment suggesting that a client is experiencing significant depressive symptoms even though she seeks help for what she describes as attacks of anxiety. Following the criteria for evidence-based assessment, the clinician would determine whether the tool or tools she used to make the diagnosis provided an accurate characterization of the woman's symptoms as they evolved over the course of treatment. Similarly, in Ben's case, the clinician must validate the findings from neuropsychological assessment carefully by obtaining multiple measures to assess possible brain injury.

3.2 Clinical Interview

Clinicians typically begin their assessment with the **clinical interview,** a series of questions that they administer in face-to-face interaction with the client. The answers the client gives to these questions provide important background information on clients, allow them to describe their symptoms, and enable clinicians to make observations of their clients that can guide decisions about the next steps, which may include further testing.

The least formal version of the clinical interview is the **unstructured interview,** which consists of a series of open-ended questions regarding the client's symptoms, health status, family background, life history, and reasons for seeking help. In addition to noting the answers to these questions, the clinician also observes the client's body language. By noting the client's nonverbal cues, the clinician can gain an understanding of whether the client is experiencing, for example, anxiety, attentional difficulties, unwillingness to cooperate, or unusual concern about testing. The clinician may also use cues from the client's appearance that give further indication of the client's symptoms, emotional state, or interpersonal difficulties. The typical clinical interview covers the areas outlined in Table 3.2. The clinician can vary the order of questions and the exact wording he or she used to obtain this information.

In Ben's case, the clinical interview provided Dr. Tobin with key information about his history including not only his educational and vocational background, but also his relationship history. She determined that, prior to the incident, he enjoyed engaging with others, so his current isolation is a change from his previous pattern of social functioning.

clinical interview
A series of questions that clinicians administer in face-to-face interaction with the client.

unstructured interview
A series of open-ended questions aimed at determining the client's reasons for being in treatment, symptoms, health status, family background, and life history.

TABLE 3.2 Areas Covered in a Clinical Interview

Topic	Purpose
Age and sex	Obtain basic demographic information.
Reason for referral	Hear client's reason for seeking treatment, in his or her own words.
Education and work history	Obtain socioeconomic status and determine whether client is still working.
Current social situation	Find out whether client is currently in a relationship and how much social support is potentially available.
Physical and mental health history	Determine whether client has any medical illnesses and whether there has been a recent change in health. Find out about history of present problem including past diagnoses and treatments and whether treatment was helpful or not.
Drug/alcohol use and current medication	Ascertain whether client is using psychoactive drugs (including alcohol and caffeine). Obtain list of medications to avoid potential interactions with any psychopharmacological interventions.
Family history	Find out whether client's family has medical and psychological disorders, particularly any relevant to client's current symptoms.
Behavioral observations	Note behaviors, including nonverbal behaviors, which indicate whether client is experiencing anxiety or altered mood. Also note whether client seems to be experiencing difficulties in attention or compliance. Attempt to determine client's mental status. Compare client's appearance with stated age. Determine whether client is oriented to time, place, and person. Observe any unusual motor behaviors.

Dr. Washington obtained more detailed information from his clinical interview with Ben. Upon further questioning about his symptoms, Ben stated that he has difficulty concentrating, but that his main symptom is the occurrence of "very strange thoughts" that have been quite troubling to him. Specifically, he feels too afraid to leave his apartment because he believes that the police will apprehend and arrest him as punishment for "what [he] did." He worries that others blame him for killing people in the incident and that if he returned to work the passengers would turn on him, thus resulting in his apprehension. He states that he spends several hours a day worrying about the consequences of the incident and sometimes hears accusatory voices blaming him for hurting people and telling him that he is a "monster." He reported that he has only heard these voices a few times in the past four weeks. As it turned out, no one was injured in the incident.

Though Ben reports that he feels distressed about his recent psychological problems, he stated that he had no thoughts of hurting or killing himself. Ben also reported that he has been unable to get a full night's sleep since the incident. At times he is unable to fall asleep, and when he does, frequent nightmares awaken him about the incident, and he feels that those he believes he killed in the incident are "haunting" him.

Ben stated that although he was worried about what he had been experiencing recently, he had been too embarrassed to tell anyone, worrying that he was "going crazy." As he had not spent time with friends or family, and had not been to work, the people in his life had been unaware of the extent of his psychological problems following the incident. Ben took a leave of absence for the first two weeks following the incident and has since been calling in sick daily. When the suggestion of psychological testing came up, Ben reports that he was hoping that it might help reveal the nature of his troubling symptoms.

As you can see, the clinical interview is a key step in the diagnostic process because of the information it provides regarding the client's current symptoms, history, and availability of social support. In addition, Dr. Washington used the interview as an opportunity to establish rapport with Ben. Over the course of a 30- to 45-minute interview, the clinician must help the client feel as relaxed as possible. Because the client is providing highly personal information, the clinician attempts to draw the client out with questioning that is respectful, but also matter-of-fact. The clinical interview is not like an ordinary conversation in that respect.

Unlike the clinical interview, the **structured interview** provides standardized questions that are worded the same way for all clients. A structured interview can either provide a diagnosis on which to further base treatment or classify the client's symptoms into a *DSM* disorder.

One of the most widely used clinical interviews is the **Structured Clinical Interview for *DSM-IV* Disorders (SCID),** presented in Table 3.3. Though the title uses the word "Structured," clinicians who administer the SCID modify the wording and order of questions to accommodate the particular individual whom they are examining. Clinicians use the SCID-I to make Axis I diagnoses and the SCID-II to make Axis II diagnoses. Both SCIDs are designed so that the clinician can adapt to the interviewee's particular answers. The questions are worded in standard form, but the interviewer chooses which questions to ask based on the client's answers to previous questions. For example, if a client states that she experiences symptoms of anxiety, the interviewer would follow up with specific questions about these symptoms. The interviewer would only ask follow-up questions if

structured interview
A standardized series of assessment questions, with a predetermined wording and order.

Structured Clinical Interview for *DSM-IV* Disorders (SCID)
A widely used clinical interview.

TABLE 3.3 Example of SCID Questions for Current Major Depressive Episode

Current Major Depressive Episode	MDE Criteria				
Now I am going to ask you some more questions about your mood	A. Five (or more) of the following symptoms have been present during the same two-week period and represent a change from previous functioning; at least one of the symptoms is either (1) depressed mood, or (2) loss of interest or pleasure.				
In the last month . . . . . . has there been a period of time when you were feeling depressed or down most of the day nearly every day? (What was that like?) If yes: How long did it last? (As long as two weeks?)	(1) depressed mood most of the day, nearly every day, as indicated either by subjective report (e.g., feels sad or empty) or observation made by others (e.g., appears tearful).	?	1	2	3
. . . what about losing interest or pleasure in things you usually enjoyed? If Yes: Was it nearly every day? How long did it last? (As long as two weeks?)	(2) markedly diminished interest or pleasure in all, or almost all, activities most of the day, nearly every day (as indicated either by subjective account or observation made by others).	?	1	2	3

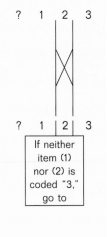

If neither item (1) nor (2) is coded "3," go to

Note: When rating the following items, code "1" if clearly due to a general medical condition, or to mood-incongruent delusions or hallucinations

SOURCE: First, M. B., & Gibbon, M. (2004). "The structured clinical interview for *DSM-IV* Axis I Disorders (SCID-I) and the structured clinical interview for *DSM-IV* Axis II Disorders (SCID-II). In M. J. Hilsenroth & D. L. Segal (Eds.), *Comprehensive handbook of psychological assessment*, Vol. 2: *Personality assessment*. (pp. 134–143). Hoboken, NJ: John Wiley & Sons Inc.

the client stated that she was experiencing anxiety symptoms. If she stated that she had different symptoms, such as depressed mood, then the follow-up questions would inquire further about her mood (First & Gibbon, 2004). The SCID-I takes 45 to 90 minutes to administer, depending on the complexity of the client's symptoms.

An advantage of a structured interview is that it is a systematic approach that is less subject to variations from clinician to clinician than an unstructured interview. Furthermore, anyone with the proper training can administer the SCID, not necessarily just licensed mental health professionals. This has practical value in that clients can receive initial screening prior to their beginning a course of therapy. Furthermore, there is a research version of the SCID that professionals can use to provide systematic diagnostic information across different investigations. Researchers can feel confident that an SCID-based diagnosis of a mood disorder means the same thing regardless of who conducted the study. A SCID for *DSM-5* is currently under development.

3.3 Mental Status Examination

mental status examination
A method of objectively assessing a client's behavior and functioning in a number of spheres, with particular attention to the symptoms associated with psychological disturbance.

A clinician uses a **mental status examination** to assess a client's current state of mind. In conducting a mental status examination, the clinician assesses a number of features of the client including appearance, attitudes, behavior, mood and affect, speech, thought processes, content of thought, perception, cognition, insight, and judgment. The outcome of the mental status examination is a comprehensive description of how the client looks, thinks, feels, and behaves.

The Mini-Mental State Examination (MMSE) is a structured tool that clinicians use as a brief screening device to assess dementia. The clinician administers a set of short memory tasks and compares the client's scores to established norms. If the client scores below a certain cutoff, the clinician then can (and should) continue to more in-depth testing of potential cognitive impairments.

In Ben's case, Dr. Washington noted that Ben was not experiencing an altered mental state at the time of the interview. He arrived on time and was alert and fully oriented. His conversational speech was normal in tone, rhythm, volume, rate, and prosody. The clinician noted that his receptive language appeared intact, and he was able to understand novel test instructions. However, his general appearance was slightly disheveled (i.e., his clothes were wrinkled and he was unshaven). His affect was appropriate, meaning that his apparent emotional state matched that expected in the situation, though he made a few jokes when he became frustrated during the administration of a test he found difficult. In general, though, throughout testing he cooperated with the examiner and appeared motivated and interested in the tests themselves. Dr. Washington decided not to administer a formal mental status examination. Instead he proceeded directly to further neuropsychological and personality testing.

3.4 Intelligence Testing

Many professions (i.e., mental health, academia, business, government agencies) use intelligence (IQ) tests for a variety of assessments, including overall cognitive evaluation, diagnosis of learning disabilities, determination of giftedness or mental retardation, and prediction of future academic achievement. Clinicians also sometimes use IQ tests in the diagnosis of neurological and psychiatric disorders, in which cases they are a component of a more comprehensive assessment procedure. Finally, human resource departments often use IQ tests in personnel selection to evaluate the potential for employees to perform in specific conditions.

Through intelligence testing, clinicians can obtain standardized scores that allow them to evaluate the cognitive strengths and weaknesses of their clients. The most commonly used intelligence tests in clinical settings are on a one-to-one basis, providing a comprehensive view of the client's abilities to perform a range of perceptual, memory, reasoning, and speeded tasks.

TABLE 3.4 Types of Abilities Assessed by the Stanford-Binet 5 (SB5)

Scale	Definition	Example
Fluid Reasoning	Ability to solve novel problems	Sort picture chips into groups of three
Knowledge	Accumulated fund of general information	Show how to perform a given action
Quantitative Reasoning	Ability to solve problems with numbers or numerical concepts	Count a set of items
Visual-Spatial Reasoning	Ability to analyze spatial relationships and geometric concepts	Assemble puzzle-like forms
Working Memory	Ability to store, transform, and retrieve information in short-term memory	Recall a sequence of taps

SOURCE: Roid & Barram, 2004.

Stanford-Binet Intelligence Test

First developed in the early 1900s by Alfred Binet, the Stanford-Binet is now in its fifth edition, known as the Stanford-Binet 5 (SB5). Children taking this test receive a **deviation intelligence (IQ)** score, calculated by converting their raw scores to standardized scores that reflect where a child stands in relation to others of similar age and gender. The average deviation IQ score is set at 100 with a standard deviation of 15. If a child receives an SB5 IQ score of 115, this means that the child stands at above the IQ of 84 percent of the population.

In addition to yielding an overall IQ score, the SB5 yields scores on measures of scales labeled Fluid Reasoning, Knowledge, Quantitative Reasoning, Visual-Spatial Reasoning, and Working Memory (Table 3.4). These scales are intended to provide greater understanding of the child's cognitive strengths and weaknesses not necessarily conveyed in an overall IQ score.

deviation intelligence (IQ)
An index of intelligence derived from comparing the individual's score on an intelligence test with the mean score for that individual's reference group.

Wechsler Intelligence Scales

The first comprehensive individual test that researchers specifically designed to measure adult intelligence was the Wechsler Adult Intelligence Scale (WAIS). Originally developed in 1939 by David Wechsler as the Wechsler-Bellevue test, the WAIS, first published in 1955, is now in its fourth edition (WAIS-IV) (D. Wechsler, 2008). Researchers subsequently developed parallel tests for children based on the same format as the adult scales. Those currently in use are the Wechsler Intelligence Scale for Children–Fourth Edition (WISC-IV) (D. Wechsler, 2003) and the Wechsler Preschool and Primary Scale of Intelligence–Third Edition (WPPSI-III) (D. Wechsler, 2002).

Wechsler originally sought to develop a tool for use in clinical settings, not just schools. He also believed that it was important to include both verbal and nonverbal tests. Originally he labeled these two categories "Verbal" and "Performance." For many years, clinicians reported the WAIS scores in terms of these two categories of subtests. However, over time it became increasingly evident that these two categorical scores didn't adequately capture the full complexity of intellectual functioning. Thus, the WAIS-III was substantially revised in 2008 to become the WAIS-IV, which now includes new tests and a different scoring system.

The WAIS-IV, like its predecessors and the SB5, produces an overall IQ score based on an age-normed mean of 100 and standard deviation of 15. However, the full scale IQ is not as useful for clinical purposes as are scores on Verbal Comprehension, Perceptual

TABLE 3.5 Scales on the Wechsler Adult Intelligence Scale-IV (WAIS-IV)

Scale	Tests	Type of Item
Verbal Comprehension	Vocabulary	Define the word "barrel"
	Information	How many minutes are there in an hour?
	Comprehension	Why do plants need water?
	Similarities	How are an elephant and a cat alike?
Perceptual Reasoning	Matrix reasoning	Choose which pattern logically follows after a set of patterns
	Visual puzzles	Indicate which pictures of shapes go together in a drawing of a puzzle
	Block design	Arrange a set of blocks so that they reproduce a design
	Picture completion	State what is missing in a picture of a common object
Working Memory	Digit span forward	Recall a series of digits in forward order
	Digit span backward	Recall a series of digits in backward order
	Letter-number sequencing	Recall a set of digits from smallest to largest
		Recall a set of mixed letters and numbers from largest to smallest
Processing Speed	Symbol search	
	Coding	Copy numbers that match symbols into appropriate boxes

Reasoning, Working Memory, and Processing Speed (Table 3.5). The intent of the WAIS-IV is to allow clinicians to examine in more depth the client's cognitive functioning along these key dimensions.

You can think of scores from the WAIS-IV as forming a triangle (see Figure 3.1). At the top is the Full Scale IQ (FSIQ), which reflects general cognitive functioning and is the best

FIGURE 3.1 Structure of the WAIS-IV

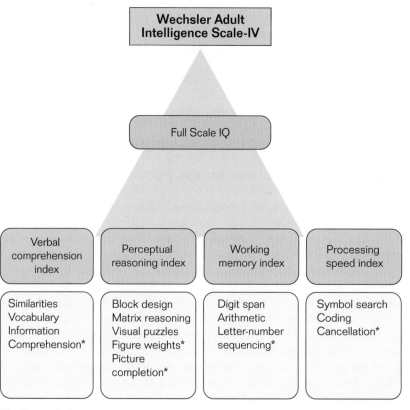

*Supplemental subtest

TABLE 3.6 Ben's WAIS-IV Scores

Full Scale:	115
Verbal Comprehension Index	132
Perceptual Reasoning Index	107
Working Memory Index	111
Processing Speed Index	97

Individual Subtests:

Vocabulary:	15	Picture Completion:	12
Similarities:	17	Coding:	7
Arithmetic:	13	Block Design:	10
Digit Span:	11	Matrix Reasoning:	14
Information:	14	Symbol Search:	12
Comprehension:	18	Figure Weights:	13
Letter-Number Seq.:	10	Visual Puzzles:	10
		Cancellation:	12

single predictor of school achievement on the WAIS-IV. Beneath the FSIQ score at the top of the pyramid are four index scores. Verbal Comprehension Index (VCI) assesses acquired knowledge and verbal reasoning skills. Perceptual Reasoning Index (PRI) measures visual-spatial and fluid reasoning. Working Memory Index (WMI) measures the capacity to hold and process information in memory. Processing Speed Index (PSI) measures the ability to process nonverbal information quickly. Beyond interpreting the index scores, clinicians propose hypotheses about individuals' performance based on an interpretation of clinical clusters, which are comprised of various combinations of individual subscale scores.

Because the WAIS-IV is given on an individual basis, clinicians have ample opportunities to observe the test-taker's behavior during the test, possibly gaining valuable diagnostic information to complement the test scores. In fact, the instructions for the WAIS-IV scoring include suggestions for the examiner to include behavioral observations such as the individual's fluency in English; physical appearance; problems with vision, hearing, or motor behavior; difficulties with attention and concentration; motivation for testing; and any unusual behaviors that the test-taker shows.

Table 3.6 shows Ben's performance on the WAIS-IV. Ben's FSIQ was 115, indicating that he has an above average level of performance (higher than 84 percent of the population). However, if you look across the entire pattern of his scores, you'll notice that Ben demonstrated high variability among the index scores that make up the FSIQ. This type of variability suggests that there is a wide range to Ben's cognitive abilities. The clinician found it noteworthy that Ben's Processing Speed cluster score was low (higher than only 40 percent of the population). This would suggest that Ben struggles with the perception of visual patterns and stimuli, particularly when speed is a factor. The appearance of this low test score where he should have performed well given his job suggests that there may be injury to the areas of his brain involved in processing of spatial information.

While administering the WAIS-IV, Dr. Washington carefully recorded Ben's behaviors, further fleshing out the picture provided by the test scores themselves. Ben stated several times throughout the testing session that "they give you fake confidence early on," referring to his frustration as the test became more difficult. Despite his frustration, Ben remained determined to complete the test. For example, he took nearly six minutes to complete the final Block Design item, and finally stated, "It doesn't make sense—there aren't enough blocks." On the Matrix Reasoning subtest, Ben took nearly one minute for each response toward the end of the task. While completing the Figure Weights subtest, Ben commented on what the shapes in the stimulus book looked like and made several jokes throughout the subtest administration. On the Letter-Number Sequencing task, before giving his response to each item, Ben described how each correlated with the name of a different type of army ship or plane. As the tests became more difficult toward the end of the testing session, Ben appeared visibly restless and began to tap his fingers and tap on his legs. On tasks requiring verbal responses, Ben provided long elaborations, and when the test required a short answer, he would sometimes respond in a sing-song voice.

3.5 Personality Testing

Clinicians use tests of personality to understand a person's thoughts, behaviors, and emotions. There are two main forms of personality tests: self-report and projective. These tests differ in the nature of their items and in the way they are scored.

Self-Report Tests

self-report clinical inventory
A psychological test with standardized questions having fixed response categories that the test-taker completes independently, self-reporting the extent to which the responses are accurate characterizations.

A **self-report clinical inventory** contains standardized questions with fixed response categories that the test-taker completes independently either on paper or on the computer. Test-takers rate the appropriateness of the item to themselves on a fixed scale. These tests are objective in the sense that the scoring does not involve any form of subjective judgment on the part of the examiner. In fact, computers can both score these tests and produce brief explanatory reports. However, clinicians need to balance the advantages of their objectivity against the possibility that these reports are subject to the Barnum Effect. Because computer programs rely on a set of algorithms to produce their reports, they run the risk of being overly generic and not tapered to the particular test-taker's idiosyncrasies.

Nevertheless, a major advantage of self-report inventories is that they are relatively easy to administer and score. Consequently, large numbers of people can take these in an efficient manner. Clinicians can take advantage of the wealth of information on the validity and reliability of the better-known self-report inventories when interpreting the scores of their own clients.

There are literally hundreds of self-report clinical inventories, many of which researchers developed specifically to investigate particular clinical problems or research areas. These inventories can range from a few dozen to several hundred items. As with tests such as the MMPI, clinicians must take care to ensure that the measures meet standards of reliability and validity before interpreting their scores.

The most popular self-report inventory by far is the Minnesota Multiphasic Personality Inventory (MMPI), originally published in 1943. The current version of the test is the 1989 revision known as the MMPI-2 (Table 3.7). There are 567 true-false items on the MMPI-2, which are all in the form of statements that describe the individual's thoughts, behaviors, feelings, and attitudes. The original intent of the MMPI was to provide scores on 10 so-called "clinical scales" corresponding to major diagnostic categories such as schizophrenia, depression, and anxiety. The text developers built an additional 3 "validity" scales into the test in order to guard against people trying to feign either exceptional psychological health or illness.

In the decades after its publication, researchers and clinicians became aware of limitations in MMPI-2 clinical scale scores. They did not correspond to the original clinical categories, meaning that they could not interpret them as the scale's developers originally planned (i.e., a high "Schizophrenia" scale score did not imply that the individual had a diagnosis of schizophrenia). Consequently, MMPI-2 users are incorporating the MMPI's newer, restructured clinical scales (RC's). In fact, the newest version of the MMPI is the MMPI-2-RF, published in 2008 (Table 3.8). The MMPI-RF is based entirely on the restructured scales. Containing only 338 items, this latest version of the MMPI-2 also provides scores for so-called "higher order" factors that indicate a client's overall emotional, cognitive, and behavioral functioning.

TABLE 3.7 Clinical and Validity Scales of the MMPI-2, with Adapted Items

Scale	Scale Name	Type of Content	Adapted Item
Clinical scales			
1	**Hypochondriasis**	Bodily preoccupations and concerns, fear of illness and disease.	I have a hard time with nausea and vomiting.
2	**Depression**	Unhappiness and feelings of low personal worth.	I wish I were as happy as others appear to be.
3	**Hysteria**	Denial of psychological problems and over-reactions to stressful situations, various bodily complaints.	Frequently my head seems to hurt everywhere.
4	**Psychopathic deviate**	Antisocial tendencies and delinquency.	I was occasionally sent to the principal's office for bad behavior.
5	**Masculinity-femininity**	Adoption of stereotypic sex-role behaviors and attitudes.	I like reading romantic tales (female item).
6	**Paranoia**	Feelings of persecution and suspiciousness of others.	I would have been a lot more successful had others not been vindictive toward me.
7	**Psychasthenia**	Uncontrollable urges to think and act; unreasonable fears.	Sometimes I think thoughts too awful to discuss.
8	**Schizophrenia**	Disturbances of thinking, mood, and behavior.	I have had some rather bizarre experiences.
9	**Hypomania**	Elevated mood, accelerated speech and motor activity.	I become excited at least once a week.
10	**Social introversion**	Tendency to withdraw from social situations.	I usually do not speak first. I wait for others to speak to me.
Validity scales (composed of items from clinical scales)			
L	**Lie scale**	Unrealistically positive self-representation	
K	**Correction**	Similar to L scale—more sophisticated indication of tendency toward positive self-presentation	
F	**Infrequency**	Presenting oneself in an unrealistically negative light	

SOURCE: *MMPI*®-2 *(Minnesota Multiphasic Personality Inventory*®-2) Manual for Administration, Scoring, and Interpretation. Copyright © 2001 by the Regents of the University of Minnesota. All rights reserved. Used by permission of the University of Minnesota Press.

TABLE 3.8 Clinical Scales of the MMPI-2-RF

Scale	Scale Name	Type of Content
RCd	Demoralization	General unhappiness and dissatisfaction
RC1	Somatic complaints	Diffuse physical health complaints
RC2	Low positive emotions	Lack of positive emotional responsiveness
RC3	Cynicism	Non self-referential beliefs expressing
RC4	Antisocial behavior	Rule breaking and irresponsible behavior
RC6	Ideas of persecution	Belief that others pose a threat to the self
RC7	Dysfunctional negative emotions	Maladaptive anxiety, anger, and irritability
RC8	Aberrant experiences	Unusual thoughts or perceptions
RC9	Hypomanic activation	Over-activation, aggression, impulsivity, and grandiosity

SOURCE: Ben-Porath, 2010.

The Personality Assessment Inventory (PAI) (Morey, 1992) consists of 344 items organized into 11 clinical scales, 5 treatment scales, 2 interpersonal scales, and 4 validity scales. One advantage of the PAI is that clinicians can use it with clients who may not have the language or reading skills to complete the MMPI-2. A second advantage is that, unlike the MMPI, one calculates the validity scale independently of any of the content scales.

The SCL-90-R (Derogatis, 1994) measures the test-taker's current experiencing of 90 physical and psychological symptoms. One advantage of the SCL-90-R is that it focuses on the client's current status rather than asking about symptoms over a previous period of time. Consequently, clinicians can track the progress of their clients over multiple occasions.

Less oriented toward clinical use is the NEO Personality Inventory (Revised) (NEO-PI-R)(Costa & McCrae, 1992), a 240-item questionnaire that measures five personality

FIGURE 3.2 Ben's MMPI-2 profile

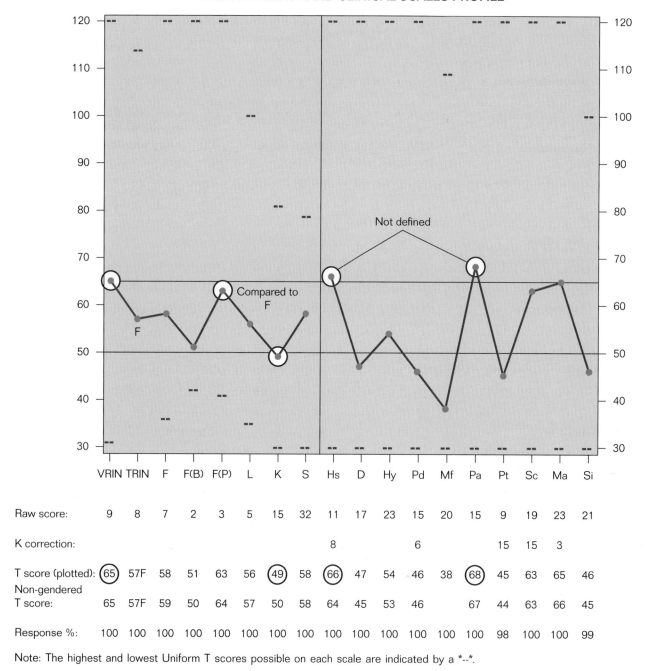

MMPI-2 VALIDITY AND CLINICAL SCALES PROFILE

	VRIN	TRIN	F	F(B)	F(P)	L	K	S	Hs	D	Hy	Pd	Mf	Pa	Pt	Sc	Ma	Si
Raw score:	9	8	7	2	3	5	15	32	11	17	23	15	20	15	9	19	23	21
K correction:									8			6			15	15	3	
T score (plotted):	65	57F	58	51	63	56	49	58	66	47	54	46	38	68	45	63	65	46
Non-gendered T score:	65	57F	59	50	64	57	50	58	64	45	53	46		67	44	63	66	45
Response %:	100	100	100	100	100	100	100	100	100	100	100	100	100	100	98	100	100	99

Note: The highest and lowest Uniform T scores possible on each scale are indicated by a *--*.

dimensions, or sets of traits. The scales are designed so the test-taker can complete them as well as individuals who know the test-taker, such as spouses, partners, or relatives (Form R). People use the NEO-PI-R less in clinical settings than in personality research or in personnel selection, although it can be of value in describing a client's "personality" as distinct from the client's symptoms.

Clinicians and researchers may also use specific self-report inventories designed to investigate specific disorders or research questions for which a general test may not be as relevant. There are literally hundreds of these developed for such specific purposes. These inventories may also supplement more general assessment methods.

You can see Ben's MMPI-2 scores in Figure 3.2. His scores on the Paranoia scale were slightly elevated and he endorsed several critical items relating directly to psychosis such

MMPI-2 RESTRUCTURED CLINICAL SCALES PROFILE

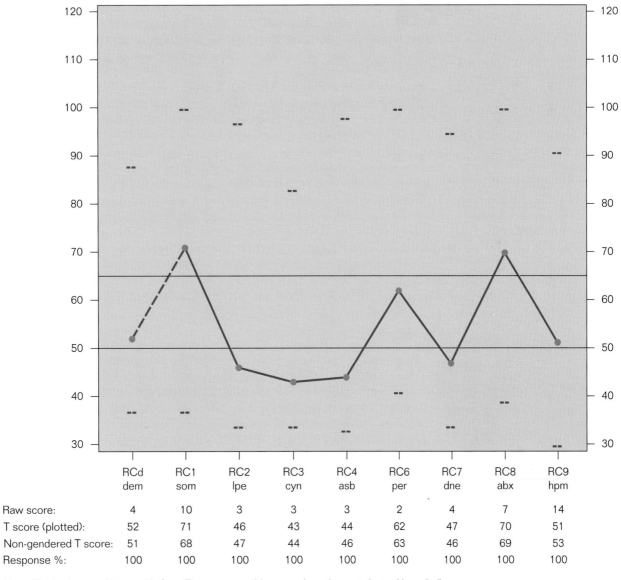

	RCd dem	RC1 som	RC2 lpe	RC3 cyn	RC4 asb	RC6 per	RC7 dne	RC8 abx	RC9 hpm
Raw score:	4	10	3	3	3	2	4	7	14
T score (plotted):	52	71	46	43	44	62	47	70	51
Non-gendered T score:	51	68	47	44	46	63	46	69	53
Response %:	100	100	100	100	100	100	100	100	100

Note: The highest and lowest Uniform T scores possible on each scale are indicated by a "--".

Legend		
dem = Demoralization	cyn = Cynicism	dne = Dysfunctional negative emotions
som = Somatic complaints	asb = Antisocial behavior	abx = Aberrant experiences
lpe = Low positive emotions	per = Ideas of persecution	hpm = Hypomanic Activation

as "I have no enemies who really wish to harm me" (False), "I have strange and peculiar thoughts" (True), and "At times my thoughts have raced ahead faster than I could speak them" (True). According to his responses, he may have unusual thought content and may often feel suspicious that others are saying bad things about him. As a result, he may feel disconnected from reality. He may believe that his feelings and thoughts are controlled by others. His abnormal thought content was evidenced at times throughout the WAIS-IV administration in his unusual reactions to certain test items. His scores on the MMPI-2, however, indicate that he does not tend to be impulsive or take physical risks and generally follows rules and laws. These may be protective factors for Ben in that he may be able to maintain some control of his abnormal thoughts, which may differentiate him from those with diagnosable psychotic disorders.

From looking at Ben's scores, Dr. Washington concluded that his limited coping resources may be a more situational than long-standing problem. Further, his clinical profile suggests that he may be excessively sensitive and overly responsive to the opinions of others. He may overemphasize rationality and be moralistic and rigid in his attitudes and opinions. As a result, he may be argumentative and have a tendency to blame others and act suspicious, hostile, and guarded in relationships. This may account for his report of having few close friends at school and his preference to be alone in his dorm room.

Based on his scores on the MMPI-2, it appears that Ben has a traditional sense of masculinity and may have stereotypically masculine preferences in work, hobbies, and other activities. In the clinical interview, he reported having had no previous significant romantic relationships with women, which may be a result of his tendency to be guarded and hostile in his relationships with others. Ben's scores on the MMPI-2-R suggest that he does endorse aberrant experiences, but his score on persecution is within the normative range. He also received scores above the norm on somatic complaints.

Clinicians typically interpret the MMPI-2 scores in the context of other test scores. They also may use the content scales to flesh out the profiles provided by the basic 10 clinical scales of the MMPI-2. The Restructured MMPI-2 also provides a different perspective on a client's current psychological state, because the content scales provide a more descriptive summary of the client's symptoms. In Ben's case, Dr. Washington noted that his score was high on the Demoralization scale, suggesting that Ben felt discouraged and hopeless about his current life situation.

projective test
A technique in which the test-taker is presented with an ambiguous item or task and is asked to respond by providing his or her own meaning or perception.

behavioral assessment
A form of measurement based on objective recording of the individual's behavior.

target behavior
A behavior of interest or concern in an assessment.

Projective Testing

A **projective test** is a technique in which the examiner asks the test-taker questions about an ambiguous item. The underlying idea behind projective tests is that people cannot or will not provide accurate statements on self-report inventories. For example, clients may not wish to say that they are experiencing unusual symptoms or have qualities that they deem negative. On projective tests, clients may be less guarded about their responses because they don't know how the assessor will interpret their answers. Projective tests are most useful when combined with self-report inventories rather than used as the sole basis for diagnosing or evaluating a client.

The most famous projective technique is the Rorschach Inkblot Test, named after Swiss psychiatrist Hermann Rorschach, who developed the method in 1911. To administer the test, the examiner shows the test-taker a set of 10 cards (5 black and white, 5 with color), one by one. The test-taker's job is to describe what the inkblot looks like. Although the method sounds simple enough, over the last century researchers and clinicians continue to refine the scoring methods.

The Thematic Apperception Test (TAT) presents test-takers with a very different task than does the Rorschach. Test-takers look at black-and-white drawings that portray people in a variety of ambiguous situations. Their task is to tell a story about what is happening in each scene, focusing on such details as what the characters in the picture are thinking and feeling. The TAT's original

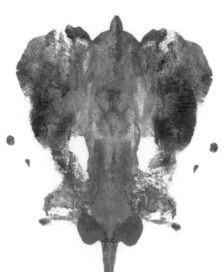

Ben's perception of this Rorschach-like inkblot was "An evil mask that's jumping out to get you. Also a seed, some kind of seed which is dividing itself into two equal halves. It could be a sign of conception and yet it's dying. It's losing part of itself, falling apart, raging."

purpose was to evaluate motivation such as the need for achievement or need for power. Like the Rorschach, its use has evolved over time and clinicians can administer it as part of a larger test battery.

In Ben's case, Dr. Washington decided not to conduct projective testing until he completed the neuropsychological assessment. Clinicians typically do not administer these instruments as part of a standard battery, particularly if there is the potential that the client's symptoms are related to a trauma or injury.

3.6 Behavioral Assessment

Unlike psychological tests, **behavioral assessments** record actions rather than responses to rating scales or questions. The **target behavior** is what the client and clinician wish to change. Behavioral assessments include descriptions of the events that precede or follow the behaviors. We call events that precede the behavior antecedents and events following the behavior consequences.

For example, a child in a classroom may be unusually disruptive immediately following recess, but not immediately following lunch. When clinicians record behavior in its natural context, such as the classroom or the home, this is called *in vivo* **observation.** However, it's not always possible or practical to conduct an *in vivo* observation. The teacher or a teacher's aide is most likely too busy to record the behavior of one child, and having a clinician in the room would create a distraction or influence the behavior he or she is observing.

Analog observations take place in a setting or context such as a clinician's office or a laboratory specifically designed for observing the target behavior. A clinician assessing the disruptive child would need to arrange a situation as comparable as possible to the natural setting of the classroom for the analog observation to be useful.

Clients may also report on their own behavior rather than having someone observe them. In a **behavioral self-report** the client records the target behavior, including the antecedents and consequences of the behavior. **Self-monitoring** is a form of behavioral self-report in which the client keeps a record of the frequency of specified behaviors, such as the number of cigarettes he or she smoked or calories he or she consumed, or the number of times in a day that a particular unwanted thought comes to the client's mind. Clinicians may also obtain information from their clients using **behavioral interviewing** in which they ask questions about the target behavior's frequency, antecedents, and consequences.

3.7 Multicultural Assessment

When psychologists conduct an assessment, they must take into account the person's cultural, ethnic, and racial background, performing a **multicultural assessment.** Clinicians evaluating clients who speak English as a second language, or do not speak English at all, must ask a number of questions: Does the client understand the assessment process sufficiently to provide informed consent? Does the client understand the instructions for the instrument? Are there normative data for the client's ethnic group? Even if clients appear as fairly fluent, they may not understand idiomatic phrases for which there are multiple meanings (Weiner & Greene, 2008).

Publishers of psychological tests are continually re-evaluating their instruments to ensure that a range of clients can understand the items. At the same time, graduate trainees in clinical programs are trained to understand the cultural backgrounds of the clients who

Patients often complete individual self-reports of behavioral patterns as part of a comprehensive psychological assessment.

in vivo observation
Process involving the recording of behavior in its natural context, such as the classroom or the home.

analog observations
Assessments that take place in a setting or context such as a clinician's office or a laboratory specifically designed for observing the target behavior.

behavioral self-report
A method of behavioral assessment in which the individual provides information about the frequency of particular behaviors.

self-monitoring
A self-report technique in which the client keeps a record of the frequency of specified behaviors.

behavioral interviewing
Assessment process in which clinicians ask questions about the target behavior's frequency, antecedents, and consequences.

multicultural assessment
Assessment process in which clinicians take into account the person's cultural, ethnic, and racial background.

It is important for psychologists to take multicultural considerations into account throughout each part of the assessment process.

neuropsychological assessment
A process of gathering information about a client's brain functioning on the basis of performance on psychological tests.

they assess. They are also learning to evaluate assessment instruments critically and to recognize when they need further consultation (Dana, 2002).

3.8 Neuropsychological Assessment

Neuropsychological assessment is the process of gathering information about a client's brain functioning on the basis of performance on psychological tests. Clinicians use neuropsychological assessment measures to attempt to determine the functional correlates of brain damage by comparing a client's performance on a particular test with normative data from individuals who are known to have certain types of injuries or disorders. There is no one set procedure for conducting a neuropsychological assessment. Particular clinicians may have preferences for certain tests, but these preferences are not set in stone. Moreover, neuropsychologists typically choose tests that will help them understand the client's presenting symptoms and possible diagnoses. The client's age is another factor that the clinician takes into account. Tests appropriate for older adults are not necessarily either appropriate or useful for diagnosing a child or adolescent.

Certain neuropsychological tests are derived from or the same as tests on the WAIS-IV, such as Digit Span (used to assess verbal recall and auditory attention) and Similarities (used to assess verbal abstraction abilities). Developers think that each of these tests is related to brain damage in particular areas. Developers have also created other tests, such as the Trail Making Tests, also called "Trails." Figure 3.3 shows a sample item from the Trail Making Test A. This test evaluates frontal lobe functioning, and focuses on attention, scanning of visual stimuli, and number sequencing.

In a neuropsychological assessment, the clinician can choose from tests that measure attention and working (short-term) memory, processing speed, verbal reasoning and comprehension, visual reasoning, verbal memory, and visual memory. A number of tests evaluate what clinicians call "executive function," the ability to formulate goals, make plans, carry out those plans, and then complete the plans in an effective way. There are a variety of available tests within each category. If a clinician wishes to investigate one area in depth for a particular client, then he or she will administer more tests from that category.

FIGURE 3.3 Trail Making Test

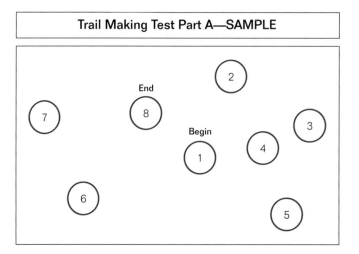

There are a large number of tests that measure visuospatial ability. Many neuropsychologists rely on the Clock Drawing Test (Sunderland et al., 1989) a simple procedure that involves giving the client a sheet of paper with a large predrawn circle on it. Then the examiner asks the client to draw the numbers around the circle to look like the face of an analog clock. Finally, the examiner asks the client to draw the hands of the clock to read "10 after 11." The clinician then rates the client's drawing according to number of errors. The most impaired clients are unable to reproduce a clock face at all, or make mistakes in writing the numbers or placing them around the clock.

The Wisconsin Card Sorting Test (WCST) (see Figure 3.4) requires that the client match a card to one of a set of cards that share various features. Originally developed using the physical cards, the clinician typically administers the test in its computerized format. The test requires that the client shift mental set because the basis for a correct match shifts from trial to trial. In the example we've shown in Figure 3.4, the client could match the card on the basis of color, number of items, or shape. The profession regards the WCST as a test of executive functioning (Rabin, Barr, & Burton, 2005) that is sensitive to injury of the frontal lobes, but also assesses damage in other cortical areas (Nagahama, Okina, Suzuki, Nabatame, & Matsuda, 2005).

What's New in the DSM-5

Section 3 Assessment Measures

DSM-5's Section 3 contains a set of assessment measures that clinicians can use to enhance their decision-making process. These tools include a "cross-cutting" interview that reviews symptoms across all psychological disorders that either the client or someone close to the client can complete. This review of symptoms would allow clinicians to draw attention to symptoms that may not fit precisely into the categorically-based diagnoses. Such questions could be incorporated into a mental status examination. One set of questions contains a brief survey of 13 domains for adults and 12 for children. The follow-up questions go into more depth in domains that seem to warrant further attention.

The *DSM-5* authors recognize that dimensional approaches are increasingly being supported by the literature due to the fact that categorical distinctions among disorders may, at times, seem arbitrary. In addition, there are disorders that combine features of two disorders. Many clients also have more than one disorder, diagnoses that do not fit easily into one category. Eventually, a dimensional approach could be combined with the DSM's categorically-based diagnoses. This approach would allow clinicians to indicate the severity of a client's disorder, making it possible to evaluate a client's progress during treatment.

In addition to these tools, Section 3 includes the WHODAS (that we presented in Chapter 2) and a section providing clinicians with tools to perform a cultural formulation. This is a comprehensive semi-structured interview that focuses on the client's experience and social context. The *DSM-5* authors emphasize that the interview should be conducted in a way that allows the client to report his or her subjective experiences. This is intended to reduce the chances that the clinician's stereotypes or pre-existing biases will affect the diagnostic process.

The *DSM-5* authors express the hope that by providing these tools and techniques, they will not only improve the diagnostic process, but also contribute to the research literature on the nature and causes of psychological disorders.

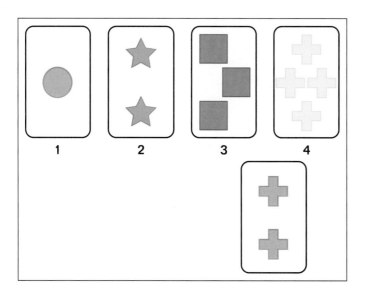

FIGURE 3.4 Sample item from the Wisconsin Card Sorting Test

Psychologists in the Legal System

Psychologists working within the legal system are frequently called on to serve as expert witnesses, and their testimony often relies on psychological assessments. Unlike the therapeutic setting, the forensic setting does not necessarily involve a positive relationship. In fact, the psychologist may face a malpractice suit from the clients if they wish to seek revenge for an assessment that led to a conviction or unfavorable decision, as in custody cases.

Knapp and VandeCreek (2001), though writing before the adoption of the 2002 APA Ethical Principles, present an interesting case history of a psychologist involved in a custody case who wrote in his report that the father had "authoritarian tendencies and could benefit from participating in parenting classes" (pp. 244–245). However, the psychologist had not actually interviewed the father; he based this statement on what the children told him. As a result, the psychologist was reprimanded by his state licensing board.

Psychologists are also mandated by the Ethics Code to practice within their field of competence. If they have not received training in forensic psychology, they are required to seek consultation from an expert colleague. A second case example presented by Knapp and VandeCreek involved the testimony by a psychologist proficient in assessment, but not forensic assessment, who testified that on the basis of elevated scores on the MMPI-2 scales 6 and 9, the defendant was indeed "insane." However, legal insanity is not the same as psychologically disordered, and therefore the psychologist's testimony was discredited in court.

Informed consent is another key ethical principle that applies not only to research but to assessment and treatment. When a defendant with a psychological disorder is interviewed for a forensic assessment, the psychologist must take all possible precautions to let the defendant know about the limits of confidentiality in this context. In another example presented by Knapp and VandeCreek, a defendant was genuinely startled to hear the psychologist report on the interview, because the defendant had not understood the nature of the informed consent.

As a final example, consider the prohibition in the Ethics Code against dual relationships. Psychologists providing therapy should not be providing information that could be used by a lawyer in a legal case. The example cited by Knapp and VandeCreek involved a psychologist treating the children of a separated couple. The children stated that they preferred to live with their mother. The mother later requested that the psychologist write a letter to her attorney. In turn, the attorney asked the psychologist to "share your opinions as to where the children should live" (p. 250).

Q: *You be the judge:* As you can see here, the APA Ethics Code clearly states the proper course of action in each case, the question here for you to judge is not which course of action is proper, as this is clearly stated in the APA Ethics Code. Instead, consider the complexities that psychologists face when interacting in the legal system. These examples are only a handful from the many possible scenarios that can ensue, placing psychologists in situations that require them to be entirely familiar with the principles that guide the profession.

Neuropsychologists use the Boston Naming Test (BNT) to assess language capacity. Containing 60 line drawings of objects ranging in familiarity, clinicians can use the test to examine children with learning disabilities and adults who suffer from brain injury or dementia. Simple items are those that have high frequency, such as a house. Each item on the BNT contains a picture of a common object that the test-taker must name (e.g., chimney, church, school, and house).

The Paced Auditory Serial Addition Test (PASAT) assesses a client's auditory information processing speed, flexibility, and calculation ability. The client hears a recording of numbers between 1 and 9 every 3 or fewer seconds. The task is to add the number just heard with the number that preceded it. If the recording was "1-3-5-2-6-7," the correct response would be "4-8-7-8-13." In addition to its usage to assess traumatic brain injury, clinicians also use the PASAT extensively in assessing the functioning of individuals with multiple sclerosis (Tombaugh, Stormer, Rees, Irving, & Francis, 2006).

Other neuropsychological tests investigate a variety of memory functions, for example, the Wechsler Memory Scale, now in its fourth edition (WMS-IV). The WMS-IV includes tests of working (short-term) and long-term memory for visual and verbal stimuli. Examiners can choose from among the WMS-IV subscales according to which areas they believe are most critical to evaluate in particular clients. For example, when testing an older adult, the examiner may use only the scales assessing Logical Memory (recall of a story), Verbal Paired Associates (remembering the second in pairs of words), and Visual Reproduction (drawing a visual stimulus). However, neuropsychologists are cautious in accepting the newer versions of both the WMS-IV and the WAIS-IV, as they are too new to have accumulated sufficient validational data.

Increasingly, neuropsychologists are relying on computerized test batteries, which are easier to administer than paper-and-pencil tests. One advantage to computerized testing is that it provides the opportunity for **adaptive testing,** in which the client's responses to earlier questions determine the subsequent questions presented to them.

The Cambridge Neuropsychological Testing Automated Battery (CANTAB) consists of 22 subtests that assess visual memory, working memory, executive function and planning, attention, verbal memory, and decision making and response control. Before deciding whether to move to a computerized test, the clinician must weigh the advantages of ease of administration and scoring against the potential disadvantages that may exist for clients who are disadvantaged in their ability to use computers, such as young children (Luciana, 2003). However, given the relatively rapid growth of this field, more extensive normative data will be available that will allow clinicians to feel more confident about their utility.

Dr. Washington chose to administer tasks that would be sensitive to the type of injury that Ben might have sustained given his low WAIS-IV Coding score, which suggested that Ben may have suffered brain damage that led to changes in his ability to focus his visual attention and perform quickly on a psychomotor speed task. Unfortunately, because Dr. Washington did not see Ben at the scene of the accident or in the ER, he could not administer the Glasgow Coma Scale (GCS), a common test that clinicians use in cases of possible traumatic brain injury. Included in the GCS are ratings, for example, of the individual's ability to hear and obey commands, open the eyes, and speak coherently.

Ben's completion time on Trail Making Test Part A was in the marginally impaired range. On the Clock Drawing Test, Ben received a score of 5 out of a possible 10, erroneously crowding the numbers at one end of the clock. He received a score within the normal range on the PASAT, suggesting that the injury did not affect his auditory attentional functioning. On the WCST, Ben showed evidence of perseverative errors, meaning that he was unable to switch mental set in categorizing the cards according to different criteria. Ben's performance on the WMS-IV was within normal range, a finding consistent with his relatively high scores on the Verbal scales of the WAIS-IV, indicating that he has not suffered either short- or long-term memory loss.

adaptive testing
Testing in which the client's responses to earlier questions determine the subsequent questions presented to them.

neuroimaging
Assessment method that provides a picture of the brain's structures or level of activity and therefore is a useful tool for "looking" at the brain.

electroencephalogram (EEG)
A measure of changes in the electrical activity of the brain.

3.9 Neuroimaging

Neuroimaging provides a picture of the brain's structures or level of activity and therefore is a useful tool for "looking" at the brain. There are several types of neuroimaging methods that vary in the types of results they provide.

The **electroencephalogram (EEG)** measures electrical activity in the brain. EEG activity reflects the extent to which an individual is alert, resting, sleeping, or dreaming. The EEG pattern also shows particular patterns of brain waves when an individual engages in particular mental tasks. Clinicians use

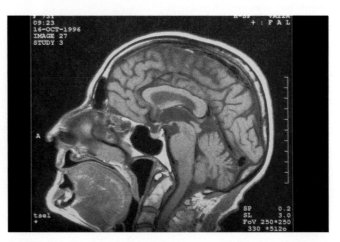

A CAT scan of a patient's brain helps neuropsychologists to find brain structure abnormalities that may be causing cognitive dysfunction.

REAL STORIES

Ludwig van Beethoven: Bipolar Disorder

"At times I was on the point of putting an end to my life—art alone restrained my hand. Oh! It seemed as if I could not quit this earth until I had produced all I felt within me . . ." (1802).

The German composer Ludwig van Beethoven is one of the most brilliant musical composers of all time. His music captures the incredibly vast range of emotions he experienced throughout his lifetime—arguably a greater range than most people experience, as scholars believe he suffered from bipolar disorder. The book *The Key to Genius* chronicles the stories from Beethoven's life based on letters from the composer and accounts from his friends who recall the emotionally chaotic and often volatile life he led. As one friend remarks in the book, "it seems unlikely that one could achieve works of emotional range and intensity comparable to those of Beethoven without such extraordinary emotional experiences."

Beethoven was raised by a father who often beat him and would reportedly lock him in the basement, and a mother whom he loved but who was more or less absent for much of the time he was growing up. When Beethoven was 17, his mother became ill and passed away, leaving behind three young sons and a husband who began abusing alcohol. Since their father was unable to care for his children, it fell upon Beethoven to take care of his two younger brothers until they were grown.

At this point in his life, Beethoven had already published his first piano composition. At 22, he left his family to study with the renowned composer Franz Joseph Haydn in Vienna, Austria, where he remained for the rest of his life. Though most composers at the time worked on commission from churches, Beethoven was a freelance composer and quickly became a successful and respected name. This success protected him from a society that would no doubt have looked upon him in a very negative light otherwise. Those close to Beethoven viewed him as an emotionally unstable man who was prone to periods of both intense irritability and paranoia, as well as lengthy periods of depression. His fiery temper often led to quarrels

Ludwig van Beethoven was believed to have suffered from bipolar disorder.

with landlords and servants, and he often moved residences as a result. His temper greatly affected his personal relationships, and he would often excommunicate friends only to later beg them for forgiveness, which they usually granted due to his generally good nature, aside from his periods of agitation and melancholy.

Remarkably, although Beethoven suffered from hearing loss and eventually became completely deaf for the last 10 years of his life, he continued to compose and perform music until the very end of his life, despite the anguish his deafness caused him. As with many creative individuals with bipolar disorder, Beethoven's mania proved to be a huge creative force in his life. In contrast, his periods of depression were usually unproductive as he typically languished in solitude until the mood passed. He was often physically ill and dealt with asthma in the winters, which undoubtedly contributed to his persistent depression and high consumption of alcohol. In turn, his alcoholism led to many more physical problems. Unfortunately, substance abuse such as alcoholism is often a secondary problem for individuals suffering from bipolar disorder, in an attempt to control their distressing mood fluctuations.

Beethoven's episodes of mania not only allowed for heightened periods of creativity, but they would also allow him to temporarily overcome any physical conditions he suffered, even in the later years of his life when he was afflicted with a multitude of painful medical problems. As one doctor noted, "often, with rare endurance, he worked at his compositions on a wooded hillside and his work done, still aglow with reflection, he would not infrequently run about for hours in the most inhospitable surroundings, denying every change of temperature, and often during the heaviest snowfalls."

Beethoven was never married and had no children of his own, though he was known as a romantic who had many amorous pursuits. When his younger brother died, he took in his 9-year-old nephew, Karl, an action that soon turned disastrous by all accounts. Beethoven was highly untrusting of Karl's mother (it was not uncommon that he was suspicious of people in his life) and took her to court over his nephew's custody. The custody dispute lasted for some time, and once Beethoven gained guardianship of Karl, he was known to constantly harangue the boy and interfere with his life. It became so hard on Karl that he attempted suicide and later decided to join the military, apparently in an effort to seek a

more stable life than the one he came to know with his uncle. It's not hard to imagine that it was difficult for Beethoven to take care of a young child when he often took very poor care of himself. His friends tell accounts in *The Key to Genius* about the composer's often complete lack of hygiene and self-care in his later years. He often appeared so disheveled that once he was imprisoned when he was mistaken for a burglar while walking around a neighborhood in Vienna, and was only released once a friend was able to identify him. Based on his appearance, the officers did not believe he was Beethoven.

Those close to Beethoven eventually tolerated his unusual, sometimes rapid shifts in mood and impulsive behaviors. Additionally, Viennese society accepted his odd behavior due to his success and musical contributions. His unbounded creativity and love for music both benefited from his emotional experiences and helped him survive through many trying

periods of his life. Wrote one friend, ". . . it may be that Beethoven survived as a creator because he was brave or because his love of music kept him going." However, his physical health was in constant compromise due in large part to the mania that caused him to push himself to the brink of limitation. When his illnesses became too much to bear, depression often would follow, and this constant cycle represents the struggles that those with bipolar disorder experience. In the end, Beethoven's passion for music was not enough to save him from succumbing to cirrhosis of the liver caused by excessive alcohol consumption in 1827 at the age of 57. Though we remember him for his music, we can hear his emotional struggles within his creations. As one friend noted, "so much of Beethoven's life was spent in sickness and pain, weakness, and depression that it is remarkable that he accomplished anything at all. Given the pervasiveness of his misery, his work is all the more miraculous."

EEGs to evaluate clients for conditions such as epilepsy, sleep disorders, and brain tumors.

Computed axial tomography (CAT or CT scan) is an imaging method that clinicians and researchers use to provide an image of a cross-sectional slice of the brain from any angle or level. CT scans provide an image of the fluid-filled areas of the brain, the ventricles. The method is useful when clinicians are looking for structural damage to the brain. **Magnetic resonance imaging (MRI)** uses radiowaves rather than X-rays to construct a picture of the living brain based on the water content of various tissues. The person is placed inside a device that contains a powerful electromagnet. This causes the nuclei in hydrogen atoms to transmit electromagnetic energy (hence the term *magnetic resonance*), and activity from thousands of angles is sent to a computer, which produces a high-resolution picture of the scanned area. The picture from the MRI differentiates areas of white matter (nerve fibers) from gray matter (nerve cells) and is useful for diagnosing diseases that affect the nerve fibers that make up the white matter. However, like the CAT scan, the MRI produces static images so it cannot monitor brain activity. **Positron emission tomography (PET) scan**, or a variant known as **single photon emission computed tomography (SPECT)**, does provide images of brain activity. Specialists inject radioactively labeled compounds into a person's veins in very small amounts. The compounds travel through the blood into the brain and emit positively charged electrons called positrons, which they can detect much like X-rays in a CT. The images, which represent the accumulation of the labeled compound, can show blood flow, oxygen or glucose metabolism, and concentrations of brain chemicals. Vibrant colors at the red end of the spectrum represent higher levels of activity, and colors at the blue-green-violet end of the spectrum represent lower levels of brain activity. **Proton magnetic resonance spectroscopy (MRS)** is

computed axial tomography (CAT or CT scan)
A series of X-rays taken from various angles around the body that are integrated by a computer to product a composite picture.

magnetic resonance imaging (MRI)
The use of radiowaves rather than X-rays to construct a picture of the living brain based on the water content of various tissues.

positron emission tomography (PET) scan
A measure of brain activity in which a small amount of radioactive sugar is injected into an individual's bloodstream, following which a computer measures the varying levels of radiation in different parts of the brain and yields a multicolored image.

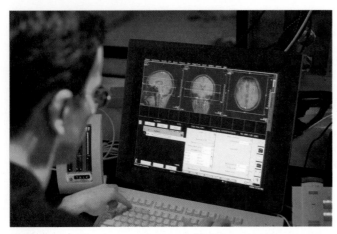

An fMRI is used to monitor changes in brain activity.

single photon emission computed tomography (SPECT)
A variant of the PET scan that permits a longer and more detailed imaging analysis.

proton magnetic resonance spectroscopy (MRS)
A scanning method that measures metabolic activity of neurons, and therefore may indicate areas of brain damage.

functional magnetic resonance imaging (fMRI)
A variant of the traditional MRI, which makes it possible to construct a picture of activity in the brain.

another scanning method that measures metabolic activity of neurons, and therefore may indicate areas of brain damage (Govind et al., 2010).

Functional magnetic resonance imaging (fMRI) provides a picture of how people react to stimuli virtually in real time, making it possible to present stimuli to an individual while the examiner monitors the individual's response. Researchers are increasingly using fMRIs to understand the brain areas involved in the processing of information. One major advantage of the fMRI is that it does not require injection of radioactive materials, like the PET or SPECT scans. However, because the fMRI uses magnetism to detect brain activity, people with artificial limbs made from metals such as titanium cannot use this testing method.

Brain scans can produce evidence of specific areas of damage, but they do not necessarily correspond to a specific loss of behavioral functioning (Meyers & Rohling, 2009). Upon evaluating Ben through neuropsychological testing, Dr. Washington decided to administer a CT scan (de Guise et al., 2010), because Ben showed some signs of frontal lobe damage (personality changes, some perseveration on the WCST, and marginal errors on the TMT). However, it was necessary to rule out parietal lobe damage, which can also contribute to this performance pattern as well as to visual attentional deficits. The CT scan revealed that Ben had suffered a traumatic brain injury as a result of the incident, perhaps in the form of a brain hemorrhage.

3.10 Putting It All Together

As we have just shown in Ben's case, clinicians face a formidable task when attempting to develop a diagnosis from the evidence that they obtain through the assessment process. They must evaluate each client on an individual basis and determine which combination of tests is most appropriate to identify as closely as possible the nature and cause of his or her behavioral symptoms. In addition, clinicians performing assessments attempt to understand a client's adaptive skills, so that they can make recommendations to build on his or her existing abilities and help address treatment to maximize his or her functioning in everyday life.

Return to the Case: Ben Robsham

Given the potential cause of his symptoms, Dr. Washington recommended that Ben will require rehabilitation to strengthen his existing skills so that he can return to his previous employment. Ben will also receive supportive therapy and possibly vocational counseling if he continues to demonstrate deficits in visual and spatial processing speed, skills that he clearly needs for his present job.

Dr. Tobin's reflections: It is somewhat reassuring to know that Ben's injury, though currently interfering with his ability to go to work, will most likely resolve on its own. A neuropsychological assessment was clearly called for in this case; unfortunately, with increases in traumatic brain injuries in recent years, this type of assessment will be increasingly necessary. Ben's injury occurred at work, but many other young people are experiencing such injuries in areas of activity as diverse as playing hockey or football to involvement in war. With the development of more sophisticated neuroimaging and computerized testing, we will be better prepared to assess individuals like Ben in the future, as well as those clients we see whose disorders are primarily psychological in nature.

SUMMARY

- A **psychological assessment** is a procedure in which a clinician provides a formal evaluation of an individual's cognitive, personality, and psychosocial functioning. Clinicians conduct assessments under a variety of conditions. In many cases, clinicians use the assessment process to provide a diagnosis, or at least a tentative diagnosis, of an individual's psychological disorder.

- To be useful, clinicians must hold assessments to standards that ensure that they provide the most reproducible and accurate results. The reliability of a test indicates the consistency of the scores it produces. The test's validity reflects the extent to which a test measures what it is designed to measure.

- Clinicians should use the best assessment methods possible. Evidence-based assessment includes (1) relying on research findings and scientifically viable theories; (2) using psychometrically strong measures; and (3) empirically evaluating the assessment process.

- The **clinical interview** is a series of questions that clinicians administer in face-to-face interaction with the client. The answers the client provides to these questions provide important background information on clients, allow them to describe their symptoms, and enable clinicians to make observations of their clients that can guide decisions about the next steps, which may include further testing. The format can be structured or unstructured.

- A clinician uses a **mental status examination** to assess a client's current state of mind. The clinician assesses a number of features of the client including appearance, attitudes, behavior, mood and affect, speech, thought processes, content of thought, perception, cognition, insight, and judgment. The outcome of the mental status examination is a comprehensive description of how the client looks, thinks, feels, and behaves.

- Intelligence tests such as the Stanford-Binet Intelligence Test, but particularly the Wechsler scales, provide valuable information about an individual's cognitive functioning.

- Clinicians use tests of personality to understand a person's thoughts, behaviors, and emotions. There are two main forms of personality tests: self-report and projective. Tests include the Minnesota Multiphasic Personality Inventory (MMPI), the Personality Assessment Inventory (PAI), the SCL-90-R, the NEO Personality Inventory, and other specific self-report inventories designed to investigate specific disorders or research questions for which a general test may not be relevant.

- Unlike psychological tests, **behavioral assessments** record actions rather than responses to rating scales or questions. The **target behavior** is what the client and clinician wish to change. Behavioral assessments include descriptions of the events that precede or follow the behaviors. **In vivo observation** takes place when clinicians record behavior in its natural context, such as the classroom or the home. **Analog observations** take place in a setting or context such as a clinician's office or a laboratory specifically designed for observing the target behavior. In a **behavioral self-report** the client records the target behavior, including the antecedents and consequences of the behavior. **Self-monitoring** is a form of behavioral self-report in which the client keeps a record of the frequency of specified behaviors.

- When psychologists conduct a **multicultural assessment,** they must take into account the person's cultural, ethnic, and racial background.

- **Neuropsychological assessment** is the process of gathering information about a client's brain functioning on the basis of performance on psychological tests. Clinicians use neuropsychological assessment measures to attempt to determine the functional correlates of brain damage by comparing a client's performance on a particular test with normative data from individuals who are known to have certain types of injuries or disorders. There are a variety of tests to assess verbal recall and auditory attention. Physiological measures include brain imaging techniques such as EEG, CT scan, MRI, fMRI, PET, and other techniques for assessing abnormalities in the body, particularly the brain.

KEY TERMS

Theoretical Perspectives

Learning Objectives

4.1 Assess the theories of the biological perspective and identify treatments

4.2 Describe trait theory

4.3 Compare and contrast Freud's theory to post-Freudian psychodynamic views and identify treatments

4.4 Assess the theories of the behavioral perspective and identify treatments

4.5 Assess the theories of the cognitive perspective and identify treatments

4.6 Assess the theories of the humanistic perspective and identify treatments

4.7 Assess the theories of the sociocultural perspective and identify treatments

4.8 Explain the biopsychosocial perspective

CHAPTER 4

Case Report: Meera Krishnan

Demographic information: 26-year-old Indian-American female.

Presenting problem: Meera self-referred to my office upon the urging of a friend. For the past three weeks she reports feeling "profoundly sad for no reason at all," lethargic, and preoccupied with thoughts of suicide, although she stated that she has no specific plan or intent to commit suicide. Her work performance has suffered. She oversleeps most days, has lost her appetite, and tries to avoid any social contact. She describes feeling that she has greatly let down her family and friends.

Relevant history: A college graduate, Meera works as a biologist in a hospital research laboratory. The younger of two daughters, Meera reported feeling that her parents favored her older sister. She feels that her parents disapprove of her current lifestyle in comparison to her sister, who married the son of family friends. Although she and her sister had once been very close, they no longer maintain regular contact, and she rarely visits her parents, although they live in a neighboring town.

Meera reported that she rarely drank alcohol and had never used any illicit drugs. She has no medical conditions and reported that, in general, her health is very good. Prior to the onset of her current depressive episode, Meera reported that she exercised regularly by participating in a long-distance running club and enjoyed cooking with her friends and listening to music.

This is Meera's third depressive episode since her junior year of high school. Each episode has lasted approximately two months or slightly longer. She has not previously sought treatment.

Symptoms: For three weeks, Meera has been experiencing overwhelming feelings of sadness, not accounted for by bereavement, substance use, or a medical condition. Her symptoms include feelings of worthlessness, tearfulness, loss of interest, sleep disturbance (oversleeping), and loss of appetite. She has experienced recurrent thoughts about death and passive suicidal ideation.

Case formulation: Meera meets *DSM*-5 criteria for Major Depressive Disorder (MDD), recurrent. The symptoms of her current depressive episode are interfering with her ability to carry out her normal daily functioning. Since Meera has experienced two previous depressive episodes that have been at least two months apart each, her diagnosis is Major Depressive Disorder, recurrent.

Treatment plan: The principles of evidence-based practice suggest that the best treatment for Meera is cognitive-behavioral therapy. Following intake, she will receive a complete psychological assessment and be referred to a psychiatrist for a medical evaluation.

Sarah Tobin, PhD

4.1 Theoretical Perspectives in Abnormal Psychology

theoretical perspective
An orientation to understanding the causes of human behavior and the treatment of abnormality.

Underlying **theoretical perspectives,** orientations to understanding the causes of human behavior and the treatment of abnormality all guide research and clinical work in abnormal psychology. In this chapter, we will explore the major theoretical perspectives that form the foundation for the book. You will read in more detail about each perspective and how it applies to specific disorders within the chapters covering the major psychological disorders. To facilitate your understanding of these perspectives, we will use Meera's case as an example to show how clinicians working within each perspective would address her treatment. Although Meera's plan calls for treatment within the cognitive-behavioral perspective, her case has many facets that each of the major theories do address. These warrant discussion.

4.2 Biological Perspective

biological perspective
A theoretical perspective in which it is assumed that disturbances in emotions, behavior, and cognitive processes are caused by abnormalities in the functioning of the body.

Psychologists working within the **biological perspective** believe that abnormalities in the body's functioning are responsible for the symptoms of psychological disorders. In particular, they deem that we can trace the causes of psychological symptoms primarily to disturbances in the nervous system or other systems that have an impact on the nervous system.

Theories

neurotransmitter
A chemical substance released from a neuron into the synaptic cleft, where it drifts across the synapse and is absorbed by the receiving neuron.

The transmission of information throughout the nervous system takes place at synapses, or points of communication between neurons. Electrical signals containing information transmit chemically across the synapse from one neuron to the next. Through this transmission, neurons form complex pathways along which information travels from one part of the nervous system to another. **Neurotransmitters** are the chemical messengers that travel across the synapse, allowing neurons to communicate with their neighbors. Table 4.1 shows the proposed role of several major neurotransmitters in psychological disorders.

Apart from disturbances in neurotransmitters, abnormalities in the brain structures themselves can also cause psychological symptoms. Although it's not always possible to link brain structures that are too large or too small to behavioral impairments, researchers believe that some disturbances in behavior have a connection to abnormally developed or functioning brain structures. Because we cannot directly observe brain structures, researchers have developed sophisticated brain scanning methods to allow them to measure how an individual's brain is structured and, more importantly, how it performs while it is processing information.

The causes of nervous system dysfunction range from genetic abnormalities to brain damage. Genetic abnormalities can come about through the inheritance of particular combinations of genes, to faulty copying when cells reproduce, or to mutations that a person acquires over the course of life. Cells do possess the ability to repair many of these mutations. If these repair mechanisms fail, however, the mutation can pass along to the altered cell's future copies.

Genes contain the instructions for forming proteins, which, in turn, determine how the cell performs. In the case of neurons, genes control the manufacturing of neurotransmitters, as well as the way the neurotransmitters behave in the synapse. Genes also determine, in part, how the brain's structures develop throughout life. Any factor that can alter the genetic code can also alter how these structures perform.

genotype
The genetic makeup of an organism.

allele
One of two different variations of a gene.

Inherited disorders come about when the genes from each parent combine in such a way that the ordinary functioning of a cell is compromised. Your **genotype** is your genetic makeup, which contains the form of each gene that you inherit, called an **allele.** Let's say that Allele A causes a protein to form that leads a neuron to form abnormally.

TABLE 4.1 Selected Neurotransmitters Involved
in Psychological Disorders

Neurotransmitter	Related disorders
Norepinephrine	Depressive disorders
	Anxiety disorders (panic disorder)
Serotonin	Depressive disorders
	Anxiety disorders
	Schizophrenia
	Anorexia nervosa
	Substance use disorders
Gamma-aminobutyric acid (GABA)	Anxiety disorders
	Substance use disorders
Dopamine	Neurocognitive disorder due to Parkinson's disease
	Schizophrenia
	Eating disorders
	Substance use disorders
Acetylcholine	Neurocognitive disorder due to Alzheimer's disease
Opioid peptides	Substance use disorders

Allele B causes the neuron to be entirely healthy. If you have inherited two genes containing Allele B, then you have no chance of developing that disease. If, on the other hand, you have inherited two genes containing Allele A, you will almost certainly get the disease. If you inherit one Allele A and one Allele B, the situation becomes more complicated. Whether or not you get the disease depends on whether Allele A is "dominant," meaning that its instructions to code the harmful protein will almost certainly prevail over those of Allele B. If Allele A is "recessive," then it alone cannot cause the harmful protein to form. However, because you are an AB combination, you are a carrier because should you produce a child with another AB carrier, that child could receive the two AAs, and therefore develop the disorder (Figure 4.1).

The dominant-recessive gene inheritance model rarely, if at all, can account for the genetic inheritance of psychological disorders. In some cases, inherited disorders come about through maternal linkages only, meaning that they transmit only through the mother. These disorders occur with defects in the mitochondrial DNA, which is the DNA that controls protein formation in the cell's mitochondria (energy-producing structures). Many psychological disorders reflect a **polygenic** model involving the joint impact of multiple gene combinations.

To complicate matters further, not only are multiple genes involved in the development of psychological disorders, but the environment plays an important role in contributing to the way our behavior reflects our genetic inheritance. Your **phenotype** is the observed and measurable characteristic that results from the combination of environmental and genetic influences. Some phenotypes are relatively close to their genotype. For example, your eye color does not reflect environmental influences. Complex organs such as the brain, however, often show a wide disparity between the genotype and phenotype because the environment to which people are exposed heavily influences brain development throughout life. Moreover, there are numerous genes that participate in building the structures in the brain and influencing their changes over time. The study of **epigenetics** attempts to identify the ways that the environment influences genes to produce phenotypes.

polygenic
A model of inheritance in which more than one gene participates in the process of determining a given characteristic.

phenotype
The expression of the genetic program in the individual's physical and psychological attributes.

epigenetics
The science that attempts to identify the ways that the environment influences genes to produce phenotypes.

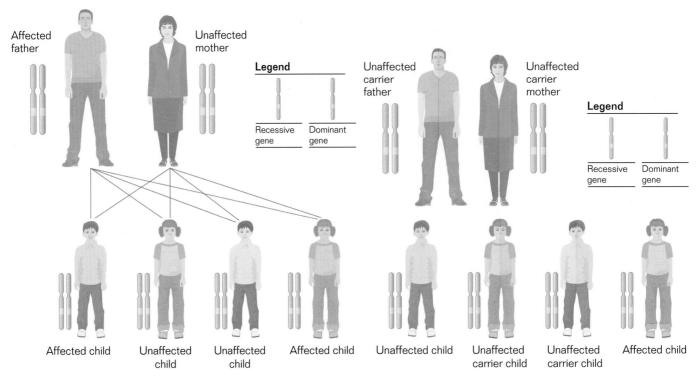

FIGURE 4.1 Pattern of Dominant-Recessive Trait Inheritance

endophenotypes
Biobehavioral abnormalities that are linked to genetic and neurobiological causes of mental illness.

Reflecting the complexity of the brain's structures and functions, leading researchers in schizophrenia (Gottesman & Shields, 1972; Gottesman & Shields, 1973) proposed the use of the term **"endophenotypes"** to characterize the combination of genetic and environmental contributors to complex behaviors. An endophenotype is an internal phenotype, that is, a characteristic that is not outwardly observable. In the case of schizophrenia, for example, there are several possible endophenotypes that may underlie the disease's outwardly observed symptoms. These include abnormalities in memory, sensory processes, and particular types of nervous system cells. The assumption is that these unobservable characteristics, which heredity and the environment influence, are responsible for the disease's behavioral expressions. The concept of endophenotypes was probably decades ahead of its time, because in the 1970s, researchers were limited in what they could study both in terms of genetics and the brain. With the development of sophisticated DNA testing and brain imaging methods, the concept is seeing a resurgence (Gottesman & Gould, 2003).

The relationships between genetic and environmental influences fall into two categories: gene-environment correlations and interactions between genes and the environment (Lau & Eley, 2010). Gene-environment correlations exist when people with a certain genetic predisposition are distributed unequally in particular environments (Scarr & McCartney, 1983). These correlations can come about in three ways. The first way is through passive exposure. Children with certain genetic predispositions can be exposed to environments that their parents create based on their genetic predispositions. For example, a child of two athletically gifted parents who participate in sports inherits genes that give this child athletic prowess. Because the parents themselves are involved in athletic activities, they have created an environment that fosters the child's own athletic development. This elicits the second gene-environment interaction and can occur when the parents treat the children with certain genetic predispositions in particular ways because their abilities bring out particular responses. Returning to our example, the school coach may recruit the athletically gifted child for sports teams starting in early life, leading the child to become even more athletically talented. We call the third gene-environment correlation "niche picking." The athletically gifted child may not wait for

MINI CASE

Biological Approaches to Treating Meera

A clinician working within a biological perspective would treat Meera's depression with antidepressant medications beginning, most likely, with SSRIs. Because these medications do not take effect for several weeks, the clinician would monitor her closely during this period to ensure that Meera remains stable. During this time, the clinician would meet with her on a weekly basis at least, to monitor Meera's progress, learn of any side effects that she is experiencing, and make adjustments as necessary particularly after four to six weeks. Meera is not a suitable candidate for more radical interventions because, although she has suicidal thoughts, she does not have plans and does not appear to be at significant risk. The clinician may also recommend that Meera attempt to resume her prior exercise routines to help augment the therapeutic effects of her medications.

recruitment, but instead seeks out opportunities to play sports, and in this process becomes even more talented. In terms of the development of psychological disorders, any three of these situations can occur, heightening the risk that children of parents with genetic predispositions are more likely to develop the disorder because of the environment's enhancing effect.

Gene-environment interactions occur when one factor influences the expression of the other. In the case of people with major depressive disorder, for example, researchers have found that people with high genetic risk are more likely to show depressive symptoms when placed under high stress than are people with low genetic risk. Thus, the same stress has different effects on people with different genetic predispositions. Conversely, the genetic risk of people exposed to higher stress levels becomes higher than that of people who live in low-stress environments. In other words, a person may have a latent genetic predisposition or vulnerability that only manifests itself when that individual comes under environmental stress. In these studies, the researchers defined genetic risk in terms of whether or not an individual had a close relative with disorder symptoms. The genetic risk presence did not predict whether or not the person developed major depressive disorder unless that individual was exposed to a high-stress environment (Lau & Eley, 2010).

Researchers studying psychopathology have long been aware of the joint contributions of genes and the environment to the development of psychological disorders. The **diathesis-stress model** proposed that people are born with a diathesis (genetic predisposition) or acquire vulnerability early in life due to formative events such as traumas, diseases, birth complications, or harsh family environments (Zubin & Spring, 1977). This vulnerability then places these individuals at risk for the development of a psychological disorder as they grow older (Johnson, Cohen, Kasen, Smailes, & Brook, 2001).

diathesis-stress model
The proposal that people are born with a predisposition (or "diathesis") that places them at risk for developing a psychological disorder if exposed to certain extremely stressful life experiences.

With advances in genetic science, researchers are now much better able to understand the precise ways in which genes and environmental factors interact. Usually, people inherit two copies of a gene, one from each parent, and both copies actively shape the individual's development. However, certain genes regulate through a process known as **epigenesis,** meaning that the environment causes them to turn "off" or "on." If the remaining working gene is deleted or severely mutated, then a person can develop an illness. The process of **DNA methylation** can turn off a gene as a chemical group, methyl, attaches itself to the gene (Figure 4.2) (http://www.nature.com/scitable/topicpage/the-role-of-methylation-in-gene-expression-1070).

epigenesis
Process through which the environment causes them to turn "off" or "on."

DNA methylation
The process that can turn off a gene as a chemical group, methyl, attaches itself to the gene.

Through the epigenetic processes of DNA methylation, maternal care, for example, can change gene expression. One study showed that during pregnancy, a mother's exposure to environmental toxins caused DNA methylation in her unborn child (Furness, Dekker, & Roberts, 2011). Studies on laboratory animals also show that stress can affect

FIGURE 4.2 Epigenesis

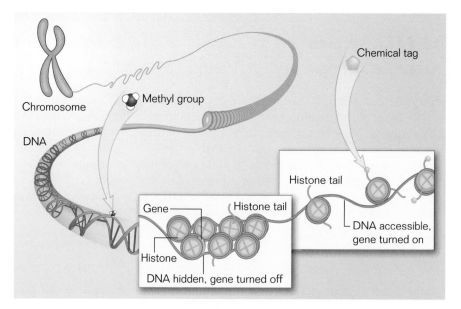

The epigenome can mark DNA in two ways, both of which play a role in turning genes off or on. The first occurs when certain chemical tags, which we call methyl groups, attach to the backbone of a DNA molecule. The second occurs when a variety of chemical tags attach to the tails of histones, which are spool-like proteins that package DNA neatly into chromosomes. This action affects how tightly DNA is wound around the histones.

(Source: NHGRI, www.genome.gov)

DNA in specific ways that alter brain development (Mychasiuk, Ilnytskyy, Kovalchuk, Kolb, & Gibb, 2011). Researchers believe that certain drugs that the mother uses during pregnancy cause DNA methylation, including nicotine, alcohol, and cocaine.

To understand the contributions of genetics to psychological disorders, researchers use three methods: family inheritance studies, DNA linkage studies, and genomics combined with brain scan technology. In family inheritance studies, researchers compare the disorder rates across relatives who have varying degrees of genetic relatedness. These studies examine disorder rates in different pairs of genetically related individuals. The highest degree of genetic relatedness is between identical or monozygotic (MZ) twins, who share 100 percent of their genotype. Dizygotic (DZ) or fraternal twins share, on the average, 50 percent of their genomes, but both types of twins share the same familial environment. Therefore, although MZ-DZ twin comparisons are useful, they do not allow researchers to rule out the impact of the environment. Similarly, studies of parents and children are confounded by the fact that the parents create the environment in which their children are raised. In order to separate the potential impact of the environment in studies comparing MZ and DZ twins, researchers turned long ago to adoption studies in which different families raised MZ twins, and therefore the twins experienced different environments.

For decades, family and twin studies were the only methods researchers had at their disposal to quantify the extent of genetic influences on psychological disorders. With the advent of genetic testing, however, researchers became able to examine specific genetic contributions to a variety of traits, including both physical and psychological disorders.

In a **genome-wide linkage study,** researchers study the families of people with specific psychological traits or disorders. The principle behind a linkage study is that characteristics near to each other on a particular gene are more likely inherited together. With refined genetic testing methods available, researchers can now carry this task out with far greater precision than was true in the past.

Although useful, linkage studies have limitations primarily because they require the study of large numbers of family members and may produce only limited findings. In **genome-wide association studies (GWAS)**, researchers scan the entire genome of individuals who are not related to find the associated genetic variations with a particular

genome-wide linkage study
Genetic method in which researchers study the families of people with specific psychological traits or disorders.

genome-wide association studies (GWAS)
Genetic method in which researchers scan the entire genome of individuals who are not related to find the associated genetic variations with a particular disease.

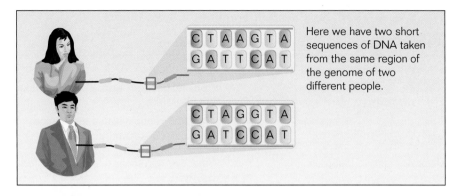

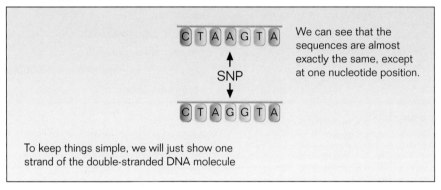

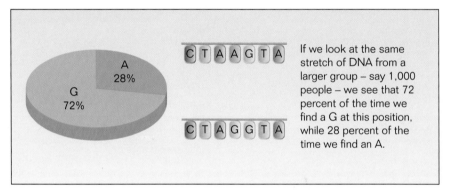

FIGURE 4.3 **SNP Detection**
This figure shows how SNP variation occurs such as when two sequences of DNA differ only by a single nucleotide ("A" vs. "G".)

disease. They are looking for a **single nucleotide polymorphism (SNP)** (pronounced "snip"), which is a small genetic variation that can occur in a person's DNA sequence. Four nucleotide letters—adenine, guanine, thymine, and cytosine (A, G, T, C)—specify the genetic code. A SNP variation occurs when a single nucleotide, such as an A, replaces one of the other three. For example, a SNP is the alteration of the DNA segment AAGGTTA to ATGGTTA, in which a "T" replaces the second "A" in the first snippet (Figure 4.3). With high-tech genetic testing methods now more readily available, researchers have more powerful tools to find SNPs that occur with particular traits (or diseases) across large numbers of people. Although many SNPs do not produce physical changes in people, researchers believe that other SNPs may predispose people to disease and even influence their response to drug regimens.

Imaging genomics is increasingly augmenting genetic studies. Researchers can combine linkage or association methods with imaging tools to examine connections between gene variants and activation patterns in the brain.

single nucleotide polymorphism (SNP) (pronounced "snip") A small genetic variation that can occur in a person's DNA sequence.

Treatment

At the present time, biologically based treatment cannot address the disorder's cause in terms of fixing genetic problems. Instead, biological therapies either involve medications, surgery, or other direct treatment forms on the brain.

TABLE 4.2 Major Psychotherapeutic Medications

Used to Treat	Category
Schizophrenia spectrum and other psychotic disorders	Antipsychotics Conventional or "typical" antipsychotic medications "Atypical" antipsychotic medications (also called "second generation")
Major depressive disorder	Selective serotonin reuptake inhibitors (SSRIs) Serotonin and norepinephrine reuptake inhibitors (SNRIs) Atypical antidepressants Tricyclic antidepressants Monoamine oxidase inhibitors (MAOIs) Mood stabilizers
Bipolar disorder	Anticonvulsants Atypical antipsychotics Antianxiety medications
Anxiety disorders	Benzodiazepines Atypical antidepressants MAOIs SSRIs SNRIs Tricyclics Stimulants
Attention-deficit/hyperactivity disorder	Stimulants Antidepressants

SOURCE: http://www.nimh.nih.gov/health/publications/mental-health-medications/complete-index.shtml

psychotherapeutic medications

Somatic treatments that are intended to reduce the individual's symptoms by altering the levels of neurotransmitters that researchers believe are involved in the disorder.

psychosurgery

A form of brain surgery, the purpose of which is to reduce psychological disturbance.

psychiatric neurosurgery

A treatment in which a neurosurgeon operates on brain regions.

Psychotherapeutic medications are intended to reduce the individual's symptoms by altering the levels of neurotransmitters that researchers believe are involved in the disorder. In 1950, a French chemist, Paul Charpentier, synthesized chlorpromazine (Thorazine). This medication gained widespread acceptance in the 1960s, and led the way toward the development of a wider range of psychotherapeutic agents.

Currently, the major categories of psychotherapeutic agents include antipsychotics, antidepressants, mood stabilizers, anticonvulsants, antianxiety medications, and stimulants (Table 4.2). As you can see from this table, some medication categories that pharmaceutical companies have designed to treat one disorder, such as antidepressants, also serve to treat other disorders, such as anxiety disorders. That clinicians use the same medications to treat different disorders suggests that abnormalities involving similar neurotransmitter actions may mediate these disorders.

Each of these medications can have serious side effects, leading patients experiencing these so-called adverse drug reactions to discontinue their use and try a different medication, perhaps from a different category. The Federal Drug Administration maintains a watch list of side effects with monthly updates (http://www.fda.gov/Safety/MedWatch/default.htm) and patients can sign up for a monthly newsletter by following a link on this website.

Biological treatments also include a second major category of interventions. **Psychosurgery**, or **psychiatric neurosurgery,** is a treatment in which a neurosurgeon operates

Psychiatric Neurosurgery

A handful of medical centers have been conducting several experimental brain surgeries as a last resort for severe obsessive-compulsive disorders that are beyond the range of standard treatment.

Cingulotomy
Probes are inserted into the brain to destroy a spot on the anterior cingulate gyrus, to disrupt a circuit that connects the emotional and conscious planning centers of the brain.

Capsulotomy
Probes are inserted deep into the brain and heated to destroy part of the anterior capsule, to disrupt a circuit thought to be overactive in people with severe OCD

Deep brain stimulation
As an alternative to capsulotomy, an electrode is permanently implanted on one or both sides of the brain. A pacemaker-like device then delivers an adjustable current.

Gamma knife surgery
An MRI-like device focuses hundreds of small beams of radiation at a point within the brain, destroying small areas of tissue.

FIGURE 4.4 Forms of Psychosurgery for Treating Severe Obsessive-Compulsive Disorder That Are Beyond the Range of Standard Treatment

on brain regions, most likely responsible for the individual's symptoms. The first modern use of psychosurgery was a prefrontal lobotomy, which the Portuguese neurosurgeon Egas Moniz developed in 1935. By severing the prefrontal lobes from the rest of the brain, Moniz found that he was able to reduce the patient's symptoms. Unfortunately, the procedure also caused severe changes in the patient's personality, including loss of motivation. The medical field considered the technique a major breakthrough at the time, leading Moniz to be honored with a Nobel Prize in 1949. In the 1960s, when psychotherapeutic medications became available, psychiatrists had an alternative to prefrontal lobotomies, allowing them to reduce a patient's symptoms without resorting to this extreme measure.

Modern psychosurgery relies on targeted interventions designed to reduce symptoms in patients who have proven otherwise unresponsive to less radical treatment (Figure 4.4). Each of these psychiatric neurosurgery forms targets a specific region of the brain that researchers believe is involved as a cause of symptoms. With higher levels of precision that reflect advances in surgical techniques, neurosurgeons can produce a lesion in a specific brain region to provide symptom relief. For individuals with severe obsessive-compulsive or major depressive disorder, the lesions target the cortex, striatum, and thalamus. **Deep brain stimulation (DBS),** also called **neuromodulation,** is another form of psychiatric neurosurgery in which permanently implanted electrodes trigger responses in specific brain circuits, as needed (Shah, Pesiridou, Baltuch, Malone, & O'Reardon, 2008).

In **electroconvulsive therapy (ECT),** attached electrodes across the head produce an electric shock that produces brief seizures. Ugo Cerletti, an Italian neurologist seeking a treatment for epilepsy, developed this method in 1937. ECT became increasingly popular in the 1940s and 1950s, but, as the movie *One Flew over the Cuckoo's Nest* depicts, staff in psychiatric hospitals also misused it as a way to restrain violent patients. Even though ECT had largely fallen into disuse by the mid-1970s, psychiatrists continued to use it to treat a narrow range of disorders. A comprehensive review of controlled studies using ECT for treatment of major depressive disorder showed that, in the short-term, ECT was more effective than medications in producing rapid improvement of symptoms. However, there are long-term ECT consequences including memory impairment (UK ECT Review Group, 2003).

deep brain stimulation (DBS)
A somatic treatment in which a neurosurgeon implants a microelectrode that delivers a constant low electrical stimulation to a small region of the brain, powered by an implanted battery.

neuromodulation
A form of psychiatric neurosurgery in which permanently implanted electrodes trigger responses in specific brain circuits, as needed.

electroconvulsive therapy (ECT)
The application of electrical shock to the head for the purpose of inducing therapeutically beneficial seizures.

4.3 Trait Theory

personality trait

An enduring pattern of perceiving, relating to, and thinking about the environment and others.

Five Factor Model (also called "Big Five")

Trait theory proposing that there are five basic dispositions in personality.

As much a theory about normal personality functioning as about psychological disorders, the trait theory approach proposes that abnormality occurs when the individual has maladaptive **personality traits.** In Chapter 3, we mentioned briefly that some assessment methods focus on measuring these qualities of personality, which we think of as stable, enduring dispositions that persist over time. For many personality trait theorists, these components of psychological functioning are long-standing qualities that are potentially biologically inherited.

It is easy for most people to relate to trait theory because it fits so closely with the use of the term "personality" in everyday life. When you think about how to describe the personality of someone you know, you will likely come up with a list of qualities that seem to fit the person's observable behavior. These characteristics typically take the form of adjectives such as "friendly," or "calm," or perhaps, "anxious" and "shy." Trait theories of personality propose that adjectives such as these capture the essence of the individual's psychological makeup. The fact that people use these adjectives in everyday life to describe themselves and others agrees with the basic principle of trait theory—namely, that personality is equivalent to a set of stable characteristic attributes.

The predominant trait theory in the field of abnormal psychology is the **Five Factor Model,** also called the "Big Five" (Figure 4.5) (McCrae & Costa, 1987). According to this theory, each of the basic five dispositions has six facets, which leads to a total of 30 personality components. The Five Factor Model includes the personality traits of neuroticism, extraversion, openness to experience, agreeableness, and conscientiousness (conveniently, they spell out "OCEAN" or "CANOE"). A complete characterization of an individual on the five factors involves providing scores or ratings on each facet.

According to trait theory, where they fall on the 30 facets strongly influences the shape of people's lives. People high on the traits that define the less psychologically healthy end of each continuum may be more likely to experience negative life events

Big Five		
	Low scorers	**High scorers**
1 Extroversion	Loner Quiet Passive Reserved	Joiner Talkative Active Affectionate
2 Agreeableness	Suspicious Critical Ruthless Irritable	Trusting Lenient Soft-hearted Good-natured
3 Conscientiousness	Negligent Lazy Disorganized Late	Conscientious Hard-working Well-organized Punctual
4 Neuroticism	Calm Even-tempered Comfortable Unemotional	Worried Temperamental Self-conscious Emotional
5 Openness to experience	Down-to-earth Uncreative Conventional Uncurious	Imaginative Creative Original Curious

FIGURE 4.5 Five Factor Model of Personality

MINI CASE

Trait Theory Approaches to Treating Meera

Because trait theory does not incorporate treatment, there are no obvious ways in which a clinician would apply this perspective to Meera's depression. However, as Dr. Tobin noted in the Case Report, Meera's Axis II diagnosis is deferred. Assessment of Meera's personality traits could assist in determining whether she in fact would receive such a diagnosis. Even if she does not have a personality disorder, it is possible that Meera's personality trait profile would be relevant to treatment. For example, she seems not to be overly introverted, as she interacts frequently with friends. Her depressive symptoms appear not to be overlaid

onto personality traits that include high neuroticism. She seems to enjoy activities that involve creativity and exploration of the outdoors, indicating a normative personality for her age in openness to experience. Prior to her depressive episode, she was, at least, average in conscientiousness, as her successful work history indicated, and there is no evidence to suggest that she is unusually low in agreeableness. Meera's clinician would most likely order an assessment that includes a personality trait-based measure to confirm these hypotheses and to determine whether or not she has a comorbid personality disorder.

because their personalities make them more vulnerable to life stresses. People high on personality traits representing riskiness (thrill-seeking) are more likely to get hurt because their personalities lead them into situations that can land them in trouble. According to the Five Factor Model, although circumstances can change personality, it's more likely that personality molds circumstances.

However, according to research using highly sophisticated data analytic designs to follow up on people over time, people can change even their fundamental personality traits. Most of the research is based on samples whose scores fall within the normal range of functioning. For example, as people get older, they are less likely to act impulsively (Terracciano, McCrae, Brant, & Costa, 2005).

The main value of understanding personality trait theory is that it provides a perspective for examining personality disorders. Research based on the Five Factor Model became the basis for the current attempts to reformulate the personality disorders in the *DSM-5*. Although the Five Factor Model does not necessarily provide a framework for psychotherapy, it has proven valuable as a basis for personality assessment within the context of understanding an individual's characteristic behavior patterns (Bastiaansen, Rossi, Schotte, & De Fruyt, 2011).

What's New in the DSM-5

Theoretical Approaches

Versions of the *DSM* prior to *DSM-III* were based almost entirely on clinical judgments framed within the psychodynamic model of abnormality. The *DSM* used terms such as "neurosis" and "psychosis," which had meaning in the psychodynamic world, to differentiate disorder categories. For example, anxiety disorders fell into the category of neurosis because their primary symptoms included irrational fears and worries. It labeled schizophrenia a psychotic disorder because its primary symptoms involve lack of contact with reality and other cognitive distortions. The *DSM-III* authors reconceptualized their approach along two major lines. First, they intended it to be atheoretical—meaning that there was no underlying theory, psychodynamic or otherwise. Second, they intended the diagnostic criteria to be ones that a variety of mental health professionals could reliably evaluate. The *DSM-III* Taskforce therefore commissioned studies in which researchers could evaluate the reliability of the diagnostic criteria. Rather than use the rather vague terminology (such as neurosis) that could be open to various interpretations, the *DSM-III* diagnostic spelled out criteria in exacting levels of detail. The *DSM-IV* and its later revision, the *DSM-IV-TR*, carried on this tradition of specifying diagnostic criteria in research-based, objective terms.

The *DSM-5* continues this empirical tradition and remains atheoretical. Critics now maintain that the authors should, instead, have developed a system that recognizes the known (to date) underpinnings of many of the disorders (Hyman, 2011). Rather than maintain the distinct categorical system of previous *DSM*s, disorders that share common features, whether in terms of symptoms, risk factors, or shared neural abnormalities, they believed that the *DSM-5* should have represented on spectrums or larger grouping systems. Although the *DSM-5* task forces considered making this radical change, they eventually decided to maintain the previous categories, albeit with some alterations. The move away from categories and toward dimensions would have required not only a massive restructuring, but also a need to retrain clinicians who were trained on the previous *DSM*s. These changes would also reinforce the medical model because they would lead to a system more similar to the diagnosis of physical diseases than psychological.

Whether future *DSM*s move away from the present system will depend largely on developments in the field of psychopathology. Section III of the *DSM-5* contains a dimensional system that clinicians can use to supplement their formal diagnoses of the personality disorders. Diagnoses are now in groups or chapters according to their presumed underlying similarities or causes. Ultimately, the authors will make decisions on empirical grounds, which will maintain the intent of *DSM* to maintain its atheoretical basis.

4.4 Psychodynamic Perspective

The **psychodynamic perspective** emphasizes unconscious determinants of behavior. Of all the psychological approaches, the psychodynamic gives greatest emphasis to the role of processes beneath the surface of awareness as influences on abnormality.

Freud's Theory

Emerging out of his interest in the cause of unusual symptoms in his patients, in the late 1800s, Sigmund Freud began to explore the idea that man could scientifically study and explain the causes of and symptoms of psychological disorders. By the time of his death in 1939, Freud had articulated a vision for psychological disorder cause and treatment with the basic tenet that most symptoms had roots buried deep within an individual's past.

According to Freud (1923), the mind has three structures: the id, the ego, and the superego. The **id** is the structure of personality hidden in the unconscious that contains instincts oriented toward fulfilling basic biological drives, including gratification of

psychodynamic perspective
The theoretical orientation in psychology that emphasizes unconscious determinants of behavior.

id
In psychoanalytic theory, the structure of personality that contains the sexual and aggressive instincts.

Sigmund Freud believed that an individual's dreams held vital information about their innermost wishes and desires that could be understood through dream analysis.

pleasure principle
In psychoanalytic theory, a motivating force oriented toward the immediate and total gratification of sensual needs and desires.

libido
An instinctual pressure for gratification of sexual and aggressive desires.

ego
In psychoanalytic theory, the structure of personality that gives the individual the mental powers of judgment, memory, perception, and decision making, enabling the individual to adapt to the realities of the external world.

reality principle
In psychoanalyic theory, the motivational force that leads the individual to confront the constraints of the external world.

secondary process thinking
In psychoanalytic theory, the kind of thinking involved in logical and rational problem solving.

superego
In psychoanalytic theory, the structure of personality that includes the conscience and the ego ideal; it incorporates societal prohibitions and exerts control over the seeking of instinctual gratification.

defense mechanisms
Tactics that keep unacceptable thoughts, instincts, and feelings out of conscious awareness and thus protect the ego against anxiety.

psychosexual stages
According to psychoanalytic theory, the normal sequence of development through which each individual passes between infancy and adulthood.

sexual and aggressive needs. The id follows the **pleasure principle,** a motivating force that seeks immediate and total gratification of sensual needs and desires. According to Freud, we can only obtain pleasure when the tension of an unmet drive reduces. The way the id attempts to achieve pleasure is not necessarily through the actual gratification of a need with tangible rewards. Instead, the id uses wish fulfillment to achieve its goals. Through wish fulfillment, the id conjures an image of whatever will satisfy the needs of the moment. We call the id's primal instincts the **libido.**

The center of conscious awareness in personality is the **ego,** which gives the individual the cognitive powers of judgment, memory, perception, and decision making. Freud (1911) described the ego as being governed by the **reality principle,** meaning that the ego uses rationality to achieve its goals. In contrast to the id's illogical primary process thinking, **secondary process thinking,** logical analytic approaches to problem solving, characterize the ego functions. The third part of the equation in psychodynamic theory is the **superego,** which is personality's seat of morality. The superego includes the conscience (sense of right and wrong), and the ego ideal, or aspirations.

According to Freud (1923), in a healthy individual's personality, the id achieves instinctual desires through the ego's ability to navigate in the external world within the confines that the superego places on it. Psychodynamics, or the interplay among the structures of the mind, is thus the basis for both normal and abnormal psychological functioning.

Freud believed that people need protection from knowing about their own unconscious desires. They do so by using **defense mechanisms** (Table 4.3). According to Freud, everyone uses defense mechanisms on an ongoing basis to prevent recognizing the existence of these desires. Although everyone uses defense mechanisms to some extent, they become problematic when an individual fails to come to terms completely with his or her true unconscious nature.

The topic of development forms an important piece of Freud's theory. In 1905, he proposed that there is a normal sequence of development through a series of what he called **psychosexual stages.** Freud claimed that children go through these stages in accordance

TABLE 4.3 Categories and Examples of Defense Mechanisms

Defense Mechanism	Definition
Displacement	Shifting unacceptable feelings or impulses from the target of those feelings to someone less threatening or to an object
Intellectualization	Resorting to excessive abstract thinking rather than focus on the upsetting aspects of response to issues that cause conflict or stress
Reaction formation	Transforming an unacceptable feeling or desire into its opposite in order to make it more acceptable
Repression	Unconsciously excluding disturbing wishes, thoughts, or experiences from awareness
Denial	Dealing with emotional conflict or stress by refusing to acknowledge a painful aspect of reality or experience that would be apparent to others
Projection	Attributing undesirable personal traits or feelings to someone else to protect one's ego from acknowledging distasteful personal attributes
Sublimation	Transferring an unacceptable impulse or desire into a socially appropriate activity or interest
Regression	Dealing with emotional conflict or stress by reverting to childish behaviors

with the development of their libido. At each stage, the libido becomes fixated on a particular "erogenous" or sexually excitable zone of the body. According to Freud, an individual may regress to behavior appropriate to an earlier stage or may become stuck, or fixated, at that stage. For example, the so-called *"anal retentive"* personality is overly rigid, controlled, and perfectionistic. Freud believed that the adult personality reflects the way in which the individual resolves the psychosexual stages in early life, though some reworking may occur at least up through middle adulthood. Freud also believed that the child's feelings toward the opposite-sex parent set the stage for later psychological adjustment. The outcome of what he called the "Oedipus Complex" (named after a tragic character in ancient Greece), determined whether the individual has a healthy ego or would spend a life marred by anxiety and repressed conflictual feelings.

Post-Freudian Psychodynamic Views

Freud developed his theory in the context of his clinical practice, but he also encouraged like-minded neurologists and psychiatrists to work together to develop a new theory of abnormality. Over a period of years, they spent many hours comparing notes about their

MINI CASE

Psychodynamic Approaches to Treating Meera

A clinician working with Meera from a psychodynamic perspective would assume that her difficulties stem from conflicts in early life. For example, the clinician would explore the resentment that she feels toward her parents for favoring her sister and her possible guilt over breaking away from the family when she established her own independent life. In treatment, the clinician would observe whether Meera re-enacts the conflicted feelings she has toward her parents onto the relationships that Meera establishes with the clinician. CCRT would seem particularly appropriate for Meera, given the possible role of these difficult relationships in triggering her depressive disorder. Meera's depressive symptoms would warrant a time-limited approach focusing on her current episode with the option that she would seek treatment in the future if her depression recurs.

Carl Jung's archetype theory would explain that popular superheroes are outward representations of universal aspects of human personality.

clinical cases and trying to come to a joint understanding of the cause of abnormality. Although they shared many of the same views when they began their discussions, several went on to develop their own unique brand of psychodynamic theory and now have their own schools of thought.

The most notable departure from Freud's school of thought came when Swiss psychiatrist Carl Jung (1875–1961) revamped the definition of the unconscious. According to Jung (1961), the unconscious is formed at its very root around a set of images common to all human experience, which he called *archetypes*. Jung believed that people respond to events in their daily lives on the basis of these archetypes, because they are part of our genetic makeup. For example, Jung asserted that archetypal characters (such as today's Batman and Superman) are popular because they activate the "hero" archetype. In addition, Jung (1916) believed that abnormality resulted from an imbalance within the mind, especially when people fail to pay proper attention to their unconscious needs.

For Alfred Adler (1870–1937) and Karen Horney (1885–1952), the ego was the most important aspect of personality. Although their theories represented distinct contributions, and each associated with it a particular type of therapy, they both gave great emphasis to the role of a healthy self-concept in normal psychological functioning. Adler talked about the negative consequences of an "inferiority complex," and Horney proposed that unhappiness comes from trying to live up to a false self. Both Adler and Horney also emphasized social concerns and interpersonal relations in the development of personality. They saw close relationships with family and friends and an interest in the life of the community as gratifying in their own right, not because a sexual or an aggressive desire is indirectly satisfied in the process (as Freud might say).

Perhaps the only psychodynamic theorist to give attention to the whole of life, not just childhood, was Erik Erikson (1902–1994). Like Adler and Horney, Erikson gave greatest attention to the ego, or what he called "ego identity." For this reason, we refer to the theories of Adler, Horney, and Erikson as the **ego psychology** group. In fact, we associate Erikson with the term "identity crisis," a task that he believed was central to development in adolescence. Erikson believed that the ego goes through a series of transformations throughout life in which a new strength or ability can mature. He also believed that each stage builds on the one that precedes it, and in turn, influences all following stages. However, Erikson proposed that any stage could become a major focus at any age—identity issues can resurface at any point in adulthood, even after a person's identity is relatively set. For example, a middle-aged

ego psychology
Theoretical perspective based on psychodynamic theory emphasizing the ego as the main force in personality.

According to Alfred Adler's theory, this person may be portraying himself negatively to others due to a sense of low self-worth and inferiority.

Karen Horney believed the ego to be a central aspect of human functioning.

woman who is laid off from her job may once again question her occupational identity as she seeks to find a new position for herself in the workforce.

Yet another group of psychodynamically oriented theorists focused on what became **object relations,** namely, the relationships that people have with the others ("objects") in their lives. In particular, the object relations theorists believed that the individual's relationship with the caregiver (usually the mother) becomes a model for all close adult relationships. These theorists included John Bowlby (1907–1990), Melanie Klein (1882–1960), D. W. Winnicott (1896–1971), Heinz Kohut (1913–1981), and Margaret Mahler (1897–1995). As with the ego psychologists, the object relations theorists each have a particular model of therapy that we associate with their theories. However, they all agree that early childhood relationships are at the root of abnormality.

The work of object relations theorists led to the development of what is now a widely recognized framework for understanding adult personality, particularly as applied to romantic relationships. Canadian psychologist Mary Salter Ainsworth (1913–1999) and her associates (1978) studied differences among infants in **attachment style,** or the way of relating to a caregiver figure. She developed the "strange situation," an experimental setting in which researchers separated infants from and then reunited them with their mothers.

Although designed as a theory of child development, later researchers have adapted the concept of attachment style to apply to adult romantic relationships. Most children develop secure attachment styles, and later in life relate to their close romantic partners without undue anxiety about whether or not their partners will care about them. Those who are insecurely attached in childhood, however, may show a pattern in adulthood of anxious attachment in which they feel they cannot rely on their partner's love and support. Alternatively, insecurely attached adults may show a dismissive or avoidant attachment style in which they fear rejection from others, and therefore try to protect themselves by remaining distant.

An individual's attachment style may also influence how he or she responds to psychotherapy. Across 19 separate studies involving nearly 1,500 clients, researchers found that attachment security was positively related to therapy outcome. Individuals with a secure attachment style, these researchers maintain, are better able

object relations
One's unconscious representations of important people in one's life.

attachment style
The way a person relates to a caregiver figure.

Attachment theorists believe that a child transfers emotional bonding from the primary caregiver to an object, such as a teddy bear, and eventually from this object to people outside the family.

to establish a positive working relationship with their therapists, which, in turn, predicts positive therapy outcomes (Levy, Ellison, Scott, & Bernecker, 2011).

Treatment

free association
A method used in psychoanalysis in which the client speaks freely, saying whatever comes to mind.

The main goal of traditional psychoanalytic treatment as developed by Freud (1913–14/1963) was to bring repressed, unconscious material into conscious awareness. To accomplish this task, he developed the therapeutic method of **free association,** in which the client literally says whatever comes to mind. Freud believed that clients needed to work through their unconscious conflicts, bringing them gradually into conscious awareness.

Current psychodynamic treatment is focused on helping clients explore aspects of the self that are "unconscious" in the sense that the client does not recognize them. Therapists focus in particular on how clients reveal and influence these aspects of the self in their relationship with the therapist. The key elements of psychodynamic therapy involve exploring the client's emotional experiences, use of defense mechanisms, close relationships with others, past experiences, and exploration of fantasy life in dreams, daydreams, and fantasies (Shedler, 2010).

behavioral perspective
A theoretical perspective in which it is assumed that abnormality is caused by faulty learning experiences.

classical conditioning
The learning of a connection between an originally neutral stimulus and a naturally evoking stimulus that produces an automatic reflexive reaction.

Unlike the stereotyped portrayal that you might see in movies or on television, clinicians need not conduct psychodynamic therapy on a couch, for years at a time, or with a silent therapist. However, given the impracticality of maintaining such a long-term and intense form of treatment, psychotherapists began developing briefer forms of psychodynamic therapy. Instead of attempting to revamp a client's entire psychic structure, psychotherapists using these methods focus their work on a specific symptom or set of symptoms for which the client is seeking help. The number of sessions can vary, but rarely exceeds 25. Unlike traditional psychodynamic therapy, the therapist takes a relatively active approach in maintaining the focus of treatment on the client's presenting problem or issues immediately relevant to that problem (Lewis, Dennerstein, & Gibbs, 2008).

In one version of brief psychodynamic therapy, the clinician identifies the client's "Core Conflictual Relationship Theme (CCRT)." The clinician assesses the client's wishes, expected responses from others, and client responses either to the responses of others or to the wish. Clients describe specific instances in their relationships with others that allow the clinician to make the CCRT assessment. The clinician then works with the clients in a supportive way to help them recognize and eventually work through these patterns (Jarry, 2010).

4.5 Behavioral Perspective

According to the **behavioral perspective,** the individual acquires maladaptive behavior through learning.

Theories

Behavioral therapists often use a fear hierarchy to gradually expose an individual to their most feared situations, such as being trapped in a smoke-filled room with no escape.

Classical conditioning accounts for the learning of emotional, automatic responses. For example, if you were trapped in a smoke-filled room with no immediate escape, you might experience fear every time you hear a loud buzzing noise that sounds like the fire alarm that blared in the background while you awaited rescue. Much of the classical conditioning that behavioral clinicians focus on involves this type of aversive conditioning in which the individual associates a maladaptive response with a stimulus that could not itself cause harm.

Evidence-Based Practice

As we discussed in Chapter 2, APA adopted principles of evidence-based practice that provide guidelines for clinicians to follow in their provision of psychological treatment. In this chapter, you've learned about the wide range of theoretical models available to clinicians, ranging from psychosurgery at one extreme, to family therapy at another. Given the recommendation that psychologists provide treatment best suited to the client's psychological disorder, the question becomes one of ensuring that each clinician has the ability to provide treatment within each of these theoretical models. However, is this a realistic assumption? Can we expect a clinician literally to be knowledgeable about each theoretical perspective thoroughly enough to be able to give clients the most effective interventions?

As research within clinical psychology and related fields continues to expand by an almost exponential rate, how can each clinician stay on top of all of the latest developments well enough to be comfortable in providing the most recent approaches to each client? According to the APA Ethical Guidelines, clinicians should work within their areas of expertise, and if they must extend outside of this area, then they should seek consultation. Moreover, each state within the United States maintains strict regulations over licensing of psychologists to ensure that they participate in continuing education. As a result, there are many safeguards to give clients protection from receiving outdated or inappropriate intervention methods.

You be the judge: As a consumer of psychology, do you feel that it is more important for potential clients to see a clinician whom they trust based on reputation, prior experience, or recommendations from other people, or should they instead find a specialist who, in the theoretical perspective, most closely matches evidence-based standards? Can a respected "generalist" provide care that is as high quality as another professional who is more narrowly trained? Ultimately, clients have protection against inadequate care by the standards that govern each profession (counseling, psychiatry, psychology, social work). However, it also benefits consumers to stay abreast of the latest developments so that they can make the most informed choices possible.

By contrast, in **operant conditioning** an individual acquires a maladaptive response by learning to pair a behavior with its consequences. The behavior's consequences are its **reinforcement**—the condition that makes the individual more likely to repeat the behavior in the future. Reinforcement can take many forms. For example, through positive reinforcement, your friends may laugh when you express outrageous opinions, making you more likely to express those opinions in the future. You might also learn through negative reinforcement to take an over-the-counter sleep medication if you find that it helps alleviate your insomnia. Both negative and positive reinforcement increase the frequency of the behaviors that precede them. In these examples, the behaviors that increase are speaking outrageous opinions and taking sleep medication.

According to the behavioral perspective, you don't have to directly experience reinforcement in order for it to modify your behavior. Psychologists who study **social learning theory** believe that people can learn by watching others. Through **vicarious reinforcement**, you become more likely to engage in these observed behaviors. You can also develop ideas about your own abilities, or sense of **self-efficacy,** by watching the results of your own actions or those of other people with whom you identify. For example, you may wonder whether you have the ability to overcome your fear of public speaking, but if you see a fellow student present successfully in class, this will build your feelings of self-efficacy, and you do well when it's your turn to get up and speak.

operant conditioning
A learning process in which an individual acquires behaviors through reinforcement.

reinforcement
The "strengthening" of a behavior.

social learning theory
Perspective that focuses on understanding how people develop psychological disorders through their relationships with others and through observation of other people.

vicarious reinforcement
A form of learning in which a new behavior is acquired through the process of watching someone else receive reinforcement for the same behavior.

self-efficacy
The individual's perception of competence in various life situations.

MINI CASE

Behavioral Approaches to Treating Meera

Following from the behavioral assumption that clients experiencing major depressive episodes have developed maladaptive responses, a behaviorally oriented clinician would give Meera the opportunity to learn new, adaptive behaviors. As you will learn in Chapter 9, behavioral approaches to major depressive disorder involve having clients increase the frequency of positively reinforcing events. Meera would keep a diary of her interactions with friends, involvement in exercise, and other enjoyable activities, which she would then show to her therapist. To increase the frequency of these behaviors, Meera and her clinician would develop a set of rewards that would occur with their completion based on rewards that Meera would find desirable. For effective intervention, the clinician would need to ensure that Meera can realistically obtain her goals so that she continues to experience success in achieving them.

Treatment

counterconditioning
The process of replacing an undesired response to a stimulus with an acceptable response.

systematic desensitization
A variant of counterconditioning that involves presenting the client with progressively more anxiety-provoking images while in a relaxed state.

Behavior therapists focus their therapeutic efforts on helping their clients unlearn maladaptive behaviors and replacing them with healthy, adaptive behaviors. In **counterconditioning,** clients learn to pair a new response to a stimulus that formerly provoked the maladaptive response. The new response is, in fact, incompatible with the old (undesirable) response. For example, you cannot be physically anxious and relaxed at the same time. Through counterconditioning, as developed by physician Joseph Wolpe (1915–1997), clients learn to associate the response of relaxation to the stimulus that formerly caused them to feel anxious. Clinicians teach clients to relax through a series of progressive steps; for example, by first relaxing the head and neck muscles, then the shoulders, arms, and so forth.

Counterconditioning often occurs in gradual stages using the **systematic desensitization** method. The therapist breaks down the maladaptive response into its smallest steps rather than exposing the client all at once to the feared stimulus. The client provides the therapist with a hierarchy, or list, of images associated with the feared

A psychologist exposes patients to a situation that would normally induce a phobic reaction. By practicing breathing exercises that reduce physiological tension and addressing the automatic thoughts that arise while in the feared situation, psychologists help patients to overcome their phobia.

Handling a stuffed toy spider → Handling a small rubber spider → Observing a live spider in an enclosed box → Observing a person handling a spider → Holding a live spider

FIGURE 4.6 **Fear Hierarchy in Systematic Desensitization**

stimulus. Starting with the least fearful situation in the hierarchy, the clinician asks the client to imagine that image and relax at the same time. After the client has established the connection between that image and relaxation, the clinician then moves up the hierarchy to the next level. Eventually, the client can confront the feared situation, while at the same time feeling entirely relaxed. At any point, though, if the client suffers a setback, the clinician moves back down the hierarchy to help the client relearn to associate relaxation with the image one level down. Figure 4.6 shows an example of a fear hierarchy that a clinician might use in systematically desensitizing a person who fears spiders.

Based on principles of operant conditioning, **contingency management** is a form of behavioral therapy in which clinicians provide clients with positive reinforcement for performing desired behaviors. The client learns to connect the outcome of the behavior with the behavior itself, in order to establish a contingency or connection. The clinician works with the client to develop a list of positive reinforcements that the client can receive only after performing the desired behavior. For example, if the client is trying to quit smoking, the clinician suggests a schedule in which the client can receive the designated reinforcement after going without a cigarette for a specific amount of time (such as permission to play video games). Gradually, the client extends the time period until he or she is able to cease smoking altogether. One contingency management form which hospitals use is the **token economy,** in which residents who perform desired activities earn tokens that they can later exchange for tangible benefits (LePage et al., 2003).

Behavioral treatments can also involve the principle of vicarious reinforcement, in which clinicians show models of people receiving rewards for demonstrating the desired behaviors (Bandura, 1971). For example, the clinician may show a video of someone who is enjoying playing with a dog to a client who is afraid of dogs. The vicarious reinforcement in this situation is the enjoyment of playing with the dog. The therapist might also use **participant modeling,** a form of therapy in which the therapist first shows the client a desired behavior and then guides the client through the behavior change.

Clinicians working within the behavioral perspective often provide their clients with homework assignments. The clinician may ask the client to keep a detailed record of the behaviors that he or she is trying to change, along with the situations in which the behaviors occur. The homework assignment might also include specific tasks that the clinician asks the client to perform with specific instructions for observing the outcome of completing those tasks.

contingency management
A form of behavioral therapy that involves the principle of rewarding a client for desired behaviors and not providing rewards for undesired behaviors.

token economy
A form of contingency management in which a client who performs desired activities earns chips or tokens that can later be exchanged for tangible benefits.

participant modeling
A form of therapy in which the therapist first shows the client a desired behavior and then guides the client through the behavioral change.

4.6 Cognitive Perspective

The **cognitive perspective** focuses on the way that people's thoughts influence their emotions.

cognitive perspective
A theoretical perspective in which it is assumed that abnormality is caused by maladaptive thought processes that result in dysfunctional behavior.

Theories

Psychological disorders, according to the cognitive perspective, are the product of disturbed thoughts. By changing people's thoughts, cognitive psychologists believe that they can also help clients develop more adaptive emotions (see Figure 4.7).

Figure 4.7 The Relationship Among Dysfunctional Attitude, Experience, Automatic Thought, and Negative Emotion

SOURCE: Adapted from A. T. Beck, A. J. Bush, B. F. Shaw, & G. Emery in *Cognitive Therapy of Depression.* Copyright © 1979 Guilford Publications, Inc. Reprinted by permission.

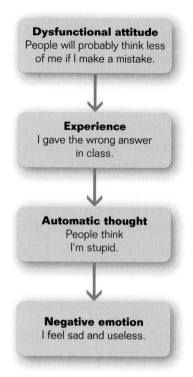

Dysfunctional attitude
People will probably think less of me if I make a mistake.

↓

Experience
I gave the wrong answer in class.

↓

Automatic thought
People think I'm stupid.

↓

Negative emotion
I feel sad and useless.

automatic thoughts
Ideas so deeply entrenched that the individual is not even aware that they lead to feelings of unhappiness and discouragement.

dysfunctional attitudes
Personal rules or values people hold that interfere with adequate adjustment.

cognitive restructuring
One of the fundamental techniques of cognitive-behavioral therapy in which clients learn to reframe negative ideas into more positive ones.

cognitive-behavioral therapy (CBT)
Treatment method in which clinicians focus on changing both maladaptive thoughts and maladaptive behaviors.

Acceptance and Commitment Therapy (ACT)
A form of cognitive therapy that helps clients accept the full range of their subjective experiences, such as distressing thoughts and feelings, as they commit themselves to tasks aimed at achieving behavior change that will lead to an improved quality of life.

Particularly problematic, according to the cognitive perspective, are **automatic thoughts**—ideas so deeply entrenched that the individual is not even aware that they lead to feelings of unhappiness and discouragement. Automatic thoughts are the product of **dysfunctional attitudes,** which are negative beliefs about the self that are also deeply engrained and difficult to articulate. Faulty logical processes contribute to the problem. Although everyone makes incorrect logical inferences from time to time, people prone to certain psychological disorders draw conclusions about themselves that are consistently detrimental to their feelings of well-being.

In the model developed by Albert Ellis, there is an "A-B-C" chain of events leading from faulty cognitions to dysfunctional emotions (Ellis, 2005). *A* refers to the "activating experience," *B* to beliefs, and *C* to consequences. In people with psychological disorders, these beliefs take an irrational form of views about the self and the world that are unrealistic, extreme, and illogical. These irrational beliefs cause people to create unnecessary emotional disturbance by sticking rigidly to the "musts" and then punishing themselves needlessly. They then engage in unnecessary self-pity and refuse to admit that they need help (see Figure 4.7).

Treatment

If dysfunctional thoughts cause dysfunctional emotions, as the cognitive perspective proposes, then changing a person's thoughts should alleviate the distress that they cause. In **cognitive restructuring,** the clinician attempts to change the client's thoughts by questioning and challenging the client's dysfunctional attitudes and irrational beliefs. The clinician also makes suggestions that the client can test in behavior outside the therapy session. For example, the clinician might give the client who is afraid of dogs the assignment to visit for five minutes with the neighbor's dog while, at the same time, practicing relaxation.

In **cognitive-behavioral therapy (CBT),** as the term implies, clinicians focus on changing both maladaptive thoughts and maladaptive behaviors. Clinicians incorporate behavioral techniques such as homework and reinforcement with cognitive methods that

MINI CASE

Cognitive Approach to Treating Meera

A clinician working within a cognitive perspective would treat Meera by helping her to develop more adaptive thoughts. From a strictly cognitive point of view, a clinician would focus on Meera's beliefs that she has let down her family and friends. The clinician would encourage Meera to challenge her conclusion and look with her at the basis for her assumption about her family's feelings toward her.

Combining the cognitive with a behaviorist approach, the clinician would also ask Meera to keep a record of her behaviors, including her participation in positively rewarding activities. However, unlike the strict behaviorist, a clinician working within the cognitive-behavioral perspective would also instruct Meera to keep a record of her dysfunctional thoughts, particularly those that exacerbate her negative emotions.

increase awareness by clients of their dysfunctional thoughts. Clients learn to recognize when their appraisals of situations are unrealistically contributing to their dysfunctional emotions. They can then try to identify situations, behavior, or people that help them counteract these emotions. The goal of CBT is to give clients greater control over their dysfunctional behaviors, thoughts, and emotions.

Cognitive theorists and therapists have continued to refine methods that target the problematic ways in which people view and deal with their psychological problems. **Acceptance and Commitment Therapy (ACT)** helps clients accept the full range of their subjective experiences, including distressing thoughts and feelings, as they commit themselves to tasks aimed at achieving behavior change that will lead to an improved quality of life (Forman, Herbert, Moitra, Yeomans, & Geller, 2007). Central to ACT's approach is the notion that, rather than fighting off disturbing symptoms, clients should acknowledge that they will feel certain unpleasant emotions in certain situations. By accepting, rather than avoiding such situations, individuals can gain perspective and, in the process, feel that they are more in control of their symptoms.

4.7 Humanistic Perspective

Psychologists who adhere to the **humanistic perspective** believe that people are motivated to strive for self-fulfillment and meaning in life. The "human" in humanistic refers to the focus of this perspective on the qualities that make each individual unique. Unlike the behavioral perspective, which translates principles from animal research to the behavior of people, the humanistic perspective focuses specifically on the values, beliefs, and ability to reflect on our own experiences that separate humans from other species.

Theories

Humanistic theorists and clinicians saw their ideas as a radical departure from the traditional focus of psychology, which minimized the role of free will in human experience. These theorists also saw human behavior in much more positive terms and viewed psychological disorders as the result of restricted growth potential. Existential psychology heavily influenced the work of humanistic theorists, a theoretical position that emphasizes the importance of fully appreciating each moment as it occurs (May, 1983). According to existential psychology, people who are tuned in to the world around them and experience life as fully as possible in each moment are the psychologically healthiest. Psychological disorders arise when people are unable to experience living in the moment. People develop disorders not due to fundamental flaws in their biology or thoughts, but modern society imposes restrictions on our ability to express our inner selves (Frankl, 1963; Laing, 1959).

By the mid-twentieth century, psychologists who were disenchanted with the major theoretical approaches to understanding human behavior and psychological disorder had come to believe that psychology had lost its contact with the human side of human behavior. These humanists joined together to form the "third force" in psychology, with the intention of challenging psychoanalysis and behaviorism. Two of the most prominent theorists within this tradition were Carl Rogers and Abraham Maslow.

Carl Rogers' (1902–1987) **person-centered theory** focuses on each individual's uniqueness, the importance of allowing each individual to achieve maximum fulfillment of potential, and the individual's need to confront honestly the reality of his or her

humanistic perspective
An approach to personality and psychological disorder that regards people as motivated by the need to understand themselves and the world and to derive greater enrichment from their experiences by fulfilling their unique individual potential.

person-centered theory
The humanistic theory that focuses on the uniqueness of each individual, the importance of allowing each individual to achieve maximum fulfillment of potential, and the need for the individual to confront honestly the reality of his or her experiences in the world.

Many psychologists today believe that early childhood experiences with primary caregivers influence how an individual behaves in interpersonal relationships throughout the life span.

client-centered
An approach based on the belief held by Rogers that people are innately good and that the potential for self-improvement lies within the individual.

self-actualization
In humanistic theory, the maximum realization of the individual's potential for psychological growth.

experiences in the world. In applying the person-centered theory to the therapy context, Rogers (1951) used the term **client-centered** to reflect his belief that people are innately good and that the potential for self-improvement lies within the individual rather than in the therapist or therapeutic techniques.

Rogers believed that a well-adjusted person's self-image should be congruent with the person's experiences. In this state of congruence, a person is fully functioning—meaning that the individual is able to put his or her psychological resources to their maximal use. Conversely, a psychological disorder is the result of a blocking of the individual's potential for living to full capacity, resulting in a state of incongruence or mismatch between self-image and reality. However, congruence is not a static state. To be fully functioning means that the individual is constantly evolving and growing.

According to Rogers, psychological disorders that develop have their origins in early life, when a person's parents are harshly critical and demanding. In this situation, people develop chronic anxiety about making mistakes that will subject them to further disapproval. Rogers used the term "conditions of worth" to refer to demands that parents place upon children. In order to be loved they feel they have to meet these criteria. As adults, they are constantly trying to meet the expectations of others instead of feeling that others will value them for their true selves.

Abraham Maslow's (1962) humanistic model centers on the notion of **self-actualization,** the maximum realization of the individual's potential for psychological growth. According to Maslow, self-actualized people have accurate self-perceptions and are able to find rich sources of enjoyment and stimulation in their everyday activities. They are capable of peak experiences in which they feel a tremendous surge of inner happiness, as if they were totally in harmony with themselves and their world. But these individuals are not simply searching for sensual or spiritual pleasure. They also have a philosophy of life that is based on humanitarian and egalitarian values.

Maslow defined the hierarchy of needs, which proposes that people are best able to experience self-actualization when they meet their basic physical and psychological needs. We call needs that are lower on the hierarchy deficit needs, because they describe a state in which the individual seeks to obtain something that is lacking. An individual who is preoccupied with meeting deficit needs cannot achieve self-actualization. For example, people who are motivated solely to make money (a lower-order need) will not be able to move up the hierarchy to self-actualization until they set their materialistic motives aside. Self-actualization is not a final end-state in and of itself, but is a process in which the individual seeks true self-expression.

Individuals who are self-actualized are able to achieve a sense of fulfillment by helping others because they have already met their own needs.

Treatment

A theory rich with implications for treatment, person-centered theory now forms the foundation of much of contemporary therapy and counseling. The client-centered model of therapy proposed specific guidelines for therapists to follow in order to ensure that clients are able to achieve full self-realization. According to Rogers, clinicians should focus on the client's needs, not on the preconceived clinician notions about what is best for the client. In fact, reflecting this emphasis on the inherent strengths of people seeking treatment, Rogers originated the use of the more collegial term "clients" rather than the illness-oriented term "patients."

Rogers believed that a clinician's job is to help clients discover their inherent goodness and in the process, to help each client achieve greater self-understanding. To counteract the problems caused by conditions of worth in childhood, Rogers recommended that therapists treat clients with **unconditional positive regard.** This method involves total acceptance of what the client says, does, and feels. As clients feel better about themselves, they become better able to tolerate the anxiety that occurs with acknowledging their own weaknesses because they no longer feel driven to see themselves as perfect. The clinician tries to be as empathic as possible and attempts to see the client's situation as it appears to the client.

unconditional positive regard
A method in client-centered therapy in which the clinician gives total acceptance of what the client says, does, and feels.

Contemporary humanistic and experiential therapists emphasize that, as much as possible, therapists can be most effective if they can see the world from the eyes of their clients. Therapists working within the client-centered model are trained in the techniques of reflection and clarification. In reflection, the therapist mirrors back what the client has just said, perhaps rephrasing it slightly. These techniques allow clients to feel that the clinician is empathetically listening and not judging them. Gradually, they feel increasingly confident to reveal their true, inner selves because they know that the clinician will not reject or label them as inadequate.

Rogers also suggested that clinicians should provide a model of genuineness and willingness to disclose their personal weaknesses and limitations. By doing so, clients realize that they don't have to put up a false front of trying to appear to be something that they're not. Ideally, the client will see that it is acceptable and healthy to be honest in confronting one's experiences, even if those experiences have less than favorable implications. For example, the Rogerian clinician might admit to having experiences similar to those the client describes, such as feeling anxious about speaking before a group.

Motivational interviewing (MI) is another client-centered technique that uses empathic understanding as a means of promoting behavioral change in clients (Miller & Rose, 2009). In motivational interviewing, the clinician collaborates with the client to strengthen the client's motivation to make changes by asking questions that elicit the individual's own arguments for change. MI, like the client-centered approach in general, emphasizes the client's autonomy.

motivational interviewing (MI)
A directive, client-centered style for eliciting behavior change by helping clients explore and resolve ambivalence.

MINI CASE

Humanistic Approaches to Treating Meera

In humanistic therapy, a clinician would treat Meera by focusing on her low feelings of self-worth. The clinician would explore how Meera was influenced by the negative comparisons her parents made when comparing her to her sister. The fact that they refused to accept Meera in the family unless she abided by their rules caused Meera to feel that people could not regard her as an individual on her own terms. The clinician would work with Meera to establish a firm therapeutic alliance by empathically listening to her descriptions of her feelings. Consistent with Carl Rogers' emphasis on becoming more aware of one's feelings, the clinician would encourage Meera to experience more fully her feelings regarding her rejection by her family and her sadness as a result of her disconnectedness from them. In this process, the clinician would help Meera identify her feelings and accept them without undue self-criticism.

4.8 Sociocultural Perspective

sociocultural perspective
The theoretical perspective that emphasizes the ways that individuals are influenced by people, social institutions, and social forces in the world around them.

family perspective
A theoretical perspective in which it is assumed that abnormality is caused by disturbances in the pattern of interactions and relationships within the family.

social discrimination
Prejudicial treatment of a class of individuals, seen in the sociocultural perspective as a cause of psychological problems.

Theorists within the **sociocultural perspective** emphasize the ways that people, social institutions, and social forces influence people in the world around them. The sociocultural perspective reaches outside the individual to include factors that may contribute to their development of psychological disorders.

Theories

Proponents of the **family perspective** see abnormality as caused by disturbances in the patterns of interactions and relationships that exist within the family. These disturbed patterns of relationships may create the "identified patient"; namely the individual in treatment whose difficulties reflect strains within the family.

Researchers within the sociocultural perspective also focus on **social discrimination** as a cause of psychological problems. Discrimination on the basis of gender, race, sexual orientation, religion, social class, and age, for example, can contribute to disorders in the realms of physical and mental health. Starting in the 1950s, researchers established the finding that psychological disorders are more commonly diagnosed among people in lower socioeconomic strata (Hollingshead & Redlich, 1958). This relationship may reflect the fact that people of lower social class experience economic hardships and have limited access to quality education, health care, and employment. Socioeconomic discrimination is further compounded by membership in ethnic or racial minorities. When people have few opportunities or when they encounter oppression because of unalterable human characteristics, they are likely to experience inner turmoil, frustration, and stress, leading to the development of psychological symptoms.

Psychological disorders can also emerge as a result of destructive historical events, such as the violence of a political revolution, the turmoil of a natural disaster, or the poverty of a nationwide depression. Since World War I, American psychologists have conducted large-scale studies of the ways in which war negatively affects psychological functioning. People who are traumatized as the result of terrorist attacks, exposure to battle, persecution, or imprisonment are at risk for developing serious anxiety disorders. Similarly, fires and natural disasters, such as earthquakes, tornadoes, and hurricanes, leave more than physical destruction in their wake.

Treatment

How do clinicians intervene with people suffering from conditions which sociocultural factors cause or exacerbate? Clearly, it is not possible to "change the world." However, clinicians can play a crucial role in helping people come to grips with problems that have developed within a family system, the immediate environment, or extended society.

According to family systems theorists, dysfunction within the family dynamic may be a main source of an individual's psychological distress.

In family therapy, the clinician encourages all family group members (however defined) to try new ways of relating to each other or thinking about their problems. The family therapist, sometimes working with a co-therapist, meets with as many family members as possible at one time. Rather than focusing on an individual's problems or concerns, family and couples therapists focus on the ways in which dysfunctional relational patterns maintain a particular problem or symptom. They also use a life-cycle perspective in which they consider the developmental issues, not only of each individual, but of the entire family or couple. Furthermore, family and couples therapists see the continuing relationships among the family members as potentially more healing than the relationship between clinicians and clients.

The particular techniques that clinicians use in family therapy depend greatly on the therapist's training and theoretical approach. An intergenerational family therapist might suggest drawing a genogram, a diagram of all relatives in the recent past, in an effort to understand the history of family relationships and to use this understanding to bring about change. A structural family therapist might suggest that a subset of the family members enact a disagreement as if they were characters in a play about the family. Strategic family therapists might work with family members to develop solutions to the issues that are causing difficulty. An experiential family therapist might work with the family members to develop insight into their relationships with each other.

In group therapy, people who share similar experiences share their stories with each other, aided by the facilitation of the therapist. According to Irvin Yalom (1995), a founder of group therapy, group therapy has a positive impact by allowing clients to find relief and hope in the realization that their problems are not unique. In the group, they can acquire valuable information and advice from people who share their concerns. Furthermore, in the process of giving to others, people generally find that they themselves derive benefit.

Clinicians use milieu therapy in treatment settings such as inpatient hospitals to promote positive functioning in clients by creating a therapeutic community. Community members participate in group activities, ranging from occupational therapy to training classes. Staff members encourage clients to work with and spend time with other residents, even when leaving on passes. Every staff person, whether a therapist, nurse, or paraprofessional, takes part in the overall mission of providing an environment that supports positive change and reinforces appropriate social behaviors. The underlying idea behind milieu therapy is that the pressure to conform to conventional social norms of behavior fosters more adaptive behavior on the part of individual clients. In addition, the normalizing effects of a supportive environment are intended to help the individual make a smoother and more effective transition to life outside the therapeutic community.

Although clinicians cannot reverse social discrimination, they can adopt a **multicultural approach** to therapy that relies on awareness, knowledge, and skills of the client's sociocultural context. For example, therapists need to be sensitive to the ways in which the client's cultural background interacts with his or her specific life experiences and family influences. A commitment to learning about the client's cultural, ethnic, and racial group and how these factors play a role in assessment, diagnosis, and treatment, characterize knowledge. Multicultural skills include mastery of culture-specific therapy techniques that are responsive to a client's unique characteristics.

multicultural approach
To therapy: therapy that relies on awareness, knowledge, and skills of the client's sociocultural context.

MINI CASE

Sociocultural Approach to Treating Meera

A clinician working within the sociocultural perspective would incorporate Meera's specific family issues within the context of her cultural background. Not only have Meera's symptoms emerged from her own construction of her family's attitude toward her work and relationship decisions, but they also reflect her cultural background, which places heavy emphasis on family obligations. By choosing a path that is different from that of her sister, Meera has, perhaps, in reality, or in her own perception, violated her family's expectations. The clinician might suggest that Meera be seen with her family, if possible, to work through these cultural and relational issues.

REAL STORIES

Sylvia Plath, Major Depressive Disorder

"I am inhabited by a cry.
Nightly it flaps out
Looking, with its hooks,
for something to love.
I am terrified by this dark thing
That sleeps in me;
All day I feel its soft,
feathery turnings, its malignity."

At the age of 30, American poet Sylvia Plath succumbed to her lifelong battle with depression. On the night of November 11, 1963, with her two infant children asleep, Sylvia carefully placed towels under the crack of the doors to her children's bedroom and her kitchen, turned on the gas to her oven, and laid her head inside. She had left milk and bread in her children's room with the window open to the chilly London night so that their breakfast would be fresh for the morning. Only days prior, she had begun a course of antidepressants, and experts believe that her suicide occurred at a dangerous time in the course of treatment with such medications, when the individual—still depressed—becomes simultaneously more active, leading to an increased risk for suicide attempts. *Bitter Fame: A Life of Sylvia Plath*, by Anne Stevenson, chronicles the entire life and writings of the notoriously tortured writer through Sylvia's journal entries, personal letters, and interviews with those who were in her life. Born and raised around Boston, Massachusetts, Sylvia began writing at the age of seven. Her life experiences would serve to inspire her until the final days of her life. Throughout her childhood and adolescence, Sylvia produced an impressive number of poems and short stories that gave rise to her ultimate dream of being a professional writer. Perhaps the most influential event of her life was the sudden death of her father shortly after her eighth birthday. The event

served to fuel her innermost fears and desires, and the loss of her father was an ever-present theme in her work. This loss also left her incredibly sensitive to depression following abandonment from others in her life, particularly romantic partners.

Sylvia grew up in the prototypical New England town of Wellesley, Massachusetts, and attended Smith College in Northampton, Massachusetts, on an academic scholarship. Although the transition to college was initially difficult for Sylvia, her intelligence and diligent work ethic helped her receive high grades and a prominent reputation at Smith. As she grew into young adulthood, Sylvia started to experience heightened moodiness and began to suffer from bouts of depression. At age 19, she attempted suicide by swallowing her mother's sleeping pills and hiding in a crawlspace in her house. It was two days before anyone discovered her in a semi-conscious and dazed state. Following the attempt, Sylvia entered a nearby psychiatric hospital for a period of four months, where she received electroconvulsive

therapy (ECT) and insulin treatment. This marked a major turning point in her life and in her writing.

"Attributable to her ECT," Stevenson writes in *Bitter Fame*, "is the unseen menace that haunts nearly everything she wrote, her conviction that the world, however benign in appearance, conceals dangerous animosity, directed particularly toward herself." We can observe her deeply introspective nature in her personal journals that she faithfully kept throughout her life. Her journals served as an important source of self-expression in which she poured her every thought and feeling. She utilized this means of self-expression particularly in times of distress, offering readers an intimate view of her darkest moments.

After her hospitalization, Sylvia returned to Smith and graduated in 1954, summa cum laude. She went on to pursue graduate studies on a prestigious Fulbright scholarship in Cambridge, England. As Sylvia matured professionally while studying at Cambridge, her romantic interests turned to a fellow poet whom she greatly admired, Ted Hughes.

After meeting at a party, the two experienced an immediate attraction and, after a whirlwind romance, married in a secret ceremony in England. At the time, Sylvia was funded by a fellowship that she feared would dissipate should news of her marriage surface. Eventually, the couple became public with their union, and spent the first few months of their married life in Spain while Ted was teaching.

In *Bitter Fame*, Stevenson describes how Sylvia's mood shifts became highly pronounced after the initial period of marital bliss had faded. "Her moods seemed to soar and sink with alarming rapidity. Sylvia recorded in her journal her volatile and intense reactions to some

Sylvia Plath in 1957.

unmentioned incident, possibly arising out of her husband's surprise at the rancor she displayed in a running tiff with the house owner, who wanted to raise the rent, or perhaps arising out of an evening when they had drinks with some English people who upset Sylvia. These moods, Ted found, were largely unaccountable: they began and ended like electric storms, and he came to learn simply to accept their occurrence."

The couple then moved overseas to Sylvia's home state of Massachusetts where Sylvia taught English courses at her alma mater, Smith College. Her initial excitement about the prestige of teaching at such a renowned institution quickly gave way to her anxiety about the amount of work entailed and particularly how this left no time for her to work on her own writing. She was further plagued by crippling periods of self-doubt that propelled her again into depression. She wrote, "Last night I felt . . . the sick, soul-annihilating flux of fear in my blood switching its current to defiant fight. I could not sleep, although tired, and lay feeling my nerves shaved to pain and the groaning inner voice: oh, you can't teach, can't do anything. Can't write, can't think. And I lay under the negative icy flood of denial, thinking that voice was all my own, a part of me, and it must somehow conquer me and leave me with my worst visions: having had the chance to battle it and win day by day, and having failed." Such thoughts of worthlessness are common to individuals suffering from major depression.

After one year of teaching, Sylvia and Ted moved to Boston where they became part of a closely knit community of poets and writers. At this point, Ted had begun to gain considerable accolades for his writing, and the couple lived mainly off of money from awards from his writing. This allowed Sylvia to spend the majority of her time developing her writing. When she was pregnant with the couple's first child, the Hugheses moved to England, settling in an apartment in London, and then a home in the countryside prior to the birth of their second child.

Although by all accounts Ted was a devoted husband and father, Sylvia was stricken with fears of his infidelity, and often accused her husband of extramarital affairs. On one occasion, Ted was late returning home from an interview with the BBC. She reacted by destroying a large portion of the materials on which he was writing, along with some of his most prized books. Eventually, the two separated (although they never divorced), and after Ted moved out of the home that they shared, Sylvia moved to a flat in London with their two children. Here, she experienced a surge of creative energy that produced many of her most famous poems. At this point Sylvia had completed her first and what was to be her only novel, *The Bell Jar*, a semi-autobiographical account of a young woman's journey through young adulthood, navigating the muddy waters of career, romance, and psychological distress. Much of the narrative of the book directly mirrors Sylvia's own experiences.

Her poetry, too, reflected her struggles as she continued to grapple with her deteriorating mental health. "As absorbed and intent as a cartographer," Stevenson writes in *Bitter Fame*, "Sylvia reported in her poems on the weather of her inner universe and delineated its two poles: 'stasis' and rage. At the depressed pole there was a turning in on herself, a longing for nonbeing . . . It was as though she looked in a glass and a huge mirror image of her traumatized childhood self stared back."

Although she was experiencing a surge of creativity, Sylvia was falling into a deep depression. She began seeing a psychiatrist who noted the severity of her condition. Unable to care for herself and her children, Sylvia stayed with friends while she tried to recuperate—too afraid to face another round of ECT in a psychiatric hospital. One day, Sylvia defiantly decided that she was ready to return to her flat with her children. Her friends, puzzled by her sudden determinism, tried in vain to persuade her to stay in their care. The very evening she went home, finally away from the watchful eyes of friends, Sylvia ended her short, yet intense life. In the years following her death, critics have come to regard Sylvia Plath as one of the most talented and influential poets of the twentieth century. Compiled by Ted Hughes, who went on to raise their two children with his second wife, *The Collected Poems*, a complete collection of Sylvia's poems, which she wrote between adolescence and the end of her life, won the Pulitzer Prize in 1982.

4.9 Biopsychosocial Perspectives on Theories and Treatments: An Integrative Approach

Now that you have read about the major perspectives on abnormal behavior, you probably can see value in each of them. Certain facets of various theories may seem particularly useful and interesting. In fact, you may have a hard time deciding which approach is the "best." However, as we have said repeatedly, most clinicians select aspects of the various models, rather than adhering narrowly to a single one. In fact, in recent decades, there has been a dramatic shift away from narrow clinical approaches that are rooted in a single theoretical model. Most clinicians use approaches that are integrative or eclectic. The therapist views the needs of the client from multiple perspectives and develops a treatment plan that responds to these particular concerns.

Following a more comprehensive psychological assessment as her treatment plan indicated, the clinician determined that Meera would benefit the most from a cognitive-behavioral approach to psychotherapy in conjunction with medication. She followed up on both of these recommendations and saw a psychiatrist who prescribed her an SSRI. She met with her psychiatrist once per week for the first month of her medication course and then began to meet once per month for a check-in. Meera also began seeing a therapist for weekly psychotherapy sessions. Using a cognitive-behavioral perspective, the beginning of the work with her therapist focused on strategies such as behavioral activation that would help her cope with the depressive symptoms that were interfering with her functioning. Once her depression remitted, the therapy began to focus on Meera's maladaptive thought patterns regarding her interpersonal relationships. With help from her therapist, Meera recognized that she had created unachievable standards for herself, which she thought that her friends and family were expressing. Looking more carefully at her relationships, she discovered that she was imposing these expectations upon herself and that her friends and family accepted her for who she was.

Dr. Tobin's reflections: Given her response to treatment, Meera's depression appears to be a result of both a biological vulnerability and a maladaptive thought process that began to emerge as she grew into adulthood. As such, it will be important for Meera to remain on the antidepressant medication to prevent future depressive episodes from occurring. Her therapist may recommend that she stay in therapy as it can take some time for individuals' thought patterns to become more adaptive. Although she was already feeling better after only two months, given that her thought pattern has seemingly been present most of her life, it will be important for Meera to remain in therapy to ensure that she adapt to a more corrective way of coping with her environment and with stress. Meera's strong commitment to recovery helped motivate her to receive the treatment that she needed, and as a result, her prognosis is quite positive.

SUMMARY

- **Theoretical perspectives** influence the ways in which clinicians and researchers interpret and organize their observations about behavior. In this chapter, we discussed five major theoretical perspectives: psychodynamic, humanistic, sociocultural, behavioral and cognitively based, and biological. We concluded the discussion with a consideration of an integrative approach in which theorists and clinicians bring together aspects and techniques of more than one perspective.

- Within the **biological perspective,** clinicians view disturbances in emotions, behavior, and cognitive processes as caused by abnormalities in the body's functioning, such as brain and nervous system, or endocrine system disorders. A person's genetic makeup can play an important role in precipitating certain disorders. In trying to assess the relative roles of nature and nurture, researchers have come to accept the notion of an interaction between genetic and environmental contributors to abnormality. Treatments that clinicians base on the biological model involve a range of somatic therapies, the most common of which is medication. More extreme somatic interventions include **psychosurgery** and **electroconvulsive treatment.**

- Trait theory proposes that abnormal behavior reflects maladaptive **personality traits.** The basic principle of trait theory is that personality is equivalent to a set of stable characteristics. In abnormal psychology, the predominant trait theory is the **Five Factor Model,** or "Big Five," which includes the personality traits of neuroticism, extraversion, openness to experience, agreeableness, and conscientiousness ("OCEAN" or "CANOE"). Although the Five Factor Model does not necessarily provide a framework for psychotherapy, it does provide a perspective for assessing for personality disorders.

- The **psychodynamic perspective** is a theoretical orientation that emphasizes unconscious determinants of behavior and is derived from Freud's psychoanalytic approach. We use the term *psychodynamics* to describe interaction among the **id,** the **ego,** and the **superego.** According to psychodynamic theorists, people use **defense mechanisms** to keep unacceptable thoughts, instincts, and feelings out of conscious awareness. Freud proposed that there is a normal sequence of development through a series of what he called **psychosexual stages,** with each stage focusing on a different sexually excitable zone of the body: oral, anal, phallic, and genital.

- Post-Freudian theorists such as Jung, Adler, Horney, and Erikson departed from Freudian theory, contending that Freud overemphasized sexual and aggressive instincts. **Object relations** theorists such as Klein, Winnicott, Kohut, and Mahler proposed that interpersonal relationships lie at the core of personality and that the unconscious mind contains images of the child's parents and of the child's relationships with the parents.

- Treatment within the psychodynamic perspective may incorporate techniques such as **free association,** dream analysis, analysis of transference, and analysis of resistance. Considerable debate about the tenets and techniques of the psychodynamic perspective continues to take place. Much of this debate focuses on the fact that psychodynamic concepts are difficult to study and measure and that some clinicians now regard Freudian notions as irrelevant in contemporary society. Newer approaches, based on object relations theory, have adapted the concept of infant **attachment style** to understanding the ways that adults relate to significant people in their lives.

- According to the **behavioral perspective,** faulty learning experiences cause abnormality. According to the cognitive-behavioral (sometimes called cognitive) perspective, maladaptive thought processes cause abnormality. Behaviorists contend that individuals acquire many emotional reactions through **classical conditioning. Operant conditioning,** with Skinner's emphasis on **reinforcement,** involves the learning of behaviors that are not automatic. **Social learning theorists** have studied the process of acquiring new responses by observing and imitating the behavior of others, which we call modeling. In interventions based on behavioral theory, clinicians focus on observable behaviors.

- Beck's cognitive theories emphasize disturbed ways of thinking. Clinicians adhering to a **cognitive perspective** work with clients to change maladaptive thought patterns.

- At the core of the **humanistic perspective** is the belief that human motivation is based on an inherent tendency to strive for self-fulfillment and meaning in life, notions that were rooted in existential psychology. Carl Rogers' person-centered theory focuses on the uniqueness of each individual, the importance of allowing each individual to achieve maximum fulfillment of potential, and the need for the individual to confront honestly the reality of his or her experiences in the world. Maslow's **self-actualization** theory focuses on the maximum realization of the individual's potential for psychological growth. In **client-centered therapy,** Rogers recommended that therapists treat clients with **unconditional positive regard** and empathy, while providing a model of genuineness and a willingness to self-disclose.

- Theorists within the **sociocultural perspective** emphasize the ways that people, social institutions, and social forces influence individuals. Proponents of the **family perspective** see the individual as an integral component of the pattern of interactions and relationships that exists within the family. The four major approaches are intergenerational, structural, strategic, and experiential. Psychological disturbance can also arise as a result of discrimination that occurs with attributes such as gender, race, or age or of pressures associated with economic hardships. General social forces, such as fluid and inconsistent values in a society and destructive historical events, such as political revolution, natural disaster, or nationwide depression also can adversely affect people. The nature of the group involved determines treatments within the sociocultural perspective. In family therapy, clinicians encourage family members to try new ways of relating to each other and thinking about their problems. In group therapy, people share their stories and experiences with others in similar situations. Milieu therapy provides a context in which the intervention is the environment, rather than the individual, usually consisting of staff and clients in a therapeutic community.

- In contemporary practice, most clinicians take an integrative approach, in which they select aspects of various models rather than adhering narrowly to a single one. Three ways in which clinicians integrate various models include technical eclecticism, theoretical integration, and the common factors approach.

KEY TERMS

Neurodevelopmental Disorders

Learning Objectives

5.1 Explain the characteristics and causes of intellectual
disability

5.2 Explain characteristics, theories, and treatment of autism
spectrum disorder

5.3 Differentiate among learning and communication and
communication disorders

5.4 Explain characteristics, theories, and treatment of ADHD

5.5 Describe motor disorders

5.6 Analyze the biopsychosocial model of neurodevelopmental
disorders

CHAPTER 5

Case Report: Jason Newman

Demographic information: Jason is an 8-year-old Caucasian male.

Presenting problem: Jason's third-grade teacher, Mrs. Brownstein, had noted his increasingly hyperactive behavior and inability to pay attention in class since the first day of school. As she did not wish to cause alarm for Jason's parents, Mrs. Brownstein observed his behavior over the first few weeks of school to determine if settling into the classroom might decrease his rowdy behavior. However, his behavior only deteriorated as the weeks went on, and Mrs. Brownstein decided to contact his parents, Pam and John, and suggest a psychological evaluation for Jason. Though they had been advised by previous teachers to bring Jason to a psychologist, the Newmans' health insurance had not covered this expense, and they were unable to afford it on their own. However, it was becoming clear that treatment for Jason would be necessary in order for him to successfully complete his schooling. Fortunately, Mrs. Brownstein's husband was a child psychologist with a private practice who agreed to evaluate Jason free of charge. Jason's mother, Pam, accompanied him to see Dr. Brownstein, who interviewed her separately before seeing Jason. Pam explained that Jason has been a "very fidgety child" from infancy but that his disruptive and often inappropriate behavior in school has been getting notably worse over the past 3 years. Since he was the first child for the couple, Pam did not perceive that his apparent abundance in energy was abnormal. The couple also has a 4-year-old child, Nicholas, whose behavior as an infant was much "calmer" in comparison, which further alerted them that something was different about Jason. Pam further explained that outside the classroom environment, Jason is usually more restless in situations where he has to sustain attention for a long period of time.

For instance, Pam noted that in church on Sundays, Jason typically starts to squirm in his seat after the first 5 minutes of the service. She remarked that this is quite embarrassing for her and her husband, who have difficulty getting Jason to sit still and as a result have stopped going to church altogether. She further described that it was often difficult to take care of Nicholas when he was an infant, because Jason would often run into the nursery when Nicholas was being fed or changed and demand that Pam pay attention to him. On several occasions Jason would grab the feeding bottle out of Pam's hand as she was feeding Nicholas.

While she attempts to be very patient with Jason, Pam reports that her husband, John, has more difficulty coping with their son's restless behavior. Pam described instances in which Jason has been particularly "rowdy" in the home and broken furniture and expensive items that were on tabletops he had climbed on. She stated that this has greatly strained the relationship between John and Jason and has been a source of tension between her and John as well, as they often disagree on how to discipline him. Pam and John have tried, unsuccessfully, to implement a system of punishment and rewards based on performance at school. However, this has only caused further frustration as Pam and John often disagree as to the appropriate amount of punishment.

Pam stated that Jason's teachers had been describing the same patterns of behavior each year, though during this current school year his ability to pay attention has severely declined, perhaps, as Pam noted, because the material presented in the classroom has become more complex and requires more attention and thought. During earlier years, the extent of Jason's inability to pay attention would manifest in his leaving classroom materials strewn about after he was finished, and he would never pick up after himself. During the current school year, when presented with difficult problems in the classroom, Mrs. Brownstein reported that Jason would bolt from his desk and go to another part of the room and begin playing with toys when she is trying to give a lesson. Pam was particularly concerned that Jason's misbehavior in school would impinge upon the quality of his education throughout the years, especially since his grades have been at the bottom of the class each year. Furthermore, it had been difficult for Jason to make friends at school, given his overly energetic demeanor and his propensity to be rude or impatient with other children. Pam stated that she feared without good peer associations at school, Jason might become isolated and subjected to ridicule from his schoolmates. She remarked that Jason and Nicholas did not get along very well either, as Jason tended to be bossy with his younger brother and was usually unwilling to play with him.

When Dr. Brownstein called Jason into his office after the interview with Pam, he had gone out into the hallway and was running up and down the staircase that leads to the office. Pam retrieved Jason and brought him back into the office and waited outside while Dr. Brownstein interviewed Jason individually. Once he was seated, Jason sat still for several minutes, but became increasingly restless, climbing out of his seat and trying to leave the office several times throughout the interview. His responses to Dr. Brownstein's questions were tangential and difficult to comprehend, as he repeatedly got out of his chair while he was talking. When asked why it was so difficult for him to sit still, Jason responded, "I'm just bored all the time. I can't help it!"

In order to observe Jason's ability to maintain attention on a task, Dr. Brownstein presented Jason with colored markers and asked him to draw a house. Jason began to draw the shape of a house but soon gave up the task and ran over to one corner of the room where he saw toy building blocks and began playing with them. When Dr. Brownstein asked Jason to return to the task, he angrily stated, "No! No! No! No! No! They make me draw in school all the time! Where is my mommy?" At this point, Jason began to cry. Being careful not to cause undue distress, Dr. Brownstein called Pam back into the office, and Jason immediately settled down and began to smile.

Relevant history: Pam reported having no birth complications during her pregnancy and that Jason has had no health problems during his development. There is no family history of childhood or attention-deficit disorders.

Case formulation: Based on the interview with Pam and observation of Jason's behavior, Dr. Brownstein determined that Jason meets *DSM-5* diagnostic criteria for Attention-Deficit/Hyperactivity Disorder, Hyperactive-Impulsive type. His symptoms have been present for longer than six months and were present before the age of 7. He displays predominantly hyperactive-impulsive symptoms, and though he does have some symptoms of inattention, they are too few to distinguish him as having combined presentation.

Treatment plan: Jason will be referred to his pediatrician for a medication consultation. He will also be referred for behavior therapy at a low-cost clinic in the area.

Sarah Tobin, PhD

Because they strike so early, disorders that begin in childhood are particularly significant in affecting the lives of individuals with the disorders, their families, the schools, and society as a whole. Interventions targeting these disorders are particularly important because they can literally reshape the direction that the individual's life will take. At the same time, clinicians, parents, and teachers struggle with the issue of whether or not to apply diagnoses of a particular disorder to the children who show behavioral disturbances. Once given a diagnosis, the potential exists for people to treat those children "differently" and hence to experience effects that go beyond their initial symptoms. For example, is it right to give a psychiatric diagnosis to a boy who frequently loses his temper, argues with his parents, refuses to obey rules, acts in annoying ways, swears, and lies? How do these behaviors differ from those of the "normal" child going through phases such as the "terrible two's" or the rebellion of early adolescence? As you will learn, clinicians attempt to define these diagnoses as restrictively as possible to avoid confusing normal with abnormal development. Invariably, however, it is possible that there are cases in which a clinician considers normal behavior as one that meets the criteria for a psychological disorder.

Disorders that begin early in life and remain with the individual throughout life are known as **neurodevelopmental disorders.** These disorders typically become evident early in children's development, often before they reach school age. The deficits associated with these disorders include impairments in personal, social, academic, or occupational functioning. Some disorders have specifiers to indicate, for example, that the disorder is linked to a genetic abnormality or environmental factors affecting the individual during the prenatal period.

It is important to keep in mind that, by definition, neurodevelopmental disorders may show important changes over time. As individuals develop from childhood through adolescence and adulthood, they may experience maturational changes that alter the way their disorder manifests in particular behaviors. Fortunately, with appropriate interventions, clinicians can help children either to learn to manage their symptoms or to overcome the symptoms entirely.

neurodevelopmental disorders
Conditions that begin in childhood and have a major impact on social and cognitive functioning, involving serious deficits in social interaction and communication skills, as well as odd behavior, interests, and activities.

5.1 Intellectual Disability (Intellectual Developmental Disorder)

Clinicians diagnose individuals with an intellectual disability if they have intellectual and adaptive deficits that first became evident when they were children. The ICD uses the term "intellectual developmental disorder," so the *DSM-5* places this term in parentheses after the term **"intellectual disability."** The *DSM-IV-TR* used the term **"mental retardation"** to apply to this group of disorders. However, in keeping with recommendations by the American Association of Intellectual and Developmental Disabilities (AAIDD), among other groups, the *DSM-5* authors adopted the terminology of "intellectual disability" (intellectual developmental disorder). For the sake of brevity, we will refer to the disorder as intellectual disability, though technically the disorder should include "intellectual developmental disorder" as well.

To receive a diagnosis of intellectual disability, the individual must meet conditions that fall into three sets of criteria. The first set of criteria include deficits in the general intellectual abilities that an intelligence test might measure, including reasoning, problem-solving, judgment, ability to learn from experience, and learning in an academic context. In making this determination, the clinician should use tests that are individualized, standardized, and psychometrically sound. Also, the tests must be culturally appropriate. This means that individuals who do not speak English as a first language, for example, and might not score well on an English-based IQ test, should receive assessment with a linguistically appropriate test. Beyond linguistic appropriateness, the test should also consider cultural differences in the ways people communicate, move, and behave. These latter considerations are consistent with those of the AAIDD. The cutoff for meeting this criterion is a measured intelligence of approximately 70 or below.

The second set of criteria for a diagnosis of intellectual disability involves impairments in adaptive functioning, relative to a person's age and cultural group, in a variety of daily life activities such as communication, social participation, and independent living. Some of these adaptive difficulties, for example, include problems in using money, telling time, and relating to other people in social settings. Clinicians should judge whether or not an individual's adaptive behavior is impaired using tests that are standardized, individualized, psychometrically sound, and culturally appropriate.

The third criterion relates to age of onset. Specifically, the disorder must begin prior to the age of 18.

Once the clinician determines that the diagnosis of intellectual disability is appropriate, the next step is to rate the degree of severity. The levels of severity are mild, moderate,

intellectual disability (intellectual developmental disorder)
Diagnosis used to characterize individuals who have intellectual and adaptive deficits that first became evident when they were children.

mental retardation
A condition, present from childhood, characterized by significantly below-average general intellectual functioning (an IQ of 70 or below).

MINI CASE

Intellectual Disability

Juanita is a 5-year-old girl with Down syndrome. Her mother was 43 when she and her husband decided to start their family. Because of her age, doctors advised Juanita's mother to have prenatal testing for any abnormalities in the chromosomal makeup of the developing fetus. Juanita's parents were shocked and distressed when they learned the test results. When Juanita was born, her parents were prepared for what to expect in terms of the child's appearance, behavior, and possible medical problems. Fortunately, Juanita needed no special medical attention. Very early in Juanita's life, her parents consulted with educational specialists, who recommended an enrichment program designed to maximize cognitive functioning. From age 6 months, Juanita attended a program each morning in which the staff made intensive efforts to facilitate her motor and intellectual development. Now that she is school-age, Juanita will enter kindergarten at the local public school, where teachers will make efforts to bring her into the mainstream of education. Fortunately, Juanita lives in a school district in which the administrators recognize the importance of providing resources for pupils like Juanita, so that they will have the opportunity to learn and grow as normally as possible.

severe, and profound. In previous classifications, these levels were based on intelligence test scores. In *DSM-5,* the levels of severity are based on how well the individual is able to adapt in conceptual, social, and practical domains (see Table 5.1). Furthermore, the *DSM-5* wording is more specific than was true of *DSM-IV-TR.* Moreover, *DSM-5* requires that clinicians use tests reflecting cultural sensitivity. The *DSM-5* bases adaptive behavior domains on areas that best determine whether or not an individual is impaired in daily life, and they are more completely delineated. The combination of improved specificity in adaptive behavior criteria and inclusion of culturally sensitive tests will result, researchers believe, in a more accurate basis for diagnosis and, ultimately, better treatment of individuals with intellectual developmental disorders.

Estimates show that approximately 1 percent of the world's population has intellectual disability, but the prevalence is higher in low-income countries (1.64%) than in countries classified as middle-income (1.59%) or high-income (1.54%). The highest prevalence occurs in urban slums or mixed rural-urban settings. Studies on children and adolescents also report higher prevalence rates than studies on adults. The costs to the economy associated with the care of these individuals can be very burdensome, with lifetime estimates as high as $51.2 billion in the United States alone. Offsetting these costs are efforts to improve maternal and child health and interventions aimed at teaching adaptive skills to children with these disorders so that they can live at higher functional levels (Maulik, Mascarenhas, Mathers, Dua, & Saxena, 2011).

Causes of Intellectual Disability

Down syndrome

A form of intellectual disability caused by abnormal chromosomal formation during conception.

Genetic abnormalities are a significant cause of intellectual disability. The three most important genetic causes are **Down syndrome,** phenylketonuria, and Fragile X syndrome. Epigenetics also appears to play an important role in increasing an individual's risk of developing an intellectual disability. Lifestyle, diet, living conditions, and age can affect the expression of a gene through mutations, deletions, or altered positions of genes on the chromosomes (Franklin & Mansuy, 2011).

Most people with Down syndrome have inherited an extra copy of chromosome 21, and therefore have 47 chromosomes instead of the typical 46. In this form of Down syndrome, called Trisomy 21, the extra chromosome interferes with the normal development of the body and brain. The symptoms of Down syndrome range from mild to severe and can vary from person to person. Down syndrome is the most common cause of birth defects in humans, and almost always is associated with intellectual disability as well as a range of physical signs.

TABLE 5.1 Diagnostic Adaptive Behavior Scale

DSM-5 specifies four severity levels for intellectual disability in each of three domains:

Conceptual

Mild: Difficulties in learning academic skills, limited executive functioning (in adults), and impaired memory.

Moderate: Significant lags throughout childhood in language, reading, and mathematics. Adults remain at an elementary school level and need ongoing assistance to complete tasks of everyday life.

Severe: Limited attainment of conceptual skills, little understanding of language, arithmetic, time, and money; needs extensive support throughout life.

Profound: Unable to think symbolically, limited understanding of how to use objects; motor and sensory impairments often present at this level, making it impossible for the individual to use objects in a functional way.

Social

Mild: Immature in social interactions, difficulties in regulating emotion and behaving in an age-appropriate manner; gullibility.

Moderate: Language less complex than that of peers, capable of social and emotional ties to others, but may not be able to read other people's social cues. Caretakers must assist with decision making.

Severe: Limited vocabulary and grammar; speech and language focused on "here and now"; able to understand simple speech and gestures; however, also capable of rewarding interpersonal relationships.

Profound: Very limited understanding of speech and gestures in social communication; can express desires and emotions in nonverbal ways; can have rewarding relationships with others, nevertheless, if they are familiar to the individual. Sensory and motor impairments, however, may prevent the individual from participating in a wide range of social activities.

Practical

Mild: May be able to perform personal care, but needs support with complex tasks in daily living such as shopping, transportation, child care, and money management. In adulthood, may be employed in jobs that do not require conceptual skills.

Moderate: Capable of caring for a range of personal needs, though considerable training is required at first. Employment in jobs requiring limited conceptual skills is possible, requires support and supervision. A small minority engage in maladaptive behavior.

Severe: Requires support and supervision for all daily living activities; cannot make decisions for self or others; as an adult, requires long-term training and support for any type of skill acquisition. A number of people at this level may engage in maladaptive behavior, including self-injury.

Profound: Dependent on other people for all aspects of daily activities; may be able to assist with some tasks at home or the workplace. Can enjoy a variety of forms of entertainment though physical and sensory impairments prevent active participation. A significant minority engage in maladaptive behavior.

The face of an individual with Down syndrome is relatively easy to recognize and includes a head that is smaller than normal and unusually shaped. Some of the characteristic features of people with Down syndrome include a flattened nose, small ears, small mouth, upward slanting eyes, excess skin at the nape of the neck, and white spots on the colored part of the eye. Showing delays in physical development, individuals with Down syndrome never reach full adult height. They also are prone to suffering from a variety of physical ailments including heart defects, eye cataracts, hearing problems, hip problems, early and massive vomiting, chronic constipation, sleep apnea,

Children with Down syndrome suffer from a genetic abnormality that severely affects their intellectual development.

phenylketonuria (PKU)
Condition in which children are born missing an enzyme called phenylalanine hydroxase.

fragile X syndrome
A genetic disorder caused by a change in a gene called FMRI.

underactive thyroid, and teeth that appear later than normal and in locations that can lead to problems with chewing. In addition to lower IQ scores, individuals with Down syndrome are more likely to show impulsive behavior, poor judgment, short attention span, and a tendency to become frustrated and angry over their limitations. They are much more likely than other individuals to develop Alzheimer's disease, and to do so at a far earlier age than would be expected (PubMedHealth, 2011b). The high levels of life stressors that they face make them potentially vulnerable to developing depressive disorders (Walker, Dosen, Buitelaar, & Janzing, 2011).

Infants born with **phenylketonuria (PKU)** are missing an enzyme called phenylalanine hydroxase, which breaks down phenylalanine, an amino acid found in foods that contain protein. As phenylalanine builds up in the body, it causes damage to the central nervous system. Untreated, PKU leads to developmental delays, a smaller than normal head size, hyperactivity, jerking arm and leg movements, seizures, skin rashes, and tremors. Fortunately, administering a simple blood test to all babies shortly after birth can diagnose PKU. Children who have inherited this condition must then follow a diet that is low in phenylalanine, particularly early in life. However, such a diet means that the individual must avoid milk, eggs, and other common foods, as well as the artificial sweetener aspartame. The child may also follow a diet that is high in fish oil, iron, and carnitine. Individuals who do not adhere to this diet may develop attention-deficit/hyperactivity disorder (PubMedHealth, 2011d). They may also show abnormalities in strategy use on verbal tasks, even if they received treatment early in life (Banerjee, Grange, Steiner, & White, 2011).

In children born with Tay-Sachs disease, deficits in intellectual functioning occur due to a lack of hexosaminidase A, an enzyme that helps break down a chemical in the nerve tissue called ganglioside. Without this enzyme, levels of ganglioside accumulate, particularly in neurons within the brain. The disease occurs due to a defective gene on chromosome 15. In order to develop the disease, both of the child's parents must have this genetic defect. If only one parent has this defect, the child becomes a carrier and could transmit the disease to his or her offspring if the other parent also has the defective gene. The disease is most common among the Ashkenazi Jews, who are of Eastern European descent.

The symptoms of Tay-Sachs disease, in addition to developmental delays, include deafness, blindness, loss of muscle tone and motor skills, dementia, delayed reflexes, listlessness, paralysis, seizures, and slow growth. Although Tay-Sachs disease can develop later in life, most individuals have the form that appears within the first 3 to 10 months after birth. The disease progresses rapidly, and most children with it do not live past the age of 4 or 5. There is no treatment. However, parents can receive genetic testing before the child is born (PubMedHealth, 2011e).

The most common form of intellectual disability in males is **fragile X syndrome**, a genetic disorder caused by a change in a gene called FMRI. A small part of the gene's code is repeated on a "fragile" area of the X chromosome, and the more the number of repeats, the greater the deficit. Because males have only one X chromosome, this genetic defect more likely affects them than females.

Children with fragile X syndrome may appear normal, but they do show some physical abnormalities including a large head circumference, subtle abnormalities of facial appearance such as a large forehead and long face, flat feet, large body size, and large testicles after they start puberty. Behavior problems that they exhibit include delays in achieving benchmarks such as crawling or walking, hyperactive or impulsive behavior, hand clapping or biting, speech and language delay, and a tendency to avoid eye contact. Girls with this disorder may show no symptoms other than premature menopause or difficulty conceiving a child (PubMedHealth, 2011c). Clinicians also associate fragile X syndrome with hyperactivity and poor attention as well as other neurodevelopmental disorders, including autism spectrum disorder. A survey of over 1,000 families who had at least one child with fragile X syndrome revealed that over half experienced significant financial burden as a direct result of the disorder, and nearly 60 percent had to stop or significantly change their work hours (Ouyang, Grosse, Raspa, & Bailey, 2010).

Environmental hazards during prenatal developing are the second category of causes of intellectual disability. These hazards, called "teratogens," include drugs or toxic chemicals, maternal malnutrition, and infections in the mother during critical phases of fetal development. Mothers who contract rubella ("German measles") during the first three months of pregnancy are likely to give birth to a child with intellectual disability. Infections, oxygen deprivation

What's New in the DSM-5

Neurodevelopmental Disorders

Many changes occurred in the organization of disorders of childhood when *DSM-5* was finalized. Perhaps the most significant was the relabeling of a large group of conditions with the term "neurodevelopmental." Critics of *DSM-5* argue that this term presumes a theoretical model by attributing many of the disorders to biological causes that in the past clinicians viewed as reflecting multiple factors. Specifically, putting ADHD into this category suggests that the appropriate treatment would, in turn, focus on changing the individual's biology through medication.

The more generic category "Specific Learning Disorder" replaced what were separate disorders such as mathematical skills disorder. The more generally accepted term "intellectual disability" replaced the term "mental retardation." "Autistic spectrum disorder" replaced autistic disorder, and the term "Asperger's disorder" was completely eliminated. People who received the diagnosis of Asperger's disorder are now included in the autistic spectrum.

There were other major category shifts in the move to *DSM-5*. Separation anxiety disorder was included in disorders originating in childhood and is now included in the category of anxiety disorders. Oppositional defiant and conduct disorders moved to "disruptive, impulse control, and conduct disorders," a category that we will discuss in Chapter 14. Pica, rumination disorder, and feeding disorder of infancy and early childhood moved to the category of "feeding and eating disorders."

By moving many of these childhood disorders to new or other existing categories, the *DSM-5* authors acknowledge the continuity of behavior from infancy through adulthood, a position that would be consistent with life-span developmental principles. However, children may be more likely than was true in *DSM-IV-TR* to receive diagnoses that clinicians previously considered appropriate only for adults.

These twin boys both have fragile X syndrome, a rare genetic disorder that causes some subtle physical abnormalities and, in many cases, behavioral problems.

Fetal alcohol syndrome causes children to be born with severe developmental and intellectual disabilities.

during birth ("anoxia"), premature birth, and brain injury during delivery can also lead to brain damage and associated intellectual deficits. We can also associate premature birth with intellectual disability. Diseases, head injuries caused by accidents or child abuse, and exposure to toxic substances such as lead or carbon monoxide can also lead older children to suffer loss of intellectual capacity.

A mother's consumption of alcohol during pregnancy can lead the prenatal child to develop **fetal alcohol syndrome (FAS),** a set of abnormalities in facial appearance, slower than average growth patterns, and most importantly, maturation of the nervous system resulting in intellectual deficits. Maternal alcohol use during all stages of pregnancy can cause damage to the developing child. The medical profession considers the level of harmful drinking more than 80 grams of alcohol per day (about 3 ounces). The greater the amount of alcohol a pregnant woman consumes, the greater the effects on the child.

Clinicians diagnose individuals with FAS if they meet the criteria listed in Table 5.2. The idea behind these guidelines is that by having objective, quantitative measures, clinicians will be able to provide more precise diagnoses, facilitating both treatment and research (Bertrand et al., 2004).

The cognitive deficits of children with FAS seem particularly pronounced in the area of executive functioning, leading them to be particularly challenged in processing and integrating information. They find it difficult to perform tasks that require them to regulate their attentional control and perform mental manipulations (Kodituwakku, 2009). Although alcohol exposure affects the entire brain, children with FAS include reduced brain volume and malformations of the corpus callosum, the tissue that connects the brain's two hemispheres (Lebel, Roussotte, & Sowell, 2011).

Epidemiologists estimate the prevalence of FAS at approximately 0.5 to 2.0 of every 1,000 children born per year (Centers

fetal alcohol syndrome (FAS)
A condition associated with intellectual disability in a child whose mother consumed large amounts of alcohol on a regular basis while pregnant.

TABLE 5.2 Diagnostic Criteria for Fetal Alcohol Syndrome (FAS)

Area of Functioning	Criteria
Facial appearance	Smooth ridge between nose and lip, thin edge around the lip, and small separation between upper and lower eyelids (based on racial norms)
Growth problems	Height, weight, or both at or below the 10th percentile (adjusted for age, sex, and race or ethnicity)
Central nervous system abnormalities	Smaller head circumference and brain abnormalities visible on imaging
	Neurological problems not due to injury or fever
	Performance on functional measures substantially below that expected for an individual's age, schooling, or circumstances
Maternal alcohol exposure	Confirmed prenatal alcohol exposure; if this information is not available, children who meet all three of the above criteria would be referred for further testing

SOURCE: Bertrand et al., 2004.

for Disease Control and Prevention, 2011). Using these estimates, this means that among the approximately 4 million infants born in the United States each year, from 1,000 to 6,000 will have FAS. However, FAS rates vary tremendously within particular subgroups of the population. Economically disadvantaged groups, Native Americans, and other minorities have rates that are as high as three to five out of every 1,000 births. Children with FAS are at risk for developing a variety of negative outcomes including dropping out of school, getting into trouble with the law, diagnoses of other mental health problems, developing substance use disorders, engaging in inappropriate sexual behavior, inability to live independently, and having difficulty staying employed (Bertrand et al., 2004).

Treatment of Intellectual Disability

People with intellectual disability can benefit from early intervention aimed at providing them with training in motor coordination, language use, and social skills. Educators can combine **mainstreaming,** which integrates them into ordinary school classrooms, with special education that provides them with assistance geared to their particular needs.

mainstreaming
A governmental policy to integrate fully into society people with cognitive and physical disabilities.

Because many people with intellectual disability have limited understanding of social situations and of how to carry out their activities of daily living, they may require treatment for these associated difficulties. Therefore, treatment for these individuals often takes the form of behavioral or social interventions that train them to cope with the demands of everyday life. This includes coordinated care that integrates behavioral treatment, outreach, and multidisciplinary assessment, as well as treatment of any related conditions that may be affecting the individual, including depression, anxiety disorder, bipolar disorder, or an autism spectrum disorder (Richings, Cook, & Roy, 2011).

When possible, prevention is of value to reduce risk of intellectual disabilities. In the case of FAS, education and counseling are of potential value. Unfortunately, there is very limited evidence to show that such programs actually reduce alcohol consumption in pregnant women or, more importantly, produce beneficial effects on children (Stade et al., 2009). Doctors can use genetic testing to detect the presence or risk of Down syndrome, Tay-Sachs, PKU, and fragile X syndrome. In the case of PKU specifically, children need to adhere to phenylalanine-restricted diets immediately after testing shows that they have inherited this condition.

Children born with FAS can benefit from several protective factors that reduce the impact of their disorder on their later adaptation and development. Early diagnosis can help educators place children in appropriate classes and receive the social services that can help them and their families. Involvement in special education focused specifically on their needs and learning styles can be particularly beneficial. The more they can receive help from a loving and stable home life, the greater their chances of avoiding secondary conditions such as criminal behavior, unemployment, and disruptions in education. Finally, they can benefit from learning ways to prevent expressing their anger or frustration so that they do not become involved in youth violence (Centers for Disease Control and Prevention, 2011).

Friendship training is one behavioral intervention that can help children with FAS learn how to interact appropriately with other children so that they can make and keep friends. This type of training involves a combination of social skills such as how to play with other children, arrange and handle play dates in the home, and work out or avoid conflicts (O'Connor et al., 2006). Cognitive interventions that focus on taking into account the specific executive function deficits of children with FAS can help improve their school performance. These methods include using concrete examples, repeating information, and breaking a problem down into parts (Kodituwakku & Kodituwakku, 2011). Parents also need to learn how better to manage their children's behaviors, which ultimately reduces their distress and therefore leads to a less stressful home environment.

5.2 Autism Spectrum Disorder

autism spectrum disorder
A neurodevelopmental disorder involving impairments in the domains of social communication and performance of restricted, repetitive behaviors

The disorder that we know familiarly as "autism," is called **autism spectrum disorder** in *DSM-5*. This disorder incorporates a range of serious disturbances in the ways that individuals interact with and communicate with others, as well as in behaviors that can include a person's interests and activity patterns. The constellation of diagnostic criteria associated with this disorder can persist for an individual's entire life, but, depending on its severity, the individual can receive help to function satisfactorily with treatment.

The *DSM-5* diagnosis replaces the *DSM-IV-TR* category of autistic disorder. The main reason for changing the term was to provide a more reliable and valid distinction between children who clearly show "typical development" and those who demonstrate a range of deficits in communication and social behaviors. The term autism spectrum disorder reflects a consensus among the scientists writing the *DSM-5* that four disorders previously considered to be separate are a single condition with differing levels of severity. These four disorders were autistic disorder, Asperger's disorder, childhood disintegrative disorder, and pervasive developmental disorder not otherwise specified.

To diagnose autism spectrum disorder, clinicians evaluate children along two core domains. The first domain includes social and communication disturbances. The second domain includes a restricted range of interests and performance of repetitive behaviors and activities. Within each domain, clinicians specify one of three severity levels: requiring support, requiring substantial support, and requiring very substantial support.

In the area of communication, children with autism spectrum disorder may show developmental delays in the use of language, but this particular aspect of the diagnosis is not unique to autism spectrum disorder. More typical of autism spectrum disorder are deficits in the social aspects of communication. Individuals with this disorder may avoid eye contact, and their facial expressions, gestures, and even posture may strike others as odd or unusual. For example, they may find it difficult to understand the body language of other people, and their own body language may strike others as odd.

The friendship patterns of children with autism spectrum disorder differ from those of children who do not have this disorder because they do not seem to enjoy playing with

MINI CASE

Autism Spectrum Disorder

Brian is a 6-year-old child currently receiving treatment at a residential school for mentally disabled children. As an infant, Brian did not respond well to his parents' efforts to play with and hold him. His mother noticed that his whole body seemed to stiffen when she picked him up out of his crib. No matter how much she tried, she could not entice Brian to smile. When she tried to play games by tickling his toes or touching his nose, he averted his eyes and looked out the window. Not until Brian was 18 months old did his mother first realize that his behavior reflected more than just a quiet temperament—that he, in fact, was developing abnormally. Brian never did develop an attachment to people; instead, he clung to a small piece of wood he carried with him everywhere. His mother often found Brian rocking his body in a corner, clinging to his piece of wood. Brian's language, though, finally indicated serious disturbance. At an age when most children start to put together short sentences, Brian was still babbling incoherently. His babbling did not sound like that of a normal infant. He said the same syllable over and over again—usually the last syllable of something that had just been said to him—in a high-pitched, monotone voice. Perhaps the most bizarre feature of Brian's speech was that he did not direct it to the listener. Brian seemed to be communicating in a world of his own.

There is a vast range of symptom presentation and level of dysfunction for children who are diagnosed with autism spectrum disorder.

others, sharing experiences, or engaging in the usual give-and-take of social interactions. In extreme cases, they may completely avoid social interactions, or at least not attempt to initiate interactions with other people. Imaginative play, an essential component of normal development, presents these children with particular challenges. They may be unable to engage in the type of imitative play patterns that characterize the ordinary social interactions of young children.

Separate from the deficient communication and social patterns of people with autism spectrum disorder are disturbances in their behavior. They may engage in restricted or repetitive behaviors, such as tapping their hands or fingers, or even twisting their bodies. The repetitive behaviors can also take the form of the symptom of **echolalia,** which is repeating the same sounds again and again. Repeating the same routines without any changes may be another manifestation of their disorder. If anyone tries to change the order in which they do something, such as eat, they can become extremely distressed.

echolalia
Repeating the same sounds over and over

Individuals with autism spectrum disorder may also develop extremely narrow and specifically focused interests beyond the typical games or amusements of other people. They may become expert in a very targeted area that engages their attentional focus.

Any of these symptoms alone would present a challenge to the families of people with autism spectrum disorder, but particularly distressing are the disturbances that these individuals may show in their sensitivity to stimuli in their environment. They may seem almost impervious to pain, heat, or cold, meaning that they can easily place themselves at risk of significant injury. On the other hand, their sensory abnormalities may take the form of hypersensitivity to sound, light, or smell.

The unusual characteristics of autism spectrum disorder become more prominent as the infant grows into the toddler and school-age years, and this disorder continues throughout the individual's life, taking one of a number of forms varying in symptoms and severity. However, the particular areas affected and the severity of symptoms vary from childhood to adolescence and then again from adolescence to adulthood. In one large cross-sectional study comparing these three age groups, the ability to interact with others was less impaired among the adolescents than among the adults, and the adults were less impaired in the area of repetitive, restricted behaviors (Seltzer et al., 2003).

Autistic savants often excel in one specific skill, such as playing an entire song on the piano from memory after hearing it only one time.

In a multi-site surveillance study in 14 states using records from educational and health settings, the Centers for Disease Control and Prevention reported an estimated prevalence rate averaging 0.66 percent or one out of approximately 150 children, a large increase from previously reported rates (Centers for Disease Control and Prevention, 2007). The publication of this report drew a great deal of media attention to what the authors regarded as a public health crisis. In the wake of this report, researchers have been trying to understand the reasons for the apparent increase in prevalence. Several possibilities stand out. One is that there have been changes in the way in which clinicians interpret the diagnostic criteria. Another pertains to the overlap between intellectual disability and autism spectrum disorder. Previously, the Centers for Disease Control and Prevention estimated that 75 percent of individuals with autism spectrum disorder also had intellectual disability; however, in the CDC study, the percentage ranged from 33 percent to 64 percent. This change reflects the fact that clinicians evaluate children with a certain constellation of dysfunctional communication behaviors under current systems of categorization differently than in previous decades. Another possible reason for the increase in estimated prevalence is that, although researchers used *DSM* criteria in identifying individuals with autism spectrum disorder, they conducted evaluations using case records rather than in-person evaluations. It is possible that individuals might interpret case records differently than face-to-face evaluations.

An unusual variant of this disorder, called autistic savant syndrome, occurs in people with autism spectrum disorder who possess an extraordinary skill, such as the ability to perform extremely complicated numerical operations—for example, correctly naming the day of the week on which a date thousands of years away would fall (Thioux, Stark, Klaiman, & Schultz, 2006). The autistic savant syndrome typically appears at an early age, when the young child with autism spectrum disorder appears to have exceptional musical skills, artistic talent, or the ability to solve extremely challenging puzzles. It is perhaps due to their tendency to focus intensely on the physical attributes of objects rather than the implications of these attributes: seeing the trees, but not the forest. However, memory for areas outside of their own areas of expertise appears to be no better than that of people with autism spectrum disorder who do not have these special memory skills (Neumann et al., 2010).

Theories and Treatment of Autism Spectrum Disorder

Evidence pointing to patterns of familial heritance supports the theory that autism spectrum disorder is biologically caused. Based on these investigations, researchers estimate the heritability of the disorder at approximately 90 percent, with genetic abnormalities suspected to exist on chromosomes 7, 2, and 15. No clear evidence exists regarding specific deficits in brain structure, but researchers have focused on the cerebellum, frontal cortex, hippocampus, and amygdala. In addition, people with autism spectrum disorder appear to have deficits in the association areas of the cortex (Minshew & Williams, 2007). There is some evidence that overall brain size is increased in some individuals (Santangelo & Tsatsanis, 2005).

Abnormalities exist in the neural circuitry of people with autism spectrum disorder, as reflected by their particular difficulty in processing facial stimuli (Batty, Meaux, Wittemeyer, Rogé, & Taylor, 2011; Dalton et al., 2005). These brain alterations may account for the fact that people with the disorder are less likely to gaze into other

With early therapeutic intervention, children who are diagnosed with autism spectrum disorder can experience significant symptom improvement.

people's eyes when communicating with them and less able to use emotional cues when processing information from other people's facial expressions (Bayliss & Tipper, 2005; Dawson et al., 2004).

Given the strong evidence favoring neurobiological abnormalities in individuals with autism spectrum disorder, the behavioral perspective is most relevant to treatment. Clinicians treating children with this disorder from a behavioral perspective base their methods on the early intervention programs devised by UCLA psychologist Ivar Lovaas in the late 1980s (Lovaas, 1987). In the original report on the program, Lovaas and his associates randomly assigned 38 children ages 3 to 4 diagnosed with autism spectrum disorder to two treatment groups. One group received intervention for at least 40 hours per week for 2 or more years. Children in the second group received treatment with the same intervention for less than 10 hours per week. Another group of children received treatment outside of the Lovaas clinic. Using IQ scores as dependent variables, nearly half (9) of the 19 children who received intensive treatment increased by over 20 points; by age 13, 8 of the children had maintained their IQ gains. By contrast, only one child in the less intensive treatment showed these IQ improvements. The Lovaas studies, as impressive as they were, received criticism from other researchers because the study never assessed the intervention's effects on social and communication skills.

The Lovaas treatment rests on principles of operant conditioning, practiced both by student therapists and parents. The behavioral aspects of the intervention consisted of ignoring the child's aggressive and self-stimulatory behaviors, using time-outs when children were disruptive, and positively attending to the children only when they engaged in socially appropriate behavior, using shaping to increase the performance of the targeted behaviors. As a last resort, when children engaged in undesirable behavior, they were given a loud "no" or a slap on the thigh.

In the first year, the treatment focused on reducing self-stimulatory and aggressive behaviors, shaping the children to comply with simple verbal requests, using imitation learning, establishing the beginnings of play with toys, and extending the treatment into the family home. In the second year of the intervention, the children learned how to use language in an expressive and abstract manner. They also learned how to play interactively with their peers. In the third year, the children learned how to express emotions appropriately, academic tasks to prepare them for school, and observational learning in which they learned by watching other children learn. The clinicians attempted to place the children in mainstream classes rather than special education classes with the idea that others would not label them as "autistic" or as a "difficult child." Children who did not recover received an additional six years of training. The others remained in contact with the project team for occasional consultation.

In the years following the Lovaas study, a number of researchers attempted to replicate his findings. Reviewing 14 of the best-controlled of these studies, Makyrgianni and Reed (2010) concluded that the weight of evidence supports the use of behavioral early intervention projects. These programs are very effective in improving the intellectual, linguistic, communication, and social abilities. The evidence also supports the effectiveness of these programs. The more intensive the program, and the longer it lasts, the stronger the impact on the children. However, intensive programs of 25 hours per week were sufficient to provide a beneficial effect, rather than the 40 hours per week of the Lovaas program. In addition, as we would expect, children who are younger and those who are higher functioning at the outset improve more through treatment. Programs are also more successful if they involve parents.

Children with autism spectrum disorder will show a decrease in disruptive and self-stimulatory behaviors if they receive reinforcement for appropriate behaviors, such as asking for help or feedback. Such reinforcement can make them less likely to engage in self-injurious or aggressive behaviors. In this type of treatment, clinicians find it more useful to focus on changing pivotal behaviors, with the goal of bringing about improvements in other behaviors, rather than focusing on changing isolated behavioral disturbances. The therapist may also help the child develop new learning skills that will give him or her some experiences of success in problem solving. For example, the therapist might teach the child to break down a large problem, such as getting dressed, into smaller tasks that the child can accomplish. As a result the child feels less frustrated and is therefore less likely to regress to problem behaviors, such as rocking and head-banging. Clinicians also focus on the need to motivate the child to communicate more effectively. The child will then be more motivated to respond to social and environmental stimuli, which is the key to treatment (Koegel, Koegel, & McNerney, 2001). Over time the children will be more motivated to regulate and initiate behaviors on their own. Even simple changes can have this impact, such as having children choose the materials, toys, and activities for the intervention rather than having the clinician choose.

Other behavioral strategies include self-control procedures, such as self-monitoring, relaxation training, and covert conditioning. Children can also learn to touch an icon of a "frowny" face to indicate their displeasure rather than by acting out aggressively when they are upset or unhappy (Martin, Drasgow, Halle, & Brucker, 2005).

An important fact to realize is that, for these behavioral programs to be effective, clinicians must carry them out intensively for a long period of time, beginning early in the child's life. A longitudinal study conducted by UCLA researchers tracked children between ages 2 and 6, showing that children who had better skills in the areas of communication and play had better language and social skills in their early preteen years (Sigman & Ruskin, 1999).

Another approach to intervention is to have peers rather than adults interact with the child. This situation approximates a more normal type of social environment, in which children typically serve a powerful role in modifying a peer's behavior. In contrast to interventions in which adults provide the reinforcement, peer-mediated interventions have the advantage of allowing children to carry on with their ordinary activities without adult interruption. The most effective of these interventions involve younger boys whose older male siblings provide the intervention, use peer modeling, attempt to generalize across situations, and involve collaboration among family members and with school staff (Zhang & Wheeler, 2011).

Rett Syndrome

In **Rett syndrome,** the child develops normally early in life (up to age 4) and then begins to show neurological and cognitive impairments including deceleration of head growth and some of the symptoms of autism spectrum disorder. Although not a separate diagnosis in *DSM-5,* Rett syndrome was a topic of clinical and research focus after its introduction in the *DSM-IV-TR.* The syndrome occurs almost exclusively in females.

Researchers identified the gene for Rett syndrome in 1999. Mutations in this gene, which has the name MECP2, lead to abnormalities in the production of a specific protein that are important in the normal functioning of neurons. Researchers do not yet know how these mutations link to the child's symptoms. However, there are promising signs that people with this condition may benefit from receiving treatments soon after birth that promote healthy brain development (Matsuishi, Yamashita, Takahashi, & Nagamitsu, 2011). Clinicians who would have diagnosed children as having Rett syndrome prior to *DSM-5*'s elimination of this diagnosis now use the autism spectrum diagnosis. However, by specifying that the children have a known genetic or medical condition, they are able to indicate that the symptoms are related to Rett syndrome.

Some children with autism spectrum disorder appear to develop normally for the first two years but, at some point before the age of 10, start to lose language and motor skills as well as other adaptive functions, including bowel and bladder control. This rare condition was formerly called **childhood disintegrative disorder,** but the diagnosis was eliminated from *DSM-5* and is now incorporated into autism spectrum disorder.

High-Functioning Autism Spectrum Disorder, Formerly Called Asperger's Disorder

Once considered to be a disorder separate from autism spectrum disorder, the diagnosis of **Asperger's disorder** was used to characterize individuals with symptoms that were of a less extreme nature. *DSM-IV-TR* differentiated autistic and Asperger's disorders on the basis of whether or not the child shows delays in language and intellectual development. In *DSM-5,* the diagnosis of Asperger's disorder was removed, and individuals with these symptoms are diagnosed with autism spectrum disorder.

Rett syndrome
A condition in which the child develops normally early in life (up to age 4) and then begins to show neurological and cognitive impairments including deceleration of head growth and some of the symptoms of autism spectrum disorder.

childhood disintegrative disorder
A disorder in *DSM-IV-TR* in which the child develops normally for the first 2 years and then starts to lose language, social, and motor skills, as well as other adaptive functions, including bowel and bladder control.

Asperger's disorder
A term once used to describe individuals with high-functioning autism spectrum disorder.

The symptoms of Rett syndrome begin to appear after about 5 months of age.

REAL STORIES

Daniel Tammet: Autism Spectrum Disorder

"I was born on January 31, 1979—a Wednesday. I know it was a Wednesday, because the date is blue in my mind and Wednesdays are always blue, like the number 9 or the sound of loud voices arguing."

In many ways, Daniel Tammet's developmental journey followed a path typical to many children. However, there are several aspects of his childhood that stand apart from the others. Daniel was 26 years old when he wrote his autobiography, *Born on a Blue Day*, which describes in vivid detail his experiences, which are both a part of any other child's development and those that are much rarer.

Daniel was the first child born to a couple living in poverty that would go on to have eight more children after him. As an infant, Daniel cried inconsolably except when eating or sleeping. The doctors believed it was simply a case of colic and that the crying was a phase that he would quickly pass through. In the book, Daniel reflects on this time in his life. "My parents tell me I was a loner, not mixing with the other children, and described by the supervisors as being absorbed in my own world. The contrast between my earliest years and that time must have been vivid for my parents, evolving as I did from a screaming, crying, head-banging baby to a quiet, self-absorbed, aloof toddler. With hindsight, they realize now that the change was not necessarily the sign of improvement they took it to be at the time. I became almost too good—too quiet and too undemanding."

When Daniel was a child, the scientific world knew little about developmental disorders, and his parents could not understand what their son was experiencing. "I think my parents must also have been afraid of the possible stigma attached to having a child with developmental problems", he writes, and describes how they did their best to provide him with a normal childhood. When friends or neighbors would question his parents, they would tell them that Daniel was just sensitive or shy.

At the age of four, Daniel began having seizures and doctors eventually diagnosed him with temporal lobe epilepsy. The condition caused major problems with his sleeping, and he took medication for about 3 years until the seizures subsided. His doctors now believe that these seizures led to savant syndrome, a rare condition from which Daniel suffers. Daniel describes that his synesthesia (a neurologically based condition in which sensory or cognitive pathway stimulation leads to automatic, involuntary experiences in a second sensory or cognitive pathway) causes a blurring of his senses and emotions when someone presents him with numbers or words. He writes, "The word *ladder*, for example, is blue and shiny, while *hoop* is a soft, white word."

Much like those with savant syndrome, Daniel also has a diagnosis of autism spectrum disorder and throughout the book he describes having many experiences during his childhood that are consistent with the diagnosis. He recalls that as a child he took comfort in the daily routines at school, and would become highly anxious should the routines be upset in any way. To this day, Daniel writes, "I have an almost obsessive need for order and routine, which affects virtually every aspect of my life." In school, many of his classmates teased him for his unusual quirks, such as uncontrollably flapping his arms. When he was feeling particularly anxious, he would bang his head against a wall, or run home to his parents' house when he felt overwhelmed during school. Looking back, Daniel wonders, "What must the other children have made of me? I don't know, because I have no memory of them at all. To me they were the background to my visual and tactile experiences."

Daniel had an especially difficult time connecting with other children at school, and describes that he spent most of his childhood in isolation, while he learned to comfort himself by making up games, thinking about numbers, or fanatically collecting small items such as chestnuts or coins. Although his parents tried hard to get him to socialize outside of the home with his siblings and other children, Daniel found it difficult to be away from home comforts. He made friends with children whom others regarded as outsiders in the classroom, but generally he preferred to keep to himself. As Daniel transitioned to high school, he continued to find it difficult to relate to others and maintained an almost obsessive interest in his studies, particularly in history. He also struggled in some areas, particularly the courses that required interaction with others.

As his body was adjusting to adulthood, Daniel recalls feeling the typical rush of hormones and increased interest in relationships, although his social skills made peer relationships excessively awkward and hard to sustain. As he recalls, "I did not understand emotions; they were things that just happened to me, often seemingly appearing from nowhere. All I knew is that I wanted to be close to someone, and not understanding closeness as being primarily emotional, I would walk up to some of the other students in the playground and stand very close to them until I could feel the warmth of their body heat against my skin. I still had no concept of personal space, that what I was doing made other people feel uncomfortable around me." During adolescence, Daniel became unquestionably aware that he was attracted to other boys, and even recalls having his first crush, and subsequently his first disappointing attempt at dating.

After finishing high school, Daniel decided not to attend college and instead took a job for Voluntary Services Overseas, a charity focused on international development. As part of the job, he lived in Lithuania for 1 year and found the experience to be a crucial part of his development into adulthood. Of what he learned from his time in Lithuania he writes, "For one thing, I had learned a great deal about myself. I could see more clearly than ever before how my 'differences' affected my day-to-day life, especially my interactions with other people. I had eventually come to understand that friendship was a delicate, gradual process that mustn't be rushed or seized upon, but allowed and encouraged to take its course over time. I pictured it as a butterfly, simultaneously beautiful and fragile, that once afloat belonged to the air and any attempt to grab at it would only destroy it. I recalled how in the past at school I had lost potential friendships because, lacking social instinct, I had tried too hard and made completely the wrong impression."

Daniel writes about struggling to find a job after returning home to England due to his difficulties functioning not only in social settings, but also in job interviews that required him to think about abstract, theoretical situations. As Daniel explains, he does not easily adjust to novel situations. Eventually, Daniel started an online program that teaches different languages, which has become successful over the years.

In *Born on a Blue Day,* Daniel Tammet describes his childhood experiences with autism spectrum disorder and savant syndrome, at a time when scientists knew very little about either condition.

Around the time that he returned home to England from Lithuania, Daniel met the man who would become his life partner, Neil. They met in an online chat group and exchanged e-mails for many months before finally meeting in person. Daniel explains that it was much easier for him to communicate electronically with Neil while they got to know each other, as it did not require complex social skills.

Through their relationship, Daniel writes that he has learned to be more open with others, and that Neil's support has been a source of immense strength that has helped him learn to cope with autism. Daniel's savant syndrome grants him the ability to see letters and numbers as colors and textures, and has led to some remarkable lifetime achievements. For example, Daniel has taught himself to speak at least ten languages, including Icelandic, which he learned in just 4 days as part of the filming for a documentary in which he participated. In 2005, Daniel set the British and European record for reciting 22,514 digits of *pi* in just over 5 hours. Although he has gained considerable media attention for his extraordinary abilities, Daniel enjoys a quiet life, which he spends mostly at home where he takes pleasure in his daily routines. He has also found strength through attending church, and especially enjoys the ritual aspect of it. From time to time he gives talks for the National Autistic Society and the National Society for Epilepsy and writes that he hopes to continue contributing to an understanding and acceptance of developmental disorders. Daniel has gone on to write another book, *Embracing the Wide Sky*, in addition to many other articles and public appearances.

People who would have received a diagnosis of Asperger's disorder in the past tended to have less severe and more focused impairments compared to individuals with autism spectrum disorder. People with Asperger's disorder may not show symptoms until they are of preschool age. At that point, when most children develop social and interactive skills, these children have difficulty reading the social cues of others, taking turns talking, and are unable to interpret language subtleties. They may avoid eye contact or, alternatively, they may stare at others. Their facial expressions or postures may appear unusual. These high-functioning individuals with autism spectrum disorder tend to become preoccupied with a narrow set of interests. They may talk extensively about these interests without realizing that such one-sided conversations are not socially appropriate. However, they are more likely than children at the lower-functioning end of the autism spectrum to try to make friends.

The term Asperger's is named after Hans Asperger, a Viennese physician who, during World War II, described a group of boys who possessed rather good language and cognitive skills, but had marked social problems because they acted like pompous "little professors" and were physically awkward.

In one case described in the literature (Volkmar, Klin, Schultz, Rubin, & Bronen, 2000), an 11-year-old boy, Robert, had the verbal abilities of a 17-year-old, but the social skills of a 3-year-old. Although Robert had a remarkable knowledge about the stars, planets, and time, his exclusive intellectual devotion to these subjects kept him from acquiring other kinds of knowledge. Peers rejected him because of his one-sided and naive overtures. The case of Robert serves to highlight the complex nature of autism spectrum disorder for individuals at the high-functioning end of the continuum. In the early years of life, parents are more likely to view their child as especially gifted rather than suffering from a serious impairment. As these children develop, their problems become more prominent. Parents and educators with responsibility for children who start to show symptoms early in life can focus on helping them to maximize their adaptive interpersonal skills.

Over time, and with support from parents and educators, individuals at the high end of the autism spectrum can develop adaptive coping strategies and may even become highly successful in their chosen field, particularly in areas such as technology and engineering. In addition, adults eventually are able to gain self-insight into their strengths and weaknesses, and can learn to acquire social skills, including how to read other people's social cues more accurately.

5.3 Learning and Communication Disorders

Specific Learning Disorder

specific learning disorder
A delay or deficit in an academic skill that is evident when an individual's achievement and skills are substantially below what would be expected for others of comparable age, education, and level of intelligence.

Children who have a **specific learning disorder** experience a delay or deficit in their ability to acquire a basic academic skill. These difficulties become evident when their achievement and skills are substantially below the level of performance based on their age, education, and measured intelligence. Within this general category, clinicians also specify which academic domain the disorder involves and its level of severity (mild, moderate, or severe).

In the United States, researchers estimate that approximately 5.3 percent of boys and 3.8 percent of girls ages 5 to 17 have a diagnosed learning disorder (Centers for Disease Control and Prevention, 2005). However, the lifetime prevalence is far higher, with estimates of 5.4 percent in the general population. The factors that appear to increase the child's risk of developing a learning disorder are coming from a home that has lower education and higher poverty rates. Growing up in a two-parent stepfamily, being adopted, and in the presence of a smoker also increase their risks. Other family risk factors include having parents who experience more difficulty in parenting, failing to share ideas with children, and not discussing openly disagreements in the home (Altarac & Saroha, 2007).

The individual with **specific learning disorder with impairment in mathematics** has difficulty with mathematical tasks and concepts. He or she may be unable to understand mathematical terms, symbols, or concepts. Individuals with specific learning disorder with impairment in mathematics may have **dyscalculia,** which refers to a pattern of difficulties in number sense, ability to learn arithmetic facts, and performing accurate calculations. A school-age child with this disorder may have problems completing home-work. An adult with this disorder might be unable to balance a checkbook because of difficulty performing simple mathematical calculations.

There are serious long-term consequences of having a specific learning disorder with impairment in mathematics. In a large-scale longitudinal study of over 17,000 individu-als followed from birth through adulthood, people with poorer mathematical skills had lower rates of full-time employment and the jobs they did have were in lower-wage manual positions. Without intervention, individuals with this disorder risk serious long-term consequences that can affect their quality of life.

In the **specific learning disorder with impairment in written expression,** the individual has difficulty spelling, properly using grammatical or punctuation errors, and organizing paragraphs. Such challenges lead them to have serious problems for children in many academic subjects. For adults, the disorder of written expression can create many interpersonal and practical problems. Fewer job opportunities will be open to them, particularly if their symptoms place them in the severe level of functioning.

Individuals with **specific learning disorder with impairment in reading** (commonly called **dyslexia**), omit, distort, or substitute words when they read. Consequently, they read in a slow, halting fashion. Their disorder can cause children to fail to show adequate progress in a variety of school subjects. As with the disorder of written expression, adults with dyslexia face restrictions in the type of employment for which they may qualify. Epidemiological studies show prevalence rates of from 5 to 10 percent of the population (PubMedHealth, 2011a).

Adolescence is the peak time during which people with learning disorders are par-ticularly susceptible to behavioral and emotional problems and are at risk of dropping out of school before finishing high school. Even outside the school context, though, many people with learning disorders have low self-esteem and feelings of incompetence and shame. The accompanying difficulties experienced by people with learning disorders can place them at risk for abusing substances including tobacco, methamphetamine, inhalants, cocaine, ecstasy and cannabis. These individuals are also more likely to expe-rience sleep difficulties (Fakier & Wild, 2011).

The core features of these disorders seems to involve deficits in the planning and programming of behavior, not with difficulties in motor execution, motor control across brain hemispheres, or any visual or visual perceptual disorders (Vaivre-Douret et al., 2011b). Practitioners believe the best approach to identifying children with learning disorders uses the "Response to Intervention" (RTI) approach in which they institute a set of evidence-based procedures that follow a series of steps. First, they use screening criteria to identify at-risk children. Next, the children identified as being at risk receive a well-established intervention for a specific period of time. Those children who do not benefit from this intervention receive an even more intensive intervention. At this point, the chil-dren who do not benefit from the treatment would be the children who the practitioners classify as having learning disorders. To aid in diagnosis, at this point the child would also undergo a comprehensive evaluation using information from multiple sources, including standardized tests (Büttner & Shamir, 2011). There are few empirically validated treatment programs to address the deficits of children with specific learning disorder with impairment in mathematics, but there are some approaches that researchers are developing. The most promising is a multi-tiered approach in which children at risk participate in general math-ematics instruction and small-group interventions. Those who do not improve then move on to more intensive one-on-one interventions (Table 5.3) (Geary, 2011). School is usually

specific learning disorder with impairment in mathematics
A learning disorder in which the individual has difficulty with mathematical tasks and concepts.

dyscalculia
A pattern of difficulties in number sense, ability to learn arithmetic facts, and performing accurate calculations.

specific learning disorder with impairment in written expression
A learning disorder in which the individual's writing is character-ized by poor spelling, grammati-cal or punctuation errors, and disorganization of paragraphs.

specific learning disorder with impairment in reading (dyslexia)
A learning disorder in which the individual omits, distorts, or sub-stitutes words when reading and reads in a slow, halting fashion.

TABLE 5.3 Recommendations for Treating Children with Specific Learning Disorder with Impairment in Mathematics

Checklist for carrying out the recommendations

Recommendation 1. Screen all students to identify those at risk for potential mathematics difficulties and provide interventions to students identified as at risk.

☐ As a district or school sets up a screening system, have a team evaluate potential screening measures. The team should select measures that are efficient and reasonably reliable and that demonstrate predictive validity. Screening should occur in the beginning and middle of the year.

☐ Select screening measures based on the content they cover, with an emphasis on critical instructional objectives for each grade.

☐ In grades 4 through 8, use screening data in combination with state testing results.

☐ Use the same screening tool across a district to enable analyzing results across schools.

Recommendation 2. Instructional materials for students receiving interventions should focus intensely on in-depth treatment of whole numbers in kindergarten through grade 5 and on rational numbers in grades 4 through 8. These materials should be selected by committee.

☐ For students in kindergarten through grade 5, tier 2 and tier 3 interventions should focus almost exclusively on properties of whole numbers and operations. Some older students struggling with whole numbers and operations would also benefit from in-depth coverage of these topics.

☐ For tier 2 and tier 3 students in grades 4 through 8, interventions should focus on in-depth coverage of rational numbers as well as advanced topics in whole number arithmetic (such as long division).

☐ Districts should appoint committees, including experts in mathematics instruction and mathematicians with knowledge of elementary and middle school mathematics curricula, to ensure that specific criteria are covered in-depth in the curriculum they adopt.

Recommendation 3. Instruction during the intervention should be explicit and systematic. This includes providing models of proficient problem solving, verbalization of thought processes, guided practice, corrective feedback, and frequent cumulative review.

☐ Ensure that instructional materials are systematic and explicit. In particular, they should include numerous clear models of easy and difficult problems, with accompanying teacher think-alouds.

☐ Provide students with opportunities to solve problems in a group and communicate problem-solving strategies.

☐ Ensure that instructional materials include cumulative review in each session.

Recommendation 4. Interventions should include instruction on solving word problems that is based on common underlying structures.

☐ Teach students about the structure of various problem types, how to categorize problems based on structure, and how to determine appropriate solutions for each problem type.

☐ Teach students to recognize the common underlying structure between familiar and unfamiliar problems and to transfer known solution methods from familiar to unfamiliar problems.

Recommendation 5. Intervention materials should include opportunities for students to work with visual representations of mathematical ideas and interventionists should be proficient in the use of visual representations of mathematical ideas.

☐ Use visual representations such as number lines, arrays, and strip diagrams.

☐ If visuals are not sufficient for developing accurate abstract thought and answers, use concrete manipulatives first. Although this can also be done with students in upper elementary and middle school grades, use of manipulatives with older students should be expeditious because the goal is to move toward understanding of—and facility with—visual representations, and finally, to the abstract.

Recommendation 6. Interventions at all grade levels should devote about 10 minutes in each session to building fluent retrieval of basic arithmetic facts.

☐ Provide about 10 minutes per session of instruction to build quick retrieval of basic arithmetic facts. Consider using technology, flash cards, and other materials for extensive practice to facilitate automatic retrieval.

☐ For students in kindergarten through grade 2, explicitly teach strategies for efficient counting to improve the retrieval of mathematics facts.

☐ Teach students in grades 2 through 8 how to use their knowledge of properties, such as commutative, associative, and distributive law, to derive facts in their heads.

TABLE 5.3 Recommendations for Treating Children with Specific Learning Disorder with Impairment in Mathematics (continued)

Recommendation 7. Monitor the progress of students receiving supplemental instruction and other students who are at risk.

☐ Monitor the progress of tier 2, tier 3, and borderline tier 1 students at least once a month using grade-appropriate general outcome measures.

☐ Use curriculum-embedded assessments in interventions to determine whether students are learning from the intervention. These measures can be used as often as every day or as infrequently as once every other week.

☐ Use progress monitoring data to regroup students when necessary.

Recommendation 8. Include motivational strategies in tier 2 and tier 3 interventions.

☐ Reinforce or praise students for their effort and for attending to and being engaged in the lesson.

☐ Consider rewarding student accomplishments.

☐ Allow students to chart their progress and to set goals for improvement.

SOURCE: Gersten et al., 2009.

the primary site of treatment for specific developmental disorders. An interdisciplinary team consisting of various professionals, such as a school psychologist, a special education teacher, the classroom teacher, a speech language therapist, and possibly a neurologist design a treatment plan. Typically, children with these disorders require more structure, fewer distractions, and a presentation of new material that uses more than one sensory modality at a time. For example, the instructor may teach math concepts by using oral presentation combined with hands-on manipulation of objects. Perhaps most important is building on the child's strengths, so that he or she can feel a sense of accomplishment and increased self-esteem.

Communication Disorders

Communication disorders are conditions characterized by impairment in language, speech, and communication. Children with **language disorder** do not have the ability to express themselves in ways appropriate to their age and developmental level. They use limited and faulty vocabulary and speak in short sentences with simplified grammatical structures, omitting critical words or phrases. They may also put words together into sentences in peculiar order. A person with this disorder may, for example, always use the present tense, saying, "I have a good time yesterday" instead of "I had." Developmental delays may cause expressive language disorders, but similar symptoms can arise from a medical illness or head injury.

The expressive difficulties of some people are characterized not by their inability to understand or express language, but by difficulties specific to speech. A person with **speech sound disorder** substitutes, omits, or incorrectly articulates speech sounds. For example, a child may use a *t* sound for the letter *k*, saying "tiss" rather than "kiss." People often regard the mispronunciations of children as cute; however, these childhood speech patterns are likely to cause academic problems as the child grows older and becomes ridiculed by other children in school.

Children who experience **childhood-onset fluency disorder (stuttering)** are unable to produce fluent speech. They may emit verbalizations such as sound repetitions and prolongations, broken words, the blocking out of sounds, word substitutions to avoid problematic words, and words expressed with an excess of tension. Although it is difficult to determine cause and effect, a team of Australian researchers demonstrated that there is a strong negative correlation between stuttering severity and educational attainment. It is possible that this relationship reflects, at least in part, the long-term consequences faced by children whose speech problems create

communication disorders Conditions involving impairment in language, speech, and communication.

language disorder A communication disorder characterized by having a limited and faulty vocabulary, speaking in short sentences with simplified grammatical structures, omitting critical words or phrases, or putting words together in peculiar order.

speech sound disorder A communication disorder in which the individual misarticulates, substitutes, or omits speech sounds.

childhood-onset fluency disorder (stuttering) A communication disorder also known as stuttering that involves a disturbance in the normal fluency and patterning of speech that is characterized by such verbalizations as sound repetitions or prolongations, broken words, the blocking out of sounds, word substitutions to avoid problematic words, or words expressed with an excess of tension.

**social (pragmatic)
communication disorder**
Disorder involving deficits in the
social use of verbal and nonverbal
communication..

negative experiences in their early school years (O'Brian, Jones, Packman, Menzies, & Onslow, 2011).

Children who have **social (pragmatic) communication disorder** have deficits in the social use of verbal and nonverbal communication. They have problems adjusting their behavior to the social context, such as knowing how to greet people or interpret the way they are greeted. In addition, they are unable to match their communication with the needs of the listener, such as talking differently to children and adults. In a conversation, they have difficulties following the ordinary conventions of taking turns when speaking. Finally, they have trouble understanding implicit or ambiguous meanings such as those used in humor and metaphors. These deficits can make it difficult not only for individuals to communicate effectively, but also to perform on the job and participate in ordinary social interactions.

5.4 Attention-Deficit/Hyperactivity Disorder (ADHD)

**attention-deficit/
hyperactivity disorder
(ADHD)**
A neurodevelopmental disorder
involving a persistent pattern of
inattention and/or hyperactivity.

One of the most commonly recognized psychological disorders in terms of popular attention, **attention-deficit/hyperactivity disorder (ADHD),** a neurodevelopmental disorder involving a persistent pattern of inattention and/or hyperactivity. The diagnostic criteria and the name of the disorder have changed significantly over the past few decades. Adding to the complications in our understanding of ADHD are debates concerning its prevalence, causes, course, and treatment.

In all likelihood, you have heard the term "ADHD" in its common sense. As is true for autism spectrum disorder, ADHD now has a broad meaning that many people use to describe a child or adult whose symptoms are readily apparent in a variety of social and educational settings. Sensitized to the disorder by media coverage of ADHD in both children and adults, parents, teachers, and friends may view children who disrupt the classroom or home environment as either having or being at risk for this disorder because they show signs of hyperarousal and distractibility. The question of what behaviors constitute a diagnosable condition, however, is not entirely clear.

Characteristics of ADHD

Individuals who fulfill the *DSM-5* diagnostic criteria for ADHD have, to an extreme degree, behavior patterns in which they are inattentive and hyperactive/impulsive. As you can see from Table 5.4, the disorder's two components are defined in terms of a set of specific behavioral criteria. Clinicians can also diagnose children with ADHD "combined type" if they meet both sets of criteria for at least 6 months. They can also diagnose them with ADHD "predominantly inattentive" type if they meet the criteria for inattentiveness, but not hyperactivity-impulsivity for the past 6 months. Alternatively, clinicians may diagnose them as "predominantly hyperactive-impulsive" if they meet the second set of criteria, but have not shown inattentiveness for the previous 6 months.

Researchers estimate the mean prevalence of ADHD around the world at 5.29 percent, but the ranges of ADHD's prevalence rates vary widely by country and region of the world (Figure 5.1) (Polanczyk, de Lima, Horta, Biederman, & Rohde, 2007). The variability in prevalence rates is due not to actual differences in prevalence, but to methodological differences across epidemiological studies. Nevertheless, from the disparity in prevalence rates, we can conclude that ADHD definitions are still very much in need of clarification and standardization.

These wide prevalence variations show us that researchers and clinicians have not yet arrived at a consistent view of the core symptoms of ADHD. Are the presence of both inattentiveness and hyperactivity-impulsivity required or should we regard only one set of symptoms as a sufficient basis for a clinician assigning the diagnosis to a particular

TABLE 5.4 *DSM-5* Criteria for ADHD

To receive the diagnosis of ADHD, an individual must show six or more of the following symptoms in either of the categories of inattentiveness and hyperactivity. These behaviors must be present for at least 6 months to a degree that is maladaptive and inconsistent with the person's developmental level.

In addition, several inattentive or hyperactive-impulsive symptoms must be present prior to the age of 12 years, the symptoms must cause impairment in two or more settings (such as school and family), there must be clear evidence of significant impairment in daily functioning, and the symptoms must not be better explained by another disorder or occur in the course of another disorder.

Inattention (6 or more of the following):

(a) often fails to give close attention to details or makes careless mistakes in schoolwork, work, or other activities

(b) often has difficulty sustaining attention in tasks or play activities

(c) often does not seem to listen when spoken to directly

(d) often does not follow through on instructions and fails to finish schoolwork, chores, or duties in the workplace (not due to oppositional behavior or failure to understand instructions)

(e) often has difficulty organizing tasks and activities

(f) often avoids, dislikes, or is reluctant to engage in tasks that require sustained mental effort (such as schoolwork or homework)

(g) often loses things necessary for tasks or activities (e.g., toys, school assignments, pencils, books, or tools)

(h) is often easily distracted by extraneous stimuli

(i) is often forgetful in daily activities

Hyperactivity and impulsivity (6 or more of the following; for those 17 and older at least 5 are required):

(a) often fidgets with hands or feet or squirms in seat

(b) often leaves seat in classroom or in other situations in which remaining seated is expected

(c) often runs about or climbs excessively in situations in which it is inappropriate (in adolescents or adults, may be limited to subjective feelings of restlessness)

(d) often has difficulty playing or engaging in leisure activities quietly

(e) is often "on the go" or often acts as if "driven by a motor"

(f) often talks excessively

(g) often blurts out answers before questions have been completed

(h) often has difficulty awaiting turn

(i) often interrupts or intrudes on others (e.g., butts into conversations or games)

child? The matter is very much under debate, as the *DSM-5* criteria shown in Table 5.4 indicate.

Moving on to understanding the clinical picture of ADHD using current diagnostic criteria, we can see that children who experience this disorder can face many challenges. During the grade school years, children with ADHD may have lower grades, repeated discipline problems, and placement in special education classes (Wilens, Faraone, & Biederman, 2004). As they reach early adulthood, they are more likely to develop substance use disorders (Wilens et al., 2011). Although researchers and clinicians once thought that ADHD symptoms subside by adolescence, they now recognize that people with ADHD continue to experience them during adolescence and adulthood. The symptom picture changes from childhood to adolescence, such that the hyperactivity that is so evident during preschool and early childhood years declines by

FIGURE 5.1 Worldwide
Prevalence of ADHD

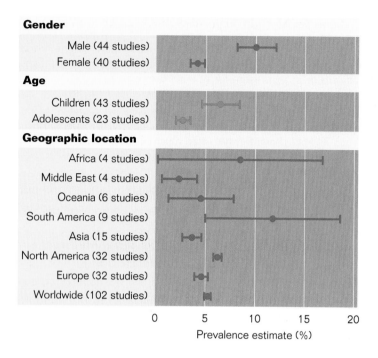

adolescence, yet attentional problems remain, and overt difficulties in executive functions become prominent. Executive functions include tasks such as self-reflection, self-control, planning, forethought, delay of gratification, affect regulation, and resistance to distraction (Wasserstein, 2005). Adults with ADHD are more likely to have deficits in working memory, sustained attention, verbal fluency, and processing speed, problems that resulted in their having lower academic achievement than adults without ADHD (Biederman et al., 2006).

Teenagers with ADHD can have a wide range of behavioral, academic, and interpersonal problems that create serious difficulties for them and problems in their relationships with family, friends, and educators. They tend to be especially immature, likely to engage in conflict with their parents, have strikingly poor social skills, and engage in more high-risk activities such as substance abuse, unprotected sex, and reckless driving (Resnick, 2005).

The diagnosis of ADHD in teenage girls is especially complicated; as a result, educators and clinicians often miss it because their symptoms tend to be less overt than the symptoms of boys. The symptoms in girls include forgetfulness, disorganization, low self-esteem, and demoralization. Unlike boys, they externalize their

MINI CASE

Attention-Deficit/Hyperactivity Disorder

Joshua's mother has just had a conference with her son's teacher, who related that Joshua, age 7, had been extremely restless and distractible in class. Every few minutes, he was up from his desk, exploring something on a bookshelf or looking out the window. When he was in his seat, he kicked his feet back and forth, drummed his fingers on the table, shifted around, and generally kept up a constant high level of movement. He might ask to go to the bathroom three times in an hour. He spoke very quickly, and his ideas were poorly organized. During recess, Joshua was aggressive and violated many of the playground rules. Joshua's mother corroborated the teacher's description of Joshua with similar stories about his behavior at home. Although Joshua is of normal intelligence, he is unable to sustain concentrated attention on any one activity for more than a few minutes.

symptoms and become anxious, depressed, and socially withdrawn. Alternatively, some teenage girls show a symptom picture in which they are hypertalkative or emotionally overreactive (Quinn, 2005), characteristics that we can mistake as reflecting typical adolescent volatility. Teenage girls with ADHD often experience an intensification of symptoms because of hormonal changes at puberty, and they are likely to act out in ways different from male counterparts and put themselves at risk for unplanned and unwanted pregnancies (Resnick, 2005). They continue to experience persistent symptoms and may remain impaired well into early adulthood (Mick et al., 2011).

ADHD in Adults

Once regarded as a disorder restricted to childhood, clinicians and researchers now view ADHD as having the potential to continue into adulthood. ADHD most likely does not show up for the first time in people of adult age, but clinicians can only properly diagnose it until that time. We can assume that clinicians overlooked or misdiagnosed adult ADHD cases, particularly in those individuals who, as children, had inattentive but not disruptive symptoms. Perhaps as many as 4 percent of American adults meet the diagnostic criteria for this disorder, with nearly equal numbers of men and women having this condition (Kessler et al., 2006).

The symptoms of ADHD appear in different forms in adults compared to children. Adults with ADHD are less likely to demonstrate hyperactivity and impulsivity, and are more likely to continue to have symptoms of inattentiveness. Their symptoms fit a picture consistent with deficits in executive functioning, meaning that they are more likely to have difficulty organizing tasks, make careless mistakes, lose things, and perform tasks that involve prioritizing activities on the basis of importance. Whereas children may show greater evidence of restlessness and impulsivity, adult ADHD involves difficulties in maintaining attentional focus (Kessler et al., 2010).

In their daily lives, then, adults with ADHD have trouble devising routines, are haphazard in their management of time and money, and find it difficult to complete academic work or follow through on job tasks. Throughout adulthood, men in particular are at higher risk of having vehicular accidents and receive moving vehicle citations (Cox, Cox, & Cox, 2011). A small percentage of adults with ADHD are able to channel their excessive energy and restlessness into creative endeavors, such as entrepreneurial ventures (Weiss & Murray, 2003), although their inability to sustain attention and commitment to a project may limit the likelihood of their succeeding for any extended period of time.

Women with ADHD are less likely to show the high-risk behaviors seen in men. Instead, they are more likely to experience dysphoria, organization problems, impulsivity, and inattention, characteristics that are of particular concern if they interfere with consistent parenting (Quinn, 2005).

Adults with ADHD typically have serious problems in relationships, whether the relationship is with an intimate partner, a co-worker, an acquaintance, or even a stranger. Somewhat ironically, because they are always seeking stimulation, they may do so by provoking conflict in their interactions with others by starting arguments, refusing to end arguments, or insisting that they have the last word. They find it difficult to listen to others, they may hear only parts of a conversation, they are prone to interrupting, and they speak while others are trying to speak. They tend to be very high-strung,

Children and adolescents who suffer from ADHD experience significant difficulties in keeping up with their schoolwork due to symptoms such as inattention and extreme restlessness. Many researchers believe that the diagnosis is influenced by environmental and sociocultural factors.

which is evident in their hypersensitive and overreactive tendencies, expressed at times in outbursts and intense moodiness. Their intimate partners become exasperated by their impulsivity, propensity for overcommitment, poor decision making, and inept management of money. Conflicts and arguments arise due to the affected individual's symptoms of disorganization, forgetfulness, chronic lateness, repeated misplacement of keys and other important items, and overall undependability (Robbins, 2005).

If they show deficiencies in the types of executive functioning tasks involved in carrying out activities of everyday life, adults with ADHD are also at greater risk of engaging in deviant or antisocial behavior (Barkley & Murphy, 2011). These tasks include self-organization (e.g., managing time), self-discipline (e.g., managing money and being able to tolerate waiting), self-motivation (taking short-cuts at work), and self-activation/concentration (being easily distracted). Adult ADHD is more than a theoretical construct; it is a highly disabling condition that can prevent individuals from achieving their life goals.

Theories and Treatment of ADHD

The biological determination of ADHD is well established, as indicated by family, twin, adoption, and molecular genetic studies. Researchers estimate ADHD heritability as high as 76 percent (Faraone et al., 2005) and is among the highest rates of all psychiatric disorders. Studies of individuals with ADHD have found evidence for the involvement of several genes related to dopamine, suggesting that deficits in reward patterns may contribute to the symptoms of this disorder (Volkow et al., 2009).

Researchers have also found structural brain abnormalities in people with ADHD, and believe that a network of interrelated brain areas is involved in the impairment of attentional-executive functions of these individuals (Wilens et al., 2004). For example, the MRIs of children with ADHD in one recent study revealed that, on average, they had 9 percent less volume in the cortex and disruptions in circuits involved in regulating motor control (Qiu et al., 2011).

Although researchers have found functional and structural abnormalities in the brains of people with ADHD, most agree that genetic vulnerability interacts with environmental exposure. These stressors include birth complications, acquired brain damage, exposure to toxic substances, infectious diseases, and even marital stress of parents (Martel et al., 2011). Researchers also suspect that there may be subtypes of ADHD, depending on comorbidity with other disorders, such as mood or anxiety disorders, learning disabilities, or conduct or oppositional defiant disorder (Adler, Barkley, Wilens, & Ginsberg, 2006). Each of these subtypes may have a different pattern of family inheritance, risk factors, neurobiology, and responses to medications (Biederman, Mick, Faraone, & Burback, 2001).

Tying together biological abnormalities and behavioral problems in ADHD, Barkley's (1997) theory of ADHD proposes that the core impairment is inability to inhibit responses due to abnormalities in the prefrontal cortex and its connections to other parts of the brain. The impairment of response inhibition manifests itself in four areas of functioning: (1) working memory, (2) internalization of self-directed speech, (3) the self-regulation of affect, motivation, and level of arousal, and (4) reconstitution—the ability to break down observed behaviors into component parts that can recombine into new behaviors directed toward a goal. In addition, according to Barkley, children with ADHD fail to develop a future orientation and sense of the self across time.

Consider how each of these impairments is expressed in a child's behavior. Problems with working memory cause the child to have difficulty keeping track of time or remembering such things as deadlines and commitments. Having an impaired internalization of self-directed speech means that these children fail to keep their thoughts to themselves or engage in private self-questioning or self-guidance. Their impaired self-regulation of mood and motivation causes them to display all their emotions outwardly without censorship, while being unable to self-regulate their drive and motivation. Their impaired ability to reconstitute causes these children to be less able to solve problems, because they are unable to analyze behaviors and synthesize new behaviors.

Barkley's theory continues to receive support. Most recently, he has devised a scale to measure executive functioning in adults that assesses self-management with regard to time, self-organization and problem-solving, self-discipline, self-motivation, and self-activation/concentration. Adults with ADHD showed impairment on these ratings. Moreover, their executive functioning ratings were related to the measures of deviant behavior in daily life including antisocial acts, diversity of crimes, and traffic offenses committed while driving (Barkley & Murphy, 2011). Sample items from the adult executive functioning scale are shown in Table 5.5.

In addition to biological and psychological factors, sociocultural influences play a role in the aggravation of the ADHD symptom picture. Many children with ADHD have grown up in a chaotic or disorganized family environment and have had failure experiences in school. However, the child's disruptive behavior may contribute further to family and school problems. Raising a child with ADHD is more difficult than raising a non-ADHD child, and this stress on the family could lead to family disturbances. Similarly, the child's experiences of failure in school may be the result, rather than the cause, of attentional disturbances.

By the time that individuals with ADHD reach adulthood, they have experienced so many frustrations in life, particularly in relationships, that they become caught in a vicious trap of dysfunction. The very nature of their disorder causes them to have difficulty relating to others, even those to whom they are closest. Partners become exasperated and may give up on the relationship, causing the individual with ADHD to become

Table 5.5 Sample Items from the Adult ADHD Executive Functioning Rating Scale

Each item is rated on a 0–3 Likert scale (1 = Rarely or not at all; 2 = Sometimes; 3 = Often; 4 = Very Often).

Scale	Sample Items
Self-Management to Time	Procrastinate or put off doing things until the last minute
	Late for work or scheduled appointments
Self-Organization and Problem-Solving	Often at a loss for words when I want to explain something to others
	Unable to "think on my feet" or respond as effectively as others to unexpected events
Self-Discipline	Make impulsive comments to others
	Trouble following the rules in a situation
Self-Motivation	Likely to take short cuts in my work and not do all that I am supposed to do
	Others tell me I am lazy or unmotivated
Self-Activation/Concentration	Easily distracted by irrelevant thoughts when I must concentrate on something
	Have trouble staying alert or awake in boring situations

SOURCE: Barkley & Murphy, 2011.

You Be the Judge

Prescribing Psychiatric Medications to Children

Research on human participants of any age requires that investigators adhere strictly to the APA Ethical Guidelines. In the case of children, however, the issues shift considerably given that they are "vulnerable populations." This means that they may be at increased risk for abuse and exploitation. Consequently, for decades, researchers avoided conducting studies to test the efficacy of psychotherapeutic medications on children to avoid exposing them to unnecessary harm during research trials. With no conclusive data about effectiveness, safety, and pharmacological action on which to base treatment recommendations, psychiatrists treated their pediatric patients using so-called "off-label" prescriptions that had not received U.S. Food and Drug Administration (FDA) approval.

The practice of prescribing these off-label medications for disorders is widespread in the United States, but because of the problems of conducting research on children, these prescriptions are often targeted toward this population. The FDA has no authority to regulate the way in which physicians practice medicine, so they must make their own decisions about whether or not to prescribe an off-label medication to a child. In the process, physicians must balance the potential benefits with the risks of the medication. With few studies of the safety and efficacy of the medications, physicians must rely on their own experience (Spetie & Arnold, 2007).

Children may therefore be at greater risk of side effects than other populations about whom extensive data exists. The situation was brought to light in a dramatic manner in 2003 when the FDA received reports showing an association between SSRI use in adolescents and a heightened risk of self-harm and suicidal thoughts. By 2007, these medications received "black box" warnings from the FDA that applied not only to children and adolescents, but also to young adults. Because the FDA did not have extensive data on the use of these medications for young people, they used the information they had at their disposal to make this ruling. There is now considerably more information about these medications present, suggesting that antidepressants may, in fact, reduce suicide risks in this population, a risk that decreases steadily with length of treatment (Dudley, Goldney, & Hadzi-Pavlovic, 2010).

Q: *You be the judge:* Should researchers conduct more research on psychotherapeutic medication with children? Do the risks of side effects that may occur during this research justify these investigations? Furthermore, if researchers discover that a medication has harmful side effects, how should prescribing health professionals weigh these against possible benefits?

---

even more depressed and more inclined to seek self-energizing behaviors that ultimately prove to be counterproductive.

Individuals with ADHD often receive medications to control their symptoms. Although there are more than a dozen brand names under which prescriptions are written, most medications are based on methylphenidate (Ritalin). Over the past few decades, pharmaceutical companies have made significant advances in developing effective medications for ADHD, such that more recently produced medications, in extended-release formulations, are longer lasting. The first class of stimulant medications, which included methylphenidate, was effective for brief durations (3 to 5 hours) and required multiple, well-timed doses throughout the day. The extended-release formulations work in one of two ways: back-loaded delivery systems and beaded 50-50 delivery systems. Concerta is a back-loaded product: 22 percent of the dose is in the immediate release overcoat, and 78 percent of the dose is delivered about 4 hours after ingestion. Adderall

XR is a 50-50 beaded delivery product and mimics the patient taking two equal doses at the right time. The duration of action is 7 to 9 hours in adults (Dodson, 2005). One advantage to long-acting medications is that they are less likely to be abused (Mao, Babcock, & Brams, 2011).

As an alternative to methylphenidate, antidepressant medications are sometimes prescribed for people with ADHD. These include buproprion (Wellbutrin SR), pemoline (Cylert), atomoxetine (Strattera), and imipramine. Clinicians use these medications to treat mild to moderate ADHD, with some effects apparent in 2 to 3 days. Clinicians typically use this group of medications for individuals with mild ADHD symptoms and co-existing symptoms, such as anxiety or depression; for individuals with medical conditions that contraindicate stimulant use; for individuals with tic disorder or Tourette's disorder (discussed later in this chapter); and for people with drug abuse histories (Dodson, 2005).

Parents are understandably concerned about the side effects that occur with stimulant use. For example, some children on the medication have trouble sleeping and have a reduced appetite. More serious side effects involve the development of uncontrollable bodily twitches and verbalizations, as well as temporary growth suppression. Critics contend that clinicians overprescribe such medications and that they use medication as the primary, and often only, intervention for dealing with individuals, particularly children, with behavior problems. Moreover, based on animal models, long-term use of stimulants such as Ritalin may provoke persistent neurobehavioral consequences that actually exacerbate ADHD symptoms (Marco et al., 2011). On the other hand, stimulants can play an important role as part of an integrated intervention (Breggin & Barkley, 2005).

In the nonpharmacological realm, a number of interventions are effective in reducing ADHD symptoms and helping individuals with this condition function better interpersonally and feel better about themselves. Murphy (2005) enumerates a multipronged approach to psychosocial treatment. Although he focuses on the treatment of teens and adults with ADHD, we can apply some of the strategies in families of children with ADHD. The eight strategies are as follows:

1. Psychoeducation is the starting point, because the more people with ADHD know about their condition and how it affects them, the better they will be able to understand the impact of this disorder on their daily functioning and to develop coping strategies. Psychoeducation instills hope and optimism as the individual frames the condition as treatable and begins to expect that life will become better once he or she begins making changes.

2. Psychological therapies, such as individual therapy, provide a context in which clinicians, along with the client can set treatment goals, resolve conflicts, solve problems, manage life transitions, and treat co-existing problems such as depression and anxiety. Specific techniques, such as cognitive-behavioral strategies, can help clients change maladaptive behavior and thought patterns that interfere with daily functioning. Maladaptive thought patterns have commonly become entrenched as the result of recurrent negative messages from teachers, parents, and peers.

3. Compensatory behavioral and self-management training provides the opportunity to build skills by incorporating more structure and routine into one's life. Simple strategies can make day-to-day tasks and responsibilities more manageable. These include making to-do lists, using appointment books, keeping notepads in useful locations, and having multiple sets of keys.

4. Other psychological therapies, such as marital counseling, family therapy, career counseling, group therapy, and college planning also provide opportunities to assess the various ways in which ADHD symptoms affect life choices and the people with whom the individual is involved.

5. Coaching, a more recently developed intervention, involves consulting with a professional who can assist the individual with ADHD to focus on the practical implementation of goals. In other words, the coach helps the person find ways to accomplish things through a pragmatic, behavioral, results-oriented approach.

6. Technology (e.g., computer programs or personal digital assistants [PDAs]) can help individuals with ADHD access tools and devices that assist them to communicate more effectively, write, spell, stay organized, remember information, stay on schedule, and keep track of time.

7. School and workplace accommodations can facilitate productivity and minimize distraction. Students or employees with ADHD usually work better in quiet, nondistracting environments. They are also more likely to succeed when they receive more frequent performance reviews to help shape their performance and establish priorities. It is important to restructure tasks in ways that capitalize on their strengths and talents.

8. Advocacy, particularly in the form of advocating for oneself, is especially important in attaining success. Although it is difficult for most people to disclose the disabling aspects of ADHD to others, they may find that explaining their condition to others improves the situation for everyone involved.

This multipronged approach is obviously most appropriate for teens and adults who can take more managerial responsibility for their lives. Clinicians, parents, and teachers treating children with ADHD can, nevertheless, adapt some of these strategies.

A therapist working with a child might use self-reinforcement to encourage the child to regulate behaviors such as settling into a task, delaying gratification, maintaining self-motivation, and monitoring progress toward goals. Implicit in the behavioral approach is the notion that the family must learn to use behavioral methods and directly involve themselves in helping the child reduce disruptive behaviors. Coordinating these efforts with comparable intervention by classroom teachers improves the odds for helping the child gain better self-control.

5.5 Motor Disorders

Developmental Coordination Disorder

developmental coordination disorder
A motor disorder characterized by marked impairment in the development of motor coordination.

The primary form of motor disorder is **developmental coordination disorder.** Children with this disorder experience marked impairment in their abilities to coordinate the movements of their hands and feet. Surprisingly common, affecting as many as 6 percent of children, this disorder can lead children to encounter problems in their academic achievement and ability to engage in ordinary tasks of daily life (Nass & Ross, 2008). There may be subtypes of developmental coordination disorder with one subtype involving hand-eye coordination and the other visual-spatial difficulties (Vaivre-Douret et al., 2011a).

In infancy and early childhood, children with developmental coordination disorder have trouble crawling, walking, and sitting. As they develop, their performance on other age-related tasks also is below average. They may be unable to tie their shoelaces, play ball, complete a puzzle, or even write legibly. Consequently, they may experience problems of low self-esteem. In addition, their lack of coordination may also lead them to be less able to participate in sports and exercise programs, leading them to become overweight. Given the complexity of their symptoms, children with motor disorder seem to benefit from an integrated approach that identifies the needs of children and their families in the early stages when the symptoms first begin to emerge. An integrated approach to assessment can then proceed in which children, families, and professionals share their perspectives on the child's symptoms and start to formulate therapeutic goals. Next, professionals, parents, and children plan how intervention will proceed, taking advantage of community resources. Here again, all must collaborate in setting goals for the child. They should base their planned interventions on evidence-supported treatments. Finally, the intervention team should plan strategies that will continue to support the children and their families as they transition to self-management within the home, school, and communities (Forsyth, Maciver, Howden, Owen, & Shepherd, 2008).

Tic Disorders

A **tic** is a rapid, recurring involuntary movement or vocalization. There are several kinds of tic disorders involving bodily movements or vocalizations. Examples of motor tics include eye blinking, facial twitches, and shoulder shrugging. Vocal tics include coughing, grunting, snorting, coprolalia (the uttering of obscenities), and tongue clicking.

Tourette's disorder is perhaps the most well-known of the tic disorders, affecting approximately 1 percent of children. People with this disorder experience a combination of chronic movement and vocal tics. The majority of individuals with Tourette's disorder are males. Their disorder begins gradually, often with a single tic, such as eye blinking, which over time grows into more complex behaviors. People with Tourette's disorder usually make uncontrollable movements of the head and sometimes parts of the upper body. In some cases, individuals engage in complex bodily movements involving touching, squatting, twirling, or retracing steps. At the same time, they utter vocalizations that sound very odd to others; for example, an individual may have a complex tic behavior in which he rolls his head around his neck while making sniffing and barking noises. In only a small percentage of cases do people with Tourette's disorder utter obscenities. This is not a passing condition but, rather, one that can be lifelong, with onset in childhood or adolescence.

Individuals with this disorder also have other psychological symptoms as well, the most common of which are obsessive-compulsive symptoms, speech difficulties, and attentional problems. Clinicians believe that deficits in brain inhibitory mechanisms in the prefrontal cortex are involved in Tourette's disorder, a feature that is shared with obsessive-compulsive disorder and ADHD (Aliane, Pérez, Bohren, Deniau, & Kemel, 2011). The condition may resolve itself by adulthood, as the brain structures involved in inhibiting the tics mature.

tic
A rapid, recurring involuntary movement or vocalization..

Tourette's disorder
A disorder involving a combination of chronic movement and vocal tics.

This child suffers from a developmental coordination disorder, making it difficult for him to learn to put objects in order at a normative developmental rate.

Children with Tourette's can benefit from educational interventions that help bolster the child's self-esteem and provide supportive counseling. However, if the tics are painful, self-injurious (such as scratching), and cause significant disability, clinicians need to intervene more systematically. These individuals can benefit from a form of cognitive-behavioral therapy using habit reversal. In this approach, the profession trains clients to monitor their tics and sensations that precede the tics and respond to them with a voluntary behavior that is physically incompatible with the tics. However, the individual may not have access to cognitive-behavioral treatment, which can be time-consuming and is unproven. Therefore, the clinician may place the client on pharmacological therapy, which can include SSRIs, atypical antipsychotic agents, and, in extreme cases, deep brain stimulation. However, each of these approaches carries risks. The only medications for Tourette's disorder that the Food and Drug Administration has approved are the classic neuroleptic antipsychotic agents haloperidol and pimozide, which block D2 dopamine receptors (Kurlan, 2010).

Stereotypic Movement Disorder

stereotypic movement disorder
A disorder in which the individual voluntarily repeats nonfunctional behaviors, such as rocking or head-banging, that can be damaging to his or her physical well-being.

Children with **stereotypic movement disorder** engage in repetitive, seemingly driven behaviors, such as waving, body rocking, head-banging, self-biting, and picking at their bodies. These behaviors can interfere with their normal functioning and cause bodily injury. As many as 60 percent of children between the ages of 2 and 5 engage in these repetitive behaviors, so they are very common, but they only receive a diagnosis when they create significant impairment. Subgroups of children are particularly likely to engage in stereotyped motor disorders, including children who are blind and those who have developmental delays. Because repetitive behaviors may be so common, and may even serve a developmental purpose, the child may not require intervention. For children who are truly impaired, or who risk serious injury as a result of their behavior, behavior modification appears to be the most efficacious to help them stop engaging in the behavior. If the behavior does not lead to physical harm, however, children may benefit from learning to cease engaging in the behavior publicly (such as in the classroom) even while they may continue engaging in the behavior privately (Freeman, Soltanifar, & Baer, 2010).

5.6 Neurodevelopmental Disorders: The Biopsychosocial Perspective

The disorders that we have covered in this chapter include a range of conditions that reflect, to differing degrees, combinations of biological, psychological, and sociocultural influences. Genetic influences on many of these disorders are clearly evident, but even so, interactions with social context play an important role. Moreover, because these disorders begin early in life, they have the potential to exert profound psychological effects on an individual's life. Family factors also play a critical role given the importance of early parenting experiences as contributor to psychological outcomes.

Just as the disorders reflect multiple influences, so do treatments. In providing interventions to children, clinicians are becoming justifiably concerned about the use of medication. Treatment from the behavioral perspective seems to have a number of advantages, because their symptoms may be particularly amenable to treatments that focus on principles of reinforcement.

The tremendous growth of interest in the conditions that can affect children within the past few decades means that there is considerably more information available on causes and interventions than was true even a few years ago. Although interventions can be efficacious on people of any age, targeting children as soon as possible can help individuals achieve favorable outcomes that can influence their lives for decades to follow.

Jason was started on a stimulant medication, and both his parents and Mrs. Brownstein noted an improvement in his ability to pay attention and to sit still for longer periods of time. Though he continued to feel restless, Jason's behavioral work with a therapist at the clinic began to help decrease his disruptive behavior at school. The therapist also worked with Pam and John to create a consistent system of rewards and punishment for Jason's behavior. Together they realized that due to their differing opinions on how strict to be with Jason, Pam and John had been sending diverging reinforcement messages to Jason. In order to facilitate an agreement on how to punish or reward Jason accordingly, they worked on creating a set system of reinforcement that they shared with Jason so that he was better informed about what to expect should he misbehave. After several months of medication and therapy, and with his parents' improved ability to discipline him, Jason became less hyperactive while in school and his grades began to improve. Jason started getting along better with his classmates and joined a basketball league, which allowed him to make friends and channel his energy appropriately.

Dr. Tobin's reflections: It can be difficult to differentiate normal overactivity in young children from more severe symptomatology that is indicative of ADHD. Dr. Brownstein made careful consideration of this when diagnosing Jason, based on Pam's description of his behavior over the years. It was clear that Jason's behavioral problems were severely interfering with his ability to lead a normal childhood and attain an education. Especially compared with his brother Nicholas, it was clear that Jason was struggling with symptoms that went beyond that of normative childhood behavior.

ADHD is typically diagnosed during the elementary school years, and though the disorder can last through adolescence, with appropriate treatment such as the kind Jason is receiving, the symptoms can begin to diminish towards adulthood. It can be a difficult ethical decision to place children on stimulant medication, though in Jason's case it was important in helping to decrease his hyperactive symptoms that were causing him problems at school and that would further make behavior therapy difficult to conduct. Hopefully, with continued therapy and behavioral strategies implemented by his parents, he will be able to discontinue medication in the near future.

SUMMARY

- **Neurodevelopmental disorders** include disorders that strike children early in life and appear to affect their behavioral functioning by creating brain abnormalities.

- **Intellectual disability** refers to intellectual and adaptive deficits that are first evident in childhood. Genetic abnormalities are a significant cause. The three most important genetic causes are **Down syndrome, phenylketonuria,** and **fragile X syndrome.** Another genetic disorder is Tay-Sachs disease.

- Environmental hazards during prenatal developing are the second category of causes of intellectual disability. These hazards, called "teratogens," include drugs or toxic channels, maternal malnutrition, and infections in the mother during critical phases of fetal development. Consumption of alcohol during pregnancy can lead to **fetal alcohol syndrome (FAS).**

- People with intellectual disability can benefit from early intervention aimed at providing them with training in motor coordination, language use, and social skills. Educators can combine **mainstreaming,** which integrates them into ordinary school classrooms, with special education that provides them with assistance geared to their particular needs.

- The *DSM-5* authors created the category of **autism spectrum disorder** to provide a more reliable and valid distinction between children who clearly show "typical development" and those who demonstrate the range of deficits in communication and social behavior that *DSM-IV-TR* attempted to differentiate. The new spectrum format for this category underscores the commonalities between disorders previously considered discrete. Disorders listed in *DSM-IV-TR* such as Asperger's, autism, Rett syndrome, **childhood disintegrative disorder,** and pervasive developmental disorder are included in autism spectrum disorder in the *DSM-5*. Symptoms that formerly differentiated these disorders from one another now are indicated by diagnostic specifiers.

- Evidence pointing to patterns of familial heritance supports the theory that autism spectrum disorder is biologically caused. Although it is evident that neurological differences exist between people with and without this autism spectrum disorder, the basis for these differences and their implications are not clear.

- Although there is strong evidence favoring neurobiological abnormalities in individuals with autism spectrum disorder, the behavioral perspective is the most relevant to treatment, particularly interventions that rest on principles of operant conditioning practiced by student therapists and parents. Disruptive and self-stimulatory behaviors will decrease if children with autism spectrum disorder receive reinforcement for appropriate behaviors, such as asking for help or feedback. In such instances, they are less likely to engage in self-injurious or aggressive behaviors.

- **Attention-deficit/hyperactivity disorder (ADHD)** involves inattentiveness or hyperactivity and impulsivity. There are many theories about the cause of this disorder, but familial heritability rates may be as high as 76 percent. Although researchers have found fundamental and structural abnormalities in the brains of people with ADHD, most agree that genetic vulnerability interacts with environmental exposure. Social-cultural influences also play a role in the aggravation of the ADHD symptom picture.

- In *DSM-5*, the new specific learning disorders category now includes specific learning disorder with impairment in reading (dyslexia), specific learning disorder with impairment in mathe-

matics, specific learning disorder with impairment in written expression, and **dyscalculia.** Communication disorders include language disorder, childhood-onset fluency disorder (stuttering), and social (pragmatic) communication disorder.

- Practitioners believe that the best approach to identifying children with learning disorders uses the "Response to Intervention" (RTI) approach in which they institute a set of evidence-based procedures that follow a series of steps.

- **Tics** are the identifying symptom for motor disorders and are characterized by rapid, recurring involuntary movements or vocalizations. Disorders formerly known as **Tourette's disorder,** developmental coordination disorder, **stereotypic movement disorder,** persistent motor or vocal tic disorder, and provisional tic disorder are now included in the *DSM-5* category motor disorders.

- The disorders covered in this chapter include a range of conditions that reflect, to differing degrees, combinations of biological, psychological, and sociocultural influences. Genetic influences on the development of many of these disorders are clearly evident, but even so, interactions with social context play an important role. Moreover, because these disorders begin early in life, they have the potential to exert profound psychological effects on an individual's life.

KEY TERMS

Schizophrenia Spectrum and Other Psychotic Disorders

Learning Objectives

6.1 Explain the characteristics of schizophrenia

6.2 Describe the key features of other psychotic disorders

6.3 Identify the theories and treatments of schizophrenia

6.4 Analyze the biopsychosocial model of schizophrenia

CHAPTER 6

Case Report: David Marshall

Demographic information: 19-year-old Asian American male.

Presenting problem: David was evaluated at an inpatient psychiatric facility following his second psychotic episode within a one-year period. He was brought to the hospital by his mother, Ann, who had noticed that David's behavior had become increasingly bizarre over the past seven months. David's mother was the main source of information during the interview, as David was unable to give an accurate personal history.

David is a college sophomore, attending a university in his hometown. Though he lived at home with Ann during his first year (she had raised David after getting a divorce when David was 5), she and David decided it would be beneficial for him to move into the dormitories in order to gain a sense of independence. Ann reported that David was doing well for the first two weeks of living in the dormitories. Ann and David typically spoke on the phone a few times per week, and David had been coming home for dinner on Sunday evenings. One Sunday evening in mid-October, Ann reported that David failed to show up for dinner as he had been planning to. She called David's best friend Mark who had not heard from him for a few days and was himself worried about David. Mark has known David since high school and lives in the same town. He noted to Ann that David didn't "quite seem to be himself lately," as he had been acting particularly aloof. Mark had been concerned that he hadn't heard from David and so he went to search for him in different parts of town where he knew David liked to spend time, and eventually found him outside of a coffee shop. When Mark approached David, David stated that he wished to be referred to as "Joey." Mark noted that David appeared particularly unkempt, which was unusual as he normally took very good care of himself. Upon approaching David, Mark also noticed that he was smiling and laughing to himself. Mark assumed that he was doing so because he was in a particularly good mood, though David's

tone became more serious when he offered to drive David back to his dorm room. David refused, stating, "I have a lot of writing to do. My poems are going to be published and they want me to write 20 more so they can publish a book of my poems." Writing had always been one of David's hobbies, and he and Mark often discussed their respective creative endeavors. Mark was alerted when he looked down at David's notebook, which was open in his lap while they were talking, and noticed only illegible scribbling. Mark noticed that throughout their conversation, David's left arm repeatedly and seemingly involuntarily extended with a jerking motion every few minutes. Mark was unable to convince David to go back to campus with him, and Mark hesitantly left the coffee shop. Upon hearing this story, Ann was shocked about her son's behavior, remarking that she had never seen David acting so oddly. Unsure of what to do, Ann decided to wait until she heard from David.

David eventually returned to his dorm room and called Ann around 3 A.M., stating, "I can't stay here because there are no poets here. They need me there. Meeting, meeting, bus, poems. I need poems for a money to go to meet. A meeting. I have to get there. I have got there. I have to go there." He repeated this last part several times. Confused, Ann asked David what he meant, at which point David hung up the phone. After that, Ann reported she didn't hear from David for about one week.

David was returned to Ann's house by the police, who had found him on campus causing a disturbance by yelling at some other students who were waiting for a bus nearby. Ann was unsure if David had actually gone to New York or if he had been on campus the whole time. She was able to extract that he had not been attending his classes. She decided to write to David's professors, asking for an incomplete grade as it was clear that David was unable to successfully complete his classes in his current state. David stayed with Ann for the next three weeks, during which time he continued to display bizarre behavior. Ann had hoped that he was going to recover at any given time, but it was becoming clear that he was not improving. When Ann would return home from work, she would find dirty laundry, dishes, pizza boxes, and cigarette ashes all around the house. Often David would stay in his room all day long, coming out only to use the bathroom or eat a meal. When Ann did see him she noticed that he appeared rather sad and withdrawn, barely speaking to her. Normally they had a very close relationship and enjoyed spending time together around the house. Though she worried about her son, she wasn't sure what she could do to help him.

By the time the next school year was about to start, Ann felt that David seemed to have made a great improvement—he was engaging more with her at home and was less messy and the content of his speech was less bizarre. He did seem much more withdrawn in general than he once had been, and was engaging in a minimal amount of activities. He was able to hold a part-time job for about one month in the spring at a gas station, but was fired due to excessively showing up late for work. Otherwise, he mostly stayed in his room listening to music and writing. He spent time with Mark occasionally, though David often cancelled their plans stating that he simply didn't feel like being around people.

David and Ann decided that he should re-enroll at the university, and at David's urging, he was sent to once again live in the dormitories. Two weeks later, David again disappeared. Ann again got a phone call one evening from David, who said he was in Manhattan. She reported that David said he had owed his landlord some money for needing a new set of keys. Ann had been unaware that David even went to New York or that he was living there. David asked for her credit card information over the phone and said that if he didn't come up with the money the landlord was threatening violence against him. When Ann asked where he was exactly, David hung up the phone, and Ann did not hear from him until he showed up at her house three days later, completely disheveled and visibly filthy. He told Ann that he was afraid his roommate was going to burn all of his belongings. While he was telling the story he was laughing. It appeared to Ann that David was once again acting bizarrely and after the previous experience she knew that this time something had to be done. Unsure of where to turn, Ann brought David to the closest general hospital, where he was admitted to the psychiatric ward.

Relevant history: David has no previous history of psychiatric treatment. His mother reported that he had experienced some mild depression earlier in his teenage years. She recalled that David had always been "somewhat different" from his peers, noting that he had only a few close friends throughout his childhood and adolescence.

In terms of family history, Ann reported that David's paternal grandfather had been diagnosed with schizophrenia though there was no other noted family history of mental illness.

Case formulation: It was clear from the presenting story that David had experienced two psychotic episodes over the past few months. His first psychotic break occurred after a major stressor—moving away from home for the first time. This is a typical stressor that occurs around the developmental period when psychotic symptoms may first begin to fully emerge, due to the high base rate of major life events that occur during this time. By Ann's report, David had perhaps displayed some prodromal symptoms as an adolescent, which is also typical in the case of individuals with schizophrenia. David meets diagnostic criteria for schizophrenia as his symptoms lasted for longer than six months, and included over one month of active symptoms. Further, his general level of functioning was greatly reduced following the first psychotic episode; he was unable to hold a job and remained withdrawn from his interpersonal relationships.

David's delusion about making a deal with a publishing company in New York for a book of poetry did not carry over into his next psychotic episode, which centralized from a different theme.

Treatment plan: David will be stabilized on antipsychotic medication while in the hospital, and his psychiatrists will aim to find a suitable maintenance dose for once he is discharged back home. He will be set up with an outpatient psychiatric facility to provide him medication and weekly psychotherapy. It is also recommended that David attain a case manager to help him with vocational activities and to decide whether continuing to pursue a higher educational degree is a possibility, given his past vulnerabilities when enrolled in college.

Sarah Tobin, PhD

6.1 Schizophrenia

The broad category of **schizophrenia** includes a set of disorders in which individuals experience distorted perception of reality and impairment in thinking, behavior, affect, and motivation. Schizophrenia is a serious mental illness, given its potentially broad impact on an individual's ability to live a productive and fulfilling life. Although a significant number of people with schizophrenia eventually manage to live symptom-free lives, many must find ways to adapt their lives to the reality of the illness. In economic terms, schizophrenia also exacts a heavy burden with an annual estimated cost in the United States (in 2002 dollars) of $62.7 billion, which includes direct costs of care and indirect costs of loss of productivity (McEvoy, 2007).

A **delusion** is a deeply entrenched false belief not consistent with the client's intelligence or cultural background. For example, a delusion of persecution is the false belief that someone or something is out to harm you (Table 6.1). A **hallucination** is a false

schizophrenia
A disorder with a range of symptoms involving disturbances in content of thought, form of thought, perception, affect, sense of self, motivation, behavior, and interpersonal functioning.

delusion
Deeply entrenched false belief not consistent with the client's intelligence or cultural background.

hallucination
A false perception not corresponding to the objective stimuli present in the environment.

TABLE 6.1 Types and Examples of Delusions

Grandeur

A grossly exaggerated conception of the individual's own importance. Such delusions range from beliefs that the person has an important role in society to the belief that the person is actually Christ, Napoleon, or Hitler.

Control

The feeling that one is being controlled by others, or even by machines or appliances. For example, a man may believe that his actions are being controlled by the radio, which is "forcing" him to perform certain actions against his will.

Reference

The belief that the behavior of others or certain objects or events are personally referring to oneself. For example, a woman believes that a soap opera is really telling the story of her life, or a man believes that the sale items at a local food market are targeted at his own particular dietary deficiencies.

Persecution

The belief that another person or persons are trying to inflict harm on the individual or on that individual's family or social group. For example, a woman feels that an organized group of politically liberal individuals is attempting to destroy the right-wing political organization to which she belongs.

Self-blame

Feelings of remorse without justification. A man holds himself responsible for a famine in Africa because of certain unkind or sinful actions that he believes he has committed.

Somatic

Inappropriate concerns about one's body, typically related to a disease. For example, without any justification, a woman believes she has brain cancer. Adding an even more bizarre note, she believes that ants have invaded her head and are eating away at her brain.

Infidelity

A false belief usually associated with pathological jealousy involving the notion that one's lover is being unfaithful. A man lashes out in violent rage at his wife, insisting that she is having an affair with the mailman because of her eagerness for the mail to arrive each day.

Thought broadcasting

The idea that one's thoughts are being broadcast to others. A man believes that everyone else in the room can hear what he is thinking, or possibly that his thoughts are actually being carried over the airwaves on television or radio.

Thought insertion

The belief that outside forces are inserting thoughts into one's mind. For example, a woman concludes that her thoughts are not her own, but that they are being placed there to control her or upset her.

MINI CASE

Catatonia, Unspecified

Maria is a 21-year-old college junior who has been psychiatrically hospitalized for a month. The resident assistant in Maria's dormitory brought her to the hospital in December, because she had grown increasingly concerned about Maria's deteriorating behavior over the course of the semester. When Maria returned to college in September, her roommate told others, including the resident assistant, that Maria was acting oddly. For example, she had a habit of repeating other people's words, she stared listlessly out the window, and she ignored her personal hygiene. As the semester's end approached, Maria retreated more and more into her own world, until her behavior reached a point such that she was completely unresponsive to others. In the hospital, she maintains rigid posturing of her body, while staring at the ceiling and spending most of the day in a trancelike state that seems impenetrable. The staff members treating her are in a quandary about what intervention to use for Maria because of her hypersensitivity to most medications. At present, the clinicians are attempting to determine if Maria has another medical condition or a psychological disorder, but for the moment they have diagnosed her as having unspecified catatonia.

incoherent
Language that is incomprehensible.

loosening of associations
Flow of thoughts that is vague, unfocused, and illogical.

catatonia
A condition in which the individual shows marked psychomotor disturbances.

active phase
A period in the course of schizophrenia in which psychotic symptoms are present.

positive symptoms
The symptoms of schizophrenia, including delusions, hallucinations, disturbed speech, and disturbed behavior, that are exaggerations or distortions of normal thoughts, emotions, and behavior.

negative symptoms
The symptoms of schizophrenia, including affective flattening, alogia, avolition, and anhedonia, that involve functioning below the level of normal behavior.

restricted affect
Narrowing of the range of outward expressions of emotions.

avolition
A lack of initiative, either not wanting to take any action or lacking the energy and will to take action.

perception not corresponding to the objective stimuli present in the environment. Disorganized speech refers to language that is **incoherent**, meaning that it is incomprehensible. The thought process underlying this type of speech reflects **loosening of associations**; namely, a flow of thoughts that is vague, unfocused, and illogical.

Although no longer a subtype of schizophrenia, clinicians diagnose **catatonia** when the individual shows marked psychomotor disturbances. These disturbances may consist of decreased, excessive, or peculiar motor activity, and not actively relating to situations in the environment. Catatonia may be diagnosed in association with another psychological disorder, a medical condition, or due to a cause that the clinician cannot determine.

Table 6.2 contains schizophrenia's six diagnostic criteria. The symptoms in Criterion A refer to the **active phase** of the disorder, that is, the period during which the individual's symptoms are most prominent. The symptoms the individual experiences during the active phase fall into two categories: positive symptoms and negative symptoms. **Positive symptoms** are exaggerations or distortions of normal thoughts, emotions, and behavior. Referring to Table 6.2, symptoms numbered 1 through 4 under Criterion A fit into this category.

The symptoms in #5 under Criterion A are **negative symptoms,** meaning that they involve functioning below the normal level of behavior. **Restricted affect,** as the term implies, refers to a narrowing of the range of outward expressions of emotions. **Avolition** is a lack of initiative, either not wanting to take any action or lacking the energy and will to take action. **Asociality** refers to a lack of interest in social relationships, including an inability to empathize and form close relationships with others.

Criterion B is consistent with other *DSM* criteria for psychological disorders involving significant impairment. However, for schizophrenia, the degree of impairment is more far-reaching. Criterion C, indicating the period of disturbance, is also carefully delineated to ensure that individuals receive this diagnosis only if they show a substantial duration of symptoms. Criteria D and E refer to other disorders that should not be present in people diagnosed with schizophrenia. In the case of Criterion D, schizoaffective disorder, which we discuss below, is particularly important to rule out.

In *DSM-IV-TR*, clinicians diagnosed an individual with schizophrenia into one of five subtypes based on which symptoms are most prominent. These were catatonic, disorganized, paranoid, undifferentiated, and residual. These subtypes disappeared in *DSM-5* because the members of the schizophrenia task force believed that they are not supported by empirical evidence. However, the catatonic type remains in *DSM-5* as a separate disorder (catatonia).

TABLE 6.2 Diagnostic Features of Schizophrenia

For an individual to be diagnosed with schizophrenia, he or she must meet all of the criteria listed in A–F.

A. Two (or more) of the following symptoms must be present for a significant portion of time during a one-month period (although this can be less if the individual is successfully treated). At least one symptom must be from the first three categories.

1. Delusions

2. Hallucinations

3. Disorganized speech

4. Grossly abnormal psychomotor behavior

5. Negative symptoms such as restricted affect, avolition, and asociality

B. Occupational dysfunction

For a significant portion of the time since the onset of the disturbance, one or more major areas of functioning such as work, interpersonal relations, or self-care are markedly below the level achieved prior to the onset (or when the onset is in childhood or adolescence, the person fails to achieve expected level of interpersonal, academic, or occupational achievement).

C. Duration of at least six months

Continuous signs of the disturbance must persist for at least six months. During at least one of these six months, the person must show the active-phase symptoms from Criterion A (or less if the person was successfully treated). The six months may include periods during which the individual had symptoms leading up to (prodromal) or following (residual) an active phase. During these periods, the person must show only negative symptoms or two or more of the active-phase symptoms but in attenuated form.

D. No evidence of schizoaffective, depressive, or bipolar disorder

E. Symptoms are not due to substance use disorder or general medical condition

F. If there is a history of autism spectrum disorder or a communication disorder of childhood onset, the additional diagnosis of schizophrenia is made only if prominent delusions or hallucinations are also present for at least a month (or less if successfully treated).

The speech of individuals with schizophrenia may be almost completely indecipherable and rambling, containing **neologisms,** which are invented ("new") words. Unlike words that eventually may become accepted words in a particular language (such as "google"), these words have highly idiosyncratic meanings that are used only by the individual. The behavior of the person with this type of schizophrenia is, as the term implies, highly disorganized and they may be unable to complete such basic tasks of everyday life as bathing. Another characteristic symptom is **inappropriate affect,** meaning that the person's emotional response does not match the social cues present in a situation, such as laughing after hearing a sad story.

asociality
Lack of interest in social relationships.

neologisms
Invented ("new") words.

inappropriate affect
The extent to which a person's emotional expressiveness fails to correspond to the content of what is being discussed.

MINI CASE

Schizophrenia, Continuous

Joshua is a 43-year-old man who stands daily near the steps of a local bank on a busy street corner. Every day, he wears a Red Sox baseball cap, a yellow T-shirt, worn-out hiking shorts, and orange sneakers. Rain or shine, day in and day out, Joshua maintains his post at the bank. Sometimes he is conversing with imaginary people. Without provocation, he sobs miserably. Sometimes he explodes in shrieks of laughter. Police and social workers keep taking him to shelters for the homeless, but Joshua manages to get back on the street before he can receive treatment. He has repeatedly insisted that these people have no right to keep bothering him.

Individuals with schizophrenia present with a wide range of symptoms. For example, they may maintain paranoid delusions that they are in danger.

paranoia
The irrational belief or perception that others wish to cause you harm.

Paranoia, the irrational belief or perception that others wish to cause you harm, may be associated with delusions or auditory hallucinations related to a theme that somebody is persecuting or harassing them. They do not, however, have symptoms of disorganized speech or disturbed behavior.

French physician Benedict Morel (1809–1873) first identified schizophrenia as a disease which he coined *démence precocé* (brain dementia of the young). German psychiatrist Emil Kraepelin (1856–1926) renamed the condition *dementia praecox*. He included in the definition a group of nine different clinical forms that shared a similar course in which the afflicted individuals ultimately experienced severe behavioral and cognitive decline. Underlying the different symptoms, Kraepelin believed, was one underlying disease process causing the "weakening" of mental processes.

Swiss psychologist Eugen Bleuler (1857–1939) proposed a dramatic change in both the name and the understanding of the disorder. According to Bleuler (1911), the disorder was not one, but instead, a set of diseases which he labeled the *schizophrenias*. The term *schizophrenia* is not a splitting of personalities (as in dissociative identity disorder), but a splitting of (schiz) the functions of the mind. Unlike Kraepelin, Bleuler thought it was possible for people with schizophrenia to recover from the disorder.

Clinicians still refer to fundamental features of the disorder that he identified as Bleuler's "Four A's," meaning that it includes:

1. Thought disorder, as might be evident through rambling and incoherent speech ("Association")

2. Disorder of the experience and expression of emotion ("Affect")

3. Inability to make or follow through on decisions ("Ambivalence")

4. Withdrawal from reality ("Autism")

In the decades following Bleuler's work, clinicians in Europe and the United States proposed further distinctions within the schizophrenia grouping. One notable contributor to the debate was the German psychiatrist, Kurt Schneider (1887–1967), who believed that clinicians should only diagnose schizophrenia when an individual has certain "first-rank symptoms." People with these symptoms believe, for example, that someone else is controlling their impulses and feelings. *DSM-III* and the ICD-10 included the first-rank symptoms as part of clinicians' attempts to develop a more precise set of diagnostic criteria than those present in earlier editions of these systems. However, evidence emerged from family inheritance studies showing that relatives of people with schizophrenia

MINI CASE

Schizophrenia, Multiple Episodes, Currently in Full Remission

Esther is a 36-year-old unmarried woman who lives with her mother. For the past 10 years, she has worked as a clerical assistant in an insurance company, and no longer shows the delusions, disorganized speech, and lack of emotional expression that originally led to her 2 prior hospitalizations within a 2-year period. At the moment, however, she is able to hold onto her job and maintain a relationship with her mother and a few friends.

developed not only schizophrenia, but also schizophrenia-like disorders. Researchers began to speak of the "schizophrenia spectrum" rather than a single disease entity, leading to new diagnostic categories that included, for example, personality and affective disorders. Toward this end, Section 3 of the *DSM-5* includes a set of symptom severity ratings (see Table 6.3). These can inform the diagnostic process as well as allow clinicians to track changes in a client's symptoms across time and over the course of treatment.

Along with the changing conceptualizations of schizophrenia, researchers and clinicians began to distinguish between the so-called "positive" symptoms of delusions and hallucinations and "negative" symptoms that included social withdrawal, loss of volition, affective flattening, and empty or meaningless speech. Researchers proposed that positive symptoms reflected activated dopamine levels in the nervous system and negative symptoms reflected abnormalities in brain structure (Jablensky, 2010). Increasingly, investigators are beginning to recognize that cognitive impairment plays an important role in this disorder (Reichenberg, 2010). Instead of focusing on the positive symptoms only, they are redefining cognitive deficits as core features of the disorder (Gur & Gur, 2010). We will talk more about these later in the chapter, under psychological perspectives.

> ## What's New in the DSM-5
>
> ### Schizophrenia Subtypes and Dimensional Ratings
>
> The *DSM-5* authors implemented major changes in their approach to diagnosing schizophrenia. As we mentioned at the beginning of the chapter, they eliminated the subtypes of schizophrenia. Instead, using a scale that is in Section 3, clinicians assign a diagnosis of schizophrenia to which they can add a rating of the individual's symptoms along a set of dimensions, as Table 6.3 shows.
>
> By eliminating the subtypes of schizophrenia, the *DSM-5* authors sought to improve both the diagnostic reliability and validity of the system. They also sought to have a more quantifiable basis for research on the disorder's causes as well as for treatment planning. For example, a clinician evaluating the results of cognitive-behavioral therapy could use the ratings of hallucination and delusion severity to determine whether the intervention is reducing the specific symptoms toward which they are targeting treatment.
>
> The *DSM-5* authors also decided to include cognitive impairment as a dimension in the Section 3 severity ratings, given the importance of cognitive deficits in current understandings of the individual's ability to carry out social and occupational activities and to carry out the tasks involved in everyday living. In this regard, a neuropsychological assessment could inform the diagnostic process (Reichenberg, 2010).
>
> The *DSM-5* authors considered, but decided not to, eliminate schizoaffective disorder as a separate entity.
>
> Although not there yet, the *DSM-5* authors believe that clinicians will eventually diagnose schizophrenia as a "spectrum" disorder. This would mean, potentially, that even diagnoses long in use in psychiatry would disappear, including schizophreniform disorder, schizoaffective disorder, and the two personality disorders associated with schizophrenic-like symptoms.
>
> The current system in the *DSM-5* represents a step in moving away from the old categorization system and toward the dimensional approach. By including severity ratings rather than subtypes in Section 3, they are making it possible for clinicians and researchers to track individuals over time in a quantifiable fashion.

Clinicians thought for many years that the lifetime prevalence of schizophrenia was 1 per 100, but several large-scale relatively recent reviews provide a lower estimated lifetime prevalence of 7 per 1,000 (i.e., 0.7 per 1,000). People with schizophrenia are two to three times more likely to die compared to others within their age group. The disparities in mortality risk between people with and without schizophrenia are significant. This is in part because the medications that clinicians use to treat people with schizophrenia may contribute to weight gain, which in turn increases the risk of life-threatening diseases. The sex ratio is tilted slightly in the direction of males. For every three men who develop schizophrenia over the course of their lives, two women are affected with the disorder.

Although the prevalence of schizophrenia is relatively low compared to other psychological disorders, a surprisingly high percentage of adults report experiencing minor psychotic symptoms. Reviewing a large number of studies on psychotic symptoms, one group of researchers estimate the lifetime prevalence as about 5% and the prevalence at any one time of about 3% (van Os, Linscott, Myin-Germeys, Delespaul, & Krabbendam, 2009).

Course of Schizophrenia

For many years, up through the early 1980s, with no comprehensive diagnostic criteria at their disposal, psychiatrists used schizophrenia as a catchall term applying to the majority of people requiring institutionalization for psychotic symptoms.

TABLE 6.3 Dimensions of Psychosis Symptom Severity in Section 3 of *DSM-5*

	Halluci-nations	Delusions	Disorganized speech	Abnormal psychomotor behavior	Negative symptoms (restricted emotional expression or avolition)	Impaired cognition	Depression	Mania
0	Not Present	Not Present	Not Present	Not Present	Not Present	Not Present	Not Present	Not Present
1	Equivocal (severity or duration not sufficient to be considered psychosis)	Equivocal (severity or duration not sufficient to be considered psychosis)	Equivocal (severity or duration not sufficient to be considered disorganization)	Equivocal (severity or duration not sufficient to be considered abnormal psychomotor behavior)	Equivocal decrease in facial expressivity, prosody, gestures, or self-initiated behavior	Equivocal (cognitive function not clearly outside the range expected for age or SES, i.e., within 0.5 SD of mean)	Equivocal (some depressed mood, but insufficient symptoms, duration, or severity to meet diagnostic criteria)	Equivocal (some inflated or irritable mood, but insufficient symptoms, duration, or severity to meet diagnostic criteria)
2	Present, but mild (little pressure to act upon voices, not very bothered by voices)	Present, but mild (delusions are not bizarre, or little pressure to act upon delusional beliefs, not very bothered by beliefs)	Present, but mild (some difficulty following speech and/or occasional bizarre behavior)	Present, but mild (occasional abnormal motor behavior)	Present, but mild decrease in facial expressivity, prosody, gestures, or self-initiated behavior.	Present, but mild (some reduction in cognitive function below expected for age and SES, 0.5–1 SD from mean)	Present, but mild (meets criteria for Major Depression, with minimum number of symptoms, duration, and severity)	Present, but mild (meets criteria for Mania with minimum number of symptoms, duration, and severity)
3	Present and moderate (some pressure to respond to voices, or is somewhat bothered by voices)	Present and moderate (some pressure to act upon beliefs, or is somewhat bothered by beliefs)	Present and moderate (speech often difficult to follow and/or frequent bizarre behavior)	Present and moderate (frequent abnormal motor behavior)	Present and moderate decrease in facial expressivity, prosody, gestures, or self-initiated behavior.	Present and moderate (clear reduction in cognitive function below expected for age and SES, 1–2 SD from mean)	Present and moderate (meets criteria for Major Depression with somewhat more than the minimum number of symptoms, duration, and/or severity	Present and moderate (meets criteria for Mania with somewhat more than the minimum number of symptoms, duration, and/or severity)
4	Present and severe (severe pressure to respond to voices, or is very bothered by voices)	Present and severe (severe pressure to act upon beliefs, or is very bothered by beliefs)	Present and severe (speech almost impossible to follow and/or behavior almost always bizarre)	Present and severe (abnormal motor behavior almost constant)	Present and severe decrease in facial expressivity, prosody, gestures, or self-initiated behavior.	Present and severe (severe reduction in cognitive function below expected for age and SES, > 2 SD from mean)	Present and severe (meets criteria for Major Depression with many more than the minimum number of symptoms and/or severity)	Present and severe (meets criteria for Mania with many more than the minimum number of symptoms and/or severity)

Note: SD = standard deviation; SES = socioeconomic status

remission
Term used to refer to the situation when the individual's symptoms no longer interfere with his or her behavior and are below those required for a *DSM* diagnosis.

Unfortunately, this meant that even for people experiencing a brief episode or a disorder other than schizophrenia, the diagnosis might remain with them for years in what was at the time called a "residual" phase. Making the situation worse was the fact that psychiatrists would prescribe their clients antipsychotic medication for life to prevent their symptoms from recurring. This situation began to change during the 1970s as researchers and clinicians developed a better understanding of the nature of psychotic disorders. We now know that schizophrenia may take one of several courses. In the most serious, the individual does not recover and continues to experience continuous positive symptoms. Clinicians define **remission** as occurring when the individual's symptoms no longer interfere with his or her behavior and are below those required for a *DSM* diagnosis (Lambert, Karow, Leucht, Schimmelmann, & Naber, 2010).

You Be the Judge

Schizophrenia Diagnosis

As we discussed in the chapter, the outcome of schizophrenia is not necessarily positive. Although many people do achieve recovery, particularly if they were treated early in the course of the disorder, people with schizophrenia nevertheless face substantial risks of relapse over the rest of their lives. Therefore, when a mental health professional provides a diagnosis to an individual with schizophrenia, this is serious news that could lead the individual to experience great distress, much as a person with cancer might feel at receiving that diagnosis.

There are other ethical issues that practitioners face when working with people diagnosed with schizophrenia (Howe, 2008). Not only must mental health professionals attempt to determine whether or not to provide a diagnosis of this serious disorder, but they also face specific questions relevant to the individual's particular symptoms. For example, the clinician may consider it more acceptable to inform clients with delusional disorder that they are receiving medication for anxiety, stress, or dysphoria rather than for having delusions. To inform the client about the actual nature of his or her symptoms might interfere with the ability to form a therapeutic alliance, which could interfere with the ultimate success of the treatment.

To overcome this obstacle, a clinician may decide to share a "partial" truth. Specifically, the clinician may reframe a client's symptoms as strengths. Rather than seeing a client's attachments to inanimate objects as a symptom, for example, the clinician may reframe the behavior as proving the client's exceptional capacity for caring.

A second ethical dilemma involves balancing a client's desire to succeed in life with the reality that due to the disorder, he or she may be unable to realize these ambitions. The stress of, for example, a competitive career might push the client over the edge into a relapse. Should the clinician try to protect the client from undertaking this venture or respect the client's autonomy to make his or her own decisions?

As if these two challenges were not enough, consider the situation in which a clinician wishes to involve the client's family in treatment. As we observed in the chapter, overinvolved and critical family members can exacerbate a client's symptoms. Should the clinician try to persuade the client to make the family part of treatment, knowing that this could potentially be helpful to the client's overall chances of recovery? Or would such persuasion be unethical, again, violating the client's autonomy?

Finally, given that people with a family history of schizophrenia have increased risk of developing the disorder, how much should clinicians warn high-risk adolescents or young adults? On the one hand, telling people who are asymptomatic that they may develop this serious illness could in and of itself provoke an episode. On the other hand, by not telling those at genetic risk about the possibility of their developing schizophrenia may mean that they don't take preventive steps.

Howe (2008) suggests that mental health professionals can navigate these ethical dilemmas by using an "ethical sliding scale." They can base their ethical decisions by taking into account the client's ability to achieve insight, the strength of their relationship with the client, and the nature of and strength of the client's relationship with family. Although respecting the client's autonomy should be the primary guiding principle, clinicians should balance this principle against the client's decision-making abilities.

Q: *You be the judge:* Do you agree with the idea of using an "ethical sliding scale"?

Researchers have long attempted to chart the long-term outcome of schizophrenia and, in particular, how to quantify the phases of the disorder. They are also concerned with how to provide consistent criteria for "recovery." How long and how well does an individual have to be in order to be completely symptom-free? An international team of scientists, the Remission in Schizophrenia Working Group, published a consensus statement in 2005 in which they defined remission according to a combination of symptoms (e.g., delusions, hallucinations, disorganized speech) and time course (a minimum of six months) (Lambert et al., 2010).

The Working Group proposed that clinicians use the remission definition as an absolute threshold, meaning that rather than comparing an individual to himself or herself at an earlier point, the clinicians would evaluate the individual according to which symptoms he or she displays and for how long. These criteria would help to reduce the variation in the way various individuals, including the client, define remission. For example, people with schizophrenia tend to judge their own remission by how well they are feeling. Psychiatrists base their judgments on whether or not the individual continues to meet *DSM-5* criteria.

Compared to other psychological disorders, the course and outcome are poorer for people with schizophrenia (Jobe & Harrow, 2010). During the first 10 to 15 years, people with schizophrenia have more recurrent episodes and their chances of completely recovering, even after the first 10 years, are worse than those of people with other disorders. Most people continue to experience psychotic symptoms and disordered thinking, as well as negative symptoms. They are less able to obtain or keep a job. On the positive side, however, if they receive current treatment during their acute phase, over 40% can recover (i.e., have no symptoms or hospitalizations and at least part-time work) for one or more years at a time. Some people with schizophrenia can even show complete recovery for the remainder of their lives.

Researchers who follow people with schizophrenia for extended periods of time propose a model in which 25 to 35 percent show chronic psychotic symptoms. However, even when they are symptom-free, they may still be impaired in their functioning and adjustment. The factors that contribute to poorer prognosis include poorer cognitive skills, a longer period of time without treatment, substance abuse, a poorer course of early development, higher vulnerability to anxiety, and negative life events. In addition, overinvolvement of family members in the individual's life, as we discuss later in the chapter, also predicts poorer outcome (Jobe & Harrow, 2010).

Single men seem to be at particularly high risk if they possess these additional characteristics (Gómez-de-Regil et al., 2010). Men also are more likely to experience negative symptoms, to have poorer social support networks, and to have poorer functioning over time than females (Willhite et al., 2008). The prognosis for individuals from developing (agricultural-based) countries is better than that for individuals from developed (industrial) nations due to greater resources for treating affected individuals (Hopper, Harrison, Janca, & Sartorius, 2007).

brief psychotic disorder
A disorder characterized by the sudden onset of psychotic symptoms that are limited to a period of less than a month.

A brief psychotic episode can last anywhere between one day and one month.

6.2 Brief Psychotic Disorder

As the term implies, **brief psychotic disorder** is a diagnosis that clinicians use when an individual develops symptoms of psychosis that do not persist past a short period of time. To receive this diagnosis, an individual must experience one of four symptoms, which include delusions, hallucinations, disorganized speech, and grossly disorganized or catatonic behavior. The diagnosis requires that the individual experience symptoms for more than a day, but recover in less than a month.

In assigning this diagnosis, the clinician must take into account the client's cultural background. As we discussed in Chapter 2, cultures vary in what the members of that culture consider an appropriate response pattern. The clinician also must take note of whether the client has experienced a recent stressor, such as a flood, the loss of a close relative, or an automobile accident. Clinicians also note if a woman develops this disorder within four weeks of giving birth.

MINI CASE

Brief Psychotic Disorder, With Marked Stressors

Anthony is a 22-year-old senior at a prestigious small college. His family has traditionally held high standards for Anthony, and his father had every expectation that his son would go on to enroll at Harvard Law School. Anthony felt intensely pressured as he worked day and night to maintain a high grade-point average, while diligently preparing for the national examination for admission to law schools. His social life became devoid of any meaningful contact. He even began skipping meals, because he did not want to take time away from studying. When Anthony received his scores for the law school admission exam, he was devastated,

because he knew that they were too low to allow him to get into any of the better law schools. He began crying uncontrollably, wandering around the dormitory hallways, screaming obscenities, and telling people that there was a plot on the part of the college dean to keep him from getting into law school. After two days of this behavior, Anthony's resident adviser convinced him to go to the infirmary, where clinicians diagnosed and treated his condition. After a week of rest and some medication, Anthony returned to normal functioning and was able to assess his academic situation more rationally.

6.3 Schizophreniform Disorder

People receive a diagnosis of **schizophreniform disorder** if they experience symptoms of schizophrenia for a period of from one to six months. If they have had their symptoms for longer than six months, the clinician would conduct an evaluation to determine whether they should receive a diagnosis of schizophrenia. People have good chances of recovering, and not developing schizophrenia, when they show a rapid development of symptoms (within a span of 4 weeks), confusion or perplexity while in the peak of the episode, and good social and personal functioning prior to the episode. They are also likely to have a good prognosis if they do not show the negative symptoms of apathy, withdrawal, and asociality.

schizophreniform disorder
A disorder characterized by psychotic symptoms that are essentially the same as those found in schizophrenia, except for the duration of the symptoms; specifically, symptoms usually last from 1 to 6 months.

6.4 Schizoaffective Disorder

In **schizoaffective disorder** individuals with depressive or bipolar disorder also have delusions and/or hallucinations. The diagnosis is made more complicated by the fact that individuals must have at least a two-week period in which they have no mood disorder

schizoaffective disorder
A disorder involving the experience of a major depressive episode, a manic episode, or a mixed episode while also meeting the diagnostic criteria for schizophrenia.

MINI CASE

Schizophreniform Disorder, With Good Prognostic Features

At the time that Edward developed a psychological disorder, he was 26 years old and worked for a convenience store chain. Although family and friends always regarded Edward as unusual, he had not experienced psychotic symptoms. This all changed as he grew more and more disturbed over the course of several months. His mother thought that he was just "stressed out" because of his financial problems, but Edward did not seem concerned about such matters. He gradually developed paranoid delusions and became preoccupied with reading the Bible. What brought his disturbance to the attention of his supervisors was the fact that he had

submitted an order to the district office for 6,000 loaves of bread. He had scribbled at the bottom of the order form, "Jesus will multiply the loaves." When his supervisors questioned this inappropriate order, Edward became enraged and insisted that they were plotting to prevent him from fighting world hunger. Paranoid themes and bizarre behaviors also surfaced in Edward's dealings with his wife and children. Following two months of increasingly disturbed behavior, Edward's boss urged him to see a psychiatrist. With rest and relatively low doses of antipsychotic medication, Edward returned to normal functioning after a few weeks of hospitalization.

MINI CASE

Schizoaffective Disorder, Bipolar Type

At the time of her admission to a psychiatric hospital, Hazel was a 42-year-old mother of three children. She had a 20-year history of schizophrenia-like symptoms, and she experienced periodic episodes of mania. Her schizophrenia-like symptoms included delusions, hallucinations, and thought disorder. These symptoms were fairly well controlled by antipsychotic medications, which she received by injection every two weeks. She was also treated with lithium to control her manic episodes; however, she often skipped her daily dose because she liked "feeling high." On several occasions following extended periods of abstinence from the lithium, Hazel became manic. Accelerated speech and bodily activity, sleepless nights, and erratic behavior characterized these episodes. At the insistence of her husband and her therapist, Hazel would resume taking her lithium, and shortly thereafter her manic symptoms would subside, although her schizophrenia-like symptoms were still somewhat evident.

symptoms, but do have psychotic symptoms. However, for the majority of the duration of their illness, they must have a major mood episode (depressive or manic) as well as symptoms of schizophrenia. In other words, they must have both a mood episode and a psychotic disorder, but at least two weeks during which their delusions and/or hallucinations are the only symptoms that they show.

6.5 Delusional Disorders

erotomanic type of delusional disorder
Delusional disorder in which individuals falsely believe that another person is in love with them.

grandiose type of delusional disorder
An exaggerated view of oneself as possessing special and extremely favorable personal qualities and abilities.

People with delusional disorders have as their only symptom delusions that have lasted for at least one month. They receive this diagnosis if they have no other symptoms of schizophrenia and have never met the criteria for schizophrenia. In fact, these individuals can function very well and they do not seem odd to others except when they talk about their particular delusion.

Based on which delusional theme is prominent, clinicians diagnose individuals with delusional disorders into one of five types. People with the **erotomanic type of delusional disorder** falsely believe that another person is in love with them. The target of their delusion is usually a person of higher status than they are. For example, a woman may be certain that a famous singer is in love with her and that he communicates secret love messages to her in his songs. Convinced that they are extremely important, in contrast, characterizes people who have the **grandiose type of delusional disorder**.

MINI CASE

Delusional Disorder, Jealous Type

Paul is a 28-year-old man who has recently experienced tremendous stress at his job. Although he has avoided dwelling on his job problems, he has begun to develop irrational beliefs about his lover, Elizabeth. Despite Elizabeth's repeated vows that she is consistently faithful in the relationship, Paul has become obsessed with the belief that Elizabeth is sexually involved with another person. Paul is suspicious of everyone with whom Elizabeth interacts, questioning her about every insignificant encounter. He searches her closet and drawers for mysterious items, looks for unexplained charges on the charge card bills, listens in on Elizabeth's phone calls, and has contacted a private investigator to follow Elizabeth. Paul is now insisting that they move to another state.

MINI CASE

Delusional Disorder, Persecutory Type

Julio met Ernesto in the company cafeteria of the accounting firm where they both worked. After a brief and very casual conversation, Julio began to develop the belief that Ernesto was secretly trying to break into his workstation to plant faulty reports. Soon Julio became convinced that Ernesto was conspiring with three others in their unit to make it appear that Julio was incompetent. Julio requested a reassignment so he would no longer have his job, in his opinion, jeopardized by the behavior of his co-workers.

For example, a man may believe that he is the Messiah waiting for a sign from heaven to begin his active ministry. In the **jealous type of delusional disorder**, individuals are certain that their romantic partner is unfaithful to them. They may even construct a plan to entrap their partner to prove the partner's infidelity. People with the **persecutory type of delusional disorder** believe that someone or someone close to them is treating them in a malevolent manner. They may, for example, become convinced that their neighbors are deliberately poisoning their water. People with the **somatic type of delusional disorder** believe that they have a medical condition. Unlike people with an anxiety disorder, people with a delusional disorder have these beliefs, but they are not anxiety based.

The *DSM-IV* listed **shared psychotic disorder** as a diagnosis for clinicians to use in cases when one or more people develop a delusional system as a result of a close relationship with a psychotic person who is delusional. When two people are involved in this disorder, clinicians referred to the situation as a *folie à deux* (folly of two) to the pair. Occasionally, three or more people or the members of an entire family are involved. Because this disorder is very rare, it is no longer included in the category of delusional disorders.

jealous type of delusional disorder
Delusional disorder in which individuals falsely believe that their romantic partner is unfaithful to them.

persecutory type of delusional disorder
Delusional disorder in which individuals falsely believe that someone or someone close to them is treating them in a malevolent manner.

somatic type of delusional disorder
Delusional disorder in which individuals falsely believe that they have a medical condition.

shared psychotic disorder
Delusional disorder in which one or more people develop a delusional system as a result of a close relationship with a psychotic person who is delusional.

People with persecutory type of delusional disorder believe, incorrectly, that someone is plotting or planning against them.

6.6 Theories and Treatment of Schizophrenia

Theories accounting for the origin of schizophrenia have traditionally fallen into two categories: biological and psychological. In the first part of this century, a debate raged between proponents of both sides. However, it's now clear that both biology and experience interact in the determination of schizophrenia and have built complex theoretical models that incorporate multiple factors (McGuffin, 2004). Researchers base these models on the concept of vulnerability, proposing that individuals have a biologically determined predisposition to developing schizophrenia, but that the disorder develops only when certain environmental conditions are in place. As we look at each of the contributions to a vulnerability model, keep in mind that no single theory contains the entire explanation.

Biological Perspectives

Theories Biological explanations of schizophrenia have their origins in the writings of Kraepelin, who thought of schizophrenia as a disease caused by a degeneration of brain tissue. Kraepelin's ideas paved the way for the later investigation of such factors as brain structure and genetics, which are now recognized as contributing to an individual's biological vulnerability to schizophrenia.

Scientists first became interested in possible brain abnormalities in people with schizophrenia in the nineteenth century. The methods available to these researchers were not up to the task, however. Instead of the sophisticated brain imaging techniques that researchers now can use, early investigators could only examine the brains from autopsied individuals. Not only were the autopsy-based measures imprecise, but researchers could not draw connections between the individual's behavior and brain abnormalities. The technologies of computerized tomography (CT, or CAT, scan) and magnetic resonance imaging (MRI) are enabling researchers in schizophrenia to take pictures of the living brain and analyze those pictures quantitatively, and in real time.

One of the earliest discoveries to emerge from neuroimaging methods was that the brains of people with schizophrenia have enlarged ventricles, which are the cavities within the brain that hold cerebrospinal fluid. This condition, called ventricular enlargement, often occurs in people with schizophrenia alongside cortical atrophy, a wasting away of brain tissue. The loss of brain volume is particularly pronounced in the prefrontal lobes, the area of the brain responsible for planning as well as for inhibiting thoughts and behaviors (Molina, Sanz, Sarramea, Benito, & Palomo, 2005). The prefrontal lobe also shows abnormal fluctuations in people who are in the early stages of the disorder (Huang et al., 2010). Over the course of the illness, the cortex shows pronounced thinning throughout the brain, but particularly in the frontal lobes and the temporal lobes, the parts of the brain that process auditory information (van Haren et al., 2011).

Neuroimaging studies using CT scans, fMRIs, and PET scans show widespread, though subtle, changes in brain structures that may affect the individual's thinking by interfering with the integration of neural and cognitive functioning (Shenton, Whitford, & Kubicki, 2010). Specifically, through fMRI studies, people with schizophrenia have a wide range of deficits including poor performance on motor tasks, difficulties in working memory, poorer attention, reduced word fluency, deficient processing of emotional information, and impaired decision making (Gur & Gur, 2010). Researchers are also using **diffusion tensor imaging (DTI),** a method to investigate abnormalities in the white matter of the brain. This method tracks the activity of water molecules as they diffuse along the length of axons, making it possible to investigate abnormalities in neural pathways (Figure 6.1). The results of DTI studies show that in addition to its association with changes in brain structures, schizophrenia is related to loss of connectivity among brain regions caused by changes in neural pathways (Coyle, Balu, Benneyworth, Basu, & Roseman, 2010).

diffusion tensor imaging (DTI) A method to investigate abnormalities in the white matter of the brain.

Structural changes alone, as important as they may be, cannot entirely explain what happens to the brain to increase the individual's susceptibility to developing schizophrenia. Based on the observation that a drug to relax surgical patients seemed to have calming effects, French physicians began to experiment with its use on patients with psychotic disorders. Physicians believed that the drug, chlorpromazine, had its effect by blocking dopamine receptors, giving rise to the dopamine hypothesis of schizophrenia (Carlsson, 1988). More specifically, the D2 receptor seems to be the one involved in schizophrenia (Hirvonen et al., 2005). Gamma-aminobutyric acid (GABA), an inhibitory neurotransmitter, also appears to be involved in schizophrenia. Changes in the N-methyl-D-aspartate (NMDA) receptors, which are GABA receptors, also seem to play a role. NMDA receptors help to promote new learning in the brain by helping to build synapses. These alterations may, in turn, be related to changes in the neurons that make them less capable of supporting memory and learning. Symptoms of schizophrenia related to increased excitation, decreased inhibition, and altered cognitive functioning would thus correspond to these changes in the neurotransmitters (Coyle et al., 2010).

Research on patterns of family inheritance supports the idea that schizophrenia is, at least in part, a genetically caused disorder with heritability estimates ranging from 64 to 81 percent (Lichtenstein et al., 2009; Sullivan, Kendler, & Neale, 2003). Having established that there is a high heritability to schizophrenia, researchers have since moved on to attempting to locate the specific genes involved and to understanding the factors that increase the genetically vulnerable person's chances of actually developing the disorder. The combination of neuroimaging and genomics shows, further, that siblings show fMRI abnormalities less severe than those that appear in the brains of affected individuals (Gur & Gur, 2010).

At present, researchers have identified at least 19 possible genes dispersed over chromosomes 1, 2, 5, 6, 8, 11, 13, 14, 19, and 22. Some of the functions served by these genes involve the neurotransmitters we've already discussed, including dopamine and GABA, as well as serotonin and glutamate. These genetic abnormalities could also affect brain development, synaptic transmission, immune functioning, and the manufacturing of important proteins involved in neurotransmission (Tiwari, Zai, Muller, & Kennedy, 2010). For example, some individuals with schizophrenia have a particular allele in the gene for the enzyme catechol-O-methyltransferase (COMT) that could be responsible for decreased activity in the prefrontal area of the cortex. People who have inherited this allele from both of their parents are less likely to engage the prefrontal cortex and hippocampus when performing memory tasks in the lab (Gur & Gur, 2010).

However, in contrast to disorders such as dementia, which cause a progressive loss of neural tissue in adulthood, researchers believe that the changes in the brains of people with schizophrenia represent an evolution over time, beginning early in life and proceeding throughout the course of the disorder.

According to the **neurodevelopmental hypothesis** (Andreasen, 2010), schizophrenia is a disorder of development that arises during the years of adolescence or early adulthood due to alterations in the genetic control of brain maturation. Individuals with schizophrenia may have a genetic vulnerability, which becomes evident if they are exposed to certain risks during early brain development. These risks can occur during the prenatal period in the form of viral infections, malnutrition, or exposure to toxins. They may also occur during or shortly after birth if they are exposed to injuries or viral infections, or if their mothers suffer birth complications. The harm to their developing

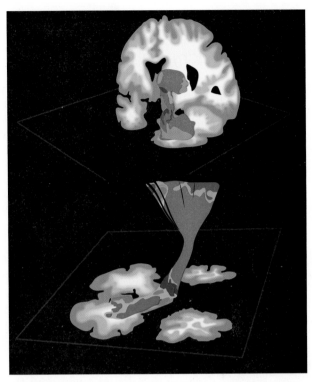

FIGURE 6.1 DTI Scan of Brain of Individual with Schizophrenia

Diffusion tensor imaging (DTI) yields images of nerve fiber tracts. Different colors indicate the organization of the nerve fibers. Here, a tract originating at the cerebellum is superimposed on a structural-MRI image of a cross section of the brain.

neurodevelopmental hypothesis
Theory proposing that schizophrenia is a disorder of development that arises during the years of adolescence or early adulthood due to alterations in the genetic control of brain maturation.

REAL STORIES

Elyn Saks: Schizophrenia

"If you are a person with mental illness, the challenge is to find the life that's right for you. But in truth, isn't that the challenge for all of us, mentally ill or no? My good fortune is not that I've recovered from mental illness. I have not, nor will I ever. My good fortune lies in having found my life."

In her memoir, *The Center Cannot Hold: My Journey through Madness*, UCLA professor Elyn Saks tells the moving story of her lifelong struggle with schizophrenia. Her story provides a unique perspective on one of the most debilitating psychological disorders, and offers a firsthand account of the experience of psychosis. Elyn begins the book by describing the first signs of her illness as a child growing up in an upper-middle class family in Miami, Florida.

"When I was about eight, I suddenly needed to do things a little differently than my parents would have wished me to do them. I developed, for loss of a better word, a few little quirks. For instance, I couldn't leave my room unless my shoes were all lined up in my closet. Or beside my bed. Some nights, I couldn't shut off my bedroom light until the books on my shelves were organized just so." Elyn also recalls early dissociative experiences that began around this same time. These experiences of "disorganization" as she refers to them initially elicited fear. This was partially because she was unable to express what was happening to her with her family who were otherwise supportive and caring.

Throughout her formative years, Elyn continued to experience what she now recognizes as prodromal symptoms of schizophrenia. At the time her experiences caused her to feel paranoid around others, afraid that they would find out her secret. She attended college at Vanderbilt University, and at first greatly enjoyed her newfound independence. However, within the first two weeks of school, away from the protective

clutches of her family and all the comforts that came along with being taken care of, as she puts it "everything slowly began to unravel." Her inability to perform self-care activities such as bathing signaled the start of her illness, and Elyn had several, very brief psychotic episodes, which resolved without intervention. In the book, she describes the insidious nature of her illness when it began to manifest itself.

"Schizophrenia rolls in like a slow fog, becoming imperceptibly thicker as time goes on. At first, the day is bright enough, the sky is clear, the sunlight warms your shoulders. But soon, you notice a haze beginning to gather around you, and the air feels not quite so warm . . . For me (and for many of us), the first evidence of that fog is a gradual deterioration of basic commonsense hygiene . . . Once away from my parents' watchful eyes, I grew inconsistent about asking myself the taken-for-granted questions."

After returning home from her freshman year, Elyn continued to

experience paranoia and occasional hallucinations though now in addition to those symptoms she was feeling depressed and lethargic. Her parents took her to see a psychiatrist whose only insight to her condition was that she "needed help." Once Elyn returned to Vanderbilt for her sophomore year, her symptoms subsided as she found comfort in her studies and with a close-knit group of friends. With strong social support, Elyn was able to remain in a relatively stable condition for the rest of her time in college. However, that comfort quickly turned to fear as graduation approached and she felt the fragile structure that kept her content was about to be shaken.

Elyn won a highly prestigious Marshall scholarship to study philosophy at Oxford University in England. She was terrified of living in a new country, so far away from everything she knew, and particularly of being away from her routine and friends at college. Indeed, after just a few weeks at Oxford, Elyn's still unnamed illness again began to take hold, and her fear of

Elyn Saks has enjoyed a successful law career despite suffering from schizophrenia

her illness turned into suicidal ideation. At the urging of a friend, she saw a psychiatrist and admitted that she had thoughts of ending her life. She entered a day treatment program at a psychiatric hospital though she had no idea just how ill she was. "This was like a bad cold, or a bout of the flu. Something had gone wrong; it was simply a matter of finding out what that something was and fixing it," she writes of her perspective on her symptoms at the time.

At the hospital, Elyn received intensive psychotherapy and spent the rest of her time working on her studies. Her program did not require her to attend classes, and so she was able to isolate herself in her apartment while she worked, which made it difficult for her to realize the extent of her psychological difficulties. She was not taking any medication at the time, and her ability to attain a firm grasp on reality slowly deteriorated. When she reported to her psychiatrist that her suicidal ideation had worsened, she was urged to become a full-time patient at the hospital where she remained for two weeks. After beginning a course of psychotherapeutic medication, Elyn eventually felt well enough to return to her studies though she soon began to decompensate. She returned to the hospital where she languished in psychosis and depression for several months. Once she was stabilized, her psychiatrist recommended that she enter psychoanalysis. Determined to finish her degree at Oxford, Elyn continued

at her studies while seeing a psychoanalyst for five days per week. Even after finishing her studies, which ended up taking 4 years instead of 2, Elyn felt that her relationship with her analyst was helping her so much so that she decided to stay in England to continue their work together for 2 more years. In the book, Elyn describes her experience of living with her illness during this time in her life. "Completely delusional, I still understood essential aspects of how the world worked. For example, I was getting my schoolwork done, and I vaguely understood the rule that in a social setting, even with the people I most trusted, I could not ramble on about my psychotic thoughts. To talk about killing children, or burning whole worlds, or being able to destroy cities with my mind was not part of polite conversation . . . At times, though, I was so psychotic that I could barely contain myself. The delusions expanded into full-blown hallucinations, in which I could clearly hear people whispering. I could hear my name being called when no one was physically around—in a corner of the library, or late at night, in my bedroom where I slept alone. Sometimes, the noise I heard was so overwhelming it drowned out almost all other sound."

After leaving England, Elyn decided to attend law school at Yale University, where she continued to struggle with psychotic episodes that resulted in several lengthy hospitalizations though she was eventually able to finish her de-

gree. She had discovered a passion for helping psychiatric patients after working in a mental health law clinic, fueled by her intimate understanding of the experience of herself being a psychiatric patient. Throughout her career she has worked toward creating a high legal standard of care for psychiatric patients in the United States.

Elyn eventually took a position at the law school at UCLA where she continues to work as a tenured faculty member. Over the years she has worked hard to keep her psychotic symptoms at bay with help from a combination of talk therapy, medication, and social support from her husband and close friends. Though Elyn struggled for many years to accept the reality of her illness, she now accepts her diagnosis and all that it entails. At the end of the book, Elyn writes that she feels grateful to be one of the lucky few able to successfully live with schizophrenia. She dispels the idea that she has had a better life because of schizophrenia, but instead states that she has been able to live her life despite it. Often throughout her career in discussing legal aspects of mental health treatment she noticed others stigmatizing those with mental illness, not believing that they could lead normal lives or even be trusted to not be violent. When explaining why she decided to write the book and "out" herself as mentally ill, she describes that she decided to write the book because "I want to bring hope to those who suffer from schizophrenia, and understanding to those who do not."

brains may show up early in life in the form of decreased head size, motor impairments, and impairments in cognition and social functioning. Support for the neurodevelopmental hypothesis also comes from the fact that individuals having their first psychotic episodes have a number of inexplicable brain abnormalities as the result of the illness. As their illness proceeds, they may show continued deleterious changes through a process of "neuroprogression" in which the effects of schizophrenia interact with brain changes caused by normal aging.

Treatments The primary biological treatment for schizophrenia is antipsychotic medication. As we discussed in Chapter 4, psychiatrists prescribe two categories of antipsychotic medication, also called neuroleptics (derived from the Greek words meaning "to seize the nerve"). In addition to their sedating qualities, neuroleptics reduce

Dementia often causes secondary physical problems when those who suffer from it are unable to take the correct dosages of their medication.

extrapyramidal symptoms (EPS)
Motor disorders involving rigid muscles, tremors, shuffling movement, restlessness, and muscle spasms affecting their posture.

tardive dyskinesia
Motor disorder that consists of involuntary movements of the mouth, arms, and trunk of the body.

Psychiatrists strive to find an appropriate regimen of medication in order to prevent individuals with psychotic disorders from experiencing highly disruptive psychotic symptoms.

the frequency and severity of the individual's psychotic symptoms. The two main categories of neuroleptics are the so-called "typical" or "first generation" and "atypical" or "second generation" antipsychotics.

As we discussed in Chapter 4, the first medication that doctors used in treating schizophrenia was the typical antipsychotic chlorpromazine (Thorazine), a sedative developed by Paul Charpentier, a French chemist. Haloperidol (Haldol) is another typical antipsychotic medication that was in widespread use. These neuroleptics seem to have their effect on reducing symptoms primarily by acting on the dopamine receptor system in areas of the brain associated with delusions, hallucinations, and other positive symptoms.

In addition to being highly sedating, causing a person to feel fatigued and listless, the typical antipsychotics also have serious undesirable consequences. These include **extrapyramidal symptoms (EPS),** which are motor disorders involving rigid muscles, tremors, shuffling movement, restlessness, and muscle spasms affecting their posture. After several years, they can also develop **tardive dyskinesia,** another motor disorder, which consists of involuntary movements of their mouth, arms, and trunk of the body.

The distressing side effects and failure of typical antipsychotics to treat negative symptoms of schizophrenia led psychiatric researchers on a search to alternatives that would both be more effective and not cause tardive dyskinesia. The atypical (second generation) antipsychotics operate on both serotonin and dopamine neurotransmitters and hence, are also called serotonin-dopamine antagonists. Clinicians thought that these later medications resulted in fewer side effects and helped in treating negative symptoms. However, doctors discovered that one of the first atypical antipsychotics, clozapine (Clozaril), had potentially lethal side effects by causing agranulocytosis, a condition that affects the functioning of the white blood cells. Clinicians now recommend it only under very controlled conditions and only when other medications do not work. Instead, clinicians can now prescribe one of a number of safer atypical antipsychotics, including risperidone (Risperdal), olanzapine (Zyprexa), and quetiapine (Seroquel).

Unfortunately, even medications in the newer group of atypical antipsychotics are not without potentially serious side effects. They can cause metabolic disturbances, particularly weight gain, increases in blood cholesterol, and greater insulin resistance, placing them at greater risk of diabetes and cardiovascular disease.

Because of the many complexities in the biological treatment of individuals with schizophrenia, researchers and clinicians increasingly recognize the need to take the individual's medical and psychiatric profile into account. For treatment-resistant clients, clozapine is the only approach that has empirical support. In other instances, clinicians may attempt to find a combination of antipsychotics or a combination of antipsychotics with other classes of medications. The next question becomes one of determining how long to maintain a client on medications balancing the value of continued treatment against the risk of relapse and possible health hazards that occur with their use over time (Kane & Correll, 2010).

Psychological Perspectives

Theories With increasing evidence suggesting specific genetic and neurophysiological abnormalities in the brains of people with schizophrenia, researchers are becoming increasingly interested in finding out more about the role of cognitive deficits in causing the disorder. As we mentioned earlier, delusions and hallucinations are obviously disruptive to a person's

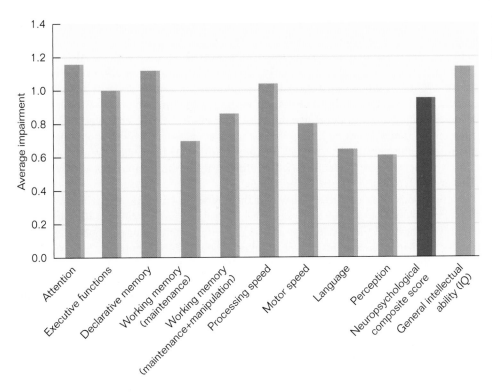

FIGURE 6.2 **Neuropsychological Performance Profile of Schizophrenia**

life and critically important to the diagnosis of the disorder. However, these symptoms, as surprising as it may seem, may not be at the core of the disorder. Instead, cognitive functions affected by schizophrenia may be more fundamental to understanding the disorder's central features.

Figure 6.2 shows the average impairment of people with schizophrenia on a variety of neuropsychological tests. They have lower than average intellectual ability, but also deficits in the specific areas of attention, declarative memory (long-term recall of information), and processing speed. Although it is possible that these abnormalities are the result of other factors that can influence how people with schizophrenia perform on these tests, such as age, educational background, use of medication, or severity or length of illness. However, people who are experiencing positive symptoms (delusions and hallucinations) perform inconsistently on these tasks. Overall, estimates of how many people with schizophrenia are cognitively impaired vary from 55 to between 70 and 80 percent (Reichenberg, 2010).

People with schizophrenia also show deficits in the area of social cognition, meaning that they have difficulty perceiving the emotions of others. This deficit in social cognition is particularly problematic when they are given the task of recognizing the emotions of fear, anger, and disgust. People with schizophrenia are, however, better at identifying mild happiness in the facial expressions of other people. Not only do they have difficulty recognizing emotions from a person's face, but their brains become less activated when given a social cognition task (Gur & Gur, 2010).

These impairments in cognitive functioning can lead to many problems in the individual's daily life, setting up a vicious cycle. Their problems in memory, planning, and processing speed, for example, interfere with their ability to hold down mentally challenging jobs. The limitations they have in social cognition make it difficult for them to work in people-oriented jobs. With an inability to maintain consistent employment, they can slip into poverty which, as we will see in the next section, further stresses their abilities to lead productive lives. Moreover, living in high-poverty areas places them at risk for becoming involved in substance abuse, which can contribute to the symptoms they experience as a result of their disorder.

Treatments For many years, the most common psychological interventions for people with schizophrenia involved behavioral treatments intended to lower the frequency of an individual's maladaptive behaviors that interfere with social adjustment and functioning. These interventions typically employed a token economy (Ayllon & Azrin, 1965), in which institutionalized individuals received rewards for acting in socially appropriate ways. The expectation was that, over time, the new behaviors would become habitual and not dependent on reinforcement by tokens. However, this form of intervention is no longer practical given that most individuals with schizophrenia receive treatment in the community. In addition, there is little data on its effectiveness, and with clinicians focusing on evidence-based treatment, the profession cannot justify its use (Dickerson, Tenhula, & Green-Paden, 2005).

More promising is cognitive-behavioral therapy when clinicians use it as an adjunct to pharmacological treatments (Wykes, Steel, Everitt, & Tarrier, 2008). Clinicians using cognitive-behavioral therapy to treat individuals with symptoms of psychosis (CBTp) do not try to change their delusions or eliminate their hallucinations, but instead try to reduce their distress and preoccupation with these symptoms. In addition, cognitive-behavioral therapists attempt to teach their clients coping skills so that they can improve their ability to live independently. Clinicians might assign homework of having their clients keep a diary of their experiences of hearing voices or a "reality check" of their delusional beliefs. CBTp was initially developed in the United Kingdom, perhaps because service providers were more interested in developing nonmedical approaches to treating the symptoms of psychosis than is true in the United States. However, the method is gaining more widespread acceptance in the United States, based on studies showing its effectiveness, particularly in conjunction with atypical antipsychotics (Pinninti, Rissmiller, & Steer, 2010).

Researchers are also developing interventions to help address the cognitive deficits of individuals with schizophrenia, particularly those who suffer from primarily negative symptoms (see Figure 6.3). Like physical fitness training, people with schizophrenia receive cognitive training that builds on their current level of functioning to restore or enhance their performance. Cognitive training is guided by the findings from neuroscience showing that people with schizophrenia have deficits in memory and sensory processing. One promising cognitive training approach involves training in speech recognition and auditory perception. By improving their memory and sensory skills, individuals with schizophrenia are then better able to take advantage of other psychologically based interventions as well as to participate more successfully in vocational rehabilitation programs. These studies are also showing that people with schizophrenia can actually show neural "plasticity," meaning that their brains undergo positive adaptive changes during training (Genevsky, Garrett, Alexander, & Vinogradov, 2010).

Sociocultural Perspectives

Theories In some of the earliest formulations about schizophrenia's causes, psychological theorists proposed that disturbed patterns of communication in a child's family environment could precipitate the development of schizophrenia. In studies on modes of communication and behavior within families with a schizophrenic member, researchers attempted to document deviant patterns of communication and inappropriate ways that parents interacted with their children. Clinicians thought that these disturbances in family relationships led to the development of defective emotional responsiveness and cognitive distortions fundamental to the psychological symptoms of schizophrenia.

Contemporary researchers have approached the issue by trying to predict outcome or recovery in adults hospitalized for schizophrenia. Instead of regarding a disturbed family as the cause of schizophrenia, these researchers view the family as a potential source of stress in the environment of the person who is trying to recover from a

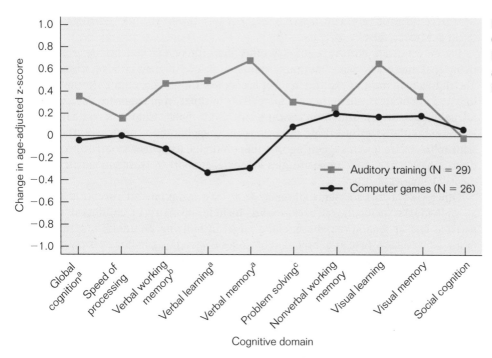

FIGURE 6.3 Change in Cognitive Performance in Patients with Schizophrenia after 50 Hours of Computerized Auditory Training

[a]Significant difference between groups (P < 0.01, repeated-measure ANOVA)
[b]Significant difference between groups (P < 0.05, repeated-measure ANOVA)
[c]Nonsignificant difference between groups (P = 0.10, repeated-measure ANOVA)

schizophrenic episode. The index of expressed emotion (EE) reflects the stress that family members create. This provides a measure of the degree to which family members speak in ways that reflect criticism, hostile feelings, and emotional overinvolvement or overconcern. Supporting the concept of EE as a source of stress, researchers found that people living in families high in EE are more likely to suffer a relapse, particularly if they are exposed to high levels of criticism (Marom, Munitz, Jones, Weizman, & Hermesh, 2005). One fMRI study showed that people with schizophrenia have higher activation of brain regions involved in self-reflection and sensitivity to social situations when hearing speech high in EE compared to neutral speech (Rylands, McKie, Elliott, Deakin, & Tarrier, 2011).

It goes without saying that research on EE could never employ an experimental design. Consequently, researchers can never draw causal links between EE and schizophrenia, even in people whose schizophrenia may have reflected genetic or neurodevelopmental vulnerability. It is also very likely that the presence of an individual with schizophrenia creates stress within the family, even if the family member is not living at home. The individual's disorder can impact parents, siblings, and even grandparents, particularly when the symptoms first begin to emerge in an individual's early adult years.

Moving beyond the family environment, researchers have also studied broader social factors, such as social class and income, in relationship to schizophrenia. In perhaps the first epidemiological study of mental illness in the United States, Hollingshead and Redlich (1958) observed that schizophrenia was far more prevalent in the lowest socioeconomic classes. A number of researchers have since replicated the finding that more individuals with schizophrenia live in the poorer sections of urban areas in the United States and Europe. One possible interpretation of this finding is that people with schizophrenia experience "downward drift," meaning that their disorder drives them into poverty, which interferes with their ability to work and earn a living. The other possibility is that the stress of living in isolation and poverty in urban areas contributes to the risk of developing schizophrenia. However, the rates of schizophrenia are higher in individuals who were born or raised in urban areas, not just those who moved there as adults (Stilo & Murray, 2010).

People who were born in a country other than the one in which they are currently living (i.e., those who have "migrant" status) also have higher rates of schizophrenia. The individuals most at risk for schizophrenia are those who migrate to lower-status jobs and urban areas where they are more likely to suffer from exposure to environmental pollutants, stress, and overcrowding (McGrath, Saha, Chant, & Welham, 2008). However, as the rates of ethnic minorities in a neighborhood increases, the rates of schizophrenia are lower, suggesting that these individuals benefit from less exposure to discrimination and more opportunities for social support in their immediate environments (Veling et al., 2007).

Other risk factors for schizophrenia, or at least symptoms of psychosis related to an individual's sociocultural background, include adversity in childhood including parental loss or separation, abuse, and a target of bullying. In adulthood, individuals more vulnerable to first or subsequent episodes of psychosis include people who have experienced severely stressful life events, including being a victim of assault (Stilo & Murray, 2010). Individuals with high genetic risk who are exposed to environmental stressors are more likely than others who experience mild psychotic symptoms to develop a full-blown disorder (van Os et al., 2009). People who use cannabis (marijuana) also show an elevated risk of developing schizophrenia. Although researchers were long aware of the cannabis-schizophrenia link, they believed that people with schizophrenia used the drug to alleviate their symptoms. Long-term follow-up studies show, instead, that people develop the disorder after continued use of cannabis. The more they use the drug, the greater their chances of having schizophrenia (McGrath et al., 2010).

Recognizing that the causes of schizophrenia are multifaceted and develop over time, Stilo and Murray (2010) proposed a "developmental cascade" hypothesis that integrates genetic vulnerabilities, damage occurring in the prenatal and early childhood periods, adversity, and drug abuse as leading, ultimately, to changes in dopamine expressed in psychosis (see Figure 6.4).

Treatments   The coordination of services is especially important in programs geared toward helping people with schizophrenia. One approach to integrating various services is **Assertive Community Treatment (ACT),** in which a team of professionals from psychiatry, psychology, nursing, and social work reach out to clients in their homes and workplaces. ACT's focus is on engendering empowerment and self-determination

Assertive Community Treatment (ACT)
Treatment approach in which a team of professionals from psychiatry, psychology, nursing, and social work reach out to clients in their homes and workplaces.

FIGURE 6.4 Developmental Cascade toward Schizophrenia

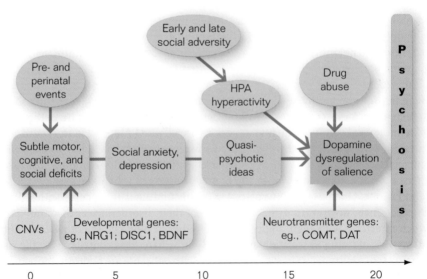

on its "consumers," the term they use to refer to their clients. Typically, a team of about a dozen professionals work together to help approximately 100 consumers with issues such as complying with medical recommendations, managing their finances, obtaining adequate health care, and dealing with crises when they arise. This approach involves bringing care to the clients, rather than waiting for them to come to a facility for help, a journey that may be too overwhelming for seriously impaired people. Although approaches such as ACT are expensive, the benefits are impressive. Researchers have conducted dozens of studies on the effectiveness of ACT and have concluded that ACT has had significant positive impact on reducing hospitalizations, stabilizing housing in the community, and lowering overall treatment costs (Bond, Drake, Mueser, & Latimer, 2001).

As effective as it can be, critics charge that ACT is not provided in a manner consistent with its goal of empowering consumers and instead is coercive and paternalistic. To address this charge, ACT researchers are investigating the possibility of combining ACT with another program, called Illness Management and Recovery (IMR). In IMR, consumers receive training in effective ways to manage their illnesses and pursue their goals for recovery. Resting on the principle of self-determination, IMR is based on the premise that consumers should be given the resources they need to make informed choices. IMR uses peers and clinicians to deliver structured, curriculum-based interventions. Although an initial investigation of ACT-IMR revealed that the providers experienced a number of difficulties in implementing the program, it appeared to reduce hospitalization rates. Moreover, even after the funding for the study ran out, the teams continued to provide services (Salyers et al., 2010).

Assertive Community Treatment involves a highly skilled and collaborative team of psychiatrists, nurses, social workers, and other mental health care professionals.

6.7 Schizophrenia: The Biopsychosocial Perspective

Definitions and diagnostic approaches to schizophrenia are undergoing significant revisions, but throughout the past decade, researchers have gained a great deal of understanding about its many possible causes. Perhaps most exciting is the evolution of an integrated approach to theories that focus on underlying brain mechanisms as expressed in cognitive deficits. Treatment is moving beyond the provision of medication to greater use of evidence-based psychological interventions. Finally, researchers appear to be gaining greater appreciation of the role of sociocultural influences. Together, these advances are increasing the chances that individuals with these disorders will receive integrated care, maximizing their chances of recovery (Sungur et al., 2011).

Clinicians, also, increasingly understand schizophrenia from a life-span perspective. The needs and concerns of individuals with this disorder vary over the years of adulthood. In addition to the fact that many actually do recover, researchers and mental health practitioners are recognizing that part of their job involves providing ways to help people with long-term schizophrenia adapt both to changes involved in the aging process, as well as changes involved in the evolution of the disease. The idea that schizophrenia is a neurodevelopmental disorder highlights this important new focus and provides a basis for interventions that take into account individual changes over time.

Return to the Case: David Marshall

David was eventually able to return to school part-time, living at home with Ann. Though he struggled with the change in his level of functioning, he was able to use therapy and case management to understand his limitations. By doing so, the aim is to avoid future stressors from occurring and from inducing psychotic episodes. It is difficult to completely avoid any instances of psychosis from occurring with a disorder as severe as schizophrenia. However, with the proper contingencies and social support the impact of his symptoms will be easier for David to tolerate.

Dr. Tobin's reflections: David's move into the dorms presented as a first major life stressor. Though he had already been attending college for one year, living with his mother seems to have provided a feeling of safety that was shattered once he moved away. It was difficult though, as David certainly wished he could attain independence and wanted to be able to. Though he was not at his same level of functioning as before, David and Ann had assumed that whatever David had been going through was finished. Returning to the dormitories, however, proved too great a stressor and so David's symptoms were brought on once again.

Luckily for David, Ann was able to take action to help David after it had become clear that he was suffering from something very serious that neither of them had quite understood. Having "caught" the disorder early on, entering a treatment program, is beneficial as it decreases the likelihood that his life will be complicated by the fallout from future psychotic episodes. However, prevention of future episodes is contingent upon his participation in therapy and his medication compliance.

SUMMARY

- **Schizophrenia** is a serious mental illness, given its potentially broad impact on an individual's ability to live a productive and fulfilling life. Although a significant number of people with schizophrenia eventually manage to live symptom-free lives, many must find ways to adapt their lives to the reality of the illness.

- There are six diagnostic criteria for schizophrenia (see Table 6.2). In addition to the diagnostic criteria for schizophrenia and related psychotic disorders, the *DSM*-5 authors provide a set of severity rating criteria in several spheres of functioning. *DSM*-5 authors conceptualize schizophrenia as a spectrum or set of related disorders characterized by dimensions.

- Using the *DSM-IV-TR*, clinicians could make subtype diagnoses to provide more information about the presenting symptoms. With *DSM*-5, these same subtypes (disorganized, paranoid, undifferentiated, and residual) have become specifiers. Specifiers serve the same purpose of providing more diagnostic information, without standing alone as discrete disorders. The exception to this change is **catatonia,** which has become its own disorder. This exception came about as a result of evidence that the symptoms of catatonia develop differently from the other specifiers.

- First identified as a disease in the 1800s by Benedict Morel, researchers, including physicians, psychiatrists, and psychologists, have been studying schizophrenia, theorizing its origin, and identifying symptoms and categories. As the years unfold, researchers attempt to develop a more precise set of diagnostic criteria.

- Schizophrenia may take one of several courses. When symptoms no longer interfere with a patient's behavior, he or she is in **remission.** Compared to other psychological disorders, the course and outcome are poorer for people with schizophrenia

- For many years, up through the early 1980s, with no comprehensive diagnostic criteria at their disposal, psychiatrists used schizophrenia as a catchall term applied to the majority of people requiring institutionalization for psychotic symptoms. Currently, the *DSM* includes a set of so-called "psychotic" disorders that share three features: (1) each is a form of psychosis representing a serious break with reality, (2) the condition is not caused by a known cognitive impairment, and (3) there is no mood disturbance as a primary symptom. These include **brief psychotic disorder, schizophreniform disorder,** and **delusional disorder (erotomanic, grandiose, jealous, persecutory,** and **somatic types**).

- Theories accounting for the origin of schizophrenia have traditionally fallen into two categories: biological and psychological. In the first part of this century, a debate raged between proponents of both sides. More recently, researchers have begun to accept that both biology and experience interact in the determination of schizophrenia and have begun to build complex theoretical models that incorporate multiple factors. This includes the **neurodevelopmental hypothesis,** which states that schizophrenia is a disorder of development that arises during the years of adolescence or early adulthood due to alterations in the genetic control of brain maturation.

- The primary biological treatment for schizophrenia is antipsychotic medication, or neuroleptics. The two main categories of neuroleptics are the so-called "typical" or "first generation" and "atypical" or "second generation" antipsychotics.

The distressing side effects and failure of typical antipsychotics to treat negative symptoms of schizophrenia have led psychiatric researchers on a search to alternatives that would both be more effective and not cause **tardive dyskinesia,** a motor disorder that consists of involuntary movements of their mouth, arms, and trunk of the body. Because of the many complexities in the biological treatment of individuals with schizophrenia, researchers and clinicians increasingly recognize the need to take the individual's medical and psychiatric profile into account.

• From a psychological perspective, with increasing evidence suggesting specific genetic and neurophysiological abnormalities in the brains of people with schizophrenia, researchers are becoming increasingly interested in finding out more about the role of cognitive deficits in causing the disorder. However, these symptoms may not be at the core of the disorder. Instead, cognitive functions affected by schizophrenia may be more fundamental to understanding the disorder's central features.

• For many years, the most common psychological interventions for people with schizophrenia involved behavioral treatments intended to lower the frequency of an individual's maladaptive behaviors that interfere with social adjustment and functioning. However, this form of intervention is no longer practical given that most individuals with schizophrenia receive treatment in the community. In addition, there is little data on its effectiveness and with clinicians focusing on evidence-based treatment, the profession cannot justify its use. More promising is cognitive-behavioral therapy when clinicians use it as an adjunct to pharmacological treatments. Clinicians using cognitive-behavioral therapy to treat individuals with symptoms of psychosis (CBTp) do not try to change their delusions or eliminate their hallucinations, but instead try to reduce their distress and preoccupation with these symptoms. Researchers are also developing interventions to help address the cognitive deficits of individuals with schizophrenia, particularly those who suffer from primarily negative symptoms.

• There have been many theories regarding schizophrenia from a sociocultural perspective. Contemporary researchers have approached the issue by trying to predict the outcome or recovery of adults hospitalized for schizophrenia. The index of expressed emotion (EE) provides a measure of degree to which family members speak in ways that reflect criticisms, hostile feelings, and emotional overinvolvement or overconcern. Moving beyond the family environment, researchers have also studied broader social factors, such as social class and income, in relationship to schizophrenia. Other risk factors for schizophrenia, or at least symptoms of psychosis related to an individual's sociocultural background, include adversity in childhood including parental loss or separation, abuse, and being a target of bullying.

• The coordination of services is especially important in programs geared toward helping people with schizophrenia.

• From a biopsychosocial perspective, an exciting development is the evolution of an integrated approach to theories that focus on underlying brain mechanisms as expressed in cognitive deficits. Treatment is moving beyond the provision of medication to greater use of evidence-based psychological interventions. Finally, researchers appear to be gaining greater appreciation of the role of sociocultural influences. Together, these advances are increasing the chances that individuals with these disorders will receive integrated care, maximizing their chances of recovery. Clinicians, also, increasingly understand schizophrenia from a life-span perspective. The idea that schizophrenia is a neurodevelopmental disorder highlights this important new focus and provides a basis for interventions that take into account individual changes over time.

KEY TERMS

Depressive and Bipolar Disorders

Learning Objectives

7.1 Explain the key features of major depressive disorder and persistent depressive disorder, including prevalence

7.2 Compare and contrast bipolar I, bipolar II, and cyclothymic disorder

7.3 Understand theories and treatments of depressive and bipolar disorders

7.4 Discuss the relationships among age, gender, and suicide

7.5 Analyze the biopsychosocial model of depressive and bipolar disorders

CHAPTER 7

Case Report: Janice Butterfield

Demographic information: 47-year-old Caucasian female.

Presenting problem: Janice was referred for psychotherapy after a recent hospitalization following a suicide attempt. Janice reported that the precipitant to her suicide attempt was the loss of her job in a real estate company, where she had worked for 25 years. She reported that although she realized her company had downsized due to the economy, she found herself feeling profoundly guilty for the negative impact her unemployment would have on her family. Janice reported she has been married for 27 years and has three daughters, one of whom lives at home. Another is in college, and her youngest will be attending college at the start of the next school year. Janice reported she had felt overwhelmed by the stress about her financial state, as her family mainly relied on her income.

Along with feelings of guilt, Janice reported she had felt so depressed and down that she spent many days in the past 2 weeks in bed, and often found herself thinking of ending her life. She stopped taking pain medication, which was prescribed for her chronic backaches "to save up if I needed them later." One evening when her husband was out of the house, she attempted suicide by taking all of her saved-up medications at once. Janice's husband returned to find her unresponsive and rushed her to the hospital just in time to save her life. She was hospitalized in an inpatient psychiatric unit and given medication until her suicidal thoughts and severe depression decreased enough so that the doctors deemed her no longer a threat to herself. She followed the referral given to her by the psychiatrists on the inpatient unit to attend weekly psychotherapy for follow-up. She had never been in therapy before.

During her first therapy session, Janice reported that she had thought about going to therapy many times before. She explained that her depressions usually lasted about 1 month, but sometimes as long as 3 months. During these periods, she missed a few days of work but she was able to struggle through these periods and go about her normal routine albeit with much difficulty. During these periods, she would go out to her car to cry, because it would be too painful to be around others. "I just didn't want anything to do with life at those points," she recalled. Her depression would eventually improve on its own, as well as her thoughts about getting treatment. She reported that she had occasionally thought about suicide in the past when she was feeling depressed, but had never before made and carried out a plan as she had during the most recent episode.

Janice went on to explain how these depressed moods always caught her "off guard," as they would occur directly after long periods when she felt happy and energetic. She stated these moods usually started after she had made a large real estate sale, and she felt "invincible" after such a sale. During these times, she described that she often needed very little sleep due to the seeming endless amount of energy she possessed, and she would begin to take on many new projects and clients at work—much more than would be expected of her. During these periods she splurged on lavish clothing or jewelry, and during her last energetic period had purchased new cars for herself and her husband. These expenditures were uncharacteristic for Janice, as she described herself as normally financially frugal. Due to her constantly moving thoughts, Janice found it very difficult to concentrate and was so distracted she was rarely able to finish anything she began to take on at work. She would feel disappointed that she had to give up some of her projects, and her joyful feelings would turn to irritability and anger. She reported that her husband usually experienced the brunt of her irritable mood, and this caused major problems in their marriage. Janice further reported that she felt like she ignored her family altogether due to her work habits when she was feeling particularly energetic. She remarked, "When I'm feeling that good, I can only think about myself and what feels good to me. I stop being a mother and a wife." Her extreme spending periods eroded her family's savings, which was especially a concern now that she had lost her job. This also contributed to her guilt about paying for her youngest daughter's college tuition. Janice had never talked with her husband or her children about her vast mood shifts. She stated she worried that if she had told her family about her personal difficulties, they would "see me as a weakling, instead of the head of the household."

Relevant history: Janice had never received psychiatric treatment or therapy in the past, though she reported she had experienced mood swings since she was 19. She estimated that she had severe mood episodes (either manic or depressive) about three to four times per year. When reflecting about the severity of her mood episodes, she stated that she felt her behaviors had been more "extreme" in more recent years than when she was younger. Janice reported that she noticed the patterns in her mood swings always began with an energetic period, directly followed by a depressive episode, and then a period of several months of stability. More recently, though, she

noted that the periods of stability had only been lasting 1 or 2 months, and her mood episodes had been lasting longer.

Case formulation: Janice's diagnosis from the psychiatric unit was a Major Depressive Episode, and her current presentation also met this criteria. However, in the initial therapy session she reported also having a history of manic episodes that were followed by periods of depression, which she had not mentioned while she had been hospitalized. The manic symptoms she described caused significant problems for Janice financially, due to her excessive spending sprees. In combination with losing her job, her financial problems caused significant stress for Janice and may have contributed to the severity of her most recent depressive episode, which eventually led to a suicide attempt. Therefore, her diagnosis is Bipolar I Disorder, most recent episode depressed.

Treatment plan: It is recommended that Janice continue to attend psychotherapy weekly. In therapy, it will be necessary to make a suicide safety plan, given her history of suicidal ideation in the past. Therapy should initially focus on psychoeducation, symptom management, and mood monitoring. She will also be referred to an outpatient psychiatrist for medication reconciliation, as psychotherapeutic medication is highly recommended in the treatment of bipolar disorder.

Sarah Tobin, PhD

People can experience day-to-day highs and lows, but when their disturbances of mood reach a point of clinical significance, they may be considered to have a depressive or bipolar disorder. In *DSM-5*, these two disorders involve a set of criteria that allow clinicians to establish alterations in mood that significantly deviate from the individual's baseline or ordinary emotional state.

7.1 Depressive Disorders

depressive disorder
Involves periods of symptoms in which an individual experiences an unusually intense sad mood.

A **depressive disorder** involves periods of symptoms in which an individual experiences an unusually intense sad mood. The disorder's essential element is an unusually elevated sad mood, known as **dysphoria.**

dysphoria
An unusually elevated sad mood.

Major Depressive Disorder

major depressive disorder
A disorder in which the individual experiences acute, but time-limited, episodes of depressive symptoms.

Major depressive disorder involves acute, but time-limited, periods of depressive symptoms that are called **major depressive episodes** (see Table 7.1). Persistent depressive disorder (dysthymia) is a chronic but less severe mood disturbance in which the individual does not experience a major depressive episode. People receive a diagnosis of recurrent major depressive disorder if they have had two or more major depressive episodes with an interval of at least two consecutive months though they may meet the criteria for a major depressive disorder for two years.

major depressive episode
A period in which the individual experiences intense psychological and physical symptoms accompanying feelings of overwhelming sadness (dysphoria).

TABLE 7.1 **Criteria for a Major Depressive Episode**

For most of the time during a two-week period, a person experiences at least five or more of the first 9 symptoms in addition to the last two. He or she must experience a change from previous functioning and at least one of the first two symptoms must be present. During this two-week period, most of these symptoms must be present nearly every day.

- Depressed mood most of the day
- Markedly diminished interest or pleasure in all or most daily activities
- Significant unintended weight loss or unusual increase or decrease in appetite
- Insomnia or hypersomnia
- Psychomotor agitation or retardation observable by others
- Fatigue or loss of energy
- Feelings of worthlessness or excessive or inappropriate guilt
- Difficulty maintaining concentration or making decisions
- Recurrent thoughts of death or having suicidal thoughts, plans, or attempts
- The symptoms are not attributable to a medical condition or use of a substance
- The symptoms cause significant distress or impairment

Major depressive disorder can be and often is diagnosed with a range of other disorders, including personality disorders, substance use disorders, and anxiety disorders, for example. Many conditions can mimic major depressive disorder, including those that are associated with disorders that we discussed in Chapter 6, which include or are related to schizophrenia. These include schizoaffective disorder, schizophrenia, schizophreniform disorder, and delusional disorder. Therefore, the clinician must rule out these specific disorders before assigning the diagnosis of major depressive disorder to the client.

The lifetime prevalence of major depressive disorder in the United States is 16.6 percent of the adult population (Kessler, Chiu, Demler, Merikangas, & Walters, 2005). Each year, 6.7 percent of the adult population receives a diagnosis of major depressive disorder, with clinicians classifying 30.4 percent of these cases (2.0 percent of the adult population) as severe. Figure 7.1 summarizes these overall prevalence statistics. The overall prevalence statistics do not tell the whole story, though, as there are significant gender and age differences. Women are 70 percent more likely than men to experience major depressive disorder at some point in life. Compared to adults 60 years of age and older, adults 59 years of age and younger are approximately twice as likely to have experienced major depressive disorder. Looking only at 12-month prevalence, 18- to 29-year-olds are 200 percent as likely as adults 60 and older to have experienced this disorder (Kessler, Berglund, et al., 2005). The average age of onset of the disorder is 32 years old (Kessler, Berglund, et al., 2005).

MINI CASE

Major Depressive Disorder, Recurrent Episode

Jonathan is a 37-year-old construction worker whose wife took him to a psychiatric facility. Although Jonathan has been functioning normally for the past several years, he suddenly became severely disturbed and depressed. At the time of admission, Jonathan was agitated, dysphoric, and suicidal, even going as far as to purchase a gun to kill himself. He had lost his appetite and had developed insomnia during the preceding 3 weeks. As each day went by, he found himself feeling more and more exhausted, less able to think clearly or to concentrate, and uninterested in anything or anyone. He had become hypersensitive in his dealings with neighbors, co-workers, and family, insisting that others were being too critical of him. This was the second such episode in Jonathan's history, the first having occurred 5 years earlier, following the loss of his job due to a massive layoff in his business.

Prevalence

- **12-month prevalence:** 6.7% of U.S. adult population

- **Severe:** 30.4% of these cases (e.g., 2.0% of U.S. adult population) are classified as "severe"

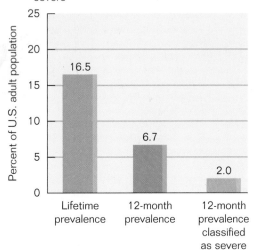

FIGURE 7.1 Prevalence of Major Depressive Disorder in the United States

✝persistent depressive disorder (dysthymia)
A depressive disorder involving chronic depression of less intensity than major depressive disorders.

✝disruptive mood dysregulation disorder
A depressive disorder in children who exhibit chronic and severe irritability and have frequent temper outbursts.

Persistent Depressive Disorder (Dysthymia)

The mood disturbance occurring with major depressive disorder may take a chronic, enduring form. People with **persistent depressive disorder (dysthymia)** have, for at least 2 years (1 year for children and adolescents), a more limited set of the symptoms of those that occur with major depressive disorder, including sleep and appetite disturbances, low energy or fatigue, low self-esteem, difficulty with concentration and decision making, and feelings of hopelessness. However, people with dysthymic disorder currently do not meet the criteria for a major depressive episode, which requires that the client meet five of the criteria in Table 7.1.

Despite the fact that people with persistent depressive disorder do not experience all the symptoms of a major depressive episode, they are never free of their symptoms for longer than 2 months. Moreover, they are likely to have other serious psychological disorders, including a heightened risk for developing major depressive disorder, personality disorder, and substance use disorder.

Approximately 2.5 percent of the adult population will develop this disorder in the course of their lives, with a peak in the 45- to 59-year-old age group (Kessler, Berglund, et al., 2005). The 12-month prevalence for dysthymic disorder is 1.5 percent of the U.S. population, with almost half of these (.8 percent of the adult population) classified as severe (Kessler, Chiu, et al., 2005). As is true for major depressive disorder, dysthymic disorder symptoms take on a different form in older adults, who are more likely to report disturbances in physical than in psychological functioning (Oxman, Barrett, Sengupta, & Williams Jr, 2000).

Disruptive Mood Dysregulation Disorder

The diagnosis of **disruptive mood dysregulation disorder** is used for children who exhibit chronic and severe irritability and have frequent temper outbursts that occur, on average, three or more times per week over at least one year and in at least two settings. These outbursts must be developmentally inappropriate. Between outbursts, children with this disorder are extremely irritable or angry. The criteria specify that the diagnosis should not be assigned to children whose first episode occurs when they are younger than 6 or older than 18. The disorder must have had its onset before the age of 10.

The authors of *DSM-5* recognized this disorder might be characterized as "temper tantrums," but they believed it was important to have a disorder earmarked for children who might otherwise be diagnosed with bipolar disorder. Follow-up data of children who show this extreme irritability and angry outbursts suggest that rather than developing bipolar disorder, they are at risk of developing depressive and/or anxiety disorders when they reach adulthood.

MINI CASE

Persistent Depressive Disorder (Dysthymia)

Miriam is a 34-year-old community college instructor who, for the past 3 years, has had persistent feelings of depressed mood, inferiority, and pessimism. She realizes that, since her graduation from college, she has never felt really happy and that, in recent years, her thoughts and feelings have been characterized as especially depressed. Her appetite is low, and she struggles with insomnia. During waking hours, she lacks energy and finds it very difficult to do her work. She often finds herself staring out the window of her office, consumed by thoughts of how inadequate she is. She fails to fulfill many of her responsibilities and, for the past 3 years, has received consistently poor teacher evaluations. Getting along with her colleagues has become increasingly difficult. Consequently, she spends most of her free time alone in her office.

Premenstrual Dysphoric Disorder

Women who experience depressed mood or changes in mood, irritability, dysphoria, and anxiety during the premenstrual phase that subside after the menstrual period begins for most of the cycles of the preceding year may be diagnosed with **premenstrual dysphoric disorder (PMDD).** This disorder was previously in the Appendix (i.e., not a diagnosable condition) in *DSM-IV-TR*. By making this disorder part of the standard psychiatric nomenclature, the *DSM-5* authors believed that better diagnosis and treatment could result for women who truly experience a highly exaggerated mood disturbance prior to their monthly menstrual cycle. Critics argue that the PMDD diagnosis pathologizes the normal monthly variations in mood that women may experience. However, the counterargument is that that the majority of women do not experience severe mood alterations on a monthly basis. By including PMDD as a diagnosis, women with these symptoms can receive treatment that might not otherwise be available to them.

premenstrual dysphoric disorder (PMDD)
Changes in mood, irritability, dysphoria, and anxiety that occur during the premenstrual phase of the monthly menstrual cycle and subside after the menstrual period begins for most of the cycles of the preceding year.

7.2 Disorders Involving Alternations in Mood

Bipolar disorder involves an intense and very disruptive experience of a **euphoric mood,** which may also occur in alternation with a major depressive episode. Cyclothymic disorder involves alternations between dysphoria and briefer, less intense, and less disruptive euphoric states called hypomanic episodes.

Bipolar Disorder

Clinicians diagnose people who have manic episodes, even if they have never had a depressive episode, as having bipolar disorder, a term that has replaced "manic depression." An individual must experience a manic episode in order for a clinician to diagnose the person with bipolar disorder, as Table 7.2 defines.

The two major categories of bipolar disorder are bipolar I and bipolar II. A diagnosis of bipolar I disorder describes a clinical course in which the individual experiences one or more manic episodes with the possibility, although not the necessity, of experiencing one or more

bipolar disorder
A mood disorder involving manic episodes—intense and very disruptive experiences of heightened mood, possibly alternating with major depressive episodes.

euphoric mood
A feeling state that is more cheerful and elated than average, possibly even ecstatic.

TABLE 7.2 Criteria for a Manic Episode

A distinct period of abnormally and persistently elevated, expansive, or irritable mood and abnormally and persistently increased activity or energy,* lasting at least 1 week and present most of the day, nearly every day (or any duration if hospitalization is necessary).

During the period of mood disturbance and increased energy or activity, three (or more) of the following symptoms (four if the mood is only irritable) are present to a significant degree, and represent a noticeable change from usual behavior:

• inflated self-esteem or grandiosity
• decreased need for sleep (e.g., feels rested after only 3 hours of sleep)
• more talkative than usual or pressure to keep talking
• flight of ideas or subjective experience that thoughts are racing
• distractibility (i.e., attention too easily drawn to unimportant or irrelevant external stimuli), as reported or observed
• increase in goal-directed activity (either socially, at work or school, or sexually) or psychomotor agitation
• excessive involvement in activities that have a high potential for painful consequences (e.g., engaging in unrestrained buying sprees, sexual indiscretions, or foolish business investments)

This episode must represent a clearly observable change in functioning but it is not severe enough to require hospitalization to prevent harm to self or others.

REAL STORIES

Carrie Fisher: Bipolar Disorder

"I outlasted my problems . . . I am mentally ill. I can say that. I am not ashamed of that. I survived that, I'm still surviving it, but bring it on. Better me than you."

Carrie Fisher is an American actress, screenwriter, novelist, and lecturer who has appeared in 37 films—most notably for her portrayal of Princess Leia Organa in the *Star Wars* trilogy. She has also written four novels, one of which, *Wishful Drinking*, has been turned into a one-woman play performed in venues across the country. In the book, she chronicles her life—from growing up in a Hollywood family, her rise to fame, her struggles with drugs and alcohol, and her battles with bipolar disorder. Carrie talks about her experiences with humor and honesty, revealing the reality of her mental illness.

Born in 1956 in Beverly Hills, California, Carrie is the daughter of actress Debbie Reynolds and singer Eddie Fisher. The product of a Hollywood marriage, Carrie seemed to have been destined to be a Hollywood star from the very beginning. When she was 2 years old, Carrie's father left her mother for Elizabeth Taylor, her mother's best friend. The media highly publicized this story, although in her book, Carrie states that she doesn't believe her childhood experiences affected any of the problems that she encountered later in life. "To complain about my childhood or even a sizeable (?) portion of my life would be as unattractive as it would be inaccurate. I had a very privileged life growing up."

Carrie first began acting at the age of 12, appearing in Las Vegas with her mother, and later dropped out of high school in order to perform on the road with her mother. In 1973, Carrie appeared with her mother in the Broadway musical *Irene*, and 2 years later, after attending drama school in London, made her film debut in the 1975 film *Shampoo* with Burt Reynolds.

Two years after that, she instantly became an international celebrity and an icon for her role in the *Star Wars* trilogy. According to Carrie, it was at this point that she began to heavily abuse cocaine and alcohol, having already experimented with marijuana at the age of 13. Looking back on her drug abuse, Carrie recalls that she used drugs as a way to self-medicate her extreme mood episodes: "I used to think I was a drug addict, pure and simple—just someone who could not stop taking drugs willfully . . . and I was that. But it turns out that I am severely manic depressive." She received this diagnosis for the first time when she was 24 years old, although she did not pursue any treatment at that time. As she describes it, ". . . [My psychiatrist] wanted to put me on medication instead of actually treating me. So, I did the only rational thing I could do in the face of such an insult—I stopped talking to the [psychiatrist], flew back to New York, and married Paul Simon a week later."

Carrie was married to singer Paul Simon from 1983 to 1984, although the two dated on and off for a total of 12 years. In 1992, Carrie had a daughter, Billie, with her partner Bryan Lourd.

Despite her chronic battles with substance abuse and bipolar disorder, Carrie continued to appear in films and television shows throughout the 1980s. Her substance abuse led to a hospitalization in the mid 1980s, inspiring her first novel, *Postcards from the Edge*,

a semi-autobiographical account of an actress suffering from substance abuse, published in 1987. The book became a successful movie for which she received critical acclaim.

Throughout the 1990s, Carrie continued to appear in films and became well-known in Hollywood for her screenwriting talents. In 1997, she suffered from a psychotic break after she sought out medication to treat her chronic depression. She describes that experience in *Wishful Drinking*: "Now, anyone who has stayed awake for six days knows that there's every chance that they'll wind up psychotic. Anyway, I did, and part of how that manifested was that I thought everything on television was about me . . . I watched CNN, and at the time Versace had just been killed by that man Cunanin, and the police were frantically scouring the Eastern seaboard for him. So, I was Cunanin, Versace, and the police. Now this is exhausting

After struggling for many years with substance abuse and bipolar disorder, Carrie Fisher is now an activist for destigmatization of mental illness.

programming." She was hospitalized for 6 days and then spent 6 months receiving outpatient treatment. Having now accepted her diagnosis of bipolar disorder and finally coming to terms with her need for treatment, Carrie set out to lecture against the stigmatization of mental illness. Since that time she has been an active voice in speaking out about the need for government funding for mental health treatment, and for the need for greater public acceptance of mental illness.

In *Wishful Drinking*, Carrie describes her experiences with switching between mania and depression. "I have two moods . . . One is Roy, rollicking Roy, the wild ride of a mood. And Pam, sediment Pam, who stands on the shore and sobs . . . sometimes the tide is in,

sometimes it's out." Carrie also describes some of the various treatments for her illness that she has received, including electroconvulsive therapy (ECT).

"Why did I feel I needed ECT? Well, it had been recommended by several psychiatrists over the years, to treat my depression. But I couldn't bring myself to consider it as it seemed too barbaric. My only exposure to it was Jack Nicholson in *One Flew Over the Cuckoo's Nest*, which wasn't exactly an enticing example. From the seizures to the biting down on a stick to the convulsions, it looked traumatic, dangerous, and humiliating. I mean, what do we know for certain about it? Aren't there a bunch of risks? What if something goes wrong and my brain blows up?

"But I'd been feeling overwhelmed and pretty defeated. I didn't necessarily feel like *dying*—but I'd been feeling a lot like not being alive. The second reason I decided to get ECT is that I was depressed. Profoundly depressed. Part of this could be attributed to my mood disorder, which was, no doubt, probably the source of the emotional intensity. That's what can take simple sadness and turn it into sadness squared."

"At times," she writes at the end of *Wishful Drinking*, "being bipolar can be an all-consuming challenge, requiring a lot of stamina and even more courage, so if you're living with this illness and functioning at all, it's something to be proud of, not ashamed of."

major depressive episodes. In contrast, a diagnosis of Bipolar II disorder means that the individual has had one or more major depressive episodes and at least one that we call a **hypomanic episode.** The criteria for a hypomanic episode, as shown in Table 7.3, are similar to those of a manic episode, but involve a shorter duration (4 days instead of 1 week).

Individuals who are in a manic, hypomanic, or major depressive episode may show features of the opposite pole, but not to an extreme enough degree to meet diagnostic criteria. For example, people in a manic episode may report feeling sad or empty, fatigued, or suicidal. *DSM-5* uses a specifier of "mixed features" to apply to cases in which an individual experiences episodes of mania or hypomania when depressive features are present, and to episodes of depression in the context of major depressive disorder or bipolar disorder when features of mania/hypomania are present. The existence of this additional "mixed" category accounts for those people whose symptoms may, either simultaneously with or close in time to, show the opposite mood symptoms.

hypomanic episode
A period of elated mood not as extreme as a manic episode.

TABLE 7.3 Criteria for a Hypomanic Episode

A distinct period of abnormally and persistently elevated, expansive, or irritable mood and abnormally and persistently increased activity or energy,* lasting at least 4 consecutive days and present most of the day, nearly every day. The episode is not severe enough to require hospitalization.

During the period of mood disturbance and increased energy and activity, three (or more) of the following symptoms have persisted (four if the mood is only irritable), represent a noticeable change from usual behavior, and have been present to a significant degree:

- inflated self-esteem or grandiosity
- decreased need for sleep (e.g., feels rested after only 3 hours of sleep)
- more talkative than usual or pressure to keep talking
- flight of ideas or subjective experience that thoughts are racing
- distractibility (i.e., attention too easily drawn to unimportant or irrelevant external stimuli), as reported or observed
- increase in goal-directed activity (either socially, at work or school, or sexually) or psychomotor agitation
- excessive involvement in pleasurable activities that have a high potential for painful consequences (e.g., the person engages in unrestrained buying sprees, sexual indiscretions, or foolish business investments)

*The increase in activity or energy is new in *DSM-5*.

MINI CASE

Bipolar I Disorder, Current Episode Manic

Isabel is a 38-year-old realtor who, for the past week, has shown signs of uncharacteristically outlandish behavior. This behavior began with Isabel's development of an unrealistic plan to create her own real estate empire. She went without sleep or food for 3 days, spending most of her time at her computer developing far-fetched financial plans. Within 3 days she put deposits on seven houses, together valued at more than $3 million, although she had no financial resources to finance even one of them. She made several visits to local banks, where she was known and respected, and made a scene with each loan officer who expressed skepticism about her plan. In one instance, she angrily pushed over the banker's desk, yanked his phone from the wall, and screamed at the top of her lungs that the bank was keeping her from earning a multimillion-dollar profit. The police were summoned, and they brought her to the psychiatric emergency room, from which she was transferred for intensive evaluation and treatment.

Bipolar disorder has a lifetime prevalence rate of 3.9 percent in the U.S. population (Kessler, Berglund, et al., 2005) and a 12-month prevalence of 2.6 percent (Kessler, Chiu, et al., 2005). Of those diagnosed with bipolar disorder in a given year, nearly 83 percent (2.2 percent of adult population) have cases classified as "severe." At least half of all cases begin before a person reaches the age of 25 (Kessler, Chiu, et al., 2005). Nevertheless, approximately 60 percent of all individuals with bipolar disorder can live symptom-free if they receive adequate treatment (Perlis et al., 2006).

Of all psychological disorders, bipolar disorder is the most likely to occur in people who also have problems with substance abuse. People with bipolar and substance use disorders have an earlier onset of bipolar disorder, more frequent episodes, greater chances of having anxiety- and stress-related disorders, aggressive behavior, problems with the law, and risk of suicide (Swann, 2010). As you can see in Figure 7.2, bipolar disorder can cause people to experience a range of moods.

Clinicians diagnose people as having **bipolar disorder, rapid cycling** if they have four or more episodes within the previous year that meet the criteria for manic, hypomanic, or major depressive disorder. In some individuals, the cycling may occur within 1 week or even 1 day. The factors that predict rapid cycling include earlier onset, higher depression scores, higher mania scores, and lower global assessment of functioning. A history of rapid cycling in the previous year and use of antidepressants also predict rapid cycling (Schneck et al., 2008). Medical conditions such as hypothyroidism, disturbances in sleep-wake cycles, and use of antidepressant medications can also contribute to the development of rapid cycling (Papadimitriou, Calabrese, Dikeos, & Christodoulou, 2005).

bipolar disorder, rapid cycling
A form of bipolar disorder involving four or more episodes within the previous year that meet the criteria for manic, hypomanic, or major depressive disorder.

Cyclothymic Disorder

Cyclothymic disorder symptoms are more chronic and less severe than those of bipolar disorder. People with this disorder have met the criteria for a hypomanic episode many times over a span of at least 2 years (1 year in children and adolescents) and also have numerous periods of depressive symptoms, but never meet the criteria for a major depressive episode. During their respective time frames, adults, children, or adolescents have never been without these symptoms for more than 2 months at a time.

cyclothymic disorder
A mood disorder with symptoms that are more chronic and less severe than those of bipolar disorder.

FIGURE 7.2 Range of Moods Present in People with Bipolar Disorder

severe depression, moderate depression, and mild low mood

normal or balanced mood

hypomania and severe mania

MINI CASE

Cyclothymic Disorder

Larry is a 32-year-old bank cashier who has sought treatment for his mood variations, which date back to age 26. For several years, co-workers, family, and friends have repeatedly told him that he is very moody. He acknowledges that his mood never feels quite stable, although at times others tell him he seems more calm and pleasant than usual. Unfortunately, these intervals are quite brief, lasting for a few weeks and usually ending abruptly. Without warning, he may experience either a somewhat depressed mood or a period of elation. During his depressive periods, his confidence, energy, and motivation are very low. During his hypomanic periods, he willingly volunteers to extend his workday and to undertake unrealistic challenges at work. On weekends, he acts in promiscuous and provocative ways, often sitting outside his apartment building, making seductive comments and gestures to women walking by. Larry disregards the urging of his family members to get professional help, insisting that it is his nature to be a bit unpredictable. He also states that he doesn't want some "shrink" to steal away the periods during which he feels fantastic.

7.3 Theories and Treatment of Depressive and Bipolar Disorder

Biological Perspectives

Long aware of the tendency for mood disorders to occur more frequently among biologically related family members, researchers working within the biological perspective are attempting to pinpoint genetic contributors to these disorders. However, there are most likely multiple genes that interact in complex ways with environmental risk factors, complicating tremendously their work (Kamali & McInnis, 2011).

Researchers estimate that first-degree relatives are 15 to 25 percent more likely to have major depressive disorder than nonrelatives. Looked at in another way, this translates into a statistic known as an "odds ratio," indicating that first-degree relatives having major depression are from two to four times as likely to develop the disorder themselves. In addition, the children of depressed parents are more likely to have major depressive disorder than are the parents of depressed children, a fact which poses a problem in family studies and shows how difficult it is to separate inherited from environmental influences. However, recall from Chapter 4 that family inheritance studies cannot separate genetic from environmental factors. Children of depressed parents grow up in households that we might imagine are different in important ways from those with children whose parents do not have major depressive disorders. Twin studies comparing identical or monozygotic (MZ) with fraternal or dizygotic (DZ) twins provide stronger evidence in favor of a genetic interpretation. Based on numerous studies involving these comparisons, researchers estimate that genetic influences on major depressive disorder are in the range of 30 to 40 percent. However, genetic predisposition interacts with environmental factors including stress, social support, and life events (Lau & Eley, 2010).

Altered serotonin functioning seems to play an important role in causing genetically predisposed individuals to develop major depressive disorder. The best evidence for serotonin's role comes from studies in which individuals are experimentally deprived of tryptophan, an amino acid that aids the body in manufacturing serotonin (Cowen, 2008). A second research area on biochemical abnormalities in people with major depressive disorder involves brain-derived neurotrophic factor (BDNF), a protein involved in keeping neurons alive and able to adapt and change in response to experience. Researchers are finding that people with major depressive disorder seem to have inherited a version of a gene that codes BDNF, resulting in lower levels in areas of the brain regions involved in controlling mood (Lau & Eley, 2010).

Antidepressant medication is commonly prescribed to individuals who suffer from major depressive disorder.

Compared to major depressive disorder, bipolar disorder has an even stronger pattern of genetic inheritance with an estimated heritability of 60 percent. In a comprehensive analysis of 367 genes possibly involved in bipolar disorder, a team of researchers from the National Institute of Mental Health narrowed the search to a defect in the "PCLO" gene (called the "piccolo" gene). This gene seems to play a role in synaptic transmission (Choi et al., 2011). Brain scan and neuropsychological testing of individuals with bipolar disorder suggest that they have difficulties in attention, memory, and executive function consistent with abnormalities in the primary visual cortex, the frontal lobes, the temporal lobes, and the cingulate cortex (Benabarre et al., 2005). Further research suggests that the inability to inhibit responses that may have a genetic component may, consequently, serve as an endophenotype for bipolar disorder (Schulze et al., 2011).

Antidepressant medication is the most common form of biologically based treatment for people with major depressive disorder. Clinicians prescribe antidepressants from four major categories of selective serotonin reuptake inhibitors (SSRIs), serotonin and norepinephrine reuptake inhibitors (SNRIs), tricyclic antidepressants, and monoamine oxidase inhibitors (MAOIs).

SSRIs block the uptake of serotonin, enabling more availabilty of this neurotransmitter for action at the receptor sites. These medications include fluoxetine (Prozac), citalopram (Celexa), escitalopram (Lexapro), paroxetine (Paxil), and sertraline (Zoloft). Compared to other antidepressants, SSRIs have fewer unpleasant side effects such as sedation, weight gain, constipation, blood pressure changes, and dry mouth. However, SSRIs are not without side effects. The most commonly reported complaints are nausea, agitation, and sexual dysfunction. SNRIs increase both norepinephrine and serotonin levels by blocking their reuptake. They include duloxetine (Cymbalta), venlafaxine (Effexor), and desvenlafaxine (Pristiq).

Compared to SSRIs, the SNRIs seem to be statistically but not clinically more efficacious, and they have a greater chance of adverse reactions (Machado & Einarson, 2010) including suicidal thoughts or attempts as well as allergic symptoms, gastrointestinal disturbances, weakness, nausea, vomiting, confusion, memory loss, irritability, and panic attacks, among other unpleasant reactions. In 2010, the manufacturer of Cymbalta (Eli Lilly) also achieved approval from the Federal Drug Administration to market the medication for chronic lower back pain, and it began extensive marketing for this purpose.

Tricyclic antidepressants (TCAs) derive their name from the fact that they have a three-ring chemical structure. These medications, such as amitriptyline (Elavil, Endep), desipramine (Norpramin), imipramine (Tofranil), and nortriptyline (Aventyl, Pamelor), are particularly effective in alleviating depression in people who have some of the more common biological symptoms, such as disturbed appetite and sleep. Although the exact process by which tricyclic antidepressants work still remains unclear, we do know that they block the premature reuptake of biogenic amines back into the presynaptic neurons, thus increasing their excitatory effects on the postsynaptic neurons.

Clinicians believe that the antidepressant effects of MAOIs, such as phenelzine (Nardil) and tranylcypromine (Parnate), occur because the medications inhibit the enzyme monoamine oxidase, which converts the biogenic amines, such as norepinephrine and serotonin, into inert substances, so that they cannot excite the postsynaptic neurons. MAOIs prolong the life of neurotransmitters, thus increasing neuronal flow. These medications are particularly effective in treating depression in people with chronic depression that dates back many years, and who have not responded to the tricyclics. However, clinicians do not prescribe MAOIs as commonly as the other two medication types, because their interactions with other substances can cause serious complications.

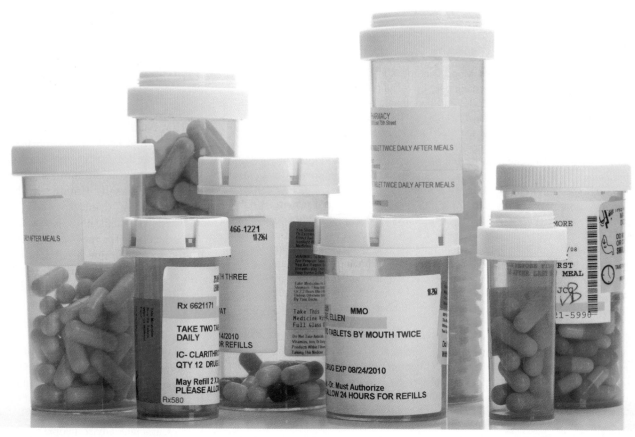

Psychotherapeutic medication offers relief to many individuals who suffer from mood disorders and are often used in combination with other modes of treatment, such as psychotherapy, to help patients manage their symptoms.

Specifically, people taking MAOIs are not able to take certain allergy medications or to ingest foods or beverages containing a substance called tyramine (for example, beer, cheese, and chocolate), because the combination can bring on a hypertensive crisis in which the person's blood pressure rises dramatically and dangerously.

Antidepressant medications take time to work—from 2 to 6 weeks before a client's symptoms begin to lift. Once the depression has subsided, the clinician usually urges him or her to remain on the medication for 4 or 5 additional months, and much longer for clients with a history of recurrent, severe depressive episodes. Because of medication side effects and client concerns, clinicians have found it helpful to develop therapeutic programs that involve regular visits early in treatment, expanded efforts to educate clients about the medications, and continued monitoring of treatment compliance.

Studies on antidepressant effectiveness suffer from the "file drawer problem" phenomenon—the fact that we are likely to file away and not even submit for publication consideration studies that fail to establish significant benefits of an intervention such as a medication. In one analysis of 74 FDA-registered studies on antidepressants, 31 percent of them, accounting for 3,349 study participants, were not published. Of the published studies, 94 percent of the medication trials reported positive findings. This bias toward publishing only positive results severely limits our ability to evaluate the efficacy of antidepressants because we are only seeing a slice of the actual data (Turner, Matthews, Linardatos, Tell, & Rosenthal, 2008). Adding further complications, some researchers have questioned whether people with less than severe depression might have experienced positive results because of their expectation of benefit, otherwise known as the placebo effect (Kirsch et al., 2008).

Although there have been media reports about the higher suicide risk that occurs with the SSRI medication category, an investigation of all suicides in the years between 1996 and 1998 revealed a lower rate of suicide among individuals who are receiving

What's New in the DSM-5

Depressive and Bipolar Disorders

Modifications to the category of Mood Disorders in *DSM-5* were intended to provide greater precision in the diagnosis by refining the criteria for major depressive episode, manic episode, and hypomanic episode. One of the major problems in the *DSM-IV-TR* was a failure to differentiate these episodes from a person's typical level of activity, sadness, or disturbance. In particular, this difficulty led to a failure to distinguish bipolar disorder from attention-deficit hyperactivity disorder, which, in turn, may have led to overdiagnosis of children and adolescents with bipolar disorder. Thus, these changes represent a slight, but important, improvement and will lead to greater specificity.

A highly controversial decision in *DSM-5* was the adding of premenstrual dysphoric disorder (PMDD). As you have learned already, the addition of the PMDD diagnosis was met with criticism for pathologizing normal experiences in women. Similarly, critics argue that disruptive mood dysregulation disorder pathologizes the "normal" experience in children of having temper tantrums. The rationale for proposing this new diagnosis was that it would reduce the frequency of diagnosing bipolar disorder in children. By separating severe chronic irritability from bipolar disorder, the authors argued that children will not be misdiagnosed.

Finally, the *DSM-5* authors angered many critics when they decided to leave out the so-called "bereavement exclusion" present in *DSM-IV-TR*. This means that an individual who meets the criteria for a major depressive episode and has lost a loved one in the past two months (which was the bereavement exclusion) would receive a psychiatric diagnosis. The argument in favor of making this change was that, in a vulnerable individual, bereavement could trigger a major depressive episode that would be appropriate to diagnose. Moreover, in a lengthly note of clarification, the *DSM-5* authors maintain that the grief associated with normal bereavement is different from the symptoms that occur in individuals who develop a true depressive disorder.

treatment with these medications compared to other forms of antidepressants. In part, this was due to the generally better medical care in facilities that prescribe SSRIs compared to the older and less effective tricyclic antidepressants (Gibbons, Hur, Bhaumik, & Mann, 2005).

The traditional treatment for bipolar disorder is lithium carbonate, referred to as lithium, a naturally occurring salt (found in small amounts in drinking water) that, when used medically, replaces sodium in the body. The medication decreases the catecholamine levels in the nervous system, which, in terms of behavior, calms the individual experiencing a manic episode. Researchers have examined the efficacy of lithium in numerous studies over the past three decades, and the conclusion seems clear that lithium is effective in treating acute mania symptoms and in preventing the recurrence of manic episodes (Shastry, 2005).

Clinicians advise people who have frequent manic episodes (i.e., two or more a year) to remain on lithium continuously as a preventive measure. The drawback is that, even though lithium is a natural substance in the body, it can have side effects, such as mild central nervous system disturbances, gastrointestinal upsets, and more serious cardiac effects. Because of these side effects, some people who experience manic episodes are reluctant or even unwilling to take lithium continuously. Furthermore, lithium interferes with the euphoria that can accompany, at least, the beginnings of a manic episode. Consequently, people with this disorder who enjoy those pleasurable feelings may resist taking the medication. Unfortunately, by the time their euphoria escalates into a full-blown episode, it's too late because their judgment is clouded by their manic symptoms of grandiosity and elation. To help overcome this dilemma, clinicians may advise their clients to participate in lithium groups, in which members who use the medication on a regular basis provide support to each other regarding the importance of staying on the medication.

Because of the variable nature of bipolar disorder, additional medication is often beneficial in treating some symptoms. For example, people in a depressive episode may need to take an antidepressant medication in addition to the lithium for the duration of the episode. However, this can be problematic for a person who is prone to developing mania, because an antidepressant might provoke hypomania or mania. Those who have psychotic symptoms may benefit from taking antipsychotic medication until these disturbing symptoms subside. People who experience rapid cycling present a challenge for clinicians because of the sudden changes that take place in their emotions and behavior.

Psychopharmacologists report that rapid cyclers, especially those for whom lithium has not been sufficient, seem to respond positively to prescriptions of anticonvulsant medication, such as carbamazepine (Tegretol) or valproate (Depakote), although these alone are not as effective as lithium (Kessing, Hellmund, Geddes, Goodwin, & Andersen, 2011).

For some clients with mood disorders, medication is either ineffective or slow in alleviating symptoms that are severe and possibly life-threatening. Even with the best of treatment, between 60 and 70 percent of individuals with major depressive disorder do not achieve symptom relief (Rush et al., 2006). A combination of genetic, physiological, and environmental factors are involved in determining response to medication. Researchers hope to improve the efficacy of medications through **pharmacogenetics,** the use of genetic testing to determine who will and will not improve with a particular medication, including antidepressants (Crisafulli et al., 2011) and lithium (McCarthy, Leckband, & Kelsoe, 2010).

pharmacogenetics
The use of genetic testing to determine who will and will not improve with a particular medication.

Clinicians, at present, have several somatic alternatives to medication for treatment-resistant depression. As we discussed in Chapter 4, one alternative is electroconvulsive therapy (ECT) (Lisanby, 2007). Clinicians and clients are not sure exactly how ECT works, but most current hypotheses center on ECT-induced changes in neurotransmitter receptors and in the body's natural opiates. As we discussed in Chapter 4, deep brain stimulation (DBS) is another somatic treatment that clinicians use to target major depressive disorder (as well as obsessive-compulsive disorder and movement disorders).

Circadian rhythms are the daily variations that regulate biological patterns such as sleep-wake cycles. Based on the hypothesis that at least some mood disorders reflect a disruption in circadian rhythms, researchers are proposing the use of treatments that "reset" the individual's bodily clock. Such treatments include light therapy, in which the individual is seated in front of a bright light for a period of time, such as 30 minutes in the morning. One distinct advantage of light therapy is that its side effects are minimal and are almost entirely gone after the reduced dosage or discontinued treatment (Pail et al., 2011). Researchers also believe that lithium may work on at least some individuals with bipolar disorder by resetting their circadian rhythms (McClung, 2007).

Although somatic interventions provide effective and sometimes lifesaving help for many people, most therapists regard these treatments as insufficient by themselves. Consequently, clinicians typically recommend individual, family, or group psychotherapy as an adjunct to help the individual understand both the etiology of the disorder and the strategies for preventing recurrences. Let's turn now to the contributions of the various perspectives that address these psychological issues.

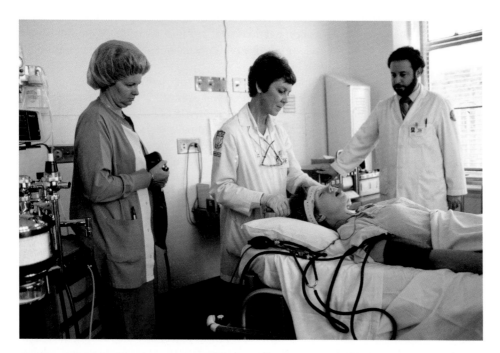

Once a risky and controversial procedure, electroconvulsive therapy is now a highly regulated and safe procedure available for individuals with severe depression who have not responded to other treatment options.

Psychological Perspectives

Psychodynamic Approaches

Early psychoanalytic theories proposed that people with depressive disorders had suffered a loss early in their lives that affected them at a deep, intrapsychic level (Abraham, 1911/1968). Attachment theory focuses on the individual's feelings of security or insecurity toward the way that their caregivers reared them in childhood. Bowlby proposed that people with an insecure attachment style have a greater risk for developing a depressive disorder in adulthood (Bowlby, 1980). Following up on Bowlby's ideas, Bemporad (1985) proposed that insecurely attached children become preoccupied with the need to be loved by others. As adults, they form relationships in which they overvalue the support of their partners. When such relationships end, they become overwhelmed with feelings of inadequacy and loss.

Psychoanalytic explanations of bipolar disorder propose that manic episodes are defensive responses through which individuals stave off feelings of inadequacy, loss, and helplessness. They develop feelings of grandiosity and elation or become hyperenergetic as an unconscious defense against sinking into a state of gloom and despair. In one investigation, the level of use of denial and narcissistic defense mechanisms was related to extent of manic symptoms (Sharma & Sinha, 2010).

Models of treatment for depressive disorders are increasingly moving toward the application of cognitive-behavioral techniques; however, there is also evidence of the beneficial effects of psychodynamically based therapy. Contemporary approaches within the psychodynamic perspective involve short (8- or 10-session) and focused treatments. A review of eight studies comparing short-term psychodynamic therapy to other methods showed this method to be as least as effective as CBT in the treatment of major depressive disorder (Lewis, Dennerstein, & Gibbs, 2008).

Behavioral and Cognitive-Behavioral Approaches

One of the earliest behavioral formulations of theories of depression regards the symptoms of depression symptoms as resulting from lack of positive reinforcement (Lazarus, 1968; Skinner, 1953). According to this view, depressed people withdraw from life because they no longer have incentives to be active. Contemporary behaviorists base their approach on Lewinsohn's (1974) model. He maintained that depressed people have a low rate of what he termed "response contingent positive reinforcement behaviors" that increase in frequency as the result of performing actions that produce pleasure. According to the behaviorist point of view, the lack of positive reinforcement elicits the symptoms of low self-esteem, guilt, and pessimism.

behavioral activation
Behavioral therapy for depression in which the clinician helps the client identify activities associated with positive mood.

In the method known as **behavioral activation** for depression, based on these behaviorist principles, the clinician helps the client identify activities associated with positive mood. The client keeps a record of the frequency of engaging in these rewarding activities and sets weekly, small goals that gradually increase the frequency and duration of these activities. These activities are preferably ones that are consistent with the client's core values. Some clients may prefer to spend time exploring the arts, and others to spend time in physical activity. Behavioral activation seems particularly well-suited for clients who are not "psychologically minded," for group therapy, and for settings such as hospitals, nursing homes, and substance-abuse treatment centers (Sturmey, 2009).

Clinicians increasingly are integrating behavioral with cognitive approaches that focus on the role of dysfunctional thoughts as causes, or at least contributors to mood disorders. Recall that the cognitive perspective is based on the idea that people's thoughts lead to their emotions. People with depressive disorders think in repetitively negative ways that maintain chronically their negative emotions. Beck (1967) defined these thoughts as the cognitive triad: a negative view of the self, the world, and the future. A sense of loss profoundly lowers their self-esteem, which causes them to feel that they cannot have what they need to feel good about themselves. They assume that they are worthless and helpless and that their efforts to improve their lives are doomed to fail. In the course of their daily experiences, they make faulty interpretations that perpetuate the cycle of negative thoughts

TABLE 7.4 Examples of Cognitive Distortions

Type of Distortion	Definition	Example
Overgeneralizing	If it's true in one case, it applies to any case that is even slightly similar.	"I failed my first English exam, so I'm probably going to fail all of them."
Selective abstraction	The only events that the person takes seriously are those that represent failures, deprivation, loss, or frustration.	"Even though I won the election for the student senate, I'm not really popular because not everyone voted for me."
Excessive responsibility	I am responsible for all bad things that happen to me or others to whom I am close.	"It's my fault that my friend didn't get the internship—I should've warned her about how hard the interview would be."
Assuming temporal causality	If it has been true in the past, then it's always going to be true.	"My last date was a wipeout, my next date will probably hate me too."
Making excessive self-references	I am the center of everyone else's attention, and they can all see when I mess up.	"When I tripped over the branch in the sidewalk, everyone could see how clumsy I am."
Catastrophizing	Always thinking the worst and being certain that it will happen.	"Because I failed my accounting exam, I will never make it in the business world."
Dichotomous thinking	Seeing everything as either one extreme or another rather than as mixed or in between.	"I can't stand people who are liars because I can never trust them."

SOURCE: Adapted from A. T. Beck, A. J. Rush, B. F. Shaw, & G. Emery in *Cognitive Therapy of Depression.* Copyright ©1979 Guilford Publications, Inc. Reprinted by permission.

and emotions (Beck, Rush, Shaw, & Emery, 1979; Beck & Weishaar, 1989). These faulty interpretations include making arbitrary inferences, incorrectly jumping to conclusions, mistakenly overgeneralizing from their experiences, and taking details out of context which they then misinterpret (see Table 7.4).

Clinicians who conduct behavioral therapy with clients who have depressive disorders follow the general principles that we outlined in Chapter 4. They begin with a careful assessment of the frequency, quality, and range of activities and social interactions in their client's life, focusing on sources of positive and negative reinforcement. Based on this analysis, behaviorally oriented clinicians help their clients make changes in their environments and teach them necessary social skills. These clinicians also encourage them to increase their involvement in activities that they find positively rewarding.

Behaviorally oriented clinicians also believe that education is an essential component of therapy. Individuals with depressive disorders perpetuate their negative emotions by setting unrealistic goals, which they are then unable to achieve. Clinicians assign homework exercises that encourage clients to make gradual behavioral changes, which will increase the probability that they can achieve their goals, and thus feel rewarded. Another technique involves behavioral contracting combined with self-reinforcement. For example, the clinician and client may agree that a client would benefit from meeting new people or going out with old friends. They would then set up a schedule of rewards in which they pair the social activity with something the client identifies as a desirable reward. Other methods the behaviorally oriented clinician would use include more extensive instruction, modeling, coaching, role playing, and rehearsal, and perhaps working with the client in a real-world setting.

Clinicians who practice cognitively based therapy (CBT), also called cognitive therapy (CT), work with their clients to try to change the nature of their thought processes so that they will be less depressed. Like behaviorally oriented therapy, CBT involves an active collaboration between the client and the clinician. In contrast to behaviorally oriented therapy, however, CBT focuses additionally on the client's dysfunctional thoughts and how to change them through cognitive restructuring. Research comparing CBT and CT to either other psychological forms of therapy or medication supports its greater effectiveness both in the short- and long-term, particularly for moderate or mild depressive disorders. Moreover, CBT can also be an effective intervention for clients with bipolar disorder to help them cope with the periods in which their symptoms are beginning to emerge, but before they are full-blown (Driessen & Hollon, 2010).

Clinicians treating people with bipolar disorder customarily turn first to pharmacological interventions. However, they are also likely to incorporate psychological interventions designed to help clients develop better coping strategies in an effort to minimize the likelihood of relapse (Bowden, 2005). Psychoeducation is an especially important aspect of treating people with bipolar disorder in order to help clients with this condition understand its nature, as well as the ways in which medication is so important in controlling symptoms. Many people who have experienced a manic episode are tempted to forgo taking their medication in the hope that they might once again experience the exciting highs of a manic episode. If they can develop insight into the risks involved in noncompliance, as well as an improved understanding of medications such as lithium, they are more likely to adhere to the treatment program.

interpersonal therapy (IPT)
A time-limited form of psychotherapy for treating people with major depressive disorder, based on the assumption that interpersonal stress induces an episode of depression in a person who is genetically vulnerable to this disorder.

Interpersonal Approaches Researchers originally developed **interpersonal therapy (IPT)** as a brief intervention, lasting between 12 and 16 weeks, which emerged from interpersonal theory. This approach adheres to a set of guidelines derived from research data. Although interpersonal therapy involves many of the techniques that most therapists use spontaneously, it frames these techniques in a systematic approach, including manuals to guide them in applying the method.

We can divide interpersonal therapy into three broad phases. The first phase involves assessing the magnitude and nature of the individual's depression using quantitative assessment measures. Interview methods also determine the factors that precipitated the current episode. At that point, depending on the type of depressive symptoms that the individual shows, the therapist considers treatment with antidepressant medications.

In the second phase, the therapist and the client collaborate in formulating a treatment plan that focuses on the primary problem. Typically, these problems are related to grief, interpersonal disputes, role transitions, and problems in interpersonal relationships stemming from inadequate social skills. The therapist then carries out the treatment plan in the third phase, with the methods varying according to the precise nature of the client's primary problem. In general, the therapist uses a combination of techniques, such as encouraging self-exploration, providing support, educating the client in the nature of depression, and providing feedback on the client's ineffective social skills. Therapy focuses on the here and now, rather than on past childhood or developmental issues. A large-scale analysis of studies conducted over 30 years on interpersonal therapy showed that, compared to cognitive-behavioral therapy and medications, interpersonal therapy was significantly more effective (Bowden, 2005).

For clients who cannot take antidepressant medications or where it is impractical to use medications, IPT is an especially valuable intervention in that nonmedical personnel can administer it or clients, with instruction, can learn it themselves (Weissman, 2007). In addition, for clients with personality disorders, IPT may be less effective than CBT, which is more structured and also focuses less on interpersonal difficulties (Carter et al., 2011).

An interpersonal therapist carefully collaborates with each client to generate a unique treatment plan, based on the client's symptoms and particular areas of concern.

Interpersonal and social rhythm therapy (IPSRT) (Frank, 2007) is a biopsychosocial approach to treating people with bipolar disorder that proposes that relapses can result from the experience of stressful life events, disturbances in circadian rhythms (e.g., sleep-wake cycles, appetite, energy), and problems in personal relationships. According to the IPSRT model, mood episodes are likely to emerge from medication nonadherence, stressful life events, and disruptions in social rhythms. Clinicians who are using this approach focus on educating clients about medication adherence, giving them a forum to explore their feelings about the disorder, and helping them develop insight about the ways in which the disorder has altered their lives. Clinicians work with clients in paying careful attention to the regularity of daily routines (including the timing of events and the stimulation that occurs with these events), and the extent to which life events, positive as well as negative, influence daily routines. The goal of IPSRT is to increase stability in a client's social rhythms.

Interpersonal and social rhythm therapy incorporates biological approaches to treatment such as light therapy to regulate an individual's circadian rhythms.

Clinicians who adhere to the IPSRT model believe that the reduction of interpersonal stress in clients with bipolar disorder is important for several reasons. First, stressful life events affect circadian rhythm because an individual feels a sense of heightened arousal of the autonomic nervous system. Second, many life events, both stressful and nonstressful, do cause changes in daily routines. Third, major life stressors affect a person's mood and also lead to significant changes in social rhythms (Frank, 2007). Clinicians help the client stabilize social rhythms or routines while improving their interpersonal relationships. Researchers employing IPSRT have found that this form of intensive psychosocial treatment enhances relationship functioning and life satisfaction among people with bipolar disorder, particularly when combined with pharmacological interventions (Frank, Maggi, Miniati, & Benvenuti, 2009).

In reviewing the results of virtually all published studies on interventions for mood disorders, Hollon and Ponniah (2010) concluded that cognitive-behavioral and behavioral therapy have received the strongest support, particularly for individuals with less severe or chronic depression. Individuals with more severe depressive or bipolar disorders also benefit from cognitive-behavioral, interpersonal, and behaviorally oriented therapy above and beyond the effects of medication, and perhaps even instead as a first-line of approach, such as therapists currently implement in England.

Sociocultural Perspectives

According to the sociocultural perspective, individuals develop depressive disorders in response to stressful life circumstances. These circumstances can involve specific events such as sexual victimization, chronic stress such as poverty and single parenting, or episodic stress such as bereavement or job loss. Women are more likely to be exposed to these stressors than are men, a fact that may account, at least in part, for the higher frequency in the diagnosis of depressive disorders in women (Hammen, 2005).

However, acute and chronic stressors seem to play a differential role in predisposing an individual to experiencing depressive symptoms. Exposure to an acute stress such as the death of a loved one or an automobile accident could precipitate a major depressive episode. However, exposure to chronic strains from poor working conditions, health problems, interpersonal problems, and financial adversities can interact with genetic predisposition and personality to lead to more persistent feelings of hopelessness. Moreover, once activated, an individual's feelings of depression and hopelessness can exacerbate exposure to stressful environments which, in turn, can increase further the individual's feelings of chronic strain (Brown & Rosellini, 2011).

On the positive side, strong religious beliefs and spirituality may combine with the social support that membership in a religious community provides to lower an individual's

Do-Not-Resuscitate Orders for Suicidal Patients

Medical professionals encourage (or sometimes require) patients, whether they are terminally ill or not, to direct them on how they wish to be treated should they require life support. Often, for such an "Advance Directive," also known as a "Living Will," patients specify whether or not they wish to have artificial life support should they be unable to survive on their own.

The issue of whether physicians should assist patients in ending their own lives, a process known as "Physician-Assisted Suicide," came to public attention in the 1990s when Dr. Jack Kevorkian, a Michigan physician, began providing terminally ill patients with the means to end their lives through pharmacological injections. Kevorkian's very public involvement in what he saw as a righteous campaign to alleviate people's suffering and allow them to "die with dignity" soon received national attention. He was imprisoned for 8 years following the televised assisted suicide that he performed on a man with amyotrophic lateral sclerosis (ALS), a terminal nervous system disease.

The purpose of a DNR is not to bring about a patient's death, but to make the patient's wishes clear regarding life support. As such, medical personnel respect the DNR when they must make life-and-death decisions. In contrast, when individuals who have psychological disorders and wish to end their lives embark upon the same plans as a medical patient with a life-threatening illness, clinicians treat them to prevent them from committing suicide. The treatment may include involuntary hospitalization.

The obligation to respect end-of-life wishes may present an ethical conflict for mental health professionals when treating suicidal individuals who complete a DNR stating that they do not wish to obtain life support. The question is whether having a serious psychological disorder that is incapacitating, resistant to treatment, and debilitating is any different from having a similarly untreatable and painful medical illness.

Q: *You be the judge:* Does the individual's right to autonomy, respected with a DNR, differ in this type of case (Cook, Pan, Silverman, & Soltys, 2010)?

---

chances of developing depression even in those with high risk. Among the adult children of individuals with major depressive disorder, those with the strongest beliefs were less likely to experience a recurrence over a 10-year period.

7.4 Suicide

Although not a diagnosable disorder, suicidality is one potential diagnostic feature of a major depressive episode. We define suicide as a "fatal self-inflicted destructive act with explicit or inferred intent to die" (Goldsmith, Pellman, Kleinman, & Bunney, 2002) (p. 27). Suicidal behavior runs from a continuum of thinking about ending one's life ("suicidal ideation") to developing a plan, to nonfatal suicidal behavior ("suicide attempt"), to the actual ending of one's life ("suicide") (Centers for Disease Control and Prevention, 2011c).

The rates of completed suicide in the United States are far lower than other reported causes of death, amounting to nearly 35,000 in the year 2007 (Xu, Kochanek, Murphy, & Tejada-Vera, 2010). However, underreporting is likely due to the difficulty of establishing cause of death as intentional rather than unintentional harm. The highest suicide rates by age are for people 45 to 54 years old (17.7 per 100,000). Individuals 75 to 84 years old have the next highest rates (16.3) and also the highest rates for suicide by discharge of firearms (12.2). However, the absolute numbers of suicides is almost twice as high in younger adults (approximately 9,400) than in the 55- to 64-year-old age group (5,069). Within the United States, white men are much more likely than are non-white men to commit suicide.

Around the world, there are approximately one million suicides each year with a global mortality rate of 16 per 100,000. The highest suicide rates around the world are for males in Lithuania (61.3 per 100,000) and for females in Republic of Korea (22.1 per 100,000), and the lowest rates (near 0) for several Latin American and Caribbean countries, Jordan,

Map of suicide rates
(per 100 000; most recent year available as of 2011)

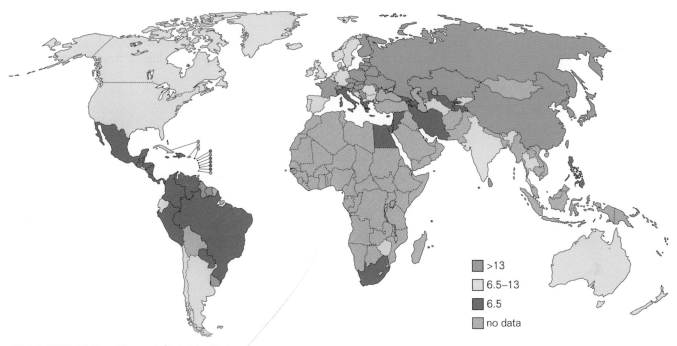

FIGURE 7.3   Map of Suicide Rates

and Iran (see Figure 7.3). In one-third of countries, young adults are at highest risk of suicide, reflecting worldwide increases in this age group compared to older adults. In Europe and North America, depression and alcohol-use disorders are a major risk factor for suicide with over 90 percent of suicides (in the United States) associated with a psychological disorder (Goldsmith et al., 2002). In contrast, impulsiveness plays a higher role in the suicides of people from Asian countries (World Health Organization, 2011).

The biopsychosocial perspective is particularly appropriate for understanding why people commit suicide and in many ways parallels the understanding provided from an integrative framework for major depressive disorders. Biological theories emphasize the genetic and physiological contributions that also contribute to the causes of mood disorders. Psychological theories focus on distorted cognitive processes and extreme feelings of hopelessless that characterize suicide victims. From a sociocultural perspective, the variations from country to country and within countries suggest that there are contributions relating to an individual's religious beliefs and values as well as to the degree to which the individual is exposed to life stresses.

The perspective of positive psychology provides a framework for understanding why individuals who are at high risk for the above reasons nevertheless do not commit suicide. The buffering hypothesis of suicidality (Johnson, Wood, Gooding, Taylor, & Tarrier, 2011) describes three aspects of resilience. First, we can distinguish resilience as a separate dimension from risk. You may be at risk of committing suicide, but if you are high on resilience, you are unlikely to do so. Second, we can view both risk and resilience as bipolar dimensions: you can be high on one, both, or neither. Third, resilience is a psychological construct such as the belief that you have the ability to overcome adversity. Resilience is not a statistical correlate of suicidality such as living in a nonstressful environment. An individual can live in a highly stressful environment (high risk), but feel that he or she can cope successfully with these circumstances (high resilience).

The factors that seem to comprise high resilience include the ability to make positive assessments of one's life circumstances and to feel in control over these circumstances. On the negative side, low resilience occurs with high levels of perfectionism and hopelessness. Also, the ability to solve problems, high levels of self-esteem, confidence in one's problem-solving ability, general feelings of social support and support from family, significant others, secure attachment, and suicide beliefs (i.e., not regarding suicide as a personal option) seem to buffer suicide risk. Religious beliefs may also play a role in resilience, but there is very little research as of yet to document this relationship. Interventions based on the resilience model would address not only the individual's specific risk factors, which may be difficult to identify given suicide's low rates in the population, but on assessing and then strengthening the individual's feelings of personal control and perceived abilities to handle stress.

7.5 Depressive and Bipolar Disorders: The Biopsychosocial Perspective

The disorders we covered in this chapter span a range of disturbances, from chronic but distressing sad moods, to rapidly vacillating alternations between mania and depression. Although these disorders clearly involve disturbances in neurotransmitter functioning, they also reflect the influences of cognitive processes and sociocultural factors. Because individuals may experience the symptoms of depressive disorders for many years, clinicians are increasingly turning to nonpharmacological interventions, particularly for cases in which individuals have mild or moderate symptoms. The situation for clients with bipolar disorder is more complicated, because life-long maintenance therapy on medications is more likely necessary.

Even in individuals whose symptoms reflect a heavy influence of biology, however, it is important for all clients with mood disorders to have access to a range of therapeutic services. With the development of evidence-based approaches, which integrate across domains of functioning, the chances are very good that individuals with these disorders will increasingly have the ability to obtain treatment that allows them to regulate their moods and lead more fulfilling lives.

Return to the Case: Janice Butterfield

After several weeks in therapy, Janice's depression had started to show improvement. Once her depression remitted however, she discontinued taking her medication. As she discussed in her initial therapy session, Janice found it important to appear strong to her family and associated psychological problems with weakness. Despite her concerns about admitting her psychological struggles, Janice continued to come to her weekly psychotherapy, and the sessions focused on her feelings about her diagnosis and the importance of taking her medication to prevent future mood swings, though she felt stable at the time. Using examples of the past consequences of her mood swings, Janice was slowly able to better understand that the impact on her family was far worse should she continue to go through mood cycles than if she worked at maintaining stability.

Dr. Tobin's reflections: Though it is a natural reaction to feel down when faced with a challenge such as losing a job and having to find a way to support your family, Janice's response went beyond the typical realm of depression most people may feel and she met diagnostic criteria for major depression. Janice's description of her past depressive episodes was also consistent with this diagnosis. Additionally, it was revealed that Janice experienced manic episodes in the past that had greatly affected not only her life but put her family at great financial risk. Unfortunately, it wasn't until Janice had attempted suicide that she finally sought the help that she needed. It is not unusual for individuals with bipolar disorder to be noncompliant with medication, as they go through long periods of feeling "normal," or what is known as their baseline. This was especially true for Janice, as she had gone her entire life without seeking treatment and had difficulty understanding the need to take medication when she was not feeling depressed or manic.

Janice described experiencing a worsening of her mood episodes with time. This is typical for individuals with bipolar disorder who go without treatment for many years. Though Janice has been hesitant to talk about her problems with her family, it will be important to include them in her treatment as they can help her understand when her mood may start to shift, because individuals with bipolar disorder may struggle to be aware of their changes in mood.

SUMMARY

- Depressive and bipolar disoders involve a disturbance in a person's emotional state, or mood. People can experience this disturbance in the form of extreme depression, excessive elation, or a combination of these emotional states. An episode is a time-limited period during which specific intense symptoms of a disorder are evident.

- **Major depressive disorder** involves acute, but time-limited, episodes of depressive symptoms, such as feelings of extreme dejection, a loss of interest in previously pleasurable aspects of life, bodily symptoms, and disturbances in eating and sleeping behavior. Individuals with major depressive disorder also have cognitive symptoms, such as a negative self-view, feelings of guilt, an inability to concentrate, and indecisiveness. Depressive episodes can be melancholic or seasonal. **Persistent depressive disorder** is a new addition to the *DSM-5* and is a consolidation of chronic major depression and dysthymic disorder. Symptoms are characterized by depression that is not as deep or intense as that experienced in major depressive disorder, but has a longer lasting course. People with dysthymic disorder have, for at least 2 years, depressive symptoms, such as low energy, low self-esteem, poor concentration, decision-making difficulty, feelings of hopelessness, and disturbances of appetite and sleep.

- **Bipolar disorder** and **cyclothymic disorder** involve alternations in mood. Bipolar disorder involves an intense and very disruptive experience of extreme elation, or **euphoria,** called a manic episode, which is characterized by abnormally heightened levels of thinking, behavior, and emotionality that cause significant impairment. Bipolar episodes in which both mania and depression are displayed can be labeled with specifiers to indicate mixed symptoms. Cyclothymic disorder involves a vacillation between **dysphoria** and briefer, less intense, and less disruptive states called **hypomanic episodes.** In bipolar I disorder, an individual experiences one or more manic episodes, with the possibility, although not the necessity, of having experienced one or more major depressive episodes. In bipolar II disorder, the individual has had one or more major depressive episodes and at least one hypomanic episode.

- Clinicians have explained depressive and bipolar disorders in terms of biological, psychological, and sociocultural approaches. The most compelling evidence supporting a biological model involves the role of genetics, with the well-established fact that these disorders run in families. Biological theories focus on neurotransmitter and hormonal functioning. Psychological theories have moved from early psychoanalytic approaches to more contemporary viewpoints that emphasize the behavioral, cognitive, and interpersonal aspects of mood disturbance. The behavioral viewpoint assumes that depression is the result of a reduction in positive reinforcements, deficient social skills, or the disruption caused by stressful life experiences. According to the cognitive perspective, depressed people react to stressful experiences by activating a set of thoughts called the cognitive triad: a negative view of the self, the world, and the future. Cognitive distortions are errors people make in the way they draw conclusions from their experiences, applying illogical rules, such as arbitrary inferences or overgeneralizing. Interpersonal theory involves a model of understanding depressive and bipolar disorders that emphasizes disturbed social functioning.

- Clinicians also base depressive and bipolar disorders treatments on biological, psychological, and sociocultural perspectives. Antidepressant medication is the most common form of somatic treatment for people who are depressed, and lithium carbonate is the most widely used medication for people who have bipolar disorder. In cases involving incapacitating depression and some extreme cases of acute mania, the clinician may recommend electroconvulsive therapy. The psychological interventions that are most effective for treating people with depressive and bipolar disorders are those rooted in the behavioral and cognitive approaches. Sociocultural and interpersonal interventions focus on the treatment of mood symptoms within the context of an interpersonal system, such as an intimate relationship.

- Although no formal diagnostic category specifically applies to people who commit suicide, many suicidal people have depressive or bipolar disorders, and some suffer from other serious psychological disorders. Clinicians explain the dramatic act of suicide from biological, psychological, and sociocultural perspectives. The treatment of suicidal clients varies considerably, depending on the context, as well as intent and lethality. Most intervention approaches incorporate support and direct therapeutic involvement.

KEY TERMS

Anxiety, Obsessive-Compulsive, and Trauma- and Stressor-Related Disorders

Learning Objectives

8.1 Distinguish between a normal fear response and an anxiety disorder

8.2 Describe separation anxiety disorder

8.3 Describe theories and treatments of specific phobias

8.4 Describe theories and treatments of social anxiety disorder

8.5 Contrast panic disorder with agoraphobia

8.6 Describe generalized anxiety disorder

8.7 Contrast obsessive-compulsive disorder with body dysmorphic disorder and hoarding

8.8 Identify the trauma- and stress-related disorders

8.9 Explain the biopsychosocial perspective on anxiety, obsessive-compulsive, and trauma- and stressor-related disorders

CHAPTER 8

Case Report: Barbara Wilder

Demographic information: Barbara is a 30-year-old Caucasian female.

Presenting problem: At the age of 18, Barbara joined the military to help pay for college. Shortly after she graduated with a bachelor's degree in business, the United States declared war on Iraq and Barbara was sent for her first tour of duty which lasted for 18 months. She returned for three more tours before she was injured in a military police raid, so severely that her lower left leg required amputation and she was forced to discontinue her service with the military.

While receiving treatment at the Veteran's Affairs (VA) Medical Center, Barbara's doctors noticed that she seemed constantly "on edge." When asked to provide details about her leg injury, she would grow very anxious and withdrawn. Barbara stated that she had difficulty sleeping because she was having frequent nightmares. Suspecting that she could be suffering from Post-Traumatic Stress Disorder (PTSD), the VA physicians referred her to the Primary Care Behavioral Health clinic. Barbara reported that she had indeed been suffering a great deal of psychological stress since returning from her final tour of duty. She described her time in Iraq as incredibly dangerous and stressful. She worked on the military police unit and was in charge of guarding prisoners of war. Her station was often attacked, and gunfire fights were a frequent occurrence. Barbara also witnessed numerous incidents in which civilians and fellow soldiers were injured and killed.

Although she was under constant threat of injury or death while in Iraq and witnessed many grotesque scenes, Barbara stated that for the first three tours she was generally able to stay focused on her work without being unduly fearful. Over time and with repeated long tours of duty, she found it increasingly difficult, however, not to be affected by the events going on around her. At the start of what was to be her last tour of duty, Barbara recalled that she felt as if she were starting to "mentally break down." When she was injured in the raid, Barbara was certain that she had been killed and remained in a state of shock for nearly 12 hours. Once she regained consciousness, Barbara describes that she "just lost it" and began screaming at the medical staff around her. She now remembers very little of that day, but recalls the feeling of total fear that overcame her, and remains with her to the present time.

In addition to the emotional difficulties Barbara faced when she came home from the war, she also was required to readjust to living in her community at home and no longer living the life of a soldier. This adjustment was difficult for Barbara not only because she had been away from her friends and family for so long, but also because she felt overwhelming distress associated with combat memories. Nevertheless, Barbara was coping well with her injury—undergoing physical therapy at the VA and getting used to life as an amputee. However, there was no denying that she was a different person than she had been before her time as a soldier, due to both her injury and the horrifying experiences she had survived during her time in Iraq.

Barbara originally planned to return to school to receive a degree in business administration when her contract with the military expired. However, since returning to the United States six months ago, Barbara has given up on this plan. She rarely leaves the house where she resides with her parents. For the first two months after her return stateside, she drank alcohol excessively on a daily basis. She noticed that drinking only seemed to make her anxiety worse, and so she stopped altogether. Though she stated she never talks about her experiences in Iraq, at least once every day she is haunted by disturbing, vivid flashbacks to violent images she witnessed while in the war. These visions also come to her in nightmares. She remarked she must have replayed the image of seeing her leg blown up thousands of times in her mind. She reported feeling as if she were in a state of constant anxiety and that she was particularly sensitive to loud, unexpected noises. As a result, Barbara reported she was often irritable and jumpy around other people, even growing angry quite easily. She expressed fears that she would never be able to make anything of her life, and that she barely felt motivated to make strides toward an independent life. Once social and outgoing, Barbara no longer has any desire to see her friends and mostly ignores her parents. Barbara described feeling emotionally "numb" and very detached from her feelings—a great departure from her usual temperament.

Relevant history: Barbara reported that she had always been "somewhat anxious," but that she never experienced this anxiety as an interference with her daily functioning. Prior to her involvement with the military, she described herself as a normal, outgoing person who was mostly content with her life. She reported no history of mental illness in her immediate family.

Symptoms: Barbara reported that since returning from Iraq, she has frequently been experiencing a number of distressing symptoms that have significantly interfered with her life. Her symptoms include difficulty sleeping, nightmares, flashbacks during the day, restlessness, feelings of detachment from others, diminished interest, feeling emotionally "numb," avoiding talking about the trauma, and feeling hypervigilance, increased anger, and irritability for the past six months.

Case formulation: Barbara's symptoms meet the required *DSM-5* criteria for Post-Traumatic Stress Disorder. During her several years in Iraq, Barbara was repeatedly exposed to dangerous, life-threatening situations and witnessed many gruesome events as a soldier. Though she was able to cope adequately at first, over time Barbara's resolve was shaken, and she began to respond to her surroundings with fear and horror, especially pertaining to the incident in which she lost part of her left leg. Her symptoms over the past six months can be categorized by the main required criteria of PTSD: intrusive recollection, avoidance/numbing, hyper-arousal, duration (at least one month), and functional significance. Barbara developed a pattern of alcohol abuse in reaction to the trauma she experienced, but with family support was able to overcome this, and her alcohol use has not recurred. Therefore, Barbara does not meet criteria for alcohol abuse.

Treatment plan: After the psychological assessment determined that Barbara was suffering from PTSD, she was referred for weekly individual psychotherapy as well as a weekly PTSD therapy group at the VA. Psychotherapy for PTSD consists of providing cognitive restructuring and some exposure to the trauma, via writing and talking about the trauma. The purpose of group therapy is to provide social support for veterans and to work on coping skills training.

Sarah Tobin, PhD

8.1 Anxiety Disorders

anxiety disorders
Disorders characterized by excessive fear and anxiety, and related disturbances in behavior.

anxiety
A future-oriented and global response, involving both cognitive and emotional components, in which an individual is inordinately apprehensive, tense, and uneasy about the prospect of something terrible happening.

The central defining feature of **anxiety disorders** is the experience of a chronic and intense feeling of **anxiety**—the sense of dread about what might happen to you in the future. The anxiety experienced by people with anxiety disorders causes them to have great difficulty functioning on a day-to-day basis. People with anxiety disorders also experience **fear,** which is the emotional response to real or perceived imminent threat. Apart from having the unpleasant feelings associated with anxiety, people with anxiety disorders go to great lengths to avoid situations that provoke this emotional response. As a result, they may have difficulty performing in their jobs, enjoying their leisure pursuits, or engaging in social activities with their friends and families.

Anxiety disorders are the most highly prevalent of all psychological disorders with the exception of substance use disorders. They have a lifetime prevalence of 28.8 percent and an overall 12-month prevalence of 18.1 percent. Of all 12-month prevalence cases, nearly 23 percent are classified as severe. The percent of people reporting lifetime prevalence across all anxiety disorders peaks between the ages of 30 and 44, with a sharp dropoff to 15.3 percent among people 60 years and older (Kessler, Chiu, Demler, Merikangas, & Walters, 2005) (Figure 8.1).

Separation Anxiety Disorder

Children with **separation anxiety disorder** have intense and inappropriate anxiety concerning separation from home or caregivers. Infants go through a developmental phase in which many of them become anxious and agitated when they are separated from their caregivers. In separation anxiety, however, these emotions continue far longer than is age appropriate.

The symptoms of separation anxiety disorder all revolve around a core of emotional distress involving situations in which they are parted from their caregivers. Even the prospect of separation causes extreme anxiety. Children with this disorder avoid situations in which they will be parted from their attachment figures. Prior to ordinary day-to-day situations, such as when their caregiver leaves for work, or even prior to going to sleep at night, they become unduly distressed. They may insist a parent stay with them until they fall asleep or may plead to sleep in their parents' bed because of nightmares involving separation. Some may refuse to sleep overnight at a friend's house or go to camp or school. When separated, they fear something terrible will happen to their parents or to themselves. Their fearful thoughts can be extreme, for example, believing if they are parted, they will be kidnapped. To avoid separation, they complain of physical symptoms such as stomachaches that would require their caregiver to stay with them. When they are not with an attachment figure, they become panicky, miserable, homesick, socially withdrawn, and sad. They are also demanding, intrusive, and in need of constant attention. Sometimes they cling so closely to a parent they will not let the parent out of their sight.

Epidemiologists estimate that 4.1 percent of children have diagnosable separation anxiety disorder and about one-third of these persist into adulthood (Shear, Jin, Ruscio, Walters, & Kessler, 2006). People with separation anxiety disorder are also at greater risk of subsequently developing other anxiety and mood disorders, such as panic disorder (Biederman et al., 2005).

The symptoms of separation anxiety seem to vary by the individual's age. Children in the age range of 5 to 8 show more signs than those who are 9 to 12. Young children report having more nightmares and excessive distress upon separation. Adolescents are more likely to report physical symptoms that keep them from going to school. Some studies show sex differences with girls reporting higher frequencies of separation anxiety symptoms and others showing an equal pattern of reporting separation anxiety symptoms. Parents tend to report the child's symptoms differently than do the children themselves. Clinicians are more likely to diagnose children with the disorder when their parents report their symptoms. However, parents and children provide different perspectives on the child's symptoms. Parents are more likely to report that the child shows symptoms of impairment, which means the child is more likely to receive a diagnosis. Children are more likely to report on the internal distress they feel. These differences in perspective mean the clinician must consider both children and caregiver perspectives when assessing the presence of this disorder in a child (Allen, Lavallee, Herren, Ruhe, & Schneider, 2010).

Theories and Treatment of Separation Anxiety Disorder A biopsychosocial model seems particularly appropriate for understanding separation anxiety disorder. There does appear to be a strong genetic component as evidenced by analyses based on twin data (Eley, Rijsdijk, Perrin, O'Connor, & Bolton, 2008).

Demographics (for lifetime prevalence)

- **Sex:** Women are 60% more likely than men to experience an anxiety disorder over their lifetime

- **Race:** Non-Hispanic blacks are 20% less likely, and Hispanics are 30% less likely, than non-Hispanic whites to experience an anxiety disorder during their lifetime

- **Age:**

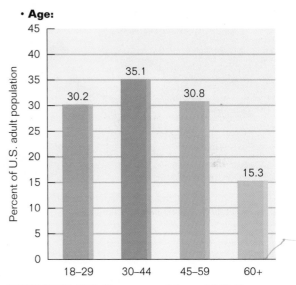

FIGURE 8.1 Demographics of Lifetime Prevalence for Anxiety Disorders

fear
The emotional response to real or perceived imminent threat.

separation anxiety disorder
A childhood disorder characterized by intense and inappropriate anxiety, lasting at least 4 weeks, concerning separation from home or caregivers.

Children with separation anxiety disorder experience extreme distress when they are apart from their primary caregivers.

However, there are also important environmental contributions to the development of this disorder. Researchers studying the risk of an adult developing internalizing symptoms, such as those seen in children with social anxiety disorder, have found the rates are higher in genetically vulnerable individuals growing up in low income environments (South & Krueger, 2011).

Children may also develop separation anxiety disorder in response to natural or manmade disasters. In the aftermath of the September 11 terrorist attacks, an estimated nearly 13 percent of New York City schoolchildren had a probable diagnosis of separation anxiety disorder (Hoven et al., 2005). It is possible that temperamental differences rooted in biology cause some children to experience heightened reactivity in these kinds of situations. From the psychodynamic and family systems perspectives, childhood anxiety disorders are the result of failing to learn how to negotiate the normal developmental tasks of separating from parents.

The majority of children diagnosed with separation anxiety disorder are completely free of symptoms within as short of a period as 18 months (Foley, Pickles, Maes, Silberg, & Eaves, 2004). However, for those who need treatment, the clinician's primary task is to help the child gain control over anxiety-provoking situations. Behavioral techniques that clinicians use for treating fears and anxieties in children include systematic desensitization, prolonged exposure, and modeling. Contingency management and self-management are also useful in teaching the child to react more positively and competently to a fear-provoking situation. The clinicians may apply behavioral techniques either individually or in combinations. For example, a child with separation anxiety disorder may learn relaxation techniques along with cognitive strategies for thinking more positively about separation (Jurbergs & Ledley, 2005).

Cognitive-behavioral therapy (CBT) seems to hold the most promise for treating children with this disorder. Researchers investigating the effectiveness of this approach have developed a form of CBT that clinicians can administer in an intensive and time-limited manner, so children do not have to commit to weeks or months of therapy. In one version of time-limited CBT, girls with separation anxiety disorder attended a one-week camp where they received intensive CBT in a group setting (Santucci, Ehrenreich, Trosper, Bennett, & Pincus, 2009) (see Table 8.1).

Selective Mutism

selective mutism
A disorder originating in childhood in which the individual consciously refuses to talk,

Refusing to talk in specific situations is the core feature of **selective mutism**. Children with this disorder are capable of using normal language, but they become almost completely silent under certain circumstances, most commonly the classroom. The estimates of this disorder's prevalence range from a low of .2 to a high of 2 percent and begin between the ages of 3 and 6, with equal frequencies among boys and girls (Kearney & Vecchio, 2007). Anxiety may be at the root of selective mutism given that children most typically show this behavior in school rather than at home (Shriver, Segool, & Gortmaker, 2011).

Behaviorist methods using shaping and exposure seem particularly well suited to treating children with selective mutism. The clinician would devise a hierarchy of desired responses beginning by rewarding the child for making any utterances, and then progressing through words and sentences, progressing from perhaps the home to the clinic and eventually to the school. Another behavioral approach uses contingency

TABLE 8.1 Summer Treatment for Girls with Separation Anxiety Disorder Program Schedule of Events

Day	Group Content	Separation	Exposure Activities
Monday 10am to 3pm	Children and Parent(s): psychoeducation; interaction between thoughts, feelings, behaviors; exposure rationale ("riding the wave" of anxiety; Subjective Units of Distress), rewards, begin cognitive restructuring (identify anxious thought; generate coping thought) Break-out Parent Group (11:30 to 12:30): differential reinforcement skills (active ignoring, creating reward system), tolerating distress in child and self, structuring of in-vivo exposures	Parents walk participants to store; separation occurs after 15 minutes of choosing beads (approx. 1:15pm)	Jewelry making (1 to 3pm)
Tuesday 10am to 3pm	Child and Parent(s): continue cognitive restructuring (identify thinking trap, evaluate evidence for worried thought) Break-out Parent Group (11am to noon): problem solving surrounding implementation of exposure or reward system, autonomy granting	At clinic, prior to departure for activity (approx. noon)	Pottery painting; eat lunch and use public transportation without parent(s)
Wednesday 10am to 3pm	Child Group: interoceptive exposure, including identification of somatic symptoms and repeated practice eliciting and habituating to relevant symptoms No Parent Group	At clinic, following homework review (approx. 10.15am)	Bowling (noon to 3pm); lunch at bowling alley
Thursday 10am to 3pm	Child Group (10am to noon): Progressive Muscle Relaxation, including measuring SUD's before and after practice and when to use PMR Parent–Group (2 to 3pm, while participants off-site at exposure activity): review of CBT skills taught to children, problem solving surrounding evening activity and sleepover, planning exposure after treatment ends	Immediately	Tour of city; lunch on way to activity; "Bravery Bingo"
Friday 6pm to 9pm	n/a	Immediately	Movie night;
Saturday 6pm–morning	n/a	Immediately	sleepover
Sunday 8am to 9am	Children and Parent(s): awards ceremony, goal setting for upcoming weeks, relapse prevention (e.g., lapse vs. relapse)	n/a	n/a

SOURCE: Santucci et al., 2009.

management, in which children receive desired rewards if they engage in the desired behavior of speaking. Contingency management seems particularly well suited for use in the home by parents. Of the two methods, shaping plus exposure therapy seems to be more effective, but contingency management in the home can nevertheless serve an important adjunct (Vecchio & Kearney, 2009).

Specific Phobias

A **phobia** is an irrational fear associated with a particular object or situation. Many people are afraid of common objects such as spiders or heights. In a **specific phobia,** however, the fear or anxiety is marked and intense. People with specific phobia go to great lengths to avoid the object or situation that is the target of their fear. If they can't get away, they endure the situation with great anxiety and distress. As is true for all anxiety disorders, a specific

phobia
An irrational fear associated with a particular object or situation.

specific phobia
An irrational and unabating fear of a particular object, activity, or situation.

A common phobia is an excessive fear of spiders.

phobia involves significant distress. Moreover, it is not a fleeting condition but must be present for at least six months in order to justify a diagnosis.

Almost any object or situation can form the target of a phobia. People can have phobias for anything from driving to syringes. The four categories of specific phobias include animals, the natural environment (storms, heights, fires), blood-injection-injury (seeing blood, having an invasive medical procedure), and engaging in activities in particular situations (driving, flying, being in an enclosed space). A fifth category of specific phobias includes a variety of miscellaneous stimuli or situations such as a child's fear of clowns or an adult's fear of contracting a particular illness.

Overall, the lifetime prevalence for specific phobia is 12.5 percent (Kessler et al., 2005). The highest lifetime prevalence rates of specific phobias involve fear of natural situations, particularly heights, estimated to be between 3.1 and 5.3 percent. Animal phobia ranges in prevalence from 3.3 to 7 percent. That these are the two most common forms of specific phobia is indicated by the fact that among people with any form of specific phobia, 50 percent have a fear of animals or a fear of heights (LeBeau et al., 2010).

Theories and Treatment of Specific Phobias

As you have just seen, there are many types of specific phobias, ranging from the common to the relatively obscure. However, the fact that they are grouped together suggests that there is a common theme or element that underlies their cause and, potentially, their treatment. As is true for panic disorder, the primary explanations of specific phobias rely on biological and psychological perspectives. Nevertheless, as is also true for panic disorder, the existence of a specific phobia in an individual can have a significant impact on those who are close to that person. Consequently, treatment sometimes involves partners and family members.

Within the biological perspective, researchers believe that the anxiety associated with specific phobias may relate to abnormalities in the anterior insular cortex (Rosso et al., 2010). This area of the brain lies between the temporal and frontal lobes associated with emotion and self-awareness. Interestingly, different specific phobias seem to show different patterns of brain activation (Lueken et al., 2011).

Treatment of specific phobias following from the biological perspective focuses on symptom management. As with panic disorder, clinicians would prescribe antianxiety medications such as benzodiazepines. However, unlike panic disorder, specific phobias are more circumscribed in nature and the situations are generally more easily avoided. Thus, clinicians would prescribe medications only when the specific phobia interferes with the individual's ability to carry on everyday activities.

The behavioral approach to specific phobias emphasizes the conditioning that occurs when the individual learns to associate unpleasant physical sensations to a certain kind of stimulus or situation. Behaviorists assume that there may be some adaptive value to having such reactions because they may truly be ones that should be feared, such as an encounter with a deadly snake. However, the maladaptive nature of the symptoms

MINI CASE

Specific Phobia, Natural Environment

Herbert is a 32-year-old lawyer seeking treatment for his irrational fear of thunderstorms. He has had this phobia since age 4, and throughout life he has developed various strategies for coping with his fear. Whenever possible, he avoids going outside when a storm is forecast. Not only will he stay within a building, but he will ensure that he is in a room with no windows and no electrical appliances. As his job has grown in responsibility, Herbert has found that he can no longer afford to take time off because of his fear, which he knows is irrational.

evolves as individuals begin to generalize this reaction to all stimuli in that category, including harmless ones. There may also be developmental aspects to specific phobias. Young children tend to fear objects or situations they can see; as they get older, the objects become more abstract in nature (such as "the bogeyman") (Davis & Ollendick, 2011). At the other end of the age spectrum, older adults with specific phobias may not report symptoms but instead misattribute their anxiety to a physical condition (Coelho et al., 2010).

According to the cognitive-behavioral view, individuals with specific phobias have overactive "alarm systems" to danger, and they perceive things as dangerous because they misinterpret stimuli. For example, the mistaken perception of an object or a situation as uncontrollable, unpredictable, dangerous, or disgusting is correlated with feelings of vulnerability. These attributions might explain the common phobia of spiders, an insect about which people have many misconceptions and apprehensions. In blood-injury-injection, by contrast, disgust and fear of contamination play a prominent role (de Jong & Peters, 2007). People with phobias also tend to overestimate the likelihood of a dangerous outcome after exposure to the feared stimulus (de Jong & Merckelbach, 2000).

Systematic desensitization is an effective behavioral method for treating specific phobia; in this method the client learns to substitute relaxation for fear through a series of graduated steps. The idea that clients learn to substitute adaptive (relaxation) for maladaptive (fear or anxiety) responses forms the basis for the four types of behavioral treatments involving exposure therapy (see Table 8.2).

In the behavioral technique called **flooding,** the client is totally immersed in the sensation of anxiety, rather than being more gradually acclimated to the feared situation. **In vivo flooding** involves exposing the client to the actual feared situation. The clinician may actually take the client to the situation that produces fear such as the top of a tall building for a client who fears heights. A variant of flooding is **imaginal flooding,** in which the clinician virtually exposes the client to the feared situation. Though requiring additional controlled studies, a number of investigations report promising findings about the ability of virtual reality exposure therapy to reduce symptoms (Parsons & Rizzo, 2008).

In vivo flooding is probably the most stressful of any of the treatments described and therefore has a high dropout rate (Choy, Fyer, & Lipsitz, 2007). An alternative is a graded *in vivo* method, involving a graduated exposure to increasingly anxiety-provoking stimuli. In the **graduated exposure** method, clients initially confront situations that cause only minor anxiety and then gradually progress toward those that cause greater anxiety. Often the therapist tries to be encouraging and to model the desired nonanxious response. In treating a client named Tan, who has a fear of enclosed spaces, the therapist could go with him into smaller and smaller rooms. Seeing his therapist showing no signs of fear could lead Tan to model the therapist's response. The therapist could also offer praise, to further reinforce the new response that Tan is learning. As illustrated in Table 8.2, behavioral treatments vary according to the nature of the client's exposure to the phobic stimulus (live or imaginal) and the degree of intensity with which the stimulus is confronted (immediate full exposure or exposure in graduated steps).

Positive reinforcement is implicit in all behavioral techniques. The therapist becomes both a guide and a source of support and praise for the client's successes.

flooding
A behavioral technique in which the client is immersed in the sensation of anxiety by being exposed to the feared situation in its entirety.

In vivo flooding
A behavioral technique in which the client is exposed to the actual feared situation.

imaginal flooding
A behavioral technique in which the client is exposed through imagination to the feared situation.

graduated exposure
A procedure in which clients gradually expose themselves to increasingly challenging anxiety-provoking situations.

TABLE 8.2 Methods of Exposure Used in Behavioral Therapy of Phobias

	Graduated Exposure	**Immediate Full Exposure**
Imagery	Systematic desensitization	Imaginal flooding
Live	Graded *in vivo*	*In vivo* flooding

The therapist may also find it useful to incorporate some techniques from the cognitive perspective into the behavioral treatment, because maladaptive thoughts are often part of the client's difficulties. Cognitive-behavioral treatment focuses on helping the client learn more adaptive ways of thinking about previously threatening situations and objects.

Cognitive restructuring can help the client view the feared situation more rationally by challenging his or her irrational beliefs about the feared stimulus. For example, a therapist may show Victor, who has an elevator phobia, that the disastrous consequences he believes will result from riding in an elevator are unrealistic and exaggerated. Victor can also learn the technique of "talking to himself" while in this situation, telling himself that his fears are ridiculous, that nothing bad will really happen, and that he will soon reach his destination.

In **thought stopping,** the individual learns to stop anxiety-provoking thoughts. In therapy, the client is supposed to alert the therapist when the anxiety-provoking thought is present; at that point, the therapist yells, "Stop!" Outside therapy, the client mentally verbalizes a similar shout each time the anxiety-provoking thought comes to mind.

thought stopping
A cognitive-behavioral method in which the client learns to stop having anxiety-provoking thoughts.

Social Anxiety Disorder

social anxiety disorder
An anxiety disorder characterized by marked, or intense, fear of anxiety of social situations in which the individual may be scrutinized by others.

The characteristic of **social anxiety disorder** is marked, or intense, fear of anxiety of social situations in which the individual may be scrutinized by others. Some people with social anxiety disorder experience their symptoms only when they are in a performance situation. But the disorder may also occur for other people when they are in ordinary social settings. Essentially, the anxiety the person experiences is centered on a desire to avoid humiliation or embarrassment. Even a simple act such as drinking can provoke symptoms of fear or anxiety. *DSM-5* introduced this as a new diagnostic term but still includes social phobia in parentheses to link it to the previous diagnosis in *DSM-IV-TR*.

The lifetime prevalence of social anxiety disorder is 12.1 percent in the United States, making it the second most common form of anxiety disorder. Of the 6.8 percent who develop this disorder over a 12-month period, nearly 30 percent are classified as severe (Kessler et al., 2005).

Theories and Treatment of Social Anxiety Disorder   As is true for the anxiety disorders we have covered already, biological approaches to social anxiety disorder are focused on abnormalities in the brain mechanisms involved in fear and anxiety. Additionally, however, studies on genetic contributions to social anxiety disorder suggest the disorder may be partially genetically based. Researchers have established some links between social anxiety disorder and the traits of shyness and neuroticism, which may be, in part, inherited (Stein & Vythilingum, 2007).

The categories of medications shown to be most effective for social anxiety disorder are SSRIs and SNRIs. Other medications used to treat this disorder that may be as effective have considerable drawbacks. Benzodiazepines have significant potential for

MINI CASE
Social Anxiety Disorder, Performance Only Type

Ted is a 19-year-old college student who reports that he is terrified at the prospect of speaking in class. His anxiety about this matter is so intense that he has enrolled in very large lecture classes, where he sits in the back of the room, slouching in his chair to make himself as invisible as possible. On occasion, one of his professors randomly calls on students to answer certain questions. When this occurs, Ted begins to sweat and tremble. Sometimes he rushes from the classroom and frantically runs back to the dormitory for a few hours and tries to calm himself down.

abuse; moreover, they may actually interfere with treatment involving psychological methods such as exposure to feared situations. MAOIs, which can also effectively manage social anxiety symptoms, have potentially dangerous side effects (Jorstad-Stein & Heimberg, 2009).

Apart from whatever genetic contributions may make some children more likely to develop social anxiety disorder, there are changes that take place in childhood and adolescence that can also heighten an individual's risk of developing this disorder. In particular, being able to think about how you are viewed by others, an ability that emerges in adolescence, may interact with physiological vulnerability to lead to the appearance of symptoms (Roberson-Nay & Brown, 2011).

The cognitive-behavioral perspective approach regards people with social anxiety disorder as unable to gain a realistic view of how others really perceive them. As with other forms of cognitive-behavioral therapy, the clinician attempts to reframe the client's thoughts in combination with real or imagined exposure. Virtually any form of cognitive-behavioral therapy seems to be highly effective, including group or individually based treatment. For clients who do not respond to psychotherapy or medication, there are promising signs about the benefits of alternative methods including motivational interviewing, acceptance and commitment therapy, and mindfulness/meditation. Treatment of social anxiety disorder can be particularly challenging, however, because clients may tend to socially isolate themselves and therefore have fewer opportunities to expose themselves in the course of their daily lives to challenging situations. Unlike people with other types of anxiety disorders, the impaired social skills of people with social anxiety disorder may lead them to experience negative reactions from others, thus confirming their fears. However, on the positive side, cognitive-behavioral therapy is an effective method on its own that can be administered across a variety of treatment settings from private practice to community mental health and counseling centers (Jorstad-Stein & Heimberg, 2009).

Social anxiety disorder causes distress by preventing an individual from engaging in social activities they would normally enjoy.

Panic Disorder and Agoraphobia

In *DSM-IV-TR*, agoraphobia was not considered a diagnosis separate from panic disorder. The *DSM-5*, consistent with emerging research and the *ICD*, now separates the two disorders although the two diagnoses may be assigned if the individual meets the criteria for both disorders. We present them in one section because the majority of research on theories and treatment was conducted on the basis of the *DSM-IV-TR* diagnostic categorization.

Panic Disorder   People with **panic disorder** experience periods of intense physical discomfort known as **panic attacks.** During a panic attack, the individual feels overwhelmed by a range of highly unpleasant physical sensations. These can include respiratory distress (shortness of breath, hyperventilation, feeling of choking), autonomic disturbances (sweating, stomach distress, shaking or trembling, heart palpitations), and sensory abnormalities (dizziness, numbness, or tingling). During a panic attack, people may also feel that they are "going crazy" or losing control. The most commonly reported symptoms of a panic attack are palpitations ("heart pounding") and dizziness (Craske et al., 2010).

Having an occasional panic attack is not enough to justify the clinician's assigning this diagnosis to the client. The panic attacks must happen more than once. Furthermore, the clinician needs to see evidence that the client was fearful of another attack for at least a month. It's also possible that the clinician would assign this diagnosis after

panic disorder
An anxiety disorder in which an individual has panic attacks on a recurrent basis or has constant apprehension and worry about the possibility of recurring attacks.

panic attack
A period of intense fear and physical discomfort accompanied by the feeling that one is being overwhelmed and is about to lose control.

establishing that the client engages in maladaptive behaviors to avoid another attack, such as deliberately staying away from situations in which another panic attack might occur. The fear of having another attack or deliberate avoidance of possible situations that may cause the client to experience a panic attack distinguishes panic disorder from other psychological disorders that may involve panic attacks. *DSM-5* includes specifiers for panic attacks, indicating the nature of the symptoms the individual experiences such as palpitations, sweating, trembling, chest pain, nausea, chills, fear of going "crazy," and fear of dying.

agoraphobia
Intense anxiety triggered by the real or anticipated exposure to situations in which they may be unable to get help should they become incapacitated.

Agoraphobia In **agoraphobia,** the individual feels intense fear or anxiety triggered by the real or anticipated exposure to situations such as using public transportation, being in an enclosed space such as a theater or an open space such as a parking lot, and being outside of the home alone. People with agoraphobia are fearful not of the situations themselves, but of the possibility that they can't get help or escape if they have panic-like symptoms or other embarrassing or incapacitating symptoms. Their fear or anxiety is out of proportion to the actual danger involved in the situation. Should the person be forced to endure such a situation, he or she is extremely fearful and anxious, or requires the presence of a companion. As with other psychological disorders, these symptoms must persist over time (in this case, at least six months), cause considerable distress, and not be due to another psychological or medical disorder.

Panic attacks are estimated to occur in 20 percent or more of adult samples; panic disorder has a much lower lifetime prevalence of between 3 and 5 percent. Across a variety of studies, settings, and diagnostic criteria, approximately 25 percent of people who have *DSM-5* panic disorder with the agoraphobia syndrome would meet diagnostic criteria for agoraphobia alone (Wittchen, Gloster, Beesdo-Baum, Fava, & Craske, 2010).

Theories and Treatment of Panic Disorder and Agoraphobia Researchers studying biological contributions to panic disorder focus on norepinephrine, the neurotransmitter involved in preparing the body to react to stressful situations. Higher levels of norepinephrine can make the individual more likely to experience fear, anxiety, and panic. Serotonin may also play a role in increasing a person's likelihood of developing panic disorder due to the role of this neurotransmitter in anxiety (Kalk, Nutt, & Lingford-Hughes, 2011). Furthermore, according to **anxiety sensitivity theory,** people who develop panic disorder have heightened responsiveness to the presence of carbon dioxide in the blood. Hence, they are more likely to panic due to the sensation that they are suffocating (Pérez Benítez et al., 2009).

anxiety sensitivity theory
The belief that panic disorder is caused in part by the tendency to interpret cognitive and somatic manifestations of stress and anxiety in a catastrophic manner.

conditioned fear reactions
Acquired associations between an internal or external cue and feelings of intense anxiety.

The most effective antianxiety medications for panic disorder and agoraphobia are benzodiazepines, which increase the availability of GABA, an inhibitory neurotransmitter. However, because they can lead clients to become dependent on them or to abuse them, clinicians may prefer to prescribe selective serotonin or norepinephrine reuptake inhibitors (SSRIs or SNRIs) (Pollack & Simon, 2009).

From a classical conditioning perspective, panic disorder results from **conditioned fear reactions** in which the individual associates unpleasant bodily sensations with memories of

MINI CASE

Panic Disorder and Agoraphobia

Frieda is a 28-year-old former postal worker who sought treatment because of recurrent panic attacks, which have led her to become fearful of driving. She has become so frightened of the prospect of having an attack on the job that she has asked for a medical leave. Although initially she would leave the house when accompanied by her mother, she now is unable to go out under any circumstances, and her family is concerned that she will become a total recluse.

In relaxation therapy, patients learn a variety of techniques that focus on breathing and relaxation in order to overcome the physiological symptoms of anxiety.

the last panic attack, causing a full-blown panic attack to develop even before measurable biological changes have occurred. Building on this notion, the cognitive-behavioral model of anxiety disorders proposes that individuals with panic disorder experience a vicious cycle that begins with the individual's feeling the unpleasant bodily sensations of a panic attack. These sensations in turn lead the person to feel that the panic attack is unpredictable and uncontrollable and that he or she doesn't have the ability to stop the panic attack from occurring (White, Brown, Somers, & Barlow, 2006).

Relaxation training is one behavioral technique used to help clients gain control over the bodily reactions involved in panic attacks. After training, the client should be able to relax the entire body when confronting a feared situation. Hyperventilation, a common symptom in panic attacks, is sometimes treated with a form of counterconditioning. In this approach, the client hyperventilates intentionally and then begins slow breathing, a response that is incompatible with hyperventilation. Following this training, the client can begin the slow breathing at the first signs of hyperventilation. Thus, the client learns that it is possible to exert voluntary control over hyperventilation. In the method known as **panic-control therapy (PCT)**, the therapist combines breathing retraining, psychoeducation, and cognitive restructuring to help individuals recognize and ultimately control the bodily cues associated with panic attacks (Hofmann, Rief, & Spiegel, 2010).

relaxation training
A behavioral technique used in the treatment of anxiety disorders that involves progressive and systematic patterns of muscle tensing and relaxing.

panic-control therapy (PCT)
Treatment that consists of cognitive restructuring, exposure to bodily cues associated with panic attacks, and breathing retraining.

Generalized Anxiety Disorder

In contrast to the forms of anxiety disorders you've just learned about, **generalized anxiety disorder** does not have a particular focus. People with generalized anxiety disorder feel anxious for much of the time, even though they can't necessarily say why. In addition to anxiety, people with this disorder worry a great deal, apprehensively expecting the worst to happen to them. Their symptoms span a range of physical and psychological experiences including general restlessness, sleep disturbances, feelings of being easily fatigued, irritability, muscle tension, and trouble concentrating to the point where their mind goes blank. There is no particular situation that they can identify as lying at the root of their anxiety, and they find it very difficult to control their worrying.

generalized anxiety disorder
An anxiety disorder characterized by anxiety and worry that is not associated with a particular object, situation, or event but seems to be a constant feature of a person's day-to-day existence.

REAL STORIES

Paula Deen: Panic Disorder and Agoraphobia

"What sickness did I have? What had happened to me? My terror had no name—least none I'd ever heard. I was alone with it. So scared about goin' *outside*. It wasn't always this way."

Paula Deen's rise to fame may never have occurred if she didn't have the courage to overcome a debilitating case of panic disorder with agoraphobia. Though Paula is now a world-famous American author of several best-selling cookbooks, owner of several successful restaurants and her own television show, her early life was plagued by unrelenting anxiety and an inability to leave her house most of the time. Her memoir, *It Ain't All About the Cookin'*, gives a charismatic and candid account of her unlikely, triumphant rise to fame after suffering from a psychological disorder she kept to herself for nearly 20 years.

Paula was born in 1947 in Albany, Georgia, and recalls having a very happy childhood, with loving parents and grandparents and a brother. In *It Ain't All About the Cookin'*, she describes having a typical adolescence with many good friends and boyfriends. It was in her youth where she first realized her love of food and cooking. "Not just the eating of it, but what it meant in life: food as comfort, food as friendship, food as sensual expression."

At 18, she married her first husband, Jimmy, who battled with alcoholism throughout their marriage. Shortly after they were married though, Paula's life was forever changed when her father died tragically at the age of 40, as a result of complications from heart surgery.

"That's the exact time my panic attacks really started," she writes in *It Ain't All About the Cookin'*. "When something snatches away that rug that you call security, you land on your ass. My daddy was my security . . . I was so frightened be-cause I had no idea why death would affect my life so early . . . I finally figured it out . . . the reason Daddy had died was because *I* was gonna die soon . . . and so at age nineteen, after that terrible time, I started waking up many mornings and wondering if this was the day I'd die. I'd get up and check my pulse, feel my heart, cough as I tried to spit up the blood that would finally tell me for sure that it was all over for me . . . I never told anybody. I just got up waiting to die by myself. And these thoughts just went on and on and on for twenty years, more or less."

Four years after her father passed away, Paula's mother discovered she had bone cancer. After a leg amputation failed to stop the cancer from spreading, her mother passed away. Though she had already been suffering from severe anxiety and frequent panic attacks, Paula recalls that it was after her mother's death when her mental health took a turn for the worse. "I was in pretty poor shape . . . at about twenty-three, an impending sense of doom really hung over me, as if I'd be living in a dark valley forever. Every day I thought I'd die, or, even worse, someone I loved would die. The blackness still didn't have a name." Though it was clear that Paula was grieving the loss of both of her parents, the "blackness" she referred to lasted for much longer than might typically be expected for a period of bereavement, and indicated that she was indeed struggling with a very serious psychological condition. In the book, she describes her symptoms, which are typical of those suffering from agoraphobia. "Almost every last time I had to go outside by myself, that panic would start in and drop me to my knees. Couldn't breathe, couldn't stop trembling. I felt weak and nauseated and dizzy, and I just knew I was gonna die in front of other people . . . So scared about goin' *outside*."

Paula had two sons, and continued to suffer from panic throughout her pregnancies and while she was raising the children. She was often unable to leave the house

Paula Deen found comfort in cooking when coping with an anxiety disorder.

without great difficulty, even to run small errands. Dealing with her troubled relationship with her husband, as well as a litany of financial struggles, she recalls this time as the darkest in her life, though she chose to keep her suffering hidden from her family. When she finally mustered the courage to seek help for her condition, being unable to afford a psychiatrist, Paula sought the help of a church minister who had a degree in psychology. She was discouraged to find the minister was unsupportive and unwilling to help her, instead urging her to support her alcoholic husband. Frustrated and mired in anxiety, often feeling "crippled by this fright I had," she found solace in her kitchen and honed in on her skill for cooking delicious, traditional southern food. "The one thing I could rely on was my stove . . . the cooking didn't give me wings to soar, but it gave me a grounding, a feeling of safety just in smellin' the good aromas of my childhood. I was in my own home, I was cooking, I was feeding my family; I was

almost like a real wife, I told myself."

Paula's family relocated to Savannah, and with the help of some neighbors, Paula was able to open up about her illness and gain the confidence to turn her life around. She finally learned the name of what she was suffering from by hearing about it on the television show *Phil Donahue*—and also learned that she was not alone in her struggling. "Finally—it finally had a name. Agoraphobia . . . he said that agoraphobics had horrible anxiety about being in places or embarrassing situations from which they might not be able to escape. *That was me.*" She immediately identified with all of the symptoms described on the show. From that point she began leaving the house for longer and longer periods of time, eventually getting a job as a bank teller. She suffered from a setback to her progress after being held up at gunpoint while working at the bank, and once again felt defenseless against her agoraphobia. It was the support of a

close friend that helped her once again begin to recover from her illness. She writes; "One day, I was lying in bed, and, well—you know what? All of a sudden Denise's words made sense to me. Simple as that. 'Get out of bed,' she'd said. So, this particular morning, I got out of my bed, stood up, and looked in the mirror. I was only forty but I was stuck in my bedroom and dying inside. Out loud, I whispered to my mirror image, 'I can't do this anymore, I just can't.'" Again, Paula slowly began to recover, step by step and day by day.

She eventually divorced her husband and thus began her steady rise to fame. Happily remarried in 2004, Paula now looks back at her struggles with agoraphobia, which helps her appreciate her good fortune and success. "You can never be too sure that success or happiness will last forever," she writes, recalling the struggle she endured to get to where she is now. One constant in her life that has helped her through is her loving family and her love of cooking.

Generalized anxiety disorder has a lifetime prevalence of 5.7 percent. Over a 12-month period, the prevalence is reported to be 3.1 percent; of these, 32 percent are classified as severe (Kessler et al., 2005).

Theories and Treatment of Generalized Anxiety Disorder

Researchers believe that people with generalized anxiety disorder experience their symptoms due to disturbances in GABA, serotonergic, and noradrenergic systems (Nutt & Malizia, 2001). Support for the notion that there is a biological component to generalized anxiety disorder is the finding of an overlap in genetic vulnerability with

MINI CASE

Generalized Anxiety Disorder

Gina is a 32-year-old single mother of two children seeking professional help for her long-standing feelings of anxiety. Despite the fact that her life is relatively stable in terms of financial and interpersonal matters, she worries most of the time that she will develop financial problems, that her children will become ill, and that the political situation in the country will make life for her and her children more difficult. Although she tries to

dismiss these concerns as excessive, she finds it virtually impossible to control her worrying. Most of the time, she feels uncomfortable and tense, and sometimes her tension becomes so extreme that she begins to tremble and sweat. She finds it difficult to sleep at night. During the day she is restless, keyed up, and tense. She has consulted a variety of medical specialists, each of whom has been unable to diagnose a physical problem.

the personality trait of neuroticism (see Chapter 3). In other words, people who are prone to developing this disorder have inherited an underlying neurotic personality style (Hettema, Prescott, & Kendler, 2004).

The symptoms of generalized anxiety disorder are perhaps best understood from a psychological standpoint as products of cognitive distortions (Aikins & Craske, 2001). People with generalized anxiety disorder become easily distressed and worried by the minor nuisances and small disruptions of life. If something goes wrong in their day-to-day existence, such as car trouble, an argument with a co-worker, or a home repair problem, they magnify the extent of the problem and become unduly apprehensive about the outcome. Their attention shifts from the problem itself to their worries, further escalating their level of worry. As a result, people with generalized anxiety disorder are less efficient in their daily tasks so that they actually have more to worry about as more goes wrong for them. Compounding the problem is their lack of confidence in their ability to control or manage their anxious feelings and reactions.

Cognitive-behavioral therapy builds on the assumption that cognitive distortions contribute to generalized anxiety (Borkovec & Ruscio, 2001). In this type of therapy, clients learn how to recognize anxious thoughts, to seek more rational alternatives to worrying, and to take action to test these alternatives. Clinicians using this approach attempt to break the cycle of negative thoughts and worries. Once this cycle is broken, the individual can develop a sense of control over the worrying behavior and become more proficient at managing and reducing anxious thoughts. Over the long run, clients may benefit more from psychotherapy rather than psychopharmacological interventions (Falsetti & Davis, 2001).

8.2 Obsessive-Compulsive and Related Disorders

obsession
An unwanted thought, word, phrase, or image that persistently and repeatedly comes into a person's mind and causes distress.

compulsion
A repetitive and seemingly purposeful behavior performed in response to uncontrollable urges or according to a ritualistic or stereotyped set of rules.

obsessive-compulsive disorder (OCD)
An anxiety disorder characterized by recurrent obsessions or compulsions that are inordinately time-consuming or that cause significant distress or impairment.

An **obsession** is a recurrent and persistent thought, urge, or image that the individual experiences as intrusive and unwanted. Individuals try to ignore or suppress the obsession, or try to neutralize it by engaging in some other thought or action. The thought or action that the person uses to try to neutralize the obsession is known as a **compulsion,** a repetitive behavior or mental act performed according to rigid rules that the person feels driven to carry out. The compulsions need not, however, be paired with obsessions.

In the disorder known as **obsessive-compulsive disorder (OCD)**, individuals experience either obsessions or compulsions to such an extent that they find it difficult to conduct their daily activities. As part of the disorder, they may experience significant distress or impairment in their occupational or social functioning. Many more individuals than those diagnosed with the disorder seek help for OCD-like symptoms (Leckman et al., 2010).

The most common compulsions involve the repetition of a specific behavior, such as washing and cleaning, counting, putting items in order, checking, or

MINI CASE

Obsessive-Compulsive Disorder, with Poor Insight

Mark is a 16-year-old high-school student referred for treatment by his teacher, who became disturbed by Mark's irrational concern about the danger posed by an electrical outlet at the front of the classroom. Mark pleaded daily with the teacher to have the outlet disconnected to prevent someone from accidentally getting electrocuted while walking by it. The teacher told Mark that his concerns were unfounded, but he remained so distressed that he felt driven, when entering and leaving the classroom, to shine a flashlight into the outlet to make sure that a loose wire was not exposed. During class time, he could think of nothing else but the outlet.

requesting assurance. Compulsions may also take the form of mental rituals, such as counting up to a certain number every time an unwanted thought intrudes. Some individuals with OCD experience tics, a pattern of abnormal motor symptoms, such as uncontrollable twitches, vocalizations, and facial grimaces.

In general, there appear to be four major dimensions to the symptoms of OCD: obsessions associated with checking compulsions, the need to have symmetry and to put things in order, obsessions about cleanliness associated with compulsions to wash, and hoarding-related behaviors (Mataix-Cols, Rosario-Campos, & Leckman, 2005). Table 8.3 lists items from the Yale-Brown Obsessive-Compulsive Symptom Checklist, an instrument commonly used for assessing individuals with OCD.

OCD has a lifetime prevalence of 1.6 percent. The 12-month prevalence is slightly lower, 1 percent; of these about half are classified as severe (Kessler et al., 2005).

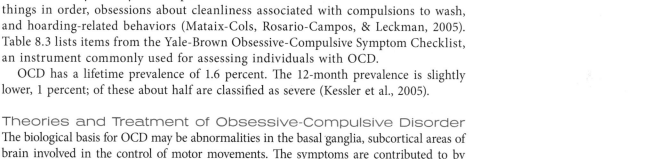

What's New in the DSM-5

Definition and Categorization of Anxiety Disorders

The *DSM-5* saw major changes in the definition and categorization of anxiety disorders. OCD is categorized with body dysmorphic disorder, hoarding disorder, trichotillomania (excessive hair-pulling), and skin-picking. Acute and post-traumatic stress disorders moved into their own category of "Trauma and Stressor-Related Disorders." Agoraphobia became a separate disorder, much as it is now in the ICD-10. In addition, social anxiety disorder had been called social phobia in *DSM-IV-TR*. The change reflects the fact that social anxiety disorder is not a "phobia," in the sense of representing fear of other people, although social phobia still appears in parentheses. Finally, several disorders formerly in the group of disorders that originated in childhood (a designation now dropped) were moved into the anxiety disorder grouping.

Theories and Treatment of Obsessive-Compulsive Disorder

The biological basis for OCD may be abnormalities in the basal ganglia, subcortical areas of brain involved in the control of motor movements. The symptoms are contributed to by failure of the prefrontal cortex to inhibit unwanted thoughts, images, or urges. Supporting this explanation are findings from brain scans showing heightened levels of activity in the brain motor control centers of the basal ganglia and frontal lobes (Cocchi et al., 2012).

Treatment with clomipramine or other serotonin reuptake inhibiting medications, such as fluoxetine (Prozac) or sertraline (Zoloft), is the most effective biological treatment available for obsessive-compulsive disorder (Kellner, 2010). In extreme cases in which no other treatments provide symptom relief, people with OCD may be treated with psychiatric neurosurgery. For example, deep brain stimulation to areas of the brain involved in motor control can help relieve symptoms by reducing the activity of the prefrontal cortex, which, in turn, may help reduce the frequency of obsessive-compulsive thoughts (Le Jeune et al., 2010).

The cognitive-behavioral perspective toward understanding OCD proposes that maladaptive thought patterns contribute to the development and maintenance of OCD symptoms. Individuals with OCD may be primed to overreact to anxiety-producing events in their environment. Such priming may place OCD in a spectrum of so-called internalizing disorders that would include other anxiety and mood disorders involving a similar pattern of startle reactivity (Vaidyanathan, Patrick, & Cuthbert, 2009). For people with OCD, these experiences become transformed to disturbing images, which they then try to suppress or counteract by engaging in compulsive rituals. Complicating their symptoms are beliefs in the danger and meaning of their thoughts, or their "metacognitions," which lead people with OCD to worry, ruminate, and feel that they must monitor their every thought (Solem, Håland, Vogel, Hansen, & Wells, 2009).

Psychological interventions provide an important supplement to or replacement for medication to treat OCD symptoms (Anand, Sudhir, Math, Thennarasu, & Janardhan Reddy, 2011). For example, clinicians may use thought stopping to help clients reduce obsessional thinking, as in exposure to situations that provoke compulsive rituals or obsessions (Bakker, 2009). The clinician

Some people with obsessive-compulsive disorder worry incessantly about germs and dirt, and feel irresistible urges to clean and sanitize.

TABLE 8.3   Sample Items from the Yale-Brown Obsessive-Compulsive Symptom Checklist

Scale	Sample items
Aggressive obsessions	Fear might harm self Fear of blurting out obscenities Fear will be responsible for something else terrible happening (e.g., fire, burglary)
Contamination obsessions	Concerns or disgust with bodily waste or secretions (e.g., urine, feces, saliva) Bothered by sticky substances or residues
Sexual obsessions	Forbidden or perverse sexual thoughts, images, or impulses Sexual behavior toward others (aggressive)
Hoarding/saving obsessions	Distinguish from hobbies and concern with objects of monetary or sentimental value
Religious obsessions	Concerned with sacrilege and blasphemy Excess concern with right/wrong, morality
Obsession with need for symmetry or exactness	Accompanied by magical thinking (e.g., concerned that another will have an accident unless things are in the right place)
Miscellaneous obsessions	Fear of saying certain things Lucky/unlucky numbers Colors with special significance Superstitious fears
Somatic obsessions	Concern with illness or disease Excessive concern with body part or aspect of appearance (e.g., dysmorphophobia)
Cleaning/washing compulsions	Excessive or ritualized hand-washing Excessive or ritualized showering, bathing, toothbrushing, grooming, or toilet routine
Checking compulsions	Checking locks, stove, appliances, etc. Checking that nothing terrible did not/will not harm self Checking that did not make mistake completing a task
Repeating rituals	Rereading or rewriting Need to repeat routine activities (e.g., in/out door, up/down from chair)
Counting compulsions	(Check for presence)
Ordering/arranging compulsions	(Check for presence)
Hoarding/collecting compulsions	Distinguish from hobbies and concern with objects of monetary or sentimental value (e.g., carefully reads junk mail, sorts through garbage)
Miscellaneous compulsions	Excessive list making Need to tell, ask, or confess Need to touch, tap, or rub Rituals involving blinking or staring

SOURCE: From W. K. Goodman, L. H. Price, S. A. Rasmussen, C. Mazure, P. Delgado, G. R. Heninger, and D. S. Charney (1989a), "The Yale-Brown Obsessive-Compulsive Scale II. Validity" in *Archives of General Psychiatry*, 46, pp. 1012–1016. Reprinted with permission of Wayne Goodman.

Psychiatric Neurosurgery

As we discussed in Chapter 4, psychiatric neurosurgery is increasingly being used to give clinicians a tool for controlling the symptoms of obsessive-compulsive disorder. However, to what extent is surgical intervention justifiable to control the existence of psychological symptoms? Moreover, this surgery is not reversible. The debate over psychosurgery goes back to the mid-twentieth century when physician Walter Freeman traveled around the country performing approximately 18,000 leucotomies in which he severed the frontal lobes from the rest of the brain to control the unmanageable behaviors of psychiatric patients. The idea was that by severing the frontal lobes from the limbic system, the patients would no longer be controlled by their impulses.

As was true in the early twentieth century, when clinicians employed lobotomies to manage otherwise intractable symptoms of psychiatric patients, is it possible that future generations will look upon cingulotomies and similar interventions as excessively punitive and even barbaric? On the other hand, with symptoms that are so severe and disabling, is any method that can control them to be used even if imperfect?

Gillett (2011) raised these issues regarding the use of current psychosurgeries. By altering the individual's brain through such radical techniques, psychiatrists are tampering with a complex system of interactions that make up the individual's personality. Just because they "work," and because no other methods are currently available, does this justify making permanent changes to the individual's brain? The victims of the leucotomies performed by Freeman "improved" in that their behavior became more docile, but they were forever changed.

Q: *You be the judge:* Is it appropriate to transform the person using permanent methods whose basis for effectiveness cannot be scientifically established? As Gillett concludes, "burn, heat, poke, freeze, shock, cut, stimulate or otherwise shake (but not stir) the brain and you will affect the psyche" (p. 43).

may combine exposure with response prevention, in which the clinician instructs the client to stop performing compulsive behaviors, and satiation therapy, in which clients confront their obsessional thoughts for so long that they lose their meaning (Khoda-rahimi, 2009).

Body Dysmorphic Disorder

People with **body dysmorphic disorder (BDD)** are preoccupied with the idea that a part of their body is ugly or defective. Their preoccupation goes far beyond the ordinary dissatisfaction that many people feel about the size and shape of their body or appearance of a bodily part. People with BDD may check themselves constantly, groom themselves to an excessive degree, or constantly seek reassurance from others about how they look. In fact, almost all perform at least one compulsive behavior (Phillips et al., 2010). They don't merely see themselves as fat or excessively heavy, but they may believe that their body build is too small or not muscular enough.

Although as many as 29 percent of college students are preoccupied with concerns about their body image, only 14 percent of those who are preoccupied meet the criteria for BDD. Overall, at any one point in time, 2.5 percent of women and 2.2 percent of men meet the criteria for BDD, though men may experience more distress over their symptoms than women. The most common areas that concern them are their skin, hair, and nose. However, men are more likely to be concerned with their body build and with thinning hair. Women are more concerned about their weight and hips. BDD is frequently accompanied by major depressive disorder, social anxiety disorder, obsessive-compulsive disorder, and eating disorders. Up to one-third may be delusional, such as being convinced that others are talking about or laughing at the imagined defect in their

body dysmorphic disorder
A disorder in which individuals are preoccupied with the idea that a part of their body is ugly or defective.

TABLE 8.4 Body Dysmorphic Disorder Modification of the Yale-Brown Obsessive-Compulsive Scale (BDD-YOCS)

This modification of the Yale-Brown Obsessive-Compulsive Scale uses the following criteria to determine the severity of the client's symptoms regarding the presumed body defect or defects:

1. Time occupied by thoughts about body defect
2. Interference due to thoughts about body defect
3. Distress associated with thoughts about body defect
4. Resistance against thoughts about body defect
5. Degree of control over thoughts about body defect
6. Time spent in activities related to body defect such as mirror checking, grooming, excessive exercise, camouflaging, picking at skin, asking others about defect
7. Interference due to thoughts about body defect
8. Distress associated with activities related to body defect
9. Resistance against compulsions
10. Degree of control over compulsive behavior
11. Insight into the nature of excessive concern over defect
12. Avoidance of activities due to concern over defect

SOURCE: http://www.veale.co.uk/wp-content/uploads/2010/11/BDD-YBOCS-Adult.pdf.

appearance. People with BDD have a rate of completed suicides that is 45 times that of the general population in the United States (Phillips, Menard, Fay, & Pagano, 2005). Table 8.4 shows the sample rating items from the Body Dysmorphic Disorder version of the Yale-Brown Obsessive-Compulsive Disorder Scale (BDD-YBOCS) with the range of associated symptoms with the disorder.

There are also cross-cultural aspects to BDD. In Japan, the belief that one's physical appearance is offensive to others is *shubo-kyufo,* a subtype of *taijin kyofusho,* or "fear of interpersonal relations." The syndrome *koro or suoyang* ("shrinkage of the penis" in

Individuals with body dysmorphic disorder often feel that their appearance is much more flawed than how they actually appear to others.

Body Dysmorphic Disorder, with Poor Insight

Lydia is a 43-year-old woman whose local surgeon referred her to the mental health clinic. For the past 8 years, Lydia has visited plastic surgeons across the country to find one who will perform surgery to reduce the size of her hands, which she perceives as "too fat." Until she has this surgery, she will not leave her house without wearing gloves. The plastic surgeon concurs with Lydia's family members and friends that Lydia's perception of her hands is distorted and that plastic surgery would be inappropriate and irresponsible.

Chinese) involves fear of genital retraction into the body. Individuals who suffer from *koro* also experience other BDD symptoms (Fang & Hofmann, 2010).

Treatment from a biological perspective involves medications, particularly SSRIs, which can reduce the associated symptoms of depression and anxiety as well as the BDD symptoms of distress, bodily preoccupations, and compulsions. Once on SSRIs, people with BDD can experience improved quality of life, overall functioning, and insight into their disorder (Bjornsson, Didie, & Phillips, 2010). Although medications help to ameliorate the symptoms of BDD, they do not address the cognitive components of the disorder, nor are they as effective (Williams, Hadjistavropoulos, & Sharpe, 2006).

From the biopsychosocial perspective, we regard people with BDD as having biological predisposition, but critical to the development of the disorder were experiences they may have had in adolescence, such as being teased about their appearance or made to feel sensitive in some other way, particularly to rejection. Once they start to believe that their bodily appearance is defective or deviates from the ideal to which they aspire, they become preoccupied with this belief. In other words, the cognitive processes underlying BDD are excessive self-focused attention on their negative body image. Reinforcing their preoccupations are the checking rituals in which they engage, which temporarily lower their anxiety levels. Similarly, they learn to avoid being with other people which, again, serves as reinforcement (Veale, 2010).

Clinicians treating clients with BDD from a cognitive-behavioral perspective focus on helping them to understand that appearance is only one aspect of their total identity, while at the same time challenging them to question their assumptions that their appearance is, in fact, defective. They may also use response prevention and exposure. We also can use cognitive restructuring at the same time. Clients look at themselves in a mirror while changing their thoughts about what they see (Wilhelm, Buhlmann, Hayward, Greenberg, & Dimaite, 2010). Additionally, interpersonal therapy can be useful to help people with BDD develop improved strategies for dealing with the distress they feel in their relationships with others, as well as addressing their low self-esteem and depressed mood (Bjornsson, et al., 2010).

Hoarding Disorder

In the compulsion known as **hoarding,** people have persistent difficulties discarding or parting with their possessions, even if they are not of much value. These difficulties include any form of discarding, including putting items into the garbage. They believe these items to have utility, to have aesthetic or sentimental value, but in reality the items often consist of old newspapers, bags, or leftover food.

When faced the prospect of discarding them, these individuals become distressed. However, in reality, their homes can become unlivable due to the clutter that accumulates over the years. The rooms in their living space fill up with a mixture of objects that are actually of value, such as collector's items, and items that ordinarily would be thrown away, such as old magazines. Unlike ordinary collectors, who organize their items in a systematic way, people with hoarding disorder accumulate items without any form of organization.

hoarding

A compulsion in which people have persistent difficulties discarding things, even if they have little value

Older adults appear to be more likely than younger adults to develop hoarding disorder. Because the disorder only became a diagnosis on its own in *DSM-5*, the only prevalence data available are the estimates the authors cite, which is from 2 to 6% of adults. A substantial percent of adults with hoarding disorder also have comorbid depressive symptoms (Hall, Tolin, Frost, & Steketee, 2013).

Treatment of hoarding disorder that follows a biopsychosocial approach appears to have the most effectiveness (Tolin, 2011). Biological treatments have traditionally included SSRIs, but researchers believe the disorder may also have a neurocognitive component that would warrant treatment through addressing cognitive function. In this regard, cognitive-behavioral therapy can not only address changes in hoarding behavior but also help clients with this disorder improve their attentional functions. Practical assistance from movers or professional organizers may be useful in supplementing medications and cognitive-behavioral treatment. Friends, family members, and local officials may also be consulted to assist in clearing the individual's living space.

Trichotillomania (Hair-Pulling Disorder)

trichotillomania (hair-pulling disorder)
The compulsive, persistent urge to pull out one's own hair.

A diagnosis of **trichotillomania (hair-pulling disorder)** is given to individuals who pull out their hair in response to an increasing sense of tension or urge. After they pull their hair, they feel relief, pleasure, or gratification. People with trichotillomania are upset by their uncontrollable behavior and may find that their social, occupational, or other areas of functioning are impaired because of this disorder. They feel unable to stop this behavior, even when the pulling results in bald patches and lost eyebrows, eyelashes, armpit hair, and pubic hair. As individuals get older, they increase the number of bodily sites from which they pull hair (Flessner, Woods, Franklin, Keuthen, & Piacentini, 2009).

People with this disorder experience significant impairment in areas of life ranging from sexual intimacy to social activities, medical examinations, and haircuts. They may also develop a range of physical symptoms including the development of hairballs (trichobezoars), which settle in their gastrointestinal tract, causing abdominal pain, nausea and vomiting, weakness, and weight loss. They can also develop skin infections, scalp pain or bleeding, and carpal tunnel syndrome. Psychologically, they may suffer low self-esteem, shame and embarrassment, depressed mood, irritability, and argumentativeness.

Their impairments appear early in life and continue through to middle and late adulthood (Duke, Keeley, Geffken, & Storch, 2010).

Diagnosable trichotillomania is relatively rare, with an estimated current prevalence rate of .6 percent of the community population. However, trichotillomania may be underreported because people with this disorder are secretive about what they are doing and tend to engage in hair-pulling only when alone (Duke, Bodzin, Tavares, Geffken, & Storch, 2009).

In *DSM-IV-TR*, trichotillomania was included in the category of impulse-control disorders, but in *DSM-5*, it moved to the category that includes obsessive-compulsive and related disorders. In addition, the name changed to hair-pulling, which the *DSM-5* authors concur would be a better description of the disorder than calling it a "mania," which they regard as inappropriate for this disorder.

There may be two types of hair-pulling. In the "focused" type, which may account for one-quarter of cases, the individual is aware of having the urge to pull, and may develop compulsive behaviors or rituals to avoid doing so. In "automatic" hair-pulling, the individual is involved in another task or is absorbed in thought while engaging in the behavior. Individuals who fall into the automatic category of hair-pulling experience pronounced stress and anxiety. For people

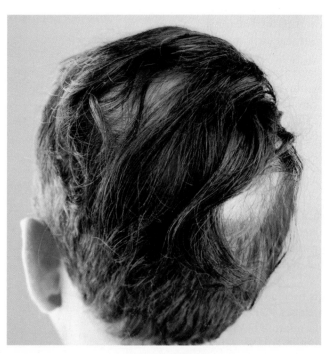

This man, like many who suffer from trichotillomania, has marked hair loss as a result of frequent and uncontrollable urges to pull his hair out.

MINI CASE

Trichotillomania (Hair-Pulling Disorder)

For most of her childhood and adolescence, 15-year-old Janet lived a fairly isolated existence, with no close friends. Although Janet never discussed her unhappiness with anyone, she often felt very depressed and hopeless. As a young child, Janet lay in bed on many nights, secretly tugging at her hair. Over time, this behavior increased to the point at which she plucked the hair, strand by strand, from her scalp. Typically, she pulled out a hair, examined it, bit it, and either threw it away or swallowed it. Because her hair was thick and curly, her hair loss was not initially evident, and Janet kept it carefully combed to conceal the bald spots. One of her teachers noticed that Janet was pulling her hair in class, and, in looking more closely, she saw the bald patches on Janet's head. She referred Janet to the school psychologist, who called Janet's mother and recommended professional help.

in the focused type, depression and disability are also likely to occur along with stress and anxiety (Duke, et al., 2010).

Heritability seems to play an important role in trichotillomania, with an estimated 80 percent heritability (Novak, Keuthen, Stewart, & Pauls, 2009). Abnormalities in a gene on chromosome 1 known as SLTRK1 may play a role in the disorder; this gene is also linked to Tourette's disorder (Abelson et al., 2005). Researchers have also identified abnormalities in SAPAP3, a gene related to glutamate which, in turn, is involved in obsessive-compulsive disorder (Zuchner et al., 2009). The neurotransmitters serotonin, dopamine, and glutamate are, in turn, thought to play a role in the development of trichotillomania (Duke, et al., 2009). Brain imaging studies of individuals with trichotillomania suggest that they may also have abnormalities in neural pathways in the brain involved in generating and suppressing motor habits; these pathways also seem to be involved in regulating affect (Chamberlain et al., 2010).

Corresponding to these abnormalities in neurotransmitter and brain functioning, the regulation model of trichotillomania suggests that individuals with this disorder seek an optimal state of emotional arousal providing them with greater stimulation when they are understimulated, and calming them when they are overstimulated. At the same time, hair-pulling may bring them from a negative to a positive affective state. Using the Trichotillomania Symptoms Questionnaire (see Table 8.5), researchers conducting an online survey found that individuals who engaged in hair-pulling experienced more difficulty controlling their emotions than those who did not. There were subgroups

TABLE 8.5 Trichotillomania Symptoms Questionnaire

1. Do you currently pull your hair out?
2. At any point in your life, including now, have you had periods of uncontrollable hair-pulling?
3. Do you (or did you in the past) experience urges to pull your hair out?
4. Do you (or did you in the past) try to resist pulling your hair out?
5. Do you (or did you in the past) feel relief when pulling your hair out?
6. Do you (or did you in the past) wish that the urge to pull your hair out would go away?
7. Have you been diagnosed with trichotillomania by a professional?
8. Do you, or did you in the past, feel shame, secrecy, or distress about your hair-pulling?

SOURCE: Shusterman et al., 2009

within those who engaged in hair-pulling. These subgroups varied in whether they were more likely to experience boredom vs. anxiety or tension and in the overall intensity of emotions they felt that seemed to drive them toward hair-pulling. The researchers suggested that these subgroups on the questionnaire seemed to correspond to the automatic vs. focused subtypes of the disorder (Shusterman, Feld, Baer, & Keuthen, 2009).

Various pharmacological treatments for trichotillomania include antidepressants, atypical antipsychotics, lithium, and naltrexone. Of these, naltrexone seems to have shown the most promising results. However, the results of controlled studies are not compelling and do not seem to justify the use of medications when weighed against the side effects that can include obesity, diabetes, neurotoxicity, delirium, encephalopathy, tremors, and hyperthyroidism, among others (Duke, et al., 2010).

The behavioral treatment of habit reversal training (HRT) is regarded as the most effective approach to treating trichotillomania. Not only does this method prevent the side effects of medication, but it is more successful in reducing the symptoms of hair-pulling (Duke, et al., 2010). However, for treatment-resistant individuals, a combination of medication and HRT may be required (Franklin, Zagrabbe, & Benavides, 2011).

In HRT, the individual learns a new response to compete with the habit of hair-pulling, such as fist-clenching. The key feature is that the new response is incompatible with the undesirable habit. When it was first developed several decades ago, HRT was given for only one session. Since that time, clinicians have extended the length of treatment and added several cognitive components, including self-monitoring and cognitive restructuring. For example, clients may learn to challenge their cognitive distortions such as their perfectionistic beliefs. Combining Acceptance and Commitment Therapy (ACT) with HRT is also shown to produce relief from hair-pulling symptoms. Cognitive-behavioral therapy can help in treating children and adolescents with trichotillomania, with very little alteration from the basic protocol used for adults. In one study, 77 percent of those who received treatment remained symptom-free after six months (Tolin, Franklin, Diefenbach, Anderson, & Meunier, 2007).

Excoriation (Skin-Picking) Disorder

excoriation (skin-picking) disorder
Recurrent picking at one's own skin.

A new diagnosis in *DSM-5,* individuals are regarded as having **excoriation (skin-picking)** disorder if they repeatedly pick at their own skin. The skin-picking may be of healthy skin, skin with mild irregularities (such as moles), pimples, calluses, or scabs. People with this disorder pick at these bodily areas either with their own fingernails or with instruments such as tweezers. These individuals spend a considerable amount of time engaging in skin-picking, perhaps as much as several hours per day. When they are not picking their skin, they think about picking it and try to resist their urges to do so. These individuals may attempt to cover the evidence of their skin-picking with clothing or bandages, and they feel ashamed and embarrassed about their behavior.

As this is a new diagnosis, epidemiological data are limited, but *DSM-5* estimates the prevalence as being at least 1.4% of adults, three-quarters of whom are female. Researchers believe that skin-picking is valid as a distinct diagnosis from trichotillomania (Lochner, Grant, Odlaug, & Stein, 2012). However, the two disorders share features in terms of causes and effective treatment approaches (Snorrason, Belleau, & Woods, 2012).

8.3 Trauma- and Stressor-Related Disorders

Individuals who are exposed to trauma or stressors may develop one of a set of disorders. These disorders include, as a diagnostic criterion, the condition that there is an actual event that precipitates the symptoms. *DSM-5* includes disorders in this group that were originally in the category of traumatic and stressor-related anxiety disorders along with disorders in childhood that can be traced to exposure to stress or trauma.

Reactive Attachment Disorder and Disinhibited Social Engagement Disorder

Children with **reactive attachment disorder** have severe disturbances in the way they relate to others. These children are emotionally withdrawn and inhibited and show little positive affect and an ability to control their emotions. When distressed, they do not seek comfort. The diagnosis of **disinhibited social engagement disorder** is used to apply to children who engage in culturally inappropriate, overly familiar behavior with people who are relative strangers.

These disorders are placed among the trauma- and stressor-related disorders because they are found in children who have experienced an abuse pattern of social neglect, repeated changes of primary caregivers, or rearing in institutions with high child-to-caregiver ratios. Consequently, such children are significantly impaired in their ability to interact with other children and adults.

Researchers conducting a longitudinal study of previously institutionalized Romanian children found these children developed as indiscriminately social/disinhibited children during early infancy as a result of poor caregiving. Their disorders did not improve, even when the quality of their caregiving improved (see Figure 8.2). Children with reactive attachment disorder have also received poorer caregiving and are more likely to have insecure attachment styles as they grow older (Gleason et al., 2011).

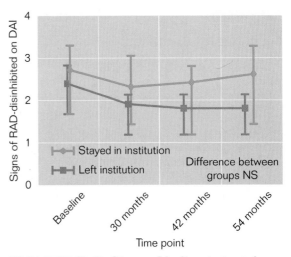

FIGURE 8.2 Signs of Indiscriminately Social/Disinhibited Reactive Attachment Disorder Across Time Points by Placement Status at 54 Months

Acute Stress Disorder and Post-Traumatic Stress Disorder

When people are exposed to the threat of death, or to actual or threatened serious injury, or sexual violation, they are at risk of developing **acute stress disorder.** Being exposed to the death of others, or to any of these events, real or threatened to others, can also lead to the development of this disorder. First responders to the scene of an accident or police officers who regularly are exposed to the details of child abuse cases may also experience this disorder.

The symptoms of acute stress disorder fall into four categories: intrusion of distressing reminders of the event, dissociative symptoms such as feeling numb or detached from others, avoidance of situations that might serve as reminders of the event, and hyper-arousal including sleep disturbances or irritability. The symptoms may persist for a few days to a month after the traumatic event.

The events that can cause acute stress disorder may lead to the longer-lasting disorder known as **post-traumatic stress disorder (PTSD).** Technically, if the individual experiences acute stress disorder symptoms for more than a month, the clinician assigns the PTSD diagnosis. Intrusions, dissociation, and avoidance remain important categories of symptoms for PTSD. In addition, however, it includes negative changes in cognition including loss of memory for the event, excessive self-blame, distancing from others, and inability to experience positive emotions.

In the 1980s, when the diagnosis of PTSD was added to the *DSM,* the media drew attention to the psychological aftereffects of combat experienced by Vietnam War veterans. The Vietnam War was the most publicized, but certainly not the only, war to produce psychological casualties. Reports of psychological dysfunction following exposure to combat emerged after the Civil War and received increasing attention following both world wars of the twentieth century, with reports of conditions called shell shock, traumatic neurosis, combat stress, and combat fatigue. Concentration camp survivors also were reported to suffer long-term psychological effects, including the "survivor syndrome" of chronic depression, anxiety, and difficulties in interpersonal relationships.

reactive attachment disorder
A disorder involving a severe disturbance in the ability to relate to others in which the individual is unresponsive to people, is apathetic, and prefers to be alone rather than to interact with friends or family.

disinhibited social engagement disorder
Diagnosis given to children who engage in culturally inappropriate, overly familiar behavior with people who are relative strangers.

acute stress disorder
An anxiety disorder that develops after a traumatic event, and lasts for up to 1 month with symptoms such as depersonalization, numbing, dissociative amnesia, intense anxiety, hypervigilance, and impairment of everyday functioning.

post-traumatic stress disorder (PTSD)
An anxiety disorder in which the individual experiences several distressing symptoms for more than a month following a traumatic event, such as a re-experiencing of the traumatic event, an avoidance of reminders of the trauma, a numbing of general responsiveness, and increased arousal.

MINI CASE

Acute Stress Disorder

Brendan is a 29-year-old paralegal clerk who was psychologically healthy until two weeks ago when he survived a wildfire that destroyed his apartment and many buildings in his neighborhood. Since the fire Brendan has been tormented by graphic images of waking to see his room filled with smoke. Although he was treated and released within several hours from the emergency room, he described himself as feeling in a daze, emotionally unresponsive to the concerns of his friends and family, and seemingly numb. He continued to experience these symptoms for several weeks, after which they gradually subsided.

The lifetime prevalence of PTSD is 6.8 percent with a yearly prevalence of 3.5 percent. Of those who develop PTSD within a given year, 37 percent experience severe symptoms (Kessler et al., 2005). Among Army soldiers returning from Afghanistan, 6.2 percent met the PTSD diagnostic criteria, with more than double that rate, 12.9 percent, among soldiers returning from Iraq (Hoge et al., 2004). As combat has continued in these two war zones, the number of soldiers developing mental health problems, particularly PTSD, has continued to climb. It is estimated that nearly 17 percent of Iraq War veterans meet the screening criteria for this disorder (Hoge, Terhakopian, Castro, Messer, & Engel, 2007).

The symptoms of PTSD and related disorders, such as depression, can persist for many years. Survivors of the North Sea oil rig disaster in 1980 continued to experience symptoms of PTSD along with anxiety disorders (not including PTSD), depressive disorders, and substance use disorders that were significantly higher than those of a matched comparison group (see Figure 8.3) (Boe, Holgersen, & Holen, 2011).

Theories and Treatment of Post-Traumatic Stress Disorder

A traumatic experience is an external event that impinges on the individual and hence does not have biological "causality." However, researchers propose that traumatic experiences in part have their impact because they lead to changes in the brain that make it primed or hypersensitive to possible danger in the future. Individuals with PTSD experience alterations in the hippocampus, the structure responsible for consolidating memory. As a result, they are unable to distinguish relatively harmful situations (such as fireworks) from the ones in which real trauma occurred (combat). They continue to re-experience the event with heightened arousal and further avoidance of the trauma (Hayes et al., 2011).

FIGURE 8.3 Percent of Long-Term Survivors of the North Sea Disaster Still Experiencing Symptoms After 27 Years

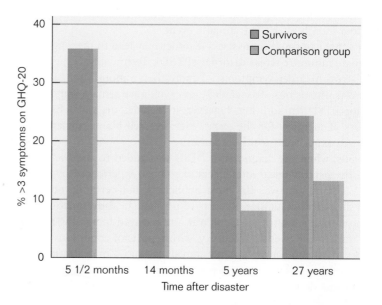

MINI CASE

Post-Traumatic Stress Disorder

For the past 10 years, Steve has suffered from flashbacks in which he relives the horrors of his 9 months of active duty in the Gulf War. These flashbacks occur unexpectedly in the middle of the day, and Steve is thrown back into the emotional reality of his war experiences. These flashbacks, and the nightmares he often suffers from, have become a constant source of torment. Steve has found that alcohol provides the only escape from these visions and from the distress he feels. Often, Steve ruminates about how he should have done more to prevent the deaths of his fellow soldiers, and he feels that his friends, rather than he, should have survived.

SSRI antidepressants are the only FDA-approved medications for people with PTSD. However, the response rates of patients with PTSD to these medications rarely are more than 60 percent, and less than 20 to 30 percent achieve full remission of their symptoms. Research does not support the use of benzodiazepines in treatment of PTSD, although these medications may relieve insomnia or anxiety (Berger et al., 2009). Although researchers believed that the antipsychotic medication respiridone might benefit individuals with PTSD, findings from a large-scale study of nearly 300 veterans did not provide empirical support for its use in reducing symptoms (Krystal et al., 2011).

From a psychological perspective, people with PTSD have a biased information processing style that, due to the trauma they experienced, causes their attention to be biased toward potentially threatening cues. They therefore feel more likely to be under threat and also are more likely to avoid situations that they perceive as potentially threatening (Huppert, Foa, McNally, & Cahill, 2009). Personality and coping style also predict responses to trauma. People more likely to experience PTSD following exposure to a trauma are found to have high levels of neuroticism, negativity, affectivity, prior psychological symptoms, and a history of childhood abuse (Baschnagel, Gudmundsdottir, Hawk, & Gayle Beck, 2009; Engelhard & van den Hout, 2007; Rademaker, van Zuiden, Vermetten, & Geuze, 2011).

Barbara seems to have been an exception in this regard; she did not appear to be high on neuroticism, negative, or a victim of childhood abuse. Her prolonged exposure to severe combat along with the loss of her leg seemed to account for her development of the disorder.

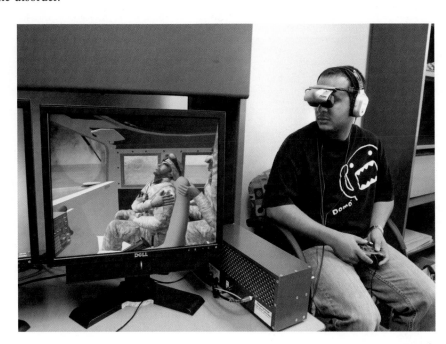

A military veteran suffering from PTSD uses virtual reality technology to expose himself to anxiety-provoking imagery as part of his treatment at a VA hospital.

Generally considered the most effective psychological treatment for PTSD, cognitive-behavioral therapy combines some type of exposure (*in vivo* or imaginal) with relaxation and cognitive restructuring. However, clinicians are reluctant to adopt these methods in treatment (Couineau & Forbes, 2011). Moreover, due to the high dropout and nonresponse rates when these methods are employed, researchers are investigating the efficacy of alternative methods including interpersonal therapy, mantra repetition, and acceptance and commitment therapy (Bomyea & Lang, 2011).

In Eye Movement Desensitization Reprocessing (EMDR), the clinician asks the client to think about a traumatic memory while focusing on rapid movement of the clinician's finger for 10 to 12 eye movements. Though being used to an increasing degree, EMDR lacks the effectiveness associated with some type of exposure therapy (Committee on Treatment of Posttraumatic Stress Disorder, 2008).

An alternative view to PTSD comes from the standpoint of positive psychology, with the proposal that people can grow through the experience of trauma. According to this approach, trauma potentially allows clients to find positive interpretations of their experiences (Helgeson, Reynolds, & Tomich, 2006). Particularly beneficial may be the personal traits of optimism and openness to new experiences (Zoellner, Rabe, Karl, & Maercker, 2008).

8.4 Anxiety, Obsessive-Compulsive, and Trauma- and Stressor-Related Disorders: The Biopsychosocial Perspective

The disorders we covered in this chapter span a broad spectrum of problems, ranging from specific, seemingly idiosyncratic responses to diffuse and undifferentiated feelings of dread. There are differences among the disorders in symptoms and causes, but there do seem to be important similarities in that they all involve regions of the brain involved in responding to fearful or threatening situations. Perhaps what determines whether an individual with a propensity toward developing an anxiety disorder is the unique combination represented in that person's life by the confluence of genetics, brain functioning, life experiences, and social context. Across these disorders, there also appear to be similarities in treatment approach, with cognitive-behavioral methods perhaps showing the greatest effectiveness.

Return to the Case: Barbara Wilder

Barbara's therapist decided not to use pharmacological interventions but instead to begin treatment with cognitive-behavioral therapy. First, Barbara learned to challenge the thoughts that she was still in danger much of the time. Then, through imaginal exposure techniques, Barbara became accustomed to discussing her experiences in Iraq without provoking fear or anxiety by relearning to associate her memories of the war with relaxation.

In addition to individual therapy, Barbara's therapist suggested that she participate in group therapy. In these sessions, Barbara met for 90 minutes a week for 10 weeks with 7 other Iraq War veterans.

Barbara was able to talk about her traumatic memories as well as provide support to other veterans as they discussed their experiences. By interacting with veterans she could relate to, she relearned how to interact with others socially, which decreased her feelings of irritability and anger around other people in her life.

Within one month of beginning her treatment at the VA, Barbara began to experience some relief from her PTSD symptoms, though she continued to have occasional nightmares. Using the coping skills she learned in therapy, Barbara was able to recover from the flashbacks and began to participate in life once again. She made a full physical recovery after receiving a prosthetic leg. Within two months, her emotional numbing, irritability, and anxious symptoms completely subsided. Barbara often remarked to her therapist that she felt that she was "herself" again. Several months later, she took a part-time job in an electronics store and enrolled in a part-time MBA program at a nearby community college. She moved into her own apartment a few towns away from her parents' home and began to reconnect with old friends who still live close by. Barbara continues to come to the VA for individual therapy every week, and though the events she experienced in Iraq continue to haunt her, she has learned to live with the memories and has begun to adjust to civilian life.

Dr. Tobin's reflections: It was clear upon her initial presentation that Barbara was presenting with classic symptoms of PTSD. Fortunately she was able to utilize the resources available for her to get help and provide relief from her suffering. Early intervention treatment for those with PTSD is critical in preventing the prolonging of symptoms throughout the life span, and Barbara was able to put her life back together as a result of addressing her PTSD early on. In the case of many veterans of wars fought in earlier eras (like Vietnam) the needed resources were not available for them when they returned home from war. These veterans currently make up a large population of the Veterans Affairs system, though the rates of PTSD continue to increase for soldiers fighting in the wars in Iraq and Afghanistan. Early intervention in those with PTSD is important in preventing the prolonging of symptoms throughout the life span.

SUMMARY

- **Anxiety disorders** are characterized by the experience of physiological arousal, apprehension, or feelings of dread, hypervigilance, avoidance, and sometimes a specific fear or phobia.

- **Separation anxiety disorder** is a childhood disorder characterized by intense and inappropriate anxiety about being separated from home or caregivers. Many infants go through a developmental phase in which they become anxious and agitated when they are separated from their caregivers. In separation anxiety disorder, these emotions continue far longer than is age appropriate. Even the prospect of separation causes extreme anxiety. Although there appears to be a strong genetic component to separation anxiety disorder, environmental factors also contribute. For children needing treatment, behavioral and cognitive-behavioral techniques may be most effective. Another childhood disorder thought to center on anxiety is **selective mutism,** in which a child refuses to speak in specific situations, such as the classroom. Behaviorist methods using shaping and exposure seem particularly well suited to treating children with selective mutism.

- **Panic disorder** is characterized by frequent and recurrent **panic attacks**—intense sensations of fear and physical discomfort. This disorder is often comorbid with agoraphobia, a disorder new to the *DSM-5*. **Agoraphobia** presents with intense anxiety around the thought or experience of being in a public place. In particular, the **fear** of being trapped or unable to escape from a public place is common. Biological and cognitive-behavioral perspectives have been particularly useful for understanding and treating this disorder. Some experts explain panic disorder as an acquired "fear of fear," in which the individual becomes hypersensitive to early signs of a panic attack, and the fear of a full-blown attack leads the individual to become unduly apprehensive and avoidant of another attack. Treatment based on the cognitive-behavioral perspective involves methods such as relaxation training and *in vivo* or **imaginal flooding** as a way of breaking the negative cycle initiated by the individual's fear of having a panic attack. Medications can also help alleviate symptoms, with the most commonly prescribed being antianxiety and antidepressant medications.

- Specific **phobias** are irrational fears of particular objects or situations. Cognitive behaviorists assert that previous learning experiences and a cycle of negative, maladaptive thoughts cause specific phobias. Treatments recommended by the behavioral and cognitive-behavioral approaches include flooding, systematic desensitization, imagery, *in vivo* exposure, and participant modeling, as well as procedures aimed at changing the individual's maladaptive thoughts, such as cognitive restructuring, coping self-statements, thought stopping, and increases in self-efficacy. Treatment based on the biological perspective involves medication.

- **Social anxiety disorder** is a fear of being observed by others while acting in a way that will be humiliating or embarrassing. Cognitive-behavioral approaches to social anxiety disorder regard the disorder as due to an unrealistic fear of criticism, which causes people with the disorder to lose the ability to concentrate on their performance, instead shifting their attention to how anxious they feel, which then causes them to make mistakes and, therefore, to become more fearful. Behavioral methods that provide *in vivo* exposure, along with cognitive restructuring and social skills training, seem to be the most effective in helping people with social anxiety disorder. Medication is the treatment recommended within the biological perspective for severe cases of this disorder.

- People who are diagnosed as having **generalized anxiety disorder** have a number of unrealistic worries that spread to various spheres of life. The cognitive-behavioral approach to generalized anxiety disorder emphasizes the unrealistic nature of these worries and regards the disorder as a vicious cycle that feeds on itself. Cognitive-behavioral treatment approaches recommend breaking the negative cycle of worry by teaching individuals techniques that allow them to feel they control the worrying. Biological treatment emphasizes the use of medication.

- In **obsessive-compulsive disorder,** individuals develop **obsessions,** or thoughts they cannot rid themselves of, and **compulsions,** which are irresistible, repetitive behaviors. A cognitive-behavioral understanding of obsessive-compulsive disorder regards the symptoms as the product of a learned association between anxiety and the thoughts or acts, which temporarily can produce relief from anxiety. A growing body of evidence supports a biological explanation of the disorder, with the most current research suggesting that it is associated with an excess of serotonin. Treatment with medications, such as clomipramine, seems to be effective, although cognitive-behavioral methods involving exposure and thought stopping are quite effective as well. **Body dysmorphic disorder, hoarding, trichotillomania (hair-pulling disorder),** and **excoriation (skin-picking) disorder** are grouped with OCD in *DSM-5.*

- Individuals who are exposed to trauma or stressors may develop one of a set of disorders. *DSM-5* includes in this group disorders that were originally in the category of traumatic and stressor-related anxiety disorders, including post-traumatic stress disorder and acute stress disorder along with the childhood disorders **reactive attachment disorder** and **disinhibited social engagement disorder.** This set of disorders include, as a diagnostic criterion, the condition that there is an actual event that precipitates the symptoms. Children with reactive attachment disorder have severe disturbances in the way they relate to others and are emotionally withdrawn and inhibited. In contrast, children with disinhibited social engagement disorder engage in culturally inappropriate, overly familiar behavior with people who are relative strangers. Both of these disorders are found in children who have experienced social neglect through repeated changes of primary caregivers or reared in instutions with high child-to-caregiver ratios. Research indicates that children with these disorders continue to have problems even if their circumstances improve.

- In **post-traumatic stress disorder,** the individual is unable to recover from the anxiety associated with a traumatic life event, such as tragedy or disaster, an accident, or participation in combat. The aftereffects of the traumatic event include flashbacks, nightmares, and intrusive thoughts that alternate with the individual's attempts to deny that the event ever took place. Some people experience a briefer but very troubling response to a traumatic event; this condition, called **acute stress disorder**, lasts from two days to four weeks and involves the kinds of symptoms that people with PTSD experience over a much longer period of time. Cognitive-behavioral approaches regard the disorder as the result of negative and maladaptive thoughts about one's role in causing the traumatic events to happen, feelings of ineffectiveness and isolation from others, and a pessimistic outlook on life as a result of the experience. Treatment may involve teaching people with PTSD new coping skills, so that they can more effectively manage stress and re-establish social ties with others who can provide ongoing support. A combination of covering techniques, such as supportive therapy and stress management, and uncovering techniques, such as imaginal flooding and desensitization, is usually helpful.

KEY TERMS

Dissociative and Somatic Symptom Disorders

Learning Objectives

9.1   Specify the symptoms of dissociative disorders

9.2   Identify symptoms and treatments of somatic symptom disorders

9.3   Recognize psychological factors affecting other medical conditions

9.4   Explain the biopsychosocial perspective for dissociative and somatic symptom disorders

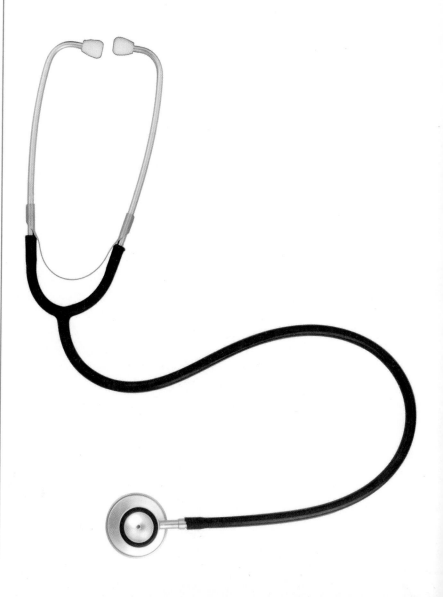

CHAPTER 9

Case Report: Rose Marston

Demographic information: 37-year-old Caucasian female.

Presenting problem: Rose was referred for a psychological evaluation by her physician, Dr. Stewart, who became concerned that she may have been suffering from symptoms of a psychological disorder. For the past year, Rose made weekly appointments with Dr. Stewart as well as other health practitioners due to her concern that she was suffering from a severe physical condition. However, Dr. Stewart was unable to detect any actual disease or syndrome that may have caused Rose's frequent stomach pains she complained of having. During the evaluation, Rose reported she was dissatisfied with Dr. Stewart's insistence that she was not suffering from a physical condition, and she consulted with alternative health care practitioners such as homeopathic physicians and even a Reiki master. She admitted she had been hoping that one of the practitioners would discover she suffered from a diagnosable medical condition, and many had even suggested she receive a psychological evaluation, which she refused. She finally agreed to Dr. Stewart's recommendation after much persistence from him.

Rose reported she had recently lost her job after calling in sick nearly every day over the past three months. She stated she felt it was more important to spend her time consulting health care practitioners and she also preferred not to leave her house for fear of exacerbating her symptoms. Rose stated she was distressed about the amount of time she had spent worrying about her stomach pain, but she also was overwhelmed by feelings of guilt if she did not direct her activities toward trying to determine the cause of her physical symptoms. Rose described that her symptoms originated as mild stomach irritation, and that over the past year they had escalated to the point where her stomach was causing her constant and severe pain. She reported having tried a multitude of remedies, all of them unsuccessful.

During the evaluation, Rose stated that she felt "devastated" about how her worry concerning her physical symptoms had interfered with her life but that she felt she had to focus on finding a diagnosis. In addition to losing her job, Rose's boyfriend of two years had recently ended their relationship, and she admitted she had distanced herself from him since the concerns about her physical symptoms began. She found, in addition, that her concern about her physical symptoms overshadowed any thoughts about her relationship.

The clinician conducting the evaluation asked Rose to describe any recent major stressors in her life, and she reported she had lost her favorite uncle to cancer in the previous year. When describing this loss, Rose immediately became tearful and admitted she felt she had never mourned her uncle and instead pushed away her feelings about his death most of the time.

Following the evaluation, the clinician contacted Dr. Stewart to consult about her case, which Rose had consented to by signing a release of information. Dr. Stewart told the clinician he believed Rose's physical symptoms seemed to be indicative of a late onset lactose intolerance, but that she had refused to accept this diagnosis. Her symptoms may have worsened as a result of a failure for her to get the proper treatment. Dr. Stewart also remarked that Rose seemed to have been acting very differently since the death of her uncle.

Relevant history: Rose had previously seen a psychiatrist for depression in her late twenties.

The depression began after Rose graduated from college, and it varied in severity until she endured an episode so intense she had contemplated suicide. She had received a course of antidepressants that had been effective. At the time of the evaluation, Rose had not been on any psychiatric medications for approximately five years because she had felt the previous course of medication had been effective enough for her to discontinue.

Case formulation: Rose meets criteria for somatic symptom disorder, moderate to severe, with predominant pain. This diagnosis is based on her heightened anxiety, which is excessive, in response to her physical symptoms, to the point where her life has been significantly disrupted (i.e., loss of her job and her romantic relationship). Her concerns about her symptoms are both persistent and disproportionate to the actual severity of her physical symptoms, and her refusal to accept a relatively mild diagnosis of lactose intolerance meets criteria for symptoms of this disorder. The anxiety about her symptoms is severe and persistent (lasting longer than six months), and she has devoted an objectively excessive amount of time and energy to her physical symptoms. The onset of Rose's symptoms possibly originates from the distress caused by the death of her uncle, due to her report that she engaged in avoidance of processing her reaction.

Treatment plan: Following the evaluation and consultation with Dr. Stewart, the clinician referred Rose to a therapist specializing in cognitive-behavioral treatment for somatic disorders. In this evidence-based approach, Rose's therapist should focus on evaluating her excessive concerns about her physical condition with cognitive restructuring and also behavioral strategies to increase her engagement with recommendations from Dr. Stewart to improve her physical symptoms.

Sarah Tobin, PhD

9.1 Dissociative Disorders

The human mind seems capable of dissociating, or separating mental functions. You can think intensively about a problem while jogging, perhaps not even realizing that you ran a mile without awareness of your surroundings. In dissociative disorders, the separation of mental functions occurs to a far more extreme degree. Dissociative disorders raise intriguing questions about the ways in which people's sense of self evolves over time, memory, and sense of reality can become fragmented. In contrast, somatic symptom disorders, which are discussed later in this chapter, raise questions about the mind-body relatiohsip.

Major Forms of Dissociative Disorders

dissociative identity disorder (DID)
A dissociative disorder, formerly called multiple personality disorder, in which an individual develops more than one self or personality.

We generally take for granted the idea that each individual has one personality and sense of self. However, in **dissociative identity disorder (DID)**, it appears that the individual has developed more than one personality with its associated sense of self. Each separate personality seems to have its own unique characteristic ways of perceiving, relating to, and thinking. By definition, people with DID have at least two distinct identities and when inhabiting the identity of one, are not aware that they also inhabit the other identity. As a result, their experiences lack continuity. They have large gaps in important memories about themselves and their lives. They may forget ordinary everyday events, but also experiences they had that are of a traumatic nature such as victimization or abuse.

dissociative amnesia
An inability to remember important personal details and experiences; is usually associated with traumatic or very stressful events.

People with **dissociative amnesia** are unable to remember information about an event or set of events in their lives. Their amnesia is not due to ordinary forgetfulness, however. What they typically forget is a specific event from their lives, most likely one of a traumatic or stressful nature. Their amnesia may involve a fugue state in which they travel or wander without knowing their identity.

MINI CASE

Dissociative Identity Disorder

Myra is a young single woman who works as a clerk in a large bookstore. She lives by herself, never goes out socially except to see her relatives, and dresses in a conservative manner, which her associates ridicule as prudish. In her early teens, she was involved in an intimate relationship with a middle-aged man who was quite abusive toward her. Although others remind her of this troubled relationship, Myra claims that she has no recollection of that person, and she has even wondered at times whether others have made up the story to annoy her. At age 25, Myra says that she is saving herself sexually for marriage, yet she seems totally uninterested in pursuing any close relationships with men. So far, this describes Myra as her work acquaintances and family know her. However, alters reside within Myra's body, and they go by other names and behave in ways that are totally incongruous with "Myra's" personality. "Rita" is flamboyant, outgoing, and uninhibited in her sexual passions. She has engaged in numerous love affairs with a variety of unsavory characters she picked up in nightclubs and discotheques. "Rita" is aware of "Myra" and regards her with extreme disdain. A third personality, "Joe," occasionally emerges from Myra's apartment. Dressed in a man's three-piece business suit, "Joe" goes downtown to do some shopping. According to "Joe," "Rita" is nothing but a "slut," who is heading for "big trouble someday." Myra's alters are oblivious to the details of her life.

Your ordinary perception of who you are involves your knowing that you live within your own body. **Depersonalization** is the condition in which people feel they are detached from their own body. They may have experiences of unreality, being an outside observer, or emotional or physical numbing. **Derealization** is a condition in which people feel a sense of unreality or detachment from their surroundings. **Depersonalization/derealization** disorder is a condition in which people have one or both of the experiences of depersonalization and derealization.

depersonalization
Condition in which people feel detached from their own body.

derealization
Condition in which people feel a sense of unreality or detachment from their surroundings.

depersonalization/derealization disorder
A dissociative disorder in which the individual experiences recurrent and persistent episodes of depersonalization.

Theories and Treatment of Dissociative Disorders

Traumatic events can lead people to experience splitting apart of their conscious experiences, sense of self, or feelings of continuity over time. In normal development, people integrate the perceptions and memories they have of themselves and their experiences. In a dissociative disorder, the individual is trying to block out or separate from conscious awareness events that caused extreme psychological, if not physical, pain.

Individuals with dissociative identity disorder have learned to cope with extremely stressful life circumstances by creating "alter" personalities that unconsciously control their thinking and behavior when they are experiencing stress.

REAL STORIES

Herschel Walker: Dissociative Identity Disorder

"In looking back on things, I can only now begin to see that I was running from something I couldn't even begin to name."

Herschel Walker is perhaps one of the most successful professional American football players of all time. He received the prestigious Heisman Trophy in his junior year of college at the University of Georgia and went on to play 11 seasons with the National Football League. Although Herschel is famous for his talents on the field, the difficulties he endured in childhood nearly prevented him from attaining any of the achievements he has accrued over the years. By developing alternate personalities as a youngster, Herschel was able to overcome the challenges in his life and go on to reach immense success as a professional athlete. By using those alternate personalities to cope with stressful situations, he eventually lost the ability to have control over when his "alters" took over his regular self and in 2001, he was diagnosed with Dissociative Identity Disorder (DID). In his autobiography, *Breaking Free: My Life with Dissociative Identity Disorder*, Herschel reveals the challenges that he faced and continues to face in his personal life due to his struggle with DID. In the book, he recounts the major moments from his life and how they were affected by his disorder. Herschel differentiates his experience with DID from more popular examples in the media. For example, his alters do not have a name or speak differently or dress differently. He admits that his case is mild when compared to some others who are afflicted with the same disorder. In fact, he states most people wouldn't even notice when he was in an altered state. He would transform his personality in the moment.

Herschel was born in 1962 in Wrightsville, Georgia, one of seven children of blue-collar parents. As a child, Herschel struggled with a weight problem and a severe stutter that rendered him almost unable to speak to others for fear of ridicule and embarrassment. Herschel recalls being teased and bullied every day at school by his peers. He was so tortured by his speech impediment that he was often afraid to speak up in class, even though he was a diligent student who enjoyed learning. Although Herschel describes his family as loving and supportive, he found it difficult to reach out to them for emotional support. Herschel also suffered from a debilitating fear of being in the dark as a result of frightening visions and nightmares that would come to him when he tried to go to sleep. In order to provide a sense of relief from the anxiety, Herschel would retreat into a fantasy world in which he felt safe and protected from any harm that his fears could cause him. Herschel told no one about these difficulties he faced, and instead he developed various personalities (or alters) in his mind to cope with the teasing that he was enduring. These personalities took on characteristics that Herschel thought he lacked in himself in order to deal with the constant embarrassment and emotional torture.

In *Breaking Free*, Herschel describes how this coping system changed him. "When the choice I made to deal with the pain worked, I used it again when a similar kind of threatening situation occurred. Through repetition, the habit of having an alter take over became a routine, and the brain is a marvelously efficient machine that likes to take any process we are engaged in—from driving a car to walking to insulating ourselves against hurtful negative comments—from the conscious to the subconscious level. That is what DID did for me, and why as I was growing up, I didn't consciously realize I was doing it."

In high school, Herschel worked hard academically, earning top honors at his school. He also began to work hard athletically, running

Football legend Herschel Walker wrote a book, *Breaking Free: My Life with Dissociative Identity Disorder*, in which he relates that he cannot remember the season he won the Heisman Trophy, let alone the day of the ceremony.

several miles per day and joining his school's football and track teams. He lost the weight that had been causing him ridicule from his peers and eventually overcame the speech impediment. Herschel excelled in both track and football, although it was his strength and prowess on the football field that gained him the most attention from college recruiters. With many offers, Herschel decided to attend the University of Georgia, helping his school earn a National Championship in his junior year. The same year he received the prestigious Heisman Trophy. Instead of going on to finish his senior year at college, Herschel joined a new professional football league that rivaled the NFL, the United States Football League. He also married his college sweetheart. Herschel played with the league for two seasons before the league dissolved and he was then drafted to the Dallas Cowboys. He played on four different teams throughout his 11-season NFL career. All the while, Herschel's DID helped him cope with the many

challenges—both physical and emotional—that came along with his career. Whenever he was faced with stress or pain, his alters took over for him. "My alters functioned as a kind of community supporting me. . . . I never wanted to experience the kind of lows that I had known as a kid," he writes in *Breaking Free,* "so I became a kind of emotional bulldozer—a machine, a powerful force, something you turn the key on, fire up the ignition, throw into gear. The machine goes, almost always forward, leveling the highs and lows of the terrain it crosses into a smooth, flat, featureless plane."

However, the alters were not always positive ways of helping Herschel cope. They often kept his emotions at arm's length, preventing him from being close with teammates and loved ones—especially his wife. He was often unable to recall certain episodes from his life when his alters had come into play. It wasn't until his marriage, and his life in general began to fall apart, that he realized he needed help. Although his

marriage was never able to recover, Herschel began to put his life in order after seeking help in 2001 from a psychologist friend, Dr. Jerry Mungadze at the Dissociative and Trauma Related Disorders Unit at Cedars Hospital in DeSoto, Texas. Herschel was diagnosed with DID and began intensive therapeutic treatment, which helped him identify and gain control over his alters, making a cohesive whole self out of the separate personalities he had been maintaining for most of his life.

Herschel has since started a career in mixed martial arts and recently appeared on a season of *Celebrity Apprentice* with Donald Trump. He lives in Dallas, Texas, and often gives motivational speeches to others who have been diagnosed with DID. In *Breaking Free,* Herschel writes, "I hope my legacy will be more than what I have achieved on the football field and on the track. I would rather be remembered for opening my heart and sharing my experience with DID so that others can understand this condition."

Clinicians, nevertheless, face a daunting task both in diagnosing and treating an individual's dissociative symptoms. In the first place, they must determine whether the condition is real or faked (either intentionally or unintentionally). People may deliberately feign a dissociative disorder to gain attention or avoid punishment. They may unwittingly develop one of these disorders, however, because they are seeking attention for having the type of diagnosis about which movies are written (such as *Sybil*, or *The Three Faces of Eve,* for example).

MINI CASE

Dissociative Amnesia with Dissociative Fugue

In a daze, Norma entered the mental health crisis center, tears streaming down her face. "I have no idea where I live or who I am! Will somebody please help me?" The crisis team helped her search her purse, but could find nothing other than a photograph of a blond-haired little girl. Norma appeared exhausted and was taken to a bed, where she promptly fell asleep. The crisis team called the local police to find out if there was a report of a missing person. As it turned out, the little girl in the photograph was Norma's daughter. She had been hit by

a car in a shopping center parking lot. Although badly injured with a broken leg, the child was resting comfortably in a hospital pediatrics ward. Her mother, however, had disappeared. Norma had apparently been wandering around for several hours, leaving her wallet and other identifying papers with the hospital social worker in the emergency room. When Norma awoke, she was able to recall who she was and the circumstances of the accident, but she remembered nothing of what had happened since.

Dissociative Identity Disorder

The possibility that an individual may not be responsible for actions committed while one's multiple personalities are in control of the person's behavior leads to fascinating legal questions. Theoretically, of course, it's possible for one alter to commit a crime while the other alters, or even the host, is not aware or in control. Obviously, however, convicting one alter means that the host (along with all the other alters) is also put in prison. At another level, however, the question becomes one related to the legal definition of insanity. Is a person with dissociative identity disorder able to control his or her own mind if part of the mind has split off and is acting independently?

There are three possible approaches to defending a client who legitimately has this diagnosis. In the "alter-in-control" approach, the defendant claims that an alter personality was in control at the time of the offense. In the "each-alter" approach, the prosecution must determine whether each personality met the insanity standard. In the "host-alter" approach, the issue is whether the host personality meets the insanity standard.

Dissociative identity disorder is rarely successful as a legal defense after a public outcry following the ruling in 1974 that serial rapist Billy Milligan was insane due to lack of an integrated personality (*State v Milligan*, 1978). Since that time, cases have had a variety of outcomes, ranging from the judgment that multiple personalities do not preclude criminal responsibility (*State v Darnall*, 1980) to the ruling that alter personalities are not an excuse for inability to distinguish right from wrong (*State v Jones*, 1998). The courts threw out two more recent cases in Washington State (*State v Greene*, 1998) and West Virginia (*State v Lockhart*, 2000) on the grounds that lack of scientific evidence and/or adequate reliability standards do not exist in the diagnosis of the disorder (Farrell, 2010). The key issue for forensic psychologists and psychiatrists is determining the difference between malingering and the actual disorder (Farrell, 2011).

There are tools now available for expert clinicians to use in aiding accurate diagnosis. The Structured Clinical Interview for *DSM–IV* Dissociative Disorders–Revised (SCID–D–R) (Steinberg, 1994; see Table 9.1), which the profession has rigorously standardized, includes a careful structuring, presentation, and scoring of questions. The professionals who developed and conducted research on this instrument emphasize that only experienced clinicians and evaluators who understand dissociative diagnosis and treatment issues must administer and score these.

The *DSM-5* considers the diagnosis of dissociative identity disorder to be valid. The precedents created by rulings that the diagnosis is not admissible due to failure to meet scientific standards may, over time, thus be overturned. Nevertheless, the diagnosis is, at best, challenging, and potentially easy to feign, particularly if a clinician inadvertently plants the idea of using the diagnosis as a defense.

Q: *You be the judge:* Should dissociative identity disorder be considered admissable in criminal cases? Why or why not?

In true cases of dissociative disorder, when the symptoms do not appear feigned, the current consensus is that these individuals were subjected to emotional or physical trauma. One large psychiatric outpatient study demonstrated that people with dissociative symptoms had high prevalence rates of both physical and sexual abuse in childhood (Foote, Smolin, Kaplan, Legatt, & Lipschitz, 2006). However, many people without a dissociative disorder can think of traumatic events from their early lives (Kihlstrom, 2005).

TABLE 9.1 Items from the SCID-D-R

Scale	Items
Amnesia	Have you ever felt as if there were large gaps in your memory?
Depersonalization	Have you ever felt that you were watching yourself from a point outside of your body, as if you were seeing yourself from a distance (or watching a movie of yourself)? Have you ever felt as if a part of your body or your whole being was foreign to you? Have you ever felt as if you were two different people, one going through the motions of life and the other part observing quietly?
Derealization	Have you ever felt as if familiar surroundings or people you knew seemed unfamiliar or unreal? Have you ever felt puzzled as to what is real and what's unreal in your surroundings? Have you ever felt as if your surroundings or other people were fading away?
Identity confusion	Have you ever felt as if there was a struggle going on inside of you? Have you ever felt confused as to who you are?
Identity alteration	Have you ever acted as if you were a completely different person? Have you ever been told by others that you seem like a different person? Have you ever found things in your possession (for instance, shoes) that belong to you, but you could not remember how you got them?

SOURCE: Steinberg, 1994.

Along similar lines, traumatic experiences in childhood can lead to other types of disorders; so why would some individuals exposed to trauma develop a dissociative disorder, but others do not?

Assuming that people with dissociative disorders are reacting to trauma with dissociative symptoms, the treatment goal becomes primarily to integrate the disparate parts

MINI CASE

Depersonalization/Derealization Disorder

Robert entered the psychiatrist's office in a state of extreme agitation, almost panic. He described the terrifying nature of his "nervous attacks," which began several years ago, but had now reached catastrophic proportions. During these "attacks," Robert feels as though he is floating in the air, above his body, watching everything he does, but feeling totally disconnected from his actions. He reports that he feels as if his body is a machine controlled by outside forces: "I look at my hands and feet and wonder what makes them move." However, Robert's thoughts are not delusions. He is aware that his altered perceptions are not normal. The only relief he experiences from his symptoms comes when he strikes himself with a heavy object until the pain finally penetrates his consciousness. His fear of seriously harming himself adds to his main worry that he is losing his mind.

within the person's consciousness of self, memory, and time. Clinicians may use hypno-therapy to help clients recall the traumatic experiences that seem to have caused the dissociation. Gradually, through post-hypnotic suggestion, clients may be able to bring those experiences back into conscious awareness. Alternatively, clinicians can use cognitive-behavioral techniques to help clients develop a coherent sense of themselves and their experiences. Clients who are dissociating traumatic experiences may be able to benefit from questioning their long-held core assumptions about themselves that are contributing to their symptoms. For example, they may believe that they are responsible for their abuse, or that it is wrong for them to show anger toward their abusers, or that they can't cope with their painful memories.

Treatment of dissociative disorders often involves not only these disorders themselves, but also associated disorders of mood, anxiety, and post-traumatic stress.

9.2 Somatic Symptom and Related Disorders

somatic symptoms
Symptoms involving physical problems and/or concerns about medical symptoms.

In the group of disorders in which **somatic symptoms** are prominent, people experience symptoms involving physical problems and/or concerns about medical symptoms. The term "somatic" comes from the Greek word "soma," meaning body. Somatic symptom disorders are psychological in nature, because although people with these disorders may or may not have a diagnosed medical condition, they seek treatment for both their physical symptoms and associated distressing behaviors, thoughts, and feelings. Though somatic symptom disorders are relatively rare, somatic symptom disorders may account for as much as 23 percent of people with medically unexplained symptoms seeking medical care may have a somatic symptom disorder (Steinbrecher, Koerber, Frieser, & Hiller, 2011). For example, over half of the patients referred to cardiologists for heart palpitations or chest pain are found, upon physical examination, not to have heart disease (Jonsbu et al., 2009).

The disorders in this category are fascinating, particularly as they make us think about the complex interplay between mind and body. They also make us realize that we may not always understand completely the role of physical conditions in contributing to psychological symptoms. These disorders also have an intriguing history, as among them were the antecedents of cases central to Freud's recognition of the role of the unconscious mind in personality.

Somatic Symptom Disorder

People with **somatic symptom disorder** have physical symptoms that may or may not be accountable by a medical condition; they also have maladaptive thoughts, feelings, and behaviors. These symptoms disrupt their everyday lives. People with this disorder think to a disproportionate degree about the seriousness of their symptoms, feel extremely anxious about them, and spend a great deal of time and energy to the symptoms or their concerns about their health.

Somatic symptom disorder is relatively rare, but is present with higher than expected frequency among patients seeking treatment for chronic pain (Reme, Tangen, Moe, & Eriksen, 2011). In a small number of cases, the individual does suffer from a diagnosable medical condition, but his or her complaints are far in excess of what we customarily associate with the condition, and the person's impairment level is also much more extreme. Although it may

Individuals with somatic symptom disorder suffer from physical ailments beyond those explained by a medical condition.

MINI CASE

Somatic Symptom Disorder, with Predominant Pain

Helen, a 29-year-old woman, is seeking treatment because her physician said there was nothing more he could do for her. When asked about her physical problems, Helen recited a litany of complaints, including frequent episodes when she could not remember what has happened to her and other times when her vision was so blurred that she could not read the words on a printed page. Helen enjoys cooking and doing things around the house, but she becomes easily fatigued and short of breath for no apparent reason. She often is unable to eat the elaborate meals she prepares, because she becomes nauseated and is prone to vomit any food with even a touch of spice. According to Helen's husband, she has lost all interest in sexual intimacy, and they have intercourse only about once every few months, usually at his insistence. Helen complains of painful cramps during her menstrual periods, and at other times says she feels that her "insides are on fire." Because of additional pain in her back, legs, and chest, Helen wants to stay in bed for much of the day. Helen lives in a large, old Victorian house, from which she ventures only infrequently "because I need to be able to lie down when my legs ache."

appear that people with this diagnosis are intentionally manufacturing symptoms, they actually are not consciously attuned to the ways in which they express these psychological problems physically.

Clients may also experience pain to such a degree that their lives become consumed by the pursuit of relief. A diagnosable medical condition may exist, but the clinician regards the amount and nature of the pain as not accountable by this condition. There are also clients with pain disorder for whom no diagnosable medical condition exists. As a result of their symptoms, people with pain as their main symptom can find themselves in an endless pursuit of relief, spending considerable time and money looking for a cure, but unable to find one because there is no apparent physical cause.

somatic symptom disorder
A disorder involving physical symptoms that may or may not be accountable by a medical condition accompanied by maladaptive thoughts, feelings, and behaviors.

Illness Anxiety Disorder

People with **illness anxiety disorder** fear or mistakenly believe that normal bodily reactions represent the symptoms of a serious illness. They easily become alarmed about their health and seek unnecessary medical tests and procedures to rule out or treat their exaggerated or imagined illnesses. Their worry is not about the symptoms themselves, but about the possibility that they have a serious disease. In addition to experiencing anxiety over their illness, people with illness anxiety disorder are preoccupied with their mistaken beliefs about the seriousness of their symptoms.

illness anxiety disorder
A somatic symptom disorder characterized by the misinterpretation of normal bodily functions as signs of serious illness.

Conversion Disorder (Functional Neurological Symptom Disorder)

The essential feature of **conversion disorder (functional neurological symptom disorder)** is that the individual experiences a change in a bodily function not due to an underlying medical condition. The term "conversion" refers to the presumed transformation of psychological conflict to physical symptoms. The forms that conversion disorder can take range from movement abnormalities, such as difficulty walking or paralysis, to sensory abnormalities such as inability to hear or see.

Clients with conversion disorder show a wide range of physical ailments including "pseudoseizures" (not real seizures, but appearing as such), disorders of movement, paralysis, weakness, disturbances of speech, blindness and other sensory disorders, and cognitive impairment. The symptoms can be so severe that clients are unable to work. Over half are bedridden or require assistive devices. Although clinicians must rule out medical diagnoses before assigning a conversion disorder diagnosis, virtually all clients with these symptoms do not have a medical condition (Rosebush & Mazurek, 2011).

conversion disorder (functional neurological symptom disorder)
A somatic symptom disorder involving the translation of unacceptable drives or troubling conflicts into physical symptoms.

MINI CASE

Conversion Disorder, with Sensory Loss

Tiffany, a 32-year-old banker, thought she had already suffered more stress than one person could handle. She had always thought of herself as a person to whom weird things usually happened, and she commonly made more out of situations than was warranted. Driving down a snowy road one night, she accidentally hit an elderly man who was walking on the side of the road, causing a near fatal injury. In the months that followed, she became caught up in lengthy legal proceedings, which distracted her from her work and caused tremendous emotional stress in her life. On awakening one Monday morning, she found herself staggering around the bedroom, unable to see anything other than the shadows of objects in the room. At first, she thought she was just having a hard time waking up. As the morning progressed, however, she realized that she was losing her vision. She waited two days before consulting a physician. When she did go for her medical appointment, she had an odd lack of concern about what seemed like such a serious physical condition.

Conversion disorder is a rare phenomenon, affecting 1 to 3 percent of those whom clinicians refer for mental health care. The disorder, which often runs in families, generally appears between ages 10 and 35, and is more frequently observed in women and people with less education. Perhaps as many as half of individuals with conversion disorder also suffer from a dissociative disorder (Sar, Akyuz, Kundakci, Kiziltan, & Dogan, 2004). In fact, the ICD-10 classifies conversion disorders as a form of dissociative disorder.

Clinicians face a significant challenge in diagnosing conversion disorder. They must ensure that a person who shows conversion-like symptoms actually does not have an underlying neurological deficit. The problem is exacerbated by the possibility that psychological factors, such as stress, translate into altered brain functioning which, in turn, affects the individual's ability to move the affected body part (Ellenstein, Kranick, & Hallett, 2011). Given the difficulties in diagnosis, *DSM-5* emphasizes the importance of a thorough neurological examination in addition to follow-up to determine whether the symptoms represent an underlying medical condition (Hurwitz, 2004).

Conditions Related to Somatic Symptom Disorders

Malingering involves deliberately feigning the symptoms of physical illness or psychological disorder for an ulterior motive such as receiving disability or insurance benefits. A diagnosis in *DSM-IV-TR*, malingering is not a diagnosis in *DSM-5*. Researchers believe that inferring the intent of the client should not be part of the diagnostic process (Berry & Nelson, 2010).

In **factitious disorder imposed on self,** people show a pattern of falsifying symptoms that are either physical, psychological, or a combination of the two. The individual falsifies these symptoms not to achieve economic gain, but for the purpose of adopting the sick role. In extreme cases, known more informally as Munchausen's syndrome, the individual's entire existence becomes consumed with the pursuit of medical care in which case it is called factitious disorder imposed on self. The individual may also feign the illness of someone else in cases of **factitious disorder imposed on another** (or Munchausen's syndrome by proxy).

Clinicians assume that clients engage in malingering in order to get a direct benefit, such as paid time off from work, insurance payments, or some other tangible reward. Some of these situations involve what we call **primary gain;** namely the direct benefits

malingering
The fabrication of physical or psychological symptoms for some ulterior motive.

factitious disorder imposed on self
A disorder in which people fake symptoms or disorders not for the purpose of any particular gain, but because of an inner need to maintain a sick role.

factitious disorder imposed on another
A condition in which a person induces physical symptoms in another person who is under that person's care.

primary gain
The relief from anxiety or responsibility due to the development of physical or psychological symptoms.

MINI CASE

Illness Anxiety Disorder, Care-Seeking Type

Beth is a 48-year-old mother of two children, both of whom have recently moved away from home. Within the past year, her menstrual periods have become much heavier and more irregular. Seeking an explanation, Beth began to spend days reading everything she could find on uterine cancer. Although medical books specified menstrual disturbance as a common feature of menopause, one newspaper article mentioned the possibility of uterine cancer. She immediately made an appointment with her gynecologist, who tested her and concluded that her symptoms were almost certainly due to menopause. Convinced that her physician was trying to protect her from knowing "the awful truth," Beth visited one gynecologist after another, in search of someone who would properly diagnose what she was certain was a fatal illness. She decided to give up her job as a department store clerk for two reasons. First, she was concerned that long hours of standing at the cash register would aggravate her medical condition. Second, she felt she could not be tied down by a job that was interfering with her medical appointments.

of occupying the sick role. The difficult issue that clinicians face in malingering cases is not trying to treat the symptoms, but to detect actual cases.

Factitious disorder presents a different clinical challenge. Clients deliberately feign or exaggerate symptoms, but they are not trying to achieve primary gain. They may be motivated by **secondary gain,** which is the sympathy and attention they receive from other people when they are ill. Unlike people with conversion disorder, then, people with factitious disorder are consciously producing their symptoms, but their motives are internally rather than externally driven. They "know" they are producing their symptoms, but they don't know why. People with conversion disorder, in other words, believe they are ill and rightfully assume the sick role. People who are malingering know that they are not ill, and therefore, any rewards they receive from sickness are illegally obtained (Kanaan & Wessely, 2010).

secondary gain
The sympathy and attention that a sick person receives from other people.

Theories and Treatment of Somatic Symptom and Related Disorders

The somatic symptom and related disorders have historical roots that go back to the time of Freud and the early psychoanalysts, many of whom attempted to explain unusual cases in which they assumed that the symptoms their patients had reflected what were underlying conflicts. At that time, they referred to conversion disorder as "hysteria" (meaning, literally, "wandering uterus"). They could not find a physiological basis for the symptoms, which tended to disappear after the individual received treatment through hypnosis or psychoanalysis, reinforcing the notion that the symptoms were caused psychologically. Current understandings of these disorders tend to focus on anxiety symptoms that we can associate with them, and the cognitive distortions present in clients' thoughts about themselves and their symptoms.

Though not physically caused per se, conversion disorder symptoms are nearly always precipitated by some form of trauma, either physical or psychological. Whatever the cause, we can most likely understand them from the psychodynamic or cognitive-behavioral perspective. In keeping with Freud's general formulation of hysteria, clinicians working from a psychodynamic approach aim to identify and bring into conscious awareness the underlying conflicts that we associate with the individual's symptoms. Through this process, the client gains insight and self-awareness and becomes able to express emotion directly, rather than through his or her physical manifestation.

Hypnotherapy can be effective in helping individuals to recount memories that are too troubling to consciously recall.

health anxiety
Worry about physical symptoms and illness.

Cognitive-behavioral therapists attempt to help their clients identify and change their thoughts linked to their physical symptoms. The underlying model is based on the premise that people catastrophize their normal bodily sensations. Once they start to exaggerate the importance of their symptoms, individuals with this disorder become even more sensitized to internal bodily cues, which in turn leads them to conclude that they are truly ill (Witthöft & Hiller, 2010). In applying cognitive-behavioral therapy to clients with somatic symptom and related disorders, clinicians help their clients gain a more realistic appraisal of their body's reactions. For example, in one study, clients who had no cardiac illness, but who complained of palpitations or chest pain were exposed to exercise on a treadmill while being taught to interpret their raised heartbeat not as a sign of disease, but as a normal reaction to exertion (Jonsbu, Dammen, Morken, Moum, & Martinsen, 2011).

Hypnotherapy and medication are two additional approaches that clinicians use in treating conversion disorder. In hypnotherapy, the therapist instructs the hypnotized client to, for example, move the paralyzed limb. The therapist then makes the post-hypnotic suggestion to enable the client to sustain the movement after the therapist brings him or her out of hypnosis. SSRIs are the medication that clinicians most likely use in treating conversion disorder, but there are almost no well-controlled investigations of its effectiveness (Rosebush & Mazurek, 2011).

The most promising approach for treating people with illness anxiety involves cognitive-behavioral therapy. Clinicians base this approach on the assumption that underlying the disorder is an unusually high level of **health anxiety,** which we define as worry about physical symptoms and illness. This kind of therapy focuses on teaching individuals to restructure their maladaptive beliefs about their physical symptoms and gain more realistic interpretations of their body's reactions. It also combines mindfulness training with cognitive-behavioral therapy. In this approach, clinicians encourage clients to gain an understanding of their symptoms. For example, clients who believe that they

Medical settings can be a source of significant anxiety for some individuals.

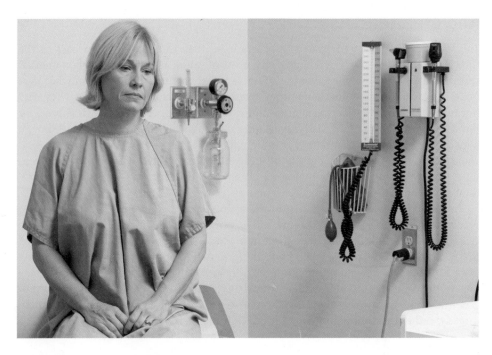

have cancer can learn to interpret their problem not as the fact that they have cancer, but that they fear having cancer (Sorensen, Birket-Smith, Wattar, Buemann, & Salkovskis, 2011).

Malingering and factitious disorder differ in important ways. As we discussed earlier, a client may be motivated to engage in malingering due to any one of several external incentives, including a desire to get out of work or school, evade criminal prosecution, obtain drugs, receive remuneration, avoid military service, or escape from an intolerable situation. People with factitious disorder don't know why they have their symptoms, even though they know that they fabricated the symptoms. In either case, the treatment of choice involves having the clinician directly confront the client (McDermott, Leamon, Feldman, & Scott, 2009).

What's New in the DSM-5

Somatic Symptom and Related Disorders

The *DSM-5* brought a number of significant changes to the entire category of what we now call somatic symptom disorders. The authors of the *DSM-5* acknowledge that the terminology for what were called somatoform disorders in *DSM-IV-TR* was potentially confusing. They also recognize that somatic symptom disorders, psychological factors affecting other medical conditions, and factitious disorders all involve the presence of physical symptoms and/or concern about medical illness. Furthermore, they recognize that the mind and body interact, so that clinicians cannot separate physical symptoms from their psychological basis, or vice versa. Further complicating the prior system, according to the *DSM-5* authors, is the fact that it is never entirely possible to determine that a psychological symptom has no physical basis.

The term "illness anxiety disorder" replaced "hypochondriasis." Clinicians will give those individuals who have no physical symptoms, but are highly anxious this diagnosis, specifying whether or not it involves care-seeking.

Conversion disorder now has functional neurological disorder in parentheses following the diagnosis. Individuals will need to have a full neurological examination before health care professionals determine that their symptoms have no neurological basis.

Other than improving the terminology, the *DSM-5* authors are hoping that their revisions will lead to improved data collection on this group of disorders. Inconsistencies in the diagnostic criteria combine with the shifting landscape from the psychodynamic to the cognitive-behavioral as the main theoretical focus to produce a situation in which there are no solid epidemiological data on a group of disorders whose prevalence may now be more accurately estimated.

9.3 Psychological Factors Affecting Other Medical Conditions

So far we have looked at disorders in which individuals are experiencing physical symptoms that do not have a physiological cause. The diagnostic category called **psychological factors affecting other medical conditions** includes conditions in which a client's physical illness is adversely affected by one or more psychological states. These can include depression, stress, denial of a diagnosis, or engaging in poor or even dangerous health-related behaviors.

In Table 9.2 we outline several examples of medical conditions that may be affected by psychological factors. Specifying the interaction of psychological factors with medical

psychological factors affecting other medical conditions
Disorder in which clients have a medical disease or symptom that appears to be exacerbated by psychological or behavioral factors.

MINI CASE

Psychological Factors Affecting Other Medical Conditions

Brenda is a 41-year-old manager of a large discount chain store. Despite her success, she struggles with an agitated depression, which causes her to feel impatient and irritable most of the time. She recognizes that her emotional problems relate to issues with her parents, and she resents the fact that she chronically suffers from an inner tension that has always been part of her personality. The youngest in a family of four children, she perceived that throughout her childhood she had to do "twice as much" as her siblings to gain her parents' attention and affection. Now, as an adult, she is caught up in a drive toward success that literally makes her physically sick. She has intense headaches and stomachaches on most days, yet she is reluctant to seek medical help, because she doesn't want to take time away from her work.

TABLE 9.2 Psychological Factors Affecting Other Medical Conditions

Medical Condition	Possible Psychological Factor
Hypertension (high blood pressure)	Chronic occupational stress increasing the risk of high blood pressure.
Asthma	Anxiety exacerbating the individual's respiratory symptoms.
Cancer	Denying the need for surgical interventions.
Diabetes	Being unwilling to alter lifestyle to monitor glucose levels or reduce intake.
Chronic tension headache	Continuing family-related stresses that contribute to worsening of symptoms.
Cardiovascular disease	Refusing to visit a cardiac specialist for evaluation despite chest discomfort.

conditions provides health professionals with a clearer understanding of how the two interact. Presumably, once the clinician identifies these, he or she can address these issues and work to help the client's medical condition improve.

Relevant Concepts for Understanding Psychological Factors Affecting Other Medical Conditions

Mental disorders, stress, emotional states, personality traits, and poor coping skills are just some of the psychological factors that can affect an individual's medical conditions. This category of disorders acknowledges the complex interactions through which psychological and physical conditions can affect each other.

Stress and Coping

stress
The unpleasant emotional reaction that a person has when an event is perceived as threatening.

stressful life event
An event that disrupts the individual's life.

coping
The process through which people reduce stress.

Within psychology, the term **stress** refers to the unpleasant emotional reaction a person has when he or she perceives an event to be threatening. This emotional reaction may include heightened physiological arousal, reflecting increased reactivity of the sympathetic nervous system. A **stressful life event** is a stressor that disrupts the individual's life. A person's efforts to reduce stress is called **coping.** It is when coping is unsuccessful, and the stress does not subside, that the individual may seek clinical attention for medical or psychological problems that have developed as a consequence of the constant physiological arousal caused by chronic stress.

What are the types of events that qualify as stressors? The most common way to describe stressors is through stressful life event rating scales, which are intended to quantify the degree to which individuals were exposed to experiences that could threaten their health. One of the best known of these is the Social Readjustment Rating Scale (SRRS) (Holmes & Rahe, 1967), which assesses life stress in terms of life change units (LCU). In developing the LCU index, researchers calculated how strongly each type of event was associated with physical illness. The rationale behind this measure is that the more an event causes you to have to adjust your life circumstances, the more deleterious it is to your health. The College Undergraduate Stress Scale (CUSS) (Renner & Mackin, 1998) is a good example of a stressful life events scale. Unlike the SRRS, which is used on adults of all ages, the CUSS assesses the kinds of stressors most familiar to traditional-age college students (90 percent of the people in the sample were under age 22). The most stressful event in the CUSS is rape, which has an LCU score of 100. Talking in front of class has a score of 72, however, which is also relatively high. Getting straight As has a moderately high score of 51. The least stressful event on the CUSS is attending an athletic event (LCU score = 20).

Life events scales have merits because they are relatively easy to complete and they present a set of objective criteria allowing us to compare people along scales having set values. However, it is not always easy to quantify stress. You and your best friend may each experience the same potentially stressful event, such as being late for class. However, you may be far more perturbed by this situation than your friend. Your day will be far less pleasant than your friend's, and if you were repeatedly late, you might be at risk for a stress-related illness.

Cognitive stress models place greater emphasis on how you interpret events rather than on whether or not you experienced a given event. According to these models, it's the appraisal of an event as stressful that determines whether it will have a negative impact on your emotional state. Not only do people differ in how they interpret events, the circumstances surrounding the event also affect them. If your friend's professor doesn't take attendance, but yours does, there's a reason why you feel more stressed about being late than your friend.

As this example shows, stress is in the eye of the beholder, or at least in the mind. Even a relatively minor event can lead you to experience stress if you interpret it negatively. The cognitive stress model assumes, furthermore, that these "little" events can have a big impact, especially when they build up in a short period of time. Events called **hassles** can have significant effects on health when there are enough of them, and you interpret them negatively. If you are not only late for class, but get into an argument with your friend, stub your toe, spill your coffee, and miss your bus home, you will have as many potentially stress-causing events in one afternoon as someone experiencing a "bigger" life event such as going out on a first date.

On the positive side, you can balance your hassles with what researchers call **uplifts,** which are events on a small scale that boost your feelings of well-being. Perhaps you open up your Facebook page and find a pleasant greeting from a former high school acquaintance. The smile this greeting brings to your face can help make up for some of the stress you might have felt at your being late, stubbing your toe, or missing your bus. Uplifts are especially important within the positive psychology movement, because we view them as contributing to people's feelings of day-to-day happiness.

hassle
A relatively minor event that can cause stress.

uplifts
Events that boost your feelings of well-being.

This woman's anger-control problems make it difficult for her to deal with everyday situations in a rational, calm manner.

problem-focused coping
Coping in which the individual takes action to reduce stress by changing whatever it is about the situation that makes it stressful.

emotion-focused coping
A type of coping in which a person does not change anything about the situation itself, but instead tries to improve feelings about the situation.

It's wonderful when life sends a few uplifts your way, but when it doesn't, you need to find other ways to reduce stress through the use of coping if you are to maintain your mental health. The two basic ways of coping are **problem-focused coping** and **emotion-focused coping** (Lazarus & Folkman, 1984). In problem-focused coping, you attempt to reduce stress by acting to change whatever it is that makes the situation stressful. If you're constantly late for class because the bus is overcrowded and tends to arrive 5 or 10 minutes after it's supposed to, then you would cope by getting an earlier bus, even if it means you have to wake up earlier than necessary. In contrast, in emotion-focused coping, you don't change the situation, but instead change the way you feel about it. Maybe your professor doesn't care if you're a little bit late so you shouldn't be so hard on yourself. Avoidance is another emotion-focused strategy. This coping method is similar to the defense mechanism of denial. Rather than think about a stressful experience, you just put it out of your mind.

Which is the better of the two ways of coping? The answer is: it depends. People cope with some situations more effectively through problem-focused coping. In changeable situations, you are most likely better off if you use problem-focused coping. If you're stressed because your grades are in a slump, rather than not think about the problem, you would be well-advised to try to change the situation by studying harder. If you're stressed because you lost your cell phone, and you truly cannot find it, then you may be better off by using emotion-focused coping such as telling yourself you needed a newer model anyhow.

As people get older, they are able to use coping strategies that more effectively alleviate their stress. In comparing a sample of community-dwelling older adults with college undergraduates, Segal, Hook, and Coolidge (2001) found that younger adults received higher scores on the dysfunctional coping strategies of focusing on and venting emotions, mentally disengaging, and using alcohol and drugs. Older adults, in contrast, were more likely to use impulse control and turn to their religion as coping strategies. These findings are in keeping with those of other researchers (Labouvie-Vief & Diehl, 2000), which indicated that older adults use more problem-focused coping and other strategies that allow them to channel their negative feeling into productive activities.

Coping strategies can play an important role in whether or not an individual will suffer health problems. A person who is able to manage stress effectively experiences fewer adverse consequences of stress. Furthermore, as you may know from personal experience, situations that create high levels of stress in a person do not always have negative consequences. Some people thrive on a lifestyle filled with challenges and new experiences, feeling energized by being under constant pressure, as shown in a classic study by DeLongis, Folkman, and Lazarus (1988).

Stress plays an important role in a variety of medical conditions through its interaction with immune status and function (Schneiderman, Ironson, & Siegel, 2005). A stressful event can initiate a set of reactions within the body that lowers its resistance to disease. These reactions can also aggravate the symptoms of a chronic, stress-related physical disorder.

There are a number of paradoxical findings from research on stress, immune functioning, and health. Both too much and too little can place the individual at risk for developing poor health outcomes, ranging from heart disease to Alzheimer's disease to some forms of cancer. Additionally, although having a large social network is generally beneficial to immune functioning, if an individual's social network is too large, life stressors may have more of a negative impact on health than they otherwise would. In terms of personality, having a generally optimistic stance toward life is usually beneficial, but in the face of difficult or long-term stressors, then optimism is associated with poorer immune functioning and, ultimately, negative health outcomes (Segerstrom, Roach, Evans, Schipper, & Darville, 2010).

Sociocultural factors also play a role in causing and aggravating stress-related disorders. For example, living in a harsh social

Drinking alcohol to cope with stress is a maladaptive coping strategy, as it can cause further problems for the stressed individuals, particularly if they drink to excess.

environment that threatens a person's safety, interferes with the establishment of social relationships, and involves high levels of conflict, abuse, and violence are conditions related to lower socioeconomic status. Chronic exposure to the stresses of such an environment can lead to a number of changes in hormones that ultimately have deleterious effects on cardiovascular health, interacting with an individual's genetic and physiological risk. Both cardiovascular health and immune system functioning seem to be sensitive to the degree of stress a person experiences as a function of being lower in socioeconomic status. The limbic system, which mediates a person's responses to stress, seems to play a large role in accounting for these connections between social class and health (McEwen & Gianaros, 2010).

Emotional Expression

Coping with stress can help you regulate the emotion of anxiety and hence reduce stress. However, there are times when expressing your emotions can improve your physical and mental well-being. Actively confronting the emotions that arise from an upsetting or traumatic event can have long-term health benefits (Pennebaker, 1997). In one classic study, researchers instructed a group of first-year college students to write about the experience of coming to college. A control group wrote about superficial topics. Those who wrote about coming to college actually reported that they were more homesick than the control subjects. However, they made fewer visits to physicians and by the end of the year, the students who wrote were doing as well as or better than the control subjects in terms of grade point average and the experience of positive moods. The researchers concluded that confronting feelings and thoughts regarding a stressful experience can have long-lasting positive effects, even though the initial impact of such confrontation may be disruptive (Pennebaker, Colder, & Sharp, 1990).

Pennebaker and his colleagues have expanded their findings to a variety of populations. In a meta-analysis of 146 randomized studies, disclosure had a positive and significant effect for people with a wide range of emotional concerns (Frattaroli, 2006). More recently, researchers have even identified positive mental health effects of writing on social media sites, including blogging (Ko & Kuo, 2009).

Children who are bullied at school may suffer long-term psychological consequences.

Stressful life events, such as moving away to college, can be damaging to physical health if the individual has difficulty coping with stress she may be experiencing.

Type A behavior pattern
Pattern of behaviors that include being hard-driving, competitive, impatient, cynical, suspicious of and hostile toward others, and easily irritated.

Type D personality
People who experience emotions that include anxiety, irritation, and depressed mood.

behavioral medicine
An interdisciplinary approach to medical conditions affected by psychological factors that is rooted in learning theory.

Personality Style

One of the most thoroughly researched areas investigating the connection between personality and health involves the **Type A behavior pattern,** a pattern of behaviors that include being hard-driving, competitive, impatient, cynical, suspicious of and hostile toward others, and easily irritated (see Table 9.3). Their constantly high levels of emotional arousal keep their blood pressure and sympathetic nervous system on overdrive, placing them at risk for developing heart disease, and at greater risk for heart attacks and stroke. Not only are people with the Type A behavior patterns at high risk because their bodies are placed under stress, but their hard-driving and competitive lifestyles often include high-risk behaviors of smoking, drinking alcohol to excess, and failure to exercise (Mainous et al., 2010).

Another significant personality risk factor for heart disease occurs among people who experience strong depressive affect, but keep their feelings hidden—the so-called **Type D Personality.** Unlike the "A" in Type A, which is not an acronym, the "D" in Type D stands for "Distressed." Type D personalities experience emotions that include anxiety, irritation, and depressed mood. These individuals are at increased risk for heart disease due to their tendency to experience negative emotions while inhibiting the expression of these emotions when they are in social situations. In addition to being at higher risk of becoming ill or dying from heart disease, these individuals have reduced quality of daily life and benefit less from medical treatments. Psychologists think that the link between personality and heart disease for these people is, in part, due to an impaired immune response to stress (Denollet & Pedersen, 2011).

Applications to Behavioral Medicine

Because psychological factors that contribute to a medical condition have such a wide range, clinicians must conduct a careful assessment of how each particular client's health is affected by their behavior. The field of **behavioral medicine** applies the growing body of scientific evidence regarding mind-body relationships to helping improve people's physical health by addressing its relationships to the psychological factors of stress, emotions, behavior patterns, and personality. In addition, clinicians working in behavioral medicine often team up with psychologists and other mental health professionals to help clients adopt strategies to learn and maintain behaviors that will maximize their physical functioning. By improving patient compliance with medical illnesses, these clinicians can help the people with whom they work to achieve better health and avoid further complications.

Psychoeducation is an important component of behavioral medicine. Clients need to understand how their behavior influences the development or worsening of the symptoms of chronic illnesses. Then, the clinician can work with the client to develop specific ways to improve his or her health habits. For example, diet control and exercise are key to preventing and reducing the serious complications of cardiovascular disease. Clinicians can teach clients ways to build these new health habits into their daily regimens. Similarly, clinicians can train people with sleep disorders to improve their sleep habits. People can manage chronic pain, which contributes to depressive symptoms, through strategies such as biofeedback.

Clients can also learn how to manage stress and improve their coping methods. For people who have a personality style that may be contributing to their symptoms, the task becomes more challenging. Psychotherapy provides a useful adjunct to medical care. In the case of people who suffer myocardial infarctions, which often trigger depression, it is crucial for health care personnel to address the client's emotional as well as physical reactions to the experience.

TABLE 9.3 Are You Type A?

The Jenkins Activity Survey assesses the degree to which a person has a coronary-prone personality and behavior pattern. People with high scores, referred to as Type A, tend to be competitive, impatient, restless, aggressive, and pressured by time and responsibilities. In the items below, you can see which responses would reflect these characteristics.

Do you have trouble finding time to get your hair cut or styled?

Has your spouse or friend ever told you that you eat too fast?

How often do you actually "put words in the person's mouth" in order to speed things up?

Would people you know well agree that you tend to get irritated easily?

How often do you find yourself hurrying to get to places even when there is plenty of time?

At work, do you ever keep two jobs moving forward at the same time by shifting back and forth rapidly from one to the other?

SOURCE: From C. D. Jenkins, S. J. Zyzanski, and R. H. Rosenman, *The Jenkins Activity Survey.* Copyright © 1965, 1966, 1969, 1979 by The Psychological Corporation, © Reprinted by permission of the author.

Behavioral medicine is also moving increasingly toward interventions that the profession once considered "alternative" (i.e., alternative to traditional medicine), including mindfulness training, relaxation, and meditation. Clinicians teach clients to monitor without judging their internal bodily states (such as heart rate and breathing), as well as their perceptions, affective states, thoughts, and imagery. By doing so, they can gain the feelings that they can control their body's reactions. With regard to their health, by observing their bodily reactions in this objective fashion, they gain a more differentiated understanding of which aspects of their experiences illness affects and which it does not. They can see their ailments as having natural roles and not impeding their ability to enjoy life in general (Carmody, Reed, Kristeller, & Merriam, 2008).

For example, people with the Type A behavior pattern can benefit from training aimed at improving their awareness of their reactions to stress, methods of coping with stressful situations, and behavioral interventions intended to improve their compliance with medical advice aimed at reducing their cardiovascular risk. Particularly important is a sense of mastery, namely, the belief that you have the ability to cope with or control the problems you encounter in life. People who feel they are in greater control over their life circumstances have a reduced risk of developing cardiovascular and related health problems (Roepke & Grant, 2011). Increasingly, clinicians are finding that efforts to improve people's health by addressing only their medical needs will not have the long-term desired effects unless the clinicians also incorporate these psychological issues into treatment.

9.4 Dissociative and Somatic Symptom Disorders: The Biopsychosocial Perspective

Although very distinct disorders, the disorders we've covered in this chapter share the features of involving complex interactions between the mind and body, questions about the nature of the self, and distinctions between "real" and "fake" psychological symptoms. We've also examined the role of stress in psychological disorders and in relation to medical illnesses and physical symptoms.

Biology clearly plays a role in making some individuals more vulnerable to psychological disorders, and particularly so in these disorders. A person may have a known or undiagnosed physical condition that certain stressors particularly affect, which then trigger the symptoms for a somatic symptom or related disorder. However, whatever the role of biology, cognitive-behavioral explanations provide useful approaches for treatment. Even people whose medical condition is clearly documented, as in chronic pain disorder, can benefit from learning how to reframe their thoughts about their disorder if not their actual health-related behaviors. At the same time, we are learning more about how stress affects physical functioning, including the impact of social discrimination on chronic conditions such as heart disease and diabetes.

It is quite likely that the mind-body connections involved in these disorders will come under even closer scrutiny as work on *DSM-5* evolves. The historical connections will fade between these so-called "neurotic" disorders that seemed to affect many of Freud's patients. Nevertheless, they will maintain, if not their nomenclature, their fascination.

Return to the Case: Rose Marston

Rose underwent 16 weekly individual therapy sessions, focusing on specific CBT techniques such as psychoeducation, self-monitoring techniques where she recorded the number of minutes spent per day thinking about her symptoms, cognitive restructuring techniques, exposure and response prevention, and perceptual retraining exercises. These exercises focused on teaching Rose to look at her body in a more holistic, objective way and taking the focus away from her stomach. During each session, Rose and her therapist discussed what happened during the previous week, reviewed "homework," and set an agenda for the session. Using this highly structured approach to treating her Rose began to feel relief from her symptoms after the first few weeks of treatment. In addition, Rose began to treat her lactose intolerance through a combination of diet control and over-the-counter medication. By the end of the 16 weeks, Rose's pain was gone, and she had, reconciled with her boyfriend, recognizing the burden put on their relationship by her constant concerns over her stomach pain. Rose's depression had also lifted, and she and her clinician agreed that she would not need to go on an antidepressant. She continued to visit her clinician once per month for check-in visits, to revisit her progress and assess for any recurrences of symptoms.

Dr. Tobin's reflections: Rose's apparent sensitivity to her rather mild physical symptoms likely contributed to her previous depression. Though her depression had been temporarily treated with antidepressants, it was clear that her concerns continued to persist until the concomitant stressors of losing her boyfriend and her job led to an exacerbation of symptoms. It was helpful in Rose's case that she was highly motivated for treatment, which contributed to her positive treatment outcome. Although individuals with somatic symptom disorder may be very uncomfortable disclosing the extent of their symptoms and thoughts about their symptoms, Rose's motivation for treatment allowed her to reveal the extent of her thoughts and beliefs about her stomach discomfort. This information allowed her clinician to successfully tailor treatment to her specific concerns. Although Rose will require constant monitoring of her lactose intake, she fortunately will be able to keep her physical symptoms under control, which will eliminate the source of her psychological preoccupation and distress.

SUMMARY

- This chapter covered three sets of conditions: dissociative disorders, somatic symptom disorders, and psychological factors affecting other medical conditions. In each of these sets of conditions, the body expresses psychological conflict and stress in an unusual fashion.

- **Dissociative disorders** occur when the human mind seems capable of dissociating, or separating mental

functions. Major forms of dissociative disorders include **dissociative identity disorder (DID), dissociative amnesia, depersonalization, depersonalization/ derealization disorder,** and **derealization.**

- Among mental health professionals, the general viewpoint regarding dissociative disorders is that some type of traumatic event leads people with these disorders to experience a splitting apart of their conscious experiences, sense of self, or feelings of continuity over time. Clinicians, nevertheless, face a daunting task both in diagnosing and treating an individual's dissociative symptoms.

- **Somatic disorders** are a group of conditions in which an individual's major symptoms involve what the individual experiences as physical problems and/or concerns about medical illness.

- **Somatic symptom disorder** involves the expression of psychological issues through bodily symptoms that any known medical condition cannot explain, or as due to the effects of a substance. The difference between somatic symptom disorder and conversion disorder is that the former involves multiple and recurrent bodily symptoms, rather than a single physical complaint.

- The essential feature of **conversion disorder (functional neurological symptom disorder)** is that the individual experiences a change in a bodily function not due to an underlying medical condition. The term "conversion" refers to the presumed transformation of psychological conflict to physical symptoms.

- Conditions related to somatic symptom disorders include **malingering,** the deliberate feigning of symptoms of physical illness or psychological disorder for an ulterior motive such as receiving disability or insurance benefits; and **factitious disorder** where people show a pattern of falsifying symptoms that are either physical, psychological, or a combination of the two.

- The diagnostic category that we call **psychological factors affecting other medical conditions** includes conditions in which a client's physical illness is adversely affected by one or more psychological states such as depression, stress, denial of a diagnosis, or engaging in poor or even dangerous health-related behaviors.

- Mental disorders, stress, emotional states, personality traits, and poor coping skills are just some of the psychological factors that can affect an individual's medical conditions. This category of disorders acknowledges the complex interactions through which psychological and physical conditions can affect each other.

- **Coping** with stress can help you regulate the emotion of anxiety and hence reduce **stress.** However, there are times when expressing your emotions can improve your physical and mental well-being. Actively confronting the emotions that arise from an upsetting or traumatic event can have long-term health benefits.

- Because psychological factors that contribute to a medical condition have such a wide range, clinicians must conduct a careful assessment of how each particular client's health is affected by their behavior. The field of **behavioral medicine** applies the growing body of scientific evidence regarding mind-body relationships to helping improve people's physical health by addressing its relationships to the psychological factors of stress, emotions, behavior patterns, and personality.

- Biology clearly plays a role in making some individuals more vulnerable to psychological disorders, and particularly so in these disorders. A person may have a known or undiagnosed physical condition that may be affected by certain **stressful life events,** which then trigger the symptoms for a somatic symptom disorder. However, whatever the role of biology, cognitive-behavioral explanations provide useful approaches for treatment.

KEY TERMS

Feeding and Eating Disorders; Elimination Disorders; Sleep-Wake Disorders; and Disruptive, Impulse-Control, and Conduct Disorders

Learning Objectives

10.1 Identify characteristics, theories, and treatments of eating disorders

10.2 Understand symptoms and theories of elimination disorders

10.3 Recognize indicators of sleep-wake disorders

10.4 Differentiate among disruptive, impulse-control, and conduct disorders

10.5 Analyze the biopsychosocial model for eating, elimination, sleep-wake, and impulse-control disorders

Case Report: Rosa Nomirez

Demographic information: Rosa is a 25-year-old Hispanic female.

Presenting problem: Rosa self-referred to a community mental health center for feelings of depression. During the intake evaluation, Rosa stated that she had been feeling down and depressed for several months, and since her depression had not remitted on its own, she decided to seek treatment. She stated this was not an easy decision for her, as she usually was able to handle difficult emotions on her own. Rosa also reported that those close to her were worried about her health and had been urging her for some time to seek treatment, although she stated that she couldn't understand why they were concerned. The clinician noted that Rosa appeared severely underweight and frail. Rosa stated she was feeling depressed, mainly because as she described, "I feel like a fat monster all of the time." Rosa estimated that these feelings originated while she was pregnant with her daughter, now 14 months old. She had stopped working after giving birth in order to focus on raising her daughter, while her husband provided for the family. Rosa stated that she had a difficult time returning to her normal weight after giving birth, and that she believed that she still appeared to look pregnant. She remarked that "all I can see in the mirror is my stomach and how enormous it makes me look all over." She reported that she did not know her current weight and that she was afraid to weigh herself for fear that she was continuing to gain weight. She exclaimed, "I feel so ashamed that I am so fat still. I feel like I'll never look normal again."

Rosa reported that she followed a diet consisting of about 300 to 400 calories per day, and that she had been "working her way down" in terms of daily caloric consumption ever since her concerns about her weight began. At that time, Rosa had searched diet tips on an Internet search engine. She discovered an online community devoted to supporting women who wanted to lose weight and stay thin. These "pro-ana" sites as she described them offered her support from other users, as well as helpful tips for not only how to restrict her caloric intake, but how to hide it from others whose concern she saw as bothersome and interfering with her goals of losing weight. She had been using the sites daily for about 6 months. Her husband discovered the sites on the computer, and recognizing the danger they posed, pleaded with Rosa to stop using them. She stated that she didn't understand why he didn't want her using the sites, as maintaining a low body weight was so important to her, and the thought of gaining weight caused her intense feelings of anxiety.

Although she stated that she rarely felt interested in sex and had not gotten her menstrual period for about 4 months, Rosa explained that she and her husband had been trying to have another child for about 6 months. The clinician asked about any other physiological changes that she had noticed. Rosa stated she felt tired much of the time, but beyond that, she denied any difficulties. "I usually just think about my daughter and about staying thin. There isn't really time to worry about much else." She further stated that while out in public, she often compares her body to others. This had become a source of overwhelming anxiety and so she typically preferred to stay home so she didn't feel "judged for being fat" as she explained.

According to Rosa, her family had been "constantly bothering" her about her weight. "They just don't understand how I feel. They try to force me to eat and it just makes me feel so uncomfortable and depressed. It feels like they are mocking because they know how disgusting I am, so I

Case Report *continued*

usually just avoid spending time with them now." She reported that her parents emigrated from Colombia when she was an infant. Since then several other relatives have moved close by and although Rosa described the family as close-knit, she explained that it was difficult for the older members of her family to understand the differences between Colombian and American culture where she felt a pressure to be thin and attractive. "It's just not that way where they are from, and so they don't know what it's like for me."

Relevant history: Rosa reported that as a teenager she occasionally had episodes of bingeing and purging by vomiting, although she found the effects of the purging aversive. She explained that she has been concerned about her body weight "for as long as I can remember," and that she generally tries to maintain a low body weight. However, her restrictive eating behaviors became more severe following the birth of her daughter. She denied a family history of eating disorders.

Case formulation: Rosa meets diagnostic criteria for anorexia nervosa, binge-eating/purging type. Criterion A states the individual must maintain a body weight significantly lower than what is expected for their age and height. With permission, the clinician obtained Rosa's weight from her most recent physician visit, and determined that her weight was below 85 percent of her expected weight. She also meets Criterion B because

she has been intensely fearful of gaining weight even though she is of lower than average body weight. Rosa meets Criterion C because she fails to recognize the seriousness of her low body weight.

Although Rosa reported feelings of depression, the clinician determined that her depressive symptoms are secondary to the anorexia. It appears that her feelings of depression are directly related to her heightened concern about her weight, therefore the clinician will not give her an additional diagnosis of depression. It is clear that Rosa's concern about her weight has alienated her from those to whom she is closest, namely her husband and her immediate family.

Treatment plan: Rosa was resistant to the clinician's advice that she should receive treatment for her anorexia. With her permission, the clinician reached out to her husband and family who agreed that treatment was crucial for her. After discussing the matter with her husband, she agreed to go for an initial consultation at a day treatment program that specializes in treatment for eating disorders. After the evaluation there, Rosa decided that pursuing treatment would be better for her and her husband's relationship and would help reduce her feelings of depression. Rosa agreed to sign a contract to participate in the treatment program for at least 2 months.

Sarah Tobin, PhD

The disorders that we cover in this chapter include eating disorders, elimination disorders, and a range of disorders in which individuals exhibit a lack of control over their impulses. Eating disorders involve difficulties that individuals have regarding food and control over their eating, dieting, or elimination of food. Elimination disorders specifically involve difficulties that affect primarily children or adolescents who are have difficulty controlling the biological functions of urination and defecation, generally due to psychological disturbances. Sleep-wake disorders similarly involve control over biological processes that often have a relationship to psychological functions. Finally, the impulse-control disorders reflect disturbances in the individual's ability to regulate one or more of a range of behaviors related to particular desires, interests, and the expression of emotions.

eating disorders
Diagnosis for people who experience persistent disturbances of eating or eating-related behavior that results in the person's altering the consumption or absorption of food.

10.1 Eating Disorders

People who have **eating disorders** experience persistent disturbances of eating or eating-related behavior that result in changes in consumption or absorption of food. These disorders significantly impair the individual's physical and psychosocial functioning.

Characteristics of Anorexia Nervosa

Clinicians diagnose an individual as having **anorexia nervosa (AN)** when he or she shows three basic types of symptoms: severely restricted eating, which leads the person to have an abnormally low body weight, intense and unrealistic fear of getting fat or gaining weight, and disturbed self-perception of body shape or weight. In other words, people with this eating disorder restrict their food intake, become preoccupied with gaining weight, and feel that they are already overweight even though they may be seriously underweight. *DSM-IV-TR* used "intense fear" of gaining weight as a criterion, but *DSM-5* emphasizes behavior ("persistent behavior that interferes with weight gain"). Within the AN category, clinicians may classify individuals as "restricting type," meaning that they do not engage in binge eating, and "binge-eating/purging type," which means that they do.

anorexia nervosa (AN)
An eating disorder characterized by an inability to maintain normal weight, an intense fear of gaining weight, and distorted body perception.

The depletion of nutrients that occurs in people with anorexia nervosa leads them to develop a series of health changes, some of which can be life threatening. Their bones, muscles, hair, and nails become weak and brittle, they develop low blood pressure, slowed breathing and pulse, and they are lethargic, sluggish, and fatigued. Their gastrointestinal system functions abnormally and they may become infertile. Most seriously, their heart and brain suffer damage and they may experience multiple organ failure. These changes can have fatal consequences. A 35-year follow-up of over 500 individuals with AN yielded a mortality estimate of 4.4 percent (Millar et al., 2005). Although the majority of deaths from AN occur in young adults, a Norwegian study of AN–related deaths found that 43 percent of the deaths occurred in women age 65 and older (Reas et al., 2005). Women with AN die not only from the complications of their disorder, but from suicide. The highest rates of suicide attempts (25 percent) occur in women who have comorbid depression and the binge-eating/purging form of the disorder (Forcano et al., 2011).

People who have AN experience a core disturbance in their body image. They are dissatisfied with their bodies and believe that their bodies are larger than they really are. In one fMRI study, women with anorexia nervosa showed distinct arousal patterns in areas of the brain involved in processing emotion (Mohr et al., 2010). Women with AN also seem to engage in social comparison processes when they view other women's bodies. An fMRI study compared women's limbic system activation with AN when seeing their own and other women's bodies. Their amgydala showed greater activation at viewing other women's bodies (Vocks et al., 2010). Women with the restrictive form of AN appear not to value thinness so much as they are repelled by the idea of being overweight (Cserjési et al., 2010).

The lifetime prevalence of AN is 0.9 percent for women and 0.3 percent for men. In addition, people with anorexia nervosa have higher rates of mood, anxiety, impulse-control,

MINI CASE

Anorexia Nervosa Restricting Type

Lorraine is an 18-year-old first-year college student who, since leaving home to go to school, has been losing weight steadily. Initially, Lorraine wanted to lose a few pounds, thinking this would make her look sexier. She stopped eating at the cafeteria, because they served too many starchy foods, choosing instead to prepare her own low-calorie meals. Within 2 months, she became obsessed with dieting and exercise and with a fear that she might gain weight and become fat. She stopped menstruating, and her weight dropped from 110 to 80 pounds. Regardless of the repeated expressions of concern by her friends that she appeared emaciated, Lorraine insisted that she was fat. When Lorraine went home for Thanksgiving break, her parents were so alarmed that they insisted that she go for professional help.

REAL STORIES

Portia de Rossi: Anorexia Nervosa

"I had lost control. I'd lost control and I could do it again without warning. If I lost control again, I could get fat again. I would have to start this thing over again. I would fail at the one thing I knew I was good at."

Born in Australia as Amanda Lee Rogers, actress Portia de Rossi has come a long way since she began her professional career at the age of 12 as a fashion model. That was the time, as she recalls in her memoir, *Unbearable Lightness: A Story of Loss and Gain*, when she began to focus obsessively on her weight. In the book, she writes; "Since I was a twelve-year-old girl taking pictures in my front yard to submit to modeling agencies, I'd never known a day where my weight wasn't the determining factor for my self-esteem. My weight was my mood, and the more effort I put into starving myself to get it to an acceptable level, the more satisfaction I would feel as the restriction and the denial built into an incredible sense of accomplishment."

After her father unexpectedly passed away when she was 9 years old, Portia and her older brother were raised by her mother. Although her mother supported her quest for perfection and helped her along in her rise to fame, Portia does not blame her for creating pressure to lose weight, writing, "it has always felt internal." She describes this internal drive as a "drill sergeant of a voice" that she developed which ordered her to keep pushing herself to lose weight, and keep a strict record of her food intake and exercise.

As a teenager, Portia remembers getting "ready" for photo shoots, which consisted of losing weight in a short amount of time before the shoot. With her mother's help, Portia would restrict her diet severely or not eat at all in the days leading up to the shoots. As she recalls, "Me losing weight before a job was like an athlete training for a competition." Before long, Portia's intense focus on dieting before photo shoots became a constant presence in her life. After unsuccessfully trying diet pills to maintain her weight, Portia followed the example which her fellow models set and began bingeing and purging. She writes, "Unlike the other girls, I didn't throw up because I had to eat to impress the client, but because I wanted to eat. Nothing was better after a modeling job than food. It was the only thing that took all the bad feelings away. Like an eraser, it allowed me to start over, to forget the feelings of insecurity and awkwardness I'd experienced that day. But the comforting ritual of rewarding myself with food started to backfire as jobs started being booked back to back. Instead of having a week of starving to counteract the weight gained from eating fries, ice cream, and candy, I was given a day or two to get back on track, to be the 34-24-35 model that they'd booked off my card. The client was expecting an image of me that wasn't who I really was. They wanted a self-confident young woman who was naturally thin, beautiful, comfortable in her skin. Who I really was, was an average-looking child staving off puberty with its acne and weight gain just waiting to expose me for the phony I was. So, I'd throw up."

After a few years of modeling, Portia discovered her love of acting. She recalls initially loving acting as she was able to escape from herself for a while. After a few high-profile appearances in Australian films, Portia moved to Los Angeles, where she eventually had her big break. At 25 years old, Portia joined the cast of the popular television series, *Ally McBeal*, playing Nelle Porter, the gutsy and outspoken new member of the law firm that the show portrayed. One of the first things she did when she landed the job was to purchase a treadmill to put in her dressing room, as she had seen her cast mates do, so she could work out during her lunch breaks.

Although she was proud of her accomplishment, joining the show marked a new chapter in her life in which she began to experience immense pressure to be thin, along with the pressure that she felt from herself to blend into the Hollywood crowd. In addition to feeling pressure to be thin, Portia was faced with the realization that she was homosexual. She became plagued by fear that the public would find out about her sexuality thus marring her image as a Hollywood star. As she hid this part of herself, she continued to struggle with her weight throughout her tenure at *Ally McBeal*.

Portia remembers enjoying her work on the show's set, but intense feelings of insecurity continued to plague her. Ironically, the hallmark of the character that she played was the confidence that she exuded, and Portia struggled to

Portia de Rossi

maintain this image on the show. Compounding her suffering was the fact that she did not share her feelings with anyone, and she remembers driving home from the set every day and crying to herself for hours.

When she started on *Ally McBeal*, Portia was bingeing and purging frequently, although this did not achieve her desired body weight, and she felt undeserving of her success. One incident on the set of a commercial she was to shoot for a beauty campaign catapulted her into what would eventually become anorexia. Portia was mortified when she was unable to fit into any of the suits that the stylists provided for her. She recalls feeling crushed when the stylists announced that she was a size 8. After this incident, Portia began seeing a nutritionist, who provided her with a list of healthy foods to eat and required her to fill out a daily food diary. The nutritionist, Suzanne, also taught Portia to measure her food portions with a scale in order to achieve successful weight loss. Portia was excited to have some direction with her dieting, although she soon took the nutritionist's recommendations to an unhealthy extreme. "Suzanne had set my calorie intake for optimum weight loss at 1,400 calories a day. I reset it to 1,000. Problem solved." This daily calorie count began to dwindle as Portia continued to lose weight. Her weight loss never left her feeling satisfied and she constantly lowered her goal weight. She began exercising frequently throughout the day, including on her drive to see her nutritionist when she would pull over so she could go for a jog as sitting in the car for a prolonged period of time made her feel anxious. Although she was faithfully seeing her nutritionist, she concealed her extreme food restriction, creating a fake food diary that mimicked what her food intake should have been.

As her weight plummeted, Portia was encouraged by the positive media attention that she was receiving, including magazine covers, and constant paparazzi coverage. Her friends' and family's reaction, however, was much different. While visiting Portia in L.A., her best friend commented that she appeared too thin. Portia recalls her reaction to this statement. "That's funny: too thin. Just this morning on the set I had to clench my buttocks as I walked through the law office on a full-length lens because if I walked normally the part where my hips meet my thighs bulged out rhythmically with each step: left fat bulge, right fat bulge, left fat bulge, and cue dialogue, 'You wanted to see me?' Too thin." This highlights the extreme and unrealistic standards Portia placed on her appearance, and that also drove her to the depths of anorexia.

Portia's weight continued to plunge, thanks to a combination of severe calorie restriction (down to a few hundred calories per day) and extreme amounts of exercise. She utilized several tricks such as keeping her apartment at 60 degrees so her body would burn more calories and not using toothpaste in order to avoid "accidentally" ingesting excess calories. She also stopped menstruating. Portia's weight loss did not go unnoticed by the media, although she didn't understand why there was cause for concern. As she writes, "Some of them said that I was anorexic. It wasn't true. At 100 pounds I was way too heavy to be anorexic."

With this distorted mindset that is typical to those suffering from anorexia nervosa, Portia continued on her path to weight loss until she was down to a frightening 82 pounds. At the time, she was shooting her first major Hollywood film as a leading actress in *Who is Cletis Tout?*. She ran into major physical difficulties while shooting the film, which required her to perform in many action shots. Due to her dietary restriction and low body weight, her joints ached to the point where she could barely move without extreme agony. She eventually collapsed while shooting a particularly challenging scene, and received immediate medical attention. The results of her medical tests indicated that she had osteoporosis, cirrhosis of the liver, and lupus. For the first time, Portia was forced to confront the reality of her obsession with weight loss. Portia had nearly starved herself to death, and so began her long and difficult journey toward recovery.

In the book, Portia equates anorexia to her first love. "We met and were instantly attracted to each other. We spent every moment of the day together . . . losing anorexia was painful—like losing your sense of purpose. I no longer knew what to do without it to consider . . . Without anorexia, I had nothing. Without it, I was nothing. I wasn't even a failure; I simply felt like I didn't exist." As she began to eat more and gain weight, she struggled once again with bulimia due to her feelings of guilt over eating foods that she had restricted herself from for over a year. Her treatment regimen included seeing a therapist, taking hormone replacement pills and antidepressants to help reduce her obsession with food. In 10 months, she gained 80 pounds. As Portia slowly recovered, she also came to terms with her sexuality. From living with a girlfriend, she learned how to eat what she wanted rather than constantly restricting her cravings, which she recognized as leading to obsessive dieting behaviors. By the time she started dating her current wife, Ellen DeGeneres, in 2004, Portia had fully recovered from anorexia. She now enjoys a healthy and active lifestyle, free from the constraints of her eating disorder. "I never wanted to think about food and weight ever again," she writes. "For me, that's the definition of recovered."

Individuals with anorexia nervosa experience distress associated with feeling "fat" despite having a low body weight.

bulimia nervosa
An eating disorder involving alternation between the extremes of eating large amounts of food in a short time, and then compensating for the added calories either by vomiting or other extreme actions to avoid gaining weight.

purging
Eliminating food through unnatural methods, such as vomiting or the excessive use of laxatives.

and substance use disorders. The majority of individuals who develop anorexia nervosa between their early teenage years and their early 20s have the disorder for 1.7 years. Men have 25 percent lower lifetime prevalence than women (Hudson, Hiripi, Pope, & Kessler, 2007).

Characteristics of Bulimia Nervosa

People with the eating disorder **bulimia nervosa** engage in **binge eating** during which they eat an excessive amount of food during a short (e.g., 2 hours) period. During these episodes, they feel a lack of control, which makes them feel that they cannot stop eating or regulate how much they eat. In order to avoid gaining weight, they then engage in **purging,** during which they compensate for the added calories through inappropriate methods such as self-induced vomiting, misuse of laxatives, diuretics or other medications, and fasting or excessive exercise. In addition to engaging in these behaviors, they base their self-evaluation on how much they weigh and their body's shape. To receive a bulimia nervosa diagnosis, these episodes must not occur exclusively during episodes of anorexia nervosa.

People with bulimia may engage in binge eating and purging once per week (Wilson & Sysko, 2009). Formerly, clinicians assigning a diagnosis of bulimia nervosa distinguished between subtypes called "purging" or "nonpurging." In *DSM-IV-TR,* people who were diagnosed with the purging type were the ones who induce vomiting, administer an enema, or take laxatives or diuretics. Those who received the nonpurging diagnosis were seen as trying to compensate for what they eat by fasting or engaging in excessive exercise. Again, though, the *DSM-5* authors found evidence that this was not a valid distinction and removed the subtypes (van Hoeken, Veling, Sinke, Mitchell, & Hoek, 2009).

Individuals with bulimia nervosa develop a number of medical problems. The most serious of these occur with purging. For example, ipecac syrup, the medication that people use to induce vomiting, has severe toxic effects when one takes it regularly and in large doses. People who induce vomiting frequently also suffer from dental decay because the regurgitated material is highly acidic. The laxatives, diuretics, and diet pills that people with bulimia use can also have toxic effects. Some people with bulimia nervosa also engage in harmful behaviors, such as using enemas, regurgitating and then rechewing their food, or overusing saunas in efforts to lose weight. In addition to the

MINI CASE

Bulimia Nervosa

Cynthia is a 26-year-old dance teacher who has struggled with her weight since adolescence. A particular problem for Cynthia has been her love of high-calorie carbohydrates. She regularly binges on a variety of sweets and then forces herself to vomit.

Over the years, Cynthia has developed a number of physical problems from the frequent cycles of bingeing and purging. She evaluates the quality of her days in terms of how "fat" or "thin" she appears to herself in the mirror.

effects of dehydration that binging and purging cause, the bulimic individual runs the risk of permanent gastrointestinal damage, fluid retention in the hands and feet, and heart muscle destruction or heart valve collapse.

The lifetime prevalence of bulimia nervosa is 1.5 percent among women and 0.5 percent among men. Researchers estimate the prevalence of bulimia nervosa at any one time at 1.3 percent among college women, but binge eating (8.5 percent), fasting (8.1 percent), and excessive exercise (14.9 percent) are far more common. The majority (59.7 percent) of college women have concerns about their weight or body shape. These estimates have remained relatively stable over the 15-year period from 1990 to 2004 (Crowther, Armey, Luce, Dalton, & Leahey, 2008). Disordered eating patterns in college tend to improve over time. A 20-year follow-up of a college student sample of men and women showed that 75 percent no longer had symptoms in early midlife. However, 4.5 percent still had a clinically significant eating disorder (Keel, Gravener, Joiner Jr, & Haedt, 2010).

Although bulimia nervosa receives more attention among, and is more prevalent in women, men also experience the disorder. An online survey of over 6,500 members of a health maintenance organization revealed that substantial percentages of men engaged in periods of uncontrolled eating (20 percent), binge eating at least once a week (8 percent), fasting (4 percent), laxatives (3 percent), exercise (6 percent) and body checking (9 percent). Women were more likely than men to show almost all of these behaviors, but there were no significant sex differences in the use of laxatives and exercise to avoid weight gain after a period of binge eating (Striegel-Moore et al., 2009).

A binge is a loss of control when eating that involves consumption of a large amount of (usually unhealthy) food in a short amount of time. Individuals with bulimia nervosa will purge following a binge, in order to avoid gaining weight from the binge.

Binge-Eating Disorder

Binge-eating disorder is a new diagnosis added to *DSM-5* that includes individuals who engage in **binge eating** in a discrete period of time, lack control over their eating, and engage in binges for at least twice a week for 6 months. To qualify as binge-eating disorder, the binges must occur with a large food intake, eating past the point of feeling full or hungry, eating while alone, and feeling self-disgust or guilt after overeating. Because the binge eating does not occur in association with compensatory behaviors, it is possible that individuals with this disorder gain a significant amount of weight.

binge eating
The ingestion of large amounts of food during a short period of time, even after reaching a point of feeling full, and a lack of control over what or how much is eaten.

Theories and Treatment of Eating Disorders

Eating disorders reflect a complex set of interactions among an individual's genetic vulnerability, experiences with eating, body image, and exposure to sociocultural influences. From a biological point of view, researchers are particularly interested in the role of dopamine, which plays a role in feelings of reward and pleasure including those feelings related to eating. According to this view, binge eaters feel relief from depression and anxiety, which, in turn, reinforces the binge-eating behavior. Like people who are dependent on substances, binge eaters experience withdrawal symptoms in between bingeing, continue to binge even though they know it is harmful, feel compelled to engage in the behavior, and feel deprived when they cannot binge. Purging, in turn, would also have positively rewarding properties to these individuals who regard their own ability to stay thin with pride and pleasure (Broft, Berner, Martinez, & Walsh, 2011).

Researchers have conducted studies of a mouse strain with a lethal recessive mutation that relates to immune functioning that leads to reduced food intake. This mutation may have a link to altered immune functioning in humans (Clarke, Weiss, & Berrettini, 2011). Research on anorexia nervosa genetics in humans has identified abnormalities involving serotonin and dopamine receptor genes that are concentrated in the limbic system and, therefore, may play a role in altering emotion regulation in individuals with anorexia nervosa. The abnormal processing of emotions in people with anorexia nervosa may also be related to variations in another gene that relates to neuroticism, depressive mood, and selective processing of emotional stimuli. Such abnormalities may be at the core of altered nonconscious emotion-related disturbances that influence the individual's thoughts, feelings, and self-regulation of eating behavior (Hatch et al., 2010).

Although clinicians have used SSRIs to treat individuals with anorexia nervosa, they appear to have limited effectiveness until they administer them after clients have reached acceptable weight levels (Holtkamp et al., 2005). Similarly, SSRIs have limited effectiveness in treating bulimia nervosa (Herpertz et al., 2011). However, obese individuals with binge-eating disorder (i.e., nonpurging bulimia) may benefit from a 6-month treatment with SSRIs (Leombruni et al., 2008).

Given the mixed evidence for pharmacological interventions for eating disorders, clinicians regard psychotherapeutic methods as the methods of choice. Psychological perspectives to eating disorders focus on the core eating disorders' symptoms of disturbances in body image, a collection of several components (Figure 10.1). The cognitive-affective component involves attitudes and affects about one's own body. The cognitive-affective component of body image includes evaluation of one's own appearance (satisfaction or dissatisfaction) and the importance of weight and shape for an individual's self-esteem. The perceptual component of body image includes the way individuals mentally represent their bodies. Individuals with eating disorders typically overestimate their own body size. The behavioral component includes body checking, such as frequent weighing or measuring body parts, and avoidance, which is the wearing of baggy clothing or avoiding social situations that expose the individual's body to viewing by others (Ahrberg, Trojca, Nasrawi, & Vocks, 2011).

Psychological treatments for eating disorders that follow this model take a multi-faceted approach to targeting changes in body image. The primary aim of treatment

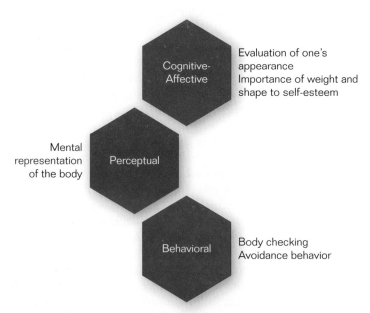

FIGURE 10.1 Components of Body Image

involves identifying and changing the individual's maladaptive assumptions that occur with his or her body shape and weight. In addition, clinicians attempt to reduce the frequency of such maladaptive behaviors as body checking and avoidance (Hrabosky, 2011). In cognitive-behavioral therapy, clinicians attempt to change what are selective biases in people with eating disorders that lead them to focus on the parts of their bodies they dislike. Second, by using exposure therapy in which clients view their own bodies ("mirror confrontation"), clinicians attempt to reduce the negative emotions that they would ordinarily experience. Behavioral interventions focus on reducing the frequency of body checking. Third, clinicians can address the component of body image involving size overestimation by helping clients view their bodies more holistically in front of a mirror, teaching them mindfulness techniques to reduce their negative cognitions and affect about their bodies, and giving them psychoeducation about the ways that their beliefs reinforce their negative body image (Delinsky, 2011).

Within the sociocultural perspective, clinicians use interventions incorporating a family component for clients with eating disorders who are

> ## What's New in the DSM-5
>
> ### Reclassifying Eating, Elimination, Sleep-Wake, and Disruptive, Impulse Control, and Conduct Disorders
>
> *DSM-5* reflects a number of changes across categories of the disorders we present in this chapter. In addition, diagnoses were added and removed to be consistent with emerging research in these important psychological disorders.
>
> With regard to eating disorders, the most significant change in *DSM-5* was to move all the eating disorders into a new category called "Feeding and Eating Disorders" that also include feeding disorders of childhood.
>
> A new category called "Binge-Eating Disorder," which was in the appendix of *DSM-IV-TR*, was added to eating disorders based on a comprehensive literature review (Wonderlich, Gordon, Mitchell, Crosby, & Engel, 2009) that showed that there was sufficient validity to the diagnosis to justify its inclusion. At the same time, the *DSM-5* eliminated the two subtypes of bulimia nervosa (with and without purging). The *DSM-5* authors decided to include binge-eating disorder to reduce the number of diagnoses given for eating disorder "not otherwise specified." They believed that there was sufficient evidence to judge its being given its own diagnosis.
>
> Other feeding disorders, formerly in the *DSM-IV-TR* section of disorders of childhood, were moved into the same category as eating disorders. Elimination disorders became its own chapter.
>
> Sleep-wake disorders received a major overhaul, as the *DSM-5* authors worked to develop a classification system that would be in greater conformity with the system used by sleep specialists. The *DSM-5* work group on sleep disorders took a "lumping vs. splitting" approach which was to put together related disorders into a single category and separate disorders that warranted their own distinct diagnoses.
>
> Finally, in the area of disruptive, impulse-control, and conduct disorders, the *DSM-5* authors moved disorders that were in the section on childhood into one chapter that also includes disorders of adulthood in which individuals have problems in regulating their emotions and/or behaviors. As you can see in this chapter, these disorders cut across the divisions in *DSM-IV-TR* in which impulse-control and childhood antisocial-like disorders were treated separately. The authors believe that these disorders are linked by dysfunctions in regulation, and therefore conceptually and practically belong together.

still in their teens and who have had symptoms for only a brief time. In the so-called "Maudsley model," families enter treatment for 10 to 20 sessions over a 6- to 12-month period. In the first phase of treatment, parents completely take charge of their child's eating and weight while they receive coaching in finding effective means of doing so. Gradually, the child can regain his or her autonomy. Although the Maudsley model has not withstood the test of controlled studies in terms of effectiveness compared to individual therapy, there are reasons for adopting this approach, particularly because it is so available on a widespread basis (Wilson, Grilo, & Vitousek, 2007).

Avoidant/Restrictive Food Intake Disorder

In **avoidant/restrictive food intake disorder,** individuals show an apparent lack of interest in eating or food. They do so because they are concerned about the aversive consequences. In addition, they may avoid food based on its sensory characteristics (color, smell, texture, temperature, or taste). People may develop this disorder as the result of a conditioned negative response to having an aversive experience while eating, such as choking.

Previously included as a feeding disorder of infancy or early childhood in the *DSM-IV-TR*, this diagnosis is now applicable to individuals of any age who do not have another eating disorder or concurrent medical condition, or who are following culturally prescribed eating restrictions. As a result of their disorder, they lose a significant amount

avoidant/restrictive food intake disorder
A disorder in which individuals avoid eating out of concern about aversive consequences or restrict intake of food with specific sensory characteristics.

of weight (or fail to achieve expected weight gain), show a significant nutritional deficiency, become dependent on feeding through a stomach tube or oral nutritional supplements, and show marked interference with their psychosocial functioning.

As a result of adding this disorder to *DSM-5,* researchers believe that the frequency of eating disorder "not otherwise specified" will be cut in half, leading to better chances of appropriate diagnosis and treatment (Ornstein et al., 2013). Young adults seem particularly prone to this disorder, with one study estimating that 25% of college-age women and 20% of college-age men engaging in significant restricted eating (Quick & Byrd-Bredbenner, 2012). Social norms may reinforce this behavior, as certain peer networks appear prone to setting expectations of restricted eating habits (Howland, Hunger, & Mann, 2012).

Eating Disorders Associated with Childhood

The authors of *DSM-5* moved the *DSM-IV-TR* eating disorders of infancy and childhood to the overall category of eating disorders in adolescents and adults. Researchers in the field hoped that reclassifying these disorders will allow them to evaluate more systematically the incidence, etiology, and treatment effectiveness of these disorders (Williams, Riegel, & Kerwin, 2009).

pica
A condition in which a person eats inedible substances, such as dirt or feces; commonly associated with mental retardation.

Children with **pica** eat inedible substances, such as paint, string, hair, animal droppings, and paper. This is a serious disorder because even one incidence can cause the child to experience significant medical consequences due to lead poisoning or injury to the gastrointestinal tract. Pica is the most serious cause of self-injury to occur in people with intellectual developmental disabilities. Clinicians treating pica must use not only a behavioral treatment strategy to reduce the individual's injurious behaviors, but must institute prevention by ridding the home of potentially dangerous substances (Williams, Kirkpatrick-Sanchez, Enzinna, Dunn, & Borden-Karasack, 2009).

rumination disorder
An eating disorder in which the infant or child regurgitates food after it has been swallowed and then either spits it out or reswallows it.

In **rumination disorder,** the infant or child regurgitates and rechews food after swallowing it. Researchers investigating rumination disorder (when it was included, with feeding disorder, as a disorder of childhood) identified five common disturbances in these children, including (1) delayed or absent development of feeding and eating skills, (2) difficulty managing or tolerating food or drink, (3) reluctance to eat food based on taste, texture, and other sensory factors, (4) lack of appetite or interest in food, and (5) the use of feeding behaviors to comfort, self-soothe, or self-stimulate. Twenty-five to 45 percent of developmentally normal children, and 80 percent of those who are intellectually disabled, have feeding problems to varying degrees. However, there are many variations in the way clinicians report these disturbances and therefore, epidemiologists do not have exact estimates of their prevalence. Further complicating the clinical picture is the fact that many different factors can contribute to eating problems in children, ranging from a choking experience to medical background, temperament, and physiological abnormalities that create eating problems (Bryant-Waugh, Markham, Kreipe, & Walsh, 2010).

10.2 Elimination Disorders

elimination disorders
Disorders characterized by age-inappropriate incontinence, beginning in childhood

Elimination disorders are characterized by age-inappropriate incontinence and are generally diagnosed in childhood. They include enuresis and encopresis. Individuals with **enuresis** wet the bed or urinate in their clothing after they have reached the age of 5 years, when they should be completely toilet trained. To receive this diagnosis, the child must show symptoms of enuresis for three consecutive months. In **encopresis,** a child who is at least 4 years old repeatedly has bowel movements either in its clothes or in another inappropriate place.

enuresis
An elimination disorder in which the individual is incontinent of urine and urinates in clothes or in bed after the age when the child is expected to be continent.

encopresis
An elimination disorder in which the individual is incontinent of feces and has bowel movements either in clothes or in another inappropriate place.

Approximately 20 to 25 percent of 4-year-old children still wet the bed, and 30 percent of children 3 years old still soil (von Gontard, 2011). By the age of 5, enuresis affects approximately 5 to 10 percent of the population and continues to decrease until the prevalence is about 1 percent in individuals 15 years and older. Boys are more likely than girls to experience this condition (Brown, Pope, & Brown, 2011). These behaviors, then, are relatively common before the period that the diagnosis specifies.

There are subtypes of enuresis based on the time of day when the child inappropriately passes urine (daytime only, night only, or both). The subtypes of encopresis distinguish between children who have constipation and then become incontinent due to overflow, and those who do not have constipation and overflow of feces. Researchers believe that these distinctions are important because they can differentiate which children do and do not have a physiological basis for their symptoms (von Gontard, 2011).

These disorders can have a negative impact on a child's subsequent adjustment due to their impact on a child's self-esteem. The best interventions for enuresis involve a multifaceted approach involving the urine alarm. Contact with urine triggers the urine alarm, leading the child to experience a small aversive stimulus. As a result of this stimulus, the child develops a conditioned avoidance response that can trigger muscular contractions in the external sphincter of the bladder. Other methods can be combined with this system, but it clearly has a central role in treatment (Brown et al., 2011).

If children have the retentive form of encopresis, they can benefit from behavioral training that rewards them for increasing their fluid intake, ensuring that they include time on the toilet as part of their daily schedules, and incorporating more fiber in their diet. To be effective, such training should encourage students to increase healthy fluids, such as water, and not fluids high in sugar content, such as juice or soda (Kuhl et al., 2010). Another more psychologically oriented approach focuses on unresolved anger that a child may be expressing in response to family issues including parental conflict, the arrival of a newborn sibling, and an older sibling who torments the child. Treatment that addresses these family system issues can help to reduce the child's symptoms by reducing the family stresses (Reid & Bahar, 2006).

10.3 Sleep-Wake Disorders

A great deal of progress is being made in the science of sleep and treatment of sleep-wake disturbances, so much so that the sleep medicine is now a field in its own right. Researchers and clinicians in sleep medicine typically take a biopsychosocial approach, examining genetic and neurophysiological contributions (e.g. Barclay & Gregory, 2013), psychological interactions, and social and cultural factors that impinge on the individual's sleep quality and quantity. In addition, people with sleep-wake disorders may also have other psychological disorders or medical illnesses. Therefore, clinicians need to be careful to perform a thorough evaluation when clients present with sleep-related disturbance. By the same token, having their sleep-wake disorder symptoms treated may help improve the overall quality of life of people who have these disorders (Morin, Savard, & Ouellet, 2013).

DSM-5 organizes the sleep-wake disorders into what the authors believe is a clinically useful system that has a basis in empirical research. This system combines sets of related disorders from the *DSM-IV-TR* in some cases and splits apart others that are best understood as separate entities. Sleep specialists have a more fine-grained diagnostic system than the *DSM-5*'s, meaning that a client seeking help from a sleep clinic may have a slightly different diagnosis than that provided by *DSM-5*.

The *DSM-5* diagnostic criteria for sleep-wake disorders also reflect progress in the availability of technology in assessment and differential diagnosis. Many of these diagnoses now use **polysomnography,** which is a sleep study that records brain waves, blood oxygen levels, heart rate, breathing, eye movements, and leg movements.

We summarize the major categories of sleep-wake disorders in Table 10.1. As you can see, they fall into the categories of insomnia disorder/hypersomnolence disorder/narcolepsy, breathing-related sleep disorders, and parasomnias. To be diagnosable, symptoms must be present for a significant period of time, occur relatively frequently, and cause the individual to experience distress. These disorders affect many individuals, perhaps as many as 30% of adults in the general population in the case of insomnia alone (Cole, 2011). If you are like many undergraduates, you most likely have already been affected by one or more of these disorders given the typical environment of the college dormitory or student-populated apartment building in which noise in the night hours interferes with both sleep quality and quantity.

polysomnography
A sleep study that records brain waves, blood oxygen levels, heart rate, breathing, eye movements, and leg movements.

TABLE 10.1 **Sleep-Wake Disorders**

Disorder (or Category)	Specific Disorders within Category	Predominant Symptoms
Insomnia disorder		Difficulty initiating or maintaining sleep, along with early-morning awakening.
Narcolepsy		Recurrent periods of an irrepressible need to sleep, lapsing into sleep, or napping within the same day. Diagnosis also requires either episodes of jaw-opening or losing facial muscle tone while laughing or showing abnormal CSF or sleep disturbances on polysomnography.
Hypersomnolence disorder		Recurrent periods of sleep or lapses into sleep during the day, prolonged main sleep episodes, or difficulty being fully awake after abruptly awakening.
Breathing Sleep-Related Disorders	Obstructive Sleep Apnea Hypopnea	Frequent episodes of **apnea** and **hypopnea** while sleeping as indicated on polysomnography along with either snoring, snorting/gaspoing, or breathing pauses during sleep and daytime sleepiness, fatigue, or unrefreshing sleep.
	Central Sleep Apnea	Frequent episodes of apnea while asleep.
	Sleep-Related Hypoventilation	Episodes of decreased breathing (ventilation) while asleep.
Circadian Rhythm Sleep-Wake Disorders		Persistent patterns of sleep disruption due primarily to altered circadian rhythm or misalignment between the individual's internal circadian rhythm and the sleep-wake schedule required by the person's environment, or work or social schedule. Includes delayed sleep phase type (delay in timing of major sleep period), advanced sleep phase type (sleep-wake cycles that are several hours earlier or conventional), irregular sleep-wake type, non-24-hour sleep-wake type, and shift work type.
Parasomnias	Non-rapid Eye Movement Sleep Arousal Disorder	Recurrent episodes of incomplete awakening from sleep accompanied by either **sleepwalking** or **sleepwalking** not associated with **rapid eye movements (REMs).**
	Nightmare disorder	Repeated occurrences of extended, dysphoric, and well-remembered dreams that typically involve threats to one's life.
	Rapid Eye Movement Sleep Behavior Disorder	Frequent episodes of arousal during sleep associated with speaking and/or motor behaviors occurring during REM sleep.
	Restless Legs Syndrome (RLS)	An urge to move the legs along with uncomfortable and unpleasant sensations in the legs, urges that begin or worsen during periods of rest or inactivity that are partially or totally relieved by movement, and are worse or only occur in the evening or night.

Samuel, Obstructive Sleep Apnea Hypopnea

Samuel is a 68-year-old married grocery store manager who seeks marriage counseling because his wife has decided she no longer wants to put up with his snoring and is insisting that they sleep in separate bedrooms. In addition, he constantly feels fatigued and sleepy during the day. The counselor sends Samuel to a sleep specialist who conducts a polysomnography, showing that Samuel goes into periods of not breathing on average every four minutes. Samuel is now being evaluated for treatment by the sleep specialist, who is exploring options, including a mechanical device that fits over the nose, that would allow Samuel and his wife to resume their previous sleeping patterns in the same bed.

10.4 Disruptive, Impulse-Control, and Conduct Disorders

This grouping of disorders includes diagnoses assigned to individuals who have difficulties regulating their emotions and behavior whose disorder violate the rights of others. Although people with a variety of other disorders also experience difficulties in self-regulating their behavior, these disorders share the quality of bringing the individuals into significant conflict with social norms or authority figures. In other words, an individual with one of these disorders is likely to "get in trouble," to put it simply.

These disorders do not necessarily share an underlying cause, and the degree to which the self-regulation difficulties relate to emotions or behavior also varies. Nevertheless, they share a tendency for individuals with these disorders to exhibit externalizing symptoms. They fall into the end of an internalizing-externalizing spectrum characterized by lack of inhibition ("disinhibition") and constraint along with high levels of negative emotionality. Again, to put it simply, individuals with these disorders are likely to be found "acting out."

apnea
Total absence of airflow.

hypopnea
Reduction in airflow.

sleepwalking
Rising from bed during sleep and walking about while seemingly asleep

sleep terrors
Abrupt terror arousals from sleep usually beginning with a panicky scream.

rapid eye movements (REM)
Phase during sleep involving frequent movements of eyes behind closed eyelids; EEG's similar to those while awake.

Oppositional Defiant Disorder

Most children go through periods of negativism and mild defiance, particularly in adolescence, and most parents complain of occasional hostility or argumentativeness in their children; however, what if such behaviors are present most of the time? Children and adolescents with **oppositional defiant disorder** angry or irritable mood, argumentative or defiant behavior, and vindictiveness that results in significant family or school problems. This disorder is much more extreme than the typical childhood or adolescent rebelliousness, and it is more than a phase. Youths with this disorder repeatedly lose their temper, argue, refuse to do what they are told, and deliberately annoy other people. They are touchy, resentful, belligerent, spiteful, and self-righteous. Rather than seeing themselves as the cause of their problems, they blame other people or insist that they are victims of circumstances. Some young people who behave in this way are more oppositional with their parents than with outsiders, but most have problems in every sphere. To the extent that their behavior interferes with their school performance and social relationships, they lose the respect of teachers and the friendship of peers. These losses can lead them to feel inadequate and depressed.

oppositional defiant disorder
A disorder characterized by angry or irritable mood, argumentative or defiant behavior, and vindictiveness that results in significant family or school problems.

Oppositional defiant disorder typically becomes evident between ages 8 and 12. Preadolescent boys are more likely to develop this disorder than are girls of the same age, but after puberty it tends to be equally common in males and females. In some cases, oppositional defiant disorder progresses to conduct disorder; in fact, most children with conduct disorder have histories of oppositional defiance. However, many children with oppositional defiant disorder outgrow the disorder by the time they reach

Boys who are diagnosed with oppositional defiant disorder may go on to develop antisocial personality disorder, though many will grow out of the disorder by the time they reach late adolescence.

adolescence, as long as they do not have another disorder such as ADHD (Mannuzza, Klein, & Moulton, 2008).

Clinicians apply some of the interventions for treating young people with ADHD when working with individuals with oppositional defiant disorder or conduct disorder. Clinicians treating conduct disorder face even greater challenges than those who treat individuals with ADHD because alcoholism and abuse characterize the home environment of many children with conduct disorder. Although not true for all children with oppositional defiant disorder, many (particularly boys) will unfortunately move toward developing antisocial personality disorder in adulthood; a small percentage of these individuals will engage in serious criminal behavior (Loeber & Burke, 2011). Girls with oppositional defiant disorder are at higher risk of developing depression, particularly if they show signs of inability to regulate their emotions and a tendency toward defiance (Hipwell et al., 2011).

A combination of behavioral, cognitive, and social learning approaches is the most useful strategy in working with youths with disruptive behavior disorders (Brown et al., 2008). The goal of treatment is to help the youth learn appropriate behaviors, such as cooperation and self-control, and to unlearn problem behaviors, such as aggression, stealing, and lying. Therapy focuses on reinforcement, behavioral contracting, modeling, and relaxation training and may take place in the context of peer therapy groups and parent training. Unfortunately, professional intervention with youths who have disruptive behavior disorders often occurs during adolescence, a developmental stage that some experts in this field consider too late. Behavioral interventions that begin during childhood are usually more promising.

intermittent explosive disorder

An impulse-control disorder involving an inability to hold back urges to express strong angry feelings and associated violent behaviors.

Intermittent Explosive Disorder   The primary features of **intermittent explosive disorder** are aggressive fail to control their aggressive impulses. They can have angry outbursts that are either verbal (temper tantrums, tirades, arguments) or physical outbursts in which individuals become assaultive or destructive in ways that are out of proportion to any stress or provocation. These physical outbursts, on at least three occasions in a 12-month period, may cause damage to the individual, other people, or property. However, even if individuals show verbal or physical aggression without causing harm, they may still receive this diagnosis.

The rage shown by people with this disorder is out of proportion to any particular provocation or stress, and their actions are not premeditated. Afterward, they feel either significantly distressed, suffer interpersonal or occupational consequences, or may suffer financial or legal consequences. The magnitude of their aggressive outbursts are out of proportion to the provocation for their anger. In addition, the outbursts are not premeditated.

An estimated 4 to 7 percent of people in the U.S. population have intermittent explosive disorder; of these, 70 percent have at least three outbursts per year with an

MINI CASE

Intermittent Explosive Disorder

Ed, a 28-year-old high-school teacher, has unprovoked, violent outbursts of aggressive and assaultive behavior. During these episodes, Ed throws whatever objects he can get his hands on and yells profanities. He soon calms down, though, and feels intense regret for whatever damage he has caused, explaining that he didn't know what came over him. In the most recent episode, he threw a coffeepot at another teacher in the faculty lounge, inflicting serious injury. After the ambulance took the injured man to the hospital, Ed's supervisor called the police. Ed was taken into custody and immediately suspended from his job.

Individuals with intermittent explosive disorder may suffer negative consequences in their interpersonal relationships due to their frequent, and unprovoked, aggressive outbursts.

average of 27 on a yearly basis (Kessler et al., 2006). People with this disorder are more vulnerable to a number of threats to their physical health, including coronary heart disease, hypertension, stroke, diabetes, arthritis, back/neck pain, ulcer, headaches, and other chronic pain (McCloskey, Kleabir, Berman, Chen, & Coccaro, 2010). People with this disorder often have co-occurring bipolar disorder, personality disorder such as antisocial or borderline, substance use disorder (particularly alcohol), and cognitive disorders.

Intermittent explosive disorder appears to have a strong familial component not accounted for by any comorbid conditions associated with the disorder (Coccaro, 2010). Researchers believe that the disorder may result from abnormalities in the serotonin system causing a loss of the ability to inhibit movement (Coccaro, Lee, & Kavoussi, 2010). Other studies show altered EEG patterns that predispose individuals to these explosive outbursts (Bars, Heyrend, Simpson, & Munger, 2001).

Faulty cognitions further contribute to the individual's development of intermittent explosive disorder. People with this disorder have a set of negative beliefs that other people wish to harm them, beliefs that they may have acquired through harsh punishments they received as children from their parents or caregivers. They feel that, therefore, their violence is justified. In addition, they may have learned through modeling that aggression is the way to cope with conflict or frustration. Adding to these psychological processes is the sanctioning of violence associated with the masculine gender role, a view that would explain in part the greater prevalence of this disorder in men.

Given the possible role of serotonergic abnormalities in this disorder, researchers have investigated the utility of SSRIs in treatment. Though effective in reducing aggressive behaviors, however, SSRIs only result in full or partial remission in less than 50 percent of cases (Coccaro, Lee, & Kavoussi, 2009). Mood stabilizers used in the treatment of bipolar disorder (lithium, oxcarbazepine, carbamazepine) also have some effects in reducing aggressive behavior but there are few well-controlled studies (Jones et al., 2011).

Cognitive-behavioral therapy can also be beneficial for individuals with this disorder. In one approach, a variant of anger management therapy uses relaxation training, cognitive restructuring, hierarchical imaginal exposure, and relapse prevention for a 12-week period in individual or group modalities. A controlled investigation of this model of therapy showed improvements in levels of anger, aggression, and depression that persisted for at least 3 months following treatment (McCloskey, Noblett, Deffenbacher, Gollan, & Coccaro, 2008).

Conduct Disorder

conduct disorder
An impulse-control disorder that involves repeated violations of the rights of others and society's norms and laws.

Individuals with **conduct disorder** violate the rights of others and society's norms or laws. Their delinquent behaviors include being aggressive to people and animals (such as bullying and acts of animal cruelty), destruction of property, deceitfulness or theft, and serious violations of rules (such as school truancy or running away from home).

Clinicians differentiate between conduct disorder with childhood onset (prior to age 10) and conduct disorder with adolescent onset (Brown et al., 2008). Around the world, rates of conduct disorder average out at 3.2 percent, with remarkable consistency across countries, although definitions of the disorder do seem to vary, at least by continent (Canino, Polanczyk, Bauermeister, Rohde, & Frick, 2010). However, conduct disorder varies in severity. More serious cases involve arrest and stable delinquent behavior and mild cases of conduct disorder involve pranks, insignificant lying, or group mischief.

Researchers believe that genetically vulnerable individuals are more likely to develop conduct disorder when they are exposed to certain harsh environments. Researchers studied the development of conduct problems in over 1,100 5-year-old twin pairs and their families as a function of the contributions of genetics and physical maltreatment by parents. Among identical twins whose co-twin had conduct problems (i.e., those at high genetic risk), the probability of a conduct disorder diagnosis was nearly 25 percent when their parents physically maltreated them. In contrast, those children at low genetic risk who were subject to physical maltreatment had only a 2 percent chance of developing conduct disorder (Jaffee et al., 2005). The specific gene that seems to be involved in conduct disorder is one that also contains a gene regulating the growth of certain tumors (Dick et al., 2011).

impulse-control disorders
Psychological disorders in which people repeatedly engage in behaviors that are potentially harmful, feeling unable to stop themselves and experiencing a sense of desperation if their attempts to carry out the behaviors are thwarted.

pyromania
An impulse-control disorder involving the persistent and compelling urge to start fires.

Unfortunately, we know that aggressive and antisocial children are likely to have serious problems as adults. In a classic longitudinal study, only one-sixth of the original sample was completely free of psychological disorders in adulthood. More than one-fourth had antisocial personality disorder (Robins, 1966). Subsequent studies have confirmed this pessimistic outlook, with results indicating that at least 50 percent of children with conduct disorder develop antisocial personality disorder (see Chapter 14), a likelihood that increases further in the presence of other diagnoses, such as major depressive disorder (Fombonne, Wostear, Cooper, Harrington, & Rutter, 2001).

Impulse-Control Disorders

People with **impulse-control disorders** repeatedly engage in behaviors, often ones that are harmful, that they feel they cannot control. Before they act on their impulses, these individuals experience tension and anxiety that they can relieve only by following through on their impulses. After acting on their impulses, they experience a sense of pleasure or gratification, although later they may regret that they engaged in the behavior.

Pyromania People with **pyromania** deliberately set fires, feel tension and arousal before they commit the act, are fascinated with and curious about fire and its situational contexts, derive pleasure, gratification, or relief when setting or witnessing fires or while participating in their aftermath. To be diagnosed with pyromania, the individual must not set fires for monetary reasons or have other medical or psychiatric conditions. Arson is deliberate firesetting for an improper purpose (e.g., monetary gain), and an arsonist does not experience the relief shown by people with pyromania.

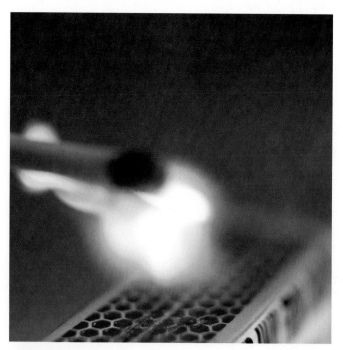

Individuals with pyromania are often fixated with every aspect of fire-setting including lighting a match.

Legal Implications of Impulse-Control Disorders

By definition, impulse-control disorders are defined as involving irresistible urges. Individuals with disorders such as kleptomania and pyromania engage in the illegal acts of, respectively, stealing and firesetting. Individuals with intermittent explosive disorder may also commit illegal acts during one of their violent outbursts. When people with these disorders encounter the justice system, then, the question arises regarding whether we should regard them as having a disorder or whether we should view their behavior as a form of illegal and deviant behavior similar to psychopathy.

People with kleptomania commit acts of stealing in response to a failure to resist impulses. The stealing may give them momentary relief from their anxiety-driven urge, but ultimately it leads only to significant distress and dysfunction in their everyday lives. A key difference between kleptomania and antisocial personality disorder lies in the feelings of guilt and remorse that accompany stealing. People with kleptomania feel intense regret; moreover, they do not seek to acquire the items that they steal for any particular monetary reason (Aboujaoude, Gamel, & Koran, 2004). Similarly, individuals with pyromania, by definition, do not seek monetary reward from their actions. Those with intermittent explosive disorder do not seek to commit violent acts, but are responding to irresistible urges. People with pathological gambling steal or cheat not for the sake of material gain, but in order to support their gambling habit.

According to one view, we should not consider impulse-control disorders to be the same as these "volitional" disorders, which should excuse an individual from moral and legal responsibility for his or her actions. A cognitive impairment that minimizes or negates memory for the negative consequences of the person's previous addictive behaviors causes the volitional disorder. Once the behavior begins, it increases the extent of the impairment (Campbell, 2003).

The terminology that the mental health profession uses to describe kleptomania and pyromania imply, however, that the individuals with these disorders are somehow attracted to the opportunities to steal and start fires. Many people outside the mental health professions do not understand the nature of these disorders. In the case of pyromania, fire agency personnel, insurance investigators, law enforcement, and even mental health professionals may fail to appreciate fully the diagnostic criteria for the disorder. Another popular belief and erroneous belief is that serial arsonists are pyromaniacs. In fact, clinicians diagnose pyromania in a very small percent of chronic firesetters. We often view people with pyromania as deriving sexual pleasure from their behavior. In reality, this occurs in only a minority of cases. According to Doley (2003), the lack of accurate information about pyromania means that it is not possible to determine whether people with pyromania even exist, let alone are responsible for their behavior.

Q: *You be the judge:* Should we treat people with impulse-control disorders, whose behavior may be illegal and potentially harmful to others, as criminals or as having psychological disorders?

Among hospitalized psychiatric patients, 3.4 percent had current symptoms and 5.9 percent had lifetime symptoms consistent with a diagnosis of pyromania (Grant, Levine, Kim, & Potenza, 2005). The majority of people with pyromania are male. Pyromania appears to be rare, however, even among arsonists. Among a sample of 90 repeated offenders, Finnish researchers found that only 3 met the *DSM-IV-TR* criteria for pyromania (Lindberg, Holi, Tani, & Virkkunen, 2005).

Pyromania appears to be a chronic condition if the individual does not receive treatment. Some individuals with pyromania, however, may switch to another addictive or impulsive behavior such as kleptomania or gambling disorder. An intensive

MINI CASE

Kleptomania

Gloria is a 45-year-old well-dressed and attractive executive with a comfortable salary and a busy lifestyle. For the past few years, she has been under considerable stress and has worked long hours as the result of reorganizations in her company. As a teenager, Gloria occasionally took small, inexpensive items, such as hair barrettes and nail polish, from the drugstore, even though she could afford to pay for them. Lately, Gloria has started shoplifting again. This time, her behavior has an intensity that she cannot control. During her lunch hour, Gloria often visits one of the large department stores near her office building, walks around until she finds something that catches her eye, and then slips it into her purse or pocket. Although she has sworn to herself that she will never steal again, every few days she finds the tension so great that she cannot stay out of the stores.

study of 21 participants with a lifetime history of pyromania described the most likely triggers for their behavior as stress, boredom, feelings of inadequacy, and interpersonal conflict (Grant & Kim, 2007).

As is true for the other impulse-control disorders, pyromania may reflect abnormalities in dopamine functioning in areas of the brain involving behavioral addictions. Treatment for pyromania that follows the cognitive-behavioral model seems to show the most promise, however. The techniques used in cognitive-behavioral therapy for pyromania include imaginal exposure and response prevention, cognitive restructuring of responding to urges, and relaxation training (Grant, 2006).

kleptomania

An impulse-control disorder that involves the persistent urge to steal.

Kleptomania   People with the impulse-control disorder **kleptomania** are driven by a persistent urge to steal. Unlike shoplifters or thieves, they don't actually wish to have the object, or the money that it's worth. Instead, they seek excitement from the act of stealing. Despite the thrill that they get from stealing, people with kleptomania would rather not be driven to this behavior and feel that their urge is unpleasant, unwanted, intrusive, and senseless. Since they don't really want or need the items that they steal, they don't have specific uses for them and they may give or throw them away. In order to receive a diagnosis of kleptomania, clinicians cannot better account for the individual's stealing by antisocial personality disorder, conduct disorder, or bipolar disorder (in a manic episode). Although shoplifting is relatively common, kleptomania appears to be far less so.

Kleptomania has a number of significant effects on the individual's life, not the least of which is the fear or actuality of arrest. In one study of 101 adults (73 percent female), 69 percent were arrested and 21 percent were incarcerated. Over half were arrested on two or more occasions. Their symptoms started when they were 19 years old, on average, and they shoplifted at least twice a week. The majority stole items of clothing, household goods, and grocery store items. To a lesser extent, they also stole from their friends, relatives, and places of employment. This study replicated those of smaller-scale investigations in reporting that people with kleptomania are likely to have high lifetime prevalence rates of co-occurring depressive disorders (43 percent), anxiety disorders (25 percent), other impulse-control disorders (42 percent), and drug abuse or dependence (18 percent). Suicide attempts are common among people with kleptomania (Grant, Odlaug, Davis, & Kim, 2009).

One reason kleptomania fits into the impulse-control disorders is that people with this disorder feel an urge or state of craving prior to stealing and a sense of gratification after

A woman with kleptomania feels the irresistible urge to steal even small, inexpensive items while in line at a coffee shop.

they steal. Researchers believe that these features of kleptomania also bear similarities to substance dependence.

Similar to tolerance, individuals with kleptomania report that they need to engage in increasingly riskier behavior in order to experience the same gratification. They also experience symptoms similar to withdrawal, in that in between episodes they experience insomnia, agitation, and irritability. Studies of the neurobiology of kleptomania suggest that, like substance use disorders, it occurs with altered dopamine, serotonin, and opioid receptor functions as well as changes in brain structures similar to those in people with cocaine dependence (Grant, Odlaug, & Kim, 2010).

Naltrexone, a therapeutic medication that clinicians use in substance dependence treatment, appears to have value in treating people with kleptomania (Grant, Kim, & Odlaug, 2009). Cognitive-behavioral treatments also are effective. These include covert sensitization, imaginal desensitization, systematic desensitization, aversion therapy, relaxation training, and helping clients find alternative sources of satisfaction (Hodgins & Peden, 2008).

10.5 Eating, Elimination, Sleep-Wake, and Impulse-Control Disorder: The Biopsychosocial Perspective

The disorders we have covered in this chapter represent a wide range of symptoms involving a combination of biological causes, emotional difficulties, and sociocultural influences. A biopsychosocial approach therefore seems appropriate in understanding each of these. Moreover, these disorders have a developmental course. Eating and oppositional/conduct disorders appear to originate early in life. Over the course of adulthood, individuals may develop impulse-control disorders, and late in life, physiological changes may predispose older adults to sleep-wake disorders.

In the case of each category of disorder, clients can benefit from a multifaceted approach in clinicians take into account these developmental and biopsychosocial influences. Some disorders, such as those in the sleep-wake category, may best be diagnosed through physiological tests such as polysomnography, even though treatment may focus on behavioral control of sleep. Individuals with symptoms of eating disorders should also be evaluated medically, but effective treatment also requires a multi-pronged and team approach among mental health and medical professionals. The psychological and sociocultural components of impulse-control disorders tend to be more prominent in both diagnosis and treatment, although there may be biological contributions to each of these as well.

This wide range of disorders provides an excellent example of why a broad-ranging and integrative approach that takes a lifespan view can be so important in understanding and treating psychological disorders. As research in these areas progress, it is likely that clients in the future will benefit increasingly interventions that take advantage of this multi-faceted view.

Return to the Case: Rosa Nomirez

Rosa maintained her involvement in the day treatment program, which consisted of twice weekly individual psychotherapy and several group therapy sessions every week. She saw a nutritionist who helped teach her the dangers of restricting her diet, and as a condition of the treatment she maintained a diet of at least 1,500 calories per day. She struggled with the change in her diet at first, which caused much anxiety for Rosa because she was concerned about becoming overweight. Her work in therapy and group therapy was aimed at maintaining a healthy body image and decreasing her unrealistic beliefs about being overweight.

As the weeks progressed, Rosa continued to gain weight and her distorted body image began to ameliorate. Her husband and family, once a source of tension and anxiety, became an important factor in her recovery from anorexia through their strong support and encouragement. Although Rosa continued to be concerned about becoming overweight, she learned the importance of nutrition and took on a more realistic view of her body. Rosa's depression remitted after the first few weeks of treatment, and she decided to stay in the program for a total of 3 months. After leaving the day treatment program, Rosa continued to see her therapist on a weekly basis.

Dr. Tobin's reflections: It is rare for an individual like Rosa to present to treatment due to actual concern about weight loss, given the typically distorted view that these individuals have that they are overweight, even when by objective standards they are in fact severely underweight. Indeed, she ignored her family's encouragement to obtain treatment in this regard. Had she been an adolescent, it would have been acceptable for her family to bring her into treatment. In this case, however, it was Rosa's experience of depression that motivated her to seek treatment. Although she was experiencing some symptoms of depression, this is not atypical for individuals suffering from an eating disorder and her symptoms did not warrant an independent diagnosis of depression. Although Rosa had experienced some eating disorder behaviors as a teenager, she was able to maintain a normal weight throughout much of her young adulthood. This fluctuating pattern is quite typical in the case of eating disorders. By her report, she continued to maintain a negative body image, although this did not manifest in any symptoms until she became pregnant with her daughter and was faced with actual weight gain. This served as a stressor that triggered a pattern of restrictive dieting that led to extreme weight loss.

Finally, the cultural aspect of this case is important to consider. Rosa's family came from a culture much less fixated on body weight and physical appearance. The gap between Rosa's experiences growing up in American society where there is pressure for women to maintain a low body weight, and her family's culture, was a great source of tension for her. Her family was unable to relate to her struggles with weight and body image, which served to increase her feelings of isolation. These differences represent the reality of the emphasis on physical appearance that is more prominent in more developed countries such as the United States, which leads to higher rates of eating disorders in these countries.

SUMMARY

- People with **anorexia nervosa** experience four kinds of symptoms: (1) they refuse or are unable to maintain normal weight; (2) they have an intense fear of gaining weight or becoming fat, even though they may be grossly underweight; (3) they have a distorted perception of the weight or shape of their body; and (4) they experience amenorrhea, if postpubertal. People with **bulimia nervosa** alternate between eating large amounts of food in a short time (**binge eating**) and then compensating for the added calories by vomiting or performing other extreme actions (**purging**). Biochemical abnormalities in the norepinephrine and serotonin neurotransmitter systems, perhaps with a genetic basis, are thought to be involved in **eating disorders.** The psychological perspective views eating disorders as developing in people who suffer a great deal of inner turmoil and pain, and who become obsessed with body issues, often turning to food for comfort and nurturance. According to cognitive theories, over time, people with eating disorders become trapped in their pathological patterns because of resistance to change. Within the sociocultural perspective, eating disorders have been explained in terms of family systems theories and, more broadly, in terms of society's attitudes toward eating and diet. Treatment of eating disorders requires a combination of approaches. While medications, particularly those affecting serotonin, are sometimes prescribed, it is also clear that psychotherapy is necessary, particularly that using cognitive-behavioral and interpersonal techniques. Family therapy, particularly when the client is a teen, can also be an important component of an intervention plan.

- **Elimination disorders** are most common in children younger than fifteen, but they can be diagnosed in individuals of any age. **Enuresis** involves incontinence of urine, and **encopresis** involves incontinence of feces.

- Sleep-wake disorders include insomnia, narcolepsy, hypersomnolence, breathing-sleeping related disorders, circadian rythm disorders, and parasomnias. Each of these disorders is characterized by a severe disturbance in sleeping patterns. Insomnia can be identified by an inability to fall asleep or to remain sleeping, while narcolepsy and hypersomnolence involve sleeping too frequently and at inappropriate times. Breathing-sleeping and circadian-rythm disorders, as well as parasomnias, can be characterized by abnormal bodily movements or behaviors, which can disrupt sleep or waking cycles.

- People with **impulse-control disorders** repeatedly engage in behaviors that are potentially harmful, feeling unable to stop themselves and experiencing a sense of desperation if they are thwarted from carrying out their impulsive behavior **Oppositional-defiant-disorder** is characterized by angry or irritable mood, argumentative or defiant behavior, and vindictiveness that results in significant family or school problems.

- People with **pyromania** are driven by the intense desire to prepare, set, and watch fires. This disorder seems to be rooted in childhood problems and firesetting behavior. In adulthood, people with pyromania typically have various dysfunctional characteristics, such as problems with substance abuse as well as relationship difficulties. Some treatment programs focus on children showing early signs of developing this disorder. With adults, various approaches are used, with the aim of focusing on the client's broader psychological problems, such as low self-esteem, depression, communication problems, and inability to control anger.

- People with **kleptomania** are driven by a persistent urge to steal, not because they wish to have the stolen objects but because they experience a thrill while engaging in the act of stealing. In addition to recommending medication, clinicians commonly treat people with kleptomania with behavioral treatments, such as covert sensitization, to help them control the urge to steal.

- People with **intermittent explosive disorder** feel a recurrent inability to resist assaultive or destructive acts of aggression. Theorists propose that an interaction of biological and environmental factors leads to this condition. In terms of biology, serotonin seems to be implicated. In terms of psychological and sociocultural factors, theorists focus on the reinforcing qualities of emotional outbursts, as well as the effects of such behaviors on family systems and intimate relationships. Treatment may involve the prescription of medication, although psychotherapeutic methods would also be included in the intervention.

KEY TERMS

Paraphilic Disorders, Sexual Dysfunctions, and Gender Dysphoria

Learning Objectives

11.1 Identify the patterns of sexual behaviors that represent psychological disorders

11.2 Compare and contrast paraphilic disorders and theories of their development

11.3 Recognize symptoms of sexual dysfunction and understand treatment methods for these dysfunctions

11.4 Comprehend theories and symptoms of gender dysphoria

11.5 Explain the biopsychosocial perspective of paraphilic disorders, sexual dysfunctions, and gender dysphoria

CHAPTER 11

Case Report: Shaun Boyden

Demographic information: 38-year-old Caucasian male.

Presenting problem: Shaun underwent a court-ordered psychological evaluation after his arrest for kidnapping and sexually assaulting a 7-year-old boy. This was Shaun's first encounter with the legal system and his first psychological evaluation. During the evaluation, Shaun admitted that from the time he was 16 years old, he had been stalking young children, sometimes having sex with them. He reported that although his desires to have sex with children never caused any distress, the fantasies, thoughts, and desires were often so intense that he felt driven to act upon them.

At the time of the evaluation, Shaun had been married for 8 years, and stated that his wife was unaware of his abnormal sexual urges. He explained that he and his wife rarely had sex, and when they did he would have to fantasize about children in order to become aroused. He only enjoyed intercourse when it involved children.

Shaun described that while he was growing up, he was rarely very interested in girls, and noticed that when he reached puberty at 16, he began to have sexual fantasies about children and became sexually aroused when he was around them, especially young boys. Eventually his attraction became exclusive to boys. Unsure of whether his peers were experiencing the same feelings, Shaun kept his powerful attraction to children to himself and distracted himself by dating women. However, as he grew older he found it more and more difficult to ignore his strong feelings and urges. Shaun graduated from high school and went on to college, where he received a degree in computer engineering. Throughout college he dated women, but recalls that he was never able to be truly sexually aroused around them. At this point he began

to fantasize about young boys in order to achieve arousal and orgasm.

After graduating from college, Shaun began his first serious relationship with a woman, the mother of a 3-year-old boy. His girlfriend often left Shaun to look after her son. Shaun reported that when his girlfriend's son was about 5 years old, he molested him for the first time, no longer able to control the urges he felt when he was alone with the boy. The molestations continued for five years, until Shaun's relationship with the mother ended. During that time, his girlfriend never found out about his behavior with her son. The breakup was very difficult for Shaun because he found he had grown dependent on the satisfaction he achieved from intercourse with the boy and he worried how he would be able to achieve this in the future. Shaun reported that he only worried about the moral implications of his having intercourse with his girlfriend's son a few times over the course of their relationship. He remarked that though he realized it was illegal, it came so naturally to him that he rarely worried about any of the possible consequences. However, due to the demands of his job, it was difficult for Shaun to find time to come into contact with children enough so that he would be able to be alone with them.

Three years after his previous relationship ended, Shaun started dating his future wife, Anne. He gleaned much satisfaction and stability from the relationship with Anne, and found that his urges to have sex with children severely dwindled for the first few years of their marriage. After about five years of marriage, Anne and Shaun began to fight frequently, and Shaun often felt anxious and worried. Anne wanted to have children, but Shaun was staunchly opposed. He knew that he would not be able to resist his urges. As their fighting got worse, Shaun noticed that his fantasies about children returned and he began to think of ways in which he could come into contact with children.

Shaun eventually quit his job at an engineering firm and took a job as an assistant at a day care center, after convincing his wife that he needed to work in a less stressful setting than the company where he had worked for years. He was hesitant to start acting on his urges at his new job right away, although he found his anxiety growing worse the more time he spent around children. He found himself using most of his free time to plan ways in which he could be alone with just one. Finally, the day care supervisor assigned Shaun to take a 7-year-old boy home after the parent was unable to retrieve him. Suspicious of a lone car in a dark parking lot, a police officer approached, and found that Shaun had molested the boy. The officer arrested Shaun and charged him with kidnapping and sexual assault of a minor.

Relevant history: Shaun had been experiencing his pedophilic urges since the age of 16. He reported that he had been sexually abused "a few times" by his father when he was 5 or 6 years old, although he was unable to recall many details.

Case formulation: As with many individuals diagnosed with pedophilic disorder, Shaun presented as a "normal" individual with no criminal history or evidence of psychological disturbance. Although he sometimes appeared mildly anxious to other people, his co-workers remarked that they never would have believed that he was a pedophile. Shaun had successfully been keeping his urges and fantasies to himself, and until he was caught by the police officer, he had maintained the cover of a normal life. It was clear from the evaluation, however, that Shaun met all the necessary criteria for pedophilic disorder, and had acted on his urges many times. Since his attractions were limited to young boys, his diagnosis specifies this.

Treatment plan: Shaun agreed to begin attending weekly psychotherapy sessions targeting his pedophilic urges by using cognitive-behavioral techniques. Shaun was also prescribed anti-androgen medication, which aims to reduce sexual urges.

Sarah Tobin, PhD

11.1 What Patterns of Sexual Behavior Represent Psychological Disorders?

When it comes to sexuality, deciding which patterns of behavior represent psychological disorders becomes more complicated, perhaps, than in other areas of human behavior. When evaluating the "normality" of a given sexual behavior, the context is extremely important, as are customs and mores, which change over time. Attitudes and behaviors related to sexuality are continually evolving. For example, although not a sexual disorder, addiction to sex over the Internet is becoming progressively prevalent, and clinicians are increasingly seeing clients with Internet-related problems. A survey of more than 1,500 mental health professionals revealed 11 categories of problematic behavior among their clients, with the second most prevalent involving Internet pornography. (see Figure 11.1).

For decades, there was little scientific research on sexual disorders. In 1886, the Austro-German psychiatrist Richard Freihurr von Krafft-Ebing wrote a comprehensive treatise called *Psychopathia Sexualis* (1886/1950), in which he documented a variety of forms of what he called "sexual perversity," which also linked sexual fantasy and the compulsion to kill.

The three individuals credited with paving the way for contemporary research on human sexuality were Alfred Kinsey, William Masters, and Virginia Johnson. Kinsey was the first to conduct a large-scale survey of sexual behavior in the United States

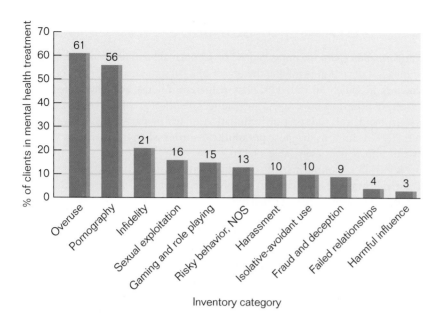

FIGURE 11.1 Percentage of Clinicians Reporting Client-Related Problematic Internet Experiences

SOURCE: Mitchell, Becker-Blease, & Finkelhor (2005).

(1948; 1953). Masters and Johnson (1966, 1970) were the first investigators to study sexual behavior in the laboratory.

In the intervening decades, psychologists, along with specialists in the emerging field of sexual medicine, have continued to expand our knowledge of human sexual behavior, but there is much still for us to learn.

Alfred Kinsey pioneered a revolutionary study about sexual behaviors that changed the way Americans viewed norms about human sexuality.

William Masters and Virginia Johnson were among the first researchers to take the study of human sexual behaviors into the lab.

11.2 Paraphilic Disorders

The term *paraphilia* (*para* meaning "faulty" or "abnormal," and *philia* meaning "attraction") literally means a deviation involving the object of a person's sexual attraction. **Paraphilias** are behaviors in which an individual has recurrent, intense sexually arousing fantasies, sexual urges, or behaviors involving (1) nonhuman objects, (2) children or other nonconsenting persons, or (3) the suffering or humiliation of self or partner. (Cantor, Blanchard, & Barbaree, 2009). Clinicians diagnose **paraphilic disorder** when the paraphilia causes intense distress and impairment (see Table 11.1).

Thus, a person's "nonnormative" (i.e., unusual) sexual behavior is not psychopathological. Furthermore, these disorders involve "recurrent and intense sexual arousal" as manifested by fantasies, urges, or behaviors.

The essential feature of a paraphilic disorder is that people with one of these disorders are so psychologically dependent on the target of desire that they are unable to experience sexual arousal unless this target is present in some form. The paraphilic disorder may be exacerbated during periods in which the individual feels especially stressed. However, paraphilic disorders are not fleeting whims or daydreams. Each represents a condition that the individual has experienced for at least 6 months.

People with these disorders are recurrently compelled to think about or carry out their unusual behavior. Even if they do not actually fulfill their urges or fantasies, they are obsessed with thoughts about carrying them out. Their attraction can become so strong and compelling that they lose sight of any goals other than achieving sexual fulfillment. By definition, paraphilic disorders cause intense personal distress or impairment in social, work, and other areas of life functioning.

Paraphilic disorders begin in adolescence and tend to be chronic, although they diminish in people who are 60 years or older (Guay, 2009). There are very poor prevalence data of these disorders because people do not voluntarily report that they have them. Moreover, although having a paraphilic disorder is not illegal, acting on paraphilic urges may be illegal and can result in the individual being subjected to arrest and the requirement, upon release, to register as a sex offender. The large majority of registered sex offenders have committed crimes against individuals under the age of 14 (70%); almost all victims (90%) are 18 or under (Ackerman, Harris, Levenson, & Zgoba, 2011).

paraphilias

Behaviors in which an individual has recurrent, intense sexually arousing fantasies, sexual urges, or behaviors involving (1) nonhuman objects, (2) children or other nonconsenting persons, or (3) the suffering or humiliation of self or partner.

paraphilic disorder

Diagnosis in which a paraphilia causes distress and impairment.

TABLE 11.1 Paraphilic Disorders

Disorder	Characteristics
Pedophilic disorder	Sexual arousal for children or adolescents
Exhibitionistic disorder	Derive sexual arousal from exposing their genitals to unsuspecting stranger
Voyeuristic disorder	Derive sexual pleasure from observing nudity or sexual activity of others
Fetishistic disorder and partialism	Fetishism is sexual arousal from an object Partialism is sexual arousal from a part of the body
Frotteuristic disorder	Sexual urges and sexually arousing fantasies of rubbing against or fondling a nonconsenting person
Sexual masochism and sexual sadism	Masochism is being aroused by being made to suffer Sadism is being aroused by inflicting suffering on another person
Transvestic disorder	Engages in cross-dressing associated with intense distress or impairment

MINI CASE

Pedophilic Disorder Nonexclusive Type

Shortly following his marriage, Kirk began developing an inappropriately close relationship with Amy, his 8-year-old stepdaughter. It seemed to start out innocently, when he took extra time to give her bubble baths and backrubs. But, after only two months of living in the same house, Kirk's behavior went outside the boundary of common parental physical affection. After his wife left for work early each morning, Kirk invited Amy into his bed on the pretext that she could watch cartoons on the television in his bedroom. Kirk would begin stroking Amy's hair and gradually proceed to more sexually explicit behavior, encouraging her to touch his genitals, saying that it would be "good" for her to learn about what "daddies" are like. Confused and frightened, Amy did as she was told. Kirk reinforced compliance to his demands by threatening Amy that, if she told anyone about their secret, he would deny everything and he would severely beat her. This behavior continued for more than two years, until one day Kirk's wife returned home unexpectedly and caught him engaging in this behavior.

We will examine the specific diagnostic criteria along with current literature on the paraphilic disorders; however, there is considerable overlap among them in terms of their association with each other and with other psychological disorders, substance use, and sexual risk taking or novelty seeking. In addition, these disorders are more prevalent in men than women (Långström & Seto, 2006).

pedophilic disorder
A paraphilic disorder in which an adult is sexually aroused by children or adolescents.

Pedophilic Disorder

People diagnosed with **pedophilic disorder** are sexually aroused by children or adolescents. Clinicians use this diagnosis for adults who are at least 18 years of age and at least 5 years older than the children to whom they are attracted. The key feature of this disorder is that the individual experiences sexual arousal when with children that may be equal to, if not greater than, that which he or she experiences with individuals who are physically mature.

We do not know the prevalence of pedophilic disorder because people with this disorder rarely step forward to receive treatment given the illegality of their behavior should they act on their urges with underage children. From the data on the prevalence of child sexual abuse cases in the United States, we can get an idea of the prevalence of pedophilic disorder. Among children about whom reports of maltreatment are made, approximately 10 percent involve cases of sexual abuse (U.S. Department of Health and Human Services, 2005). Looked at from a different perspective, approximately two-thirds of all sexual assault victims are children and adolescents. Nearly two-thirds of the victims are females, the vast majority of perpetrators are males, and approximately one-third of the offenders are relatives of the victimized children (Snyder, 2000).

Addiction to Internet sex with children and adolescents and involvement in "chat rooms" is recently coming under scrutiny by mental health professionals. In one study, a police sting operation caught 51 Internet chat room sex offenders who met the criteria for diagnoses of major depressive disorder, adjustment disorder, and substance use disorders. None was diagnosed with pedophilic disorder. The Internet offenders fell into two groups. Those who were "contact driven" used Internet chat rooms to arrange meetings with the potential victims. The "fantasy driven" offenders

Individuals with pedophilic disorder suffer from uncontrollable urges to engage in sexual activity with young children.

MINI CASE

Exhibitionistic Disorder, Sexually Aroused by Exposing Genitals to Physically Mature Individuals

Ernie is in jail for the fourth time in the past two years for public exposure. As Ernie explained to the court psychologist who interviewed him, he has "flashed" much more often than he has been apprehended. In each case, he has chosen as his victim an unsuspecting college-age woman, and he jumps out at her from behind a doorway, a tree, or a car parked at the sidewalk. He has never touched any of these girls, instead fleeing the scene after having exposed himself. On some occasions, he masturbates immediately after the exposure, fantasizing that his victim was swept off her feet by his sexual prowess and pleaded for him to make love to her. This time, his latest victim responded by calling the police to track him down. Ernie felt crushed and humiliated by an overwhelming sense of his sexual inadequacy.

engaged their victims in some type of online cybersex intending to achieve sexual climax while online. The majority did not fit the criteria for antisocial personality disorder, and 94% were facing their first encounter with the criminal justice system. The majority were white, had some college education, and had middle-class or higher occupational status (Briggs, Simon, & Simonsen, 2011).

Exhibitionistic Disorder

exhibitionistic disorder
A paraphilic disorder in which a person has intense sexual urges and arousing fantasies involving the exposure of genitals to a stranger.

People who engage in exhibitionism have fantasies, urges, and behaviors suggesting that they derive sexual arousal from exposing their genitals to an unsuspecting stranger. In **exhibitionistic disorder,** these fantasies, urges, and behaviors cause significant distress or impairment.

Exhibitionistic disorder begins early in adulthood and persists throughout life. In one study of a small sample of male outpatients with this disorder (Grant, 2005), researchers found that almost all also had another psychiatric disorder including major depressive disorder and substance abuse. Over half experienced suicidal thoughts. This was one of the few studies in a clinical setting of people with the disorder who were not criminal offenders. In another investigation of men from a police sample, approximately one-quarter also suffered from another psychological disorder (Bader, Schoeneman-Morris, Scalora, & Casady, 2008). The data from these samples are consistent with the findings from the Swedish national sample of nonclinical, noncriminal offenders, whose exhibitionism was also related to the presence of other psychological disorders (Långström & Seto, 2006).

The existence of comorbid conditions such as major depressive disorder and substance abuse, along with the reluctance of people with the disorder to come forward, present numerous challenges both for developing an understanding of the causes of the disorder and for planning its treatment (Murphy & Page, 2008). The most important step in treatment is accurately assessing both the disorder itself and these comorbid conditions (Morin & Levenson, 2008).

Voyeuristic Disorder

voyeuristic disorder
A paraphilic disorder in which the individual has a compulsion to derive sexual gratification from observing the nudity or sexual activity of others.

People who engage in voyeurism derive sexual pleasure from observing the nudity or sexual activity of others who are unaware of being watched. People with **voyeuristic disorder** are sexually aroused by observing an unsuspecting person who is naked, in the process of disrobing, or engaging in sexual activity. Voyeurism, the most common paraphilia, is related to exhibitionism, and people with either of these disorders are likely to engage in sadomasochistic behaviors and cross-dressing (Långström, 2010; Långström & Seto, 2006).

This man obtains sexual excitement by engaging in voyeuristic activities, such as looking at unsuspecting victims with binoculars

Unfortunately, there is very little data on voyeuristic disorder. Unlike exhibitionistic disorder, law officials are unlikely to apprehend individuals with this disorder and these individuals are even less likely to seek treatment.

Fetishistic Disorder

People with **fetishistic disorder** are sexually aroused by an object. In a related disorder, **partialism,** the individual is sexually aroused by the presence of a specific body part. Again, as with all paraphilic disorders, the attraction to objects or body parts must be recurrent, intense, and have lasted at least 6 months. There is a wide range of objects and a number of different body parts that people with fetishistic disorder can develop. However, they do not include articles of clothing associated with cross-dressing or objects such as vibrators that people use in tactile genital stimulation.

In a large-scale Internet study, a team of Swedish researchers investigated the frequency of specific fetishes among 381 "Yahoo! Groups" devoted to the topic (Scorolli, Ghirlanda, Enquist, Zattoni, & Jannini, 2007). They estimated frequency by counting numbers of groups, numbers of members of groups, and numbers of messages within groups. Nearly half of all fetishes counted in this manner involved the feet and toes, and of all preferred objects, the most frequent involved objects worn on the legs or feet. In

fetishistic disorder
A paraphilic disorder in which the individual is preoccupied with an object and depends on this object rather than sexual intimacy with a partner for achieving sexual gratification.

partialism
A paraphilic in which the person is interested solely in sexual gratification from a specific body part, such as feet.

MINI CASE

Fetishistic Disorder, Nonliving Objects

For several years, Tom has been breaking into cars and stealing boots or shoes, and he has come close to being caught on several occasions. Tom takes great pleasure in the excitement that he experiences each time he engages in the ritualistic behavior of procuring a shoe or boot and going to a secret place to fondle it and masturbate. In his home, he has a closet filled with dozens of women's shoes, and he chooses from this selection the particular shoe with which he will masturbate. Sometimes he sits in a shoe store and keeps watch for women trying on shoes. After a woman tries on and rejects a particular pair, Tom scoops the pair of shoes from the floor and takes them to the register, explaining to the clerk that the shoes are a gift for his wife. With great eagerness and anticipation, he rushes home to engage once again in his masturbatory ritual.

Individuals with a fetish gain sexual excitement from everyday, nonsexual objects such as feet.

trying to interpret these findings, the study's authors noted that they are consistent with Freud's view that feet are a penis symbol. A preference for feet and foot-related objects may, according to this view, reflect the adult consequences of castration complex associated with the Oedipus phase of development. The simpler behavioral explanation is that the person acquired this fetish through simple conditioning in which the person learned to associate sexual release with the presence of the specific body part or object.

Frotteuristic Disorder

The term "frotteurism" derives from the French word *frotter* (meaning "to rub") and *frotteur* (the person who does the rubbing). The person with **frotteuristic disorder** has recurrent, intense sexual urges and sexually arousing fantasies of rubbing against or fondling a nonconsenting person. Among men diagnosed with paraphilic disorders, approximately 10 to 14 percent have committed acts of frotteurism (Långström, 2010).

Men with frotteuristic disorder seek out crowded places in which they can safely rub up against their unsuspecting victims. Should they be caught, they can pretend that the act was not intentional. There is very little known about the disorder, in part, because the act is difficult to detect. Should someone suspect the individual of having engaged in this behavior, he or she can easily disappear into the crowd before a law official apprehends him or her.

frotteuristic disorder
A paraphilic disorder in which the individual has intense sexual urges and sexually arousing fantasies of rubbing against or fondling an unsuspecting stranger.

sexual masochism disorder
A paraphilic disorder marked by an attraction to achieving sexual gratification by having painful stimulation applied to one's own body.

Sexual Masochism and Sexual Sadism Disorders

The term "masochism" refers to seeking pleasure from being in pain. People with **sexual masochism disorder** are sexually aroused by being beaten, bound, or otherwise made to suffer. Conversely, people with **sexual sadism disorder** become sexually aroused from the physical or psychological suffering of another person.

As is true for several of the paraphilic disorders, there is very little in the way of scientific research on sexual masochism and sexual sadism disorders. In addition to the fact that people with these disorders tend not to seek treatment because they feel no need to change, they tend to carry out these behaviors in a great deal of secrecy, and because they often involve consensual behavior.

MINI CASE

Frotteuristic Disorder

Bruce, who works as a delivery messenger in a large city, rides the subway throughout the day. He thrives on the opportunity to ride crowded subways, where he becomes sexually stimulated by rubbing up against unsuspecting women. Having developed some cagey techniques, Bruce is often able to take advantage of women without their comprehending what he is doing. As the day proceeds, his level of sexual excitation grows, so that by the evening rush hour he targets a particularly attractive woman and only at that point in the day allows himself to reach orgasm.

MINI CASE

Sexual Sadism and Sexual Masochism Disorder

For a number of years, Ray has insisted that his wife, Jeanne, submit him to demeaning and abusive sexual behavior. In the early years of their relationship, Ray's requests involved relatively innocent pleas that Jeanne pinch him and bite his chest while they were sexually intimate. Over time, however, his requests for pain increased and the nature of the pain changed. At present, they engage in what they call "special sessions," during which Jeanne handcuffs Ray to the bed and inflicts various forms of torture. Jeanne goes along with Ray's requests that she surprise him with new ways of inflicting pain, so she has developed a repertoire of behaviors, ranging from burning Ray's skin with matches to cutting him with razor blades. Jeanne and Ray have no interest in sexual intimacy other than that involving pain.

Transvestic Disorder

Transvestism, also called "cross-dressing," refers to the behavior of dressing in the clothing of the other sex. The term most commonly refers to men, who are the large majority of individuals who show this behavior. A clinician would diagnose an individual with **transvestic disorder** only if he showed the symptoms of a paraphilic disorder, namely distress or impairment. Psychologists would consider a man who frequently cross-dresses and derives sexual pleasure from this behavior a transvestite, but they would not diagnose him with a disorder (Blanchard, 2010).

sexual sadism disorder
A paraphilic disorder in which sexual gratification is derived from activities that harm, or from urges to harm, another person.

transvestic disorder
Diagnosis applied to individuals who engage in transvestic behavior and have the symptoms of a paraphilic disorder.

Theories and Treatment of Paraphilic Disorders

As we mentioned at the outset of this section, deciding what is "normal" in the area of sexuality is an issue fraught with difficulty and controversy. Critics of the *DSM* argued against including several of the paraphilic disorders in *DSM-5* because to do so pathologizes so-called "deviant" (i.e., infrequent) sexual behavior. Moreover, they maintained that breaking the law is not a sufficient basis for determining that an individual engaging in a paraphilic behavior has a psychological disorder. This criticism is particularly leveled at exhibitionistic, voyeuristic, and frotteuristic disorder, which don't involve "victims" in the same sense as do the other paraphilic disorders (Hinderliter, 2010).

Researchers and advocates within the field of sexual sadism and sexual masochism were critical of including these disorders in *DSM-5* at all, arguing instead that they do not share the qualities of the other paraphilias because they involve consenting adults (Wright, 2010). In any case, researchers argue that clinicians should base decisions about psychiatric diagnoses on empirical evidence rather than on political or moral considerations (Shindel & Moser, 2011).

By defining the disorders in this area as involving intense distress or impairment, however, the authors of the *DSM-5* hoped to avoid the issue of judging on a behavior's normality and instead base the criteria for a disorder on an individual's subjective experience of distress or degree of impairment in everyday life. Yet, there are many challenges facing researchers who attempt to understand the causes of a disorder that enacts so much damage and has so many legal ramifications. Apart from identifying people with the disorder, the problem is made far more difficult because even those who are available for scrutiny by researchers

Cross-dressing is considered a psychological disorder only when it causes the individual to feel distress as a result of the cross-dressing behaviors. Cross-dressing is also distinct from transgenderism in that individuals who engage in cross-dressing typically identify with their biological gender.

MINI CASE

Transvestic Disorder, with Autogynephilia

In the evenings, when his wife leaves the house for her part-time job, Phil often goes to a secret hiding place in his workshop. In a locked cabinet, Phil keeps a small wardrobe of women's underwear, stockings, high heels, makeup, a wig, and dresses. Closing all the blinds in the house and taking the phone off the hook, Phil dresses in these clothes and fantasizes that he is being pursued by several men. After about two hours, he usually masturbates to the point of orgasm, as he imagines that a sexual partner is pursuing him. Following this ritual, he secretly packs up the women's clothes and puts them away. Though primarily limiting his cross-dressing activities to the evenings, he thinks about it frequently during the day, which causes him to become sexually excited and to wish that he could get away from work, go home, and put on his special clothes. Knowing that he cannot, he wears women's underwear under his work clothes, and he sneaks off to the men's room to masturbate in response to the sexual stimulation he derives from feeling the silky sensation against his body.

may not represent the population from which they are drawn. For example, most of the people who are available for studying disorders involving criminal acts such as pedophilic disorder are likely to have been arrested. Others who were not arrested are simply not available for study.

Biological Perspectives Given these qualifications, what do we know about people with paraphilic disorders? The most information in this area is based on research involving people with pedophilic disorder, perhaps because they are most likely to enter the criminal justice system. Clearly, this disorder has unique features, but information about how individuals develop this disorder may be helpful in understanding others.

From a biological perspective, paraphilic disorders involve a combination of influences including genetic, hormonal, and sensory factors in interaction with cognitive, cultural, and contextual influences (Guay, 2009). One theory of pedophilic disorders is that it results from early neurodevelopmental disorders, involving particularly the temporal lobe, which researchers believe is involved in altered sexual arousal. However, these changes could also be the result of early physical abuse or sexual victimization. Researchers have also identified altered serotonin levels in people with this disorder; however, these alterations may also be related to the presence of other psychological disorders in these individuals (Hall, 2007).

Castration as a treatment for men with paraphilic disorder, particularly pedophilic disorder, is intended to destroy the body's production of testosterone through surgical castration (removal of the testes) or chemical castration, in which the individual receives medications that suppress the production of testosterone. The cost of chemical castration is high, ranging from $5,000 to $20,000 U.S. dollars per year. Due to the expense of this maintenance treatment, the state of Texas continues to use surgical castration as the only option. Eight other states in the United States can order offenders to submit to chemical or surgical castration. Although castration might seem to be an effective method, one-third of castrated males can continue to engage in intercourse. There are also side effects that may increase the individual's risk of cancer or heart disease (Guay, 2009). There are also significant ethical issues involved that must be balanced against the need to protect the public from sex offenders (Thibaut, De La Barra, Gordon, Cosyns, & Bradford, 2010).

Clinicians treating paraphilic disorders based on the biological perspective may instead use psychotherapeutic medications intended to alter the individual's neurotransmitter levels. Researchers have tested the effectiveness of antidepressants, including fluoxetine, sertraline, phenelzine, and mirtazapine for nearly all of the paraphilic disorders. The other categories of tested psychotherapeutic medications include anticonvulsants, anxiolytics, mood stabilizers, neuroleptics, and opioid antagonists. Other medications that involve GABA or glutamate receptors may work by decreasing the activity of dopamine, a neurotransmitter involved in sexual arousal (Hall, 2007). Unfortunately, most of these studies, including those involving chemical castration, are based on small samples lacking experimental controls. Moreover, many of the participants in these studies had more than one paraphilic disorder and/or another psychiatric diagnosis. However, for individuals who are at moderate or high risk of reoffending, the available data support the use of SSRIs in combination with female hormones that produce a form of chemical castration (Guay, 2009).

The World Federation of Societies of Biological Psychiatry has proposed guidelines for the treatment of people with paraphilic disorder that are staged according to the severity of the individual's symptoms. The aim of treatment is to control sexual fantasies, compulsions, and behavior without impact on the individual's conventional sexual activity and sexual desire. Psychotherapy is the recommended treatment at the first level. If unsuccessful, clinicians add psychotherapeutic medications (SSRIs). At increasing levels of severity defined according to whether treatment is effective or not, clinicians add hormonal treatment starting with antiandrogens, progressing to progesterone, and finally, neurohormones that act on the areas in the pituitary gland that control the release of sex hormones. At this point in treatment, appropriate only for the most severe cases, the goal is complete suppression of sexual desire and activity (Thibaut et al., 2010).

What's New in the DSM-5

The Reorganization of Sexual Disorders

The sexual disorders underwent major rethinking in the *DSM-5*. The most significant changes involved declaring that clinicians do not consider paraphilias disorders unless they involve distress or impairment. This change recognizes the continuum along which sexual behavior falls and removes the stigma attached to sexual behaviors that do not cause distress or impairment or harm to others.

The sexual dysfunctions underwent significant shifts. Hypoactive sexual desire disorder is diagnosed only for men; women receive a diagnosis of hypoactive sexual interest/arousal. The previously separate disorders of vaginismus (inability to allow penetration) and dyspareunia (pain with intercourse) were combined into one disorder, called genito-pelvic pain/penetration disorder, because they are difficult to distinguish from one another.

In other changes, the term "early" was added in parentheses after "premature" ejaculation, and male orgasmic disorder was relabeled "delayed" ejaculation. Both of these terms reflect a desire, once again, to de-stigmatize a variant on human sexuality.

Finally, the relabeling of what was called "gender identity disorder" in *DSM-IV-TR* to the new term of "gender dysphoria," along with other changes within this category, provide a revamped view of these disorders that not only is more consistent with the research evidence, but also brings a greater understanding to people who experience the emotional distress of a mismatch between their biological sex and their own sense of identity.

Though based on empirical evidence, then, the *DSM-5* changes in the area of sexual disorders also clarify in important ways the many varieties of "normal" human sexuality. As these changes take hold in the psychological and psychiatric communities, they will provide directions for successful approaches to the treatment of people whose sexuality causes them to experience distress.

Psychological Perspectives   Freud's psychoanalytic understanding of the paraphilias was the dominant psychological perspective throughout the twentieth century. He believed that these disorders were perversions representing both biological and psychological factors in early development (Thibaut et al., 2010). According to John Money (1973/1996), in contrast, paraphilias are the expression of **lovemaps**—the representations of an individual's sexual fantasies and preferred practices. People form lovemaps early in life, during what Money considers a critical period of development: the late childhood years, when an individual first begins to discover and test ideas regarding sexuality. "Misprints" in this process can result in the establishment of sexual habits and practices that deviate from the norm. A paraphilia, according to this view, is due to a lovemap gone awry. The individual is, in a sense, programmed to act out fantasies that are socially unacceptable and potentially harmful.

The majority of the psychological literature on paraphilic disorders focuses on pedophilic disorder. A common theme in this literature is the idea of a "victim-to-abuser cycle" or "abused-abusers phenomena," meaning that abusers were themselves abused at some point in their lives, probably when they were young. Arguing against these explanations is the fact that most abuse victims do not go on to abuse or molest children. On the other hand, some people with pedophilic disorder who

lovemap

The representations of an individual's sexual fantasies and preferred practices.

The World Federation of Societies of Biological Psychiatry has proposed guidelines for the treatment of people with paraphilic disorder that are staged according to the severity of the individual's symptoms.

were abused as children show an age preference that matches their age when they were abused, suggesting that they are replicating the behaviors that were directed toward them as children.

Treatments within the psychological perspective seem most effective when combining individual with group therapy. The cognitive-behavioral perspective is particularly useful in helping clients recognize their distortions and denial. At the same time, these clients benefit from training in empathy, so that they can understand how their victims are feeling. Adding to the equation within the psychological perspective, clinicians may also train clients in learning to control their sexual impulses. Relapse prevention, much as it is used in treating clients with addictive disorders, helps clients accept that even if they slip, this does not mean that they cannot overcome their disorder. Clinicians no longer recommend aversion training, in which they teach clients to associate negative outcomes with sexual attraction toward children and masturbatory reconditioning to change their orientation away from children (Hall, 2007).

Most recently, researchers believe that the most effective treatment involves a combination of hormonal drugs intended to reduce androgen (male sex hormone levels) and psychotherapy (Hughes, 2007). Even so, under the best of circumstances, it appears that the most that we can hope for is that the individuals can manage their urges, but they cannot change their attraction to children (Hall, 2007).

11.3 Sexual Dysfunctions

Sexual arousal leads to a set of physiological changes throughout the body often culminating in orgasm. A **sexual dysfunction** involves a marked divergence of an individual's response in the sexual response cycle along with feelings of significant distress or impairment. To consider it a sexual dysfunction, clinicians must not be able to attribute this divergence to psychological disorder, effects of a substance such as a drug of abuse or medication, or a general medical condition.

sexual dysfunction
An abnormality in an individual's sexual responsiveness and reactions.

Clinicians rate a person's sexual dysfunction according to whether it is lifelong or acquired, and generalized or situational. An individual with a lifelong dysfunction has experienced it since he or she became sexually active. People with acquired sexual dysfunctions were at some earlier point asymptomatic. Those dysfunctions that are situational occur with only certain types of sexual stimulation, situations, or partners. Generalized dysfunctions affect the individual in all sexual situations.

Masters and Johnson (1966, 1970), based on systematically observing the sexual responses of men and women under controlled laboratory conditions, identified four phases of the sexual response cycle—excitement (arousal), plateau, orgasm, and resolution. During the excitement (or arousal) stage, the individual's sexual interest heightens, and the body prepares for sexual intercourse (vaginal lubrication in the female, penile erection in the male). Sexual excitement continues to build during the plateau phase, and during the orgasm phase the individual experiences muscular contractions in the genital area that bring intense sensations of pleasure. The resolution phase is a period of return to a physiologically normal state. People differ in their typical patterns of sexual activity, however; some people progress more readily through the phases and others progress at a slower pace. Not every sexual encounter necessarily involves all phases, however, and arousal and desire may arise simultaneously from the processing of sexual stimuli (Basson, 2001).

Physiological factors and chronic health conditions are strongly related to risk of developing sexual disorders. We will outline these where they apply to the specific disorders below, but several risk factors seem to apply generally including diabetes, cardiovascular disease, other genitourinary diseases, psychological disorders, other chronic diseases, and smoking. In the case of some of these conditions, it is the medication and not the condition itself that places the individual at risk, such as anti-hypertensive drugs (Lewis et al., 2010).

There are very few reliable prevalence data on these disorders (Lewis et al., 2010). The reason for this is that the definitions of many of these disorders are highly variable. Only recently are researchers systematically beginning to arrive at measurable criteria based on the unique assessment methods that they require. Fortunately, work toward the *DSM-5* is leading to improved and more rigorous diagnostic procedures that eventually will lead to more reliable data sources.

The Female Sexual Function Index (Rosen et al., 2000) is an empirical measure used in a number of studies to investigate prevalence of sexual dysfunctions in women and as a measure of the efficacy of treatment. You can see sample items from this measure in Table 11.2.

Arousal Disorders

People whose sexual disorders occur during the initial phases of the sexual response cycle have low or no sexual desire, or are unable to achieve physiological arousal. As a result, they may avoid having or be unable to have sexual intercourse.

The man with **male hypoactive sexual desire disorder** has an abnormally low level of sexual activity or may have no interest in sexual activity. In addition, a man with this disorder either has relatively few or no sexual fantasies. A woman with

male hypoactive sexual desire disorder
A sexual dysfunction in which the individual has an abnormally low level of interest in sexual activity.

MINI CASE

Female Interest/Arousal Disorder, Acquired

With the pressures of managing a full-time advertising job and raising 3-year-old twins, Carol says that she has "no time or energy" for sexual relations with her husband, Bob. In fact, they have not been sexually intimate since the birth of their children. Initially, Bob tried to be understanding and to respect the fact that Carol was recovering from a very difficult pregnancy and delivery. As the months went by, however, he became increasingly impatient and critical. The more he pressured Carol for sexual closeness, the more angry and depressed she became. Carol feels that she loves Bob, but she does not think about sex and can't imagine ever being sexual again. She is saddened by the effect that this change has had on her marriage, but feels little motivation to try to change.

TABLE 11.2 Scales and Sample Items from the Female Sexual Function Index (FSFI)

Desire scale

Over the past 4 weeks, how **often** did you feel sexual desire or interest?

- Almost always or always
- Most times (more than half the time)
- Sometimes (about half the time)
- A few times (less than half the time)
- Almost never or never

Arousal scale

Over the past 4 weeks, how **often** did you feel sexually aroused ("turned on") during sexual activity or intercourse?

- No sexual activity
- Almost always or always
- Most times (more than half the time)
- Sometimes (about half the time)
- A few times (less than half the time)
- Almost never or never

Lubrication scale

Over the past 4 weeks, how **often** did you become lubricated ("wet") during sexual activity or intercourse?

- No sexual activity
- Almost always or always
- Most times (more than half the time)
- Sometimes (about half the time)
- A few times (less than half the time)
- Almost never or never

Orgasm scale

Over the past 4 weeks, when you had sexual stimulation or intercourse, how **difficult** was it for you to reach orgasm (climax)?

- No sexual activity
- Extremely difficult or impossible
- Very difficult
- Difficult
- Slightly difficult
- Not difficult

Satisfaction scale

Over the past 4 weeks, how **satisfied** have you been with your sexual relationship with your partner?

- Very satisfied
- Moderately satisfied
- About equally satisfied and dissatisfied
- Moderately dissatisfied
- Very dissatisfied

TABLE 11.2 (Continued)

Pain scale

Over the past 4 weeks, how would you rate your **level** (degree) of discomfort or pain during or following vaginal penetration?

- Did not attempt intercourse
- Very high
- High
- Moderate
- Low
- Very low or none at all

SOURCE: (Rosen et al., 2000) http://www.fsfi-questionnaire.com/.

female sexual interest/arousal disorder is interested in having intercourse, but her body does not physiologically respond during the arousal phase.

In *DSM-IV-TR*, the definition of this disorder referred to "desire" instead of interest/arousal. This presented a challenge in the diagnosis of women, according to researchers in this field. Some reports indicate that low sexual desire is relatively prevalent among women, with estimates in some samples ranging as high as 55 percent, although the majority of studies from around the world place the prevalence at closer to 40 percent. However, the percent of women who are distressed about having low sex desire is far lower. Thus, the issue for women is that loss of desire might not be the best or only criterion to use in diagnosing a sexual dysfunction. Instead, as in *DSM-5*, it may be more accurate to characterize the disorder as one involving a range of behaviors, including loss of interest, arousal, erotic thoughts, enjoyment of sexual activity, or intensity of sensations during sexual activity (Brotto, 2010).

Men with **erectile disorder** cannot attain or maintain an erection during sexual activity that is sufficient to allow them to initiate or maintain sexual activity. Even if they are able to achieve an erection, they are unable to penetrate or to experience pleasure during a sexual encounter. Although once thought of as either physiologically or psychologically caused, clinicians and researchers now understand erectile disorder as having multiple causes that they cannot clearly separate into these two categories (Segraves, 2010). A very rough estimate of the prevalence of erectile disorder is 26 to 28 per 1,000 man-years, with higher rates among older men (Lewis et al., 2010).

female sexual interest/ arousal disorder
A sexual dysfunction characterized by a persistent or recurrent inability to attain or maintain normal physiological and psychological arousal responses during sexual activity.

erectile disorder
Sexual dysfunction in which a man cannot attain or maintain an erection during sexual activity that is sufficient to allow him to initiate or maintain sexual activity.

MINI CASE

Erectile Disorder, Acquired

Brian is 34 years old and has been dating the same woman for more than a year. This is his first serious relationship and the first person with whom he has been sexually intimate. During the past 6 months, they have frequently tried to have intercourse, but each time they have become frustrated by Brian's inability to maintain an erection for more than a few minutes. Every time this happens, Brian becomes very upset, despite his girlfriend's reassurance that things will work out better next time. His anxiety level heightens every time he thinks about the fact that he is in his mid-thirties, sexually active for the first time in his life, and encountering such frustrating difficulties. He fears he is "impotent" and will never be able to have a normal sex life.

Advertisements for male erectile enhancement drugs such as this are widely found on the Internet.

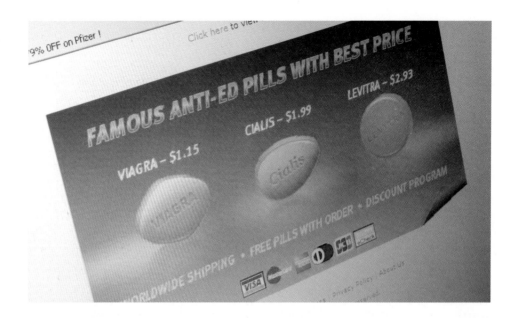

Disorders Involving Orgasm

female orgasmic disorder
A sexual dysfunction in which a woman experiences problems having an orgasm during sexual activity.

Inability to achieve orgasm, a distressing delay in achieving orgasm, or reduced intensity of orgasm constitutes **female orgasmic disorder.** Although previous versions of the *DSM* regarded orgasm resulting from clitoral stimulation as distinct from that resulting from intercourse, the *DSM-IV-TR* removed this criterion, recognizing that women can experience orgasm through a wide variety of types of stimulation. The *DSM-5* similarly does not distinguish between sources of orgasm in defining the criteria for this disorder. These changes reflect the recognition that not all women similarly experience the sexual response cycle described by Masters and Johnson (1966).

The factors relating to a woman's reporting of female orgasmic disorder include stress, anxiety, depression, relationship satisfaction, and age-related changes in the genital area that can lead to pain, discomfort, irritation, or bleeding (Laumann & Waite, 2008). Women are more likely than men to report sexual difficulties involving the subjective quality of the experience. Men are more likely to report physical problems in achieving or maintaining erection.

MINI CASE

Female Orgasmic Disorder, Lifelong

Like many of her friends, when Margaret was a teenager she often wondered what intercourse and orgasm would feel like. When she later became sexually active in college, Margaret realized that she was probably still missing something, since she did not feel "rockets going off" as she had imagined. In fact, she never could experience orgasm when she was with a man in any kind of sexual activity. When Margaret fell in love with Howard, she fervently hoped that things would improve. However, even though he made her feel more sensual pleasure than anyone else, her response to him always stopped just short of climax. She approached every sexual encounter with anxiety, and, afterward, tended to feel depressed and inadequate. To avoid making Howard worry, however, Margaret decided it would be better to fake orgasm than to be honest with him. After 5 years together, she still has not told him that she is not experiencing orgasms, and she feels too embarrassed to seek professional help, despite her ongoing distress.

Treatment for Sex Offenders

The paraphilic disorders present an ethical challenge to psychologists because of their potential link to the harm of others, particularly children and young teenagers. Treatment must be balanced with a range of ethical dilemmas involving the rights of the clients, including confidentiality, informed consent, and the right to self-determination. These rights must also be balanced against the clinician's duty to prevent harm, both to others and to the client. Since treatment is often court-mandated, the question becomes whether this represents punishment rather than therapy.

Social workers David Prescott and Jill Levenson (2010), both of whom have extensive background in treating sex offenders, suggest that clinicians can conduct mandated treatment in a manner that is consistent with the clinician's code of ethics. Mandated treatment, rather than representing punishment, they argue, is intended to assist offenders to correct the behaviors that were of harm to others and themselves. Moreover, the ethical standards that clinicians abide by regarding confidentiality are consistent with the "duty to warn" component of sex offender therapy: "Mandatory reporting trumps privilege" (Prescott & Levenson, 2010, p. 278). Second, regarding the issue of the client's right to self-determination, sex offenders are not the only individuals whom the law mandates to receive therapy. Child abusers and drivers arrested for operating a vehicle while intoxicated are two examples, but there are other cases in which the justice system gives family members, for example, an ultimatum to receive treatment for such behaviors as compulsive gambling.

Individuals who choose to work with sex offenders, according to Prescott and Levenson (2010), do so out of compassion and a desire to rehabilitate their clients so that they can become functioning members of society. They have found a way to empathize with clients who have committed sexually violent acts without judging the offenders and overcome the "natural human reaction" of "disdain" (p. 282) to these individuals.

Q: *You be the judge:* Do you agree that the principles of human rights and the ethical guidelines presented by professional associations serve to protect sex offenders when they enter into therapy? Should the justice system even offer sex offender therapy or should these individuals simply be incarcerated? On the other hand, is rehabilitation a realistic goal, as Prescott and Levenson claim, or are sex offenders beyond help?

The distinction between the nature of orgasmic difficulties for men and women led a group of clinicians and social scientists called "The Working Group for a New View of Women's Sexual Problems" to criticize the *DSM* for failing to take into account the greater focus in women on relational aspects of sexuality and individual variations in women's sexual experiences. They proposed that the profession define sexual problems as difficulties in any aspect of sexuality—emotional, physical, or relational. Researchers also believe that more work is needed to understand the experiences of women from a variety of cultures, across different age groups, and from women of differing sexual orientations (Graham, 2010).

Men with a marked delay in ejaculation or who rarely, if at all, experience ejaculations have **delayed ejaculation.** Men with **premature (early) ejaculation** reach orgasm in a sexual encounter with minimal sexual stimulation before, on, or shortly after penetration and before wishing to do so (within one minute). Regardless of what we call these disorders, clinicians prefer to apply a psychiatric diagnosis only when the individual is distressed about the condition. The prevalence rate for premature ejaculation varies widely, from 8 to 30 percent, and seems to depend on age group and country (Lewis et al., 2010).

delayed ejaculation
A sexual dysfunction in which a man experiences problems having an orgasm during sexual activity; also known as inhibited male orgasm.

premature (early) ejaculation
A sexual dysfunction in which a man reaches orgasm well before he wishes to, perhaps even prior to penetration.

MINI CASE

Premature (Early) Ejaculation, Lifelong

Jeremy is a 45-year-old investment broker who has struggled with the problem of premature ejaculation for as long as he can remember. Since his first experience with sexual intercourse as a college student, he has been unable to control his orgasms. He customarily ejaculates seconds after penetration. Because of this problem, his relationships over the years have been strained and difficult. In each instance, the person he was dating at the time became frustrated, and Jeremy felt too embarrassed to continue the relationship. For a period lasting several years, he avoided sexual relations completely, knowing that each experience of failure would leave him feeling depressed and furious.

Disorders Involving Pain

**genito-pelvic pain/
penetration disorder**
A sexual dysfunction affecting
both males and females that
involves recurrent or persistent
genital pain before, during, or
after sexual intercourse.

Clinicians diagnose sexual pain disorders, which involve the experience of difficulty in a sexual relationship due to painful sensations in the genitals from intercourse, **genito-pelvic pain/penetration disorder.** Genito-pelvic pain/penetration can affect both males and females. The individual experiences recurrent or persistent genital pain before, during, or after sexual intercourse.

Theories and Treatment of Sexual Dysfunctions

We can best view sexual dysfunctions as an interaction of complex physiological, psychological, and sociocultural factors, which clinicians who work in the field from a biopsychosocial perspective understand. In attempting to help a client with a sexual dysfunction, the clinician must first conduct a comprehensive assessment that includes a physical exam and psychological testing, including the client's partner, if appropriate. In addition, the clinician must assess the individual's use of substances including not only drugs and alcohol, but also all medications, including psychotherapeutic ones.

Biological Perspectives Perhaps one of the best-researched sexual dysfunctions is erectile disorder, which the profession increasingly views as having strong biological contributors. In 1970, Masters and Johnson claimed that virtually all men (95 percent) with erectile disorder (ED) had psychological problems such as anxiety and job stress, boredom with long-term sexual partners, and other

MINI CASE

Genito-Pelvic Pain/Penetration Disorder, Lifelong

Shirley is a 31-year-old single woman who has attempted to have sex with many different men over the past 10 years. Despite her ability to achieve orgasm through masturbation, she has found herself unable to tolerate penetration during intercourse. In her own mind, she feels a sense of readiness, but her vaginal muscles inevitably tighten up and her partner is unable to penetrate. It is clear to Shirley that this problem has its roots in a traumatic childhood experience. She was sexually abused by an older cousin. Although she recognizes that she should seek professional help, Shirley is too embarrassed and has convinced herself that the problem will go away if she can find the right man who will understand her problems.

relationship difficulties. Since that time, researchers have arrived at very different conclusions as a result of new and more sophisticated assessment devices sensitive to the presence of physiological abnormalities. Health care professionals view more than half the cases of erectile disorder as attributable to physical problems of a vascular, neurological, or hormonal nature, or to impaired functioning caused by drugs, alcohol, and smoking.

Medications to treat erectile disorder include the prescription drugs Viagra, Levitra, and Cialis. These are all in the category of phosphodiesterase (PDE) inhibitors, which work by increasing blood flow to the penis during sexual stimulation. What makes such medications appealing is the fact that they are so much less invasive than previous treatments for erectile disorder, such as surgery and implants, and so much less awkward than vacuum pumps or penile injections. These medications work when accompanied by the experience of sexual excitement, unlike other treatments in which the man achieves an erection artificially and independent of what is going on sexually with the man or his partner.

The hormonal changes take place with the climacteric, the gradual loss of reproductive potential that occurs in men and women, but is more pronounced in women during menopause. Changing estrogen levels can lead to a number of physical symptoms that affect sexuality, including vaginal dryness and gradual shrinking of vaginal size and muscle tone, but these changes do not affect the woman's ability for arousal during sexual activity. Women also experience a decline in free testosterone, the male sex hormone, but it is not clear whether this decline is related to changes in sexual desire and satisfaction. A variety of chronic diseases can also interfere with a woman's sexual desire and

Sexual dysfunctions can be disruptive and frustrating for intimate couples.

response including diabetes, spinal cord injury, multiple sclerosis, hypothyroidism (low thyroid levels), and the aftermath of cancer surgery involving the uterus. Medications that act on the serotonin and dopamine systems can also interfere with sexual responsiveness in women (Both, Laan, & Schultz, 2010).

The treatment of female sexual interest/arousal disorder that follows from the biological perspective incorporates hormonal replacement therapy (estrogen and progesterone), estrogen cream applied directly to the vagina, and testosterone therapy (Traish, Feeley, & Guay, 2009). Doctors may also give women a PDE inhibitor, but its efficacy remains undemonstrated (Both et al., 2010).

Genito-pelvic pain/penetration disorder presents a different set of challenges. From a biological perspective, the physical symptoms can come from a variety of sources, including disturbances in the muscle fibers in the pelvic area (called the "pelvic floor"). When treating these disorders, however, the clinician may be unable to trace the exact cause of the individual's pain. The best approach appears to be multifaceted, including application of corticosteroids and physical therapy to promote muscle relaxation and improved blood circulation. The clinician may also use electrical nerve stimulation to relieve the individual's pain and prescribe pharmacological agents such as amitriptylene and pregabalin (Lyrica®) (Bergeron, Morin, & Lord, 2010).

Psychological Perspectives Recognizing the role of physiological factors, the psychological perspective emphasizes the further contributing effects, if not causal role, of cognitions, emotions, and attitudes toward sexuality. Associations between sexual stimuli and pleasurable feelings also play an important role in sexual excitability. In the case of erectile disorder, for example, one team of researchers recently identified as a predisposing factor a man's belief in the "macho myth" of

REAL STORIES

Sue William Silverman: Sex Addiction

"I can't change all my behaviors in a month. All I can do is keep working on myself, keep moving forward, keep trying."

In *Love Sick: One Woman's Journey Through Sexual Addiction*, author Sue William Silverman tells the story of her battle with sexual addiction, and documents her stay at an intensive, 28-day inpatient hospital treatment program where she begins to battle her addiction for the first time. Sue joined the treatment program only at the urging of her therapist, Ted, who had recognized that her addiction had slowly been destroying every aspect of her life.

The hospital unit that Sue attended was populated with other women struggling with sexual addiction. She describes, "The only other time I was surrounded by women (girls, really) was when I lived in a college dorm. Except I didn't feel surrounded by girls then, either. For my attention was always drawn outside my bay window, to men disturbing the nights of Boston." Sue's interactions with the other women helped her gain a different perspective on her addiction, in seeing how other women were affected by sexual addiction from a more objective point of view.

In the hospital, Sue is required to maintain a rigid, daily schedule that includes group and individual therapy with Ted, regular meal times, and time for personal reflection. Much like Alcoholics Anonymous, she is required to go through a 12-step program toward recovery. As Sue makes her way through the workbook she uses throughout treatment, she reflects on many past sexual encounters with men and how she repeatedly sought out sexual affection in the hope of feeling a sense of genuine fulfillment, though the encounters only left her needing more.

Sue realizes that as a result of her constant need for sexual fulfillment and a propensity to shift her identity based on which man's attention she was seeking, she never took the time to understand her own identity. She describes that rather than her true self, it was a different version of herself—an addict persona, who had sought out all those men. She writes, "When I'm fully in the power of that addict-woman, when I am *most* sick, I am, ironically, totally capable of swimming, going to parties, socializing: *being what appears to be normal*. Yes, all these years I've convinced not only myself, but also others, that my behavior is normal because, in the strength of the addiction, I can *seem* normal. . . . Now, however, when the addiction is receding, when I'm in withdrawal, even though I'm getting better, everything scares me and I appear to be a wreck. Except I'm not; I'm in the process of becoming normal." She is in the process of not only recovering from her addiction, but becoming herself.

In the book, Sue describes how therapy helped her to recognize the danger of her addiction and the consequences of her behaviors. "For months, like a mantra, my therapist has told me, 'These men are killing you.' I don't know if he means emotionally, spiritually, or physically. I don't ask. He explains that I confuse sex with love, compulsively repeating this destructive pattern with one man after another. I do this because as a girl I learned that sex is love from my father, the first dangerous man who sexually misloved me." Sue explains that her father sexually abused her from the time she was a young girl until she left home to go to college in Boston. Once she was in college, Sue found herself spending the majority of her time thinking about and seeking out men for sex. She began a string of sexual affairs that continued until the time she entered the hospital. Each affair began soon after meeting each man, and she would attain an intense feeling of satisfaction during each sexual encounter, followed by feelings of emptiness and then the immediate desire to seek out another sexual encounter.

"The intensity is an addict's 'high,'" my therapist says. "Not love." To numb the shame and fear associated both with the past and with my current sexual behavior, I medicate, paradoxically, by using sex, he explains. "But sometimes that 'high' stops working. Usually after a scary binge."

Sue also suffered from eating disordered behavior, and was dangerously thin when she entered the treatment program. Some of the therapy groups in the treatment program focused on the connection between her body image and her addiction, and she reflects on her thoughts about her body: ". . . But *it* is not *me*—although my body is part of me—the thinner, the better. Less body, less trouble. No body. *No* trouble. If no man is able to see my body, then I won't have to keep having sex."

Throughout the book Sue talks about her marriage, which at the time of her entering treatment had dissolved to the point where she and her husband barely spoke and slept in separate bedrooms. She writes that she married her husband as a way to seek out normalcy and stability. Her husband, Andrew, is not aware of her battles with sexual addiction, and when she comes to the inpatient program she only tells him that she is seeking treatment for depression. Sue visits with her husband briefly while she is in the hospital, and their relationship offers her a sense of security that helps her through the difficulty of becoming, and staying, sober. In the program Sue finds that she longs to achieve a sense of balance and stability in her life. She calls it "a state of nothingness: I won't be drunk; nor will I have to struggle so hard to be sober." Although with her therapist, she

Author Sue William Silverman chronicles her struggle with sexual addiction in *Love Sick: One Woman's Journey Through Sexual Addiction*.

comes to realize that stability means more than not giving into her addictive behaviors, but finding out who she is and genuinely being that person.

When she leaves the hospital, Sue continues to attend individual therapy and a weekly Sex Addicts Anonymous group. Through the strength and insight that she attained in the hospital, Sue begins the slow process of recovery. The book ends by describing Sue's first day at home from the hospital. Although she finds herself missing the safety of the unit and the women she came to know, she finds comfort in doing ordinary things like making dinner with her husband and begins to plan for her future. "Now I must learn that love is where I carve out my own life," she writes.

sexual infallibility. Their belief in this myth makes them more prone to developing dysfunctional thoughts (e.g., "I'm incompetent") when they have an unsuccessful sexual experience. Once the man activates these thoughts, they impair his ability to process erotic stimuli and have sexual thoughts and images. By turning his attentional focus away from the encounter and toward his feelings of incompetence and sadness, he then is less able to achieve and maintain an erection during future sexual encounters (Nobre, 2010).

Both men and women may hold negative "sexual self-schemas" such as feeling unloved, inadequate, and unworthy, which they transfer onto sexual situations, causing them to become anxious when they feel that an inability to achieve an orgasm will cause their partner to become tired. The underlying feature that applies both to men and women who have sexual dysfunctions is the belief in their own incompetence in sexual situations (Nobre & Pinto-Gouveia, 2009). In Table 11.3, we have reproduced a portion of the scale that assesses men's responses to unsuccessful sexual situations.

The quality of the relationship may also contribute to sexual dysfunction, particularly for women, whose sexual desire is sensitive to interpersonal factors, including the frequency of positive interactions (Both et al., 2010). Researchers are also discovering the cognitive factors involved in genito-pelvic pain/penetration disorder that compound the physical causes, such as catastrophizing about pain and having low levels of self-efficacy.

The core treatment of sexual dysfunctions involving disturbances of arousal and orgasm follows from the principles that Masters and Johnson (1970) established, namely, treating both partners in a couple, reducing anxiety about sexual performance, and the development of specific skills such as **sensate focus,** in which the interaction is not intended to lead to orgasm, but to experience pleasurable sensations during the phases prior to orgasm. This procedure reduces the couple's anxiety levels until eventually they are able to focus not on their feelings of inadequacy but

sensate focus
Method of treating sexual dysfunction in which the interaction is not intended to lead to orgasm, but to experience pleasurable sensations during the phases prior to orgasm.

TABLE 11.3 Questionnaire of Cognitive Schema Activation in Sexual Context: Male Version

Read carefully each one of the episodes presented below and indicate the extent to which they usually happened to you by circling a number (1-never to 5-often)

I'm alone with my partner. She looks as if she wants to have sex, and she's going to extraordinary lengths to try to arouse me. However, I don't feel like it at all. So instead, I pretend to be tired and change the subject. Yet, she persists. She looks disappointed, and says that I don't love her as much as I used to.						
never happened	1	2	3	4	5	happened often

I'm caressing my partner, and she is enjoying it and seems to be ready for intercourse. Upon attempting penetration, I notice that my erection isn't as firm as it normally is and full penetration seems impossible. I try to no avail, and finally quit.						
never happened	1	2	3	4	5	happened often

My partner is stimulating me, and I'm becoming very aroused. I'm getting very excited and I immediately try to penetrate her. I feel out of control and reach orgasm very quickly, at which point intercourse stops. She looks very disappointed, as if she expected much more from me.						
never happened	1	2	3	4	5	happened often

I'm completely involved in lovemaking and I start to penetrate my partner. In the beginning everything is going fine, but time passes and I can't seem to reach orgasm. She seems to be getting tired. No matter how hard I try, orgasm seems to be farther and farther out of my reach.						
never happened	1	2	3	4	5	happened often

Circle all emotions you felt when you imagined the episode that most often happens to you.

Worry Sadness Disillusionment Fear Guilt Shame Anger Hurt Pleasure Satisfaction

SOURCE: Nobre & Pinto-Gouveia, 2009.

instead on the sexual encounter itself. Clinicians may also teach the partners to masturbate or to incorporate methods of sexual stimulation other than intercourse, such as clitoral stimulation alone.

Expanding on these methods, therapists are increasingly using principles derived from cognitive-behavioral therapy that restructure the individual's thoughts that can inhibit sexual arousal and desire. Both partners may also promote their interpersonal communication and have more positive intimate experiences (Both et al., 2010). For sexual pain disorders, cognitive-behavioral therapy alone does not seem to be effective, but is most beneficial when integrated with muscle relaxation, biofeedback, and education (Bergeron et al., 2010).

biological sex
The sex determined by a person's chromosomes.

gender identity
A person's inner sense of maleness or femaleness.

gender dysphoria
Distress that may accompany the incongruence between a person's experienced or expressed gender and that person's assigned gender.

11.4 Gender Dysphoria

We turn now to disorders that involve difficulties that individuals experience due to feeling a mismatch between their **biological sex** (i.e., the sex determined by their chromosomes) and their inner sense of maleness or femaleness, called **gender identity**. In the *DSM-5*, the term **gender dysphoria** refers to distress that may accompany the incongruence between a person's experienced or expressed gender and that person's assigned gender. Not everyone experiences distress as the result of this incongruence but, importantly, many people are distressed if they are unable to receive treatment through hormones and/or surgery. Thus, in the current criteria for disorder, the individual experiences identification with the other sex. The feeling that they are "in the wrong body" causes feelings of discomfort and a sense of inappropriateness

MINI CASE

Gender Dysphoria

Dale describes himself as a woman living in a man's body. His memories back to age 4 are of feeling discomfort with his assigned sex. When he was a young child, people often mistook him for a girl, because his mannerisms, style of play, and clothes were stereotypically feminine. He was glad he had an ambiguous name, and throughout adolescence he led others to believe he really was a girl. Schoolmates teased him at times, but this did not bother him, because he took pride in his feminine attributes. Dale's parents became increasingly alarmed, and they sent him to a psychologist when he was 15. The psychologist recognized that Dale had gender dysphoria, and she explained to Dale that he could not pursue sex reassignment surgery until adulthood, because a surgeon would insist that Dale have the maturity and life experience necessary for making such a dramatic decision. Now, at age 25, Dale is about to follow through on his wish to

have the body of a woman and is consulting sex reassignment specialists at a major medical school to prepare for the surgery. After an initial evaluation, the psychologist told Dale that he needed to begin a pre-surgery evaluation process that would last for at least a year and a half. During this time, he would live publicly as a woman. This would involve dressing as a woman and changing all documentation that referred to him as a male (such as voting records, credit card applications, and driver's license). He would have to enter psychotherapy to evaluate his psychological health and readiness for surgery. Dale also had to begin taking hormones that would cause him to develop female secondary sex characteristics. After successfully completing the evaluation process, Dale would be able to enter the next phase of the sex reassignment process, which would start the transformation of his physical characteristics.

about their assigned gender. Both of these conditions must be present for a clinician to assign the diagnosis. Thus, the clinical problem is the dysphoria, not the individual's gender identity.

Another term that relates to the feeling of cross-gender identification is **transsexualism,** which also refers to this phenomenon in which a person has an inner feeling of belonging to the other sex. Some people with gender dysphoria disorders wish to live as members of the other sex, and they act and dress accordingly. Unlike individuals with transvestic disorder, these people do not derive sexual gratification from cross-dressing.

The *DSM-5* authors presented a strong case for using the term gender dysphoria to replace gender identity disorder, specifying whether the individual is a child or post-adolescent. One reason for this proposed change was to take away the stigma attached to the label of the condition as a "disorder." Having cross-gender identification does not necessarily imply that an individual is distressed or has a "disorder" (Cohen-Kettenis & Pfafflin, 2010). Only if that person feels dysphoria toward having this sex would a diagnosis be applied. Moreover, although some groups would advocate for the notion of removing gender dysphoria entirely from the diagnostic nomenclature, to do so could potentially preclude individuals who wish to seek sex reassignment surgery from insurance coverage because there would be no diagnosis for the clinician to give (Corneil, Eisfeld, & Botzer, 2010).

A small number of individuals with gender dysphoria seek sex reassignment surgery. The procedure is lengthy, expensive, and carries with it a number of stringent conditions, such as requiring that the individual receive a comprehensive psychological assessment and course of psychotherapy prior to acceptance for surgery. However, based on a 5-year follow-up investigation of 42 Swedish adults, the results appear to lead to favorable outcomes, and none of the participants regretted their decision (Johansson, Sundbom, Höjerback, & Bodlund, 2010).

transsexualism
A term sometimes used to refer to gender dysphoria, specifically pertaining to individuals choosing to undergo sex reassignment surgery.

After initially coming out as a lesbian and then as transgender, Chaz Bono underwent the process of female-to-male gender conversion between 2008 and 2010.

Theories and Treatment of Gender Dysphoria

The psychology of the transgendered experience is undergoing radical shifts. Whereas in the past, the profession equated transgenderism with a "disorder," the new terminology is reflecting a theoretical perspective that does not focus specifically on what is "wrong" with people whose self-identification differs from their biological characteristics or social roles. Clinicians who work with transgendered individuals experiencing gender dysphoria take a three-pronged approach to psychotherapy including psychological, hormonal, and potentially sex reassignment surgery. Ideally, according to the World Professional Association for Transgender Health (WPATH), clinicians would provide an assessment of a client's well-being without regard to diagnostic criteria. However, because a clinician must make a diagnosis so that clients can receive insurance, the clinicians take on a "gatekeeper" role, potentially interfering with their ability to establish healthy therapeutic relationships (Corneil et al., 2010).

Given that clinicians will continue to treat individuals with gender dysphoria, however, new approaches are emerging based on transgender theory that emphasizes a more fluid view of gender than the binary male-female dichotomy (Nagoshi & Brzuzy, 2010). Clinicians can challenge this view by using the gender terminology that the client prefers. Rather than assume that people's motivations, behaviors, and attitudes are based on their socially defined identities, clinicians can recognize that these categories are conditional. For example, the clinician can avoid using terms like "real" or "biological" gender. We have summarized the American Psychological Association's Standards of Care for the Treatment of Gender Identity Disorders (written before the *DSM-5* was published) in Table 11.4.

Even though transgenderism is depathologized in *DSM-5*, clients will, nevertheless, continue to face transphobia, the negative stereotyping and fear of people who are transgendered. Rather than recommend sex reassignment surgery to help clients cope with social pressures to conform to one gender or another, clinicians can instead let their clients create their own gender identities. As a result, transgendered individuals may feel an improved sense of well-being as they are allowed to explore more openly and without bias their multiple, intersecting identities.

11.5 Paraphilic Disorders, Sexual Dysfunctions, and Gender Dysphoria: The Biopsychosocial Perspective

The sexual disorders constitute three discrete sets of difficulties involving varying aspects of sexual functioning and behavior. Although there are many unanswered questions concerning their causes, we need a biopsychosocial perspective to understand how individuals acquire and maintain these diverse problems over time. Moreover, researchers and clinicians are increasingly developing models that incorporate integrated treatment. Professionals in the area of sexual medicine are expanding the scope of their work. The growing research base that the *DSM-5* authors used reflects not only expansion of the empirical approaches to sexual disorders, but adoption of a broader, more inclusive, and socioculturally sensitive approach to their understanding and treatment.

TABLE 11.4 **APA Standards of Care for the Treatment of Gender Identity Disorders**

Guidelines for Providers	Mental Health Professional	Physician Prescribing Hormones	Surgeon Performing Sex Reassignment Surgery
Competence	• Master's or doctoral degree • Documented supervised training in psychotherapy • Specialized training in the treatment of sexual disorders • Continuing education in the treatment of gender identity disorders	• Well versed in the relevant medical and psychological aspects of treating patients with gender identity disorders	• Board-certified urologist, gynecologist, plastic or general surgeon competent in urological diagnosis • Documented supervised training in sex reassignment surgery • Continuing education in sex reassignment surgery

Guidelines for Applicants	Eligibility Criteria		Readiness Criteria
Hormone therapy	• Legal age of majority • Completion of 3 months of real-life experience OR psychotherapy for a duration specified by a mental health professional (usually 3 months) • Demonstrable knowledge of effects and side effects, social benefits, and risks of hormones and documented informed consent		• Further consolidation of gender identity during psychotherapy or the real-life experience • Progress in mastering other identified problems leading to stable mental health • The patient is likely to take hormones in a responsible manner
Female-to-male chest surgery	• Legal age of majority • Completion of 3 months of real-life experience OR psychotherapy for a duration specified by a mental health professional (usually 3 months) • Demonstrable knowledge of the potential risks and benefits of chest surgery and documented informed consent		• Further consolidation of gender identity during psychotherapy or the real-life experience • Progress in mastering other identified problems leading to stable mental health
Male-to-female breast surgery	• Legal age of majority • Completion of 3 months of real-life experience OR psychotherapy for a duration specified by a mental health professional (usually 3 months) • Hormonal breast development has been achieved (usually after 18 months) • Demonstrable knowledge of the potential risks and benefits of breast surgery and documented informed consent		• Further consolidation of gender identity during psychotherapy or the real-life experience • Progress in mastering other identified problems leading to stable mental health
Genital reconstructive surgery and surgery affecting the reproductive system	• Legal age of majority • At least 12 months of continuous full-time real-life experience • At least 12 months of continuous hormone therapy • Demonstrable knowledge of the cost, required lengths of hospitalizations, likely complications, and postsurgical rehabilitation requirements of the various surgical approaches and documented informed consent • Awareness of different competent surgeons		• Demonstrable progress in consolidating one's gender identity • Demonstrable progress in dealing with work, family, and interpersonal issues resulting in a significantly better state of mental health

SOURCE: http://www.apa.org/pi/lgbt/resources/policy/gender-identity-report.pdf

Return to the Case: Shaun Boyden

As was evident in Shaun's case, individuals with pedophilic disorder often do not feel distressed as a result of their urges. Thus, the first issue to address in psychotherapy was to engage Shaun in therapy by helping him realize the harm he had done through his actions; in other words, making his disorder "ego-dystonic." Essentially, the point was to make it difficult for Shaun to continue to deny the problems his urges caused. Some of the consequences addressed were the emotional trauma he had caused the children he had molested, the negative effect on his marriage, and perhaps most salient to Shaun at the time, legal ramifications. Therapy also focused on Shaun's distorted thinking about children, and used empathy training and sexual impulse control training. Further, Anne had decided to stay with Shaun and they began to attend couples therapy to work on their relationship.

Though at first Shaun was hesitant to put forth any effort in therapy, he was eventually able to realize the harm he had done to others with his actions. With that realization, he was able to begin working toward controlling his urges and fantasies about children. In combination with the antiandrogen medication,

therapy began to help Shaun effectively cut down on his frequent fantasies, and he began to experience fewer and fewer urges to have sex with children. Though Shaun began to recognize that he would have to work to control his urges throughout the rest of his life, he was able to accept that his disorder was harmful to others and to his relationship with his wife.

Dr. Tobin's reflections: Shaun's story is similar to that of many other individuals with pedophilic disorder. Though at some level he realized what he was doing to children was immoral and illegal, his thoughts and actions were not associated with a sense of distress. Like others with pedophilic disorder, Shaun had to develop special plans for getting access to children, and his pedophilic behavior became more intense at times of stress, such as when his relationship with his wife was going through a difficult period. Shaun's history of sexual abuse from his own father was likely a contributing factor to his disorder, and once Shaun's symptoms have significantly reduced, it may be appropriate to explore the impact of this history.

Sarah Tobin, PhD

SUMMARY

- When it comes to sexual behavior, the distinction between normal and abnormal becomes even more complicated, perhaps, than in other areas of human behavior. When evaluating the normality of a given sexual behavior, the context is extremely important, as are customs and mores, which change over time.

- **Paraphilias** are behaviors in which an individual has recurrent, intense sexually arousing fantasies, sexual urges, or behaviors involving (1) nonhuman objects, (2) children or other nonconsenting persons, or (3) the suffering or humiliation of self or partner.

- When a paraphilia causes intense distress and impairment, clinicians may diagnose **paraphilic disorder.** Paraphilic disorders include **pedophilic disorder, exhibitionistic disorder, fetishistic disorder, frotteuristic disorder, sexual masochism disorder, sexual sadism disorder,** and **transvestic disorder.**

- Critics of the *DSM* argued against including several of the paraphilic disorders in *DSM-5* because to do so pathologizes nonnormative sexual behavior. By defining these disorders as resulting in intense distress or impairment, the authors of the *DSM-5* hope to avoid judging a behavior's "normality" and instead base the criteria for a disorder on an individual's

subjective experience of distress or degree of impairment in everyday life.

- From a biological perspective, paraphilic disorders involve a combination of influences including genetic, hormonal, and sensory factors in interaction with cognitive, cultural, and contextual influences. One theory of pedophilic disorders is that it results from early neurodevelopmental disorders, involving particularly the temporal lobe, which researchers believe is involved in altered sexual arousal. However, these changes could also be the result of early physical abuse or sexual victimization. Researchers have also identified altered serotonin levels in people with this disorder; however, these alterations may also be related to the presence of other psychological disorders in these individuals. Clinicians treating paraphilic disorders based on the biological perspective may use psychotherapeutic medications intended to alter the individual's neurotransmitter levels.

- The majority of studies on paraphilic disorders focus on pedophilic disorder. A common theme in the psychological literature is the idea of a "victim-to-abuser cycle" or "abused-abusers phenomena," meaning that abusers were themselves abused at some point in their lives, probably when they were young. Treatments within the psychological perspective seem most effective when combining individual with group therapy. The cognitive-behavioral perspective is particularly useful in helping clients recognize their distortions and denial. At the same time, these clients benefit from training in empathy, so that they can understand how their victims are feeling. Adding to the equation within the psychological perspective, clinicians may also train clients in learning to control their sexual impulses. Researchers believe that the most effective treatment involves a combination of hormonal drugs intended to reduce androgen (male sex hormone) levels and psychotherapy.

- Sexual arousal leads to a set of physiological changes throughout the body often culminating in orgasm. A **sexual dysfunction** involves a marked divergence of an individual's response in the sexual response cycle along with feelings of significant distress or impairment.

- **Arousal disorders** may be diagnosed in individuals who have low or no sexual desire, or are unable to achieve physiological arousal during the initial phases of the sexual response cycle. As a result, they may avoid or be unable to have sexual intercourse. These disorders include **male hypoactive sexual desire disorder, female sexual interest/arousal disorder,** and **erectile disorder.**

- There are also disorders involving orgasm. Inability to achieve orgasm, a distressing delay in achieving orgasm, or reduced intensity of orgasm constitutes **female orgasmic disorder.** Men with a marked delay in ejaculation or who rarely, if at all, experience ejaculations may have **delayed ejaculation.**

- Clinicians diagnose sexual pain disorders, which involve difficulties in sexual relationships due to painful sensations in the genitals from intercourse as **genito-pelvic pain/ penetration disorder.** This disorder can affect both males and females.

- We can best view sexual dysfunctions through a biopsychosocial lens as an interaction of complex physiological, psychological, and sociocultural factors. To help a client with a sexual dysfunction, the clinician must first conduct a comprehensive assessment that includes a physical exam and psychological testing, including the client's partner, if appropriate. In addition, the clinician must assess the individual's use of substances, including not only drugs and alcohol, but also all medications, including psychotherapeutic ones.

- The *DSM-5* authors use the term **gender dysphoria** instead of gender identity disorder, specifying whether the individual is a child or post-adolescent. In the current criteria for gender dysphoria, the individual experiences identification with the other sex. The feeling that they are "in the wrong body" causes feelings of discomfort and a sense of inappropriateness about their assigned gender. Both of these conditions must be present for a clinician to assign the diagnosis. Another term that relates to the feeling of cross-gender identification is **transsexualism,** which also refers to this phenomenon in which a person has an inner feeling of belonging to the other sex.

- Theoretical perspectives on the transgendered experience are undergoing radical shifts in the field of psychology. Whereas in the past, the profession equated transgenderism with a "disorder," the new terminology does not focus specifically on what is "wrong" with people whose self-identification differs from their biological characteristics or social roles.

- Paraphilic disorders, sexual dysfunctions, and gender dysphoria constitute three discrete sets of difficulties involving varying aspects of sexual functioning and behavior. Although there are many unanswered questions concerning their causes, we need a biopsychosocial perspective to understand how individuals acquire and maintain these diverse problems over time.

KEY TERMS

Substance-Related and Addictive Disorders

Learning Objectives

12.1 Explain key features of substance disorders

12.2 Differentiate among disorders related to specific substances

12.3 Explain theories and treatment of substance use disorders

12.4 Identify symptoms of non-substance-related disorders

12.5 Analyze the biopsychosocial perspective on the development
of substance disorders

Case Report: Carl Wadsworth

CHAPTER 12

Demographic information: Carl is a 32-year-old African American male.

Presenting problem: Carl's sister Janice made an appointment for him to see a therapist at a local outpatient therapy clinic following an arrest for public intoxication. Janice stated that the family was "sick of being worried" about him. She reported that Carl had been drinking much more frequently over the past few years than ever before, culminating in his recent arrest for public intoxication. Janice also reported that Carl has bipolar disorder, although he is not on medication currently, about which she and the family were concerned.

During the intake session, the therapist noticed that Carl appeared intoxicated. She decided not to confront him about this during the appointment. When he presented for the next appointment intoxicated again, the therapist asked him directly if he had been drinking prior to the session, as she was concerned that his alcohol usage would interfere with therapy. Carl's reply was, "Maybe . . . just a little." The therapist asked Carl to refrain from drinking before their next appointment, to which he agreed. When he showed up to the third appointment intoxicated yet again, the therapist decided that she needed to address his alcohol use before he could make any progress in therapy. Carl had expressed that he was ashamed of his alcohol use, but that he found himself unable to cut down on his drinking. He described symptoms of withdrawal such as shaking and feeling nauseous if he did not have a drink within the first few hours of waking up in the morning. Carl stated that he had been working in a liquor store for the past 4 years, and it was difficult for him to refrain from drinking when he could so easily access alcohol. He agreed with the therapist that it would be important to address his issues with alcohol before beginning psychotherapy.

Janice called the therapist the following week to tell her that Carl had been in a car accident and was arrested for driving while under the influence of alcohol. Carl had driven into a lamppost near her home and reportedly had a blood alcohol level over three times the legal limit at the time of the accident. Janice reported that Carl sustained only a minor concussion and a few scratches. While he was in the hospital for observation, he told Janice that he was ready to quit drinking for good and wanted to go to therapy. Janice explained that Carl had lost his job after his first arrest for public intoxication, and he and the family were "willing to try anything" to help him quit drinking. The therapist agreed to see Carl, and he attended the following session sober.

Carl told his therapist about his experiences with bipolar disorder and with lithium, a medication that clinicians typically prescribe to treat the disorder. Carl described that he preferred drinking to taking medication because he did not experience side effects, and he found weekly blood testing while on lithium "annoying." Carl stated that he had never really drunk much alcohol, as his parents are both former alcoholics and he worried that he might be susceptible to alcoholism. His drinking began 4 years prior when he began working at a liquor store. At the time, he was stable on medication and had not experienced any significant psychological impairment for several years. "I wasn't planning on drinking at work ever, but my boss sure liked to, so we started getting drunk together after closing up for the night," Carl reported. Since he found it difficult to drink heavily while on lithium, he decided to stop taking his medication so that he could drink with his boss, who would taunt Carl to drink if he declined his offer. Since Carl was drinking mostly at night and was living by himself, no one in Carl's family had noticed that he was drinking. After a few months of drinking every day at work, Carl reported that he started to experience withdrawal symptoms when he woke up in the morning, and so he began drinking immediately when he woke up and while he was at work. He continued with this routine for the next 2 years. Although he was working during this time, he was essentially unable to perform any activities outside of work. His family grew increasingly worried, especially when he repeatedly showed up intoxicated at his parents' house. They urged him to try AA and warned him of the dangers of his drinking, although Carl denied that he was having any problems. To show his family that he did not have a problem, Carl would stop drinking for 1 or 2 weeks, although his desire to drink was too intense to allow him to go any longer than that. Carl grew increasingly depressed as he went without medication, and his drinking grew more severe; however, instead of seeking treatment, Carl only drank more when he was feeling particularly depressed.

While at work one day, Carl was arrested for public intoxication for verbally haranguing a customer. Occasionally he would get into an argument at work, although his boss typically did not take much notice. However, during this particular incident he threatened violence against a customer, and Carl's boss had no choice but to fire him and report him to the police. The police held Carl overnight and released him the next day, as the customer chose not to press charges. Without an income, Carl was forced to move out of his apartment and move in with Janice, who luckily for Carl lived nearby. Worried that Carl had spun out of control and unsure how she could help him, Janice called the clinic for an appointment.

"She had me on lockdown," Carl stated about living with his sister during this time. After Carl showed up for therapy intoxicated, Janice removed all alcohol from her home and forbade Carl to leave the house unaccompanied. At first, Carl struggled with severe withdrawal symptoms, "and then all of a sudden," he said, "I felt great. I felt invincible, actually. It was then that I knew that I was becoming manic." He described pacing around the house and an inability to sleep for 3 days due to racing thoughts and an abundance of energy. After convincing Janice that he needed to borrow her car to go to the grocery store, Carl drove to a nearby liquor store, purchased a bottle of whiskey, and drank the entire bottle within a

matter of minutes. On his way back to Janice's home, he drove into a lamppost and was subsequently arrested.

Relevant history: Carl reported that clinicians diagnosed him with bipolar disorder when he was 18 years old, following a manic episode in which he had slept for about 4 hours over a period of 6 days. "I was living on my own, so no one noticed what was going on," he stated. He eventually checked himself into the hospital, convinced that he was having a heart attack. He entered the hospital psychiatric unit for 1 week and began taking lithium. Over the next 10 years, Carl occasionally struggled with some mood symptoms such as depression or racing thoughts, although these symptoms did not significantly interfere with his life. Of note, however, is the fact that Carl has had limited interpersonal and adult romantic relationships. "I'm too messed up to have any friends, so I just like to keep to myself," he explained.

When Carl was 28, the telecom company for which he worked downsized and he lost his job. Carl became so depressed that he attempted suicide at his parents' home, where his mother discovered him. He re-entered the hospital for about 1 month and began receiving disability, which allowed him to receive medication and therapy. While relaying his history, Carl noted that he rarely drank alcohol during this time, due mainly to the medication he took, but also because his parents were both former alcoholics and he reported feeling worried that he would follow the same path should he start drinking. His heavy drinking only began after starting the job at the liquor store. Because Carl made enough money at the job to afford his own apartment, he felt hesitant to let his boss down by refusing to drink with him.

Case formulation: An important distinction to make in Carl's case is whether his alcohol use occurred secondarily, as a result of his bipolar disorder, or whether it arose independently, which would qualify for a dual diagnosis. As Carl stated regarding the episode of drinking that occurred while at his sister's, he began drinking heavily while he was manic, believing that he could handle drinking a large quantity of alcohol and still be able to drive safely. However, this was the only instance in which he reported drinking while experiencing mood symptoms.

After careful consideration of his case, it appears that Carl's initial problems with alcohol began in the absence of mood symptoms. Additionally, his alcohol consumption did not appear to cause his mood symptoms. Because of these two distinctions, Carl qualifies for a dual diagnosis of Alcohol Use Disorder, Severe, and Bipolar Disorder. Furthermore, Carl meets the criteria for Bipolar I Disorder due to the presence of manic, rather than hypomanic, episodes, which required hospitalization and severely impacted his functioning.

Treatment plan: Carl agreed to attend a local Alcoholics Anonymous (AA) meeting on a daily basis in conjunction with weekly psychotherapy. Carl also agreed to see a psychiatrist for a medication evaluation.

Sarah Tobin, PhD

12.1 Key Features of Substance Disorders

A **substance** is a chemical that alters a person's mood or behavior when the person smokes, injects, drinks, inhales, snorts, or swallows it in pill form. Substance-related disorders reflect patterns of use (and abuse), intoxication, and withdrawal.

The line demarcating substance use from abuse is a difficult line to draw. The *DSM-III* and *DSM-IV-TR* defined substance "abuse" as distinct from substance "dependence" and delineated two parallel sets of disorders for each type of substance. The diagnosis of substance abuse carried with it no implication that the individual is addicted to the substance.

DSM-5 combines abuse and dependence into a single dimensional rating. Individuals receive a diagnosis based on meeting only two criteria, but they are rated according to the degree of severity of their symptoms. A person in a state of substance **withdrawal** shows physiological and psychological changes that vary according to the actual substance involved. **Tolerance** occurs when an individual requires increasingly greater amounts of the substance in order to achieve its desired effects or when the person feels less of an effect after using the same amount of the substance.

A **substance use disorder** is a cluster of cognitive, behavioral, and physiological symptoms indicating that the individual continues using a substance even though it causes significant problems in his or her life. Clinicians diagnose substance use disorders by assessing the individual in four categories of symptoms: impaired control, social impairment, risky use, and pharmacological changes. They then count the number of symptoms the individual demonstrates and use this number to assign a severity rating of from mild to severe.

Although many people commonly refer to these disorders as representing an "addiction," the *DSM-5* authors prefer the more neutral term of "substance use disorder." They believe that substance use disorder, specifying mild to moderate, is more precise and has fewer negative connotations than the term "addiction." Similarly, people with these disorders are not referred to as "addicts," but instead as individuals with substance use disorders. People still use these terms in common language, of course, but from the *DSM-5* perspective, they are not included as official diagnostic terminology. The term "addictive" appears in the chapter name as a descriptive term only.

People with substance use disorders suffer a range of significant effects on their daily life. Often they neglect obligations at work, and their commitments to home and family start to erode. In addition to letting their work and family life slide, they may begin to take risks that are personally dangerous and put others in jeopardy, such as driving or operating machinery while intoxicated. Legal problems can arise for people who abuse substances. In addition to arrests for driving while intoxicated, they may face charges of disorderly conduct or assaultive behavior. These disorders also frequently involve

substance
A chemical that alters a person's mood or behavior when it is smoked, injected, drunk, inhaled, or swallowed in pill form.

withdrawal
Physiological and psychological changes that occur when an individual stops taking a substance.

tolerance
The extent to which the individual requires larger and larger amounts of a substance in order to achieve its desired effects, or the extent to which the individual feels less of its effects after using the same amount of the substance.

substance use disorder
A cluster of cognitive, behavioral, and physiological symptoms indicating that the individual uses a substance despite significant substance-related problems.

What's New in the DSM-5

Combining Abuse and Dependence

DSM-5's authors combined abuse and dependence into what is now termed a "substance use disorder." Individuals receive a diagnosis based on meeting only two criteria, but are rated according to the degree of severity of their symptoms. Critics believe that the revised system may result in too many individuals with mild symptoms who do not have an "addiction" receiving a diagnosis of a substance-related disorder (Martin, Steinley, Vergés, & Sher, 2011). However, the dimensional rating theoretically allows clinicians to allow for gradations of from mild to severe levels of the disorder. A second major change in *DSM-5* was the transition of caffeine withdrawal from a research-only to a clinical diagnosis. The *DSM-5* authors argued that there was sufficient evidence from large enough populations to warrant recognition of this condition as a psychiatric diagnosis. They believed, furthermore, that by placing a diagnosis on the condition, clinicians will be more likely to recognize, and then correctly treat, individuals who have these symptoms. Many caffeine users who suffer from caffeine withdrawal attribute their symptoms to other disorders, leading to unnecessary health care utilization and associated costs. The inclusion of this diagnosis may help them receive needed interventions.

substance intoxication
The temporary maladaptive experience of behavioral or psychological changes that are due to the accumulation of a substance in the body.

interpersonal problems due to the fact that abuse and dependence on drugs create strains on relationships with family, friends, and co-workers. In extreme cases, these disorders can also lead to health problems and even premature death.

Substance-related disorders also include substance-induced disorders, which are disorders involving the effects of the substance itself.

People receive a diagnosis of **substance intoxication** when they experience a drug's effects on their physiological functioning and show signs of significant impairment. The extent of substance intoxication that an individual may experience depends on the specific drug, how rapidly it acts, and the duration of its effects. Efficient absorption of intravenous or smokable drugs into the bloodstream is likely to lead to a more intense kind of intoxication than are drugs taken in pill form.

The second category of substance-induced disorders include those that reflect the effects of withdrawal in which individuals develop behavioral changes that are specific to the particular substance. These changes include physiological and cognitive alterations that are associated with the discontinuation of the particular substance in question. Other disorders can also be associated with substance use including psychotic disorder, mood disorder, anxiety disorder, sexual dysfunction, and sleep disorder. People may also show comorbidity of the substance-related disorder with another condition, such as an anxiety disorder or a mood disorder.

12.2 Disorders Associated with Specific Substances

According to the U.S. government's Substance Abuse and Mental Health Administration (SAMHSA), in 2010 an estimated 22.6 million Americans ages 12 and older used illicit drugs at least once in the preceding 30 days (i.e., were current users) (Substance Abuse and Mental Health Services Administration, 2011). This number translates to an estimated 8.9 percent of the population. Marijuana is the most commonly used illicit drug, with 17.4 million Americans reporting use within the past month. We can see the numbers of users of all illicit drugs in Figure 12.1.

Rates of current illicit drug use reported by SAMHSA (2011) vary considerably by demographic group. The three most significant grouping characteristics are race/ethnicity, age, and gender. The rate of past month illicit drug use is 10.7 percent among people who identify as Black or African American followed by 9.1 percent for Whites, 8.1 percent for Hispanic or Latino, and 3.5 percent for Asian. The rates of illicit drug use generally decline linearly with age from the peak of 23 percent at ages 18 to 20 to 1 percent at ages 65 and older, although there was a slight increase for adults 50 to 59 years old in just the 2 years between 2008 and 2010 from 4.3 to 7.2 percent. This increase reflects the aging of the Baby Boom generation (born between 1946 and 1962) in which the rate of drug use is higher than that of older cohorts. Males have a higher rate of drug use (11.2 percent) than females (6.8 percent). Illicit drug use tends to be lower in college graduates, the employed, Southerners, and people living in rural areas.

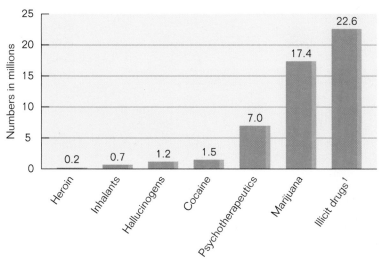

[1] Illicit drugs include marijuana/hashish, cocaine (including crack), heroin, hallucinogens, inhalants, or prescription-type psychotherapeutics used nonmedically.

Most drugs of abuse directly or indirectly target the reward center of the brain by flooding its circuits with dopamine, as you can see illustrated in Figure 12.2. Over-stimulation of the reward system produces the euphoric effects that abusers seek and leads them to repeat the behavior in order to repeat the experience. Drugs are more addictive than natural "highs" produced by such activities as eating and sex because they release far more dopamine (2 to 10 times as much) than do natural rewards, and the effects last much longer. Over time, the neurons in these dopamine pathways "down-regulate" in response to these surges in dopamine, meaning that they produce less dopa-mine themselves or reduce the number of dopamine receptors. Users then need to take drugs to raise their dopamine levels back up to normal. In order to experience the effects they experienced initially from the drugs, they also need to take higher and higher levels; in other words, they develop tolerance.

Because users learn to associate the pleasurable feelings of using the drug with the cues in the environment that were there when they took the drug, they develop classically conditioned responses that maintain their addiction. In addition to involving dopamine, some drugs of abuse involve glutamate, a neurotransmitter involved in memory and learning. Consequently, long-term drug abuse can lower the individual's level of glutamate and therefore lead the individual to experience impairments in memory.

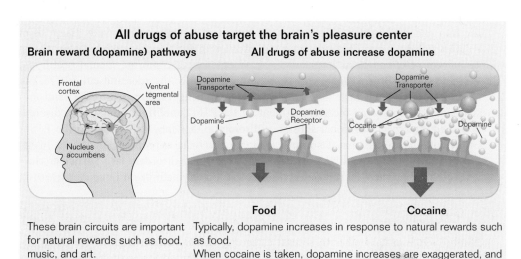

FIGURE 12.2 Effects of Drugs of Abuse on Dopamine Pathways

FIGURE 12.3 Comorbidity of Substance Use and Psychological Disorders

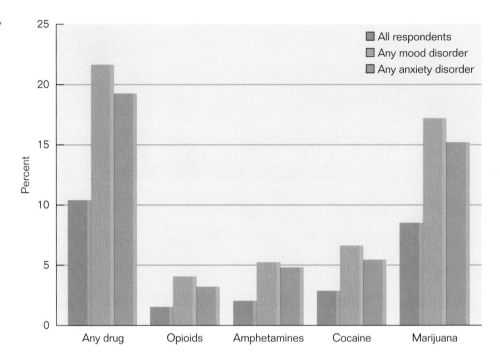

Individuals with mood and anxiety disorders are more likely to abuse substances, as we can see from Figure 12.3. Because we do not know whether the disorder led to drug abuse or vice versa, we cannot draw cause-and-effect conclusions. The three possibilities for this comorbidity are (1) drugs of abuse lead users to experience symptoms, such as psychosis in marijuana users; (2) psychological disorders can lead to drug abuse as individuals attempt to self-medicate; (3) similar factors, such as genetic predisposition, early exposure to stress and trauma, or structural brain abnormalities, cause both drug abuse and psychological disorders (National Institute on Drug Abuse, 2010).

Drug use typically begins in adolescence, which is also the time of heightened vulnerability to other psychological disorders. Early drug use is also a risk factor for later substance use disorder and may also be a risk factor for the subsequent development of other disorders. The risks are particularly likely to occur in individuals who have high genetic vulnerability. In one study following adolescents into early adulthood, only the heavy marijuana users with a particular gene variant had significantly higher risk of developing schizophreniform disorder (Caspi et al., 2005).

Higher rates of substance use disorders also occur in physically or emotionally traumatized individuals. This is a matter of particular concern for the veterans returning from the Iraq and Afghanistan Wars. As many as half of veterans who have a diagnosis of PTSD, also have a comorbid substance use disorder. In addition, researchers estimate that 45 percent of offenders in state and local prisons have a comorbid mental health and substance use disorder. People with a comorbid substance disorder and either PTSD or a criminal history may have difficulty receiving treatment. Veterans with PTSD and substance disorders may not receive treatment for the PTSD until the substance use disorder is treated; however, traditional substance disorder clinics may defer treating the PTSD. Incarcerated criminals may also have difficulty receiving appropriate treatment in the prison system. Consequently, individuals with comorbid disorders face particular challenges in treating their substance use disorders (National Institute on Drug Abuse, 2010).

Alcohol

Alcohol use is associated with several categories of disorders including use disorders, intoxication, and withdrawal. Statistics based on the United States show that alcohol is a commonly used substance. More than half (51.8 percent) of Americans over age 12

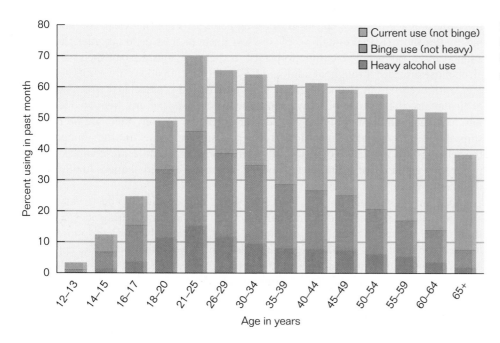

FIGURE 12.4 Current, Binge, and Heavy Alcohol Use among Persons Aged 12 or Older, by Age: 2010

reported that they had had at least one drink in the month prior to being surveyed. Nearly one-quarter (23.1 percent) of Americans 12 and older reported that they engaged in binge drinking, meaning that they had had five drinks on one occasion in the past 30 days. Heavy drinking, defined as consuming five or more drinks on the same occasion on at least 5 days in the month, was found in 6.7 percent of Americans 12 and older. Variables associated with higher rates of alcohol consumption were as follows: being male, white, married, a smoker, employed, and having a higher educational level and a higher income (Moore et al., 2005).

Patterns of alcohol use are also associated with age (Figure 12.4). Young adults ages 18 to 25 have the highest rates of binge drinking and heavy drinking. Of that group, adults ages 21 to 25 have the highest rates of drinking, with 45.5 percent engaging in binge drinking. The rates of binge and heavy drinking decline sharply throughout adulthood; among people 65 and older, 7.6 percent engage in binge drinking and 1.6 percent in heavy drinking.

The decline in binge and heavy drinking are part of a larger picture of "maturing out," similar to the maturation hypothesis of age and personality disorders. However,

MINI CASE

Alcohol Use Disorder

Rhona is a 55-year-old homemaker married to a successful builder. Every afternoon, she makes herself the first in a series of daiquiris. On many evenings, she passes out on the couch by the time her husband arrives home from work. Rhona lost her driver's license a year ago after being arrested three times on charges of driving while intoxicated. Although Rhona's family has urged her to obtain treatment for her disorder, she denies that she has a problem because she can "control" her drinking. The mother of three grown children, Rhona began to drink around age 45, when her youngest child left for college. Prior to this time, Rhona kept herself extremely busy through her children's extracurricular activities. When she found herself alone every afternoon, she took solace in having an early cocktail. Over a period of several years, the cocktail developed into a series of five or six strong drinks. Rhona's oldest daughter has begun lately to insist that something be done for her mother. She does not want to see Rhona develop the fatal alcohol-related illness that caused the premature death of her grandmother.

the pattern of age-related changes in drinking patterns is not that clear-cut. Longitudinal studies show that, although people are less likely to start drinking after the young adult years, many people continue to persist in their previously established patterns of alcohol use disorder throughout adulthood. Certain life transitions are associated, however, with decreases in alcohol use. For men, parenthood is associated with lower rates of alcohol use after the age of 38; women show the opposite pattern. Men who lose their jobs have the highest rates of alcohol use after age 38; for women, there are no relationships between job status and alcohol-use persistence. These findings suggest that the relationships among alcohol use, life transitions, and gender are complex so that maturation alone is not sufficient for understanding age-related changes in alcohol use disorders. (Vergés et al., 2011).

depressant
A psychoactive substance that causes the depression of central nervous system activity.

Clinicians classify alcohol as a nervous system **depressant.** Its effects vary by the amount that the drinker ingests. In small amounts, alcohol has sedating effects, leading users to feel relaxed. As people ingest more alcohol, they may begin to feel more outgoing, self-confident, and uninhibited. As people drink beyond that point, the depressant effects become apparent, leading users to experience sleepiness, lack of physical coordination, dysphoria, and irritability. Continuing past this point, excessive drinking can be fatal as the individual's vital functions completely shut down. More severe effects also occur when the individual mixes alcohol with other drugs, a situation referred to as **potentiation,** meaning that the effects of two drugs taken together are greater than the effect of either substance alone. Combining alcohol with another depressant, for example, can be a fatal outcome of such potentiation.

potentiation
The combination of the effects of two or more psychoactive substances such that the total effect is greater than the effect of either substance alone.

The rate at which alcohol absorption occurs in the bloodstream depends in part on a number of factors, including how much a person consumes, over what time period, and whether the person has food present in the digestive system. Another factor is the drinker's metabolic rate (the rate at which the body converts food substances to energy). The average person metabolizes alcohol at a rate of one-third of an ounce of 100 percent alcohol per hour, which is equivalent to an ounce of whiskey per hour. Following a bout of extensive intake of alcohol, a person is likely to experience an abstinence syndrome, or the phenomenon commonly called a "hangover." The symptoms of abstinence syndrome include a range of phenomena including nausea and vomiting, tremors, extreme thirst, headache, tiredness, irritability, depression, and dizziness. As with alcohol absorption, the extent of abstinence syndrome reflects the amount and rate of alcohol consumption and the individual's metabolic rate.

Alcohol affects almost every organ system in the body, either directly or indirectly. Long-term use of alcohol can lead to permanent brain damage, with symptoms of dementia, blackouts, seizures, hallucinations, and damage to the peripheral parts of the nervous system. Two forms of dementia are associated with long-term, heavy alcohol use: **Wernicke's disease** and **Korsakoff's syndrome.**

Wernicke's disease
A form of aphasia in which the individual is able to produce language but has lost the ability to comprehend, so that these verbal productions have no meaning.

Wernicke's disease is an acute and potentially reversible condition involving delirium, eye movement disturbances, difficulties in movement and balance, and deterioration of the peripheral nerves to the hands and feet. It is not the alcohol but a deficiency of thiamine (Vitamin B_1) that causes Wernicke's disease. Long-term heavy use of alcohol has deleterious effects on the body's ability to metabolize nutrients, and such alcohol users often have an overall pattern of poor nutrition. Adequate thiamine intake can reverse Wernicke's disease.

Korsakoff's syndrome
A permanent form of dementia associated with long-term alcohol use in which the individual develops retrograde and anterograde amnesia, leading to an inability to remember recent events or learn new information.

Korsakoff's syndrome is a permanent form of dementia in which the individual develops **retrograde amnesia,** an inability to remember past events, and **anterograde amnesia,** the inability to remember new information. The chances of a person recovering from Korsakoff's syndrome are less than one in four, and about another one in four people who have this disorder require permanent institutionalization.

retrograde amnesia
Amnesia involving loss of memory for past events.

Chronic heavy alcohol consumption also causes a number of harmful changes in the liver, gastrointestinal system, bone density, muscles, and immune system. When people abruptly stop ingesting alcohol after periods of chronic usage, they can experience sleep disturbances, profound anxiety, tremors, hyperactivity of the sympathetic nervous system, psychosis, seizures, or death.

anterograde amnesia
Amnesia involving the inability to remember new information.

Theories and Treatment of Alcohol Use Disorders

Clinicians who design interventions targeting individuals who have alcohol use disorders begin by conducting an assessment of the alcohol use patterns of their clients. The "AUDIT," or Alcohol Use Disorders Identification Test, shown in Table 12.1, is one such instrument (National Institute on Alcohol Abuse and Alcoholism, 2007).

Biological Perspectives   Twin, family, and adoption studies consistently point to the importance of genetic factors as contributors to alcohol-related disorders, with an estimated heritability of 50 to 60 percent. However, trying to pinpoint the genes involved in alcohol-related disorders is a great challenge to researchers, particularly for those who want to find genes that control the amount of alcohol consumption (Heath et al., 2011). The greatest success in studying the genetics of alcohol-related disorders comes from studies examining associations with genes involved in alcohol metabolism and neural transmission. Researchers are attempting to connect variations in some of these genes not only with patterns of alcohol use, but also with psychological factors, such as personality traits, and physiological factors, such as alcohol-related organ damage (Kimura & Higuchi, 2011). Large-scale analyses using genome-wide association studies are beginning to identify a large number of potential genes associated with alcohol use disorder that may pave the way toward understanding how the disorder develops (Wang et al., 2011). Using these new discoveries, researchers have already identified a relatively large number of genes, suggesting that alcohol use will not show a simple pattern of genetic transmission (Frank et al., 2012).

Physicians prescribe medications increasingly as biological treatment for alcohol use disorder if not as the sole form of treatment, then in conjunction with psychologically based therapies. A large number of well-controlled studies support the use of naltrexone as an aid in preventing relapse among people with alcohol use disorder. As an opioid receptor antagonist, it blocks the effects of the body's production of alcohol-induced opioids, perhaps through involving dopamine (Hillemacher, Heberlein, Muschler, Bleich, & Frieling, 2011). The individual who takes naltrexone is less likely to experience pleasurable effects of alcohol and even less likely to feel pleasure thinking about alcohol. As a result, people taking naltrexone feel less of an urge to drink and therefore will be less likely to suffer a relapse in which they engage in heavy drinking. An injectable form of naltrexone called nalmefene seems to be effective in promoting total abstinence (Garbutt et al., 2005).

Disulfiram is a medication that operates by the principles of aversion therapy. An individual taking disulfiram who consumes alcohol within a two-week period will experience a variety of unpleasant physical reactions, including flushing, palpitations, increased heart rate, lowered blood pressure, nausea and vomiting, sweating, and dizziness. Disulfiram works primarily by inhibiting the action of an enzyme that normally breaks down acetaldehyde, a toxic product involved in ethanol metabolism. Although not as effective as naltrexone, highly motivated individuals, particularly those treated in supervised settings who are also older, have a longer drinking history, and participate in Alcoholics Anonymous meetings, have used disulfiram effectively (Arias & Kranzler, 2008).

The third medication shown to be effective in treating alcohol use disorders is acamprosate, an amino acid derivative. Acamprosate reduces the risk of relapse by reducing the individual's urge to drink and thereby reducing the drive to use alcohol as a way of reducing anxiety and other negative psychological states. Acamprosate appears to work by modulating glutamate receptors and other reactions within the cell. Individuals who seem to benefit the most from acamprosate are those who are older when they become dependent on alcohol, have physiological signs of higher dependence, and have higher levels of anxiety, although in general, the evidence in favor of acamprosate is positive (Arias & Kranzler, 2008). People who are more highly motivated to become fully abstinent at the start of treatment are more likely

disulfiram

Known popularly as Antabuse, a medication used in the treatment of alcohol use disorder that inhibits aldehyde dehydrogenase (ALDH) and causes severe physical reactions when combined with alcohol.

TABLE 12.1 The Alcohol Use Disorders Identification Test ("AUDIT")

Scoring the AUDIT

Record the score for each response in the blank box at the end of each line, then total these numbers. The maximum possible total is 40.

Total scores of 8 or more for men up to age 60 or 4 or more for women, adolescents, and men over 60 are considered positive screens. For patients with totals near the cut-points, clinicians may wish to examine individual responses to questions and clarify them during the clinical examination.

PATIENT: Because alcohol use can affect your health and can interfere with certain medications and treatments, it is important that we ask some questions about your use of alcohol. Your answers will remain confidential, so please be honest.

Place the number from 0 to 4 that best describes your answer to each question in the box on the right.

Questions	0	1	2	3	4	
1. How often do you have a drink containing alcohol?	Never	Monthly or less	2 to 4 times a month	2 to 3 times a week	4 or more times a week	☐
2. How many drinks containing alcohol do you have on a typical day when you are drinking?	1 or 2	3 or 4	5 or 6	7 to 9	10 or more	☐
3. How often do you have 5 or more drinks on one occasion?	Never	Less than monthly	Monthly	Weekly	Daily or almost daily	☐
4. How often during the last year have you found that you were not able to stop drinking once you had started?	Never	Less than monthly	Monthly	Weekly	Daily or almost daily	☐
5. How often during the last year have you failed to do what was normally expected of you because of drinking?	Never	Less than monthly	Monthly	Weekly	Daily or almost daily	☐
6. How often during the last year have you needed a first drink in the morning to get yourself going after a heavy drinking session?	Never	Less than monthly	Monthly	Weekly	Daily or almost daily	☐
7. How often during the last year have you had a feeling of guilt or remorse after drinking?	Never	Less than monthly	Monthly	Weekly	Daily or almost daily	☐
8. How often during the last year have you been unable to remember what happened the night before because of your drinking?	Never	Less than monthly	Monthly	Weekly	Daily or almost daily	☐
9. Have you or someone else been injured because of your drinking?	No		Yes, but not in the last year		Yes, during the last year	☐
10. Has a relative, friend, doctor, or other health care worker been concerned about your drinking or suggested you cut down?	No		Yes, but not in the last year		Yes, during the last year	☐
					Total	

SOURCE: National Institute on Alcohol Abuse and Alcoholism, 2007.

Note: This questionnaire (the AUDIT) is reprinted with permission from the World Health Organization. To reflect standard drink sizes in the United States, the number of drinks in question 3 was changed from 6 to 5. A free AUDIT manual with guidelines for use in primary care settings is available online at www.who.org.

to comply with remaining on the medication and therefore more likely to improve (Koeter, van den Brink, & Lehert, 2010).

Researchers consider other medications used in the treatment of alcohol use disorders as less effective based on the available evidence. These include anticonvulsant medications, SSRIs, lithium, and baclofen, which works on GABA receptors (Arias & Kranzler, 2008).

Psychological Perspectives   Current psychological approaches to alcohol use disorders focus on the cognitive systems that guide people's drinking behavior. According to **dual-process theory,** one system involves fast, automatic processes that generate an impulse to drink alcohol. The more positive the associations that people have to alcohol, the more likely they are to consume it. The second system involves the controlled, effortful processing that regulates these automatic impulses. The more the individual can inhibit the automatic impulse, the less likely the individual is to consume excessive amounts of alcohol (Bechara, Noel, & Crone, 2006). Dual-process theory predicts that as individuals become better able to inhibit the automatic impulse to consume alcohol, they should also reduce their drinking behavior. Although the results show promise, researchers have only applied this theory in an experimental setting (Houben, Nederkoorn, Wiers, & Jansen, 2011).

In general, alcohol expectancies involve an "if–then" set of contingencies: if I consume alcohol, then I can expect certain behaviors and effects to follow. Individuals develop alcohol expectancies early in life, even before they first taste alcohol. These expectancies can include the potential for alcohol to reduce tension, cope with social challenges, feel better, feel sexier, and become more mentally alert. Based on the notion of self-efficacy, expectancies about alcohol can also include people's beliefs in their ability to resist or control their drinking (Young, Connor, & Feeney, 2011).

Cognitive factors also can influence what happens when a person consumes alcohol, particularly whether he or she engages in impulsive and potentially harmful behaviors, such as high-risk sexual activities. The high prevalence of binge drinking on college campuses presents a particular concern for this reason. According to **alcohol myopia theory,** as individuals consume greater amounts of alcohol, they are more likely to make risky choices because the immediate temptation of the moment (such as risky sex) overcomes the long-term consequences of the behavior (such as developing a sexually transmitted disease) (Griffin, Umstattd, & Usdan, 2010).

There are several well-tested psychological approaches to treating alcohol use disorders. The most successful approaches involve cognitive-behavioral interventions, motivational approaches, and expectancy manipulation (Arias & Kranzler, 2008). Part of effective treatment for alcohol use disorders also involves **relapse prevention,** in which the clinician essentially builds "failure" into treatment. If the client recognizes that occasional slips from abstinence are bound to occur, then he or she will be less likely to give up on therapy altogether after suffering a temporary setback.

The COMBINE project developed the most comprehensive protocol for psychological treatment as part of a project funded by the National Institute on Alcohol Abuse and Alcoholism (NIAAA). In this treatment, known as Combined Behavioral Intervention (CBI) (Miller, 2002), participants receive up to 20 sessions, according to their needs, beginning semiweekly and then eventually biweekly or less, for up to 16 weeks. The primary emphasis of CBI is on enhancing reinforcement and social support for abstinence. Clinicians assign motivational enhancement therapy at the outset, meaning that the clinician attempts to draw out the client's own motivation to change. The clinical style used in CBI follows from the motivational interviewing perspective (Table 12.2), in which the clinician uses a client-centered but directive style.

Clinicians expect and encourage families and significant others to participate throughout treatment, and they also encourage mutual help and involvement among clients including participation in Alcoholics Anonymous (AA). CBI includes content

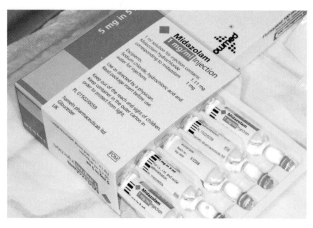

Anticonvulsant medications, such as Midazolam, can help treat individuals with alcohol use disorders.

dual-process theory
A theory regarding alcohol use proposing there are automatic processes that generate an impulse to drink alcohol and controlled, effortful processing that regulates these automatic impulses.

alcohol myopia theory
Proposes that as individuals consume greater amounts of alcohol, they are more likely to make risky choices because the immediate temptation of the moment overcomes the long-term consequences of the behavior.

relapse prevention
A treatment method based on the expectancy model, in which individuals are encouraged not to view lapses from abstinence as signs of certain failure.

TABLE 12.2 **Comparisons Among Reflective Listening and Other Therapist Responses to Client Statements**

CLIENT: I guess I do drink too much sometimes, but I don't think I have a *problem* with alcohol.
CONFRONTATION: Yes you do! How can you sit there and tell me you don't have a problem when . . .
QUESTION: Why do you think you don't have a problem?
REFLECTION: So on the one hand you can see some reasons for concern, *and* you really don't want to be labeled as "having a problem."
CLIENT: My wife is always telling me that I'm an alcoholic.
JUDGING: What's wrong with that? She probably has some good reasons for thinking so.
QUESTION: Why does she think that?
REFLECTION: And that really annoys you.
CLIENT: If I quit drinking, what am I supposed to do for friends?
ADVICE: I guess you'll have to get some new ones.
SUGGESTION: Well, you could just tell your friends that you don't drink anymore, but you still want to see them.
REFLECTION: It's hard for you to imagine how life would be without alcohol.

SOURCE: Miller, 2002, p. 13.

modules focusing on coping skills (e.g., coping with cravings and urges), refusing drinks and avoiding social pressure to drink, communication skills, assertiveness skills, management of moods, social and recreational counseling, social support for sobriety, and job-seeking skills. As needed, clinicians may also monitor sobriety, provide telephone consultation, and provide crisis intervention. They also put procedures in place to work with clients who resume drinking during treatment. Toward the end of the treatment period, clients enter a maintenance phase and then complete treatment in a termination session.

The COMBINE study evaluated the efficacy of naltrexone and acamprosate alone and in combination with CBI using placebos and medical management as control conditions. Although CBI alone was not as effective in producing abstinent days as was CBI plus medication and management immediately after treatment, 1 year after treatment ended, the CBI-only group did not differ significantly from those receiving medication (Anton et al., 2006).

Sociocultural Perspective Researchers and theorists working within the sociocultural perspective regard stressors in the family, community, and culture as factors that, when combined with genetic vulnerability, lead the individual to develop alcohol use disorder. Researchers gave support to the sociocultural perspective in a landmark longitudinal study in the early 1980s. Researchers followed individuals from childhood or adolescence to adulthood, the time when most individuals who become alcohol dependent make the transition from social or occasional alcohol use to have an alcohol use disorder (Zucker & Gomberg, 1986). Those most likely to develop alcohol use disorder in adulthood had a history of childhood antisocial behavior, including aggressive and sadistic behavior, trouble with the law, rebelliousness, lower achievement

Peer pressure and poor grades in school contribute to high rates of alcohol consumption in teenagers.

in school, completion of fewer years of school, and a higher truancy rate. These individuals also showed a variety of behaviors possibly indicative of early neural dysfunction, including nervousness and fretfulness as infants, hyperactivity as children, and poor physical coordination. Researchers concluded that these characteristics reflected a genetically based vulnerability, which, when combined with environmental stresses, led to the development of alcohol use disorder.

More recent studies have continued to support the role of family environment as influenced by larger sociocultural factors. In a two-year study of more than 800 sub-urban adolescents, the teenagers who received high levels of social support from their families were less likely to consume alcohol. The effect of social support seemed to be due primarily to the fact that families providing high levels of social support were also more likely to have a strong religious emphasis in the home. School grades also correlated with lower teen use of alcohol. Teens receiving good grades were more likely to receive higher levels of social support from their families, which in turn was associated with lower rates of alcohol use. The teens who used alcohol were more likely to show poorer school performance over the course of the study (Mason & Windle, 2001).

Stimulants

The category of drugs called **stimulants** includes substances that have an activating effect on the nervous system. These differ in their chemical structure, their specific physical and psychological effects, and their potential danger to the user. Stimulants are associated with disorders involving use, intoxication, and withdrawal.

Amphetamines **Amphetamine** is a stimulant that affects both the central nervous and the autonomic nervous systems. In addition to waking or speeding up the central nervous system, it also causes elevated blood pressure, heart rate, decreased appetite, and physical activity. It may be used for medical purposes, such as to treat ADHD or as a diet pill. Even when used for medical purposes, however, amphetamine drugs can cause dependence and have unpleasant or dangerous side effects. In

stimulant
A psychoactive substance that has an activating effect on the central nervous system.

amphetamine
A stimulant that affects both the central nervous and the auto-nomic nervous systems.

Eroding the Mind
Researchers have mapped brain decay caused by methamphetamine use. The damage affected memory, emotion, and reward systems.

Average difference in brain tissue volume of methamphetamine users, as compared with non-users;

Areas of greatest loss
Emotion, reward (limbic system)
Memory (hippocampus)

0   3% Loss   5% Loss

FIGURE 12.5 Long-term Effects of Methamphetamine on the Brain

methamphetamine
An addictive stimulant drug that is related to amphetamine but provokes more intense central nervous system effects.

cocaine
A highly addictive central nervous system stimulant that an individual snorts, injects, or smokes.

increasingly large doses, users can become hostile, violent, and paranoid. They may also experience a range of physiological effects including fever, sweating, headache, blurred vision, dizziness, chest pain, nausea, vomiting, and diarrhea.

Methamphetamine is an addictive stimulant drug that is related to amphetamine but it provokes more intense central nervous system effects. Whether taken orally, through the nose, intravenously, or by smoking, methamphetamine causes a rush or feeling of euphoria and becomes addictive very quickly. Methamphetamine overdose can cause overheating of the body and convulsions, and, if not treated immediately, it can result in death. Long-term use of methamphetamine can lead users to develop mood disturbances, violent behavior, anxiety, confusion, insomnia, severe dental problems ("meth mouth"), and a heightened risk of infectious diseases including hepatitis and HIV/AIDS. The long-term effects of methamphetamines include severe brain damage, as Figure 12.5 shows.

In 2010, 353,000 adults ages 12 and older in the United States (0.1 percent) were current users of methamphetamines. These numbers represented a slight downward trend from most previous years, during which the percentages ranged from 0.3 to 0.2 of the U.S. population ages 12 and older (Substance Abuse and Mental Health Services Administration, 2011). However, methamphetamine use begins at a relatively young age, with 2010 rates of 1 percent among high school students in the United States stating that they were current users. Approximately 1.5 percent of high school seniors stated that they engaged in nonmedical use of Ritalin. The lifetime prevalence rates among high school seniors were far higher for amphetamine (11.1 percent) and methamphetamine (2.3 percent) use (Johnston, O'Malley, Bachman, & Schulenberg, 2011).

Cocaine **Cocaine** is a highly addictive central nervous system stimulant that an individual snorts, injects, or smokes. Users can snort the powdered hydrochloride salt of cocaine or dissolve it in water and then inject it. Crack is the street name given to the form of cocaine that is processed to form a rock crystal which, when heated, produces vapors that the individual smokes. The effects of cocaine include feelings of euphoria, heightened mental alertness, reduced fatigue, and heightened energy. The faster the bloodstream absorbs the cocaine and delivers it to the brain, the more intense the user's high. Because this intense high is relatively short (5 to 10 minutes), the user may administer the drug again in a binge-like pattern.

MINI CASE

Stimulant Use Disorder, Amphetamine-type Substance

Catherine is a 23-year-old salesperson who tried for 3 years to lose weight. Her physician prescribed amphetamines but cautioned her about the possibility that she might become dependent on them. She did begin to lose weight, but she also discovered that she liked the extra energy and good feelings the diet pills caused. When Catherine returned to her doctor after having lost the desired weight, she asked him for a refill of her prescription to help her maintain her new figure.

When he refused, Catherine asked around among her friends until she found the name of a physician who was willing to accommodate her wishes for ongoing refills of the prescription. Over the course of 1 year, Catherine developed a number of psychological problems, including depression, paranoid thinking, and irritability. Despite the fact that she realizes that something is wrong, she feels driven to continue using the drug.

Like amphetamines, cocaine increases bodily temperature, blood pressure, and heart rate. Cocaine's risks include heart attack, respiratory failure, stroke, seizures, abdominal pain, and nausea. In rare cases, the user can experience sudden death on the first use of cocaine or unexpectedly afterwards. Other adverse effects on the body develop over time and include changes within the nose (loss of sense of smell, chronically runny nose, and nosebleeds), as well as problems with swallowing and hoarseness. Users may also experience severe bowel gangrene due to a reduction of blood flow to the digestive system. Cocaine users may also have severe allergic reactions and increased risk of developing HIV/AIDS and other blood-borne diseases. When people use cocaine in binges, they may develop chronic restlessness, irritability, and anxiety. Chronic users may experience severe paranoia in which they have auditory hallucinations and lose touch with reality (National Institute on Drug Abuse, 2011b).

As Figure 12.1 illustrated, 1.5 percent of adults 12 and older used cocaine in 2010. The rates of cocaine use are about double for men compared to women. The average age of first use of cocaine is 21.2 years; approximately 1,700 people per day are initiated into the use of cocaine. Among illicit drugs, cocaine (and illicit use of pain relievers) is second only to marijuana in the rate of past year dependence (Substance Abuse and Mental Health Services Administration, 2011). An estimated 5.5 percent of high school seniors have used cocaine at some point in their lives (Johnston et al., 2011).

We can see the impact of cocaine at the synapse in Figure 12.6. Like other drugs of abuse, cocaine has its effects by stimulating dopamine receptors. Researchers believe that cocaine specifically targets an area in the midbrain called the ventral tegmental area (VTA). Pathways from the VTA extend to the nucleus accumbens, a key area of the brain involved in reward. Cocaine's effects appear to be due to blocking the removal of dopamine from the synapse, which results in an accumulation of dopamine that amplifies the signal to the receiving neurons. The euphoria that users report appears to correspond to this pattern of dopamine activity (National Institute on Drug Abuse, 2011h). In addition to dopamine, serotonin appears to play a role in the motivational and reinforcing effects of the drug and may also mediate, to at least some extent, cocaine's aversive effects (Nonkes, van Bussel, Verheij, & Homberg, 2011).

Cannabis

Cannabis is associated with disorders involving use, intoxication, and withdrawal. **Marijuana** is a mix of flowers, stems, and leaves from the hemp plant *Cannabis sativa*, a tall, leafy, green plant that thrives in warm climates. Although the plant contains more than 400 chemical constituents, the primary active ingredient in marijuana is delta-9-tetrahydrocannabinol (THC). Hashish, containing a more concentrated form of THC, comes from the resins of the plant's flowers. The marijuana and hashish that reaches the street is never pure THC; other substances, such as tobacco, are always mixed in with it. Individuals use synthetic forms of THC for medicinal purposes, such as treating asthma and glaucoma and reducing nausea in cancer patients undergoing chemotherapy.

A police officer holds a sample of crack cocaine that has been confiscated from a user. Crack is highly addictive because it produces a very intense but brief "high."

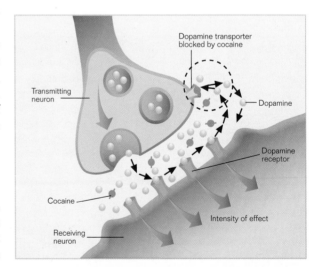

FIGURE 12.6 Cocaine in the Brain In the normal communication process, dopamine is released by a neuron into the synapse, where it can bind to dopamine receptors on neighboring neurons. Normally, dopamine is then recycled back into the transmitting neuron by a specialized protein called the dopamine transporter. If cocaine is present, it attaches to the dopamine transporter and blocks the normal recycling process, resulting in a buildup of dopamine in the synapse, which contributes to the pleasurable effects of cocaine.

MINI CASE

Cannabis Use Disorder

Gary, age 22, has lived with his parents since dropping out of college 3 years ago, midway through his freshman year. Gary was an average student in high school and, although popular, was not involved in many extracurricular activities. When he entered college, Gary became interested in the enticing opportunities for new experiences, and he began to smoke marijuana casually with his roommates. However, unlike his roommates, who limited their smoking to parties, Gary found that a nightly hit helped him relax. He started to rationalize that it also helped him study, because his thinking was more creative. As his first semester went by, he gradually lost interest in his studies, preferring to stay in his room and listen to music while getting high. He realized that it was easy to support his habit by selling marijuana to other people in the dorm. Although he convinced himself that he was not really a dealer, Gary became one of the primary suppliers of marijuana on campus. When he received his first semester grades, he did not feel particularly discouraged about the fact that he had flunked out. Rather, he felt that he could benefit from having more time to himself. He moved home and became friendly with some local teenagers who frequented a nearby park and shared drugs there. Gary's parents have all but given up on him, having become deeply discouraged by his laziness and lack of productivity. They know that he is using drugs, but they feel helpless in their efforts to get him to seek professional help. They have learned that it is better to avoid discussing the matter with Gary, because violent arguments always ensue.

marijuana

A psychoactive substance derived from the hemp plant whose primary active ingredient is delta-9-tetrahydrocannabinol (THC).

Most people who use marijuana smoke it as a cigarette or in a pipe. Marijuana users can also mix the drug in food or serve it as a tea. The most common way to take marijuana is to smoke it, but users may also eat it or inject the drug intravenously. When a person smokes marijuana, he or she reaches peak blood levels in about 10 minutes, but the subjective effects of the drug do not become apparent for another 20 to 30 minutes. The individual may experience the effects of intoxication for 2 to 3 hours, but the metabolites of THC may remain in the body for 8 or more days.

People take marijuana in order to alter their perceptions of their environment and their bodily sensations. The effects they seek include euphoria, a heightened sense of sensuality and sexuality, and an increased awareness of internal and external stimuli. However, marijuana use also carries with it a number of other unpleasant effects including impaired short-term memory, slowed reaction time, and impaired physical coordination, altered judgment, and poor decision making. Instead of feeling euphoric and relaxed, users may experience paranoia and anxiety, particularly when they ingest high doses.

As mentioned earlier in the chapter, marijuana is the most commonly used illicit drug in the United States. In 2010, slightly more than one in five adults (21.5 percent) ages 18 to 25 were users. The majority of first-time drug users (61.8 percent) chose marijuana, more than double the number who began with psychotherapeutic medications, and the highest percentage age of any who began to use an illicit drug. The average age of initiating marijuana use in 2010 was 18.4 years. Marijuana also has the highest levels of past year dependence (4.5 million in 2010 in the United States) (Substance Abuse and Mental Health Services Administration, 2011). As of 2010, nearly half (43.8 percent) of U.S. high school seniors reported marijuana use at least once during their lifetime, and about two-thirds said that marijuana made them moderately or very high (Johnston et al., 2011).

Marijuana, shown here in its plant form, is the most frequently used illicit drug in the United States.

TABLE 12.3 Summary of Effects of Cannabis on Executive Functions

Executive Function Measured	Acute Effects	Residual Effects	Long-Term Effects
Attention/concentration	Impaired (light users) Normal (heavy users)	Mixed findings	Largely normal
Decision making and risk taking	Mixed findings	Impaired	Impaired
Inhibition/impulsivity	Impaired	Mixed findings	Mixed findings
Working memory	Impaired	Normal	Normal
Verbal fluency	Normal	Mixed findings	Mixed findings

Acute effects denote 0–6 hours after last cannabis use; residual effects denote 7 hours to 20 days after last cannabis use; and long-term effects denote 3 weeks or longer after last cannabis use.

SOURCE: Crean, Crane, & Mason, 2011, p. 3. American Society of Addiction Medicine.

THC produces its effects by acting upon specific sites in the brain, called cannabinoid receptors. The brain regions with the highest density of cannabinoid receptors are the areas that influence pleasure, but also are involved in memory, thinking and concentration, perception of time, sensory responses, and ability to carry out coordinated movement. Many of these acute effects on cognitive functioning are reversible as long as the individual does not engage in chronic use.

Heavy and continued use of marijuana can produce a number of deleterious effects on bodily functioning, including higher risk of heart attack and impaired respiratory functioning. In addition to developing psychological dependence on marijuana, long-term users may experience lower educational and occupational achievement, psychosis, and persistent cognitive impairment. Particularly at risk are individuals who begin using marijuana at an early age and continue to use it throughout their lives (Pope & Yurgelun-Todd, 2004). Table 12.3 summarizes the research findings on the effects of cannabis use on the cognitive processes that make up executive functioning.

Hallucinogens

Included in hallucinogen-related disorders are use and intoxication, but not withdrawal. **Hallucinogens** are drugs that cause people to experience profound distortions in their perception of reality. Under the influence of hallucinogens, people see images, hear

hallucinogens
Psychoactive substances that cause abnormal perceptual experiences in the form of illusions or hallucinations, usually visual in nature.

MINI CASE

Other Hallucinogen Use Disorder

Candace is a 45-year-old artist who has used LSD for a number of years, because she feels that doing so enhances her paintings and makes them more visually exciting. Although she claims to know how much LSD she can handle, she is occasionally caught off guard and experiences disturbing side effects. She begins sweating, has blurred vision, is uncoordinated, and shakes all over. She commonly becomes paranoid and anxious, and she may act in strange ways, such as running out of her studio and into the street, ranting incoherently. On more than one occasion, the police have picked her up and taken her to the emergency room, where doctors prescribed antipsychotic medication.

439
379

sounds, and feel sensations that they believe to be real but are not. In some cases, users experience rapid, intense mood swings. Some people who use hallucinogens develop a condition called hallucinogen persisting perception disorder, in which they experience flashbacks or spontaneous hallucinations, delusions, or disturbances in mood similar to the changes that took place while they were intoxicated with the drug. The specific effects and risks of each hallucinogen vary among the four major categories of hallucinogens (National Institute on Drug Abuse, 2011c).

lysergic acid diethylamide (LSD)

A form of a hallucinogenic drug that users ingest in tablets, capsules, and liquid form.

People take **lysergic acid diethylamide (LSD)** in tablets, capsules, and occasionally liquid form. Users show dramatic changes in their sensations and emotions. They may feel several emotions at once or swing rapidly from one emotion to another. At larger doses, users can experience delusions and visual hallucinations. In addition, they may feel an altered sense of time and self. Users may also experience synesthesia in which they "hear" colors and "see" sounds. These perceptual and mood alterations may be accompanied by severe, terrifying thoughts and feelings of despair, panic, fear of losing control, going insane, or dying. Even after they stop taking LSD, users may experience flashbacks, leading them to be significantly distressed and impaired in their social and occupational functioning.

Unlike other substances, LSD does not seem to produce compulsive drug-seeking behavior, and most users choose to decrease or stop using it without withdrawal. However, LSD produces tolerance, so users may need to take larger doses to achieve the effects they desire. Given the unpredictable nature of LSD's effects, such increases in doses can be dangerous. LSD can also affect other bodily functions, including increasing body temperature, blood pressure, and heart rate, sweating, loss of appetite, dry mouth, sleeplessness, and tremors.

peyote

A form of a hallucinogenic drug whose primary ingredient is mescaline.

Peyote is a small, spineless cactus whose principal active ingredient is mescaline. In addition to its naturally occurring form, individuals can also produce mescaline artificially. Users chew the mescaline-containing crown of the cactus, or soak it in water to produce a liquid; some prepare a tea by boiling the cactus in water to rid the drug of its bitter taste. Used as part of religious ceremonies by natives in northern Mexico and the southwestern United States, its long-term effects on these and recreational users are not known. However, its effects on the body are similar to LSD, with increases in body temperature and heart rate, uncoordinated movements, extreme sweating, and flushing. In addition, peyote may cause flashbacks, much like those associated with LSD.

psilocybin

A form of a hallucinogenic drug found in certain mushrooms.

Psilocybin (4-phosphoryloxy-N,N-dimethyltryptamine), and its biologically active form, psilocin (4-hydroxy-N,N-dimethyltryptamine), is a substance found in certain mushrooms. Users brew the mushrooms or add them to other foods to disguise their bitter taste. The active compounds in psilocybin-containing mushrooms, like LSD, alter the individual's autonomic functions, motor reflexes, behavior, and perception. Individuals may experience hallucinations, an altered sense of time, and an inability to differentiate between fantasy and reality. Large doses may cause users to experience flashbacks, memory impairments, and greater vulnerability to psychological disorders. In addition to the risk of poisoning if the individual incorrectly identifies the mushroom from other mushrooms, the bodily effects can include muscle weakness, loss of motor control, nausea, vomiting, and drowsiness.

phencyclidine (PCP)

A form of a hallucinogenic drug originally developed as an intravenous anesthetic.

Researchers developed **phencyclidine (PCP)** in the 1950s as an intravenous anesthetic, but it is no longer used medically because patients became agitated, delusional, and irrational while recovering from its effects. Users can easily mix the white crystalline powder with alcohol, water, or colored dye. PCP may be available on the illegal drug market in pill, capsule, or colored powder forms that users can smoke, snort, or take orally. When individuals smoke PCP, they may apply the drug to mint, parsley, oregano, or marijuana.

PCP causes users to experience a sense of dissociation from their surroundings and their own sense of self. It has many adverse effects including symptoms that mimic schizophrenia, mood disturbance, memory loss, difficulties with speech and thinking, weight loss, and depression. Although these negative effects led to its diminished popularity as a street drug, PCP appeals to those who still use it because they feel that it makes them stronger, more powerful, and invulnerable. Furthermore, despite PCP's adverse effects, users can develop strong cravings and compulsive PCP-seeking behavior.

The physiological effects of PCP are extensive. Low to moderate doses produce increases in breathing rate, a rise in blood pressure and pulse, general numbness of the extremities, and loss of muscular coordination, as well as flushing and profuse sweating. At high doses, users experience a drop in blood pressure, pulse rate, and respiration, which may be accompanied by nausea, vomiting, blurred vision, abnormal eye movements, drooling, loss of balance, and dizziness. They may become violent or suicidal. In addition, at high doses users may experience seizures, coma, and death. Users who combine PCP with other central nervous system depressants (such as alcohol) may become comatose.

Within MDMA-related disorders, the chemical named **MDMA** (3,4-methylenedioxy-methamphetamine), known on the street as **ecstasy,** is a synthetic substance chemically similar to methamphetamine and mescaline. Users experience feelings of increased energy, euphoria, emotional warmth, distorted perceptions and sense of time, and unusual tactile experiences. Taken as a capsule or tablet, MDMA was once most popular among white teens and young adults at weekend-long dances known as "raves." The drug is now used by a broader range of ethnic groups including urban gay males. Some users combine MDMA with other drugs including marijuana, cocaine, methamphetamine, ketamine, and sildanefil (Viagra), among other substances.

In 2010, 1.2 million U.S. individuals ages 12 and older (0.5 percent of the population) used hallucinogens; of these individuals, nearly 700,000 (0.3 percent) used MDMA. Among high school seniors, 7.3 percent reported using MDMA at least once in their lives, compared to nearly 2 percent who used PCP and 4 percent who used LSD.

Users of MDMA may experience a range of unpleasant psychological effects, including confusion, depression, sleep problems, cravings for the drug, and severe anxiety. The drug may be neurotoxic, which means that, over time, users may experience greater difficulty carrying out cognitive tasks. Like stimulants, MDMA can affect the sympathetic nervous system, leading to increases in heart rate, blood pressure, muscle tension, nausea, blurred vision, fainting, chills or sweating, and involuntary teeth

ecstasy (MDMA)
A hallucinogenic drug made from a synthetic substance chemically similar to methamphetamine and mescaline.

MDMA, also known as ecstasy, is a purely chemical drug that is often combined with other chemicals to produce long-lasting euphoria for users.

FIGURE 12.7 The Impact of Ecstasy (MDMA) on Serotonergic Neurons

clenching. Individuals also risk severe spikes in body temperature, which, in turn, can lead to liver, kidney, or cardiovascular system failure. Repeated dosages over short periods of time may also interfere with MDMA metabolism, leading to significant and harmful buildup within the body (National Institute on Drug Abuse, 2011f).

The main neurotransmitter involved with MDMA is serotonin. As Figure 12.7 shows, MDMA binds to the serotonin transporter that is responsible for removing serotonin from the synapse. As a result, MDMA extends the effects of serotonin. In addition, MDMA enters the neuron, where it stimulates excessive release of serotonin. MDMA has similar effects on norepinephrine, which leads to increases in autonomic nervous system activity. The drug also releases dopamine, but to a lesser extent.

Researchers find it difficult to investigate the long-term effects of MDMA use on cognitive functioning because users typically take MDMA with other substances. However, significant negative effects of MDMA use alone do occur on verbal memory (Thomasius et al., 2006). Moreover, when combined with alcohol, MDMA produces a number of long-term adverse psychological effects including paranoia, poor physical health, irritability, confusion, and moodiness. However, the longer the period of abstinence from the drug, the less often users experienced these effects (Fisk, Murphy, Montgomery, & Hadjiefthyvoulou, 2011).

Opioids

opioid

A psychoactive substance that relieves pain.

Within opioid-related disorders are opioid use, intoxication, and withdrawal. An **opioid** is a substance that relieves pain. Many legally prescribed medications fall within this category, including hydrocodone (e.g., Vicodin), oxycodone (e.g., OxyContin, Percocet), morphine (e.g., Kadian, Avinza), codeine, and related drugs. Clinicians prescribe hydrocodone products most commonly for a variety of painful conditions, including dental and injury-related pain. Physicians often use morphine before and after surgical procedures to alleviate severe pain. Clinicians prescribe codeine, on the other hand, for mild pain. In addition to prescribing these drugs for their pain-relieving properties, physicians prescribe some of them—codeine and diphenoxylate (Lomotil), for example—to relieve coughs and severe diarrhea.

When people take these medications as prescribed, the medications are very effective for managing pain safely. However, because of their potential to produce euphoria as well as physical dependence, these medications are among the most frequently abused prescription drugs. For example, people who abuse Oxycontin may snort or inject it, and, as a result, suffer a serious overdose reaction.

An estimated 201.9 million prescriptions were written for opioid painkillers in 2009; most were for hydrocodone- and oxycodone-containing products issued on a short-term (2 to 3 weeks) basis. Of all opioid prescriptions, 11.7 percent (9.3 million) were for patients 10 to

MINI CASE

Opioid Use Disorder

Jimmy is a 38-year-old homeless man who has been addicted to heroin for the past 10 years. He began to use the drug at the suggestion of a friend who told him it would help relieve the pressure Jimmy was feeling from his unhappy marriage and financial problems. In a short period of time, he became dependent on the drug and got involved in a theft ring in order to support his habit. Ultimately, he lost his home and moved to a shelter, where workers assigned Jimmy to a methadone treatment program.

Prescribing Prescription Drugs

Patients who suffer from chronic pain present a tremendous challenge to health care professionals. Long-term treatment of chronic pain through prescription medications carries with it the risk that patients will develop dependence. Moreover, because patients need escalating doses to achieve the same degree of relief, their pain sensitivity and levels of pain might actually increase. At the same time, patients may fear taking an opioid medication that could benefit them due to the fear of developing an addiction. These patients may suffer unduly if their condition is one that could benefit from pain medication, especially if they are terminally ill. Ironically enough, some health care professionals as well as patients worry about the risks of addiction among patients who are in their last few months of life.

Addressing the national crisis in overuse of prescription pain medication, representatives of the National Institute on Drug Abuse (2011g) propose several remedies. First, to mitigate addiction risk, they advise physicians to screen patients for potential risk factors, including personal or family history of drug abuse or psychological disorder. Second, they suggest that health care professionals monitor patients for signs of abuse using such indicators as early or frequent requests for prescription pain medication.

Clearly, as NIDA urges, the development of effective, nonaddicting pain medications is a public health priority. A growing population of older adults and an increasing number of injured military personnel only add to the urgency of this issue. Researchers need to explore alternative medications that can alleviate pain but have less abuse potential. At the same time, researchers and practitioners in psychology can step in and provide a greater understanding of effective chronic pain management, including identifying factors that predispose some patients to addiction and developing measures to prevent abuse.

Q: *You be the judge*: What is the best way to balance the patient's need for pain relief with the growing national and international crisis in abuse of prescription pain medications?

29 years old. Furthermore, over half (56 percent) of opioid prescriptions were filled by patients who had recently received another opioid medication (Volkow, McLellan, Cotto, Karithanom, & Weiss, 2011). The risk of death by overdose among patients receiving opioid prescriptions is significant. In one nationwide study of Veterans Administration patients, the risk of overdose death was directly related to the maximum prescribed daily dose of opioids (Bohnert et al., 2011). In 2007, drug overdose deaths were second only to motor vehicle accidents as the leading cause of unintentional injury death. The number of deaths involving opioid analgesics was nearly twice the number involving cocaine and nearly six times the number involving heroin (Figure 12.8) (Centers for Disease Control and Prevention, 2012).

Heroin is a form of opioid. It is a pain-killing drug synthesized from morphine, a naturally occurring substance extracted from the seed pod of the Asian opium poppy plant. Users inject, snort, sniff, or smoke heroin. Once ingested, the body converts heroin to morphine and then it binds to the opioid receptors located in areas throughout the brain and body, particularly those involved in reward and pain perception. Opioid receptors are also located in the brain stem, which contains structures that control breathing, blood pressure, and arousal.

Users experience a surge of euphoric feelings along with a dry mouth, warm flushing of the skin, heaviness in the arms and legs, and compromised mental functioning. Shortly afterward, they alternate between feeling wakeful and drowsy. If users do not inject the drug, they may not feel euphoria at all. With continued use of heroin, users develop tolerance, meaning that they need larger amounts of the drug to feel the same effect. Heroin has a high potential for addiction with estimates as high as 23 percent of all users developing dependence (National Institute on Drug Abuse, 2011d).

heroin
A psychoactive substance that is a form of opioid, synthesized from morphine.

FIGURE 12.8 Unintentional Drug Overdose Deaths by Major Type of Drug, United States, 1999–2007

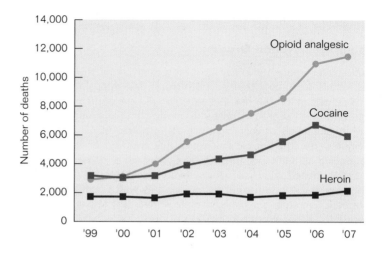

There are many serious health consequences of heroin use, including fatal overdoses, infectious diseases (related to needle sharing), damage to the cardiovascular system, abscesses, and liver or kidney disease. Users are often in poor general health, and therefore are more susceptible to pneumonia and other pulmonary complications, as well as damage to the brain, liver, and kidneys resulting from the toxic contaminants often added to heroin.

Chronic heroin users experience severe withdrawal should they discontinue its use. Withdrawal symptoms may include restlessness, muscle and bone pain, insomnia, diarrhea, vomiting, cold flashes, and kicking movements. During withdrawal, users experience severe cravings which can begin 2 to 3 days after they discontinue use and last for as long as a week, although cravings for the drug may occur for years when the individual experiences certain triggers or stress. There are also dangers to sudden withdrawal, particularly in long-term users who are in poor health.

As Figure 12.2 shows, current users in the United States report heroin to be one of the least likely illegal substances to be abused. However, 359,000 adults in the United States reported heroin dependence or abuse in 2010, an increase from 214,000 in 2009 (Substance Abuse and Mental Health Services Administration, 2011). In 2010, researchers estimated the lifetime prevalence among high school seniors in the United States to be 1.6 percent, a slight rise from the previous year's 1.2 percent (Johnston et al., 2011).

Sedatives, Hypnotics, and Anxiolytics

sedative
A psychoactive substance that has a calming effect on the central nervous system.

hypnotic
A substance that induces sedation.

anxiolytic
An antianxiety medication.

The category of sedatives, hypnotics, and anxiolytics (antianxiety medications) includes prescription medications that act as central nervous system depressants. A **sedative** has a soothing or calming effect, a **hypnotic** induces sleep, and an **anxiolytic** is used to treat anxiety symptoms. These central nervous system depressant drugs can be useful for treating anxiety and sleep disorders. Their sedating effects are due to the fact that they increase the levels of the neurotransmitter GABA, which inhibits brain activity and therefore produces a calming effect. Disorders within this category include use disorder, intoxication, and withdrawal.

These medications are among the most commonly abused drugs in the United States. They include benzodiazepines, barbiturates, nonbenzodiazepine sleep medications such as zolpidem (Ambien), eszopiclone (Lunesta), and zaleplon (Sonata). In 2010, 7 million people ages 12 and older in the United States (0.5 percent) used these and other prescription drugs nonmedically. Although safe when used as prescribed, these medications have high potential for abuse and dependence. The longer the person uses these drugs, the greater the amount they need to take in order to experience their sedating effects. In addition to the risk of dependence, these medications also can cause harmful effects on individuals taking other prescription and over-the-counter medications (National Institute on Drug Abuse, 2011g). Among high school seniors in 2010, 7.5 percent reported using (nonmedically) barbiturates, and 8.5 percent reported using tranquilizers at some point in their lives (Johnston et al., 2011).

For older adults, the risk of abuse of these prescription drugs is also high, particularly given the fact that they may interact with alcohol and other prescription and over-the-counter medications. Moreover, older adults with cognitive decline may improperly take their medication, which, in turn, can lead to further cognitive decline (Whitbourne & Whitbourne, 2011).

Caffeine

Disorders included in the caffeine-related category are intoxication and withdrawal, but not caffeine use disorder. **Caffeine** is a stimulant found in coffee, tea, chocolate, energy drinks, diet pills, and headache remedies. By activating the sympathetic nervous system through increasing the production of adrenaline, caffeine increases an individual's perceived level of energy and alertness. Caffeine also increases blood pressure and may lead to increases in the body's production of cortisol, the stress hormone.

Energy drinks such as Red Bull, introduced in Austria in 1987 and in the United States in 1997, are becoming an increasing problem due to the high levels of caffeine they may contain. Red Bull contains 80 mg of caffeine, but Wired X505 contains 505 mg per can. In comparison, a can of Coca Cola contains 34.5 mg of caffeine. In 2006, worldwide energy drink consumption increased by 17 percent to 906 million gallons, and the market for them continues to grow exponentially. In the United States, at least 130 energy drinks exceed the FDA-recommended limit of 0.02 percent of caffeine, and the FDA has not aggressively pursued manufacturers to seek compliance, nor does it require warning labels. Although caffeine is such a common feature of everyday life that people tend not to be aware of its dangers, caffeine from energy drinks and other sources can lead to many adverse reactions, and can become a gateway to other forms of substance dependence (Reissig, Strain, & Griffiths, 2009).

Already a diagnosis in ICD 10, *DSM-5* was the first psychiatric manual in the United States to include caffeine withdrawal as a diagnosis. The symptoms of caffeine withdrawal include headache, tiredness and fatigue, sleepiness and drowsiness, dysphoric mood, difficulty concentrating, depression, irritability, nausea, vomiting, muscle aches, and stiffness. Caffeine withdrawal is estimated to cause significant distress and impairment in daily functioning among 13 percent of people in experimental studies (Juliano & Griffiths, 2004).

Energy drinks such as Red Bull contain high amounts of caffeine and other additives such as Taurine to boost energy. These drinks put consumers at risk from consuming excess amounts of caffeine, which can lead to major health problems.

caffeine
A stimulant found in coffee, tea, chocolate, energy drinks, diet pills, and headache remedies.

MINI CASE

Caffeine Intoxication

Carla is a 19-year-old college sophomore who felt compelled to excel at every endeavor and to become involved in as many activities as time and energy would permit. As her commitments increased and her studies became more burdensome, Carla became more and more reliant on coffee, soda, and over-the-counter stimulants to reduce her need for sleep. During final examination week, Carla overdid it. For 3 days straight, she consumed approximately 10 cups of coffee a day,

along with a few bottles of Aeroshot. In addition to her bodily symptoms of restlessness, twitching muscles, flushed face, stomach disturbance, and heart irregularities, Carla began to ramble when she spoke. Her roommate became distressed after seeing Carla's condition and insisted on taking her to the emergency room, where the intake worker recognized her condition as caffeine intoxication.

REAL STORIES

Robert Downey Jr.: Substance Use Disorder

Set against a Hollywood backdrop, Robert Downey Jr.'s story resembles that of many other individuals struggling with substance use disorder. As a child, his father Robert Downey Sr., an actor, producer and film director, raised Robert in an environment rich in drug and alcohol use due to his own struggles with substance abuse. Robert himself began using substances at the age of 6, when his father gave him marijuana. Regarding this time in his life, Robert has said, "When my dad and I would do drugs together, it was like him trying to express his love for me in the only way he knew how." This bond between son and father led to Robert's substance dependence later in life.

As a teenager, Robert started acting in small roles in his father's films and on Broadway until he began acting in feature films. During the 1980s he gained considerable attention in his roles in several of the "Brat Pack" movies including *Weird Science* and *The Pick-up Artist* with Molly Ringwald. His major break came in 1987 in a role in *Less than Zero* in which he played a wealthy young man whose life became consumed by drug use. He received considerable praise for his portrayal of the character of which he stated, "The role was like the ghost of Christmas future," regarding his steady increase in drug usage which caused years of turmoil for the gifted actor.

As Robert began landing bigger roles in films, his substance use-related problems began to take over his life and largely impede his professional career. Between 1996 and 2001, Robert was repeatedly arrested for drug use including heroin, cocaine, and marijuana. He was drinking daily and spending large amounts of time in obtaining and doing drugs. In one instance in April of 1996, Robert was pulled over for speeding on Sunset Boulevard in Los Angeles and was arrested for possession of heroin and cocaine as well as a gun in his car. One month later while he was on parole, he trespassed into a neighbor's home while under the influence and passed out in one of the beds. He was subsequently placed on 3 years' probation with mandatory drug testing. When he missed one of his court-appointed drug tests, he was placed in prison for 4 months.

Similar to those struggling with substance use disorders who are attempting to break free of the cycle of addiction, Robert had many unsuccessful stays in rehab. He often cited his early drug use and bonding with his father over drugs as a reason it was difficult for him to quit, though he did realize the enormity of his problems. In 1999 he stated to a judge, "It's like I've got a shotgun in my mouth with my finger on the trigger, and I like the taste of gun metal."

In 2000, Robert spent a year in a California substance abuse treatment facility. Upon his release he joined the cast of the hit television show *Ally McBeal*. Though his role was a huge success that led to a boost in ratings, he was written out of the show after he was arrested again for drug possession.

In an interview with Oprah Winfrey in 2004, Robert stated, "When someone says, 'I really wonder if maybe I should go to rehab?' Well, uh, you're a wreck, you just lost your job, and your wife left you. Uh, you might want to give it a shot . . . I finally said 'you know what? I don't think I can continue doing this.' And I reached out for help, and I ran with it . . . you can reach out for help in kind of a half-assed way and you'll get it and you won't take advantage of it. It's not that difficult to overcome these seeming ghastly problems . . . what's hard is to decide to actually do it."

Though he was court-ordered to go to rehab, this attitude helped him be successful in becoming abstinent from drug use. After obtaining sobriety, Robert came back to Hollywood and after several years of starring in smaller roles in independent films, his career skyrocketed following his turn in the blockbuster *Iron Man*. Following this success, he has gone on to enjoy lead roles in several major Hollywood films, a feat that had seemed unimaginable at the lowest points in his life.

Particularly dangerous is the combination of caffeine and alcohol, a problem that is most severe on college campuses. In one survey of undergraduates, over one-quarter reported that they had mixed alcohol and energy drinks in the past month; of these, almost half used more than three energy drinks at once (Malinauskas, Aeby, Overton, Carpenter-Aeby, & Barber-Heidal, 2007). When users combine alcohol and caffeine, they may not realize how intoxicated they are and may as a result have a higher prevalence of alcohol-related consequences (Reissig et al., 2009).

Tobacco

The health risks of tobacco are well known; these risks are primarily associated with smoking cigarettes, which contain tar, carbon monoxide, and other additives. **Nicotine** is the psychoactive substance found in cigarettes. Readily absorbed into the bloodstream, nicotine is also present in chewing tobacco, pipe tobacco, and cigars. The typical smoker takes 10 puffs of a cigarette over a 5-minute period; an individual who smokes 1-1/2 packs of cigarettes therefore gets 300 "hits" of nicotine per day (National Institute on Drug Abuse, 2011a). Individuals can be diagnosed with tobacco use disorder or tobacco withdrawal, but not tobacco intoxication.

When nicotine enters the bloodstream, it stimulates the release of adrenaline (norephinephrine), which activates the autonomic nervous system and increases blood pressure, heart rate, and respiration. Like other psychoactive substances, nicotine increases the level of dopamine, affecting the brain's reward and pleasure centers. Substances found in tobacco smoke, such as acetaldehyde, may further enhance nicotine's effects on the central nervous system. The withdrawal symptoms associated with quitting tobacco use include irritability, difficulties with concentration, and strong cravings for nicotine.

Although rates of cigarette smoking are decreasing in the United States from the 2002 high of 26 percent of the population ages 12 and older to the 2010 rate of 23 percent, there remained as of 2010 a rate of 40.8 percent among young adults 18 to 25 years old. The rate among youths ages 12 to 17 in 2010 was 10.7 percent (Substance Abuse and Mental Health Services Administration, 2011). Among high school seniors, however, the estimated lifetime prevalence rate is 42.2 percent (Johnston et al., 2011).

nicotine
The psychoactive substance found in cigarettes.

Inhalants

Inhalants are a diverse group of substances that cause psychoactive effects by producing chemical vapors. These products are not in and of themselves harmful; in fact, they are all products commonly found in the home and workplace. There are four categories of inhalants: volatile solvents (paint thinners or removers, dry-cleaning fluids, gasoline, glue, and lighter fluid), aerosols (sprays that contain propellants and solvents), gases (butane lighters and propane tanks, ether, and nitrous oxide), and nitrites (a special category of products that individuals use as sexual enhancers). Young teens (ages 12 to 15) tend to inhale glue, shoe polish, spray paint, gasoline, and lighter fluid. Older teens (ages 16 to 17) inhale nitrous oxide, and adults (ages 18 and older) are most likely to inhale nitrites. Within the category of inhalant disorders, individuals can be diagnosed as having inhalant use disorder or intoxication, but not inhalant withdrawal.

The effects of an inhalant tend to be short-lived; consequently, users try to extend their high by inhaling repeatedly over a period of several hours. Inhalants have similar effects as alcohol including slurring of speech, loss of coordination, euphoria, dizziness, and, over time, loss of inhibition and control. Users may experience drowsiness and headaches but, depending on the substance, may also feel confused and nauseous. The vapors displace the air in the lungs, causing hypoxia (oxygen deprivation), which is particularly lethal to neurons in the central nervous system. Long-term use may also cause the myelin sheath around the axon to deteriorate, leading to tremors, muscle spasms, and perhaps permanent muscle damage. The chemicals in inhalants can also cause heart failure and sudden death (National Institute on Drug Abuse, 2011e).

As Table 12.2 shows, less than 1 percent of the 12 and older population in the United States were current inhalant users. However, an estimated 3.6 percent of high school seniors reported lifetime inhalant use in 2010 (Johnston et al., 2011).

inhalants
A diverse group of substances that cause psychoactive effects by producing chemical vapors.

Theories and Treatment of Substance Use Disorders

Since all psychoactive substances operate on the reward and pleasure systems in the brain, similarities exist between the mechanisms through which individuals develop dependence on substances other than alcohol and the mechanisms involved in alcohol dependence itself. However, there are important differences related to the specific substance; for example, which receptor pathways the substance involves, the psychosocial factors associated with how users acquire dependence, and, ultimately, which methods are best suited to treatment.

Biological Perspectives Research evidence clearly supports the importance of genetics in the development of serious substance problems. Extensive studies on humans and laboratory animals (mice) suggest possible genetic abnormalities in the opioid receptor on chromosome 1 *(OPRM1)* that may be involved in susceptibility to alcohol and other substances as well as sensitivity to pain. A second genetic abnormality appears on chromosome 15 in a cluster of nicotinic receptor subunits *(CHRNA-3, -5,* and *-4)* involved in nicotine dependence. The third is a widely studied abnormality affecting catechol-O-methyltransferase *(COMT),* which is associated with pain sensitivity, anxiety, and substance abuse (Palmer & de Wit, 2011). Researchers have linked alterations in the gene that codes the adenosine A2A receptor on chromosome 22 to individual differences in the consumption of caffeine and caffeine's effects on sleep, EEGs, and anxiety (Reissig et al., 2009).

Compared to biological treatments for alcohol dependence, weak evidence exists for the efficacy of pharmacotherapies (Arias & Kranzler, 2008). There are no FDA-approved treatments for dependence on cocaine, methamphetamines, marijuana, hallucinogens, ecstasy, or prescription opioids. There are, however, several treatments for heroin dependence that are particularly effective when combined with behavioral interventions.

Medically assisted detoxification is the first step in treatment of heroin dependence. During detoxification, individuals may receive medications to minimize withdrawal symptoms. To prevent heroin relapse, clinicians may use one or more of three different medications. **Methadone** is a synthetic opioid that blocks the effects of heroin by binding to the same receptor sites in the central nervous system. The proper use of methadone involves specialized treatment that includes group and/or individual counseling along with referrals for other medical, psychological, or social services. Developed over 30 years ago, methadone is not considered an ideal treatment because of its potential for dependence, even when combined with psychosocial interventions. **Buprenorphine**, approved by the FDA in 2002, produces less physical dependence, a lower risk of overdose, and fewer withdrawal effects. Originally developed as a pain medication, buprenorphine is also approved for treatment of opiate dependence. The FDA has also approved **Naltrexone** for heroin dependence, but it is not widely used because patients are less likely to comply with treatment.

For nicotine dependence, clinicians may use biologically based treatments. Nicotine replacement therapies (NRTs), including nicotine gum and the nicotine patch, were the first FDA-approved pharmacological treatments. These deliver controlled doses of nicotine to the individual to relieve symptoms of withdrawal. Other FDA-approved products include nasal sprays, inhalers, and lozenges. However, the ability of the nicotine patch to treat nicotine dependence has come under question. In a follow-up study of almost 800 smokers, there were no differences in relapse rates among those who did and did not use the patch (Alpert, Connolly, & Biener, 2012). Other biological approaches to nicotine dependence are medications that do not involve delivery of nicotine, including bupropion (Wellbutrin), an antidepressant, and Varenicline tartrate (Chantix), which targets nicotine receptors in the brain.

Psychological Perspectives The cognitive-behavioral approach to understanding substance use disorders provides an important counterpart to biological theories and treatments. Whether or not individuals with dependence on substances other than alcohol receive biologically based treatment, cognitive-behavioral therapy (CBT) is now widely understood to be a crucial component of successful treatment (Arias & Kranzler, 2008).

The principles of treating substance use disorders other than alcohol through CBT are similar to those involved in treating alcohol dependence. As noted earlier in the chapter, there is also a high degree of comorbidity between alcohol and substance dependence. Well-

methadone
A synthetic opioid that produces a safer and more controlled reaction than heroin and that is used in treating heroin addiction.

buprenorphine
A medication used in the treatment of heroin addiction.

Naltrexone
A medication used in the treatment of heroin addiction.

controlled studies support the efficacy of CBT for populations dependent on a wide range of substances. Clinicians may combine CBT with motivational therapies, as well as with behavioral interventions that focus on contingency management. In addition, clinicians can readily adapt CBT to a range of clinical modalities, settings, and age groups. Given the limitations of medication-only treatment, CBT also provides an effective adjunct in both inpatient and outpatient clinics. The ability to help clients develop coping skills is also useful in fostering compliance with pharmacotherapies such as methadone and naltrexone. Because these interventions are relatively brief and highly focused, they are adaptable to clients treated within managed care who may not have access to longer-term treatment (Carroll, 2011).

12.3 Non-Substance-Related Disorders

Gambling Disorder

People who have **gambling disorder** are unable to resist recurrent urges to gamble despite knowing that the gambling will bring about negative consequences to themselves or others. The diagnosis of gambling disorder in *DSM-IV-TR* included gambling disorder as an impulse-control disorder. In *DSM-5*, it is included with substance use disorders as it is now conceptualized as showing many of the same behaviors, such as cravings, increasing needs to engage in the behavior, and negative social consequences. The unique features of gambling disorder include behaviors seen when people engage in chasing a bad bet, lying about how much they have lost, seeking financial bailouts, and committing crimes to support their gambling.

As venues for gambling continue to become available on a more widespread basis, including online gambling, the incidence of gambling disorder appears to be on the increase. Among countries with legalized gambling, lifetime prevalence estimates range from about .5 to as high as 3.5 percent of the adult population (Stucki & Rihs-Middel, 2007). In the United States, although the large majority of adults have gambled at some point in their lives, gambling disorder was estimated to be diagnosable in .6 percent. Moreover, the greater the number of occasions on which people gambled, the higher their chances of developing gambling disorder—with the highest prevalence occurring after people had gambled 1,000 times in their lives.

Gambling disorder often co-occurs with other psychological disorders. The highest risk of developing gambling disorder occurs among people who engage in gambling on games involving mental skill (such as cards), followed by sports betting, gambling machines, and horse races or cock/dog fights (Kessler et al., 2008). People with gambling disorder who bet on sports tend to be young men who have substance use disorders. Those who bet on slot machines are more likely to be older women who have higher rates of other psychological disorders and begin gambling at a later age (Petry, 2003). In general, women are less likely than men to engage in the type of gambling that depends on strategy, such as poker (Odlaug, Marsh, Kim, & Grant, 2011).

People with gambling disorder also have high rates of other disorders, particularly nicotine dependence (60 percent), dependence on other substances (58 percent), mood disorder (38 percent), and anxiety disorder (37 percent). Mood and anxiety disorders are more likely to precede, rather than follow, the onset of gambling disorder (Lorains, Cowlishaw, & Thomas, 2011). Unfortunately, the likelihood of an individual always having symptoms of gambling disorder continue to predict gambling behavior. A follow-up of Vietnam War veterans showed that even after controlling for family genetics, education, substance use, and other disorders, the men most likely to have symptoms were the ones who showed symptoms 10 years earlier (Scherrer et al., 2007).

Abnormalities in multiple neurotransmitters including dopamine, serotonin, noradrenaline, and opioid may contribute to gambling disorder. The repetitive behaviors characteristic of this disorder may be viewed as resulting from an imbalance between two competing and relatively separate neurobiological mechanisms—those involved in

gambling disorder
A non-substance-related disorder involving the persistent urge to gamble.

Individuals with gambling disorder often experience severe financial problems due to their inability to stop betting money, no matter how much they try to stop.

urges and those involved in cognitive control (Grant, Chamberlain, Odlaug, Potenza, & Kim, 2010). There may also be genetic contributions, perhaps involving abnormalities in dopamine receptor genes (Lobo et al., 2010).

From a behavioral perspective, gambling disorder may develop in part because gambling follows a variable ratio reinforcement schedule when rewards occur, on average, every "X" number of times. This pattern of reinforcement produces behaviors that are highly resistant to extinction. Slot machines, in particular, produce payoffs on this type of schedule, maintaining high rates of responding by gamblers. Classical conditioning is also involved in maintaining this behavior, because gamblers learn to associate certain cues to gambling including their internal states or moods and external stimuli such as advertisements for gambling.

Cognitive factors also play an important role in gambling disorder. People with this disorder seem to engage in a phenomenon known as "discounting of probabilistic rewards," in which they discount or devalue rewards they could obtain in the future compared to rewards they could obtain right away (Petry, 2011). They also engage in other cognitive distortions many of which involve poor judgment of the probabilities that their gambling will lead to successful outcomes, as shown in Table 12.4.

The biopsychosocial perspective seems particularly relevant for understanding gambling disorder. According to the **pathways model,** the genetic vulnerability interacts with the poor coping and problem-solving skills of the person with gambling disorder to make the individual particularly susceptible to early gambling experiences, such as having early gambling luck ("the big win"). These, combined with sociocultural factors can propel the individual into more serious symptoms. The pathways model predicts that there are three main paths leading to three subtypes of people with gambling disorder. The behaviorally conditioned subtype had few symptoms prior to developing the disorder but through frequent exposure to gambling, develops positive associations, distorted cognitions, and poor decision-making about gambling. The emotionally vulnerable subtype had pre-existing depression, anxiety, and perhaps a history of trauma; gambling helps this individual feel better. The third type of person with pathological gambling has pre-existing impulsivity, attentional difficulties, and antisocial

pathways model
Approach to gambling disorder that predicts that there are three main paths leading to three subtypes.

TABLE 12.4 Common Cognitive Distortions in People with Gambling Disorder

Type of Heuristic	Cognitive Distortions Derived from Heuristics	Example
Representativeness	Gambler's Fallacy	When events generated by a random process have deviated from the population average in a short run, such as a roulette ball falling on red four times in a row, individuals may erroneously believe that the opposite deviation (e.g., ball falls on black) becomes more likely.
	Overconfidence	Individuals express a degree of confidence in their knowledge or ability that is not warranted by objective reality.
	Trends in number picking	Lottery players commonly try to apply long-run random patterns to short strings in their picks such as avoiding duplicate numbers and adjacent digits in number strings.
Availability	Illusory correlations	Individuals believe events that they expect to be correlated, due to previous experience or perceptions, have been correlated in previous experience even when they have not been, such as wearing a "lucky hat" they wore when they won previously.
	Availability of others' wins	When individuals see and hear other gamblers winning, they start to believe that winning is a regular occurrence, which reinforces their belief that they will win if they continue to play.
	Inherent memory bias	Individuals are biased to recollect wins with greater ease than losses. They then reframe their memories regarding gambling experiences in a way that focuses on positive experiences (wins) and disregards negative experiences (losses). This causes them to rationalize their decision to continue gambling.
Additional cognitive distortions	Illusion of control	Individuals have a higher expectancy for success than objective probability would warrant.
	Switching and double switching	Individuals recognize errors and process gambling-related situations in a rational way when they are not actively participating, but abandon rational thought when they personally take part in gambling.

SOURCE: Fortune & Goodie, 2011.

characteristics. For this individual, the risk of gambling provides thrills and excitement (Hodgins & Peden, 2008).

Researchers are beginning to investigate the possibility of treating gambling disorder with medications that target particular neurotransmitters. One set of medications are the opioid-acting medications to reduce the urge to drink in people with alcohol dependence, such as naltrexone and its long-acting form, nalmefine (Grant, Odlaug, Potenza, Hollander, & Kim, 2010). Another medication that shows promise is memantine, used as a treatment for Alzheimer's disease. People with gambling disorder showed improved cognitive control presumably due to the medication's effect on glutamate receptors (Grant, Chamberlain, et al., 2010).

Based on the pathways model, even if a medication is found that can reduce gambling disorder, individuals with this disorder would nevertheless require psychosocial interventions. Although many gamblers turn to help from Gamblers Anonymous, there are few studies of its efficacy. The most thoroughly studied intervention is cognitive-behavioral therapy. A typical cognitive-behavioral treatment would involve these steps. First, the clinician teaches clients to understand the triggers for their gambling by having them describe their pattern of gambling behaviors. For example, common triggers include unstructured or free time, negative emotional states, reminders such as watching sports or advertisements, and having some available money. The clinician would also ascertain the times when clients do not gamble. Clinicians use this information to help their clients analyze the times they gamble and the times they do not. Following this assessment, clinicians continue in subsequent sessions to work on helping their clients increase pleasant activities, think of ways to handle cravings or urges, become more assertive, and correct their irrational cognitions. At the end of treatment, clinicians would help prepare their clients for setbacks using relapse-prevention methods (Morasco, Ledgerwood, Weinstock, & Petry, 2009)

In addition to classifying gambling disorder as a non-substance-related disorder, the *DSM-5* authors considered adding internet gaming disorder to the non-substance-related disorder category. But for the present time, they have included it in Section 3 as a disorder requiring further study. Although there is ample evidence to indicate that internet gaming is becoming a problematic behavior in its own right, the available research was not considered sufficiently well-developed to justify inclusion in the diagnostic system at the present time. Much of the data in support of this condition was produced by studies conducted in Asia and used inconsistent definitions of the phenomenon. Therefore, the *DSM-5* work group believed that further investigations are required to produce reliable prevalence estimates. Other disorders that the work group considered adding were "sex addiction," "exercise addiction," and "shopping addiction," to name a few. However, the work group believed there were even fewer empirical studies in peer-reviewed articles to justify their inclusion even in Section 3.

12.4 Substance Disorders: The Biopsychosocial Perspective

As we have seen in this chapter, the biopsychosocial model is extremely useful for understanding substance use disorder and approaches to treatment. Genetics clearly plays a role in the development of these disorders, and the action of substances on the central nervous system also plays a role in the maintenance of dependence. Developmental issues in particular are critical for understanding the nature of these disorders, which often have their origins during the years of late childhood and early adolescence. Moreover, because alcohol, drugs, and medications with high abuse potential continue to be widely available, sociocultural factors play a strong role in maintaining dependence among users. Addictions have characterized human behavior throughout the millennia; however, with more widespread public education in conjunction with advances in both genetics and psychotherapeutic interventions, it is possible that we will also see advances in prevention, as well.

Return to the Case: Carl Wadsworth

Carl initially had some difficulties in finding an AA meeting to attend in which he felt comfortable, although once he found the "right" group for him, he looked forward to attending on a daily basis and remained highly motivated to refrain from drinking. He connected with many members of the group, and for the first time in his life, Carl felt that he had a supportive group of friends. Carl began a course of mood-stabilizing medication that did not require weekly blood tests and resulted in significantly lower side effects than lithium, which was helpful in encouraging him to continue taking his medication regularly. In psychotherapy, Carl and his therapist focused on processing what he was learning in AA as well as mood-monitoring techniques for his bipolar disorder. He will continue to live with Janice until he feels stable enough to look for a job and begin to support himself again.

Dr. Tobin's reflections: Carl's case is somewhat unusual, as many individuals who experience substance abuse and/or dependence begin abusing substances earlier in life. It is interesting that Carl had been able to refrain from drinking for many years until he was tempted by his boss. Until that point, he showed good insight in his awareness that he may be genetically predisposed to alcohol use disorder, based on his parents' history. In therapy, Carl can explore the reasons why he began drinking in order to gain approval from his boss.

Carl's case is a good example of the destructive combination of alcohol use disorder and a psychological disorder. Unfortunately, the occurrence of such comorbidity is not rare, especially among those suffering from mood disorders, due to the self-medicating effects that alcohol sometimes offers. Carl's lapse in judgment when he agreed to drink with his boss was unfortunate, and it demonstrates the destructive power of alcohol addiction, as well as how quickly it can take over one's life. Fortunately, alcohol use disorders typically have a good prognosis after appropriate intervention, and they are not incurable. Carl will have to work hard at staying sober and monitoring his bipolar disorder. Much of the focus of his treatment will be on keeping his mood stable in order to prevent relapsing into alcohol abuse in the future. Fortunately, Carl appears highly motivated to remain abstinent from alcohol and get his life back in order. Finding a supportive AA group in which Carl feels he can trust the other members is a crucial aspect of his treatment and will be a wonderful source of support that will help him through his recovery.

SUMMARY

- A **substance** is a chemical that alters a person's mood or behavior when smoked, injected, drunk, inhaled, or ingested. **Substance intoxication** is the temporary maladaptive experience of behavioral or psychological changes that are due to the accumulation of a substance in the body. When some substances are discontinued, people may experience symptoms of substance **withdrawal** that involve a set of physical and psychological disturbances. To counteract withdrawal symptoms, people are inclined to use more of the substance, causing them to develop **tolerance. Substance use disorder** is a cluster of cognitive, behavioral, and physiological symptoms indicating that the individual uses a substance despite significant substance-related problems.

- Approximately one in seven Americans has a history of alcohol abuse or dependence. The short-term effects of alcohol use are appealing to many people because of the sedating qualities of this substance, although side effects such as hangovers cause distress. The long-term effects of heavy use are worrisome and involve serious harm to many organs of the body, resulting in medical problems and possibly dementia. Researchers in the field of alcohol dependence were among the first to propose the biopsychosocial model to explain the development of a psychological disorder. In the realm of biological contributors, researchers have focused on the role of genetics in light of the fact that dependence runs in families. This line of research has focused on markers and genetic mapping. Psychological theories focus on concepts derived from behavioral theory, as well as cognitive-behavioral and social learning perspectives. For example, according to the widely accepted expectancy model, people with alcohol use disorder develop problematic beliefs about alcohol early in life through reinforcement and observational learning. Researchers and theorists working within the sociocultural perspective regard stressors within the family, community, and culture as factors that lead the person to develop alcohol use disorder.

- Clinicians may derive treatment for alcohol problems in varying degrees from each of the three perspectives. In biological terms, medications may be used to control symptoms of withdrawal, to control symptoms associated with co-existing conditions, or to provoke nausea following alcohol ingestion. Clinicians use various psychological interventions, some of which are based on behavioral and cognitive-behavioral techniques. Alcoholics Anonymous is a 12-step recovery program built on the premise that alcoholism is a disease.

- **Stimulants** have an activating effect on the nervous system. **Amphetamines** in moderate amounts cause euphoria, increased confidence, talkativeness, and energy. In higher doses, the user has more intense reactions and, over time, can become addicted and develop psychotic symptoms. **Cocaine** users experience stimulating effects for a shorter period of time that are nevertheless quite intense. In moderate doses, cocaine leads to euphoria, sexual excitement, potency, energy, and talkativeness. At higher doses, psychotic symptoms may develop. In addition to disturbing psychological symptoms, serious medical problems can arise from the use of cocaine. **Cannabis,** or marijuana, causes altered perception and bodily sensations, as well as maladaptive behavioral and psychological reactions. Most of the acute effects of cannabis intoxication are reversible, but a long period of abuse is likely to lead to dependence and to have adverse psychological and physical effects. **Hallucinogens** cause abnormal perceptual experiences in the form of illusions and hallucinations. Opioids include naturally occurring substances (e.g., morphine and opium) as well as semisynthetic (e.g., heroin) and synthetic (e.g., methadone) drugs. **Opioid** users experience a rush, involving a range of psychological reactions as well as intense bodily sensations, some of which reflect life-threatening symptoms, particularly during episodes of withdrawal. **Sedatives, hypnotics,** and **anxiolytics** are substances that induce relaxation, sleep, tranquility, and reduced awareness. Although not typically regarded as an abused substance, high levels of **caffeine** can cause a number of psychological and physical problems. **Nicotine,** the psychoactive chemical found in tobacco, is highly addictive. Withdrawal from nicotine can result in mood and behavior disturbances.

- **Gambling disorder** is characterized by the persistent urge to gamble. Individuals with this disorder may feel unable to stop themselves from participating in gambling events or games, even after they have experienced significant financial and material losses.

- Various treatment programs for people with substance-related disorders have emerged within the biopsychosocial perspective. Biological treatment may involve the prescription of substances that block or reduce cravings. Behavioral treatment involves techniques such as contingency management, while clinicians utilize cognitive-behavioral techniques to help clients modify their thoughts, expectancies, and behaviors associated with drug use. Detailed **relapse prevention** plans are an important part of alcohol treatment programs.

KEY TERMS

Neurocognitive Disorders

Learning Objectives

13.1 Describe characteristics of neurocognitive disorders

13.2 Identify the symptoms of delirium

13.3 Understand the symptoms, theories, and treatment of neurocognitive disorder due to Alzheimer's disease

13.4 Explain the differences among neurocognitive disorders that are unrelated to Alzheimer's disease

13.5 Identify neurocognitive disorders due to traumatic brain injury (TBI)

13.6 Describe neurocognitive disorders due to substances/ medications and HIV infection

13.7 Explain neurocognitive disorders due to another general medical condition

13.8 Analyze neurocognitive disorders through the biopsychosocial perspective

Case Report: Irene Heller

Demographic information: Irene is a 76-year-old Caucasian female.

Presenting problem: Irene was referred for neuropsychological testing from her primary care physician, who noted a significant decline in her memory and motor functioning from the previous year. During a routine physical evaluation, Irene's doctor reported that she displayed cognitive impairments and abnormal reflexes. She was referred for neuropsychological testing to a private specialty practice.

During the initial interview before neuropsychological testing was conducted, Irene was asked about her cognitive functioning. Her daughter Jillian accompanied her to the appointment. Irene had difficulty answering some of the questions in the interview, and thus Jillian provided most of the information for the interview. Jillian reported that her mother's visit to the doctor was not the first sign of any recent abnormalities in her behavior, and that over the past month both she and her other siblings noticed that their mother was acting strangely. Irene currently lives by herself in the town where her two grown children live. On two separate occasions Irene's neighbors had reportedly found her in the parking lot of the apartment complex where she lives late at night in her nightgown looking "totally out of it." The neighbors had brought her back into her home, though Irene did not recall these incidents occurring.

When asked about any physical changes she had noticed recently, Irene stated that was having difficulty writing because she was unable to grasp pens or other writing instruments. As a result she stated she hadn't been able to pay her bills and sometimes had trouble preparing food for herself. In fact, she noted that she had lost about 10 pounds over the past two months because of this.

Jillian also reported that she had noticed her mother was having significant walking difficulties recently. Irene preferred to stay at home as a result and had begun to miss out on many activities that she had previously enjoyed, including spending time with her family and weekly bridge games.

Jillian added that Irene typically called either her or her brother at least once per day, and that they had family meals together once or twice every week. Jillian reported that during the past two months when she or her brother called their mother on the phone, her speech was sometimes difficult to understand, and that Irene would forget to whom she was speaking in the middle of the conversation. All of this was very troubling to Jillian, though Irene wasn't able to acknowledge much of what Jillian was reporting. "I guess I sometimes have a hard time paying my bills or calling my children. I guess I just don't feel like it these days."

Jillian stated that she and her brother thought that perhaps Irene's behavior was due to medical reasons. Irene has been diagnosed with Type II Diabetes and according to Jillian, had forgotten to check her blood sugar and take insulin for two days in a row. Since Jillian and her brother Steve hadn't been talking to their mother, they were unaware that this was occurring. When they didn't hear from their mother, Jillian and Steve went to Irene's house to check on her, finding her nearly unconscious in her living room. After giving her insulin, the siblings made an appointment with Irene's primary care physician for the next day.

After the clinical interview, Irene completed neuropsychological testing, which consisted of a battery of cognitive tests aimed at measuring her overall cognitive functioning.

Relevant history: Irene reported that she has remained relatively healthy throughout her life and that she has never experienced any major medical, emotional, or cognitive problems. Two years prior to the interview, Jillian stated that her mother was diagnosed with Type II Diabetes and has been taking insulin to regulate her blood sugar. Jillian reported that until her recent decline, Irene had remained quite active and participated in many social activities and was able to carry out all of her activities of daily living without difficulty.

Case formulation: The rather sudden onset of Irene's symptoms is typical of neurocognitive disorder due to vascular disease. Though the onset varies, typically it occurs suddenly. Since Irene had stopped taking her medication, she was putting herself at significant medical risk. Further, consistent with diagnostic criteria, Irene's functioning was significantly impaired—she had ceased

her previous activities and had even stopped paying her bills due to her motor difficulties.

The results of the neuropsychological testing indicated that Irene indeed was experiencing a significant impairment in her short-term memory and her ability to speak fluently and coherently, and also evidenced difficulties in her executive functioning, including organizing and sequencing information that was presented to her. Taken together with the physical examination from her doctor, Irene is given a diagnosis of Neurocognitive Disorder due to Vascular Disease although until she has an MRI to confirm the existence of brain lesions, the diagnosis will be tentative.

Treatment plan: Irene will be referred for an MRI in order to confirm her diagnosis, upon which she will be given a referral for medication and follow-up home care, if needed.

Sarah Tobin, PhD

13.1 Characteristics of Neurocognitive Disorders

neurocognitive disorder
Disorder characterized by acquired cognitive decline in one or more domains of cognition based upon concerns of the client or someone who knows the client well, and performance on objective assessment measures.

The brain's functioning affects our abilities to think, remember, and pay attention. The **neurocognitive disorders** that we will discuss in this chapter have two main characteristics: they involve cognitive decline acquired in life in one or more domains of cognition based upon concerns of the client or someone who knows the client well, and performance on objective assessment measures. There are many sources of insults or injuries that can affect an individual's brain, including trauma, disease, or exposure to toxic substances, including drugs. The *DSM-5* provides descriptions to help clinicians provide a diagnosis that indicates both the fact that the individual has a neurocognitive disorder and, where known, the possible cause.

As the seat of all thoughts, actions, motivations, and memories, the brain, when damaged, can cause a variety of symptoms. Some of these symptoms may mimic schizophrenia, mood disorders, and personality disorders. People can develop delusions, hallucinations, mood disturbances, and extreme personality changes due to brain changes resulting from disease, reactions to medication, and exposure to toxic substances. Although we may think of these symptoms as "psychological," they must, by necessity, have a physiological basis. In the cognitive disorders, we can clearly identify this physiological basis.

Clinicians use neuropsychological testing and neuroimaging techniques, as well as an individual's medical history, to decide whether an individual's symptoms fall into the category of a cognitive disorder. Neuropsychological testing helps clinicians identify specific patterns of responses that fit known disease profiles. They combine this knowledge with their client's medical histories to see if a specific event triggered the symptoms. In addition, neuroimaging provides clinicians with an inside look at the brain to help them connect symptoms with specific illnesses or injuries. Both are required for an individual to receive a diagnosis of one of these disorders.

Table 13.1 shows the domains covered in the neurocognitive disorders and types of abilities included in each. Clinicians would incorporate additional tests from neuropsychological batteries as needed to help determine the client's level of functioning in each of these domains. Furthermore, clinicians rate the client as showing major or mild neurocognitive disorder based on criteria indicated within each domain. They conduct the ratings of major or mild on the basis of interviews with the client and with the client's families or significant others. For example, a mild level of memory impairment would involve the individual's reliance on notes or reminders in everyday tasks. Major impairment would be represented by the individual's inability to keep track of short lists, including completing a task within a single sitting.

In *DSM-5,* the term *neurocognitive disorder* replaces *dementia,* used in *DSM-IV-TR* to refer to a form of cognitive impairment in which individuals undergo progressive loss of cognitive functions severe enough to interfere with their normal daily activities and social relationships. Clinicians still use the term "dementia," and the *DSM-5* work group considered dementia to be useful in settings where medical personnel are familiar with the term.

Major neurocognitive disorders are diagnosed when individuals show significant cognitive decline from a previous level of performance in the six domains of Table 13.1 based on either concern of the individual or a knowledgeable informant or, preferably, a standardized neuropsychological or other quantified clinical assessment. In addition, these cognitive deficits must interfere with the individual's ability to perform necessary tasks in everyday living, do not occur exclusively with delirium, and cannot be better explained by another psychological disorder. The diagnosis of **mild neurocognitive disorder** is applied when the individual shows modest levels of cognitive decline. These declines are not severe enough to interfere with the individual's capacity for living independently.

major neurocognitive disorders
Disorders involving significant cognitive decline from a previous level of performance.

mild neurocognitive disorders
Disorders involving modest cognitive decline from a previous level of performance.

TABLE 13.1 Neurocognitive Domains in *DSM-5*

Domain	Examples of Relevant Abilities	Assessment Task Examples
Complex attention	Sustained attention	Maintaining attention over time
	Selective attention	Separating signals from distractors
	Divided attention	Attending to two or more tasks at once
Executive function	Planning	Deciding on a sequence of actions
	Decision making	Performing tasks that require choosing between alternatives
	Working memory	Being able to hold information in memory while manipulating stimuli
	Mental/cognitive flexibility	Switching between two concepts, tasks, or response rules (e.g., picking odd numbers, then picking even numbers)
Learning and memory	Immediate memory span	Remembering a series of digits or words
	Recent memory	Encoding new information such as word lists or a short story
Language	Expressive language	Being able to name objects
	Grammar and syntax	Speaking without errors while performing other tasks
	Receptive language	Being able to understand word definitions and instructions
Perceptual-motor	Visual perception	Assessing whether a figure can be "real" based on its depiction in two-dimensional space
	Visuoconstructional	Being able to assemble items requiring hand-eye coordination
	Praxis	Ability to engage in common motor skills, use common tools, imitate the use of tools, and imitate gestures
	Gnosis	Recognizing faces and colors
Social cognition	Recognition of emotions	Identifying emotions in images of faces
	Theory of mind	Being able to consider another person's mental state based on pictures or stories

After diagnosing the level of cognitive impairment, the clinician then specifies which disease appears to be responsible for the cognitive symptoms. When one specific disease cannot be diagnosed, the clinician can use codes that indicate this or that there are multiple diseases contributing to the symptoms.

13.2 Delirium

delirium
A neurocognitive disorder that is temporary in nature involving disturbances in attention or awareness.

People who experience **delirium** temporarily experience disturbances in their attention and awareness. The symptoms tend to appear abruptly and fluctuate over the course of the time that they have the disorder. *DSM-IV-TR* defined delirium in terms of a disturbance of "consciousness," but *DSM-5* uses the criterion of a disturbance in attention or awareness, given the vague nature of the term consciousness. The core of the disorder involves an acute state of confusion or impairment in cognitive processing that affects memory, orientation, executive functioning, ability to use language, visual perception, and learning. To receive a diagnosis of delirium, the individual must show these changes in consciousness or awareness over a very short period of time, on the order of hours or days, and tending to fluctuate over the course of the day. Finally, a general medical condition must cause the disturbance. In addition, clinicians specify whether the delirium results from substance intoxication, substance withdrawal, a medication, or another medical condition or conditions. The clinician also rates the delirium as acute (a few hours or days) or persistent (weeks or months).

Delirium can develop for a variety of reasons, including substance intoxication or withdrawal, head injury, high fever, and vitamin deficiency. People of any age can experience delirium, but it is more common among medically or psychiatrically hospitalized older adult patients, particularly among surgical patients with pre-existing cognitive impairment and depressive symptoms (Minden et al., 2005). In addition to age, the risk factors for delirium include a previous history of stroke, dementia, sensory impairment, and use of multiple prescription medications ("polypharmacy"). People at risk may develop delirium following infections, urinary retention or use of catheters, dehydration, loss of mobility, and disorders involving heart rate. Changes in neurotransmitters may be involved in delirium. People who develop delirium following a stroke may do so due to loss of neuron oxygenation in the brain (Dahl, Rønning, & Thommessen, 2010). Increases in immune system inflammatory responses may also contribute to delirium (Simone & Tan, 2011).

Infection is another precipitating factor in at-risk individuals. In a survey of nearly 1.3 million patients studied over the years 1998 to 2005, researchers found that the most frequent causes were infections, including respiratory infections, cellulitis, and urinary tract and kidney infections. The next largest cause of delirium consisted of some type of central nervous system disorder, including cancer, dementia, strokes, and seizures. The third most frequent cause of delirium included metabolic disorders, cardiovascular disease, and orthopedic procedures. However, over the course of the study, drug-induced delirium increased in prevalence among older adults, suggesting that either hospital workers became more attuned to this diagnosis or that people in this age group are becoming more and more likely to receive delirium-inducing medications. Making health professionals aware of adverse drug effects may ultimately help to reduce the prevalence of delirium in high-risk individuals (Lin, Heacock, & Fogel, 2010).

Apart from the cognitive symptoms of inattention and memory loss, individuals experiencing delirium may also have hallucinations, delusions, abnormalities in sleep/wake cycles, changes in mood, and movement abnormalities (Jain, Chakrabarti, & Kulhara, 2011). Once they experience this condition, people who had delirium are more

Delirium is a temporary condition that can have a wide range of physiological causes. Individuals who experience this condition suffer from several sensory disturbances simultaneously.

likely to experience medical complications that can cause rehospitalization and a higher risk of mortality (Marcantonio et al., 2005). People who experience delirium following a stroke also have higher rates of developing dementia within 2 years (van Rijsbergen et al., 2011).

There are several specialized tests to assess delirium. The Delirium Rating Scale-Revised (DRS-R-98) (Trzepacz et al., 2001) is a widely used measure that has been translated into several languages (Table 13.2) and has well-established validity and reliability (Grover, Chakrabarti, Shah, & Kumar, 2011). The advantage of using this scale is that although designed for

TABLE 13.2 Delirium Rating Scale-Revised-98 (DRS-R-98)

1. Sleep-wake cycle disturbance
   0. Not present
   1. Mild sleep continuity disturbance at night or occasional drowsiness during the day
   2. Moderate disorganization of sleep/wake cycle (e.g., falling asleep during conversations, napping during the day, or several brief awakenings during the night with confusion/behavioral changes or very little nighttime sleep)
   3. Severe disruption of sleep/wake cycle (e.g., day-night reversal of sleep/wake cycle or severe circadian fragmentation with multiple periods of sleep and wakefulness or severe sleeplessness)

2. Perceptual disturbances and hallucinations
   0. Not present
   1. Mild perceptual disturbances (e.g., feelings of derealization or depersonalization; or patient may not be able to discriminate dreams from reality)
   2. Illusions present
   3. Hallucinations present

3. Delusions
   0. Not present
   1. Mildly suspicious, hypervigilant, or preoccupied
   2. Unusual or overvalued ideation that does not reach delusional proportions or could be plausible
   3. Delusional

4. Lability of affect (outward presentation of emotions)
   0. Not present
   1. Affect somewhat altered or incongruent to situation; changes over the course of hours; emotions are mostly under self-control
   2. Affect is often inappropriate to the situation and intermittently changes over the course of minutes; emotions are not consistently under self-control, although they respond to redirection by others
   3. Severe and consistent disinhibition of emotions; affect changes rapidly, is inappropriate to context, and does not respond to redirection by others

5. Language
   0. Normal language
   1. Mild impairment including word-finding difficulty or problems with naming or fluency
   2. Moderate impairment including comprehension difficulties or deficits in meaningful communication (semantic content)
   3. Severe impairment including nonsensical semantic content, word salad, muteness, or severely reduced comprehension

6. Thought process abnormalities
   0. Normal thought processes
   1. Tangential or circumstantial
   2. Associations loosely connected occasionally, but largely comprehensible
   3. Associations loosely connected most of the time

7. Motor agitation
   0. No restlessness or agitation
   1. Mild restlessness of gross motor movements or mild fidgeting
   2. Moderate motor agitation including dramatic movements of the extremities, pacing, fidgeting, removing intravenous lines, etc.
   3. Severe motor agitation, such as combativeness or a need for restraints or seclusion

TABLE 13.2 Delirium Rating Scale-Revised-98 (DRS-R-98) (continued)

8. Motor retardation

 0. No slowness of voluntary movements
 1. Mildly reduced frequency, spontaneity or speed of motor movements, to the degree that may interfere somewhat with the assessment
 2. Moderately reduced frequency, spontaneity, or speed of motor movements to the degree that it interferes with participation in activities or self-care
 3. Severe motor retardation with few spontaneous movements

9. Orientation

 0. Oriented to person, place, and time
 1. Disoriented to time (e.g., by more than 2 days or wrong month or wrong year) or to place (e.g., name of building, city, state), but not both
 2. Disoriented to time and place
 3. Disoriented to person

10. Attention

 0. Alert and attentive
 1. Mildly distractible or mild difficulty sustaining attention, but able to refocus with cueing. On formal testing makes only minor errors and is not significantly slow in responses
 2. Moderate inattention with difficulty focusing and sustaining attention. On formal testing, makes numerous errors and requires prodding either to focus or to finish the task
 3. Severe difficulty focusing and/or sustaining attention, with many incorrect or incomplete responses or inability to follow instructions. Distractible by other noises or events in the environment

11. Short-term memory (Defined as recall of information [e.g., 3 items presented either verbally or visually] after a delay of about 2 to 3 minutes)

 0. Short-term memory intact
 1. Recalls 2/3 items; may be able to recall third item after category cueing
 2. Recalls 1/3 items; may be able to recall other items after category cueing
 3. Recalls 0/3 items

12. Long-term memory

 0. No significant long-term memory deficits
 1. Recalls 2/3 items and/or has minor difficulty recalling details of other long-term information
 2. Recalls 1/3 items and/or has moderate difficulty recalling other long-term information
 3. Recalls 0/3 items and/or has severe difficulty recalling other long-term information

13. Visuospatial ability

Assess informally and formally. Consider patient's difficulty navigating one's way around living areas or environment (e.g., getting lost). Test formally by drawing or copying a design, by arranging puzzle pieces, or by drawing a map and identifying major cities, etc. Take into account any visual impairments that may affect performance.

 0. No impairment
 1. Mild impairment such that overall design and most details or pieces are correct; and/or little difficulty navigating in his/her surroundings
 2. Moderate impairment with distorted appreciation of overall design and/or several errors of details or pieces; and/or needing repeated redirection to keep from getting lost in a newer environment despite trouble locating familiar objects in immediate environment
 3. Severe impairment on formal testing; and/or repeated wandering or getting lost in environment

SOURCE: Trzepacz et al., 2001.

psychiatrists, other professionals (physicians, nurses, psychologists) and researchers can also use it. When completing the instrument, the clinician can use information gathered from family members, visitors, hospital staff, physicians, medical charts, and even hospital roommates.

To treat delirium, clinicians may use a pharmacological approach in which they administer antipsychotics. The standard approach involves using haloperidol, but clinicians may use "off-label" antipsychotics such as respiridone. This combination appears to help resolve symptoms in as many as 84 percent of cases over a period of 4 to 7 days (Boettger, Breitbart, & Passik, 2011).

MINI CASE

Delirium due to Another Medical Condition, Acute

Jack is a 23-year-old carpenter whose co-workers brought him to the emergency room when he collapsed at work with a high fever accompanied by chills. When told that he would be rushed to the hospital, Jack repeatedly responded with the nonsensical answer, "The hammer's no good." Jack's co-workers were startled and perplexed by his bizarre suggestions that they were trying to steal his tools and by his various other paranoid-sounding remarks. Grabbing at things in the air, Jack insisted that people were throwing objects at him. Jack couldn't remember the name of anyone at the site; in fact, he was unsure of where he was. Initially, he resisted his co-workers' attempts to take him to the hospital because of his concern that they had formed a plot to harm him.

However, given the potential long-term negative consequences even of delirium that is treated, clinicians aim to direct their efforts toward prevention. In one pioneering program, a multidisciplinary team targeted at-risk patients experiencing cognitive, sleeping, motor, or sensory impairments by involving professionals from areas including recreation therapy, physical therapy, and geriatrics, as well as trained volunteers. For those individuals suffering from cognitive impairment, for example, the team focused on providing cognitively stimulating activities such as discussions of current events or word games. Each at-risk group received specialized interventions directed at their particular risk factors. Over an 11-day period, the incidence of delirium in the treatment group was significantly lower than that of a matched group who received usual hospital care (Inouye et al., 1999). Subsequent studies validate the effectiveness of intervention particularly when aimed at a population selected to be at high risk (Hempenius et al., 2011).

13.3 Neurocognitive Disorder due to Alzheimer's Disease

Neurocognitive disorder due to Alzheimer's disease is a neurocognitive disorder associated with progressive, gradual declines in memory, learning, and at least one other cognitive domain. We show the diagnostic criteria in Table 13.3. The first symptoms of memory loss precede a cascade of changes that eventually end in death due to a complication such as pneumonia.

Alzheimer's disease was first reported in 1907 by a German psychiatrist and neuropathologist, Alois Alzheimer (1864–1915), who documented the case of "Auguste D.," a 51-year-old woman complaining of poor memory and disorientation regarding time and place (Alzheimer, 1907/1987). Eventually, Auguste became depressed and began to hallucinate. She showed the classic cognitive symptoms now understood as part of the diagnostic criteria for the disorder. Alzheimer was unable to explain this process of deterioration until after she died, when an autopsy revealed that most of the tissue in her cerebral cortex had undergone severe degeneration. Upon examining the brain tissue under a microscope, Alzheimer also found that individual neurons had degenerated and had formed abnormal clumps of neural tissue. Ninety years later, a discovery of brain slides from this woman confirmed that the changes seen in her brain were similar to those typically found in current cases of the disease (Enserink, 1998) (see Figure 13.1).

Although there is still no explanation for what causes the process of brain deterioration that forms the core of this disease, we have come to associate the term Alzheimer's disease with the severe cerebral atrophy seen in Auguste D., as well as the characteristic microscopic changes in brain tissue. Throughout the remainder of the chapter, we will refer to neurocognitive disorder due to Alzheimer's disease as "Alzheimer's disease" or "AD." Where not otherwise noted, we also will be describing characteristics of major neurocognitive disorder rather than mild neurocognitive disorder.

Very early Alzheimer's

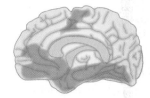

Mild to moderate Alzheimer's

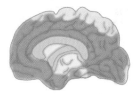

Severe Alzheimer's

As Alzheimer's disease progresses, neurofibrillary tangles spread throughout the brain (shown in blue). Plaques also spread throuhgout the brain, starting in the neocortex. By the final stage, damage is widespread, and brain tissue has shrunk significantly.

FIGURE 13.1 Changes in the Brain Associated with Alzheimer's Disease

TABLE 13.3 Diagnostic Criteria for Neurocognitive Disorder due to Alzheimer's Disease

The diagnostic criteria for neurocognitive disorder due to Alzheimer's disease include the diagnostic criteria for major or mild neurocognitive disorder as well as the following:

For major neurocognitive disorder, because Alzheimer's disease cannot be definitively diagnosed until autopsy, clinicians can assign the diagnosis as either "probable" (when both 1 and 2 are met) or "possible" (when only one of the two is met):

1. Evidence of a genetic mutation known to be associated with Alzheimer's disease from family history or genetic testing

2. All three of these symptoms:
   A. Clear evidence of decline in memory and learning and at least one other cognitive domain
   B. Steadily progressive, gradual decline in cognitive functions
   C. No evidence of another neurodegenerative disease or other disease that can contribute to cognitive decline.

For minor neurocognitive disorder, "probable" is diagnosed if either genetic testing or family history provide evidence of a genetic mutation, and "possible" if there is no genetic indication, but all three of the above symptoms in criterion 2 are present.

neurocognitive disorder due to Alzheimer's disease
A neurocognitive disorder associated with progressive, gradual declines in memory, learning, and at least one other cognitive domain.

Prevalence of Alzheimer's Disease

The popular press widely but inaccurately reports the prevalence of Alzheimer's disease as 5 to 5.5 million, which would constitute 12 percent of the population over age 65 and 50 percent of those over age 85. The World Health Organization (2001) provides a far lower prevalence estimate of 5 percent of men and 6 percent of women worldwide. The incidence rate of new cases is less than 1 percent a year in those ages 60 to 65, or possibly as high as 6.5 percent in those 85 and older (Kawas, Gray, Brookmeyer, Fozard, & Zonderman, 2000).

Autopsy studies confirm the lower estimate. In one rural Pennsylvania community, researchers found Alzheimer's disease as the cause of death in 4.9 percent of people age 65 and older (Ganguli, Dodge, Shen, Pandav, & DeKosky, 2005). Of course, this estimate includes only those whose deaths are confirmed to have resulted from Alzheimer's disease. In many cases, another disease, such as pneumonia, is actually the immediate cause of death in people with advanced Alzheimer's disease. Nevertheless, this percentage is substantially lower than what we would expect on the basis of figures published in the media. Perhaps somewhat amazingly, among the 100-year-old and older participants in the New England Centenarian Study, approximately 90 percent were symptom-free until age 92 (Perls, 2004).

The overestimation of Alzheimer's disease reinforces the notion in the minds of the public that any cognitive changes experienced by people in later life (or earlier) reflect the disease's onset. Loss of working memory occurs normally in later life for most individuals. Once people become self-conscious about their memory, however, they tend to exaggerate even small losses, thinking that they have Alzheimer's disease. Unfortunately, this self-consciousness only worsens their memory, which further perpetuates the cycle. Rather than taking preventive steps, such as engaging in memory exercises or other cognitively challenging activities, people in this situation are likely to give into despair (Jones, Whitbourne, Whitbourne, & Skultety, 2009).

What appears to be the overestimation of Alzheimer's disease in epidemiological reports occurs for several reasons. Most importantly, the authors of these reports tend to include other forms of neurocognitive disorder due to Alzheimer's disease in their overall estimates. Neurocognitive disorders caused by other diseases can account for as many as 55 percent of cases (Jellinger & Attems, 2010) including 20 percent caused solely by cardiovascular disease (Knopman, 2007). Consequently, the "5.5 million" actually includes, perhaps, as many as 2 to 3 million people who have some form of vascular disease or other neurological disorder. Because cardiovascular disease is related to hypertension (Sharp, Aarsland, Day, Sønnesyn,

& Ballard, 2011) and diabetes (Knopman & Roberts, 2010), both of which people can control or prevent through diet and exercise, it is particularly important for older adults and their families to receive accurate diagnoses of any neurocognitive symptoms that they experience. Other reasons for the inaccurate data on Alzheimer's disease include failure to take into account the education level of individuals who participate in epidemiological surveys, variations in the measurement of symptoms, and failure to account adequately either for health status or for other possible forms of dementia (Whitbourne & Whitbourne, 2011).

Stages of Alzheimer's Disease

By definition, the symptoms of Alzheimer's disease become progressively worse over time. Table 13.4 shows the sequence of progression from the early through late stages.

What's New in the DSM-5

Recategorization of Neurocognitive Disorders

Revisions in the *DSM*-5 resulted in major categorization changes in the former set of disorders that included delirium and dementia. The revisions divided the disorders into two broad groups consisting of major and mild neurocognitive disorders. Among the many controversial diagnoses added in *DSM*-5, that of mild neurocognitive disorder due to Alzheimer's disease was one of the most heavily criticized. Mild neurocognitive disorder involves minor cognitive changes from previous functioning that do not interfere with an individual's ability to live independently. However, they may be noticeable enough so that the individual must engage in compensatory strategies in response to these changes.

Critics of this new category argue that it applies a diagnostic label to behaviors that clinicians would not otherwise consider diagnosable. Moreover, if the deficits do not impact an individual's ability to live independently in the community, the benefits of assigning a diagnosis are not all that clear. Although eliminating the term "dementia" helps to reduce the stigma that we associate with memory deficits, the labeling as a mental disorder of what may be minor normal age-related changes negates this advantage, according to critics.

Secondly, the *DSM*-5 now allows for the diagnosis of "probable" to be applied in the absence of any abnormalities in memory and learning, but only some loss of abilities and a family history of Alzheimer's disease. The distinction between "probable" and "possible" may be a difficult one for the general public, if not professionals, to grasp. Although the *DSM*-5 authors clearly wish to indicate that probable is less serious than possible, individuals hearing the terms out of context may not discern the nuance and come to the wrong conclusion about their own, or a relative's condition.

TABLE 13.4 Stages of Alzheimer's Disease

Not Alzheimer's	Early-stage	Middle-stage	Late-stage
• Forgetting things occasionally	• Short-term memory loss, usually minor	• Short-term memory loss deepens, may begin to forget conversations completely or name of street where you live, names of loved ones or how to drive a car	• Severe cognitive impairment and short-term memory loss
• Misplacing items, like keys, eye glasses, bills, paper work	• Being unaware of the memory lapses		• Speech impairment
• Forgetting the names or titles of some things, like movies, books, people's names	• Some loss, usually minor, in ability to retain recently learned information	• Mental confusion deepens, trouble thinking logically	• May repeat conversations over and over
• Some reduction in ability to recall words when speaking	• Forgetting things and unable to dredge them up, such as the name of a good friend or even family member	• Some loss of self-awareness	• May not know names of spouse, children, or care-givers, or what day or month it is
• Being "absent-minded" or sometimes hazy on details	• Function at home normally with minimal mental confusion, but may have problems at work or in social situations	• Friends and family notice memory lapses	• Very poor reasoning ability and judgment
• "Spacing things out," such as appointments	• Symptoms may not be noticeable to all but spouse or close relatives/friends	• May become disoriented, not know where you are	• Neglect of personal hygiene
		• Impaired ability to perform even simple arithmetic	• Personality changes; may become abusive, highly anxious, agitated, delusional, or even paranoid
		• May become more aggressive or passive	• May need extensive assistance with activities of daily living
		• Difficulty sleeping	
		• Depression	

SOURCE: Consumer Reports, 2009.

FIGURE 13.2 Charting the Course of Healthy Aging, Mild Neurocognitive Disorder, and AD

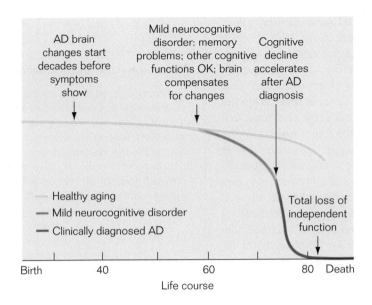

However, not all people who show early symptoms of Alzheimer's disease actually have the disease. As you can see from Figure 13.2, some individuals remain healthy until death. Some experience memory problems (referred to here as "amnestic mild neurocognitive disorder"), but are able to compensate for them and never develop Alzheimer's disease. In those individuals who develop Alzheimer's disease, however, the loss of independent function continues in a progressive manner until death. Factors related to more rapid decline in the early stages of the disease include being younger at the age of onset, having higher education, and poorer cognitive status when one first identifies the disease's symptoms (Lopez et al., 2010).

Diagnosis of Alzheimer's Disease

Because of the importance of early diagnosis to rule out treatable neurocognitive disorders, researchers and clinicians devote significant energy and attention to the development of behavioral tests for diagnosing Alzheimer's disease in its initial stages. An erroneous diagnosis would be a fatal mistake if the person had a neurocognitive disorder that would have been reversible if the clinician had applied proper treatment when the symptoms first became evident. Similarly, if the individual had a disorder with a strictly psychological basis, the clinician would have missed a crucial opportunity to intervene. Unfortunately, the early symptoms of Alzheimer's do not provide a sufficient basis for diagnosis.

Only an autopsy can make a definitive diagnosis of Alzheimer's disease by allowing pathologists to observe the characteristic changes in brain tissue, leaving clinicians with the only option of conducting diagnosis by exclusion. However, in the later stages of the disease, there are diagnostic guidelines that the clinician can apply that have 85 to 90 percent accuracy. A joint commission of the National Institute of Neurological and Communicative Disorders and Stroke and the Alzheimer's Disease and Related Diseases Association developed these guidelines in 1984. We refer to them as the NINCDS/ADRDA Guidelines (McKhann et al., 1984). The diagnosis of Alzheimer's disease, which at present is based on the NINCDS/ADRDA criteria, involves thorough medical and neuropsychological screenings. Even with these very stringent and complete guidelines, the diagnoses to which they lead is at best one of "probable" Alzheimer's disease, again reflecting the fact that only through an autopsy can clinicians obtain a certain diagnosis.

Clinicians are using brain imaging techniques increasingly for diagnosing Alzheimer's disease. The continued improvement of MRI has resulted in a virtual explosion of studies on the diagnosis of Alzheimer's disease through brain imaging. In addition to using brain imaging, clinicians are investigating the feasibility of diagnosing the disease from the amount of amyloid in spinal fluid.

In order to be diagnosed with Alzheimer's disease, individuals who show symptoms must undergo a series of neurocognitive assessments including memory tests.

Many psychologists, nevertheless, remain firm that accurate diagnosis of Alzheimer's disease must ultimately rest upon neuropsychological testing. They cite the expense, invasiveness, and lack of clear-cut connections to behavior of these biologically based diagnostic methods. Some argue that until there are effective treatments, early diagnosis does not help clients or their families, but only increases their anxiety.

In 2011, a group of researchers and clinicians convened to revise the 1984 NINCDS/ADRDA Guidelines, taking into account improved knowledge of the clinical manifestations and biological changes involved in Alzheimer's disease (McKhann et al., 2011). They also believed that it is important to acknowledge the fact that memory changes may or may not occur in individuals whose brains show signs of the disease. Their goal was to develop diagnostic criteria not dependent on the expensive and potentially invasive brain scans used in research. The group recognized that there is still no infallible way of diagnosing the disorder in a living individual, proposing that clinicians diagnose an individual as having "probable" or "possible" Alzheimer's disease. They also suggested that there be a third diagnostic category, "probable or possible," with evidence of brain pathology. This would not be a clinical diagnosis, but would be intended only for research purposes. However, the authors of *DSM-5* adopted this terminology, which is now used to indicate level of certainty of the diagnosis.

The clinical tool that clinicians most commonly use for diagnosing Alzheimer's disease is a specialized form of the mental status examination, which we call the MiniMental State Examination (MMSE) (Folstein, Folstein, & McHugh, 1975) (Table 13.5). People with Alzheimer's disease respond in certain ways to several items on this instrument. They tend to be circumstantial, repeat themselves, and lack richness of detail when describing objects, people, and events. As a screening tool, the MMSE can provide preliminary indications that an individual has neurocognitive disorder, if not Alzheimer's disease, but it is only a very rough screening tool and clinicians should not use it alone for diagnosis purposes.

Adding to the complexity of separating the causes of neurocognitive disorder in disorders other than Alzheimer's is the fact that depression can lead to symptoms that are similar to those apparent in the early stages of Alzheimer's disease. Depression may also co-exist with Alzheimer's disease, particularly during the early to middle phases, when the individual is still cognitively intact enough to be aware of the onset of the disorder and to foresee the deterioration that lies ahead. Although depressive symptoms are distinct from Alzheimer's disease, these symptoms may serve to heighten the risk of developing Alzheimer's disease, particularly among men. In a 40-year longitudinal study of

TABLE 13.5 MiniMental State Examination

Orientation to time	"What is the date?"
Registration	"Listen carefully. I am going to say three words. You say them back after I stop. Ready? Here they are . . . HOUSE (pause), CAR (pause), LAKE (pause). Now repeat those words back to me."
	[Repeat up to 5 times, but score only the first trial.]
Naming	"What is this?" (NAME A COMMON OBJECT.)
Reading	"Please read this and do what it says." [Show examinee the words on the stimulus form.] CLOSE YOUR EYES

SOURCE: Reproduced by special permission of the Publisher, Psychological Assessment Resources, Inc., 16204 North Florida Avenue, Lutz, Florida 33549, from the MiniMental State Examination, by Marshal Folstein and Susan Folstein. Copyright 1975, 1998, 2001 by MiniMental LLC. Published 2001 by Psychological Assessment Resources, Inc. Further reproduction is prohibited without special permission of PAR, Inc. The MMSE can be purchased from PAR, Inc. by calling (813) 968-3003.

pseudodementia
Literally, false dementia, a set of symptoms caused by depression that mimic those apparent in the early stages of Alzheimer's disease.

nearly 1,400 older adults, men who were depressed had twice the risk of developing Alzheimer's disease as men who were not depressed (Dal Forno et al., 2005). Interestingly, the brain autopsies of 90 of the participants who died during the course of the study did not show the characteristic brain changes that occur with Alzheimer's disease (Wilson et al., 2007). A study linking loneliness to the development of Alzheimer's disease in both men and women showed similar findings. Such findings strengthen the idea that loneliness can trigger depression, which in time may lead to brain deterioration and symptoms of neurocognitive disorder similar to those in people with diagnosable Alzheimer's disease.

In assessing neurocognitive disorder-like symptoms, clinicians must be aware of the condition **pseudodementia,** or false dementia, a severe form of depression. Distinguishing between pseudodementia and neurocognitive disorder is important because one can successfully treat depression. Several indicators can help the clinician differentiate depression from neurocognitive disorder. For example, depressed individuals are more keenly aware of their impaired cognition and frequently complain about their faulty memory. In contrast, individuals with Alzheimer's usually try to hide or minimize the extent of impairment or to explai it away when they cannot conceal the loss. As the disorder progresses, people with Alzheimer's disease lose awareness of the extent of their cognitive deficits and may even report improvement as they lose their capacity for critical self-awareness. The order of symptom development also differs between Alzheimer's disease and depression. In depressed elderly people, mood changes precede memory loss. The reverse is true for people with Alzheimer's disease. People with depression are anxious, have difficulty sleeping, show disturbed appetite patterns, and experience suicidal thoughts, low self-esteem, guilt, and lack of motivation. People with neurocognitive disorder, in contrast, experience unsociability, uncooperativeness, hostility, emotional instability, confusion, disorientation, and reduced alertness. People with pseudodementia also are likely to have a history of prior depressive episodes that may have been undiagnosed. Their memory problems and other cognitive complaints have a very abrupt onset, compared with those of people with neurocognitive disorder, who experience a slower downward course. Another clue that can help clinicians distinguish between Alzheimer's and pseudodementia is to explore the individual's recent past to determine whether a stressful event has occurred that may have precipitated the onset of depression. Sensitive tests of memory also may enable the clinician to distinguish pseudodementia from Alzheimer's disease. People with pseudodementia are likely to not respond when they are unsure of the correct answer. In contrast, individuals with Alzheimer's disease adopt a fairly liberal criterion for making responses and, as a result, give many incorrect answers. A wide range of influences may produce symptoms that are similar to those of Alzheimer's disease, as Figure 13.6 shows.

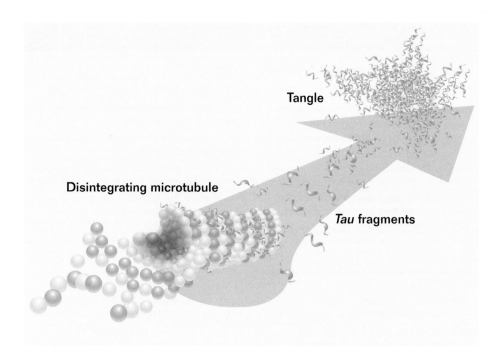

FIGURE 13.3 Neurofibrillary Tangle

Finally, as we saw earlier, Alzheimer's disease may occur along with other neurocognitive disorders, or these other disorders may occur on their own. Because these other disorders may be treatable, clinicians must attempt to rule them out before arriving at a final diagnosis of Alzheimer's disease which, as you will soon learn, is essentially untreatable.

Theories and Treatment of Alzheimer's Disease

All theories regarding the cause of Alzheimer's disease focus on biological abnormalities involving the nervous system. However, approaches to treatment incorporate other perspectives, recognizing that at present, there are no biological treatments that have more than brief effects on reducing symptom severity.

Theories The biological theories of Alzheimer's disease attempt to explain the development of two characteristic abnormalities in the brain: neurofibrillary tangles and amyloid plaques. **Neurofibrillary tangles** are made up of a protein called **tau** (Figure 13.3), that seems to play a role in maintaining microtubule stability, which forms the axon's internal support structure. The microtubules are like train tracks that guide nutrients from the cell body down to the axon's ends. The tau proteins are like the railroad ties or crosspieces of the microtubule train tracks. In Alzheimer's disease, the tau changes chemically and loses its ability to separate and support the microtubules. With their support gone, the tubules begin to wind around each other and they can no longer perform their function. This collapse of the transport system within the neuron may first result in malfunctions in communication between neurons and may eventually lead to the neuron's death. The development of neurofibrillary tangles appears to occur early in the disease process and may progress quite substantially before the individual shows any behavioral symptoms.

Amyloid plaques can develop 10 to 20 years before behavioral symptoms become noticeable and are one of the first events in the disease's pathology. Amyloid is a generic name for protein fragments that collect together in a specific way to form insoluble deposits (meaning that they do not dissolve). The amyloid form most closely linked with Alzheimer's disease consists of a string of 42 amino acids, thus we call it beta-amyloid-42. Beta amyloid forms from a larger protein that is located in the normal brain called amyloid precursor protein (APP). As APP is manufactured, it

neurofibrillary tangles
A characteristic of Alzheimer's disease in which the material within the cell bodies of neurons becomes filled with densely packed, twisted protein microfibrils, or tiny strands.

tau
A protein that normally helps maintain the internal support structure of axons.

amyloid plaques
A characteristic of Alzheimer's disease in which clusters of dead or dying neurons become mixed together with fragments of protein molecules.

Early Diagnosis of Alzheimer's Disease

As you've learned in the chapter, there are no treatments of Alzheimer's disease for anything other than its symptoms, and even these treatments only stave off decline for a matter of months. These problems raise the question of whether early diagnosis of Alzheimer's disease through potentially invasive methods such as spinal taps and brain scans are worth the expense and effort.

On the one hand, early diagnosis that rules out Alzheimer's disease is beneficial to individuals who have a treatable form of a neurocognitive disorder. By identifying one of the many other conditions that can lead to severe cognitive changes, clinicians can then diagnose surgical, medical, or other rehabilitative procedures to allow these individuals to resume their previous levels of activity and involvement with work, family, and social roles. On the other hand, because the methods of diagnosis are not 100 percent accurate, clinicians might incorrectly tell people who do not have Alzheimer's disease that their condition is untreatable.

In a related issue, genetic testing can potentially identify who is at risk of developing Alzheimer's disease. Again, there are no treatments for the disease, so if the person is asymptomatic what might be the benefits of informing the person that he or she has a genetic risk? The individual could potentially try methods of intervention that seem to have some benefits such as physical exercise, participation in mentally challenging activities, or avoidance of potentially harmful environmental toxins. However, these are behaviors that benefit mostly older individuals, not just those with a genetic marker for Alzheimer's disease.

Advocates of early diagnosis argue that this knowledge can be helpful to allow individuals to make plans with their families for the future. On the other hand, if the information were available to insurance companies, including those administered by the government, at-risk individuals may face increases in their premiums or restrictions on how they can spend their assets. For example, if you knew that you were going to develop Alzheimer's disease and therefore require expensive private care, you might divest yourself of your assets by putting money into a trust fund for your children.

These are only a few of the practical and ethical questions raised by the question of whether or not individuals should receive a diagnosis of a disease that, at best, can only be made as "probable," and at worst, has no known treatment.

Q: *You be the judge:* Under these conditions, would you want to know if you were at risk for developing Alzheimer's disease?

secretases
Enzymes that trim part of the amyloid precursor protein molecule remaining outside the neuron so that it is flush with the neuron's outer membrane.

embeds itself in the neuron's membrane. A small piece of APP lodges inside the neuron and a larger part of it remains outside. In healthy aging, enzymes called **secretases** trim the part of APP remaining outside the neuron so that it is flush with the neuron's outer membrane. In Alzheimer's disease, something goes wrong with this process so that the APP snips at the wrong place, causing beta-amyloid-42 to form. The cutoff fragments of beta-amyloid-42 eventually clump together into beta-amyloid plaques, the abnormal deposits that the body cannot dispose of or recycle (Figure 13.4).

Although researchers are testing various theories to determine the causes of Alzheimer's disease, the most probable is that an underlying defect in the genetic programming of neural activity triggers whatever changes may take place within the brain as a result of degenerative processes. The genetic theory was given impetus from the discovery that a form of the disease called early-onset familial Alzheimer's disease, which begins at the unusually young ages of 40 to 50, occurs with higher than expected prevalence in certain families. Other genes appear to be involved in a form of late-onset familial Alzheimer's disease that starts at the more expected ages of 60 to 65. Researchers postulate that these genes lead to excess amounts of beta-amyloid protein.

With the discovery of familial patterns of early-onset Alzheimer's disease along with advances in genetic engineering, researchers have identified several genes that may hold the key to understanding the cause of the disease. The apoE gene on chromosome 19 has three common forms: e2, e3, and e4. Each produces a corresponding form of apolipoprotein E (apoE) called E2, E3, and E4. The presence of the e4 allele sets up the mechanism for production of the E4 form of apoE, which researchers believe damages the microtubules within the neuron, which probably play an essential role in the cell's activity. Ordinarily, apoE2 and apoE3 protect the tau protein, which helps stabilize the microtubules. The theory is that, if the tau protein is unprotected by apoE2 and apoE3, the microtubules will degenerate, eventually leading to the neuron's destruction.

Most early-onset familial Alzheimer's disease cases occur with defects in the so-called presenilin genes (PS1 and PS2), which, as the name implies, are most likely involved in causing the brain to age prematurely. The mean age of onset in families with mutations in the PS1 gene is age 45 (ranging from 32 to 56) and age 52 for people with PS2 gene mutations (from 40 to 85). The pattern of inheritance for the presenilin genes is autosomal dominant, meaning that, if one parent carries the allele that occurs with the disease, the offspring has a 50 percent chance of developing the disorder. Researchers are attempting to determine how presenilin genes 1 and 2 interact with APP, beta amyloid, plaques, and tangles. Researchers estimate that the four genes, presenilin 1 and 2, APP, and apoE, account for approximately half the genetic risk for Alzheimer's disease (St. George-Hyslop & Petit, 2005).

While the genetic theory is compelling, we need other theories to account for the other 50 percent of people who develop the disease, but do not have genetic risk. Researchers are viewing increasingly health-related behaviors as important moderators of genetic risk (Savica & Petersen, 2011). One important behavioral risk factor is cigarette smoking, which doubles the risk of both vascular neurocognitive disorder and Alzheimer's disease. We do not know the exact mechanisms for smoking's effect on the brain, but diffuse tensor imaging documents a loss of structural integrity in the white matter of the brains of smokers (Gons et al., 2011).

Another behavioral risk factor is obesity, perhaps due to abnormalities in leptin, the obesity-regulating hormone (Doherty, 2011). People who have metabolic syndrome, a condition that places them at risk for diabetes and heart disease, also have higher rates of Alzheimer's disease. Researchers also link metabolic syndrome to depression and cerebrovascular disease (stroke) (Farooqui, Farooqui, Panza, & Frisardi, 2012). Conversely, people who eat healthy diets have a lower risk of Alzheimer's disease. The Mediterranean diet includes foods that are high in tomatoes and olive oil, with low amounts of red meat and an occasional glass of red wine. Individuals who follow this diet have a lower risk of developing Alzheimer's disease (Gu, Luchsinger, Stern, & Scarmeas, 2010).

Lack of physical exercise is increasingly gaining support as another contributor to an individual's risk of developing Alzheimer's disease by operating on the nervous and cardiovascular systems, and perhaps even by altering gene expression in people at high risk for the disease (Archer, 2011). Similarly, engaging in mentally challenging exercises can help reduce the risk of Alzheimer's disease, as well as help to reduce normal age-related changes in memory and other cognitive functions.

There are two main implications of research documenting the behavioral risk factors for Alzheimer's disease. First, people can reduce their risk of Alzheimer's disease by taking advantage of behaviors that contribute to its development. Second, these risk factors also increase the likelihood of an individual developing cerebrovascular disease, depression, and other causes of neurocognitive disorder. Consequently, this supports the contention that estimates of Alzheimer's prevalence statistics are inflated by the existence of other, preventable, neurocognitive disorders related to risk factors within the aging population. Advances in public health efforts intended to reduce obesity, diabetes, and smoking should lead to a decrease in the estimates of Alzheimer's disease, if not actual reductions in the numbers of people who truly have the disorder.

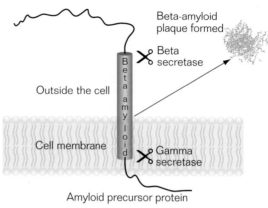

FIGURE 13.4 Development of Amyloid Plaques

Older adults who exercise regularly can prevent the onset of many age-related physical problems.

Treatment Clearly, the ultimate goal of the intense research on Alzheimer's disease is to find effective treatment, if not a prevention or cure. There is a great deal of optimism in the scientific community that this treatment, when discovered, will also benefit those with other degenerative brain diseases. As the search for the cause of Alzheimer's disease proceeds, researchers are attempting to find medications that will alleviate its symptoms.

The U.S. Food and Drug Administration-approved medications for treating mild to moderate Alzheimer's disease symptoms include galantamine (Razadyne), rivastigmine (Exelon), and donepezil (Aricept) (Table 13.6). Clinicians only rarely prescribe another medication, tacrine (Cognex), due to concerns about its safety. These medications inhibit the action of acetylcholinesterase, the enzyme that normally destroys acetylcholine after its release into the synaptic cleft. Because these slow the breakdown of acetylcholine, they allow higher levels to remain in the brain, thus facilitating memory. All have significant side effects. Memantine falls into a separate category of FDA-approved medications for treatment of Alzheimer's disease in the moderate to severe stages. An NMDA antagonist, memantine regulates glutamate, which, in excessive amounts, may destroy neurons.

The side effects that Table 13.6 shows include those that clinicians consider mild and therefore tolerable. However, the anticholinesterases can have serious side effects that include fainting, depression, anxiety, severe allergic reactions, seizures, slow or irregular heartbeat, fever, and tremor. Memantine's side effects can include hallucinations, seizures, speech changes, sudden and severe headache, aggressiveness, depression, or anxiety. When prescribing these medications, clinicians must weigh any benefits against these side effects, which themselves may interact with other medications that the individual is receiving for other health conditions, such as aspirin and nonsteroidal anti-inflammatory

TABLE 13.6 Mechanism of Action and Side Effects of Alzheimer's Medications

Drug Name	Drug Type and Use	How It Works	Side Effects
Namenda® **(memantine)**	N-methyl D-aspartate (NMDA) antagonist prescribed to treat symptoms of moderate to severe AD	Blocks the toxic effects associated with excess glutamate and regulates glutamate activation	Dizziness, headache, constipation, confusion
Razadyne® **(galantamine)**	Cholinesterase inhibitor prescribed to treat symptoms of mild to moderate AD	Prevents the breakdown of acetylcholine and stimulates nicotinic receptors to release more acetylcholine in the brain	Nausea, vomiting, diarrhea, weight loss, loss of appetite
Exelon® **(rivastigmine)**	Cholinesterase inhibitor prescribed to treat symptoms of mild to moderate AD	Prevents the breakdown of acetylcholine and butyryl-choline (a brain chemical similar to acetylcholine) in the brain	Nausea, vomiting, diarrhea, weight loss, loss of appetite, muscle weakness
Aricept® **(donepezil)**	Cholinesterase inhibitor prescribed to treat symptoms of mild to moderate, and moderate to severe AD	Prevents the breakdown of acetylcholine in the brain	Nausea, vomiting, diarrhea

drugs (NSAIDs), Tagamet (used to treat heartburn), certain antibiotics, antidepressants, and medications that improve breathing.

The benefits of the current medications to treat Alzheimer's disease symptoms are short-lived. Memantine, prescribed for moderate to severe Alzheimer's disease, shows positive effects for up to 12 weeks (Schulza et al., 2011). Although donepezil may reduce symptoms by as much as 39 to 63 percent (Lopez et al., 2010), past the first 12 weeks of treatment its benefits begin to diminish. After 3 years, individuals on any of the three anticholinesterases show poorer performance on the MMSE than they did at the beginning of treatment (Figure 13.5). Administering higher levels of anticholinesterases may slow the progression somewhat, but does not prevent deterioration in cognitive functioning over 3 years of treatment (Wattmo, Wallin, Londos, & Minthon, 2011). Donepezil may reduce the perception by caregivers of their burden and of the other symptoms shown by the patients they care for, but these effects have not been studied past 12 weeks of treatment (Carrasco, Aguera, Gil, Morinigo, & Leon, 2011). Another medication, galantamine (Razadyne), acts as an anticholinesterase and may have positive effects for up to 3 years, but also has a higher death rate associated with its use (Scarpini et al., 2011). Medications that address the deleterious changes in tau are being developed, but at present are not suitable for use in humans (Navarrete, Pérez, Morales, & Maccioni, 2011).

Other approaches to treating neurocognitive disorder due to Alzheimer's disease target the free radicals, which are molecules that form when beta amyloid breaks into fragments. Free radicals most likely damage neurons in the surrounding brain tissue. Antioxidants can disarm free radicals and, therefore, may be another treatment for Alzheimer's disease. Bioflavonoid, a substance that occurs naturally in wine, tea, fruits, and vegetables, is one such antioxidant. Researchers view naturally occurring bioflavonoids (in, for example, blueberries) as having important preventive roles in reducing the extent of memory loss in later adulthood (Joseph, Shukitt-Hale, & Casadesus, 2005). A longitudinal study of over 1,300 French people found that bioflavonoids were beneficial in reducing the risk of Alzheimer's disease (Commenges et al., 2000).

Given that no medical treatments exist to cure the disease, behavioral psychologists are developing strategies to maximize the daily functioning of people with Alzheimer's disease. They often target these efforts at the caregivers, who are the people (usually family members) primarily responsible for caring for the person with the disease. Caregivers often suffer adverse effects from the constant demands placed on them, effects

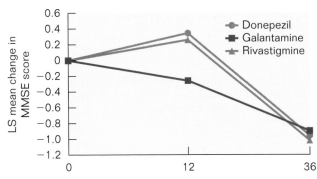

FIGURE 13.5 Comparison of Alzheimer's Medications

MINI CASE

Major Neurocognitive Disorder due to Alzheimer's Disease, Probable

Ellen is a 69-year-old woman whose husband took her to her family physician as he was becoming increasingly concerned by her failing memory and strange behavior. Ellen's husband had first become concerned a few months earlier when Ellen couldn't remember the names of basic household items, such as spoon and dishwasher. Her day-to-day forgetfulness became so problematic that she would repeatedly forget to feed or walk the dog. As the weeks went by, Ellen seemed to get worse. She would leave food burning on the stove and water overflowing the bathtub. However, Ellen had no family history of relatives diagnosed with early-onset Alzheimer's disease. Ellen's physician sought consultation from a neuropsychologist who determined that Ellen showed significant impairments in memory, learning, and language. In addition, a complete medical examination identified no other possible causes of Ellen's cognitive symptoms, and she did not meet the criteria for major depressive disorder.

REAL STORIES

Ronald Reagan: Alzheimer's Disease

"I didn't know then to what degree Alzheimer's would be a slow prelude to dying, a blurring of everything that was uniquely, essentially my father."

—Patti Reagan Davis

Born in 1911, Ronald Reagan was the oldest American president to take the oath of office, at 70 years old. He served two terms between 1981 and 1989, and is remembered as one of the most popular presidents of recent history. His political and economic policies changed the face of the nation and as president he helped, in part, to end the Cold War between the United States and the former Soviet Union. In 1994, four years after leaving office, Reagan publicly disclosed that he had been diagnosed with Alzheimer's disease. He passed away in 2004, after spending the final 3 years of his life confined to a hospital bed in his California home.

A native of Illinois, Reagan attended college in Eureka before moving to Iowa to begin his career in radio broadcasting. He soon moved to Los Angeles and launched his acting career, starring in many popular films and television shows. Following a turn as a spokesman for General Electric, Reagan became involved in politics. He served as governor of California for 10 years before he was elected president in 1980, having run unsuccessfully twice before and beating out the incumbent President Jimmy Carter.

A *New York Times* article from 1997 described Reagan's life just a few short years after coming forward with his diagnosis. At the time of the article, Reagan appeared unchanged, although he was on the verge of showing some of the more severe signs of Alzheimer's. The article stated, "If, at the age of 86, the old movie actor still looks the image of vigorous good health, the truth is that the man behind the firm handshake and barely gray hair is steadily, surely ebbing away." Although the signs were becoming clear, Reagan was still able to perform activities of daily living such as dressing himself and he continued to partake in his regular routine, which involved playing golf, exercising, and making occasional public appearances. Despite his healthy exterior and extensive support network, at this point Reagan's condition began to deteriorate.

During his presidency, Ronald Reagan notoriously struggled with his memory, particularly when it came to remembering people's names. By 1997, this difficulty was much more pronounced and the only person he was able to remember on a consistent basis was his wife, Nancy. Following the revelation of his diagnosis, there was much controversy as to whether or not he had symptoms of Alzheimer's disease during his presidency. The *New York Times* article cites Reagan's doctor who confirmed that he did not actually start showing any symptoms until at least 3 years following the end of his final term.

"Alzheimer's is often said to involve a family of victims," the article states. "As it inexorably shuts off communication, the disease breeds loneliness, frustration and confusion not just for the patient, but for the spouse, relatives and friends. Many longtime friends and aides say they find it too painful to compare the Ronald Reagan afflicted with Alzheimer's with his former self."

In 2001, 4 years after the article appeared, Reagan suffered a fall in his home and broke his hip. Although his hip was repaired, he became homebound as his condition had greatly deteriorated. In her book, *The Long Goodbye*, Reagan's daughter Patti Davis recalls that doctors had given him just months to live. In the end, he lived another 4 years. Her book poignantly depicts the heartache and struggle that haunts not only the patients, but the families of those dying from Alzheimer's disease. Patti highlights that the most painful aspect of the process of watching a loved one suffer from Alzheimer's is the length of the process of physical and mental deterioration and the psychological effect this has on the family.

"I am a daughter who lived her life missing her father." Patti describes her father as a man who had little time to be involved in the lives of his children as he spent 8 years of his life as leader of a powerful nation. The turmoil of watching their father's long and slow death was made all the more excruciating due to Reagan's guarded personal disposition. As Patti describes in the book, "Even my mother has admitted there was a part of him—a core—that she could never touch."

The book started as a collection of diary entries that Patti had written about her experiences watching her father succumb to his disease. The second youngest of Reagan's five children, Patti was often at odds with her father's social and political views. In the book she writes about how

Ronald Reagan began to show pronounced signs of Alzheimer's disease just a few short years after completing two consecutive terms as President of the United States.

their relationship changed as the years went on and as she stuck by his side throughout the progression of his illness. Not only did her father's relationship with her change with the course of his disease, but the entire family dynamic shifted as the differences between them drifted away in light of their desire to be together through this difficult time. This is not uncommon as families come together to cope with the slow loss of a loved one to Alzheimer's.

"Alzheimer's disease locks all the doors and exits. There is no reprieve, no escape. Time becomes the enemy, and it seemed to stretch out in front of us like miles of fallow land." Patti goes on to describe the insidious nature of the disease and its slow progression throughout the years as she witnessed in her father. Alongside observations of her father as he grew older and as Alzheimer's increasingly took its toll, Patti recalls the memories of him throughout her life—giving a speech on her wedding day, swimming with her in the ocean, singing together in church. These memories were important in helping the family cope with the pain of slowly losing their father. "You breathe life into your

own memories because right there, in front of you, sitting in the chair he always goes to, or walking down the hall, or gazing out the window, is a reminder of the hollowness that's left when memories are erased. So you welcome it when images come back, or bits of conversations. You seize them, dust them off, and pray they'll stay as bright."

In her book, Patti describes the process that her mother endured as she slowly lost her husband of over 40 years. "My mother speaks of the loneliness of her life now. He's here, but in so many ways he's not. She feels the loneliness in small ways—he used to put lotion on her back; now he doesn't. And in the huge, overwhelming ways—a future that will be spent missing him."

Patti also addresses the issue of Nancy Reagan's decision to keep the details of her husband's suffering private from the watchful eye of the media. "My mother has called it a long goodbye—the way Alzheimer's slowly steals a person away. It's been one of her only public comments; upon agreement, we have chosen the cloak of respectful silence when it comes to the subject of my father's condition. It's a heartbreaking

phrase, and she's told me she won't say it again because it ushers in tears." Even on the day that her father passed away on June 5, 2004, Patti recalls a reporter hovering around the home, as rumors that he was nearing the end of his life had surfaced to the public. As the family gathered around Reagan's bed during his final moments of life, Patti remembers hearing news reports in the next room that his condition was grave and how more reporters began calling and coming to the house. In the end, the family was prepared for their father to pass away, although this did not erase the pain that they shared when his battle with Alzheimer's finally ended.

"There will be times," Patti writes of their reaction to his death, "when we are lifted up on the back of memories, and other times when sorrow drives us to our knees. Especially my mother, who will have moments of wondering why he had to leave first. We will wait for him to enter our dreams. We will look for him in every breeze that drifts through every open window. We will breathe deep and wait for his whisper to stream into us—tell us secrets and make us smile."

that we call caregiver burden (Table 13.7). However, we can teach caregivers behavioral strategies that can promote the patient's independence and reduce his or her distressing behaviors. Support groups can also provide a forum in which caregivers learn ways to manage the emotional stress that occurs with their role.

Behavioral strategies aimed at increasing the patient's independence include giving prompts, cues, and guidance in the steps involved in self-maintenance. For example, the clinician can encourage the patient to relearn the steps involved in getting dressed and then positively reward him or her with praise and attention for having completed those steps. Through modeling, the patient relearns previous skills through imitation. We can also teach the caregiver time management, which involves following a strict daily schedule. As a result, the patient is more likely to fall into a regular routine of everyday activities. All of these methods benefit both the patient and the caregiver. The patient regains some measure of independence, which reduces the caregiver's burden to the extent that the patient can engage in self-care tasks (see Table 13.7).

Behavioral strategies can also eliminate, or at least reduce the frequency of, wandering and aggression in an Alzheimer's patient. One possible approach, which is not always practical, involves extinction. The caregiver ignores certain disruptive behaviors, with the intention of eliminating the reinforcement that has helped maintain them. However, extinction is not practical for behaviors that may lead to harm to the patient, such as wandering if it involves leaving the house and walking into the street. One possibility is to give the patient positive reinforcement for staying within certain boundaries. However, this may not be sufficient, and, at that point, the caregiver needs to install protective

Table 13.7 **APA Caregivers Briefcase**

In 2011, the American Psychological Association launched the Caregivers Initiative under the leadership of then-president Carol Goodheart. The Caregivers Briefcase summarizes resources, facts, and tips for caregivers: http://www.apa.org/pi/about/publications/caregivers/index.aspx.

This summary of five tips suggests helpful strategies for family caregivers, whether parents are caring for children, partners for partners, or children for parents:

1. **Recognize how widespread caregiving situations are.** Although everyone's situation is unique, you're not alone in experiencing burden.

2. **Take advantage of support services.** Sharing your experiences with others can give you both practical and emotional help.

3. **Focus on positive coping strategies.** Adapt the self-statements and coping strategies mentioned above until you find the ones that work for you.

4. **Take care of your own needs.** You need to focus on your health, both mental and physical, if you're going to be an effective caregiver. You'll also feel better.

5. **Ask for help when you need it.** You don't have to be a martyr. Reaching out to others will alleviate your stress. You may be surprised at the willingness of others to offer you assistance.

SOURCE: Whitbourne, S. K. (March, 2011). Family caregiving across the generations. *Psychology Today,* http://www.psychologytoday.com/blog/fulfillment-any-age/201103/family-caregiving-across-the-generations.

barriers. Another possible approach is for the caregiver to identify situations that are particularly problematic for the patient, such as in the bathtub or at the table. The caretaker can then use behavioral methods in these circumstances. For example, if the problem occurs while eating, it may be that the caretaker can encourage the patient to relearn how to use a knife and fork, rather than feeding him or her. Again, such an intervention can reduce caregiver burden, as well as increase the patient's functional skills (Callahan et al., 2006).

The caregiver can implement behavioral interventions through individual therapy or in a support group. The support group facilitator can teach these methods to participants. Furthermore, caregivers can share strategies among themselves based on their experiences. The emotional support that caregivers can provide for each other can be just as valuable as the actual instruction that they receive. Ultimately, the Alzheimer's patient receives better quality care when caregiver burden is minimized.

You can see, then, that although the prospect of Alzheimer's is frightening and painful for all individuals involved, a number of interventions are available. However, until researchers find a cure for the disorder, clinicians must be content to measure their gains less as progress toward a cure and more as success in prolonging the period of maximum functioning for the individual and the individual's family.

13.4 Neurocognitive Disorders due to Neurological Disorders Other than Alzheimer's Disease

The symptoms of neurocognitive disorder can have a number of causes that include degenerative neurological conditions other than Alzheimer's disease. Each of these disorders has a separate diagnosis associated with it. Figure 13.6 shows the overlap among symptoms of these neurological disorders. Rather than involving a decline in memory, as we see in Alzheimer's disease, **frontotemporal neurocognitive disorder** is reflected in personality changes, such as apathy, lack of inhibition, obsessiveness, and loss of judgment. Eventually, the individual becomes neglectful of personal habits and loses the ability to communicate. The onset of the disorder is slow and insidious. On autopsy, the brain shows atrophy in the frontal and temporal cortex, but there are no amyloid plaques or arterial damage.

frontotemporal neurocognitive disorder Neurocognitive disorder that involves the frontotemporal area of the brain.

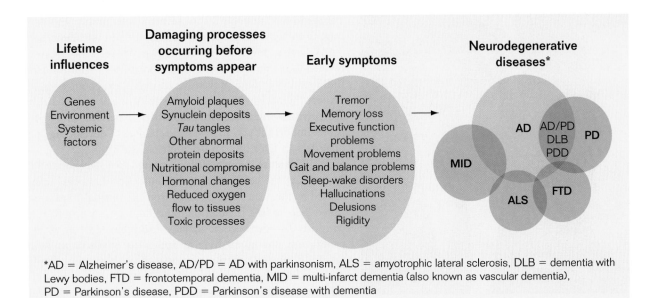

*AD = Alzheimer's disease, AD/PD = AD with parkinsonism, ALS = amyotrophic lateral sclerosis, DLB = dementia with Lewy bodies, FTD = frontotemporal dementia, MID = multi-infarct dementia (also known as vascular dementia), PD = Parkinson's disease, PDD = Parkinson's disease with dementia

As shown here, a variety of lifetime influences and damaging processes ranging from nutritional influences to toxins can lead to symptoms that appear to mimic Alzheimer's disease. These disorders may occur along with Alzheimer's disease (shown in the overlapping circles) or may occur entirely independently of Alzheimer's.

FIGURE 13.6 Other Diseases That Can Cause Deterioration in Cognitive Function

SOURCE: National Institute of Aging (2005). Progress report on Alzheimer's disease 2004–2005: U.S. Department of Health and Human Services.

Neurocognitive disorder with Lewy bodies, which researchers first identified in 1961, is very similar to Alzheimer's disease, with progressive loss of memory, language, calculation, and reasoning, as well as other higher mental functions. However, the progress of the illness may be more rapid than what we see in Alzheimer's disease. Lewy bodies are tiny, spherical structures consisting of protein deposits in dying nerve cells found in damaged regions deep within the brains of people with Parkinson's disease. A clinician diagnoses this condition when Lewy bodies are more diffusely dispersed throughout the brain. It is not clear whether the condition called neurocognitive disorder with Lewy bodies is a distinct illness or a variant of Alzheimer's or Parkinson's disease (Serby & Samuels, 2001), although some claim that this is the second most common form of neurocognitive disorder (McKeith et al., 2004). Based on neurological evidence, researchers are beginning to differentiate neurocognitive disorder with Lewy bodies from Alzheimer's disease. In one study, using both PET scan and autopsies, investigators found that deficits in the visual cortex were specific to the brains of people with neurocognitive disorder due to Lewy bodies (Gilman et al., 2005).

Another possible cause of neurocognitive disorder is cardiovascular disease affecting the supply of blood to the brain. This condition, called **vascular neurocognitive disorder** is highly prevalent and researchers link it to a variety of cardiovascular risk factors. The most common form is referred to as **multi-infarct dementia (MID),** caused by transient attacks in which blood flow to the brain is interrupted by a clogged or burst artery. The damage to the artery deprives the surrounding neurons of blood and oxygen, which causes the neurons to die. Although each infarct is too small to be noticed at first, over time the progressive damage caused by the infarcts leads the individual to lose cognitive abilities. Their memory impairment appears to be similar to that involved in Alzheimer's disease. However, there are some significant differences between these two forms of disorders. People with vascular neurocognitive disorder show a particular set of physical abnormalities, such as walking difficulties and weakness in the arms and legs. Furthermore, people with vascular show a pattern of cognitive functioning that is distinctly different from that in people with Alzheimer's.

In the typical clinical picture of vascular neurocognitive disorder, certain cognitive functions remain intact and others show significant loss, a pattern that neuropsychologists call patchy deterioration. Another unique feature of vascular neurocognitive disorder is that it shows a stepwise deterioration in cognitive functioning: a function that was relatively

neurocognitive disorder due to Lewy bodies
A form of neurocognitive disorder with progressive loss of memory, language, calculation, and reasoning, as well as other higher mental functions resulting from the accumulation of abnormalities called Lewy bodies throughout the brain.

vascular neurocognitive disorder
A form of neurocognitive disorder resulting from a vascular disease that causes deprivation of the blood supply to the brain.

multi-infarct dementia (MID)
A form of neurocognitive disorder caused by transient attacks in which blood flow to the brain is interrupted by a clogged or burst artery.

As one of the most notable individuals known to suffer from neuro-cognitive disorder due to Parkinson's disease, Michael J. Fox has brought public attention to the reality of this disabling condition.

Pick's disease
A relatively rare degenerative disease that affects the frontal and temporal lobes of the cerebral cortex and that can cause neurocognitive disorders.

neurocognitive disorder due to Parkinson's disease
A neurocognitive disorder that involves degeneration of neurons in the subcortical structures that control motor movements.

akinesia
A motor disturbance in which a person's muscles become rigid and movement is difficult to initiate.

bradykinesia
A motor disturbance involving a general slowing of motor activity.

neurocognitive disorder due to Huntington's disease
A hereditary condition causing neurocognitive disorder that involves a widespread deterioration of the subcortical brain structures and parts of the frontal cortex that control motor movements.

unimpaired is suddenly lost or severely deteriorates. This is in contrast to the gradual pattern of deterioration in Alzheimer's disease.

As is true for Alzheimer's disease, there is no treatment to reverse the cognitive losses in neurocognitive disorder. However, individuals can take preventive actions throughout adulthood to protect themselves from the subsequent onset of vascular neuro-cognitive disorder. Reducing the risk of hypertension and diabetes is one important way to lower the chances of developing cognitive disorders in later life (Papademetriou, 2005).

Pick's disease is a relatively rare progressive degenerative disease that affects the cerebral cortex's frontal and temporal lobes. It is caused by the accumulation in neurons of unusual protein deposits called Pick bodies. In addition to having memory problems, people with this disorder become socially disinhibited, acting either inappropriately and impulsively or appearing apathetic and unmotivated. In contrast to the sequence of changes that people with Alzheimer's disease show, people with Pick's disease undergo personality alterations before they begin to have memory problems. For example, they may experience deterioration in social skills, language abnormalities, flat emotionality, and a loss of inhibition.

Neurocognitive disorder due to Parkinson's disease involves neuronal degeneration of the basal ganglia, the subcortical structures that control motor movements. Deterioration of diffuse areas of the cerebral cortex may occur. Cognitive changes do not occur in all people with Parkinson's disease, but researchers estimate rates as high as 60 percent, mostly involving those who are older and at a more advanced stage of the disease. Parkinson's disease is usually progressive, with various motor disturbances the most striking feature of the disorder. At rest, the person's hands, ankles, or head may shake involuntarily. The person's muscles become rigid, and it is difficult for him or her to initiate movement, a symptom called **akinesia.** A general slowing of motor activity, known as **bradykinesia,** also occurs, as does a loss of fine motor coordination. For example, some people with Parkinson's disease walk with a slowed, shuffling gait. They have difficulty starting to walk and, once they start, they have difficulty stopping. In addition to these motor abnormalities, they show signs of cognitive deterioration, such as slowed scanning on visual recognition tasks, diminished conceptual flexibility, and slowing on motor response tests. The individual's face also appears expressionless and speech becomes stilted, losing its normal rhythmic quality. They have difficulty producing words on tests that demand verbal fluency. However, many cognitive functions, such as attention, concentration, and immediate memory, remain intact.

Although primarily a disease involving loss of motor control, **neurocognitive disorder due to Huntington's disease** is a degenerative neurological disorder that can also affect personality and cognitive functioning. Researchers have traced Huntington's disease to an abnormality on chromosome 4 that causes a protein, now known as huntingtin, to accumulate and reach toxic levels. The symptoms first appear during adulthood, between ages 30 and 50. The disease involves the death of neurons in subcortical structures that control motor behavior.

A number of disturbances occur with Huntington's disease, ranging from altered cognitive functioning to social and personality changes. We associate the disease with mood disturbances, changes in personality, irritability and explosiveness, suicidality, changes in sexuality, and a range of specific cognitive deficits. Because of these symptoms, clinicians may incorrectly diagnose the disorder as schizophrenia or a mood disorder, even if the individual has no history suggestive of these disorders. People with Huntington's disease can also appear apathetic because of their decreased ability to plan, initiate, or carry out complex activities. Their uncontrolled motor movement interferes with sustained performance of any behavior, even maintaining an upright posture, and eventually most people with Huntington's disease become bedridden.

Neurocognitive disorder due to prion disease, also known as **Creutzfeldt-Jakob disease,** is a rare neurological disorder known as a **prion disease,** which researchers believe is caused by an infectious agent and that results in abnormal protein accumulations in the brain. Initial symptoms include fatigue, appetite disturbance, sleep problems, and concentration difficulties. As the disease progresses, the individual shows increasing signs of neurocognitive loss and eventually dies. Underlying these symptoms is widespread damage known as spongiform encephalopathy, meaning that large holes develop in brain tissue. The disease appears to be transmitted to humans from cattle that have eaten the body parts of dead farm animals infected with the disease (particularly sheep, in which the disease is known as scrapie). In 1996, an epidemic in England of "mad cow disease," along with reported cases of the disease in humans, led to a ban on importation of British beef. Concerns about this disease continue to exist in European countries, as well as in the United States.

neurocognitive disorder due to prion disease (also known as Creutzfeld-Jakob disease)
A neurological disease transmitted from animals to humans that leads to dementia and death resulting from abnormal protein accumulations in the brain.

prion disease
A disease caused by an abnormal protein particle that infects brain tissue.

13.5 Neurocognitive Disorder due to Traumatic Brain Injury

Trauma to the head that results in an alteration or loss of consciousness, or post-traumatic amnesia is called **traumatic brain injury,** or **TBI.** The diagnostic criteria for **neurocognitive disorder due to traumatic brain injury** require evidence of impact to the head along with loss of consciousness, amnesia following the trauma, disorientation and confusion, and neurological abnormalities such as seizures. The symptoms must occur immediately after the trauma or after recovering consciousness, and past the acute post-injury period.

According to the Centers for Disease Control and Prevention (2011), an estimated 1.7 million people a year in the United States experience TBI (See Figure 13.7). Children aged 0 to 4 years, adolescents aged 15 to 19 years, and adults 65 years and older have the greatest risk of TBI. The highest rates of hospitalization and death due to TBI occur in adults 75 years of age and older. People within these age groups sustain accidental TBIs for different reasons. Children and adolescents are most likely to receive TBIs through falls, sports injuries, and accidents. In older adults, falls are the most common cause of TBIs.

As many as 12 to 20 percent of the veterans of the Iraq and Afghanistan wars may have experienced TBIs resulting from injuries from improvised explosive devices (IEDs). Most of these cases are relatively mild in severity, meaning that they involved loss of consciousness for 30 minutes or less, or post-traumatic amnesia of 24 hours or less. Most of these TBI victims recover within 6 months of their injury, but a subgroup of veterans do not. Another group may have undetectable symptoms until after their deployment. Not only does TBI carry with it significant health risks, but veterans who experienced TBIs are at higher risk of developing PTSD, anxiety, and adjustment disorders (Carlson et al., 2010). Unlike previous combat veterans, those who fought in the Iraq and Afghanistan wars were more likely to have head injuries because their modern helmets offered better protection than those worn by soldiers in previous wars. Thus, they survived the blast only to develop head (and other) serious injuries.

traumatic brain injury (TBI)
Damage to the brain caused by exposure to trauma.

neurocognitive disorder due to traumatic brain injury
A disorder in which there is evidence of impact to the head along with cognitive and neurological symptoms that persist past the acute post-injury period.

post-concussion syndrome (PCS)
A disorder in which a constellation of physical, emotional, and cognitive symptoms persists from weeks to years.

People undergoing mild TBI may experience a related condition known as **post-concussion syndrome (PCS)** in which they continue to have symptoms such as fatigue, dizziness, poor concentration, memory problems, headache, insomnia, and irritability. Individuals most at risk of developing PCS are those who had an anxiety or depressive disorder prior to their injury and acute post-traumatic stress for approximately 5 days after their injury. However, PCS may also develop in traumatized individuals with these characteristics who do not actually suffer a mild TBI (Meares et al., 2011).

Professional athletes may also suffer mild TBIs, particularly those who play contact sports such as football and hockey. Their injuries may not be properly assessed when they occur, leading them to return to play before they are fully ready to do so. Although they may appear to have recovered enough to go

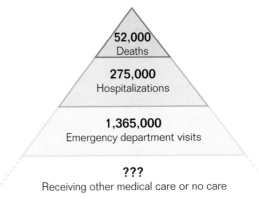

FIGURE 13.7 Prevalence Estimates and Associated Risks of Traumatic Brain Injury

back onto the field, they may nevertheless suffer mental impairments that are only evident later. In one study of male and female college athletes involved in high-contact sports, researchers found memory impairments even in those players who did not appear to have suffered a concussion (Killam, Cautin, & Santucci, 2005). However, unlike trauma victims, athletes are more likely to return to pre-injury functioning within 2 days to 2 weeks (Iverson, 2005).

13.6 Neurocognitive Disorders due to Substances/Medications and HIV Infection

A wide range of infectious diseases can cause the changes that occur with neurocognitive disorder. These include neurosyphilis, encephalitis, tuberculosis, meningitis, and localized infections in the brain. People who experience kidney failure may have symptoms of neurocognitive disorder as a result of the toxic accumulation of substances that the kidneys cannot cleanse from the blood. People with certain kinds of brain tumors also experience cognitive impairments and other symptoms of neurocognitive disorder.

The individual's cognitive functioning can also be negatively affected by anoxia (oxygen deprivation to the brain), which may occur during surgery under general anesthesia or may result from carbon monoxide poisoning. Anoxia can have severe effects on many brain functions because neurons quickly die if they are deprived of oxygen. Because brain neurons do not replace themselves, significant neuron loss can lead to impairments in concrete thinking and functions such as new learning ability, attention, concentration, and tracking. The emotional effects of brain damage due to anoxia can include affective dulling and disinhibition, as well as depression. This can drastically reduce the person's ability to plan, initiate, and carry out activities.

Exposure to certain drugs and environmental toxins can cause brain damage and result in a condition called substance/medication induced neurocognitive disorder. These toxins include intense fumes from house paint, styrene used in plastics manufacturing, and fuels distilled from petroleum.

Nutritional deficiencies can also cause cognitive decline. People who are severely undernourished are prone to develop a deficiency of folate, a critical nutrient, leading to progressive cerebral atrophy. If the deficiency is not corrected by dietary improvements, the individual can become depressed and show various cognitive impairments, such as poor memory and impaired abstract reasoning.

The cognitive losses that occur with physical disorders and toxic reactions may be reversible if the person receives prompt and appropriate medical treatment. However, if the person fails to receive intervention for a treatable dementia in the early stages, the brain damage becomes irreversible. The more widespread the structural damage to the brain, the lower the chances that the person will ever regain lost functions.

Prior to the introduction of antiretroviral therapies for AIDS, dementia in the late stages of the disease was a common and devastating complication (Gisslen et al., 2007). With improvements in treatment, this condition, known as AIDS dementia complex, has become less prevalent. However, cases continue to arise among people who go undiagnosed and untreated, a situation that is particularly true in developing countries (Wu, Zhao, Tang, Zhang-Nunes, & McArthur, 2007).

13.7 Neurocognitive Disorders due to Another General Medical Condition

amnesia
Inability to recall information that was previously learned or to register new memories.

major neurocognitive disorder due to another medical condition
Cognitive disorders involving the inability to recall previously learned information or to register new memories.

Amnesia is the inability to recall information that was previously learned or to register new memories. In *DSM-5*, people with amnesia receive a diagnosis of **major neurocognitive disorder due to another general medical condition.** People with major neurocognitive

MINI CASE

Major Neurocognitive Disorder due to Another General Medical Condition

Harvey is a 57-year-old bookstore owner living in a small town. While bicycling to work one day, he was struck by a car and was rushed to the emergency room. In addition to receiving a broken leg, Harvey suffered a head injury and was unable to remember anything that had happened during the preceding 2 weeks. Furthermore, he had no idea how old he was, where he was born, or whether he was married. This inability to remember his personal past was a source of great distress to Harvey. In contrast, Harvey had no trouble remembering the ambulance ride to the hospital or the name of the emergency room physician who first examined him. Following a 3-day hospital stay, Harvey was transferred to a rehabilitation facility for 3 months, where memory therapy helped him learn mnemonic strategies for recalling important information.

disorder due to a general medical condition are unable to recall previously learned information or to register new memories. In previous editions of the *DSM,* the term "amnesia" was used to refer to this type of memory loss. In *DSM-5,* this form of neurocognitive disorder is indicated as being caused by a general medical condition. They can result from a wide variety of medical problems, including head trauma, loss of oxygen, or herpes simplex. When drugs or medications cause serious memory impairment, we refer to the condition as substance-induced persisting amnestic disorder. An array of substances may cause this condition, including medications, illicit drugs, or environmental toxins such as lead, mercury, insecticides, and industrial solvents. The most common cause of this form of neurocognitive disorder is chronic alcohol use. The memory loss must persist over time for the clinician to assign the diagnosis of neurocognitive disorder due to another general medical condition. For some people, especially chronic abusers of alcohol, the neurocognitive disorder due to another general medical condition persists for life, causing such severe impairment that the individual may require custodial care. For others, such as those whose condition results from medications, full recovery is possible.

13.8 Neurocognitive Disorders: The Biopsychosocial Perspective

We can best understand the cognitive impairments that occur with the disorders that we discussed in this chapter, by definition, from a biological perspective. However, the biological perspective has not yet produced a viable treatment for one of the most devastating of these disorders, Alzheimer's disease. Until researchers find a cure, individuals and their families whose lives are touched by the disease must be willing to try a variety of approaches to alleviate the suffering. Many research programs are currently underway to explore strategies for reducing the stress placed on caregivers. Some of these strategies involve innovative, high-technology methods, such as computer networks. Others take the more traditional approach of providing emotional support to individuals with Alzheimer's disease and their families. The application of cognitive-behavioral and other methods of therapy to help people cope with Alzheimer's is another useful approach. It seems that the bottom line in all this research on understanding and treating those affected by Alzheimer's disease is that it is not necessary for psychologists to wait until biomedical researchers discover a cure. They can do quite a bit to improve the quality of life for people with Alzheimer's and to help them maintain their functioning and their dignity as long as possible.

Irene's MRI showed multiple vascular legions on her cerebral cortex and the subcortical structures of her brain, confirming her diagnosis of neurocognitive disorder due to vascular disease. The qualifier of "with behavioral disturbance" was added to her diagnosis due to her history of wandering spells that had occurred with the onset of her symptoms.

Following her diagnosis, Irene was immediately started on medication, and after a few weeks she and her family began noticing that she had returned to her "premorbid" (previous) level of functioning. Upon a recommendation made by the neuropsychologist she saw for testing, Irene began to attend a support group for those who have been diagnosed with neurocognitive disorder due to vascular disease offered in a community center in her town. Irene avidly attends every week and has reported benefiting due to the social support aspect of the group as well as learning more about the disease and how it affects each person differently. The support group has also educated Irene to be mindful of any changes in her cognition or motor movements, and to seek consultation immediately with her physician should any new difficulties arise. Due to her improved memory, Irene's health remained stable as she

was remembering to take her insulin as prescribed. Irene enjoyed taking part in her regular activities again and spending time with her family, no longer burdened by motor difficulties. Irene will undergo a brief battery of neuropsychological testing every 6 months to monitor for any further deterioration in her cognition and to assess efficacy of her treatment regimen.

Dr. Tobin's reflections: Neurocognitive disorder due to vascular disease can result from a stroke. Due to the patchy and irregular deterioration of Irene's symptoms it is more likely that her symptoms resulted from a more gradual process of cerebrovascular disease. In many cases, adults live for some time with mild symptoms of neurocognitive disorder. Irene was fortunate to have attentive children who noticed her symptoms relatively soon after they arose and she was able to seek treatment that I hope will slow the development of this disorder. She was also fortunate that her diagnosis was based on careful consideration of multiple sources of testing, as many older adults with neurocognitive disorder due to vascular disease are incorrectly diagnosed with Alzheimer's disease, which is irreversible and requires a different course of treatment and case planning.

SUMMARY

- **Neurocognitive disorders** (formally called "delirium, dementia, amnestic, and other cognitive disorders") are those in which the central characteristic is cognitive impairment that results from causes such as brain trauma, disease, or exposure to toxic substances.

- **Delirium** is a temporary state in which individuals experience a clouding of consciousness in which they are unaware of what is happening and are unable to focus or pay attention. They experience cognitive changes in which their memory is foggy and they are disoriented, and they may have various other symptoms, such as rambling speech, delusions, hallucinations, and emotional disturbances. Delirium, which is caused by a change in the brain's metabolism, can result from various factors, including substance intoxication or withdrawal, head injury, high fever, and vitamin deficiency. The onset is generally rapid and the duration brief.

- The best-known neurocognitive disorder is **neurocognitive disorder due to Alzheimer's disease.** Symptoms are characterized by progressive cognitive impairment involving a person's memory, communication abilities,

judgment skills, motor coordination, and ability to learn new information. In addition to experiencing cognitive changes, individuals with this condition undergo changes in their personality and emotional state. Clinicians specify Alzheimer's disease according to subtypes: with delirium, with delusions, with depressed mood, or uncomplicated. It is challenging to make this diagnosis due to the fact that some conditions, such as **vascular neurocognitive disorder** and major depressive disorder, mimic the symptoms of Alzheimer's disease.

- **Major neurocognitive disorder due to another medical condition** is a disorder in which people are unable to recall previously learned information or to register new memories, a condition referred to as **amnesia** in *DSM-IV-TR*. This disorder is due either to the use of substances or to medical conditions such as head trauma, loss of oxygen, and herpes simplex.

- Researchers are increasingly recognizing **traumatic brain injury (TBI)** as an important cause of mental and physical dysfunction. Symptoms include headaches, sleep disturbances, sensitivity to light and noise, and diminished cognitive performance on tests of attention, memory, language, and reaction time. These individuals may also suffer depression, anxiety, emotional outbursts, mood changes, or inappropriate affect.

- The biological perspective is predominant among theories regarding the cause of Alzheimer's. Current research focuses on abnormalities in the nervous system—specifically, two types of structure changes in the brain. The first is the formation of **neurofibrillary tangles,** in which the cellular material within the cell bodies of neurons becomes replaced by densely packed, twisted microfibrils, or tiny strands, of protein. The second change involves the development of **amyloid plaques,** which are clusters of dead or dying neurons mixed with fragments of protein molecules. Although there is no cure for this disease, medications, such as anticholinesterase agents can slow the progress of cognitive decline. In the absence of a biological cure, psychological perspectives have led to the use of psychopharmacological medication to alleviate secondary symptoms, such as depression. Researchers are exploring social contributors, such as the role of certain behaviors in preventing the development of the disease. Additionally, experts are refining behavioral techniques for managing symptoms and developing strategies for alleviating caregiver burden.

KEY TERMS

Akinesia   342

Amnesia   344

Amyloid plaques   333

Bradykinesia   342

Delirium   324

Frontotemporal neurocognitive
disorder   340

Major neurocognitive disorders   323

Major neurocognitive disorder due to
another medical condition   344

Mild neurocognitive disorders   323

Multi-infarct dementia (MID)   341

Neurocognitive disorder   322

Neurocognitive disorder due to
Alzheimer's disease   328

Neurocognitive disorder
due to Huntington's disease   342

Neurocognitive disorder due to Lewy
bodies   341

Neurocognitive disorder due to
Parkinson's disease   342

Neurocognitive disorder due to prion
disease (also known as Creutzfeld-
Jakob disease)   343

Neurocognitive disorder due to
traumatic brain injury   343

Neurofibrillary tangles   333

Pick's disease   342

Post-concussion
syndrome (PCS)   343

Prion disease   343

Pseudodementia   332

Secretases   334

Tau   333

Traumatic brain injury (TBI)   343

Vascular neurocognitive
disorder   341

Personality Disorders

Learning Objectives

14.1 Understand the nature of personality disorders and the alternative diagnostic system in the *DSM*-5

14.2 Identify the characteristics, theories, and treatments of Cluster A personality disorders

14.3 Identify the characteristics, theories, and treatments of Cluster B personality disorders

14.4 Identify the characteristics, theories, and treatments of Cluster C personality disorders

14.5 Analyze the biopsychosocial perspective on personality disorders

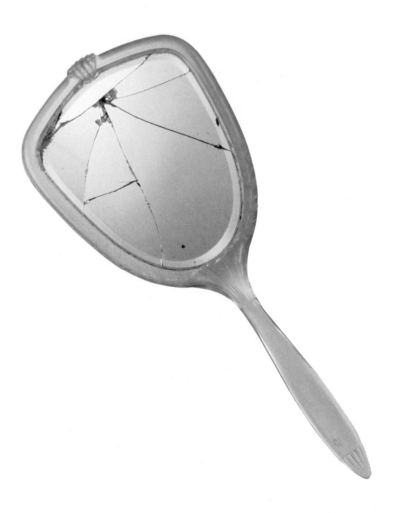

CHAPTER 14

Case Report: Harold Morrill

Demographic information: Harold is a 21-year-old Caucasian male.

Presenting problem: Harold presented for an emergency intake evaluation at his university's counseling center due to self-reported suicidal ideation. He reported to the intake counselor that he had a strong, pervasive desire to kill himself. He presented as angry and emotionally distraught, and he grew easily frustrated with the counselor several times throughout the interview. Harold reported that this was not the first time he had wanted to kill himself, and without being prompted showed the counselor a large, vertical scar down his left forearm indicating a previous suicide attempt. He stated that he was 17 at the time he slit his wrist, and that he had been under the influence of alcohol and cocaine at the time. He remarked that he barely remembered the incident. Following this suicide attempt, Harold had been admitted to an inpatient psychiatric unit and was stabilized on medication, though he discontinued his medication on his own once he was discharged, against the recommendations of his doctors.

Harold became highly agitated when asked questions about his past during the evaluation, at one point yelling at the counselor and threatening to storm out of the room. Once the counselor was able to calm him down, he tearfully stated, "I'm just so sick of feeling this way," and agreed to continue with the evaluation. This was in contrast to his initial presentation as pleasant and polite, even as he described his thoughts about ending his life.

Harold reported having few close interpersonal relationships. He stated that he didn't have any close friends at school and had switched dormitories four times during his freshman year alone. He was vague in describing the reasoning behind this,

remarking only that "all my roommates have been total jerks." Harold went on to discuss his various romantic relationships during the past four years, when he began dating. He stated that each relationship lasted a few weeks, the longest lasting for two months. When describing the relationships, he reported that they usually ended due to "blow out" arguments. When asked about the nature of the arguments, he stated in each case he had accused the woman of infidelity and would immediately end the relationship. Harold elaborated that he felt "no one could ever make me happy. I don't know why I even try. Nothing that I ever do makes me feel better, so I keep trying new things and looking for new people. But none of it works." He related this to his recurrent thoughts of suicide and past suicide attempts. When asked about his family, Harold reported that he was "disgusted" with them and how they treated him as a child (see Relevant history, next page).

Harold reported that he frequently abuses alcohol—as many as seven days per week—and that he typically drinks to the point of blacking out. He described that he mostly enjoys going to bars and did so with a "fake ID" before he turned 21. He explained that he enjoyed meeting new people, and that drinking "helps me to not be so bored all of the time." Harold also reported a history of drug abuse including marijuana, cocaine, and ecstasy since the age of 13. Harold stated that he had been caught with substances by the police on campus, though he had avoided being arrested. He was arrested for a DUI during his freshman year and had attended alcohol education classes, which he called "a complete waste of my time." Following the arrest, Harold lost his driver's license which greatly upset him, as he typically enjoyed driving to the bars in town or other towns nearby when he was feeling tired of his own town. He regained his license and had been frequenting bars and drinking heavily until three weeks prior to the current intake evaluation.

Harold stated that for the past three weeks he had been spending most of his time alone in his room, saying, "why would anyone want to spend time with such a lousy person. That's why I wanted to die." He had also quit his part-time job at a grocery store and was attending only a few classes per week. He was unable to recall a specific event that brought on his current depression. While being asked about his current depression, Harold burst into tears and pleaded with the evaluator for help. "I just know I'm going to kill myself." He showed the evaluator burn marks on his legs that appeared to be recently inflicted. The evaluator asked Harold about his current suicidal ideology, and he was able to contract for safety, meaning he agreed not to hurt himself and affirmed that if his thoughts about death grew stronger he would call the emergency room or the counseling center. Then Harold asked the evaluator if she could be his therapist. The evaluator described the counseling center's policy, that the intake evaluator could not see clients being evaluated for psychotherapy. "Just like a typical woman," he retorted. "You don't want to be with me. I think you're terrible at your job, anyway."

Relevant history: Harold stated that he had attended psychotherapy sessions in the past, but that he "hated every single one of them," referring to his therapists, when describing why he never stayed in therapy long. He had seen about five different therapists since the age of 14, but described the experiences as "uncomfortable and just weird. They didn't get me." When the counselor asked Harold why he had gone to therapy as an adoles-

cent, he stated, "I think my mom thought I was messed up. I didn't think I needed it." He described his childhood as "a disaster" and his father as a severe alcoholic, who was often emotionally abusive and sometimes physically abusive. He reported that his mother worked two jobs to support the family, and so he spent much of his time alone as a child.

Case formulation: Harold's behaviors and reported history during the evaluation match the criteria for a Personality Disorder as defined by the *DSM-5*, and his symptoms meet criteria for Borderline Personality Disorder. Although he often abused substances, Harold's personality disorder was not a result of substance use, and instead is a reflection of his impulsivity and inability to cope with strong emotions that is typical of Borderline individuals.

His symptoms of depression for the past three weeks meet criteria for a Major Depressive Episode, though it is unknown whether these have been recurrent for Harold or whether this was a singular intense episode. It might be that it is recurrent, given his prior suicide attempts, though these may be related to the instability that is a feature of his Borderline symptoms, and Major Depressive Disorder was ruled out as a diagnosis.

Treatment plan: Dialectical Behavior Therapy or DBT is currently the preferred treatment for Borderline Personality Disorder. Once Harold made a safety plan with the counselor, he was referred to a private DBT outpatient program two miles from his college campus. Harold was also referred to the psychiatrist on campus for a medication consultation.

Sarah Tobin, PhD

In this chapter, our focus shifts to the set of disorders that represent long-standing patterns of impairments in an individual's self-understanding, ways of relating to others, and personality traits. As we discussed in Chapter 4, a personality trait is an enduring pattern of perceiving, relating to, and thinking about the environment and others, a pattern that characterizes the majority of a person's interactions and experiences. Most people are able to draw upon their personality traits in a flexible manner, adjusting their responses to the needs of the situation. However, when people become rigidly fixed on one particular trait or set of traits, they may place themselves at risk for developing a personality disorder.

14.1 The Nature of Personality Disorders

When does a personality trait become a disorder? What may be a characteristic way of responding can develop into a fixed pattern that impairs a person's ability to function satisfactorily. Perhaps you're the type of person who likes to have your room look "just so." If someone moves your books around or changes the arrangement of your clothes on the hanger, you feel a little bothered. At what point does your unhappiness with a change in the order of your possessions become so problematic that you have crossed over from a little finicky to having a personality disorder involving extreme rigidity? Should this behavioral pattern place you into a diagnostic category with a distinct set of criteria that separates you from people with other personality traits and related behaviors?

Personality Disorders in *DSM*-5

A **personality disorder** is an ingrained pattern of relating to other people, situations, and events with a rigid and maladaptive pattern of inner experience and behavior, dating back to adolescence or early adulthood. As conceptualized in the *DSM*-5, the personality disorders represent a collection of distinguishable sets of behavior, falling into 11 distinct categories. Fitting the general definition of a psychological disorder, a personality disorder deviates markedly from the individual's culture and leads to distress or impairment. The types of behavior that these disorders represent can involve, for example, excessive dependency, overwhelming fear of intimacy, intense

What's New in the DSM-5

Dimensionalizing the Personality Disorders

The area of personality disorders received, perhaps, the greatest attention from clinicians and researchers as they waited for the unveiling of the final revisions to the *DSM*-5. Clinicians began to challenge the categorization system in the early *DSM*s even when the American Psychiatric Association was developing the *DSM-IV*. The *DSM*-5 authors proposed a compromise system to accommodate both the critics and supporters of the categorical system. The proposed *DSM*-5 revision would have retained six of the disorders but added a dimensional rating system of pathological personality traits. These changes would address the criticism that we cannot easily divide personality into separate and discrete chunks. However, these changes were not implemented, and when the American Psychiatric Association's Board of Directors took the final vote on approving *DSM*-5's changes, they rejected the idea of revamping the personality disorders and retained the *DSM-IV-TR* system. Along with the vote, the Board decided to move the new dimensional rating system to Section 3 of the *DSM*-5, where it could receive continued testing.

DSM-5 supporters and critics are already discussing a *DSM*-5.1 that will eliminate all categories entirely and instead use the dimensional system that allows clinicians to rate the personality traits of all their clients.

The history of personality disorders, which are not so much "illnesses" as characteristics of an individual's core ways of relating to others and experiencing the self, further complicates these diagnostic issues. How do you summarize the many complex facets of personality in a discrete set of units? Unlike mood and anxiety disorders, which people may "overcome," the personality disorders are by definition (in the minds of many psychologists) enduring features of the individual. Personality traits can, and do, change over time. However, clinicians are used to thinking of these disorders as deeply seated, and many of the disorders were framed within a psychoanalytic perspective having a long tradition and history. It is convenient for clinicians to describe their "borderline" clients rather than to list all the personality traits that particular individuals display.

The tension between the categorical and dimensional approaches to disorders will most likely persist for the foreseeable future. Researchers are hopeful that they can provide a system that will have diagnostic and empirical utility, ultimately improving the nature of treatment that they can offer clients with these forms of psychopathology.

worry, exploitative behavior, or uncontrollable rage. With their current definitions, these behavior patterns, to fit the diagnostic criteria, must manifest themselves in at least two of these four areas: (1) cognition, (2) affectivity, (3) interpersonal functioning, and (4) impulse control. As a result of these behaviors, the individual experiences distress or impairment.

The *DSM*-5 groups the 10 diagnoses into three clusters based on shared characteristics. Cluster A includes paranoid, schizoid, and schizotypal personality disorders, which share features involving odd and eccentric behavior. Cluster B includes antisocial, borderline, histrionic, and narcissistic personality disorders, which share overdramatic, emotional, and erratic or unpredictable attitudes and behaviors. Cluster C includes avoidant, dependent, and obsessive-compulsive personality disorders, which share anxious and fearful behaviors. These clusters are not based on empirical data, as the *DSM*-5 authors point out. They are perhaps best thought of as a rough categorization system, possibly of use in some clinical or educational settings.

Because the personality disorders fall into separate categories, clinicians evaluating individuals for a possible diagnosis must decide how many of the criteria a client meets within each category and assign a diagnosis on that basis. Either the client has the disorder or not. The clinician may start by trying to match the most prominent symptoms that the individual shows with the diagnostic criteria. If the client does not fit the

personality disorder
An ingrained pattern of relating to other people, situations, and events with a rigid and maladaptive pattern of inner experience and behavior, dating back to adolescence or early adulthood.

criteria for that disorder, the clinician may either move to another disorder or decide that the client has a personality disorder "not otherwise specified" (technically the eleventh personality disorder category).

Currently, studies in both the United States and the United Kingdom yield an overall prevalence among nationally representative samples of 9 to 10 percent. Personality disorders are highly comorbid with drug dependence. For example, among people with antisocial personality disorder, the lifetime prevalence rate of alcohol dependence is 27 percent and 59 percent for nicotine dependence (Trull, Jahng, Tomko, Wood, & Sher, 2010).

Alternative Personality Disorder Diagnostic System in Section 3 of the *DSM-5*

Even as the authors were writing *DSM-IV*, a number of prominent researchers went on record stating that the categorical diagnostic system was flawed. They maintained that there were too many fine distinctions that the diagnoses required. These distinctions, they maintained, were not sufficiently clear and there were many overlapping criteria. Consequently, clinicians could not empirically justify the diagnoses. Clinicians found that they were using most commonly the less than precise diagnosis of "personality disorder not otherwise specified" (Widiger & Trull, 2007). A second major flaw with the categorical rating system is that it did not allow for the possibility of a client's "somewhat" antisocial or narcissistic behavior. Clients either did or did not fit into a diagnostic category.

In the process of revising the *DSM-IV-TR*, the personality disorders panels developed a number of alternative models to get away from the categorical diagnostic system. At one time, researchers proposed eliminating the categories entirely and replacing them with dimensional ratings, such as scales based on the Five Factor Model. Nevertheless, the categories seemed to hold worth and, as long as the researchers could delineate distinct empirically based criteria, the *DSM-5* authors proposed a possible compromise. They revamped the original 12 personality disorders (11 categories plus "not otherwise specified") into 6 (plus an additional category for individuals who did not fit into the 6). Within each personality disorder, the authors set empirically based criteria (Livesley, 2011) along the dimensions of self and interpersonal relationships. This dimensional system is shown in Table 14.1. In addition, in this framework, clinicians would have evaluated all clients on a consistent set of five personality traits. In the end, they decided that the dimensional system would move to Section 3 where it would receive further study and then, in the future, the issue would be revisited.

In the Section 3 dimensional ratings shown in Table 14.1, clinicians can assign ratings along four sets of criteria. The first two reflect personality "functioning," meaning how the individual expresses personality in his or her identity and self-direction. The second two reflect the individual's personality as reflected in relationships with other people in terms of the ability to understand other people's perspectives and form close relationships. Clinicians rate individuals from mild to extreme in these domains. The third set of criteria involves ratings of the individual's specific personality traits. A person must have significant impairment in both areas of personality functioning to receive a diagnosis of personality disorder in this framework. With respect to the personality traits, the individual must have pathological traits in at least one of five trait domains: antagonism, disinhibition, detachment, negative affectivity, and compulsivity (see Table 14.3). Clinicians can rate all clients on these personality traits if such an assessment is conceptually helpful. The new diagnostic system reduces the set of 79 criteria in *DSM-IV-TR* to 25 core criteria. Clinicians can use the remaining category of "personality disorder trait specified" for people who show significant impairment in personality functioning, but who rate at the maladaptive end of one or more personality traits.

In this alternative model, the individual would have to meet the general criteria for personality disorder shown in Table 14.2. The trait model in Table 14.3 is oriented toward abnormal, not normal, personality and so is not the same as the Five Factor Model. For

TABLE 14.1 DSM-5 Section 3 Personality Disorder Framework

	Personality Functioning		Interpersonal Functioning		Personality Traits
	Identity	**Self-direction**	**Empathy**	**Intimacy**	
Antisocial	Egocentrism; self-esteem derived from personal gain, power, or pleasure	Goal-setting based on personal gratification; absence of prosocial internal standards associated with failure to conform to lawful or culturally normative ethical behavior	Lack of concern for feelings, needs, or suffering of others; lack of remorse after hurting or mistreating another	Incapacity for mutually intimate relationships, as exploitation is a primary means of relating to others, including by deceit and coercion; use of dominance or intimidation to control others	**Antagonism:** Manipulativeness Deceitfulness Callousness Hostility **Disinhibition:** Irresponsibility Impulsivity Risk taking
Avoidant	Low self-esteem associated with self-appraisal as socially inept, personally unappealing, or inferior; excessive feelings of shame or inadequacy	Unrealistic standards for behavior associated with reluctance to pursue goals, take personal risks, or engage in new activities involving interpersonal contact	Preoccupation with, and sensitivity to, criticism or rejection, associated with distorted inference of others' perspectives as negative	Reluctance to get involved with people unless certain of being liked; diminished mutuality within intimate relationships because of fear of others shaming or ridiculing	**Detachment** Withdrawal Intimacy Avoidance Anhedonia **Negative affectivity** Anxiousness
Borderline	Markedly impoverished, poorly developed, or unstable self-image, often associated with excessive self-criticism; chronic feelings of emptiness; dissociative states under stress	Instability in goals, aspirations, values, or career plans	Compromised ability to recognize the feelings and needs of others associated with interpersonal hypersensitivity (i.e., prone to feel slighted or insulted); perceptions of others selectively biased toward negative attributes or vulnerabilities	Intense, unstable, and conflicted close relationships, marked by mistrust, neediness, and anxious preoccupation with real or imagined abandonment; close relationships often viewed in extremes of idealization and devaluation and alternating between over involvement and withdrawal	**Negative affectivity** Emotional lability Anxiousness Separation Hostility Depressivity **Disinhibition** Impulsivity Risk taking **Antagonism** Hostility
Narcissistic	Excessive reference to others for self-definition and self-esteem regulation; exaggerated self-appraisal may be inflated or deflated, or vacillate between extremes; emotional regulation mirrors fluctuations in self-esteem	Goal-setting is based on gaining approval from others; personal standards are unreasonably high in order to see oneself as exceptional, or too low based on a sense of entitlement; often unaware of own motivations	Impaired ability to recognize or identify with the feelings and needs of others; excessively attuned to reactions of others, but only if perceived as relevant to self; over- or underestimate own effect on others	Relationships largely superficial and exist to serve self-esteem regulation; mutuality constrained by little genuine interest in others' experiences and predominance of a need for personal gain	**Antagonism** Grandiosity Attention seeking

(continued)

TABLE 14.1 DSM-5 Section 3 Personality Disorder Framework (*Continued*)

Obsessive-Compulsive Personality Disorder	Sense of self derived predominantly from work or productivity; constricted experience and expression of strong emotions	Difficulty completing tasks and realizing goals associated with rigid and unreasonably high and inflexible internal standards of behavior; overly conscientious and moralistic attitudes	Difficulty understanding and appreciating the ideas, feelings, or behaviors of others	Relationships seen as secondary to work and productivity; rigidity and stubbornness negatively affect relationships with others	**Compulsivity** Rigid perfectionism **Negative affectivity** Perseveration
Schizotypal Personality Disorder	Confused boundaries between self and others; distorted self-concept; emotional expression often not congruent with context or internal experience	Unrealistic or incoherent goals; no clear set of internal standards	Pronounced difficulty understanding impact of own behaviors on others; frequent misinterpretations of others' motivations and behaviors	Marked impairments in developing close relationships associated with mistrust and anxiety	**Psychoticism** Eccentricity Cognitive and perceptual dysregulation Unusual beliefs and experiences **Detachment** Restricted affectivity Withdrawal **Negative affectivity** Suspiciousness

example, detachment in this system is a pathological variant of introversion (or low extraversion). In developing these factors for the *DSM-5*, the authors made clear that although these are bipolar (i.e., two-way) dimensions, people with one of these disorders would score at the maladaptive end of the domains of detachment, antagonism, disinhibition, and negative affectivity. However, the fifth trait in the Five Factor Model, openness to experience, does not fit into this framework because it is not a feature of any of the personality disorders. Instead, authors have introduced the dimension of psychoticism into the *DSM-5* that they associate with schizotypal personality disorder.

TABLE 14.2 General Criteria for a Personality Disorder in Section 3

This description summarizes the Section 3 personality trait criteria from *DSM-5*.

- Moderate or greater impairment in personality as reflected in self and interpersonal functioning (Table 14.1)
- One or more pathological personality traits (Table 14.3)
- These impairments are relatively inflexible, pervasive across a range of situations, stable across time and can be traced back at least to adolescence or early adulthood.
- Another psychological disorder does not better explain these impairments, nor are they attributable to the physiological effects of a substance or another medical condition.
- The impairments are not better understood as normal for an individual's developmental level or social and cultural context.

TABLE 14.3 Personality Domains in the DSM-5 Section 3 Rating System

Negative Affectivity involves experiencing negative emotions frequently and intensely.

Trait facets: Emotional lability, anxiousness, separation insecurity, perseveration, submissiveness, hostility, depressivity, suspiciousness, restricted affectivity (−).

Detachment involves withdrawal from other people and from social interactions.

Trait facets: Restricted affectivity, depressivity, suspiciousness, withdrawal, anhedonia, intimacy avoidance.

Antagonism involves behaviors that put the person at odds with other people.

Trait facets: Manipulativeness, deceitfulness, grandiosity, attention seeking, callousness, hostility.

Disinhibition involves engaging in behaviors on impulse, without reflecting on potential future consequences. Compulsivity is the opposite pole of this domain.

Trait facets: Irresponsibility, impulsivity, distractibility, risk taking, rigid perfectionism (−).

Psychoticism involves unusual and bizarre experiences.

Trait facets: Unusual beliefs & experiences, eccentricity, cognitive & perceptual dysregulation.

14.2 Cluster A Personality Disorders

Cluster A of the personality disorders in *DSM-5* include those disorders characterized by eccentric behavior. In other words, individuals with these disorders show characteristics that might lead others to view them as slightly odd, unusual, or peculiar.

Paranoid Personality Disorder

People with **paranoid personality disorder** are extremely suspicious of others and are always on guard against potential danger or harm. Their view of the world is very narrowly focused, in that they seek to confirm their expectations that others will take advantage of them, making it virtually impossible for them to trust even their friends and associates. They may accuse a spouse or partner of unfaithfulness, even if no substantiating evidence exists. For example, they may believe that an unexplained toll call that appears on a telephone bill is proof of an extramarital affair. They are unable to take responsibility for their mistakes and, instead, project blame onto others. If others criticize them, they become hostile. They are also prone to misconstrue innocent comments and minor events as having a hidden or threatening meaning. They may hold grudges for years, based on a real or an imagined slight by another person. Although

paranoid personality disorder
A personality disorder whose outstanding feature is that the individual is unduly suspicious of others and is always on guard against potential danger or harm.

MINI CASE

Paranoid Personality Disorder

Anita is a computer programmer who constantly worries that other people will exploit her knowledge. She regards as "top secret" the new database management program she is writing. She even fears that, when she leaves the office at night, someone will sneak into her desk and steal her notes. Her distrust of others pervades all her interpersonal dealings. Her suspicions that she is being cheated even taint routine transactions in banks and stores. Anita likes to think of herself as rational and able to make objective decisions; she regards her inability to trust other people as a natural reaction to a world filled with opportunistic and insincere corporate ladder climbers.

individuals with this disorder may be relatively successful in certain kinds of jobs requiring heightened vigilance, their emotional life tends to be isolated and constrained.

A certain amount of paranoid thinking and behavior might be appropriate in some situations, such as in dangerous political climates in which people must be on guard just to stay alive; however, people with paranoid personality disorder think and behave in ways that are unrelated to their environment. Particularly frustrating to relatives and acquaintances of these people is their refusal to seek professional help because they don't acknowledge the nature of their problem. In the unlikely event they do seek therapy, their rigidity and defensiveness make it very difficult for the clinician to make progress and work toward any kind of lasting change.

Research on the divorce rates of people with histrionic and paranoid personality disorder suggests that these disorders interfere with the quality of interpersonal relationships (Disney, Weinstein & Oltmanns, 2012). With their guardedness and suspiciousness, it seems evident that these individuals would have difficulty establishing the type of interpersonal closeness that helps maintain the quality of a long-term intimate relationship.

Schizoid Personality Disorder

schizoid personality disorder
A personality disorder primarily characterized by an indifference to social relationships, as well as a very limited range of emotional experience and expression.

An indifference to social and sexual relationships characterizes **schizoid personality disorder,** as well as a very limited range of emotional experience and expression. Individuals with this disorder prefer to be by themselves rather than with others, and they appear to lack any desire for acceptance or love, even by their families. Sexual involvement with others holds little appeal. As you might expect, others perceive them as cold, reserved, withdrawn, and seclusive, yet the schizoid individual is unaware of, and typically insensitive to, the feelings and thoughts of others.

Throughout their lives, people with schizoid personality disorder seek out situations that involve minimal interaction with others. Those who are able to tolerate work are usually drawn to jobs in which they spend all of their work hours alone. They rarely marry, but rather choose solitary living, possibly in a single room, where they guard their privacy and avoid any dealings with neighbors. They do not appear particularly distressed or a risk to others. However, their self-imposed isolation and emotional constriction is maladaptive to their social functioning.

Both paranoid and schizoid personality disorders would have been eliminated in the new *DSM-5* system, bringing the total number of personality disorders down to six. Researchers believed that existing research did not support their continued inclusion in the psychiatric nomenclature as they could not be uniquely identified (Hopwood & Thomas, 2012); however, for the present, they remain as diagnoses.

MINI CASE

Schizoid Personality Disorder

Pedro, who works as a night security guard at a bank, likes his job because he can enter the private world of his thoughts without interruptions from other people. Even though his numerous years of service make him eligible for a daytime security position, Pedro has repeatedly turned down these opportunities because daytime work would require him to deal with bank employees and customers. Pedro has resided for more than 20 years in a small room at a boarding house. He has no television or radio, and he has resisted any attempts by other house residents to involve him in social activities. He has made it clear he is not interested in small talk and he prefers to be left alone. Neighbors, coworkers, and even his family members (whom he also avoids) perceive Pedro as a peculiar person who seems strikingly cold and detached. When his brother died, Pedro decided not to attend the funeral because he did not want to be bothered by all the carrying on and sympathetic wishes of relatives and others.

MINI CASE

Schizotypal Personality Disorder

Joe is a college junior who has devised an elaborate system for deciding which courses to take, depending on the course number. He will not take a course with the number 5 in it, because he believes that, if he does so, he might have to "plead the Fifth Amendment." Rarely does he talk to people in his dormitory, believing that others are intent on stealing his term paper ideas. He has acquired a reputation for being somewhat of a "flake" because of his odd manner of dress, his reclusive tendencies, and his ominous drawings of sinister animals displayed on the door of his room. The sound of the nearby elevator, he claims, is actually a set of voices singing a monastic chant.

Schizotypal Personality Disorder

Confusions and distortions in the individual's basic sense of self are a core feature of **schizotypal personality disorder.** Such individuals lack a clear sense of direction or motivation, and do not have a clear set of standards against which to measure their behavior. Not only do they have difficulty understanding their own sense of self and motivation, but people with schizotypal personality disorder also have difficulty understanding the motives and behaviors of others. They associate the confusion that they feel about themselves and others with a lack of trust, causing them difficulty in establishing close relationships.

The pathological personality traits of people with schizotypal personality disorder fall along the extremely maladaptive end of the psychoticism dimension. They may hold eccentric ideas, have unusual beliefs and experiences, and have difficulty in forming accurate perceptions and cognitions about their world. As we show in Table 14.1, they also have restricted affect and have withdrawal tendencies, which reflect the pathological personality trait of detachment. They express negative affectivity as extreme suspiciousness.

The social isolation, eccentricity, peculiar communication, and poor social adaptation that come with schizotypal personality disorder place it within the schizophrenic spectrum (Camisa et al., 2005). According to this view, schizotypal personality disorder symptoms represent a latent form of schizophrenia, meaning that people with schizotypal symptoms are vulnerable to developing a full-blown psychosis if exposed to difficult life circumstances that challenge their ability to maintain contact with reality. Supporting this position, researchers found that adolescents with schizotypal personality disorder and those with a particular genetic defect linked to schizophrenia showed similar patterns of performance on measures of prodromal syndromes such as disorganized symptoms, problems with focused attention, and impaired tolerance to stress (Shapiro, Cubells, Ousley, Rockers, & Walker, 2011).

Treatment for people with schizotypal personality disorder parallels the interventions that clinicians commonly use in treating schizophrenia. Specifically, medications that act on dopamine are most effective and can help alleviate cognitive deficits in memory and executive functioning (McClure et al., 2010).

schizotypal personality disorder
A personality disorder that primarily involves odd beliefs, behavior, appearance, and interpersonal style. People with this disorder may have bizarre ideas or preoccupations, such as magical thinking and beliefs in psychic phenomena.

14.3 Cluster B Personality Disorders

Cluster B personality disorders include those that are marked by dramatic, emotional, or erratic behaviors. These behaviors include impulsivity, an inflated (or apparently inflated) sense of self, and a tendency to seek stimulation.

Antisocial Personality Disorder

Synonymous in the past with "psychopaths" or "sociopaths," the *DSM-5* defines people who receive the diagnosis of **antisocial personality disorder** as highly impulsive and lacking in the capacity for regret over their actions. Television depicts serial killers as

antisocial personality disorder
A personality disorder characterized by a lack of regard for society's moral or legal standards and an impulsive and risky lifestyle.

MINI CASE

Antisocial Personality Disorder

Tommy was the leader of a teenage street gang that had the reputation as the most vicious in the neighborhood. He grew up in a chaotic home atmosphere, his mother having lived with a series of violent men who were heavily involved in drug dealing and prostitution. At age 18, Tommy was jailed for brutally mugging and stabbing an older woman. This was the first in a long series of arrests for offenses ranging from drug trafficking to car thefts to counterfeiting. At one point, between jail terms, he met a woman at a bar and married her the next day. Two weeks later, he beat her when she complained about his incessant drinking and involvement with shady characters. Tommy left her when she became pregnant, and he refused to pay child support. From his vantage point now as a drug trafficker and leader of a child prostitution ring, Tommy shows no regret for what he has done, claiming that life has "sure given me a bum steer."

having these qualities, and then some. However, we can find people with antisocial personality operating in much more mundane situations. The phenomenon of the "psychopath in the boardroom" describes corporate executives who ruthlessly exploit investors and employees alike, seeking their own gain at the expense of the bank accounts and livelihood of their victims (Jonson, 2011). Such individuals also commit acts of bullying in the workplace, increasing the risk of unfair supervision (Boddy, 2011).

Characteristics of Antisocial Personality Disorder

The diagnosis of antisocial behavior has its origins in the work of Hervey Cleckley, whose 1941 book, *The Mask of Sanity*, represented the first scientific attempt to list and categorize the behaviors of the "psychopathic" personality. Cleckley (1976) developed a set of criteria for **psychopathy,** a cluster of traits form the core of the antisocial personality. The specific traits in psychopathy include lack of remorse or shame for harmful acts committed to others; poor judgment and failure to learn from experience; extreme egocentricity and incapacity for love; lack of emotional responsiveness to others; impulsivity; absence of "nervousness"; and unreliability, untruthfulness, and insincerity. Cleckley used the term "semantic dementia" to capture the psychopath's inability to react appropriately to expressions of emotionality. Other people may find it difficult to see the psychopath's true colors because they are able to disguise their egocentric and impulsive behaviors beneath a veneer of superficial charm and seeming intelligence.

Cleckley's notion of psychopathy remains a key concept in descriptions of antisocial personality disorder. Building on Cleckley's work, Canadian psychologist Robert D. Hare developed the Psychopathy Checklist–Revised (PCL-R) (Hare, 1997), an assessment instrument whose two factors are the core psychopathic personality traits and an antisocial lifestyle (Table 14.4). The core personality traits include glibness and superficial charm, a grandiose sense of self-worth, pathological lying, a lack of empathy for others, lack of remorse or guilt, and an unwillingness to accept responsibility for one's actions. The antisocial-lifestyle trait revolves around impulsivity, a characteristic that can lead to behaviors expressed in an unstable lifestyle, juvenile delinquency, early behavioral problems, lack of realistic long-term goals, and a need for constant stimulation (Hare & Neumann, 2005).

The diagnostic criteria in the *DSM-5* require that an individual show a pervasive pattern of three out of seven possible behaviors including failure to conform to social norms, deceitfulness, impulsivity, aggressiveness, disregard for safety of self or others, irresponsibility, and lack of remorse. Although people with this personality disorder do not actually experience feelings of remorse, they may feign their regret for harming others in order to get themselves out of a difficult situation when they get caught. These

psychopathy
A cluster of traits that form the core of the antisocial personality.

TABLE 14.4 Items and Factors in the PCL-R Scales

PCL-R	PCL:YV	PCL:SV
F1		**P1**
Interpersonal	**Interpersonal**	**Interpersonal**
1. Glibness–superficial charm	1. Impression management	1. Superficial
2. Grandiose sense of self-worth	2. Grandiose sense of self-worth	2. Grandiose
4. Pathological lying	4. Pathological lying	3. Deceitful
5. Conning–manipulative	5. Manipulation for personal gain	
Affective	**Affective**	**Affective**
6. Lack of remorse or guilt	6. Lack of remorse	4. Lacks remorse
7. Shallow affect	7. Shallow affect	5. Lacks empathy
8. Callous–lack of empathy	8. Callous–lack of empathy	6. Does not accept responsibility
16. Failure to accept responsibility	16. Failure to accept responsibility	
F2		**P2**
Lifestyle	**Behavioural**	**Lifestyle**
3. Need for stimulation	3. Stimulation seeking	7. Impulsive
9. Parasitic lifestyle	9. Parasitic orientation	9. Lacks goals
13. Lack of realistic, long-term goals	13. Lack of goals	10. Irresponsibility
14. Impulsivity	14. Impulsivity	
15. Irresponsibility	15. Irresponsibility	
Antisocial	**Antisocial**	**Antisocial**
10. Poor behavioural controls	10. Poor anger control	8. Poor behavioural controls
12. Early behavioural problems	12. Early behaviour problems	11. Adolescent antisocial behaviour
18. Juvenile delinquency	18. Serious criminal behaviour	12. Adult antisocial behaviour
19. Revocation of conditional release	19. Serious violations of release	
20. Criminal versatility	20. Criminal versatility	

The PCL-R, PCL:YV, and PCL:SV items are from Hare,[14,20] Forth et al,[24] and Hart et al,[23] respectively. Reprinted by permission of the copyright holders, RD Hare and Multi-Health Systems. Note that the item titles cannot be scored without reference to the formal criteria contained in the published manuals. PCL-R items 11, Promiscuous sexual behaviour and 17, Many short-term marital relationships, contribute to the total score but do not load on any factors. PCL:YV items 11, Impersonal sexual behaviour, and 17, Unstable interpersonal relationships, contribute to the total score but do not load on any factor. F1 and F2 are the original PCL-R factors, but with be addition of item 20. Parts 1 and 2 (P1 and P2) are described in the PCL:SV manual[23].
SOURCE: Hare & Neumann, 2009.

individuals also try hard to present themselves in as favorable a light as possible. You might think of them as the "smooth talkers" who can con anyone out of anything, such as asking someone for money or favors that they have no intention of repaying.

There is a difference between antisocial personality disorder and antisocial behavior. Stealing, lying, and cheating are examples of antisocial behavior. There is also a difference between antisocial and criminal behavior. The term "criminal" has meaning in the legal system, but is not a psychological concept. Still, many individuals who land in prison meet the psychological criteria for antisocial personality disorder. At the same time, not all individuals with antisocial personality disorder engage in explicitly criminal behavior, but instead their disorder may manifest itself in behaviors such as job problems, promiscuity, and aggressiveness.

Antisocial personality disorder seems to emerge in childhood, both in terms of the development of psychopathic traits and rates of breaking the law. We may

Typical antisocial behaviors include lying, cheating, and stealing.

consider a certain degree of antisocial behavior normative in teenagers; however, this behavior can have lifelong consequences if it leads teenagers to drop out of school, accumulate a criminal record and incarceration, and develop an addiction to drugs (Salekin, 2008).

Over the course of their adult years, people with antisocial personality disorder seem to become less likely to commit criminal acts (Moran, 1999). The rate of homicide offenses for people over the age of 35 is lower than for people under the age of 34 and even lower for people 50 and older (Bureau of Justice Statistics, 2011). Overall, the rates for violent crime drop from approximately 1,000 per 100,000 for people aged 35 to 39 to 93 per 100,000 for people 60 and older (Federal Bureau of Investigation, 2004). Less than 1 percent of all prisoners, federal and state, are over 65 and 5 percent are 55 to 64 (Glaze, 2011). The components of psychopathy involving impulsivity, social deviance, and antisocial behavior are less prominent in prison inmates who are in their mid-forties and older (Harpur & Hare, 1994). Perhaps antisocial individuals experience burnout or have become more adept at avoiding detection, or perhaps some of the more extreme cases are eliminated from the population, because these people are killed or arrested in the course of their criminal activities.

Another possibility is that aging brings with it a reduction of the acting-out and impulsive behaviors that we associate with antisocial, as well as with histrionic and borderline personality disorders. The **maturation hypothesis** suggests that older individuals are better able to manage their high-risk tendencies (Segal, Coolidge, & Rosowsky, 2000). A longitudinal study of men from adolescence to middle adulthood supports this hypothesis. Personality traits related to antisocial behavior decreased in a large majority of men in midlife (Morizot & Le Blanc, 2005).

maturation hypothesis
The proposition that people with antisocial personality and the other Cluster B disorders become better able to manage their behaviors as they age.

Theories of Antisocial Personality Disorder

As you have seen, antisocial personality disorder represents a deeply entrenched pattern of behavior, with wide-ranging effects on both the individual and the people with whom the individual comes into contact. In this section, we will consider the most compelling explanations for the development of this personality disorder. It is important to remember

Antisocial Personality Disorder and Moral Culpability

If antisocial personality disorder is a psychological disorder, should people who meet the diagnosis be held responsible for criminal acts that they may commit? What about people who have the personality trait of psychopathy? Are they somehow more or less culpable? The question of criminal responsibility permeates the ethical literature on ASPD and the related personality trait of psychopathy. According to Robert Hare, when the judicial system applies the term "psychopathy" rather than "antisocial personality disorder" to an offender, that offender is likely to receive a harsher sentence because the court perceives the person (usually a male) as lacking any redeeming qualities. Canadian philosopher Ishtiyaque Haji challenges the idea that people high in psychopathy are mentally healthy and thus, responsible for their crimes (Haji, 2010). He suggests that these individuals have less moral responsibility for their crimes than do people who are not high on the psychopathy trait. According to Haji, the emotional insensitivity that is a hallmark of psychopathy makes an individual less able to appreciate the moral consequences of his or her actions.

Carrying this argument further, consider the factors that may lead an individual to develop high levels of the trait of psychopathy. Perhaps their lack of emotional sensitivity relates to an abnormality of brain development, as some researchers suggest. If they truly cannot experience empathy, how can they relate to the harm that they may be causing a victim? Similarly, if they lack the neurological basis for learning fear, and thus are less likely to avoid the negative consequences of criminal activity, is this flaw of brain development a fact that makes them similar to people who have a physical illness? Without the ability to appreciate the punishment that may follow a crime, people high in psychopathy cannot learn from their experiences and seem doomed to continue to become "emotionally depraved" (in Haji's words).

The question of whether people high in psychopathy have a true impairment that prevents them from recognizing the moral implications of their actions will, no doubt, continue. Each case of a serial murderer committed by an individual with antisocial personality disorder or one who is high on psychopathy seems to raise the issue all over again. With increasingly sophisticated evidence on the neurodevelopmental factors that predispose individuals to developing this disorder, we may eventually understand the issue with greater clarity.

Q: *You be the judge*: Should people with antisocial personality disorder be considered responsible for their illegal behaviors?

that some of these investigations pertain to criminals, who may or may not have been diagnosed specifically with antisocial personality disorder.

Biological Perspectives Family inheritance studies provide strong evidence in favor of genetic explanations of antisocial personality disorder, the personality trait of psychopathy, and antisocial behavior with heritability estimates as high as 80 percent. To explain this genetic variation, their attention is focused on genes related to the activity of serotonin and dopamine. One in particular is monoamine oxidase A, an enzyme coded by the MAOA gene. A mutation in this gene results in insufficient amounts of monoamine oxidase in the nervous system, which results in abnormally high levels of dopamine, serotonin, and norepinephrine. High levels of these neurotransmitters are linked to greater impulsivity. Researchers also believe that dependence of the mother during pregnancy can lead to epigenetic influences through DNA methylation (Gunter, Vaughn, & Philibert, 2010). Malnutrition in early life may serve as another risk factor for the development of antisocial personality disorder. In

REAL STORIES

Ted Bundy: Antisocial Personality Disorder

"...the most cold-hearted son of a bitch you'll ever meet."

Infamous serial killer Ted Bundy was born in 1946 in Burlington, Vermont. Although the identity of his father is unknown, various sources have suspected that it may be his grandfather who was abusive and violent toward Ted's mother. This caused Ted to harbor a lifelong resentment toward his mother for never revealing who his father was. In turn, Ted looked up to his grandfather who was known for his bigotry and propensity toward violence. As a child, Ted's mother recalls him engaging in strange behaviors, including placing knives around his mother's bed while she slept, waking to find him standing over her and smiling.

Ted and his mother moved to Washington State, where his mother married Johnny Bundy, who formally adopted him. The couple had four children of their own and although they made a point to include Ted in all of their activities, Ted preferred to stay out of the family's affairs and kept mostly to himself. Ted described varying accounts of his early life to biographers, although in general it appears that he presented himself as a charming, outgoing young man. However, on the inside he felt no desire to make any connection with others and had difficulty keeping friends and romantic partners.

After dropping out of college, Ted began working at a suicide hotline and enrolled in a community college where he studied psychology. Eventually, he went to law school at the University of Utah, although by the end of his first year he had stopped attending classes. He moved back to the Pacific Northwest and worked on political campaigns, and around this time, young women had begun disappearing. Profilers on the cases of the murdered women had Ted on their suspect list, although they had difficulty believing that such an engaging and motivated young man could be capable of such crimes. Between the years of 1974 and 1978, Ted was responsible for the grisly murders of at least 30 women in Utah, Washington, Oregon, Idaho, and Florida. The details of these murders are gruesome. In his book *The Bundy Murders*, Kevin M. Sullivan describes that "The planning, hunting, taking, and subsequent killing of his victims (not to mention his penchant for necrophilia) would prove to be a time-consuming process." Ted would reportedly approach his young female victims in public places, often in broad daylight, and pretend to either be an authority figure, or to be injured before taking them to a more secluded area where he would molest, assault, and eventually murder them.

Ted escaped from prison following his first arrest. He was finally convicted for the murder of Kimberly Leach. In his book *The Bundy Murders*, Kevin M. Sullivan describes this murder: "He was intoxicated, but not with alcohol. His intoxication was the deep and vicious craving to which he had surrendered himself long ago. This craving, which had so utterly taken control and superseded every other aspect of his life, would never stop seeking victims as long as he was alive."

After his conviction, Bundy was sentenced to death by electrocution in the state of Florida in 1989. *The Bundy Murders* described how Ted gained a very high profile status in the media during his trial and subsequent time spent on death row. During his trial, Ted attempted to use his law school experience to argue his way out of a guilty conviction.

Dr. Emmanuel Tanay, a professor of psychiatry at Wayne State University conducted a clinical interview with Ted with an aim to find Ted not guilty by reason of insanity. A report of the interview goes as follows:

"Bundy is a 32-year-old, handsome-looking man, dressed with the casual elegance of a young college professor. He was meticulously groomed with well-cared-for fingernails to freshly washed hair. He was in total command of the situation. The deputy sheriffs appeared more like a part of his entourage than policemen guarding a prisoner ... At the outset of the interview, Mr. Bundy commented on the security precautions, saying that they were the result of 'the Bundy mystique,' which has developed as a result of news media activities. This was presented in the manner of a complaint; it was however my impression that Mr. Bundy was taking pride in his

Executed in 1989 for murder, Ted Bundy admitted to being responsible for the deaths of at least 30 people.

celebrity status. In the nearly three hours which I spent with Mr. Bundy, I found him to be in a cheerful even jovial mood; he was witty but not flippant, he spoke freely; however, meaningful communication was never established. He was asked about his apparent lack of concern so out of keeping with the charges facing him. He acknowledged that he is facing a possible death sentence, however, 'I will cross that bridge when I get to it.' Mr. Bundy has an incapacity to recognize the significance of evidence held against him. It would be simplistic to characterize this as merely lying inasmuch as he acts as if his perception of the significance of evidence was real . . . In his decision-making process, Mr. Bundy is guided by his emotional needs, sometimes to the detriment of his legal interests. The pathological need of Mr. Bundy to defy authority, to manipulate his associates and adversaries, supplies him with 'thrills' to the detriment of his ability to cooperate with his counsel."

In the end, Ted decided not to plead insanity. As Sullivan writes, "In Bundy's mind, everything he'd ever done was apparently outside the realm of 'insanity.' The removal and sequestering of his victims' heads and having sex with the dead did not, in his mind, constitute mental aberration. He would refer to this sort of thing only as 'my problem.' Committing murder, Ted Bundy once told a writer, was nothing more than 'acting out.'"

After the court rejected his final appeal, Ted Bundy was executed by electric chair on the morning of January 24, 1989. Of his execution, Sullivan writes, "Apparently, Bundy was free of any feelings of animosity towards those who helped put him there as he had conciliatory body gestures (head nods, etc.) for others entering the room. But when it came to his last statement, he spoke only of giving his 'love to my family and friends,' leaving the living victims of Bundy's homicidal rage little more than a final slap in the face."

---

a study of children tested from ages 3 to 17, those who experienced poor nutrition at age 3 showed more aggressiveness and motor activity as they grew up. By age 17 they had a higher likelihood of conduct disorder, a precursor to antisocial personality disorder (Liu, Raine, Venables, & Mednick, 2004).

The hippocampus, the brain structure involved in short-term memory processing, seems to function abnormally in individuals with psychopathy. Although the volume of the hippocampus does not seem to differ between psychopath and nonpsychopath samples, these brain structures seem to have abnormal shapes in people with psychopathy (Boccardi et al., 2010). Neuroimaging studies also suggest that people high in psychopathy have deficits in frontal lobe functioning, meaning that they are less able to inhibit input from subcortical areas of the brain that are involved in aggression (Pridmore, Chambers, & McArthur, 2005).

Psychological Perspectives   Closely related to the biological perspective is the hypothesis that antisocial personality disorder causes neuropsychological deficits reflected in abnormal patterns of learning and attention. Recall that Cleckley believed that psychopathic individuals lack emotional reactivity. David Lykken (1957) took this idea into the lab and demonstrated that psychopathic individuals exposed to aversive stimuli indeed failed to show the normal fear response. Consequently, they do not learn from their negative experiences. We call this deficit of classical conditioning passive avoidance, meaning that the correct responses involve learning to avoid responding to a previously punished stimulus. Poor passive avoidance learning in people high in the personality trait of psychopathy may be related to deficits in the activation of limbic system circuits responsible for emotional processing (Birbaumer et al., 2005).

People high in psychopathy also have difficulty processing negative emotional stimuli such as sad facial expressions (Sommer et al., 2006). Researchers believe that this emotional processing deficit could relate to the inability that these individuals have to develop a sense of morality. Since they can't empathize with their victims, they do not feel remorse over harming them.

The response modulation hypothesis attempts to explain the failure of individuals high in psychopathy to learn from negative

Individuals with antisocial personality disorder may engage in manipulative behaviors due to a lack of remorse about hurting other people.

experience and to process emotional information (Glass & Newman, 2009). According to this explanation, people have a dominant and nondominant focus of their attention in any given situation. For example, you may be focusing your attention now on your reading, but at the same time, in the background, you are surrounded by noises such as music, other students talking, or the sound of traffic. Although your primary responses right now are to try to understand what you are reading, you might switch over to the secondary cues if something changes to require your attention, such as another student talking directly to you. You need to pay enough attention to those secondary cues to switch if necessary, but not so much that you are unable to carry out your primary task.

According to the response modulation hypothesis, individuals high on the trait of psychopathy are unable to pay enough attention to secondary cues to switch (i.e., modulate) their attention when necessary. Therefore, in a passive avoidance task, they pay attention only to the trials in which they will receive a reward and do not learn from trials in which they incur punishment. In their behavior in the outside world, this pattern would translate into a tendency to focus only on what they can get from a situation (money, power, or other desired goals) and not consider that if they pursue these rewards that punishment might result. Similarly, they focus on their own pleasure, but not on the pain that they may cause the people that they hurt.

The majority of research on psychopathy is focused on men and, in fact, researchers primarily developed and tested the response modulation hypothesis on male populations. Interestingly, when researchers examined both emotion processing and passive avoidance learning in women, they did not find differences between women high and low in psychopathy. It is possible that women are better able to attend to nondominant responses compared to men (Vitale, MacCoon, & Newman, 2011).

Early life experiences can also serve as important influences on whether an individual develops antisocial personality disorder. The parents of individuals with this disorder are more likely to have been overburdened, lack parenting skills, and themselves exhibit antisocial behaviors (Lykken, 2000).

Treatment of Antisocial Personality Disorder

The accepted wisdom for many years in the field of abnormal psychology was that people with antisocial personality disorder are untreatable. Their traits of inability to learn from negative experiences and to experience empathy would seem to make them resistant to approaches involving either insight or behavioral interventions. The problems of working with these individuals include the very characteristics of the disorder itself: a seeming lack of motivation to change, a tendency toward deception and manipulation, and lack of deep or lasting emotion. In investigating psychotherapy outcomes, researchers must attempt to arrive at reasonable treatment goals. Should they measure the effectiveness of therapy in terms of re-arrest or recidivism (return of symptoms), or should researchers focus instead on changes in job performance, relationships with others, and involvement in noncriminal activities (such as sports or hobbies) (Salekin, Worley, & Grimes, 2010)?

Despite these challenges to successful treatment, the most effective interventions are those that are less focused on developing empathy and conscience or personality. Instead, effective treatment should convince participants that they are responsible for their own behavior. In addition, therapists should help clients to develop more prosocial ways to satisfy their needs by using their strengths. Cognitive-behavioral therapy seems well-suited for both adolescents and adult offenders (Hare & Neumann, 2009).

Borderline Personality Disorder

The term "borderline" in this personality disorder relates to its origins in the 1930s as a condition on the "border" between neurotic and psychotic forms of psychopathology, on the edge of schizophrenia. The criteria are very different now than they were at the time, reflecting continuing revisions of the criteria of this disorder, but the terminology remains with us today.

MINI CASE

Borderline Personality Disorder

Lisa is a 28-year-old account executive with a long history of interpersonal problems. At the office, her co-workers view her as intensely moody and unpredictable. On some days, she is pleasant and high-spirited, but on others she exhibits uncontrollable anger. People are often struck by her inconsistent attitudes toward her supervisors. She vacillates between idealizing them and devaluing them. For example, she may boast about the brilliance of her supervisor one day, only to deliver a burning criticism the next day. Her co-workers keep their distance from her, because they have become annoyed with her constant demands for attention. She has also gained a reputation in the office for her promiscuous involvements with a variety of people, male and female. On several occasions, colleagues have reprimanded her for becoming inappropriately involved in the personal lives of her clients. One day, after losing one of her accounts, she became so distraught that she slashed her wrists. This incident prompted her supervisor to insist that Lisa obtain professional help.

Characteristics of Borderline Personality Disorder (BPD) The diagnosis of **borderline personality disorder (BPD)** rests on the individual's demonstration of at least five out of a possible nine behaviors, including frantic efforts to avoid abandonment, unstable and intense relationships, identity disturbance, impulsivity in areas such as sexuality, spending, or reckless driving, recurrent suicidal behavior, affective instability, chronic feelings of emptiness, difficulty controlling anger, and occasional feelings of paranoia or dissociative symptoms. In the dimensional rating system in Section 3, clinicians will evaluate individuals along the dimensions of personality and interpersonal functioning, as well as on the extent to which they show negative personality traits.

People with this disorder go beyond being insecure. They literally rely on other people to help them feel "whole." Even after they have passed through the customary time of identity questioning in adolescence, they remain unsure and conflicted about their life's goals. Their chronic feelings of emptiness also lead individuals with BPD almost to

borderline personality disorder (BPD)
A personality disorder characterized by a pervasive pattern of poor impulse control and instability in mood, interpersonal relationships, and sense of self.

Men who suffer from borderline personality disorder are more likely to present with antisocial symptoms than women.

morph their identities into those of the people to whom they are close. Unfortunately for them, the more that they seek the reassurance and closeness of others, the more they drive these people away. As a result, their disturbed feelings only become more intense, and they become more and more demanding, moody, and reckless. In this way, the symptoms of the disorder become cyclical and self-perpetuating, often escalating to the point at which the individual requires hospitalization.

A term that the profession often uses to describe the way that people with BPD relate to others is *splitting.* This means that their preoccupation with feelings of love for the object of their desire and attention can readily turn to extreme rage and hatred when that love object rejects them. They may apply this all-good vs. all-bad dichotomy to other experiences and people as well. The intense despair into which they can become thrust may also lead them to perform suicidal gestures, either as a way to gain attention, or to derive feelings of reality from the physical pain that this action causes. These so-called "parasuicides" may lead to hospitalization, where clinicians detect that the act was, in fact, a gesture and not a true desire to die.

Individuals who have BPD improve over time, at least in terms of the severity of their symptoms. In a 10-year longitudinal study of 175 individuals with this disorder, a team of leading researchers in the field found that 85 percent no longer had symptoms, although they improved at slower rates than did people with either major depressive disorder or other personality disorders. However, their overall social functioning and Global Assessment of Functioning (GAF) scores remained lower over time than those of individuals with other personality disorders. Thus, although people may experience improved functioning in terms of their psychiatric disorder, they remain challenged when it comes to their employment and interpersonal relationships (Gunderson et al., 2011).

BPD's lifetime prevalence in the United States is 7 percent. The prevalence is much higher (15 to 20 percent) in psychiatric hospitals and outpatient community settings (Gunderson, 2011). At one time, researchers believed that women were more likely to have BPD than were men, but they consider the prevalence equal between the genders. However, there are gender differences in specific symptoms and in other disorders that occur in conjunction with a diagnosis of BPD. Men with BPD are more likely to have substance use disorder and antisocial personality characteristics. Women have higher rates of mood and anxiety disorders, eating disorders, and post-traumatic stress disorder. These differences in the nature of their associated disorders may account for the previous estimates of higher rates of the disorder in women, who clinicians more likely encountered in mental health settings. In contrast, clinicians are more likely to see men in substance use disorder programs (Sansone, Dittoe, Hahn, & Wiederman, 2011).

Theories and Treatment of BPD   BPD symptoms are tied to a number of biological factors, including high heritability (42 to 68 percent) and abnormalities in the amygdala and prefrontal cortex, areas of the brain involved in emotional processing and regulation. People with BPD may also have abnormalities in neurotransmitters and hormones involved in regulating emotional responses and sensitivity to pain (Gunderson, 2011). Although biological factors may certainly create a vulnerability to developing BPD, the psychological perspective is more prominent in the approach taken by clinicians who provide treatment. Disturbances in emotional functioning form an important component of the diagnosis of BPD and correspondingly, researchers have focused their efforts on identifying the specific psychological processes that contribute to these emotional disturbances. People with BPD seem to have an inability to regulate emotions (**emotional dysregulation**), limitations in ability to withstand distress (distress tolerance), and avoidance of emotionally uncomfortable situations and feelings (experiential avoidance).

You might be able to imagine how these difficulties can translate into the symptoms of BPD in everyday life when individuals with BPD encounter stressful situations. More so than other people, these individuals dislike emotionally tense situations, feel uncomfortable when distressed, and have great difficulty handling their anger when something does go wrong. Researchers investigating the relationships among these three types of emotional disturbance in a sample of young adult outpatients found that, after controlling

splitting
A defense, common in people with borderline personality disorder, in which individuals perceive others, or themselves, as being all good or all bad, usually resulting in disturbed interpersonal relationships.

emotional dysregulation
Lack of awareness, understanding, or acceptance of emotions; inability to control the intensity or duration of emotions; unwillingness to experience emotional distress as an aspect of pursuing goals; and inability to engage in goal-directed behaviors when experiencing distress.

for depressive symptoms, it was experiential avoidance that had the highest relationship to BPD symptoms (Iverson, Follette, Pistorello, & Fruzzetti, 2011).

Early childhood experiences play an important role in the development of BPD. These include childhood neglect or traumatic experiences, and marital or psychiatric difficulties in the home. Additionally, children who were insecurely attached are more likely to develop into adults with BPD (Gunderson, 2011).

As we pointed out earlier, people with BPD experience significant challenges in social functioning, but they can achieve significant relief of their symptoms. The treatment with the greatest demonstrated effectiveness is **dialectical behavior therapy (DBT),** a form of psychotherapy. Psychologist Marsha Linehan developed this type of behavior therapy specifically to treat individuals with BPD (Linehan, Cochran, & Kehrer, 2001). In DBT, the clinician integrates supportive and cognitive behavioral treatments with the goal of reducing the frequency of the client's self-destructive acts and to increase his or her ability to handle emotional distress.

The term "dialectical" in DBT refers to the back-and-forth process in which the clinician accepts clients as they are, but also confronts them about their problematic behavior, moving them slowly toward greater control over their feelings and behaviors. Therapists working from this perspective help their clients find new ways to analyze their problems and to develop healthier solutions. Clinicians help clients regulate their emotions, develop greater effectiveness in handling social relationships, tolerate emotional distress, and develop self-management skills. Using a process called core mindfulness, DBT clinicians teach their clients to balance their emotions, reason, and intuition as they approach life's problems.

Another evidence-based treatment for BPD, transference-focused psychotherapy, uses the client-clinician relationships as the framework for helping clients achieve greater understanding of their unconscious feelings and motives (Levy et al., 2006). Psychiatrically based management incorporates psychodynamic therapy as developed for BPD treatment, along with family interventions and pharmacologic treatment (Gunderson & Links, 2008).

Regardless of the specific treatment approach that they use, clinicians have the greatest success if they follow a set of basic principles (Table 14.5). These principles set the

dialectical behavior therapy (DBT)
Treatment approach for people with borderline personality disorder that integrates supportive and cognitive-behavioral treatments to reduce the frequency of self-destructive acts and to improve the client's ability to handle disturbing emotions, such as anger and dependency.

Table 14.5 Needs Involved in Basic Principles of Effective Treatment for Clients with BPD

Need for Clinicians to:	Explanation
Take over a primary role in treatment	One clinician discusses diagnosis, assesses progress, monitors safety, and oversees communication with other practitioners and family.
Provide a therapeutic structure	The clinician establishes and maintains goals and roles, particularly outlining limits on his or her availability and a plan to manage the client's possible suicidal impulses or other emergencies.
Support the client	The clinician validates the client's emotions of distress and desperation, providing hopeful statements that change is possible.
Involve the client in the therapeutic process	The clinician recognizes that progress depends on the client's active efforts to take control over his or her behavior.
Take an active role in treatment	The clinician is active in therapy, focuses on situations in the here-and-now, and helps the client connect his or her feelings to events in the past.
Deal with the client's suicidal threats or self-harming acts	The clinician expresses concern about and listens patiently to threats, but behaves judiciously (i.e., not always recommending hospitalization).
Be self-aware and ready to consult with colleagues	The clinician may require consultation when the client-clinician relationship becomes problematic.

SOURCE: Adapted from Gunderson, 2011.

MINI CASE

Histrionic Personality Disorder

Lynnette is a 44-year-old high school teacher who is notorious for her outlandish behavior and inappropriate flirtatiousness. Several of her students have complained to the principal about her seductive behavior during individual meetings. She often greets students with overwhelming warmth and apparent concern over their welfare, which leads some to find her appealing and engaging at first; however, they invariably become disenchanted when they realize how shallow she is. To her colleagues, she brags about her minor accomplishments as if they were major victories, yet if she fails to achieve a desired objective, she sulks and breaks down into tears. She is so desperate for the approval of others that she will change her story to suit whomever she is talking to at the time. Because she is always creating crises and never reciprocates the concern of others, people have become immune and unresponsive to her frequent pleas for help and attention.

stage for the clinician to help the client because they focus on providing key features that can be therapeutic for people with this specific disorder. Although many of these principles could generalize beyond clients with BPD, the need to establish clear boundaries, expectations, structure, and support are particularly important for individuals with this diagnosis. The last principle encourages clinicians to seek support themselves when the client's symptoms lead to difficulties within therapy. For example, the symptom of splitting shown by individuals with BPD may lead them alternatively to devalue and idealize the clinician. In these cases, the clinician may experience complicated reactions and would benefit from obtaining the outside perspective of a supervisor or consultant.

Histrionic Personality Disorder

histrionic personality disorder
A personality disorder characterized by exaggerated emotional reactions, approaching theatricality, in everyday behavior.

Clinicians diagnose **histrionic personality disorder** in people who show extreme pleasure as the center of attention and who behave in whatever way necessary to ensure that this happens. They are excessively concerned with their physical appearance, often trying to draw attention to themselves in such extreme ways that their behavior seems ludicrous. Furthermore, people perceive them as flirtatious and seductive, and they demand reassurance, praise, and approval of others and become furious if they don't get it. They want immediate gratification of their wishes and overreact to even minor provocations, usually in an exaggerated way, such as by weeping or fainting. Although their relationships are superficial, they assume them to be intimate and refer to acquaintances as "dear friends." They are easily influenced by others, lack analytical ability, and see the world in broad, impressionistic terms. This disorder was at one time regarded as synonymous with Freud's characterization of the "hysteric" individual (typically a woman). With the decline in psychoanalytic thinking, this disorder has fallen out of use (Blashfield, Reynolds, & Stennett, 2012) and, in fact, was almost eliminated in the proposed reworking of *DSM-5*.

Nevertheless, researchers continue to investigate personality traits associated with this disorder (e.g., Tomiatti et al., 2012). There do seem to be connections between this disorder and outcomes in people's everyday lives. For example, as is suggested in the description of the disorder, individuals with histrionic personality disorder may have difficulties in their close personal relationships. Their flightiness, tendency to flirt, and shallowness lead to instability in their close relationships, including higher divorce rates (Disney et al., 2012).

Narcissistic Personality Disorder

narcissistic personality disorder (NPD)
A personality disorder primarily characterized by an unrealistic, inflated sense of self-importance and a lack of sensitivity to the needs of other people.

People who meet the criteria for the diagnosis of **narcissistic personality disorder (NPD)** base their self-esteem excessively on the views of other people. They see themselves as exceptional and have a strong sense of entitlement. Because they see themselves

MINI CASE

Narcissistic Personality Disorder

Chad is a 26-year-old man who has been desperately trying to succeed as an actor. However, he has had only minor acting jobs and has been forced to support himself by working as a waiter. Despite his lack of success, he brags to others about all the roles he rejects because they aren't good enough for him. Trying to break into acting, he has been selfishly exploitive of any person whom he sees as a possible connection. He has intense resentment for acquaintances who have obtained acting roles and devalues their achievements by commenting that they are just lucky, yet, if anyone tries to give him constructive criticism, Chad reacts with outrage, refusing to talk to the person for weeks. Because of what he regards as his terrific looks, he thinks he deserves special treatment from everyone. At the restaurant, Chad has recurrent arguments with his supervisor, because he insists that he is a "professional" and that he should not have to demean himself by clearing dirty dishes from the tables. He annoys others because he always seeks compliments on his clothes, hair, intelligence, and wit. He is so caught up in himself that he barely notices other people and is grossly insensitive to their needs and problems.

as exceptional, they may set their personal standards as unrealistically high. Conversely, they may regard themselves as entitled to whatever they want and therefore set their personal standards far too low. Their impairments in goal setting also include a constant attempt to gain approval from other people.

In terms of their own sense of identity, people with NPD derive their self-definition and self-esteem from the way that they believe other people view them. However, although sensitive to others' opinions, they are unable to empathize with other people. They entirely direct whatever concern they have for others toward determining whether people like them or not. In their special personal relationships, they cannot establish true closeness with an intimate partner because they are so focused on themselves, their feelings, and how people perceive them. Their sense of entitlement translates into personality traits of grandiosity, and their desire for admiration leads them to seek out recognition whenever possible.

Although people with NPD may appear to think of themselves as better than others, this grandiosity may mask an underlying vulnerability in their sense of self. Some individuals with NPD may have a truly inflated and grandiose sense of self; hence, clinicians refer to them as high on grandiose narcissism. However, clinicians more accurately characterize others as high on vulnerable narcissism. These are the individuals who rely excessively on other people to confirm their worth. Those high on vulnerable narcissism are more sensitive to rejection, more likely to feel a sense of shame, and are less able to bolster their fragile sense of self by making up grandiose fantasies. They may appear shy and even empathic. When they feel that they have not lived up to their standards, they are more likely to become socially withdrawn. People who are higher on grandiose narcissism are more threatened by failure in the realm of personal accomplishments. Those high on vulnerable narcissism, by contrast, react more negatively when they feel that someone who is important to them is humiliating or betraying them (Besser & Priel, 2010). The *DSM-5* does not explicitly make this distinction, but clinicians and researchers maintain that it is an important differentiation (Pincus, 2011).

Prevalence studies reveal a wide variation in estimates of NPD's prevalence in the population. Averaging across these studies, researchers believe that NPD may occur in approximately 1 percent of the population. However, the rates are far higher in populations of individuals seeking clinical treatment, with those estimates ranging from 2 to as high as 36 percent (Dhawan, Kunik, Oldham, & Coverdale, 2010).

The traditional Freudian psychoanalytic approach regards narcissism as the individual's failure to progress beyond the early, highly self-focused stages of psychosexual development. Theorists operating within the object relations framework regard the narcissistic individual as having failed to form a cohesive, integrated, sense of self. The narcissistic individual expresses insecurity, paradoxically, in an inflated sense of self-importance as he or she tries to make up for early parental support (Kohut, 1966, 1971). Lacking a firm foundation of a healthy self, these individuals develop a false self that they precariously base on grandiose and unrealistic notions about their competence and desirability (Masterson, 1981). We can understand narcissistic personality disorder, then, as the adult's expression of this childhood insecurity and need for attention.

Clinicians who work within the psychodynamic perspective attempt to provide a corrective developmental experience, using empathy to support the client's search for recognition and admiration. At the same time, the clinician attempts to guide the client toward a more realistic appreciation that no one is flawless. As clients feel that their therapists increasingly support them, they become less grandiose and self-centered (Kohut, 1971).

Cognitive-behavioral theorists focus on the maladaptive ideas that their clients hold, including the view that they are exceptional people who deserve far better treatment than ordinary humans. These beliefs hamper their ability to perceive their experiences realistically, and they encounter problems when their grandiose ideas about themselves clash with their experiences of failure in the real world. Correspondingly, clinicians working in the cognitive-behavioral perspective structure interventions that work with, rather than against, the client's self-aggrandizing and egocentric tendencies. For example, rather than try to convince the client to act less selfishly, the therapist might try to show that there are better ways to reach important personal goals. At the same time, the therapist avoids capitulating to the client's demands for special favors and attention. When the therapist establishes and follows an agenda with clear treatment goals, the client may learn how to set limits in other areas of life (Beck, Freeman, & Davis, 2004).

Cutting across these theoretical perspectives, the most effective approach that clinicians can use in treating people with NPD is to provide reassurance while at the same time encouraging them to develop a more realistic view of themselves and other people. Unfortunately, people with NPD are difficult to treat because they tend not to have insight into their disorder. Moreover, the therapists who treat them may experience strong negative reactions to them due to the very nature of their symptoms of grandiosity and entitlement, making them critical and demeaning of their therapists (Dhawan et al., 2010). Their extreme perfectionism can also obstruct treatment. They have filled their lives with success and accomplishments that preserve their self-esteem and ward off their insecurities. As a result, it is particularly difficult for them to confront their anxieties and inner securities (Ronningstam, 2011).

Individuals with narcissistic personality disorder often devote their lives to seeking approval from others despite having very little concern for the well-being of other people.

14.4 Cluster C Personality Disorders

In Cluster C of the *DSM-5* personality disorders, we find a set of disorders that involve people who appear anxious or fearful and may seem highly restricted. They tend to be inner-directed and may draw little attention to themselves, in contrast to those individuals with personality disorders in Cluster B.

Avoidant Personality Disorder

People with **avoidant personality disorder** define themselves as lacking in social skills and having no desirable qualities that would make others want to be with them. They are more than "shy." Instead, their feelings of shame and inadequacy are so strong that they prefer not to be around others. They stay away almost entirely from social encounters, and are especially likely to avoid any situation with the potential for them to feel embarrassed. They may set unrealistically high standards for themselves, which, in turn, lead them to avoid encountering situations in which they feel doomed to fail. Convinced that they are socially inferior to others, people with avoidant personality disorder become extremely sensitive to rejection and ridicule, interpreting the most innocent remark as criticism. Rather than risk people making fun of them or rejecting them, they prefer to be by themselves. Involvement in an intimate relationship presents a severe threat because they fear shame or ridicule should they expose their flaws to a partner. People with avoidant personality disorder are high on the negative pole of the personality traits of detachment and negative affectivity. They are withdrawn, unlikely to experience intimacy, and unable to feel pleasure. Their negative affectivity takes the form of chronic and extreme anxiety.

Researchers believe that avoidant personality disorder exists along a continuum extending from the normal personality trait of shyness to social anxiety disorder. According to this view, avoidant personality disorder is a more severe form of social anxiety disorder (Rettew, 2000). Data from a longitudinal study involving over 34,000 adults found people with avoidant personality disorder were more likely to continue to experience symptoms of social anxiety disorder even after adjusting for a number of demographic factors (Cox, Turnbull, Robinson, Grant, & Stein, 2011). It is possible that the link between social anxiety disorder and avoidant personality disorder is that both involve excessive self-criticism.

Contemporary psychological explanations of this disorder include the psychodynamic approach's emphasis on the individual's fear of attachment in relationships (Sheldon & West, 1990). Cognitive-behavioral approaches regard avoidant personality disorder as reflecting the individual's hypersensitivity to rejection due to childhood experiences of extreme parental criticism (Carr & Francis, 2010). According to this approach, the dysfunctional attitudes that these individuals hold center on the core belief that they are

avoidant personality disorder
A personality disorder in which people have a low estimation of their social skills and are fearful of disapproval, rejection, and criticism or being ashamed or embarrassed.

MINI CASE

Avoidant Personality Disorder

Max is a delivery person for a large equipment corporation. His co-workers describe Max as a loner, because he does not spend time in casual conversation and avoids going out to lunch with others. Little do they know that every day he struggles with the desire to interact with them, but is too intimidated to follow through. Recently, he turned down a promotion to become manager because he realized that the position would require a considerable amount of day-to-day contact with others. What bothered him most about this position was not just that it would require interaction with people, but also that he might make mistakes that others would notice. Although he is 42, Max has hardly ever dated. Every time he feels interested in a woman, he becomes paralyzed with anxiety over the prospect of talking to her, much less asking her for a date. When female co-workers talk to him, he blushes and nervously tries to end the conversation as soon as possible.

A man with avoidant personality disorder stays at home by himself and avoids social contact of any kind for a significant portion of the time due to excessive fears of embarrassment or rejection by others.

flawed and unworthy of other people's regard. Because of their perceived unworthiness, they expect that people will not like them; therefore, they avoid getting close to others to protect themselves from what they believe is inevitable rejection. Contributing to their dilemma are their distorted perceptions of experiences with others. Their sensitivity to rejection causes them to misinterpret seemingly neutral and even positive remarks. Hurt by this presumed rejection, they retreat inward, placing further distance between themselves and others.

The main goal of therapists working in the cognitive-behavioral framework is to break the client's negative cycle of avoidance. Clients learn to articulate the automatic thoughts and dysfunctional attitudes that interfere with their ability to establish relationships with others. Although clinicians point out the irrationality of these beliefs, they do so in a supportive atmosphere. In order for these interventions to be successful, however, the client must learn to trust the therapist rather than see the therapist as yet another person who may ridicule or reject the client.

Cognitive-behavioral therapists may also use graduated exposure to present the client with social situations that are increasingly more difficult for them to confront. They may also train the client in specific skills intended to improve his or her intimate relationships. Therapists, regardless of orientation, must be extremely patient in their attempts to build a therapeutic relationship. The very nature of the avoidant condition makes the treatment prognosis poor, primarily because these clients tend to be intensely sensitive to the possibility of any form of negative evaluation (Millon, Davis, Millon, Escovar, & Meagher, 2000).

Dependent Personality Disorder

dependent personality disorder
A personality disorder whose main characteristic is that the individual is extremely passive and tends to cling to other people, to the point of being unable to make any decisions or to take independent action.

Individuals with **dependent personality disorder** are strongly drawn to others. However, they are so clinging and passive that they may achieve the opposite of their desires as others become impatient with their lack of autonomy. Convinced of their inadequacy, they cannot make even the most trivial decisions on their own. Others may characterize individuals with this disorder as "clingy." When they are alone, people with dependent personality disorder feel despondent and abandoned. They become preoccupied with the fear that close ones will leave them. They cannot initiate new

MINI CASE

Dependent Personality Disorder

Betty has never lived on her own; even while a college student 30 years ago, she commuted from home. She was known by her classmates as someone who was dependent on others. Relying on others to make choices for her, she did whatever her friends advised, whether it involved the choice of courses or the clothes she should wear each day. The week after graduation, she married Ken, whom she had dated all senior year. She was particularly attracted to Ken because his domineering style relieved her of the responsibility to make decisions. As she has customarily done with all the close people in her life, Betty goes along with whatever Ken suggests, even if she does not fully agree. She fears that he will become angry with her and leave her if she rocks the boat. Although she wants to get a job outside the home, Ken has insisted that she remain a full-time homemaker, and she has complied with his wishes. However, when she is home alone, she calls friends and desperately pleads with them to come over for coffee. The slightest criticism from Ken, her friends, or anyone else can leave her feeling depressed and upset for the whole day.

activities on their own because they feel that they will make mistakes unless others guide their actions. They go to extremes to avoid having people dislike them—for example, by agreeing with others' opinions, even when they believe that these opinions are misguided. Sometimes they take on responsibilities that no one else wants, so that others will approve of and like them. If anyone criticizes them, they feel shattered. They are likely to throw themselves wholeheartedly into relationships and, therefore, become devastated when relationships end. This extreme dependence causes them to urgently seek another relationship to fill the void.

Research on the personality traits of individuals with dependent personality disorder suggests that they have unusually high levels of agreeableness. Although we tend to think of agreeableness as an adaptive trait, at high levels, agreeableness can become a tendency to be overly docile, self-sacrificing, and clinging (Samuel & Gore, 2012).

Obsessive-Compulsive Personality Disorder

People with **obsessive-compulsive personality disorder (OCPD)** define their sense of self and self-worth in terms of their work productivity. We have just seen that people with NPD may also become excessively oriented toward work accomplishments to bolster their sense of self. People with OCPD are not looking for approval from their work accomplishments, but instead throw themselves into their work to the exclusion of their social relationships. Unfortunately, the extreme perfectionism that people with OCPD have about their work makes it difficult for them to complete a task because they can always see a flaw in what they have done. Their work products are never good enough to meet their unrealistic standards. They can also be overly moralistic because they stick to overly conscientious standards that almost anyone would find difficult to meet.

People with OCPD have a great deal of difficulty understanding how other people feel, particularly when those feelings differ from their own. Other people, in turn, perceive them as rigid and stubborn. Because they have such high standards for themselves, people with OCPD are very critical of other people who they see as not matching their own expectations.

The pathological personality trait of compulsivity that people with OCPD have to an excessive degree reflects this rigid perfectionism. Things must be "just so," or they are miserable. They also experience a great deal of negative affect and tend to go back over and over what they've done, looking for flaws. This is the quality of perseveration.

The words "obsessive" and "compulsive" as applied to the OCPD personality disorder have a different meaning than in the context of obsessive-compulsive disorder. People with

obsessive-compulsive personality disorder (OCPD)
A personality disorder involving intense perfectionism and inflexibility manifested in worrying, indecisiveness, and behavioral rigidity.

MINI CASE

Obsessive-Compulsive Personality Disorder

For as long as he can remember, Trevor has been preoccupied with neatness and order. As a child, his room was meticulously clean. Friends and relatives chided him for excessive organization. For example, he insisted on arranging the toys in his toy closet according to color and category. In college, his rigid housekeeping regimens both amazed and annoyed his roommates. He was tyrannical in his insistence on keeping the room orderly and free from clutter. Trevor has continued this pattern into his adult life. He is unhappy that he has not found a woman who shares his personal habits, but consoles himself by becoming immersed in his collection of rare record albums featuring music of the 1940s.

Trevor, a file clerk, prides himself on never having missed a day of work, regardless of health problems and family crises. However, his boss will not offer Trevor a promotion because she feels he is overly attentive to details, thus slowing up the work of the office as he checks and rechecks everything he does. He enhances his sense of self-importance by looking for opportunities in the office to take control. For example, when his co-workers are planning a party, Trevor tends to slow down matters because of his annoying concerns about every detail of the event. More often than not, his co-workers try to avoid letting him get involved because they object to his rigidity, even in such trivial matters.

OCPD do not experience obsessions and compulsions. The hyphenated term in OCPD refers to this rigidly compulsive (i.e., fixated on certain routines) personality tendency and also obsessive concern with perfectionism. This may seem like splitting hairs, but it is an important distinction for you to keep in mind. Moreover, OCPD is a disturbance of personality, not a disturbance involving anxiety or even out-of-control behaviors, as reflected in the *DSM-5* authors' proposal to remove OCD from the anxiety disorders.

It is important to keep in mind that there is a difference between the hard-working, well-organized person with high standards and a concern about getting a job done right and the person with an obsessive-compulsive personality disorder. People with this disorder are unproductive, and their pursuit of perfection becomes self-defeating rather than constructive.

A woman with obsessive-compulsive personality disorder is so highly driven for order and perfection that she is unable to tolerate the anxiety she feels when objects in her vicinity are disorganized.

From a psychodynamic standpoint, Freud believed that people with an obsessive-compulsive style have not progressed from, or are constantly returning to, the anal stage of psychosexual development. Psychodynamic theorists no longer focus entirely on psychosexual stages, but instead give more attention to cognitive factors and prior learning experiences as central to the development of OCPD.

From the standpoint of cognitive-behavioral theory, people with this disorder have unrealistic expectations about being perfect and avoiding mistakes (Beck et al., 2004). Their feelings of self-worth depend on their behaving in ways that conform to an abstract ideal of perfectionism. If they fail to achieve that ideal (which, inevitably, they must), they regard themselves as worthless. In this framework, obsessive-compulsive personality disorder is based on a problematic way of viewing the self.

Clinicians using cognitive-behavioral treatment for clients with OCPD face challenges due to characteristic features of this personality disorder. The person with OCPD tends to intellectualize, to ruminate over past actions, and to worry about making mistakes. Cognitive-behavioral therapy, with its focus on examining the client's thought processes, may reinforce this ruminative tendency. Consequently, therapists may use more traditional behavioral techniques, such as thought stopping with the intention of having the client "stop" when he or she is overtaken by ruminative worry (Millon et al., 2000). Clinicians might also find it useful to use metacognitive interpersonal therapy, a procedure that causes patients to "think about their thinking." In this procedure, clinicians help their clients take a step back and learn to identify their problematic ruminative thinking patterns in the context of a building a supportive therapeutic alliance (Dimaggio et al., 2011).

14.5 Personality Disorders: The Biopsychosocial Perspective

The personality disorders represent a fascinating mix of long-standing personal dispositions and behavior patterns and disturbances in identity and interpersonal relationships.

Although we tend to focus on these disorders as they appear at one point in time, clearly they evolve over an individual's life. The *DSM* authors will very likely continue to refine and elaborate on their scientific base if not their classification. We may hope that mental health professionals will develop, not only a better understanding of this form of disturbance, but also, perhaps, a richer appreciation for the factors that contribute to normal personality growth and change through life.

Return to the Case: Harold Morrill

Harold was enrolled for a year-long contract at a local DBT center where he attended twice-weekly psychotherapy and three therapy groups per week. The program focused on teaching emotion regulation and social skills. By fostering a supportive relationship with Harold, his therapist was able to model correct emotional regulation and validation of a wide range of emotions, so that Harold would not feel the need to resort to extreme measures in order to gain attention from others.

Dr. Tobin's reflections: Like many individuals with borderline personality disorder, Harold grew up in what is known as an invalidating environment—with parents who were more or less absent in his upbringing. He found that acting in an extreme manner was the only way he was able to get attention from his parents, and so this became the only way for him to connect with others. He even displayed this in the intake evaluation by showing the evaluator the marks of his self-mutilation, threatening to storm out of the room, and spontaneously bursting into tears. Further, he showed interpersonal instability in his requesting the evaluator to be his therapist and then immediately turning on her (or "devaluing") when told that she could not see him for therapy. Unlike females with borderline personality disorder (who make up the majority of borderline individuals) who often present with depression, males tend to present with more of an angry affect and are more likely to engage in substance abuse as a coping mechanism. Females are more likely to be sexually promiscuous or to engage in eating disordered behaviors in order to cope with their extreme emotions.

It is typical for an individual with Borderline Personality Disorder to present for treatment only after a suicide attempt or having strong suicidal ideation, as the disorder is ego-syntonic—meaning that the individual rarely understands that their behavior is abnormal. With the appropriate treatment, Harold's

chances of continuing to experience highly unstable and shifting mood and relational patterns greatly decreases. You may be wondering why Harold was not referred for substance abuse treatment. It was the opinion of the intake evaluator that his substance abuse, especially his alcohol use, was secondary to his personality disorder. It is typical for DBT treatment programs to require their clients to abstain from abusing substances during the course of treatment. Further, with more appropriate mood regulation skills, Harold's substance abuse may remit. Should he continue to abuse substances throughout his treatment, he will then be referred for a specific substance use disorder treatment program.

SUMMARY

- A **personality disorder** is an ingrained pattern of relating to other people, situations, and events with a rigid and maladaptive pattern of inner experience and behavior, dating back to adolescence or early adulthood. In the *DSM-5*, personality disorders represent a collection of distinguishable sets of behavior, falling into 11 distinct categories. These 11 diagnoses are grouped into three clusters based on shared characteristics. Cluster A includes **paranoid, schizoid,** and **schizotypal personality disorders,** which share the features of odd and eccentric behavior. Cluster B includes **antisocial, borderline, histrionic,** and **narcissistic** personality disorders, which share overdramatic, emotional, and erratic or unpredictable attitudes and behaviors. Cluster C includes **avoidant, dependent,** and **obsessive-compulsive personality disorders,** which share anxious and fearful behaviors.

- Because the personality disorders are grouped into discrete categories, clinicians evaluating individuals for a possible diagnosis must decide how many of the criteria a client meets within each category and assign a diagnosis on that basis. Either the client has the disorder or not. The clinician may start by trying to match the most prominent symptoms that the individual shows with the diagnostic criteria. If the client does not fit the criteria for that disorder, the clinician may either move to another disorder or decide that the client has a personality disorder "not otherwise specified."

- The diagnosis of antisocial behavior has its origins in the work of Hervey Cleckley, whose 1941 book, *The Mask of Sanity*, represented the first scientific attempt to list and categorize the behaviors of the "psychopathic" personality. Cleckley (1976) developed a set of criteria for **psychopathy,** a cluster of traits that includes lack of remorse or shame for harmful acts committed against others; poor

judgment and failure to learn from experience; extreme egocentricity and incapacity for love; lack of emotional responsiveness to others; impulsivity; absence of "nervousness"; and unreliability, untruthfulness, and insincerity. Building on Cleckley's work, Canadian psychologist Robert D. Hare developed the Psychopathy Checklist–Revised (PCL-R) (Hare, 1997), an assessment instrument whose two factors are the core psychopathic personality traits and an antisocial lifestyle. The core personality traits include glibness and superficial charm, a grandiose sense of self-worth, pathological lying, a lack of empathy for others, lack of remorse or guilt, and an unwillingness to accept responsibility for one's actions.

- There is a difference between antisocial personality disorder and antisocial behavior. Antisocial personality disorder represents a deeply entrenched pattern of behavior, with wide-ranging effects on both the individual and the people with whom the individual comes into contact. From a biological perspective, family inheritance studies provide strong evidence in favor of genetic explanations of antisocial personality disorder, the personality trait of psychopathy, and antisocial behavior with heritability estimates as high as 80 percent. Closely related to the biological perspective is the hypothesis that antisocial personality disorder causes neuropsychological deficits reflected in abnormal patterns of learning and attention. The accepted wisdom for many years in the field of abnormal psychology was that personality disorders were untreatable. Despite these challenges to successful treatment, the most effective interventions are those that are less focused on developing empathy and conscience or personality. Instead, effective treatment should convince participants that they are responsible for their own behavior.

KEY TERMS

Ethical and Legal Issues

Learning Objectives

15.1 Explain ethical standards including competence, informed consent, confidentiality, relationships with clients/students/ research collaborators, and record keeping

15.2 Explain ethical and legal issues in providing services, including commitment of clients, right to treatment, and refusal of treatment and least restrictive alternatives

15.3 Understand forensic issues in psychological treatment, such as the insanity defense, competency to stand trial, and the purpose of punishment

CHAPTER 15

Case Report: Mark Chen

Demographic information: Mark is a 19-year-old Asian American male.

Presenting problem: Mark has been attending individual psychotherapy at a private outpatient clinic on a weekly basis for 8 months after initially presenting to treatment following a Major Depressive Episode. Mark had never received previous psychiatric treatment, and after confiding to the resident director of his dormitory that he had been having a difficult time with his transition to college, she gave him information on nearby therapy clinics, as the small college had no counseling center of its own. Shortly after beginning therapy, the clinician referred him to a psychiatrist who prescribed an SSRI. Mark responded well to both therapy and the antidepressant, and his symptoms had remitted within about 4 weeks, although he still experienced a persistently low mood. He continued to come for weekly psychotherapy sessions to work on the issues underlying his depression. His mood has been relatively stable and he has few complaints about depressive symptomatology for the majority of the time since starting therapy. Mark started to become more involved with extracurricular activities at school and began attending more social events. Over the past three sessions however, Mark has been presenting with increased depressive symptoms. He reported sleeping about 10 to 12 hours per night and still does not feel rested. He is eating only once per day, having difficulty concentrating, and experiences frequent, unprovoked crying episodes. These symptoms are similar to those that he reported when he initially presented for therapy. Mark also admitted that he had not left his dorm room except to come to his therapy session. During his most recent therapy session, Mark's affect was markedly depressed and despondent. He was tearful as he reported that he was feeling increasingly hopeless and was having recurrent thoughts about ending his life. He was unable to identify a particular stressor for this current episode, remarking that "all of a sudden things just feel so . . . pointless." He stated that he had been having thoughts about suicide for about 2 weeks, but that the thoughts had become much more pervasive over the past few days.

During the session, Mark's therapist responded to his report of suicidality by performing a safety evaluation. He asked if Mark had thought about how he would commit suicide, to which Mark responded that he was in possession of a rope at home and planned on hanging himself in his dorm room from a ceiling beam. He then asked Mark about how strong his intention was to commit suicide, to which Mark responded that he had planned on hanging himself that morning, but decided to come in for one last therapy session and to "say goodbye."

Recently in therapy Mark had been discussing how he felt significant pressure from his family to achieve high grades in college. As a double major in Economics and Political Science, Mark explained that he had been finding it difficult to keep up with all of his coursework and attain "acceptable" grades. Much of his work in therapy had focused on his low self-image and propensity to undervalue not only his achievements, but also his abilities to perform well in school and in other areas. Mark had been working with his therapist to learn strategies to help generate feelings of self-worth and to take pride in his accomplishments so far. During this work, Mark often struggled to find ways to take pride in himself and his work. He attributed this to his family, and how, as he explained, "they never think I'm good enough, no matter what I do. I always have to be doing better. They're never satisfied." He stated that his parents had been a source of constant pressure for his entire life.

Mark has no siblings, and so he believed this added to their "excessive nagging." Although Mark recognized that this was a source of distress, he found it difficult to "fight back" and value himself as he had never learned to do this on his own. Throughout therapy, Mark and his clinician discussed ways to improve the relationship with his family. Mark found this difficult given that he and his parents got into arguments when they spoke on the phone. Several times, he had thought about cutting off contact with them altogether. However, this presented a challenge, given that Mark's parents supported him financially. Due to his intensive focus on schoolwork, Mark had little time in college to make friends and was often by himself in his dorm room. He reported that even when he had down time, he was constantly worrying about his schoolwork and found it quite difficult to relax.

Relevant history: Mark has experienced three depressive episodes prior to starting therapy. His first depressive episode lasted for approximately 8 months, and remitted without intervention. The other two subsequent episodes lasted for approximately 2 to 3 months each and also remitted on their own. Although these episodes were much shorter than the first, the period in between episodes had greatly decreased. The period between starting therapy and his current depressive episode was the longest period of time in between episodes to date. Although he reported thoughts of suicide during his prior depressive episodes, he had never had a plan or clear intent to commit suicide. Mark reported that he wasn't sure if his family had any history of depression or mood disorders.

Case formulation: Due to his prior depressive episodes and absence of a manic episode, Mark carries a diagnosis of Major Depressive Disorder, Recurrent. In addition, he currently meets criteria for a Major Depressive Episode. We add the qualifier of "Severe" to the diagnosis, due to his intent and plan to commit suicide.

Treatment plan: Mark's clinician determined that he posed a significant threat to himself, based on his report that he had a plan and intent to commit suicide. The clinician asked Mark if he could agree to make a contract to protect his safety. He would allow Mark to leave the session only if Mark agreed to call 911 should he feel an increase in intent to commit suicide. Mark was unable to state that he would be safe should he go home, and the clinician informed Mark that he would have to go to the hospital immediately. The clinician called 911, and an ambulance transported Mark to a nearby psychiatric hospital for stabilization.

Sarah Tobin, PhD

Psychologists are guided in both their clinical and research work by the professional guidelines established by the major professional organization, the American Psychological Association (APA). These guidelines do not hold legal power, but individual states and territories in the United States establish strict codes required for psychologists and other mental health professionals to obtain and keep their licenses. Not only are health professionals required to follow these standards, but they must regularly recertify their ability to provide services by obtaining continuing education to ensure that they are able to practice according to the highest standards.

15.1 Ethical Standards

To be considered a "psychologist," many states require that the individual pass a rigid set of licensing requirements. All states in the United States have a board of psychologists that carry out the legal requirements for obtaining and retaining a psychology license. These requirements typically include passing an examination, obtaining a certain number of hours of supervised training, receiving recommendations from other licensed psychologists, and, to remain licensed, participation in a certain number of hours of continuing education.

As we discussed in Chapter 2, psychologists follow the APA Ethical Principles of Psychologists and Code of Conduct (Ethics Code) (2010). The "general principles" are not enforceable rules, but are intended for psychologists to consider in arriving at an ethical course of action. In contrast, the "Ethical Standards" are enforceable rules.

Failure to follow these rules could result in sanctions, including loss of membership in APA and loss of a state professional license. In making decisions about their professional behavior, psychologists must consider this Ethics Code as well as any applicable laws and regulations of their state psychology boards.

There are ten standards contained within the Ethics Code, which we summarize in Table 15.1. Since writing the first version in 1953, APA has rewritten the Ethics Code to keep up with changes in electronic communication and, most recently, to set forth codes that psychologists in the military should follow to ensure that they do not participate in unethical conduct during the course of interrogating military prisoners. APA is also active in developing codes of conduct for the provision of Internet-based psychotherapy (Fisher & Fried, 2008). We will focus here on several key components of the Ethics Code that generalize across several of the specific areas.

TABLE 15.1 Summary of APA Ethics Code

Standard	Summary
1: Resolving Ethical Issues	How psychologists should resolve ethical conflicts, report ethical violations, and cooperate with professional ethics committees.
2: Competence	Establishes the fact that psychologists must work within their boundaries of competence based on their training, experience, consultation, and supervision; describes what psychologists should do in emergencies; sets forth criteria for delegating work to others; describes how to resolve personal problems and conflicts that might interfere with their ability to provide services.
3: Human Relations	Provides criteria that psychologists must follow when they relate to employees, clients, and trainees; describes how psychologists should avoid conflict of interest; regulates the nature of informed consent in research, clinical practice, or consulting, including administering psychological services through corporations.
4: Privacy and Confidentiality	Sets forth the principles for protecting research participants and clients; mandates that any public information (such as published research) includes reasonable steps to disguise the person or organization.
5: Advertising and Other Public Statements	Instructs psychologists not to provide false statements through advertising or other public outlets, in media presentations, and testimonials; sets forth limits to in-person solicitation from potential clients or people in need of care.
6: Record Keeping and Fees	Provides conditions that psychologists must follow in maintaining their records, charging clients for services, and providing reports to payors of service or sources of research funding.
7: Education and Training	Regulates the activities of psychologists in the classroom, as supervisors or trainers, and as developers of education and training programs.
8: Research and Publication	Offers specific guidelines for psychologists who conduct research including informing participants about their rights to offering inducements for research participation, using deception in research, debriefing participants, providing humane care for animals, reporting research results, avoiding plagiarism, and taking precautions in publishing of research articles.
9: Assessment	Describes the code for psychologists in conducting assessments, including how assessment data should be collected, use of informed consent, release of test data, principles of test construction, scoring and interpretation of test results, and maintenance of test security.
10: Therapy	Sets forth code for psychologists who provide therapy including obtaining informed consent, conducting therapy with individuals, couples, families and groups, interrupting and terminating therapy, and avoiding sexual intimacies with clients, relatives of clients, and former clients.

What's New in the DSM-5

Ethical Implications of the New Diagnostic System

Following release of the *DSM*-5 draft in late 2011, a number of mental health professional organizations composed a joint response to what they perceived as potentially disastrous consequences of addition of some diagnoses and removal of others. For example, by eliminating the category of "Asperger's Syndrome," critics contend that they will be leaving potentially untreated many thousands of individuals who suffer from its symptoms. In Chapter 13, we discussed the potential problems involved in broadening the dementia diagnosis to include individuals with mild cognitive impairments. Such changes would create the opposite problem of potentially mislabeling individuals who are experiencing normal age-related changes in memory.

The *DSM*-5 was written in a manner intended to reflect the latest scientific evidence in the most objective manner possible. Inevitably, however, there will be room for debate as researchers and clinicians examine the available research studies and the evidence they infer from working with their clients. There are also social and political implications of changes in the diagnostic system. If individuals do not receive a diagnosis, as may happen with children formerly diagnosed with autistic disorder, then they cannot qualify for certain types of insurance to cover the costs of their education, treatment, and medications. Politicians then are faced with making decisions about how to allocate public funding for treatment, education, and research.

Another significant change in the *DSM*-5 that has widespread implications is the shift from diagnosing major depressive disorder in the cases of people who are suffering from bereavement after the loss of a loved one. In the *DSM-IV-TR*, people who suffered the symptoms of bereavement were excluded from the diagnosis of major depressive disorder, a situation called the "bereavement exclusion." The elimination of the bereavement exclusion could mean that a clinician would diagnose an individual experiencing depressive symptoms following the death of someone close to him or her with major depressive disorder. That person will now have a psychiatric diagnosis that could potentially interfere with his or her ability to find employment in certain sectors.

However, if they don't assign a diagnosis to a client with clinically significant symptoms, does this mean their clients will be unable to obtain medication to treat their symptoms? Conversely, in order to continue to provide services to their clients who may no longer qualify for a diagnosis, should they find ways around the changing guidelines to ensure their clients do receive the diagnosis?

Unfortunately, because psychological symptoms are more difficult in many cases to identify than are physical symptoms, the debate about appropriate diagnostic categories and criteria will no doubt continue throughout each subsequent edition of the *DSM*. Maintaining your awareness of these continued debates can ultimately help you and the people you know receive the best care possible. If you continue in a professional career in mental health, it will be vital for you to stay on top of both the latest literature and the latest diagnostic issues to provide the best treatment possible for your own clients.

Competence

As you can see from Standard 2, psychologists are expected to have appropriate competence to carry out therapy, consulting, teaching, and research. They achieve this competence, first of all, in their post-baccalaureate training. APA provides accreditation to clinical doctoral training programs in the United States to ensure that these programs provide future psychologists with sufficient breadth and depth to form the basis for their career in providing mental health services. Upon completing their coursework, PhD and PsyD (Doctor of Psychology) graduates must obtain intensive supervision as interns and postdoctoral trainees. They must then pass a state licensing exam. To maintain their license, they must take and complete a required number of continuing education courses within each year or two after licensure.

The result of this intensive training is that psychologists have the competence to assess, conceptualize, and provide interventions for clients whom they accept into treatment. On a related note, Standard 5 also instructs psychologists to be truthful about their areas of expertise. Clinicians who claim to be, for example, sports psychologists should have received training in this field, preferably with supervision under a professional with appropriate training credentials. When clinicians advertise their specialty, they should have suitable expertise, including current familiarity with a field, in order to be able to offer those services.

The clinician should also have what we might call "emotional competence" to be able to provide services to their clients. Within a range of acceptable variations, they should be free of a diagnosable psychological disorder. Should they develop such a disorder, they should receive treatment and consider suspending their practice until their symptoms are in remission or minimally, under control. To ensure that mental health professionals meet these standards of competence, they are expected to conduct regular self-scrutiny, in which they objectively evaluate their competence to carry out their work. They can also benefit from seeking supervision or consultation from another professional, perhaps one with more experience or expertise.

A witness testifies in a court hearing to protect a relative with a psychological disorder.

In a court of law, counsel often asks psychologists to give expert testimony, such as providing testimony about the limits of eyewitness memory or the nature of a psychiatric diagnosis. If they do, they must make clear the limits of their areas of expertise. If they do not have expertise in a particular area, they must obtain consultation from an expert who does.

Even more complicated than the role of expert witness is the task of conducting evaluations in child protection cases. Such evaluations are necessary in situations in which there are concerns about the child's welfare. For example, if there has been evidence or charges involving abuse, a court might call a mental health professional to make recommendations about the child's care. A judge might appoint a clinician as an agent of the court or a child protection agency, or one of the parents might hire the clinician. In some instances, the clinician is a **guardian *ad litem*,** a person whom the court appoints to represent or make decisions for a person (e.g., minor or incapacitated adult) who is legally incapable of doing so in a civil legal proceeding.

Other challenges present themselves when clients seek the services of clinicians whose needs are beyond the clinician's area of competence. In these cases, the clinician should either make a referral or obtain appropriate supervision. For example, a clinician who does not treat older adults with dementia may receive a referral from a middle-aged client seeking help with her mother who is experiencing memory problems. Unless the clinician is qualified to provide assessments of cognitive functioning in older adults, the clinician should recommend that someone else evaluate the mother.

To assist psychologists in evaluating their competencies in areas that may be outside of their areas of expertise, APA has developed guidelines in specific areas of treatment. APA has approved a variety of practice guidelines and related criteria as APA policy in such areas as treatment of gay, lesbian, and bisexual clients (Table 15.2), child protection

guardian ad litem
A person appointed by the court to represent or make decisions for a person (e.g., a minor or an incapacitated adult) who is legally incapable of doing so in a civil legal proceeding.

TABLE 15.2 Guidelines for Psychotherapy with Lesbian, Gay, and Bisexual Clients

1. Psychologists understand that homosexuality and bisexuality are not indicative of mental illness.

2. Psychologists are encouraged to recognize how their attitudes and knowledge about lesbian, gay, and bisexual issues may be relevant to assessment and treatment and seek consultation or make appropriate referrals when indicated.

3. Psychologists strive to understand the ways in which social stigmatization (i.e., prejudice, discrimination, and violence) poses risks to the mental health and well-being of lesbian, gay, and bisexual clients.

4. Psychologists strive to understand how inaccurate or prejudicial views of homosexuality or bisexuality may affect the client's presentation in treatment and the therapeutic process.

5. Psychologists strive to be knowledgeable about and respect the importance of lesbian, gay, and bisexual relationships.

6. Psychologists strive to understand the particular circumstances and challenges faced by lesbian, gay, and bisexual clients.

7. Psychologists recognize that the families of lesbian, gay, and bisexual people may include people who are not legally or biologically related.

8. Psychologists strive to understand how a person's homosexual or bisexual orientation may have an impact on his or her family of origin and the relationship to that family of origin.

9. Psychologists are encouraged to recognize the particular life issues or challenges that are related to multiple and often conflicting cultural norms, values, and beliefs that lesbian, gay, and bisexual members of racial and ethnic minorities face.

10. Psychologists are encouraged to recognize the particular challenges that bisexual individuals experience.

11. Psychologists strive to understand the special problems and risks that exist for lesbian, gay, and bisexual youth.

12. Psychologists consider generational differences within lesbian, gay, and bisexual populations and the particular challenges that lesbian, gay, and bisexual older adults may experience.

13. Psychologists are encouraged to recognize the particular challenges that lesbian, gay, and bisexual individuals experience with physical, sensory, and cognitive-emotional difficulties.

14. Psychologists support the provision of professional education and training on lesbian, gay, and bisexual issues.

15. Psychologists are encouraged to increase their knowledge and understanding of homosexuality and bisexuality through continuing education, training, supervision, and consultation.

16. Psychologists make reasonable efforts to familiarize themselves with relevant mental health, educational, and community resources for lesbian, gay, and bisexual people.

Ethical Issues

Even though a person may be in extreme distress, on his or her admission to a psychiatric hospital, the clinician must obtain informed consent.

SOURCE: American Psychological Association, 2012b.

evaluations (Table 15.3), psychological practice with older adults (Table 15.4), psychological practice with girls and women (Table 15.5), and assessment of and intervention with people with disabilities (Table 15.6). These guidelines are intended to educate practitioners and provide recommendations about professional conduct. As such, they are useful tools for psychologists in practice to develop and maintain competencies and/or learn about new practice areas. APA also serves a credentialing role in the profession, providing accreditation of clinical training programs, approval of so-called "specialty" fields (such as neuropsychology or geropsychology), as well as curriculum standards for programs ranging from high school to post-graduate training in psychology.

Informed Consent

Although we typically think only of research when we hear the term "informed consent," this criterion for ethical behavior applies to other contexts, including therapy. The reason for this is that clinical psychologists are expected to provide their clients with knowledge ahead of time about what they can expect to occur in treatment. At the outset of therapy, clinicians should provide clients with a written statement that outlines the goals of treatment, the process of therapy, the client's rights, the therapist's

Table 15.3 Guidelines for Psychological Evaluations in Child Protection Matters

1. The primary purpose of the evaluation is to provide relevant, professionally sound results or opinions in matters where a child's health and welfare may have been and/or may in the future be harmed.

2. In child protection cases, the child's interest and well-being are paramount.

3. The evaluation addresses the particular psychological and developmental needs of the child and/or parent(s) that are relevant to child protection issues, such as physical abuse, sexual abuse, neglect, and/or serious emotional harm.

4. The role of the psychologist conducting evaluations is that of a professional expert who strives to maintain an unbiased, objective stance.

5. The serious consequences of psychological assessment in child protection matters place a heavy burden on psychologists.

6. Psychologists gain specialized competence.

7. Psychologists are aware of personal and societal biases and engage in nondiscriminatory practice.

8. Psychologists avoid multiple relationships.

9. Based on the nature of the referral questions, the scope of the evaluation is determined by the evaluator.

10. Psychologists performing psychological evaluations in child protection matters obtain appropriate informed consent from all adult participants and, as appropriate, inform the child participant. Psychologists need to be particularly sensitive to consent issues.

11. Psychologists inform participants about the disclosure of information and the limits of confidentiality.

12. Psychologists use multiple methods of data gathering.

13. Psychologists neither overinterpret nor inappropriately interpret clinical or assessment data.

14. Psychologists conducting a psychological evaluation in child protection matters provide an opinion regarding the psychological functioning of an individual only after conducting an evaluation of the individual adequate to support their statements or conclusions.

15. Recommendations, if offered, are based on whether the child's health and welfare have been and/or may be seriously harmed.

16. Psychologists clarify financial arrangements.

17. Psychologists maintain appropriate records.

SOURCE: American Psychological Association, 1999.

responsibilities, the treatment risks, the techniques that he or she will use, what the client should pay, and the limits of confidentiality. If the treatment involves medication, the clinician should make the client aware of possible short-term and long-term side effects. The clinician has a responsibility to ensure that the client is aware of these issues, receives answers to any questions, and has the opportunity to refuse treatment. The client is then prepared to decide whether or not to continue in treatment.

There are possible complications. Psychotherapy is an imprecise procedure, and it is not always possible to predict its course, risks, or benefits. The clinician's job, however, is to give a best estimate at the onset of therapy and to provide further information as therapy proceeds. Most people are able to discuss these matters with the clinician and to make an informed choice. There are special cases, however, when prospective clients are unable to understand the issues in order to make informed consent. These cases include children and people who are unable to understand the full nature of the treatment that they might enter due to cognitive or other psychological disabilities. In these cases, the clinician must work with the individual's family or other legally appointed guardians.

Confidentiality

Several of the standards in the APA Ethics Code cover the issue of confidentiality. This means that the client can expect that what takes place in therapy is private. Confidentiality is long regarded as a sacred part of the clinician-client relationship and is strictly maintained by licensed psychologists (Fisher & Vacanti-Shova, 2012). Safeguards against

TABLE 15.4 Guidelines for Psychological Practice with Older Adults

Attitudes

Guideline 1. Psychologists are encouraged to work with older adults within their scope of competence, and to seek consultation or make appropriate referrals when indicated.

Guideline 2. Psychologists are encouraged to recognize how their attitudes and beliefs about aging and about older individuals may be relevant to their assessment and treatment of older adults, and to seek consultation or further education about these issues when indicated.

General Knowledge about Adult Development, Aging, and Older Adults

Guideline 3. Psychologists strive to gain knowledge about theory and research in aging.

Guideline 4. Psychologists strive to be aware of the social/psychological dynamics of the aging process.

Guideline 5. Psychologists strive to understand diversity in the aging process, particularly how sociocultural factors such as gender, ethnicity, socioeconomic status, sexual orientation, disability status, and urban/rural residence may influence the experience and expression of health and of psychological problems in later life.

Guideline 6. Psychologists strive to be familiar with current information about biological and health-related aspects of aging.

Clinical Issues

Guideline 7. Psychologists strive to be familiar with current knowledge about cognitive changes in older adults.

Guideline 8. Psychologists strive to understand problems in daily living among older adults.

Guideline 9. Psychologists strive to be knowledgeable about psychopathology within the aging population and cognizant of the prevalence and nature of that psychopathology when providing services to older adults.

Assessment

Guideline 10. Psychologists strive to be familiar with the theory, research, and practice of various methods of assessment with older adults, and knowledgeable of assessment instruments that are psychometrically suitable for use with them.

Guideline 11. Psychologists strive to understand the problems of using assessment instruments created for younger individuals when assessing older adults, and to develop skill in tailoring assessments to accommodate older adults' specific characteristics and contexts.

Guideline 12. Psychologists strive to develop skill at recognizing cognitive changes in older adults, and in conducting and interpreting cognitive screening and functional ability evaluations.

Intervention, Consultation, and Other Service Provision

Guideline 13. Psychologists strive to be familiar with the theory, research, and practice of various methods of intervention with older adults, particularly with current research evidence about their efficacy with this age group.

Guideline 14. Psychologists strive to be familiar with and develop skill in applying specific psychotherapeutic interventions and environmental modifications with older adults and their families, including adapting interventions for use with this age group.

Guideline 15. Psychologists strive to understand the issues pertaining to the provision of services in the specific settings in which older adults are typically located or encountered.

Guideline 16. Psychologists strive to recognize issues related to the provision of prevention and health promotion services with older adults.

Guideline 17. Psychologists strive to understand issues pertaining to the provision of consultation services in assisting older adults.

Guideline 18. In working with older adults, psychologists are encouraged to understand the importance of interfacing with other disciplines, and to make referrals to other disciplines and/or to work with them in collaborative teams and across a range of sites, as appropriate.

Guideline 19. Psychologists strive to understand the special ethical and/or legal issues entailed in providing services to older adults.

Education

Guideline 20. Psychologists are encouraged to increase their knowledge, understanding, and skills with respect to working with older adults through continuing education, training, supervision, and consultation.

SOURCE: From Guidelines for Psychological Practice with Older Adults, 2004 (published report). Copyright © by the American Psychological Association. Reprinted by permission.

TABLE 15.5 Guidelines for Psychological Practice with Girls and Women

Guideline 1.   Psychologists strive to be aware of the effects of socialization, stereotyping, and unique life events on the development of girls and women across diverse cultural groups.

Guideline 2.   Psychologists are encouraged to recognize and utilize information about oppression, privilege, and identity development as they may affect girls and women.

Guideline 3.   Psychologists strive to understand the impact of bias and discrimination upon the physical and mental health of those with whom they work.

Guideline 4.   Psychologists strive to use gender and culturally sensitive, affirming practices in providing services to girls and women.

Guideline 5.   Psychologists are encouraged to recognize how their socialization, attitudes, and knowledge about gender may affect their practice with girls and women.

Guideline 6.   Psychologists are encouraged to employ interventions and approaches that have been found to be effective in the treatment of issues of concern to girls and women.

Guideline 7.   Psychologists strive to foster therapeutic relationships and practices that promote initiative, empowerment, and expanded alternatives and choices for girls and women.

Guideline 8.   Psychologists strive to provide appropriate, unbiased assessments and diagnoses in their work with women and girls.

Guideline 9.   Psychologists strive to consider the problems of girls and women in their sociopolitical context.

Guideline 10. Psychologists strive to acquaint themselves with and utilize relevant mental health, education, and community resources for girls and women.

Guideline 11. Psychologists are encouraged to understand and work to change institutional and systemic bias that may impact girls and women.

SOURCE: Guidelines for Psychological Practice with Girls and Women, American Psychological Association, February 2007. http://www.apa.org/about/division/girlsandwomen.pdf. Copyright © by the American Psychological Association. Reprinted with permission.

the disclosure of confidential information exist within the laws of most states. In order to adhere to the highest standards of professional practice, clinicians should have a clearly articulated protocol regarding the way in which they will inform clients about the nature, extent, and limits of confidentiality.

The content of therapy is privileged communication. In other words, the clinician may not disclose any information about the client in a court of law without the client's expressed permission. The protection offered by confidentiality allows clients in therapy to discuss freely their symptoms, problems in relationships with others, and early childhood history, all of which may contain extremely personal and delicate information. Confidentiality also protects research subjects from having the information they disclose to an investigator revealed to the public without their express consent.

There are, however, exceptions to confidentiality. Legally, there are instances in which the court is entitled to receive information that emerges within the context (Barsky & Gould, 2002). These include child custody cases, trials in which a defendant is using mental disability as a defense in a criminal trial, and when a court appoints a psychologist to determine whether the defendant is competent to stand trial. Court-ordered assessments are an exception to the confidentiality standard. Defendants must be informed of this limitation in writing and acknowledge their understanding.

The principle of confidentiality also has limits in cases involving abuse. Every state requires some form of mandated reporting by professionals when they learn firsthand of cases involving child abuse or neglect. Abuse, which may be physical or sexual, is an act by a caretaker that causes serious physical or emotional injury. Neglect is the intentional withholding of food, clothing, shelter, or medical care. The purpose of mandated reporting is to protect victims from continuing abuse and neglect, to initiate steps toward clinical intervention with the abused individual, and to deter, punish, and rehabilitate abusers. Psychologists include individuals who are vulnerable people, those who are handicapped or intellectually disabled. Vulnerable individuals also include impaired

TABLE 15.6 Guidelines for Assessment of and Intervention with Persons with Disabilities

Disability Awareness, Training, Accessibility, and Diversity

Guideline 1.   Psychologists strive to learn about various disability paradigms and models and their implications for service provision.

Guideline 2.   Psychologists strive to examine their beliefs and emotional reactions toward various disabilities and determine how these might influence their work.

Guideline 3.   Psychologists strive to increase their knowledge and skills about working with individuals with disabilities through training, supervision, education, and expert consultation.

Guideline 4.   Psychologists strive to learn about federal and state laws that support and protect people with disabilities.

Guideline 5.   Psychologists strive to provide a barrier-free physical and communication environment in which clients with disabilities may access psychological services.

Guideline 6.   Psychologists strive to use appropriate language and respectful behavior toward individuals with disabilities.

Guideline 7.   Psychologists strive to understand both the common experiences shared by persons with disabilities and the factors that influence an individual's personal disability experience.

Guideline 8.   Psychologists strive to recognize social and cultural diversity in the lives of persons with disabilities.

Guideline 9.   Psychologists strive to learn how attitudes and misconceptions, the social environment, and the nature of a person's disability influence development across the life span.

Guideline 10. Psychologists strive to recognize that families of individuals with disabilities have strengths and challenges.

Guideline 11. Psychologists strive to recognize that people with disabilities are at increased risk for abuse and address abuse-related situations appropriately.

Guideline 12. Psychologists strive to learn about the opportunities and challenges presented by assistive technology.

Testing and Assessment

Guideline 13. In assessing people with disabilities, psychologists strive to consider disability as a dimension of diversity together with other individual and contextual dimensions.

Guideline 14. Depending on the context and goals of assessment and testing, psychologists strive to apply the assessment approach that is most psychometrically sound, fair, comprehensive, and appropriate for clients with disabilities.

Guideline 15. Psychologists strive to determine whether accommodations are appropriate for clients to yield a valid test score.

Guideline 16. Consistent with the goals of the assessment and disability-related barriers to assessment, psychologists in clinical settings strive to appropriately balance quantitative, qualitative, and ecological perspectives and articulate both the strengths and limitations of assessment.

Guideline 17. Psychologists in clinical settings strive to maximize fairness and relevance in interpreting assessment data of clients who have disabilities by applying approaches which reduce potential bias and balance and integrate data from multiple sources.

Interventions

Guideline 18. Psychologists strive to recognize that there is a wide range of individual response to disability, and collaborate with their clients who have disabilities, and when appropriate, with their clients' families to plan, develop, and implement psychological interventions.

Guideline 19. Psychologists strive to be aware of the therapeutic structure and environment's impact on their work with clients with disabilities.

Guideline 20. Psychologists strive to recognize that interventions with persons with disabilities may focus on enhancing well-being as well as reducing distress and ameliorating skill deficits.

Guideline 21. When working with systems that support, treat, or educate people with disabilities, psychologists strive to keep the clients' perspectives paramount and advocate for client self-determination, integration, choice, and least restrictive alternatives.

Guideline 22. Psychologists strive to recognize and address health promotion issues for individuals with disabilities.

SOURCE: American Psychological Association, 2012a.

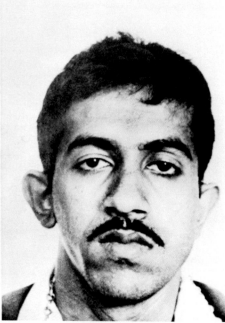

Tatiana Tarasoff (left), a junior at the University of California, was stabbed to death on the doorstep of her home by Prosenjit Poddar (right), who had told his therapist that he intended to kill her.

elders who cannot otherwise protect themselves. Some states require that psychologists report not only financial, emotional, physical, or sexual abuse, but also self-neglect by persons age 60 or older who do not attend to their needs for food, clothing, safe and secure shelter, personal care, and medical treatment.

Another exception to the principle of confidentiality involves instances in which the clinician learns that a client is planning to hurt another person. These cases face the psychologist with a **duty to warn** (or **otherwise protect**). The duty to warn mandate requires that the clinician inform the intended victim about possible dangers posed by the client's behavior.

Duty-to-warn laws have their origins in a famous Tarasoff v. Regents of the University of California ("Tarasoff v The Regents of the University of California 551 P 2d 334, [California 1976]") case, which involved a community college student named Tatiana Tarasoff who was shot and fatally stabbed by a man named Prosenjit Poddar, a graduate student who came from India in 1967 to study electronics and naval architecture at the University of California, Berkeley. Poddar met Tarasoff, a young woman who lived with her parents near campus. He began to pursue her romantically, but she was not interested in him, rejecting his marriage proposal. This was in March of 1969. Poddar became despondent and told his roommate that he wanted to blow up Tarasoff's house. The roommate advised Poddar to seek treatment and in June of 1969, Poddar saw a psychiatrist at the university health services who then prescribed antipsychotic medications and referred him to a psychologist for therapy. In August 1969, Poddar told the psychologist, repeatedly announcing his homicidal thoughts, about Tarasoff. After the psychologist warned Tarasoff that he would restrain him if he continued to express these thoughts, Poddar abruptly discontinued therapy. Although the psychologist and psychiatrist told the police about Poddar's intentions and they then confronted him, Poddar denied this intention, and the law took no further actions. Poddar began to stalk Tarasoff and in October 1969, found her home alone and killed her. He then turned himself over to the police. Tarasoff's parents sued the University and the police and, finally, in December 1976, the California Supreme Court ruled in favor of the parents. The essential question was "whether a psychotherapist must, on pain of a civil suit for damages, recognize that a patient poses a risk of serious harm or death to an identified third party and then must warn or otherwise protect that third party" (Herbert, 2002) (p. 419).

duty to warn (or otherwise protect)
The clinician's responsibility to notify a potential victim of a client's harmful intent toward that individual.

The 2007 shooting at Virginia Tech by a student there brought national attention to not only the importance of treating college students with mental health disorders but the implications of the "duty to warn" rule.

The ramifications of this landmark decision continue to be felt by psychologists who struggle to differentiate between their clients' serious threats and random fantasies. In trying to make these distinctions, clinicians recurrently weigh the client's right of confidentiality against concern for the rights of other people. In a more recent case, in April 2007, a student at Virginia Polytechnic Institute and State University named Seung-Hui Cho killed 32 people and wounded 25 others. He had received treatment from a mental health facility after having demonstrated threatening and harassing behavior on campus. In Virginia's version of the Tarasoff duty-to-warn statute, mental health caregivers must "take charge" of an individual in order to implicate duty-to-warn liability. Although Cho named no specific victims, the case once again raised questions about the legal responsibilities of mental health professionals when their clients express homicidal or suicidal intensions.

Relationships with Clients, Students, and Research Collaborators

APA's Ethics Code makes clear that psychologists must take steps to ensure that they conduct all dealings with other individuals, including other psychologists, with the utmost of professionalism. In therapy, clear roles and boundaries are essential in order for the client to feel safe and trusting, and for the clinician to maintain objectivity and effectiveness. When a clinician violates boundaries within a therapeutic relationship, the consequences can be catastrophic for clients.

The most extreme form of violation of the therapeutic relationship involves sexual intimacy with clients, which is explicitly forbidden in the ethical codes of the mental health professions. In fact, psychologists are prohibited from becoming sexually involved with a client for at least two years after treatment discontinues (or longer in many cases).

Psychologists must also refrain from **multiple relationships,** particularly with their clients in a therapy context. The APA Ethics Code defines multiple relationships as occurring when a psychologist is in a professional role with a person and has

multiple relationships
Unethical relationships occurring when a psychologist is in a professional role with a person and has another role with that person that could impair the psychologist's "objectivity, competence, or effectiveness in performing his or her functions as a psychologist" or otherwise risks exploiting or harming the other person.

Multiple Relationships Between Clients and Psychologists

The APA Ethics Code explicitly prohibits most multiple relationships between psychologists and their clients. However, given the nature of the therapist-client relationship, it is almost inevitable that potential multiple relationships can develop. In evaluating the ethics of a multiple relationship, we should distinguish between sexual and nonsexual. Sexual relationships are prohibited for at least 2 years after the ending of a therapeutic relationship. The boundaries around sexual relationships, however, can be much murkier. In rural communities or small towns, for example, psychologists may find it almost impossible to avoid such dilemmas in situations ranging from retail sales to education to provision of other professional services. Social interactions between therapists and their clients may also prove difficult, even in larger communities with multiple intersection social circles. In Chapter 3, we discussed the ethics facing psychologists in the legal system. Here we will look more generally at multiple relationships as they affect psychologists in their clinical practice.

According to research on multiple relationships (Lamb, Catanzaro, & Moorman, 2004), social interactions, in fact, are the largest group of situations in which psychologists find themselves potentially facing complications from encountering their clients. Psychologists also reported relationships in the spheres of business, financial dealings, and religious affiliations. These relationships were more likely to occur between psychologists and their former clients than with their current clients. In the area of sexual intimacy, the researchers asked the psychologists to indicate whether the potential had ever existed for them to have relationships with their clients. However, even though they may have been tempted, these psychologists did not follow through on their interest due to their personal ethics, values, and morals. They also were highly unlikely to pursue a sexual relationship with a former client. At least half of the psychologists also indicated that they wished to avoid dual relationships and/or did not want to take advantage of the unequal power dynamics between themselves and clients. Relatively few respondents mentioned that they refrained from these relationships due to possible legal repercussions or from having their peers or professional associations sanction them.

The results of this survey suggest that psychologists adhere to high ethical standards in their relationships with current and former clients. As the study's authors acknowledge, however, it is possible that the participants who were the guiltiest of multiple relationships were the least likely to respond.

Q: *You be the judge*: Turning back to the ethical issue, consider the pros and cons of multiple relationships. Once a professional relationship is over, is it absolutely necessary for the psychologist not to become involved with a former client, particularly if he or she had a close connection during the course of treatment? On the other hand, you can argue that the very nature of the client-therapist relationship is such that each should respect the boundaries, even for years after treatment has ended. Should ethics codes be as stringent as they are in the area of multiple relationships?

another role with that person that could impair the psychologist's "objectivity, competence, or effectiveness in performing his or her functions as a psychologist" or otherwise risks exploiting or harming the other person. However, multiple relationships that we reasonably would not expect to cause impairment or risk exploitation or harm are not unethical.

There are other boundaries around psychologists in relating to others, including avoiding harm to others, refraining from conflict of interest, and exploiting other people with whom they have a professional relationship. When psychologists collaborate on research, they should give or take credit only for work that they have actually performed.

Record Keeping

In an age of increasing use of electronic health care records (including maintenance of files on portable tablets), the need to protect clients becomes even more critical. These concerns led in 1996 to passage by the U.S. Congress of a complex series of rules governing patient records. This legislation, the **Health Insurance Portability and Accountability Act of 1996 (HIPAA),** went into effect in several stages beginning in 2003 and ending in 2008. To enforce the new HIPAA rules, there are civil monetary penalties for failure on the part of the employer, health care provider, or the insurance company.

Title I of HIPAA protects workers and their families from loss of health care insurance when they change or lose their jobs. Prior to HIPAA, people moving from one job to another were vulnerable to losing their health insurance if they had a history of serious illness. For example, if a man who was treated for a cancerous condition took a new job, he might have encountered the disturbing fact that he could not receive insurance coverage because of his illness.

Title II is intended to regulate the ways in which providers and insurance companies maintain and transmit medical records, called protected health information. In an electronic age, when organizations often send health records and billing information via the Internet, health care professionals must take special care to protect confidential medical records.

The Ethics Code also governs the way in which psychologists charge fees for their services. They must inform clients about the fees that they charge prior to beginning any interventions and should reach an agreement with clients about arrangements for billing. Fee practices must also be consistent with the law. Surprisingly, psychologists can barter with their clients for services, i.e., accept goods, services, or other nonmonetary remuneration in return for psychological services. However, they cannot do so if this arrangement would be clinically counterindicated or exploitative of their clients.

Health Insurance Portability and Accountability Act of 1996 (HIPAA)
U.S. legislation intended to ensure adequate coverage and protect consumers from loss of insurance coverage when they change or lose their jobs.

15.2 Ethical and Legal Issues in Providing Services

Psychologists and other mental health professionals face a number of issues in ensuring that clients receive the best possible treatment. At the same time, clinicians must balance the rights of clients with those of the community, issues that create ethical and legal dilemmas.

Commitment of Clients

In the best of all possible situations, clients who are in need of psychological treatment seek it themselves. However, clients are not always in a position to judge when they need the care of a psychologist. In these cases, the mental health professional may consider recommending **commitment,** an emergency procedure for involuntary hospitalization. Clinicians begin commitment proceedings in the cases of people who, if not hospitalized, are likely to create harm for self or other people as a result of mental illness.

The concept of commitment stems from the legal principle that the state has the authority to protect those who are unable to protect themselves. The law refers to this authority as ***parens patriae.*** This responsibility is vested in various professionals, such as psychologists, physicians, and nurse specialists, who are authorized to sign an application for a time-limited commitment (usually 10 days). If a health professional is not accessible, a police officer may file commitment papers. In this application, the professional states why the failure to hospitalize the individual would result in the likelihood of serious harm due to mental illness. In some instances, application goes to a district court judge, perhaps by a family member. After hearing the reasons for commitment, the judge may issue a warrant to apprehend the mentally ill person in order for that individual to receive a qualified professional assessment. Once the individual is hospitalized, subsequent applications and hearings may be necessary to extend the period of commitment.

commitment
An emergency procedure for involuntary psychiatric hospitalization.

parens patriae
The state's authority to protect those who are unable to protect themselves.

A court hearing is held to determine if a client should receive involuntary psychological treatment. These hearings involve expert testimony from psychologists who have evaluated the client.

More than two dozen states now give courts, police officers, psychiatrists, mental health professionals, and families the option to coerce mentally ill individuals who have broken the law into treatment rather than to arrest them. Those supporting legislation permitting outpatient commitment assert that the benefits to society, in addition to the therapeutic benefits for the individual, outweigh the risks. In 1999, New York State enacted "Kendra's Law," which provides for the state's court-ordered involuntary outpatient commitment program, termed assisted outpatient treatment (AOT). The law is named after the tragic death of Kendra Webdale, who was pushed in front of a subway train in Manhattan by a stranger who had untreated schizophrenia. Recent evidence shows that the program has resulted in decreased hospitalization and improved service engagement and medication adherence (Swartz et al., 2010).

Right to Treatment

The admission to psychiatric hospitals, whether voluntary or involuntary, is only the beginning of the story for people entering these facilities. Once admitted, the client enters a world that is unfamiliar to most people causing them to feel frightened and confused. If hospitalized against their will, they may feel outraged. To minimize these reactions, health professionals try to ensure that they give clients appropriate care and that they understand their legal rights immediately upon entry to a facility. We have already discussed the importance of obtaining informed consent, when possible, prior to beginning treatment to ensure that clients understand the nature of treatment, the options available, and the client's rights.

Perhaps the most important legal right of the person entering a psychiatric hospital is the **right to treatment.** It may seem odd that we need laws to ensure that patients in hospitals receive treatment, but, as you read the legal history of these statutes, you will understand why they are necessary. The right to treatment emerged as the outcome of a landmark legal case, Wyatt v. Stickney ("Wyatt v. Stickney, 325 F. Supp. 781 (M.D. Ala. 1971); 344 F. Supp. (M.D. Ala. 1972)"). In this case, a patient named Ricky Wyatt instituted a class action suit against the commissioner of mental health for the state of Alabama, Dr. Stickney, in response to the horrifying conditions in psychiatric and mental retardation facilities. These institutions failed to provide even a minimum of treatment, and were so inhumane that

right to treatment
Legal right of person entering psychiatric hospital to receive appropriate care.

they were actually detrimental to the patient's mental health. At the time, the court relied on a principle put forth by a legal scholar invoking the constitutional right to due process in making the ruling against Alabama. In other words, the court ruled that mental health professionals cannot commit people to an institution that is supposed to help them unless they can guarantee that institutionalization will help them. Otherwise, their commitment constitutes the equivalent of imprisonment without a trial. Similarly, people with psychiatric disorders are, therefore, entitled to treatment in the community, rather than relegation to institutions. In order to fulfill the conditions of this act, the government is obligated to provide funding for community-based treatment.

Patients also have the right to a humane environment, including privacy, appropriate clothing, opportunities for social interaction, mail, telephone, and visitation privileges, comfortable furnishings, physical exercise, and adequate diet. A related right is that of liberty and safety ("Youngberg v. Romeo, 457 U.S. 307 (1982)"), which includes the right to move about the ward and receive protection from violent patients. Seclusion and mechanical restraints are forbidden unless medically indicated and, when clinicians use them, they can only use them for a limited amount of time and only for appropriate purposes (La Fond, 1994).

Refusal of Treatment and Least Restrictive Alternative

substituted judgment
A subjective analysis of what the client would decide if he or she were cognitively capable of making the decision.

least restrictive alternative
A treatment setting that provides the fewest constraints on the client's freedom.

Just as clients have a right to treatment, they also have a right to refuse unwanted treatment. It is accepted in our society that competent adults have the right to either accept or decline medical treatment. In view of the serious side effects of certain psychotherapeutic medications, states in the United States have enacted laws that give the client the right to refuse unwanted medications. In these cases, the clinician must obtain a written order from a court of law, documenting the need for medication.

Similarly, clients may regard as harsh, or even punitive, treatments such as the application of aversive noise or unpleasant shock and therefore refuse such treatment if they are capable of giving or withholding informed consent. However, cognitively compromised clients incapable of making informed decisions about such interventions may require protection by the law. A court can, in these cases, apply a doctrine called **substituted judgment** for people deemed incompetent of making such treatment decisions themselves. Substituted judgment is a subjective analysis of what the client would decide if he or she were cognitively capable of making the decision. For example, a judge might have to imagine whether he or she would willingly approve the administration of aversive shock as a treatment designed to stop the client from engaging in life-threatening head-banging behavior.

Clients also have the right for placement in what we call the **least restrictive alternative** to treatment in an institution, meaning that adult protective services provided in a manner no more restrictive of a vulnerable adult's liberty and no more intrusive than necessary to achieve and ensure essential services. This right was established in 1975 by a landmark ruling in the U.S. Supreme Court ("O'Connor v. Donaldson (1975) 95 S. Ct. 2486"). In 1943, Kenneth Donaldson was a 34-year-old father of three working in a General Electric defense plant when he showed what appeared to be symptoms of paranoid schizophrenia. Sent to a state hospital, he was given 23 electro-shock treatments and resumed normal life. In the mid-1950s he developed paranoid delusions that he was being poisoned. At the instigation of his father, he was committed to Florida's Chattahoochee State Hospital in 1956, where he remained for 15 years. Steadfastly denying he was ill, he refused all treatment once he was

This woman is a patient in an eating disorder day-treatment facility, where part of her treatment involves ingesting a certain amount of calories per day. Since she has decision-making capacity, she reserves the right to refuse this treatment, even if her care providers do not think this is in her best interest.

hospitalized. However, Donaldson never exhibited signs of threatening behavior. His disorder, which clinicians diagnosed as paranoid schizophrenia, went into remission soon after his commitment. Nevertheless, Donaldson was kept in the hospital for nearly two decades, during which time he was denied many fundamental privileges.

The evidence showed that Donaldson's confinement was a simple regime of enforced custodial care, not a program designed to alleviate or cure his supposed illness. Numerous witnesses had testified that Donaldson had received nothing but custodial care while at the hospital. For substantial periods, Donaldson was simply kept in a large room that housed 60 patients, many of whom were under criminal commitment. Donaldson's requests for ground privileges, occupational training, and an opportunity to discuss his case with the hospital superintendent, D.J.B. O'Connor, or other staff members were repeatedly denied.

The Supreme Court's ruling in Donaldson's favor, along with several less-known cases, paved the way for major changes in the mental health system. This case established the legal principle that the presence of mental illness in a person is not sufficient reason for confinement to a mental hospital.

15.3 Forensic Issues in Psychological Treatment

At the interface between psychology and the law, forensic psychologists provide advice to the judicial system in many ways. We have already seen that psychologists may serve as expert witnesses. More generally, forensic issues in psychological treatment involve determining whether an individual who commits a crime should be incarcerated or be treated in a mental health facility.

The Insanity Defense

Insanity is a legal term that refers to the individual's lack of moral responsibility for committing criminal acts. The **insanity defense** is the argument a lawyer presents acting on behalf of the client that, because of the existence of a mental disorder, the client should not be held legally responsible for criminal actions. Criminal law is based on the principle that people have free choice in their actions and that, if they break the law, they must be held responsible. We judge people determined to be "insane" to lack freedom of choice over controlling their behavior, as well as the mental competence to distinguish right from wrong. The insanity defense originated as an attempt to protect people with mental disorders from punishment for harmful behavior resulting from their disturbed psychological state.

The insanity defense emerged from various legal precedents and the legal profession's attempts at clarification. In 1843, the court handed down the **M'Naghten Rule** in a landmark case involving a Scottish woodcutter named Daniel M'Naghten. Under the delusional belief that God was commanding him, M'Naghten killed an English government official. When M'Naghten went to trial, the defense argued that he should not be held responsible for the murder because his mental disorder prevented him from knowing the difference between right and wrong. He believed that he was following the commands of a higher power and, therefore, saw nothing wrong in his behavior. This is why the M'Naghten Rule is referred to as the "right-wrong test."

Most jurisdictions in the United States adopted the M'Naghten Rule, but legislatures and courts eventually modified and expanded the definition. Legislators later added the "irresistible impulse test" to the M'Naghten Rule to take into account the possibility that some disturbed behaviors may result from people's inability to inhibit actions that they feel compelled to carry out. Although they may know that an act is wrong, they are unable to stop themselves from acting on their impulses.

The **Durham Rule** later expanded the insanity defense after a court decision in 1954 asserted that a person is not criminally responsible if the "unlawful act was the product of mental disease or defect." Its intent was to protect individuals with disturbed

insanity
A legal term that refers to the individual's lack of moral responsibility for committing criminal acts.

insanity defense
The argument, presented by a lawyer acting on behalf of the client, that, because of the existence of a mental disorder, the client should not be held legally responsible for criminal actions.

M'Naghten Rule
The "right-wrong test" used in cases of the insanity defense to determine whether a defendant should be held responsible for a crime.

Durham Rule
An expansion of the insanity defense based on determining that the individual was not criminally responsible if the unlawful act was due to the presence of a psychological disorder.

REAL STORIES

Susanna Kaysen: Involuntary Commitment

"Don't you think you need a rest?"

"Yes," I said.

He strode off to the adjacent room, where I could hear him talking on the phone.

I have thought often of the next 10 minutes—my last 10 minutes. I had the impulse, once, to get up and leave through the door I'd entered, to walk the several blocks to the trolley stop and wait for the train that would take me back to my troublesome boyfriend, my job at the kitchen store. But I was too tired.

He strutted back into the room, busy, pleased with himself.

"I've got a bed for you," he said. "It'll be a rest. Just for a couple of weeks, okay?" He sounded conciliatory, or pleading, and I was afraid.

"I'll go Friday," I said. It was Tuesday, maybe by Friday I wouldn't want to go.

He bore down on me with his belly. "No. You go now."

I thought this was unreasonable. "I have a lunch date," I said.

"Forget it," he said. "You aren't going to lunch. You're going to the hospital." He looked triumphant.

In 1967, Susanna Kaysen, then 19 years old, was committed to McLean Hospital in Belmont, Massachusetts, following a suicide attempt in which she consumed 50 aspirin pills along with vodka. In her book, *Girl, Interrupted*, Susanna provides her own insight into her experience contrasted with actual documents from her commitment that she later obtained. Throughout the book, Susanna questions the judgment of her psychiatrist who decided to commit her, a decision that resulted in a hospitalization lasting nearly 2 years. Susanna discusses mental illness from a philosophical standpoint, and uses her experience, as well as the experiences of her fellow patients, as a way of questioning whether she was really in need of inpatient treatment, whether she was really "crazy." As

you can note from the passage above, the book also underscores the changes that have taken place over the past 50 years in procedures and laws regarding involuntary psychiatric hospitalizations. Although perhaps her doctor at the time felt that Susanna was a threat to herself, given her suicide attempt as well as a history of some self-harming behaviors (cutting and wrist-banging), his process of commitment did not include a thorough risk assessment, and was solely based on his clinical judgment.

When Susanna was admitted to McLean, clinicians diagnosed her with Borderline Personality Disorder. Looking back at her case now, it appears that her symptoms point more to a diagnosis of major depressive episode. In *Girl, Interrupted*, Susanna contemplates the meaning of her diagnosis at the time and whether her symptoms as described in the *DSM* matched up with her true experience. 'So these were the charges against me,' she writes. "I didn't read them until twenty-five years later. 'A character disorder' is what they'd told me then . . . It's a fairly accurate picture of me at eighteen, minus a few quirks like reckless driving and eating binges. It's accurate but it isn't profound. Of course, it doesn't aim to be profound. It's not even a case study. It's a set of guidelines, a generalization. I'm tempted to try refuting it, but then I would be open to the further charges of 'defensiveness' and 'resistance.'"

In the book, Susanna discusses her transition back to living independently following her hospitalization, and the stigma that she faced when applying for jobs, as she had to list the address of the hospital, which was well known to belong to McLean.

"In Massachusetts, 115 Mill Street is a famous address. Applying for a job, leasing an apartment, getting a driver's license: all problematic. The driver's license appli-

cation even asked, 'Have you been hospitalized for mental illness?' Oh, no, I just loved Belmont so much I decided to move to 115 Mill Street."

'You're living at One fifteen Mill Street?' asked a small, basement-colored person who ran a sewing-notions shop in Harvard Square, where I was trying to get a job.

'Uh-huh.'

'And how long have you been living there?'

'Oh, a while.' I gestured at the past with one hand.

'And I guess you haven't been working for a while?' He leaned back, enjoying himself.

'No,' I said. 'I've been thinking things over.'

I didn't get the job.

As I left the shop my glance met his, and he gave me a look of such terrible intimacy that I cringed. I know what you are, said his look.

What were we, that they could know us so quickly and so well?"

Susanna Kaysen wrote about her experience in an inpatient psychiatric facility in *Girl, Interrupted*. In the book, she questions the validity of her diagnosis and if she should have been hospitalized for her symptoms.

In her time at McLean, Susanna thought at length about the implications of her hospitalization for her own mental health. At times throughout the book it appears that she is trying to reason with herself and make a case for committing herself. We could argue that this was actually harmful to her, that she had to make herself believe that she needed to be there. By today's standards, we would deem this unethical, given that her treatment was causing more harm than good. Also by current ethical standards, mental health professionals would consider her length of stay almost unimaginable, given that the average length of stay is now closer to about 1 week for most inpatient hospitalizations. At the time of the book, however, a patient's stay was dictated by the family's ability to pay for hospitalization. Currently, clinicians focus on stabilizing the patient as efficiently as possible so that he or she may safely return to the community. In the end, the hospital allowed Susanna to sign herself out and she moved into her own apartment.

"Maybe I was just flirting with madness the way I flirted with my teachers and my classmates. I wasn't convinced I was crazy, though I feared I was. Some people say that having any conscious opinion on the matter is a mark of sanity, but I'm not sure that's true. I still think about it. I'll always have to think about it . . . It's a common phrase I know. But it means something particular to me: the tunnels, the security screens, the plastic forks, the shimmering, ever-shifting borderline that like all boundaries beckons and asks to be crossed. I do not want to cross it again."

---

psychological functioning due to any of a variety of conditions, including personality disorders. This expansion of the insanity defense put the burden on mental health experts to prove whether or not a defendant was mentally disturbed, even when there was no evidence of overt psychosis.

In an attempt to develop uniform standards for the insanity defense, the **American Law Institute's (ALI) guidelines** in 1962 (Sec. 4.01) took a middle position between the pre-Durham Rule codes and the liberal standing which the Durham Rule takes. According to the ALI, people are not responsible for criminal behavior if their mental disorder prevents them from appreciating the wrongfulness of their behavior (a variation of the M'Naghten Rule) or from exerting the necessary willpower to control their acts (the irresistible impulse rule). The important term here is "appreciating." In other words, knowing what is right and wrong is not equivalent to understanding that one's behavior is wrong. An important feature of the ALI code is the exclusion from the insanity defense of people whose only maladaptive behavior is repeated criminal or otherwise antisocial

American Law Institute's (ALI) guidelines
Guidelines proposing that people are not responsible for criminal behavior if their mental disorder prevents them from appreciating the wrongfulness of their behavior.

conduct. The ALI guideline is a more viable standard of insanity than the Durham Rule, because it takes the question of guilt or innocence away from mental health experts and places it in the hands of the jury, who can then make a determination based on the evidence related to the crime itself.

In the years following the publication of the ALI standards, the courts applied the insanity defense much more widely. However, the situation changed once again after John Hinckley attempted to assassinate President Ronald Reagan in 1981. Hinckley was obsessed with actress Jodie Foster believing that, if he killed the president, Jodie Foster would be so impressed that she would fall in love with him and marry him. When the case went to trial, the jury determined that Hinckley's actions justified the insanity defense. He was sent to St. Elizabeth's Hospital in Washington, D.C., where he remains to this day. This case brought to the nation's attention the rarely used but controversial insanity plea as it had been broadened through the Durham and ALI standards. The public was particularly outraged about the possibility that an assassin could potentially get away with murder on the grounds of having a mental disorder.

In response to the Hinckley case, Congress passed the Insanity Defense Reform Act of 1984, which added the criterion of "severe disturbance" to the insanity defense. This meant that people with personality disorders would no longer be able to plead insanity. The law also moved the burden of proof. Previously, the defense

The case of John Hinckley, who in 1981 tried to assassinate President Ronald Reagan, raised public concern over possible misuse of the insanity defense. Hinckley, who was declared insane by the courts, was not imprisoned; instead he was committed to treatment at St. Elizabeth's Hospital in Washington, D.C., where he still resides.

needed to provide reasonable doubt regarding the prosecution's argument that the defendant was sane. The Reform Act meant that the defense must now prove that the defendant fit the legal definition of insanity, which is a more difficult argument to make.

Individual states vary in the nature of the insanity defense that they use in criminal proceedings. Some states have moved toward separating the question of guilt from that of mental disorder by allowing the plea of "guilty, but mentally ill." The court does not exonerate defendants who use this plea from the crime, but gives them special consideration in sentencing.

Partly because of the storm of criticism following the Hinckley case, however, the court took a very different route in 1992. This time, the case involved a 31-year-old man, Jeffrey Dahmer, who confessed to murdering and dismembering 17 boys and young men and explained that he was driven to kill out of a compulsion to have sex with dead bodies. The trial took place in Milwaukee for the 15 murders that Dahmer claimed to have committed in Wisconsin. Dahmer's defense attorney argued that Dahmer's crimes could only have been committed by someone who fit the legal definition of insane. The jury rejected his guilty but mentally ill plea as they believed him to be responsible for his crimes and able to appreciate the wrongfulness of his conduct. He was sentenced to consecutive life terms for the murder of each of his victims. In 1994, Dahmer was killed at the age of 34 by another inmate.

Other highly publicized cases since Dahmer's have brought out other subtleties in the insanity defense as we currently construe it. In California, the Menendez brothers admitted to the premeditated murder of their parents in response, they claimed, to years of sexual and emotional abuse. The brothers, 23 and 26 at the time of the crime, admitted to the killings, but claimed they had acted in self-defense. Their defense attorneys presented the argument of "imperfect self-defense," asserting that they acted out of the mistaken belief that their parents were about to kill them, a belief that stemmed from a lifelong history of physical, emotional, and sexual abuse. The defense claimed that, on the night of the killings one of the brothers, in an altered mental state, retrieved his shotgun, loaded it, and burst in on his parents. The prosecution, which proved its case, claimed that the brothers instead were motivated by the $14 million they stood to inherit after the death of their parents.

The irresistible impulse defense came to light in the highly publicized case of Lorena Bobbitt, a Virginia woman who claimed to be temporarily insane as the result of years of physical and psychological abuse by her husband, leading her to cut off his penis. She

Lyle and Erik Menendez continue to serve life sentences in prison for murdering their parents in 1989.

claimed that at that point she was overcome with what she called "pictures," or mental images, of his abusive actions toward her. The jury concluded that she was temporarily insane and acquitted her of all charges of malicious and unlawful wounding. As mandated by Virginia law, the judge in the case committed Lorena Bobbitt to a state psychiatric hospital to determine whether or not she posed a danger to herself or others. After the 45-day period, she was released.

Yet another variant of the insanity defense occurred in the case of Andrea Yates who, in June 2001, drowned her five children in the bathtub of her Texas home. Yates had a history of profound postpartum depression following the births of her fourth and fifth children. Although her case seemed to merit the insanity plea, the court convicted her of capital murder in March 2002. In 2006, an appeals court overturned the verdict on the basis of the fact that one of the trial expert witnesses had presented false testimony relevant to her mental state at the time of the killings. In July 2006, the court moved her from a high-security mental health facility to a low-security state mental hospital.

The trials of Lee Boyd Malvo and John Allen Muhammed presented the case of two individuals who had committed homicides in which one individual but not the other committing the same crimes qualified for the insanity defense. The pair was arrested in October 2002 after committing sniper attacks in which they murdered 10 people in the Washington, D.C., area. The prosecution asserted that Muhammed, a man in his 40s, had undertaken the shooting spree and ordered 17-year-old Malvo to help him. Malvo's defense attorneys pleaded the insanity defense on the grounds that he was indoctrinated and therefore had a form of mental illness. Because he was a teenager under the power of a much older man, he did not know right from wrong. However, the jury rejected this version of the insanity defense.

The opposite situation occurred in the case of Theodore Kaczynski, known as the "Unabomber." Over an 18-year period, Kaczynski mounted a campaign from his cabin in Montana against the "industrial-technological system." He admitted that he killed three people and had maimed many others by sending package bombs to government addresses. From his history and extensive clinical evaluation, there was compelling evidence that he had schizophrenia, paranoid type. However, he refused to use the insanity defense as he did not consider himself to have a psychological disorder.

When Lee Boyd Malvo was 17, he and John Allen Muhammed shot and killed 10 people at random in the Washington, D.C., area in what were known as the "Beltway sniper attacks." Malvo's insanity plea was rejected by a jury and he was sentenced to six consecutive life sentences in prison.

Competency to Stand Trial

competency to stand trial
A prediction by a mental health expert of the defendant's cognitive and emotional stability during the period of the trial.

The determination of **competency to stand trial** pertains to the question of whether a defendant is aware of and able to participate in criminal proceedings against him or her. This determination is based on the principle that people should be able to participate in their own defense. To make this determination, a forensic expert evaluates the defendant's cognitive capacity, emotional stamina, and ongoing symptoms. In some cases, the court may demand postponing the trial until the defendant's symptoms subside, if necessary, by mandating that the individual receive medication. Although structured instruments are available for the purpose of making these determinations, the majority of forensic experts rely on their clinical judgment (Bartol & Bartol, 2012).

Understanding the Purpose of Punishment

Separate from the issue of competency to stand trial is the question of whether a mentally ill person who is convicted of a capital offense is able to understand the nature and purpose of a death sentence. The case of Scott Louis Panetti, which the U.S. Supreme Court heard in 2007, highlights some of the complexities of this question.

In 1992, Panetti killed his in-laws while holding hostage his estranged wife and their 3-year-old daughter. Even though Panetti had a lengthy history of mental illness and psychiatric hospitalizations, the Texas court sentenced him to death. In 2003, Panetti petitioned the Texas state appeals court to determine his competency for execution. Panetti asserted his belief that satanic forces had sought his execution to prevent him from preaching the Gospel. His defense lawyers claimed that since Panetti could not understand why the jury sentenced him to death, the death penalty would constitute cruel and unusual punishment and therefore violate the Eighth Amendment of the Constitution. The Texas Department of Criminal Justice objected to this argument, contending that capital punishment in such cases should not rest on whether or not a convict has rational understanding of the reasons for execution, but rather on the convict's moral culpability at the time he or she committed the crime.

In 2007, the U.S. Supreme Court blocked Panetti's execution and returned the case to the U.S. District Court in Austin, Texas. The court based this decision in part on arguments that the American Psychological Association, the American Psychiatric Association, and the National Alliance on Mental Illness put forward. These organizations jointly submitted a brief stating that individuals with psychotic conditions, such as Panetti, may experience delusions and a disrupted understanding of reality. Also, these individuals may be unable to connect events or understand cause and effect, namely, the connection between the murder and the punishment.

For almost two decades the case of Scott Louis Panetti has been the focus of legal debate and controversy. Panetti's death sentence in Texas was overturned by the U.S. Supreme Court on the premise that Panetti lacked understanding of why he was being put to death.

Concluding Perspectives on Forensic Issues

As you can see from our discussion of forensic issues, there is an entire body of knowledge forming on the border between psychology and the law. Mental health professionals are playing an increasingly important role in the legal system and, at the same time, are finding that they must familiarize themselves with an array of forensic issues. Clearly, the areas of intersection between psychology and the law will continue to grow as society looks for interventions that are humane, ethical, and effective.

Return to the Case: Mark Chen

Mark was hospitalized for 5 days. While on the unit, health care professionals thoroughly assessed Mark, focusing on his suicidality and depressive symptoms. He attended group therapy and worked with a psychiatrist to change his medication regimen. Once he had stabilized and was no longer suicidal, he was released from the hospital. His parents picked him up and he decided to stay with them for the rest of the semester and to return to school for the following year.

Prior to his hospitalization, Mark's parents were not aware that their son was experiencing psychological difficulties. Much to Mark's surprise, they stated that they understood his need to stay home to recuperate. Since his parents lived several hours away from where he attended school, Mark and his therapist decided to have weekly telephone sessions in order to continue their work together. Their work focused on the relationship between Mark and his parents, and Mark used his time at home to learn to discuss how he felt that the pressure they had placed on him had been a source of much stress.

Dr. Tobin's reflections: Clinicians are sometimes faced with the difficult decision of hospitalizing their therapy clients. Mark's clinician performed the appropriate steps to determine his level of safety. He was in great need of hospitalization as he appeared to be an immediate threat to his life, thus the clinician was ethically bound to break confidentiality and commit Mark to the hospital.

Luckily, Mark and his clinician had a strong enough alliance that Mark felt he should come in for "one last session" rather than ending his life. This may have been a "cry for help," because Mark knew that the clinician would be able to help him.

Mark's first depressive episode was severe, lasting around 8 months. Usually, the more severe the initial episode, the more persistent and severe subsequent episodes will become. Considering that the current work with his clinician is the first time that Mark has received psychological treatment, a part of the treatment will be to help Mark gain a sense of insight into his psychological struggles. For instance, in the future, should Mark begin to notice the same pattern of symptoms that led to his current depressive episode, he may then recognize that his symptoms may turn more severe if he does not bring them to the attention of his therapist or psychiatrist.

Finally, conducting psychotherapy over the phone, or "teletherapy," is becoming increasingly a more common way of performing therapy and is covered by APA's Ethics Code. If both parties agree that it will be the best way to maintain the therapeutic alliance over a certain period of time, as in Mark's case, it may be a suitable alternative to stopping therapy altogether. Since Mark did plan on returning to school and continuing to work with his therapist, it appears that teletherapy was an appropriate way to continue with their work to that point and avoid a rupture in his progress.

SUMMARY

- Clinicians have various roles and responsibilities. We expect them to have the intellectual competence to assess, conceptualize, and treat clients whom they accept into treatment, in addition to having the emotional capability of managing the clinical issues that emerge. When beginning work with clients, they should obtain the client's informed consent to ensure that the client understands the goals of treatment, the therapy process, the client's rights, the therapist's responsibilities, the treatment risks, the techniques that the clinician will use, financial issues, and the limits of confidentiality.

- Confidentiality is the principle that the therapist must safeguard disclosures in therapy as private. With only a few exceptions, the content of therapy is privileged communication; that is, the clinician may not disclose any information about the client in a court without the client's expressed permission. Exceptions to confidentiality include instances involving mandated reporting and **duty to warn (or otherwise protect).** Mental health professionals are mandated by law to report information involving the abuse or neglect of children or other people who are unable to protect themselves. The duty to warn involves the clinician's responsibility to take action to inform a possible victim of a client's intention to do harm to that person.

- In their relationships with clients, we expect clinicians to adhere to the highest standards of ethical and professional conduct. They are to avoid inappropriate relationships, such as sexual intimacy with clients, and must maintain neutrality and distance in their dealings with clients. In overseeing the business aspects of psychotherapy practice, mental health professionals face various challenges, particularly when operating within managed health care delivery systems. Sometimes clinicians must serve in roles that present unique ethical challenges (e.g., expert witness, child custody evaluations, and evaluations of people with dementia).

- Clinicians are sometimes involved in the process of **commitment,** an emergency procedure for the involuntary hospitalization of a person who, if not hospitalized, is likely to create harm for self or others as a result of mental illness. Hospitalized clients have the **right to treatment**—the right to a humane environment with appropriate amenities, in addition to liberty and safety. Clients also have the right to refuse unwanted treatment, unless a court deems that the client is at risk of harming self or others without needed intervention. Clients also have the right for placement in the **least restrictive alternative** to treatment in an institution.

- The major forensic issues that pertain to the field of mental health involve the **insanity defense** and the **competency to stand trial.** The insanity defense is the argument that the lawyer acting on behalf of the client presents, which states that, because of the existence of a mental disorder, the law should not hold the client legally responsible for criminal actions. Various controversies have emerged during the past two decades regarding the insanity defense, as courts have struggled with issues of assessing a defendant's responsibility in well-publicized cases involving violent assault and murder. The determination of competency to stand trial pertains to the question of whether a defendant is aware of and able to participate in criminal proceedings against him or her.

KEY TERMS

American Law Institute's (ALI) guidelines   397
Commitment   392
Competency to stand trial   400
Durham Rule   395
Duty to warn (or otherwise protect)   389

Guardian *ad litem*   383
Health Insurance Portability and Accountability Act of 1996 (HIPAA)   392
Insanity   395
Insanity defense   395
Least restrictive alternative   394

M'Naghten Rule   395
Multiple relationships   390
Parens patriae   392
Right to treatment   393
Substituted judgment   394

A

Acceptance and Commitment Therapy (ACT): A form of cognitive therapy that helps clients accept the full range of their subjective experiences, such as distressing thoughts and feelings, as they commit themselves to tasks aimed at achieving behavior change that will lead to an improved quality of life.

active phase: A period in the course of schizophrenia in which psychotic symptoms are present.

acute stress disorder: An anxiety disorder that develops after a traumatic event, and lasts for up to 1 month with symptoms such as depersonalization, numbing, dissociative amnesia, intense anxiety, hypervigilance, and impairment of everyday functioning.

adaptive testing: Testing in which the client's responses to earlier questions determine the subsequent questions presented to them.

agoraphobia: Intense anxiety triggered by the real or anticipated exposure to situations in which they may be unable to get help should they become incapacitated.

akinesia: A motor disturbance in which a person's muscles become rigid and movement is difficult to initiate.

alcohol myopia theory: Proposes that as individuals consume greater amounts of alcohol, they are more likely to make risky choices because the immediate temptation of the moment overcomes the long-term consequences of the behavior.

allele: One of two different variations of a gene.

American Law Institute's (ALI) guidelines: Guidelines proposing that people are not responsible for criminal behavior if their mental disorder prevents them from appreciating the wrongfulness of their behavior.

amnesia: Inability to recall information that was previously learned or to register new memories.

amphetamine: A stimulant that affects both the central nervous and the autonomic nervous systems.

amyloid plaques: A characteristic of Alzheimer's disease in which clusters of dead or dying neurons become mixed together with fragments of protein molecules.

analog observations: Assessments that take place in a setting or context such as a clinician's office or a laboratory specifically designed for observing the target behavior.

anorexia nervosa: An eating disorder characterized by an inability to maintain normal weight, an intense fear of gaining weight, and distorted body perception.

anterograde amnesia: Amnesia involving the inability to remember new information.

antisocial personality disorder: A personality disorder characterized by a lack of regard for society's moral or legal standards and an impulsive and risky lifestyle.

anxiety: A future-oriented and global response, involving both cognitive and emotional components, in which an individual is inordinately apprehensive, tense, and uneasy about the prospect of something terrible happening.

anxiety disorders: Disorders characterized by excessive fear and anxiety, and related disturbances in behavior.

anxiety sensitivity theory: The belief that panic disorder is caused in part by the tendency to interpret cognitive and somatic manifestations of stress and anxiety in a catastrophic manner.

anxiolytic: An antianxiety medication.

apnea: Total absence of airflow.

asociality: Lack of interest in social relationships.

Asperger's disorder: A term once used to describe individuals with high-functioning autism spectrum disorder.

Assertive Community Treatment (ACT): Where a team of professionals from psychiatry, psychology, nursing, and social work reach out to clients in their homes and workplaces.

attachment style: The way a person relates to a caregiver figure.

attention-deficit/hyperactivity disorder (ADHD): A neurodevelopmental disorder involving a persistent pattern of inattention and/or hyperactivity.

autism spectrum disorder: A neurodevelopmental disorder involving impairments in the domains of social communication and performance of restricted, repetitive behaviors.

automatic thoughts: Ideas so deeply entrenched that the individual is not even aware that they lead to feelings of unhappiness and discouragement.

avoidant personality disorder: A personality disorder in which people have low estimation of their social skills and are fearful of disapproval, rejection, and criticism or being ashamed or embarrassed.

avoidant/restrictive food intake disorder: A disorder in which individuals avoid eating out of concern about aversive consequences or restrict intake of food with specific sensory characteristics.

avolition: A lack of initiative, either not wanting to take any action or lacking the energy and will to take action.

axis: A class of information in *DSM-IV* regarding an aspect of the individual's functioning.

B

behavioral activation: Behavioral therapy for depression in which the clinician helps the client identify activities associated with positive mood.

behavioral assessment: A form of measurement based on objective recording of the individual's behavior.

behavioral interviewing: Assessment process in which clinicians ask questions about the target behavior's frequency, antecedents, and consequences.

behavioral medicine: An interdisciplinary approach to medical conditions affected by psychological factors that is rooted in learning theory.

behavioral perspective: A theoretical perspective in which it is assumed that abnormality is caused by faulty learning experiences.

behavioral self-report: A method of behavioral assessment in which the individual provides information about the frequency of particular behaviors.

binge eating: The ingestion of large amounts of food during a short period of time, even after reaching a point of feeling full, and a lack of control over what or how much is eaten.

biological perspective: A theoretical perspective in which it is assumed that disturbances in emotions, behavior, and cognitive processes are caused by abnormalities in the functioning of the body.

biological sex: The sex determined by a person's chromosomes.

biopsychosocial: A model in which the interaction of biological, psychological, and sociocultural factors is seen as influencing the development of the individual.

bipolar disorder: A mood disorder involving manic episodes—intense and very disruptive experiences of heightened mood, possibly alternating with major depressive episodes.

bipolar disorder, rapid cycling: A form of bipolar disorder involving four or more episodes within the previous year that meet the criteria for manic, hypomanic, or major depressive disorder.

body dysmorphic disorder: A disorder in which individuals are preoccupied with the idea that a part of their body is ugly or defective.

borderline personality disorder (BPD): A personality disorder characterized by a pervasive pattern of poor impulse control and instability in mood, interpersonal relationships, and sense of self.

bradykinesia: A motor disturbance involving a general slowing of motor activity.

brief psychotic disorder: A disorder characterized by the sudden onset of psychotic symptoms that are limited to a period of less than a month.

bulimia nervosa: An eating disorder involving alternation between the extremes of eating large amounts of food in a short time, and then compensating for the added calories either by vomiting or other extreme actions to avoid gaining weight.

buprenorphine: A medication used in the treatment of heroin addiction.

C

caffeine: A stimulant found in coffee, tea, chocolate, energy drinks, diet pills, and headache remedies.

case formulation: A clinician's analysis of the factors that might have influenced the client's current psychological status.

case study: An intensive study of a single person described in detail.

catatonia: A condition in which the individual shows marked psychomotor disturbances.

childhood disintegrative disorder: A disorder in *DSM-IV-TR* in which the child develops normally for the first 2 years and then starts to lose language, social, and motor skills, as well as other adaptive functions, including bowel and bladder control.

childhood-onset fluency disorder (stuttering): A communication disorder also known as stuttering that involves a disturbance in the normal fluency and patterning of speech that is characterized by such verbalizations as sound repetitions or prolongations, broken words, the blocking out of sounds, word substitutions to avoid problematic words, or words expressed with an excess of tension.

classical conditioning: The learning of a connection between an originally neutral stimulus and a naturally evoking stimulus that produces an automatic reflexive reaction.

client: A person seeking psychological treatment.

client-centered: An approach based on the belief held by Rogers that people are innately good and that the potential for self-improvement lies within the individual.

clinical interview: A series of questions that clinicians administer in face-to-face interaction with the client.

clinical psychologist: A mental health professional with training in the behavioral sciences who provides direct service to clients.

clinician: The person providing treatment.

cocaine: A highly addictive central nervous system stimulant that an individual snorts, injects, or smokes.

cognitive-behavioral therapy (CBT): Treatment method in which clinicians focus on changing both maladaptive thoughts and maladaptive behaviors.

cognitive perspective: A theoretical perspective in which it is assumed that abnormality is caused by maladaptive thought processes that result in dysfunctional behavior.

cognitive restructuring: One of the fundamental techniques of cognitive-behavioral therapy in which clients learn to reframe negative ideas into more positive ones.

commitment: An emergency procedure for involuntary psychiatric hospitalization.

communication disorders: Conditions involving impairment in language, speech, and communication.

community mental health center (CMHC): Outpatient clinic that provides psychological services on a sliding fee scale to serve individuals who live within a certain geographic area.

comorbid: The situation that occurs when multiple diagnostic conditions occur simultaneously within the same individual.

competency to stand trial: A prediction by a mental health expert of the defendant's cognitive and emotional stability during the period of the trial.

compulsion: A repetitive and seemingly purposeful behavior performed in response to uncontrollable urges or according to a ritualistic or stereotyped set of rules.

computed axial tomography (CAT or CT scan): A series of X-rays taken from various angles around the body that are integrated by a computer to produce a composite picture.

concordance rate: Agreement ratios between people diagnosed as having a particular disorder and their relatives.

conditioned fear reactions: Acquired associations between an internal or external cue and feelings of intense anxiety.

conduct disorder: An impulse-control disorder that involves repeated violations of the rights of others and society's norms and laws.

contingency management: A form of behavioral therapy that involves the principle of rewarding a client for desired behaviors and not providing rewards for undesired behaviors.

conversion disorder (functional neurological symptom disorder): A somatic symptom disorder involving the translation of unacceptable drives or troubling conflicts into physical symptoms.

coping: The process through which people reduce stress.

counterconditioning: The process of replacing an undesired response to a stimulus with an acceptable response.

cultural formulation: Includes the clinician's assessment of the client's degree of identification with the culture of origin, the culture's beliefs about psychological disorders, the ways in which the culture interprets particular events, and the cultural supports available to the client.

culture-bound syndromes: Recurrent patterns of abnormal behavior or experience that are limited to specific societies or cultural areas.

cyclothymic disorder: A mood disorder with symptoms that are more chronic and less severe than those of bipolar disorder.

D

day treatment program: A structured program in a community treatment facility that provides activities similar to those provided in a psychiatric hospital.

deep brain stimulation (DBS): A somatic treatment in which a neurosurgeon implants a microelectrode that delivers a constant low electrical stimulation to a small region of the brain, powered by an implanted battery.

defense mechanisms: Tactics that keep unacceptable thoughts, instincts, and feelings out of conscious awareness and thus protect the ego against anxiety.

delayed ejaculation: A sexual dysfunction in which a man experiences problems having an orgasm during sexual activity; also known as inhibited male orgasm.

delirium: A neurocognitive disorder that is temporary in nature involving disturbances in attention and awareness.

delusion: Deeply entrenched false belief not consistent with the client's intelligence or cultural background.

dependent personality disorder: A personality disorder whose main characteristic is that the individual is extremely passive and tends to cling to other people, to the point of being unable to make any decisions or to take independent action.

dependent variable: The variable whose value is the outcome of the experimenter's manipulation of the independent variable.

depersonalization: Condition in which people feel detached from their own body.

depersonalization/derealization disorder: A dissociative disorder in which the individual experiences recurrent and persistent episodes of depersonalization.

depressant: A psychoactive substance that causes the depression of central nervous system activity.

depressive disorder: Involves periods of symptoms in which an individual experiences an unusually intense sad mood.

derealization: Condition in which people feel a sense of unreality or detachment from their surroundings.

developmental coordination disorder: A motor disorder characterized by marked impairment in the development of motor coordination.

deviation intelligence (IQ): An index of intelligence derived from comparing the individual's score on an intelligence test with the mean score for that individual's reference group.

Diagnostic and Statistical Manual of Mental Disorders (DSM): A book published by the American Psychiatric Association that contains standard terms and definitions of psychological disorders.

dialectical behavior therapy (DBT): Treatment approach for people with borderline personality disorder that integrates supportive and cognitive-behavioral treatments to reduce the frequency of self-destructive acts and to improve the client's ability to handle disturbing emotions, such as anger and dependency.

diathesis-stress model: The proposal that people are born with a predisposition (or "diathesis") that places them at risk for developing a psychological disorder if exposed to certain extremely stressful life experiences.

differential diagnosis: The process of systematically ruling out alternative diagnoses.

diffusion tensor imaging (DTI): A method to investigate abnormalities in the white matter of the brain.

disinhibited social engagement disorder: Diagnosis given to children who engage in culturally inappropriate, overly familiar behavior with people who are relative strangers.

disruptive mood dysregulation disorder: A depressive disorder in children who exhibit chronic and severe irritability and have frequent temper outbursts.

dissociative amnesia: An inability to remember important personal details and experiences; is usually associated with traumatic or very stressful events.

dissociative identity disorder (DID): A dissociative disorder, formerly called multiple personality disorder, in which an individual develops more than one self or personality.

disulfiram: Known popularly as Antabuse, a medication used in the treatment of alcoholism that inhibits aldehyde dehydrogenase (ALDH) and causes severe physical reactions when combined with alcohol.

DNA methylation: The process that can turn off a gene as a chemical group, methyl, attaches itself to the gene.

double-blind: An experimental procedure in which neither the person giving the treatment nor the person receiving the treatment knows whether the participant is in the experimental or control group.

Down syndrome: A form of mental retardation caused by abnormal chromosomal formation during conception.

dual-process theory: A theory regarding alcohol use proposing there are automatic processes that generate an impulse to drink alcohol and controlled, effortful processing that regulates these automatic impulses.

Durham Rule: An expansion of the insanity defense based on determining that the individual was not criminally responsible if the unlawful act was due to the presence of a psychological disorder.

duty to warn (or otherwise protect): The clinician's responsibility to notify a potential victim of a client's harmful intent toward that individual.

dyscalculia: A pattern of difficulties in number sense, ability to learn arithmetic facts, and performing accurate calculations.

dysfunctional attitudes: Personal rules or values people hold that interfere with adequate adjustment.

dysphoria: An unusually elevated sad mood.

E

eating disorders: Diagnosis for people who experience persistent disturbances of eating or eating-related behavior that result in person's altering the consumption or absorption of food.

echolalia: Repeating the same sounds over and over.

ecstasy (MDMA): A hallucinogenic drug made from a synthetic substance chemically similar to methamphetamine and mescaline.

ego: In psychoanalytic theory, the structure of personality that gives the individual the mental powers of judgment, memory, perception, and decision making, enabling the individual to adapt to the realities of the external world.

ego psychology: Theoretical perspective based on psychodynamic theory emphasizing the ego as the main force in personality.

electroconvulsive therapy (ECT): The application of electrical shock to the head for the purpose of inducing therapeutically beneficial seizures.

electroencephalogram (EEG): A measure of changes in the electrical activity of the brain.

elimination disorders: Disorders characterized by age-inappropriate incontinence, beginning in childhood

emotional dysregulation: Lack of awareness, understanding, or acceptance of emotions; inability to control the intensity or duration of emotions; unwillingness to experience emotional distress as an aspect of pursuing goals; and inability to engage in goal-directed behaviors when experiencing distress.

emotion-focused coping: A type of coping in which a person does not change anything about the situation itself, but instead tries to improve feelings about the situation.

encopresis: An elimination disorder in which the child is incontinent of feces and has bowel movements either in clothes or in another inappropriate place.

endophenotypes: Biobehavioral abnormalities that are linked to genetic and neurobiological causes of mental illness.

enuresis: An elimination disorder in which the child is incontinent of urine and urinates in clothes or in bed after the age when the child is expected to be continent.

epigenesis: Process through which the environment causes genes to turn "off" or "on."

epigenetics: The science that attempts to identify the ways that the environment influences genes to produce phenotypes.

erectile disorder: Sexual dysfunction in which a man cannot attain or maintain an erection during sexual activity that is sufficient to allow him to initiate or maintain sexual activity.

erotomanic type of delusional disorder: Delusional disorder in which individuals falsely believe that another person is in love with them.

euphoric mood: A feeling state that is more cheerful and elated than average, possibly even ecstatic.

evidence-based practice in psychology: Clinical decision making that integrates the best available research evidence and clinical expertise in the context of the cultural background, preferences, and characteristics of clients.

excoriation (skin-picking) disorder: Recurrent picking at one's own skin.

exhibitionistic disorder: A paraphilic disorder in which a person has intense sexual urges and arousing fantasies involving the exposure of genitals to a stranger.

extrapyramidal symptoms (EPS): Motor disorders involving rigid muscles, tremors, shuffling movement, restlessness, and muscle spasms affecting their posture.

F

factitious disorder imposed on self: A disorder in which people fake symptoms or disorders not for the purpose of any particular gain, but because of an inner need to maintain a sick role.

factitious disorder imposed on another: A condition in which a person induces physical symptoms in another person who is under that person's care.

family perspective: A theoretical perspective in which it is assumed that abnormality is caused by disturbances in the pattern of interactions and relationships within the family.

family therapy: Psychological treatment in which the therapist works with several or all members of the family.

fear: The emotional response to real or perceived imminent threat.

female orgasmic disorder: A sexual dysfunction in which a woman experiences problems having an orgasm during sexual activity.

female sexual interest/arousal disorder: A sexual dysfunction characterized by a persistent or recurrent inability to attain or maintain normal physiological and psychological arousal responses during sexual activity.

fetal alcohol syndrome (FAS): A condition associated with intellectual disability in a child whose mother consumed large amounts of alcohol on a regular basis while pregnant.

fetishistic disorder: A paraphilic disorder in which the individual is preoccupied with an object and depends on this object rather than sexual intimacy with a partner for achieving sexual gratification.

Five Factor Model (also called "Big Five"): Trait theory proposing that there are five basic dispositions in personality.

flooding: A behavioral technique in which the client is immersed in the sensation of anxiety by being exposed to the feared situation in its entirety.

fragile X syndrome: A genetic disorder caused by a change in a gene called FMRI.

free association: A method used in psychoanalysis in which the client speaks freely, saying whatever comes to mind.

frontotemporal neurocognitive disorder: Neurocognitive disorder that involves the frontotemporal area of the brain.

frotteuristic disorder: A paraphilic disorder in which the individual has intense sexual urges and sexually arousing fantasies of rubbing against or fondling an unsuspecting stranger.

functional magnetic resonance imaging (fMRI): A variant of the traditional MRI, which makes it possible to construct a picture of activity in the brain.

G

gambling disorder: A non-substance-related disorder involving the persistent urge to gamble.

gender dysphoria: Distress that may accompany the incongruence between a person's experienced or expressed gender and that person's assigned gender.

gender identity: A person's inner sense of maleness or femaleness.

gene mapping: The attempt by biological researchers to identify the structure of a gene and the characteristics it controls.

generalized anxiety disorder: An anxiety disorder characterized by anxiety and worry that is not associated with a particular object, situation, or event but seems to be a constant feature of a person's day-to-day existence.

genito-pelvic pain/penetration disorder: A sexual dysfunction affecting both males and females that involves recurrent or persistent genital pain before, during, or after sexual intercourse.

genome-wide association studies (GWAS): Genetic method in which researchers scan the entire genome of individuals who are not related to find the associated genetic variations with a particular disease.

genome-wide linkage study: Genetic method in which researchers study the families of people with specific psychological traits or disorders.

genotype: The genetic makeup of an organism.

graduated exposure: A procedure in which clients gradually expose themselves to increasingly challenging anxiety-provoking situations.

grandiose type of delusional disorder: An exaggerated view of oneself as possessing special and extremely favorable personal qualities and abilities.

group therapy: Psychological treatment in which the therapist facilitates discussion among several clients who talk together about their problems.

guardian *ad litem*: A person appointed by the court to represent or make decisions for a person (e.g., a minor or an incapacitated adult) who is legally incapable of doing so in a civil legal proceeding.

H

halfway house: A community treatment facility designed for deinstitutionalized clients leaving a hospital who are not yet ready for independent living.

hallucination: A false perception not corresponding to the objective stimuli present in the environment.

hallucinogens: Psychoactive substances that cause abnormal perceptual experiences in the form of illusions or hallucinations, usually visual in nature.

hassle: A relatively minor event that can cause stress.

health anxiety: Worry about physical symptoms and illness.

Health Insurance Portability and Accountability Act of 1996 (HIPAA): U.S. legislation intended to ensure adequate coverage and protect consumers from loss of insurance coverage when they change or lose their jobs.

heroin: A psychoactive substance that is a form of opioid, synthesized from morphine.

histrionic personality disorder: A personality disorder characterized by exaggerated emotional reactions, approaching theatricality, in everyday behavior.

hoarding: A compulsion in which people have persistent difficulties discarding things, even if they have little value.

humanistic perspective: An approach to personality and psychological disorder that regards people as motivated by the need to understand themselves and the world and to derive greater enrichment from their experiences by fulfilling their unique individual potential.

humanitarian explanations: Regard psychological disorders as the result of cruelty, stress, or poor living conditions.

hypnotic: A substance that induces sedation.

hypomanic episode: A period of elated mood not as extreme as a manic episode.

hypopnea: Reduction in airflow.

I

id: In psychoanalytic theory, the structure of personality that contains the sexual and aggressive instincts.

illness anxiety disorder: A somatic symptom disorder characterized by the misinterpretation of normal bodily functions as signs of serious illness.

imaginal flooding: A behavioral technique in which the client is immersed through imagination into the feared situation.

impulse-control disorders: Psychological disorders in which people repeatedly engage in behaviors that are potentially harmful, feeling unable to stop themselves and experiencing a sense of desperation if their attempts to carry out the behaviors are thwarted.

inappropriate affect: The extent to which a person's emotional expressiveness fails to correspond to the content of what is being discussed.

incidence: The frequency of new cases within a given time period.

incoherent: Language that is incomprehensible.

independent variable: The variable whose level is adjusted or controlled by the experimenter.

individual psychotherapy: Psychological treatment in which the therapist works on a one-to-one basis with the client.

inhalants: A diverse group of substances that cause psychoactive effects by producing chemical vapors.

insanity: A legal term that refers to the individual's lack of moral responsibility for committing criminal acts.

insanity defense: The argument, presented by a lawyer acting on behalf of the client, that, because of the existence of a mental disorder, the client should not be held legally responsible for criminal actions.

intellectual disability (intellectual developmental disorder): Diagnosis used to characterize individuals who have intellectual and adaptive deficits that first became evident when they were children.

intermittent explosive disorder: An impulse-control disorder involving an inability to hold back urges to express strong angry feelings and associated violent behaviors.

International Classification of Diseases (ICD): The diagnostic system of the World Health Organization (WHO).

interpersonal therapy (IPT): A time-limited form of psychotherapy for treating people with major depressive disorder, based on the assumption that interpersonal stress induces an episode of depression in a person who is genetically vulnerable to this disorder.

***in vivo* flooding:** A behavioral technique in which the client is immersed to the actual feared situation.

***in vivo* observation:** Process involving the recording of behavior in its natural context, such as the classroom or the home.

J

jealous type of delusional disorder: Delusional disorder in which individuals falsely believe that their romantic partner is unfaithful to them.

K

kleptomania: An impulse-control disorder that involves the persistent urge to steal.

Korsakoff's syndrome: A permanent form of neurocognitive disorder associated with long-term alcohol use in which the individual develops retrograde and anterograde amnesia, leading to an inability to remember recent events or learn new information.

L

language disorder: A communication disorder characterized by having a limited and faulty vocabulary, speaking in short sentences with simplified grammatical structures, omitting critical words or phrases, or putting words together in peculiar order.

least restrictive alternative: A treatment setting that provides the fewest constraints on the client's freedom.

libido: An instinctual pressure for gratification of sexual and aggressive desires.

loosening of associations: Flow of thoughts that is vague, unfocused, and illogical.

lovemap: The representations of an individual's sexual fantasies and preferred practices.

lysergic acid diethylamide (LSD): A form of a hallucinogenic drug that users ingest in tablets, capsules, and liquid form.

M

magnetic resonance imaging (MRI): The use of radiowaves rather than X-rays to construct a picture of the living brain based on the water content of various tissues.

mainstreaming: A governmental policy to integrate fully into society people with cognitive and physical disabilities.

major depressive disorder: A disorder in which the individual experiences acute, but time-limited, episodes of depressive symptoms.

major depressive episode: A period in which the individual experiences intense psychological and physical symptoms accompanying feelings of overwhelming sadness (dysphoria).

major neurocognitive disorders: Disorders involving significant cognitive decline from a previous level of performance.

major neurocognitive disorder due to another medical condition: Cognitive disorders involving the inability to recall previously learned information or to register new memories.

male hypoactive sexual desire disorder: A sexual dysfunction in which the individual has an abnormally low level of interest in sexual activity.

malingering: The fabrication of physical or psychological symptoms for some ulterior motive.

marijuana: A psychoactive substance derived from the hemp plant whose primary active ingredient is delta-9-tetrahydrocannabinol (THC).

maturation hypothesis: The proposition that people with antisocial personality and the other Cluster B disorders become better able to manage their behaviors as they age.

mental retardation: A condition, present from childhood, characterized by significantly below-average general intellectual functioning (an IQ of 70 or below).

mental status examination: A method of objectively assessing a client's behavior and functioning in a number of spheres, with particular attention to the symptoms associated with psychological disturbance.

methadone: A synthetic opioid that produces a safer and more controlled reaction than heroin and that is used in treating heroin addiction.

methamphetamine: An addictive stimulant drug that is related to amphetamine but provokes more intense central nervous system effects.

mild neurocognitive disorders: Disorders involving modest cognitive decline from a previous level of performance.

milieu therapy: A treatment approach, used in an inpatient psychiatric facility, in which all facets of the milieu, or environment, are components of the treatment.

M'Naghten Rule: The "right-wrong test" used in cases of the insanity defense to determine whether a defendant should be held responsible for a crime.

modality: Form in which the clinician offers psychotherapy.

molecular genetics: The study of how genes translate hereditary information.

motivational interviewing (MI): A directive, client-centered style for eliciting behavior change by helping clients explore and resolve ambivalence.

multiaxial system: A multidimensional classification and diagnostic system in the *DSM-IV-TR* summarizing relevant information about an individual's physical and psychological functioning.

multicultural approach: To therapy: therapy that relies on awareness, knowledge, and skills of the client's sociocultural context.

multicultural assessment: Assessment process in which clinicians take into account the person's cultural, ethnic, and racial background.

multi-infarct dementia (MID): A form of neurocognitive disorder caused by transient attacks in which blood flow to the brain is interrupted by a clogged or burst artery.

multiple relationships: Unethical relationships occurring when a psychologist is in a professional role with a person and has another role with that person that could impair the psychologist's "objectivity, competence,

or effectiveness in performing his or her functions as a psychologist" or otherwise risks exploiting or harming the other person.

N

Naltrexone: A medication used in the treatment of heroin addiction.

narcissistic personality disorder (NPD): A personality disorder primarily characterized by an unrealistic, inflated sense of self-importance and a lack of sensitivity to the needs of other people.

negative symptoms: The symptoms of schizophrenia, including affective flattening, alogia, avolition, and anhedonia, that involve functioning below the level of normal behavior.

neologisms: Invented ("new") words.

neurocognitive disorder: Disorder whose primary clinical deficit is in cognition that represents a decline from previous functioning.

neurocognitive disorder: A form of cognitive impairment involving generalized progressive deficits in a person's memory and learning of new information, ability to communicate, judgment, and motor coordination.

neurocognitive disorder due to Alzheimer's disease: A neurocognitive disorder associated with progressive, gradual declines in memory, learning, and at least one other cognitive domain.

neurocognitive disorder due to Huntington's disease: A hereditary condition causing neurocognitive disorder that involves a widespread deterioration of the subcortical brain structures and parts of the frontal cortex that control motor movements.

neurocognitive disorder due to Lewy Bodies: A form of neurocognitive disorder with progressive loss of memory, language, calculation, and reasoning, as well as other higher mental functions resulting from the accumulation of abnormalities called Lewy bodies throughout the brain.

neurocognitive disorder due to prion disease (also known as Creutzfeldt-Jakob disease): A neurological disease transmitted from animals to humans that leads to neurocognitive disorder and death resulting from abnormal protein accumulations in the brain.

neurocognitive disorder due to traumatic brain injury: A disorder in which there is evidence of impact to the head along with cognitive and neurological symptoms that persist past the acute post-injury period.

neurocognitive disorder due to Parkinson's disease: A neurocognitive

disorder that involves degeneration of neurons in the subcortical structures that control motor movements.

neurodevelopmental disorder: Conditions that begin in childhood and have a major impact on social and cognitive functioning, involving serious deficits in social interaction and communication skills, as well as odd behavior, interests, and activities.

neurodevelopmental hypothesis: Theory proposing that schizophrenia is a disorder of development that arises during the years of adolescence or early adulthood due to alterations in the genetic control of brain maturation.

neurofibrillary tangles: A characteristic of Alzheimer's disease in which the material within the cell bodies of neurons becomes filled with densely packed, twisted protein microfibrils, or tiny strands.

neuroimaging: Assessment method that provides a picture of the brain's structures or level of activity and therefore is a useful tool for "looking" at the brain.

neuromodulation: A form of psychiatric neurosurgery in which permanently implanted electrodes trigger responses in specific brain circuits, as needed.

neuropsychological assessment: A process of gathering information about a client's brain functioning on the basis of performance on psychological tests.

neurotransmitter: A chemical substance released from a neuron into the synaptic cleft, where it drifts across the synapse and is absorbed by the receiving neuron.

nicotine: The psychoactive substance found in cigarettes.

O

object relations: One's unconscious representations of important people in one's life.

obsession: An unwanted thought, word, phrase, or image that persistently and repeatedly comes into a person's mind and causes distress.

obsessive-compulsive disorder (OCD): An anxiety disorder characterized by recurrent obsessions or compulsions that are inordinately time-consuming or that cause significant distress or impairment.

obsessive-compulsive personality disorder (OCPD): A personality disorder involving intense perfectionism and inflexibility manifested in worrying, indecisiveness, and behavioral rigidity.

operant conditioning: A learning process in which an individual acquires behaviors through reinforcement.

opioid: A psychoactive substance that relieves pain.

oppositional defiant disorder: A disorder characterized by angry or irritable mood, argumentative or defiant behavior, and vindictiveness that results in significant family or school problems.

P

panic attack: A period of intense fear and physical discomfort accompanied by the feeling that one is being overwhelmed and is about to lose control.

panic-control therapy (PCT): Treatment that consists of cognitive restructuring, exposure to bodily cues associated with panic attacks, and breathing retraining.

panic disorder: An anxiety disorder in which an individual has panic attacks on a recurrent basis or has constant apprehension and worry about the possibility of recurring attacks.

paranoia: The irrational belief or perception that others wish to cause you harm.

paranoid personality disorder: A personality disorder whose outstanding feature is that the individual is unduly suspicious of others and is always on guard against potential danger or harm.

paraphilias: Behaviors in which an individual has recurrent, intense sexually arousing fantasies, sexual urges, or behaviors involving (1) nonhuman objects, (2) children or other nonconsenting persons, or (3) the suffering or humiliation of self or partner.

paraphilic disorder: Diagnosis in which a paraphilia causes distress and impairment.

parens patriae: The state's authority to protect those who are unable to protect themselves.

partialism: A paraphilic disorder in which the person is interested solely in sexual gratification from a specific body part, such as feet.

participant modeling: A form of therapy in which the therapist first shows the client a desired behavior and then guides the client through the behavioral change.

pathways model: Approach to gambling disorder which predicts that there are three main paths leading to three subtypes.

patient: In the medical model, a person who receives treatment.

pedophilic disorder: A paraphilic disorder in which an adult is sexually aroused by children or adolescents.

persecutory type of delusional disorder: Delusional disorder in which individuals falsely believe that someone or someone close to them is treating them in a malevolent manner.

persistent depressive disorder (dysthymia): Chronic but less severe mood disturbance in which the individual does not experience a major depressive episode.

personality disorder: Ingrained patterns of relating to other people, situations, and events with a rigid and maladaptive pattern of inner experience and behavior, dating back to adolescence or early adulthood.

personality trait: An enduring pattern of perceiving, relating to, and thinking about the environment and others.

person-centered theory: The humanistic theory that focuses on the uniqueness of each individual, the importance of allowing each individual to achieve maximum fulfillment of potential, and the need for the individual to confront honestly the reality of his or her experiences in the world.

peyote: A form of a hallucinogenic drug whose primary ingredient is mescaline.

pharmacogenetics: The use of genetic testing to determine who will and will not improve with a particular medication.

phencyclidine (PCP): A form of a hallucinogenic drug originally developed as an intravenous anesthetic.

phenotype: The expression of the genetic program in the individual's physical and psychological attributes.

phenylketonuria (PKU): Condition in which children are born missing an enzyme called phenylalanine hydroxase.

phobia: An irrational fear associated with a particular object or situation.

pica: A condition in which a person eats inedible substances, such as dirt or feces; commonly associated with mental retardation.

Pick's disease: A relatively rare degenerative disease that affects the frontal and temporal lobes of the cerebral cortex and that can cause neurocognitive disorders.

placebo condition: Condition in an experiment in which participants receive a treatment similar to the experimental treatment, but lacking the key feature of the treatment of interest.

pleasure principle: In psychoanalytic theory, a motivating force oriented toward the immediate and total gratification of sensual needs and desires.

polygenic: A model of inheritance in which more than one gene participates in the process of determining a given characteristic.

polysomnography: A sleep study that records brain waves, blood oxygen levels, heart rate, breathing, eye movements, and leg movements.

positive psychology: Perspective that emphasizes the potential for growth and change throughout life.

positive symptoms: The symptoms of schizophrenia, including delusions, hallucinations, disturbed speech, and disturbed behavior, that are exaggerations or distortions of normal thoughts, emotions, and behavior.

positron emission tomography (PET) scan: A measure of brain activity in which a small amount of radioactive sugar is injected into an individual's bloodstream, following which a computer measures the varying levels of radiation in different parts of the brain and yields a multicolored image.

post-concussion syndrome (PCS): A disorder in which a constellation of physical, emotional, and cognitive symptoms persists from weeks to years.

post-traumatic stress disorder (PTSD): An anxiety disorder in which the individual experiences several distressing symptoms for more than a month following a traumatic event, such as a reexperiencing of the traumatic event, an avoidance of reminders of the trauma, a numbing of general responsiveness, and increased arousal.

potentiation: The combination of the effects of two or more psychoactive substances such that the total effect is greater than the effect of either substance alone.

premature (early) ejaculation: A sexual dysfunction in which a man reaches orgasm well before he wishes to, perhaps even prior to penetration.

premenstrual dysphoric disorder (PMDD): Changes in mood, irritability, dysphoria, and anxiety that occur during the premenstrual phase of the monthly menstrual cycle and subside after the menstrual period begins for most of the cycles of the preceding year.

prevalence: The number of people who have ever had a disorder at a given time or over a specified period.

primary gain: The relief from anxiety or responsibility due to the development of physical or psychological symptoms.

principal diagnosis: The disorder that is considered to be the primary reason the individual seeks professional help.

prion disease: An abnormal protein particle that infects brain tissue.

problem-focused coping: Coping in which the individual takes action to reduce stress by changing whatever it is about the situation that makes it stressful.

projective test: A technique in which the test-taker is presented with an ambiguous item or task and is asked to respond by providing his or her own meaning or perception.

proton magnetic resonance spectroscopy (MRS): A scanning method that measures metabolic activity of neurons, and therefore may indicate areas of brain damage.

pseudodementia: Literally, false dementia, or a set of symptoms caused by depression that mimic those apparent in the early stages of Alzheimer's disease.

psilocybin: A form of a hallucinogenic drug found in certain mushrooms.

psychiatric neurosurgery: A treatment in which a neurosurgeon operates on brain regions.

psychiatrists: People with degrees in medicine (MDs) who receive specialized advanced training in diagnosing and treating people with psychological disorders.

psychodynamic perspective: The theoretical orientation in psychology that emphasizes unconscious determinants of behavior.

psychological assessment: A broad range of measurement techniques, all of which involve having people provide scorable information about their psychological functioning.

psychological factors affecting other medical conditions: Disorder in which clients have a medical disease or symptom that appears to be exacerbated by psychological or behavioral factors.

psychologist: Health care professional offering psychological services.

psychopathy: A cluster of traits that form the core of the antisocial personality.

psychosexual stages: According to psychoanalytic theory, the normal sequence of development through which each individual passes between infancy and adulthood.

psychosurgery: A form of brain surgery, the purpose of which is to reduce psychological disturbance.

psychotherapeutic medications: Somatic treatments that are intended to reduce the individual's symptoms by altering the levels of neurotransmitters that researchers believe are involved in the disorder.

purging: Eliminating food through unnatural methods, such as vomiting or the excessive use of laxatives.

Q

qualitative research: A method of analyzing data that provides research with methods of analyzing complex relationships that do not easily lend themselves to conventional statistical methods.

R

rapid eye movements (REM): Phase during sleep involving frequent movements of eyes behind closed eyelids; EEG's similar to those while awake.

reactive attachment disorder: A disorder involving a severe disturbance in the ability to relate to others in which the individual is unresponsive to people, is apathetic, and prefers to be alone rather than to interact with friends or family.

reality principle: In psychoanalyic theory, the motivational force that leads the individual to confront the constraints of the external world.

reinforcement: The "strengthening" of a behavior.

relapse prevention: A treatment method based on the expectancy model, in which individuals are encouraged not to view lapses from abstinence as signs of certain failure.

relaxation training: A behavioral technique used in the treatment of anxiety disorders that involves progressive and systematic patterns of muscle tensing and relaxing.

reliability: When used with regard to diagnosis, the degree to which clinicians provide diagnoses consistently across individuals who have a particular set of symptoms.

remission: Term used to refer to the situation when the individual's symptoms no longer interfere with his or her behavior and are below those required for a *DSM* diagnosis.

restricted affect: Narrowing of the range of outward expressions of emotions.

retrograde amnesia: Amnesia involving loss of memory for past events.

Rett syndrome: A condition in which the child develops normally early in life (up to age 4) and then begins to show neurological and cognitive impairments including deceleration of head growth and some of the symptoms of autism spectrum disorder.

right to treatment: Legal right of person entering psychiatric hospital to receive appropriate care.

rumination disorder: An eating disorder in which the infant or child regurgitates food after it has been swallowed and then either spits it out or reswallows it.

S

schizoaffective disorder: A disorder involving the experience of a major depressive episode, a manic episode, or a mixed episode while also meeting the diagnostic criteria for schizophrenia.

schizoid personality disorder: A personality disorder primarily characterized by an indifference to social relationships, as well as a very limited range of emotional experience and expression.

schizophrenia: A disorder with a range of symptoms involving disturbances in content of thought, form of thought, perception, affect, sense of self, motivation, behavior, and interpersonal functioning.

schizophreniform disorder: A disorder characterized by psychotic symptoms that are essentially the same as those found in schizophrenia, except for the duration of the symptoms; specifically, symptoms usually last from 1 to 6 months.

schizotypal personality disorder: A personality disorder that primarily involves odd beliefs, behavior, appearance, and interpersonal style. People with this disorder may have bizarre ideas or preoccupations, such as magical thinking and beliefs in psychic phenomena.

scientific explanations: Regard psychological disorders as the result of causes that we can objectively measure, such as biological alterations, faulty learning processes, or emotional stressors.

secondary gain: The sympathy and attention that a sick person receives from other people.

secondary process thinking: In psychoanalytic theory, the kind of thinking involved in logical and rational problem solving.

secretases: Enzymes that trim part of the APP remaining outside the neuron so that it is flush with the neuron's outer membrane.

sedative: A psychoactive substance that has a calming effect on the central nervous system.

selective mutism: A disorder originating in childhood in which the individual consciously refuses to talk.

self-actualization: In humanistic theory, the maximum realization of the individual's potential for psychological growth.

self-efficacy: The individual's perception of competence in various life situations.

self-monitoring: A self-report technique in which the client keeps a record of the frequency of specified behaviors.

self-report clinical inventory: A psychological test with standardized questions having fixed response categories that the test-taker completes independently, self-reporting the extent to which the responses are accurate characterizations.

sensate focus: Method of treating sexual dysfunction in which the interaction is not intended to lead to orgasm, but to experience pleasurable sensations during the phases prior to orgasm.

separation anxiety disorder: A childhood disorder characterized by intense and inappropriate anxiety, lasting at least 4 weeks, concerning separation from home or caregivers.

sexual dysfunction: An abnormality in an individual's sexual responsiveness and reactions.

sexual masochism disorder: A paraphilic disorder marked by an attraction to achieving sexual gratification by having painful stimulation applied to one's own body.

sexual sadism disorder: A paraphilic disorder in which sexual gratification is derived from activities that harm, or from urges to harm, another person.

shared psychotic disorder: Delusional disorder in which one or more people develop a delusional system as a result of a close relationship with a psychotic person who is delusional.

single case experimental design (SCED): Design in which the same person serves as the subject in both the experimental and control conditions.

single nucleotide polymorphism (SNP) after (pronounced "snip"): A small genetic variation that can occur in a person's DNA sequence.

single photon emission computed tomography (SPECT): A variant of the PET scan that permits a longer and more detailed imaging analysis.

sleep terrors: Abrupt terror arousals from sleep usually beginning with a panicky scream.

sleepwalking: Rising from bed during sleep and walking about while seemingly asleep.

social anxiety disorder: An anxiety disorder characterized by marked, or intense, fear of anxiety of social situations in which the individual may be scrutinized by others.

social (pragmatic) communication disorder: Disorder involving deficits in the social use of verbal and nonverbal communication.

social discrimination: Prejudicial treatment of a class of individuals, seen in the sociocultural perspective as a cause of psychological problems.

social learning theory: Perspective that focuses on understanding how people develop psychological disorders through their relationships with others and through observation of other people.

sociocultural perspective: The theoretical perspective that emphasizes the ways that individuals are influenced by people, social institutions, and social forces in the world around them.

somatic symptom disorder: A disorder involving physical symptoms that may or may not be accountable by a medical condition accompanied by maladaptive thoughts, feelings, and behaviors.

somatic symptoms: Symptoms involving physical problems and/or concerns about medical symptoms.

somatic type of delusional disorder: Delusional disorder in which individuals falsely believe that they have a medical condition.

specific learning disorder: A delay or deficit in an academic skill that is evident when an individual's achievement and skills are substantially below what would be expected for others of comparable age, education, and level of intelligence.

specific learning disorder with impairment in mathematics: A learning disorder in which the individual has difficulty with mathematical tasks and concepts.

specific learning disorder with impairment in reading (dyslexia): A learning disorder in which the individual omits, distorts, or substitutes words when reading and reads in a slow, halting fashion.

specific learning disorder with impairment in written expression: A learning disorder in which the individual's writing is characterized by poor spelling, grammatical or punctuation errors, and disorganization of paragraphs.

specific phobia: An irrational and unabating fear of a particular object, activity, or situation.

speech sound disorder: A communication disorder in which the individual misarticulates, substitutes, or omits speech sounds.

spiritual explanations: Regard psychological disorders as the product of possession by evil or demonic spirits.

splitting: A defense, common in people with borderline personality disorder, in which individuals perceive others, or

themselves, as being all good or all bad, usually resulting in disturbed interpersonal relationships.

standardization: A psychometric criterion that clearly specifies a test's instructions for administration and scoring.

stereotypic movement disorder: A disorder in which the individual voluntarily repeats nonfunctional behaviors, such as rocking or head-banging, that can be damaging to his or her physical well-being.

stigma: A label that causes certain people to be regarded as different, defective, and set apart from mainstream members of society.

stimulant: A psychoactive substance that has an activating effect on the central nervous system.

stress: The unpleasant emotional reaction that a person has when an event is perceived as threatening.

stressful life event: An event that disrupts the individual's life.

Structured Clinical Interview for _DSM-IV_ Disorders (SCID): A widely used clinical interview.

structured interview: A standardized series of assessment questions, with a predetermined wording and order.

substance: A chemical that alters a person's mood or behavior when it is smoked, injected, drunk, inhaled, or swallowed in pill form.

substance intoxication: The temporary maladaptive experience of behavioral or psychological changes that are due to the accumulation of a substance in the body.

substance use disorder: A cluster of cognitive, behavioral, and physiological symptoms indicating that the individual uses a substance despite significant substance-related problems.

substituted judgment: A subjective analysis of what the client would decide if he or she were cognitively capable of making the decision.

superego: In psychoanalytic theory, the structure of personality that includes the conscience and the ego ideal; it incorporates societal prohibitions and exerts control over the seeking of instinctual gratification.

survey: A research tool used to gather information from a sample of people considered representative of a particular population, in which participants are asked to answer questions about the topic of concern.

systematic desensitization: A variant of counterconditioning that involves presenting the client with progressively more anxiety-provoking images while in a relaxed state.

T

tardive dyskinesia: Motor disorder that consists of involuntary movements of the mouth, arms, and trunk of the body.

target behavior: A behavior of interest or concern in an assessment.

tau: A protein that normally helps maintain the internal support structure of the axons.

theoretical perspective: An orientation to understanding the causes of human behavior and the treatment of abnormality.

thought stopping: A cognitive-behavioral method in which the client learns to stop having anxiety-provoking thoughts.

tic: A rapid, recurring, involuntary movement or vocalization.

token economy: A form of contingency management in which a client who performs desired activities earns chips or tokens that can later be exchanged for tangible benefits.

tolerance: The extent to which the individual requires larger and larger amounts of a substance in order to achieve its desired effects, or the extent to which the individual feels less of its effects after using the same amount of the substance.

Tourette's disorder: A disorder involving a combination of chronic movement and vocal tics.

transsexualism: A term sometimes used to refer to gender dysphoria, specifically pertaining to individuals choosing to undergo sex reassignment surgery.

transvestic disorder: Diagnosis applied to individuals who engage in transvestic behavior and have the symptoms of a paraphilic disorder.

transvestic fetishism: A paraphilia in which a man has an uncontrollable craving to dress in women's clothing in order to derive sexual gratification.

traumatic brain injury (TBI): Damage to the brain caused by exposure to trauma.

treatment plan: The outline for how therapy should take place.

trichotillomania (hair-pulling disorder): An impulse-control disorder involving the compulsive, persistent urge to pull out one's own hair.

Type A behavior pattern: Pattern of behaviors that include being hard-driving, competitive, impatient, cynical, suspicious of and hostile toward others, and easily irritated.

Type D personality: People who experience emotions that include anxiety, irritation, and depressed mood.

U

unconditional positive regard: A method in client-centered therapy in which the clinician gives total acceptance of what the client says, does, and feels.

unstructured interview: A series of open-ended questions aimed at determining the client's reasons for being in treatment, symptoms, health status, family background, and life history.

uplifts: Events that boost your feelings of well-being.

V

validity: The extent to which a test, diagnosis, or rating accurately and distinctly characterizes a person's psychological status.

vascular neurocognitive disorder: A form of neurocognitive disorder resulting from a vascular disease that causes deprivation of the blood supply to the brain.

vicarious reinforcement: A form of learning in which a new behavior is acquired through the process of watching someone else receive reinforcement for the same behavior.

voyeuristic disorder: A paraphilic disorder in which the individual has a compulsion to derive sexual gratification from observing the nudity or sexual activity of others.

W

Wernicke's disease: A form of aphasia in which the individual is able to produce language but has lost the ability to comprehend, so that these verbal productions have no meaning.

withdrawal: Physiological and psychological changes that occur when an individual stops taking a substance.

REFERENCES

A

Abelson, J. F., Kwan, K. Y., O'Roak, B. J., Baek, D. Y., Stillman, A. A., Morgan, T. M., . . . State, M. (2005). Sequence variants in SLITRK1 are associated with Tourette's syndrome. *Science, 310*(5746), 317–320.

Aboujaoude, E., Gamel, N., & Koran, L. M. (2004). Overview of kleptomania and phenomenological description of 40 patients. *Primary Care Companion Journal of Clinical Psychiatry, 6*(6), 244–247.

Abraham, K. (1911/1968). Notes on the psychoanalytic investigation and treatment of manic-depressive insanity and allied conditions. In K. Abraham (Ed.), *Selected papers of Karl Abraham*. New York: Basic Books.

Ackerman, A. R., Harris, A. J., Levenson, J. S., & Zgoba, K. (2011). Who are the people in your neighborhood? A descriptive analysis of individuals on public sex offender registries. *International Journal of Law and Psychiatry, 34*, 149–159.

Adler, L. A., Barkley, R. A., Wilens, T. E., & Ginsberg, D. L. (2006). Differential diagnosis of attention-deficit/hyperactivity disorder and comorbid conditions. *Primary Psychiatry, 13*(5), 1–14.

Ahrberg, M., Trojca, D., Nasrawi, N., & Vocks, S. (2011). Body image disturbance in binge eating disorder: A review. *European Eating Disorders Review, 19*(5), 375–381.

Aikins, D. E., & Craske, M. G. (2001). Cognitive theories of generalized anxiety disorder. *Psychiatric Clinics of North America, 24*(1), 57–74, vi.

Ainsworth, M. D. S., Blehar, M. C., Waters, E., & Wall, S. (1978). *Patterns of attachment: A psychological study of the strange situation*. Oxford, England: Lawrence Erlbaum.

Aliane, V., Pérez, S., Bohren, Y., Deniau, J.-M., & Kemel, M.-L. (2011). Key role of striatal cholinergic interneurons in processes leading to arrest of motor stereotypes. *Brain: A Journal of Neurology, 134*(1), 110–118.

Allen, J. L., Lavallee, K. L., Herren, C., Ruhe, K., & Schneider, S. (2010). *DSM-IV* criteria for childhood separation anxiety disorder: Informant, age, and sex differences. *Journal of Anxiety Disorders, 24*(8), 946–952.

Alpert, H. R., Connolly, G. N., & Biener, L. (2012). A prospective cohort study challenging the effectiveness of population-based medical intervention for smoking cessation. *Tobacco Control*.

Altarac, M., & Saroha, E. (2007). Lifetime prevalence of learning disability among US children. *Pediatrics, 119 Suppl 1*, S77–83.

Alzheimer, A. (1907/1987). About a peculiar disease of the cerebral cortex. *Alzheimer's Disease and Associated Disorders, 1*, 7–8.

American Psychiatric Association. (2000). *DSM-IV: Diagnostic and Statistical Manual of Mental Disorders Text Revision*. Washington, DC: American Psychiatric Association.

American Psychiatric Association. (2013). *DSM-5: Diagnostic and Statistical Manual of Mental Disorders*. Washington, DC: American Psychiatric Association.

American Psychological Association Presidential Task Force on Evidence-Based Practice. (2006). Evidence-based practice in psychology. *American Psychologist, 61*(4), 271–285.

American Psychological Association. (1999). Guidelines for psychological evaluations in child protection matters. *American Psychologist, 54*(8), 586–593.

American Psychological Association. (2002). Guidelines on multicultural education, training, research, practice, and organizational change for psychologists, American Psychological Association, from http://www.apa.org/pi/oema/resources/policy/multicultural-guidelines.aspx

American Psychological Association. (2004). Guidelines for psychological practice with older adults. *American Psychologist, 59*(4), 236–260.

American Psychological Association. (2007). Guidelines for psychological practice with girls and women. *American Psychologist, 62*(9), 949–979.

American Psychological Association. (2010). Ethical principles of psychologists and code of conduct. Retrieved 1/20/2012, from http://www.apa.org/ethics/code/index.aspx

American Psychological Association. (2012a). Guidelines for assessment of and intervention with persons with disabilities. *American Psychologist, 67*(1), 43–62.

American Psychological Association. (2012b). Guidelines for psychological practice with lesbian, gay, and bisexual clients. *American Psychologist, 67*(1), 10–42.

Anand, N., Sudhir, P. M., Math, S. B., Thennarasu, K., & Janardhan Reddy, Y. C. (2011). Cognitive behavior therapy in medication non-responders with obsessive-compulsive disorder: A prospective 1-year follow-up study. *Journal of Anxiety Disorders, 25*(7), 939–945.

Andreasen, N. C. (2010). The lifetime trajectory of schizophrenia and the concept of neurodevelopment. *Dialogues in Clinical Neuroscience, 12*, 409–415.

Anton, R. F., O'Malley, S. S., Ciraulo, D. A., Cisler, R. A., Couper, D., Donovan, D. M., . . . Zweben, A. (2006). Combined pharmacotherapies and behavioral interventions for alcohol dependence: The COMBINE study: A randomized controlled trial. *Journal of the American Medical Association, 295*(17), 2003–2017.

Archer, T. (2011). Physical exercise alleviates debilities of normal aging and Alzheimer's disease. *Acta Neurologica Scandinavica, 123*(4), 221–238.

Arias, A. J., & Kranzler, H. R. (2008). Treatment of co-occurring alcohol and other drug use disorders. *Alcohol Research & Health, 31*(2), 155–167.

Ayllon, T., & Azrin, N. H. (1965). The measurement and reinforcement of behavior of psychotics. *Journal of Experimental Analysis of Behavior, 8*, 351–383.

B

Bader, S. M., Schoeneman-Morris, K. A., Scalora, M. J., & Casady, T. K. (2008). Exhibitionism: Findings from a Midwestern police contact sample. *International Journal of Offender Therapy and Comparative Criminology, 52*, 270–279.

Bakker, G. M. (2009). In defense of thought stopping. *Clinical Psychologist, 13*(2), 59–68.

Bakkevig, J. F., & Karterud, S. (2010). Is the Diagnostic and Statistical Manual of Mental Disorders, Fourth Edition, histrionic personality disorder category a valid construct? *Comprehensive Psychiatry, 51*, 462–470.

Bandura, A. (1971). Psychotherapy based upon modeling principles. In A. E. Bergin & S. L. Garfield (Eds.), *Handbook of psychotherapy and behavior change* (pp. 653–708). New York: Wiley.

Banerjee, P., Grange, D. K., Steiner, R. D., & White, D. A. (2011). Executive strategic processing during verbal fluency performance in children with phenylketonuria. *Child Neuropsychology, 17*(2), 105–117.

Barclay, N. L., & Gregory, A. M. (2013). Quantitative genetic research on sleep: A review of normal sleep, sleep disturbances and associated emotional, behavioural, and health-related difficulties. *Sleep Medicine Reviews, 17*(1), 29–40. doi:10.1016/j.smrv.2012.01.008.

Barkley, R. A. (1997). *ADHD and the nature of self-control*. New York, NY: Guilford Press.

Barkley, R. A., & Murphy, K. R. (2011). The nature of executive function (EF) deficits in daily life activities in adults with ADHD and their relationship to performance on EF tests. *Journal of Psychopathology and Behavioral Assessment, 33*(2), 137–158.

Bars, D. R., Heyrend, F. L., Simpson, C. D., & Munger, J. C. (2001). Use of visual-evoked potential studies and EEG data to classify aggressive, explosive behavior of youths. *Psychiatric Services, 52*(1), 81–86.

Barsky, A. E., & Gould, J. W. (2002). *Clinicians in court: A guide to subpoenas, depositions, testifying, and everything else you need to know.* New York: Guilford Press.

Bartol, C. R., & Bartol, A. M. (2012). *Introduction to forensic psychology: Research and application.* Los Angeles, CA: Sage Publications.

Baschnagel, J. S., Gudmundsdottir, B., Hawk, L. W., Jr., & Gayle Beck, J. (2009). Post-trauma symptoms following indirect exposure to the September 11th terrorist attacks: The predictive role of dispositional coping. *Journal of Anxiety Disorders, 23*(7), 915–922.

Basson, R. (2001). Using a different model for female sexual response to address women's problematic low sexual desire. *Journal of Sex and Marital Therapy, 27,* 395–403.

Bastiaansen, L., Rossi, G., Schotte, C., & De Fruyt, F. (2011). The structure of personality disorders: Comparing the *DSM-IV-TR* Axis II classification with the five-factor model framework using structural equation modeling. *Journal of Personality Disorders, 25*(3), 378–396.

Batty, M., Meaux, E., Wittemeyer, K., Rogé, B., & Taylor, M. J. (2011). Early processing of emotional faces in children with autism: An event-related potential study. *Journal of Experimental Child Psychology, 109*(4), 430–444.

Bayliss, A. P., & Tipper, S. P. (2005). Gaze and arrow cueing of attention reveals individual differences along the autism spectrum as a function of target context. *British Journal of Psychology, 96*(Pt 1), 95–114.

Bechara, A., Noel, X., & Crone, E. A. (2006). Loss of willpower: Abnormal neural mechanisms of impulse control and decision making in addiction. In R. W. Wiers & A. W. Stacy (Eds.), *Handbook of implicit cognition and addiction* (pp. 215–232). Thousand Oaks, CA: Sage Publications, Inc.

Beck, A. T. (1967). *Depression: Clinical, experimental, and theoretical aspects.* New York: Harper & Row.

Beck, A. T., & Weishaar, M. (1989). Cognitive therapy. In A. Freeman, K. M. Simon, L. E. Beutler, & H. Arkowitz (Eds.), *Comprehensive handbook of cognitive therapy* (pp. 21–36). New York: Plenum Press.

Beck, A. T., Freeman, A., & Davis, D. D. (2004). *Cognitive therapy of personality disorders* (2nd ed.). New York: Guilford Press.

Beck, A. T., Rush, A. J., Shaw, B. F., & Emery, G. (1979). *Cognitive therapy of depression: A treatment manual.* New York: Guilford Press.

Bemporad, J. R. (1985). Long-term analytic treatment of depression. In E. E. Beckham & W. R. Leber (Eds.), *Handbook of depression: Treatment, assessment, and research* (pp. 82–89). Homewood, IL: Dorsey Press.

Ben-Porath, Y. (2010). *An introduction to the MMPI-2-RF (Reconstructed Form).* University of Minnesota.

Benabarre, A., Vieta, E., Martínez-Arán, A., Garcia-Garcia, M., Martín, F., Lomeña, F., . . . Valdés, M. (2005). Neuropsychological disturbances and cerebral blood flow in bipolar disorder. *Australian and New Zealand Journal of Psychiatry, 39*(4), 227–234.

Berger, W., Mendlowicz, M. V., Marques-Portella, C., Kinrys, G., Fontenelle, L. F., Marmar, C. R., et al. (2009). Pharmacologic alternatives to antidepressants in posttraumatic stress disorder: A systematic review. *Progress in Neuro-Psychopharmacology & Biological Psychiatry, 33*(2), 169–180.

Bergeron, S., Morin, M., & Lord, M.-J. (2010). Integrating pelvic floor rehabilitation and cognitive-behavioural therapy for sexual pain: What have we learned and were do we go from here? *Sexual and Relationship Therapy, 25,* 289–298.

Berry, D. T. R., & Nelson, N. W. (2010). *DSM-5* and malingering: A modest proposal. *Psychological Injury and the Law.*

Bertrand, J., Floyd, R. L., Weber, M. K., O'Connor, M., Riley, E.P., Johnson, K. A., & Cohen, D.E. (2004). National Task Force on FAS/FAE. Fetal Alcohol Syndrome: Guidelines for Referral and Diagnosis. Atlanta, GA.

Besser, A., & Priel, B. (2010). Grandiose narcissism versus vulnerable narcissism in threatening situations: Emotional reactions to achievement failure and interpersonal rejection. *Journal of Social and Clinical Psychology, 29,* 874–902.

Biederman, J., Mick, E., Faraone, S. V., & Burback, M. (2001). Patterns of remission and symptom decline in conduct disorder: A four-year prospective study of an ADHD sample. *Journal of the American Academy of Child & Adolescent Psychiatry, 40*(3), 290–298.

Biederman, J., Petty, C., Faraone, S. V., Hirshfeld-Becker, D. R., Henin, A., Rauf, A., . . . Rosenbaum, J. F. (2005). Childhood antecedents to panic disorder in referred and nonreferred adults. *Journal of Child and Adolescent Psychopharmacology, 15*(4), 549–561.

Biederman, J., Petty, C., Fried, R., Fontanella, J., Doyle, A. E., Seidman, L. J., & Faraone, S. V. (2006). Impact of psychometrically defined deficits of executive functioning in adults with attention deficit hyperactivity disorder. *The American Journal of Psychiatry, 163*(10), 1730–1738.

Birbaumer, N., Veit, R., Lotze, M., Erb, M., Hermann, C., Grodd, W., & Flor, H. (2005). Deficient fear conditioning in psychopathy: A functional magnetic resonance imaging study. *Archives of General Psychiatry, 62,* 799–805.

Bjornsson, A. S., Didie, E. R., & Phillips, K. A. (2010). Body dysmorphic disorder. *Dialogues Clin Neurosci, 12*(2), 221–232.

Blanchard, R. (2010). The *DSM* diagnostic criteria for transvestic fetishism. *Archives of Sexual Behavior, 39,* 363–372.

Blashfield, R. K., Reynolds, S. M., & Stennett, B. (2012). The death of histrionic personality disorder. In T. A. Widiger (Ed.), *The Oxford handbook of personality disorders* (pp. 603–627). New York: Oxford University Press. doi:10.1093/oxfordhb/9780199735013.013.0028

Bleuler, E. (1911). *Dementia praecox oder gruppe der schizophrenien. (Dementia praecox or the group of schizophrenias).* Leipzig: F. Deuticke.

Boccardi, M., Ganzola, R., Rossi, R., Sabattoli, F., Laakso, M. P., Repo-Tiihonen, E., . . . Tiihonen, J. (2010). Abnormal hippocampal shape in offenders with psychopathy. *Human Brain Mapping, 31,* 438–447.

Boddy, C. R. (2011). Corporate psychopaths, bullying and unfair supervision in the workplace. *Journal of Business Ethics, 100,* 367–379.

Boe, H. J., Holgersen, K. H., & Holen, A. (2011). Mental health outcomes and predictors of chronic disorders after the North Sea oil rig disaster: 27-year longitudinal follow-up study. *Journal of Nervous and Mental Disease, 199*(1), 49–54.

Boettger, S., Breitbart, W., & Passik, S. (2011). Haloperidol and risperidone in the treatment of delirium and its subtypes. *The European Journal of Psychiatry, 25*(2), 59–67.

Bohnert, A. S., Valenstein, M., Bair, M. J., Ganoczy, D., McCarthy, J. F., Ilgen, M. A., & Blow, F. C. (2011). Association between opioid prescribing patterns and opioid overdose-related deaths. *Journal of the American Medical Association, 305*(13), 1315–1321.

Bomyea, J., & Lang, A. J. (2011). Emerging interventions for PTSD: Future directions for clinical care and research. *Neuropharmacology.*

Bond, G. R., Drake, R. E., Mueser, K. T., & Latimer, E. (2001). Assertive community treatment for people with severe mental illness: Critical ingredients and impact on patients. *Disease Management and Health Outcomes, 9,* 141–159.

Borkovec, T. D., & Ruscio, A. M. (2001). Psychotherapy for generalized anxiety disorder. *Journal of Clinical Psychiatry, 62*(Suppl11), 37–42.

Both, S., Laan, E., & Schultz, W. W. (2010). Disorders in sexual desire and sexual arousal in women, a 2010 state of the art. *Journal of Psychosomatic Obstetrics & Gynecology, 31,* 207–218.

Bowden, C. L. (2005). Treatment options for bipolar depression. *Journal of Clinical Psychiatry, 66*(Suppl1), 3–6.

Bowlby, J. (1980). *Attachment and loss: Volume III: Loss: Sadness and depression.* New York: Basic Books.

Breggin, P. R., & Barkley, R. A. (2005). Issue 11: Is Ritalin overprescribed? In R. P. Halgin

(Ed.), *Taking sides: Clashing views on controversial issues in abnormal psychology,* 3rd ed. (pp. 176–195). New York: McGraw-Hill.

Briggs, P., Simon, W. T., & Simonsen, S. (2011). An exploratory study of Internet-initiated sexual offenses and the chat room sex offender: Has the Internet enabled a new typology of sex offender? *Sexual Abuse: Journal of Research and Treatment, 23,* 72–91.

Broft, A. I., Berner, L. A., Martinez, D., & Walsh, B. T. (2011). Bulimia nervosa and evidence for striatal dopamine dysregulation: A conceptual review. *Physiology & Behavior, 104*(1), 122–127.

Brotto, L. A. (2010). The *DSM* diagnostic criteria for hypoactive sexual desire disorder in women. *Archives of Sexual Behavior, 39,* 221–239.

Brown, M. L., Pope, A. W., & Brown, E. J. (2011). Treatment of primary nocturnal enuresis in children: A review. *Child: Care, Health and Development, 37*(2), 153–160.

Brown, R. T., Antonuccio, D. O., DuPaul, G. J., Fristad, M. A., King, C. A., Leslie, L. K., . . . Vitiello, B. (2008). Oppositional defiant and conduct disorders. In R. T. Brown, D. O. Antonuccio, G. J. DuPaul, M. A. Fristad, C. A. King, L. K. Leslie, G. S. McCormick, W. E. Pelham, Jr., J. C. Piacentini & B. Vitiello (Eds.), *Childhood mental health disorders: Evidence base and contextual factors for psychosocial, psychopharmacological, and combined interventions* (pp. 33–41). Washington, DC: American Psychological Association.

Brown, T. A., & Rosellini, A. J. (2011). The direct and interactive effects of neuroticism and life stress on the severity and longitudinal course of depressive symptoms. *Journal of Abnormal Psychology, 120*(4), 844–856.

Bryant-Waugh, R., Markham, L., Kreipe, R. E., & Walsh, B. T. (2010). Feeding and eating disorders in childhood. *International Journal of Eating Disorders, 43*(2), 98–111.

Bureau of Justice Statistics. (2011). Homicide trends in the U.S. Retrieved 12/20/2011, from http://bjs.ojp.usdoj.gov/content/homicide/tables/oagetab.cfm

Büttner, G., & Shamir, A. (2011). Learning disabilities: Causes, consequences, and responses. *International Journal of Disability, Development and Education, 58*(1), 1–4.

C

Callahan, C. M., Boustani, M. A., Unverzagt, F. W., Austrom, M. G., Damush, T. M., Perkins, A. J., . . . Hendrie, H. C. (2006). Effectiveness of collaborative care for older adults with Alzheimer disease in primary care: A randomized controlled trial. *Journal of the American Medical Association, 295*(18), 2148–2157.

Camisa, K. M., Bockbrader, M. A., Lysaker, P., Rae, L. L., Brenner, C. A., & O'Donnell, B. F. (2005). Personality traits in schizophrenia and related personality disorders. *Psychiatry Research, 133,* 23–33.

Campbell, W. G. (2003). Addiction: A disease of volition caused by a cognitive impairment. *Canadian Journal of Psychiatry, 48*(10), 669–674.

Canino, G., Polanczyk, G., Bauermeister, J. J., Rohde, L. A., & Frick, P. J. (2010). Does the prevalence of CD and ODD vary across cultures? *Social Psychiatry and Psychiatric Epidemiology, 45*(7), 695–704.

Cantor, J. M., Blanchard, R., & Barbaree, H. (2009). Sexual disorders. In P. H. Blaney & T. Millon (Eds.), *Oxford textbook of psychopathology* (2nd ed.) (pp. 527–548). New York: Oxford University Press.

Carlson, K. F., Nelson, D., Orazem, R. J., Nugent, S., Cifu, D. X., & Sayer, N. A. (2010). Psychiatric diagnoses among Iraq and Afghanistan war veterans screened for deployment-related traumatic brain injury. *Journal of Traumatic Stress, 23*(1), 17–24.

Carlsson, A. (1988). The current status of the dopamine hypothesis of schizophrenia. *Neuropsychopharmacology, 1,* 179–186.

Carmody, J., Reed, G., Kristeller, J., & Merriam, P. (2008). Mindfulness, spirituality, and health-related symptoms. *Journal of Psychosomatic Research, 64*(4), 393–403.

Carr, S. N., & Francis, A. J. P. (2010). Do early maladaptive schemas mediate the relationship between childhood experiences and avoidant personality disorder features? A preliminary investigation in a non-clinical sample. *Cognitive Therapy and Research, 34,* 343–358.

Carrasco, M. M., Aguera, L., Gil, P., Morinigo, A., & Leon, T. (2011). Safety and effectiveness of donepezil on behavioral symptoms in patients with Alzheimer disease. *Alzheimer Dis Assoc Disord, 25*(4), 333–340.

Carroll, K. M. (2011). Cognitive-behavioral therapies. In M. Galanter & H. D. Kleber (Eds.), *Psychotherapy for the treatment of substance abuse* (pp. 175–192). Arlington, VA: American Psychiatric Publishing, Inc.

Carter, J. D., Luty, S. E., McKenzie, J. M., Mulder, R. T., Frampton, C. M., & Joyce, P. R. (2011). Patient predictors of response to cognitive behaviour therapy and interpersonal psychotherapy in a randomised clinical trial for depression. *Journal of Affective Disorders, 128*(3), 252–261.

Caspi, A., Moffitt, T. E., Cannon, M., McClay, J., Murray, R., Harrington, H., . . . Craig, I. W. (2005). Moderation of the effect of adolescent-onset cannabis use on adult psychosis by a functional polymorphism in the catechol-O-methyltransferase gene: Longitudinal evidence of a gene X environment interaction. *Biological Psychiatry, 57*(10), 1117–1127.

Centers for Disease Control and Prevention. (2005). QuickStats: Percentage of children aged 5–17 years ever having diagnoses of Attention Deficit/Hyperactivity Disorder (ADHD) or Learning Disability (LD), by sex and diagnosis—United States, 2003. *Morbidity and Mortality Weekly Report, 54*(43), 1107. Atlanta, GA.

Centers for Disease Control and Prevention. (2007). Prevalence of autism spectrum disorder—Autism and developmental disabilities monitoring network, six sites, United States, 2000; Prevalence of autism spectrum disorder—Autism and developmental disabilities monitoring network, 14 sites, United States, 2002; and Evaluation of a methodology for a collaborative multiple source surveillance network for autism spectrum disorders—Autism and developmental disabilities monitoring network, 14 sites, United States, 2002. *Morbidity and Mortality Weekly Report, 56*(SS-1), 1–40.

Centers for Disease Control and Prevention. (2011). Fetal alcohol spectrum disorders Retrieved 10/29/2011, from http://www.cdc.gov/ncbddd/fasd/data.html

Centers for Disease Control and Prevention. (2011). How many people have TBI? Retrieved 11/22/2011, from http://www.cdc.gov/traumaticbraininjury/statistics.html

Centers for Disease Control and Prevention. (2011). Suicide: Definitions, from http://www.cdc.gov/violenceprevention/suicide/definitions.html

Centers for Disease Control and Prevention. (2012). CDC Grand Rounds: Prescription drug overdoses — a U.S. epidemic. *Morbidity and Mortality Weekly Report, 61, No. 1.*

Chamberlain, S. R., Hampshire, A., Menzies, L. A., Garyfallidis, E., Grant, J. E., Odlaug, B. L., . . . Sahakian, B. J. (2010). Reduced brain white matter integrity in trichotillomania: A diffusion tensor imaging study. *Arch Gen Psychiatry, 67*(9), 965–971.

Choi, K. H., Higgs, B. W., Wendland, J. R., Song, J., McMahon, F. J., & Webster, M. J. (2011). Gene expression and genetic variation data implicate PCLO in bipolar disorder. *Biological Psychiatry, 69*(4), 353–359.

Choy, Y., Fyer, A. J., & Lipsitz, J. D. (2007). Treatment of specific phobia in adults. *Clinical Psychology Review, 27*(3), 266–286.

Clarke, T. K., Weiss, A. R., & Berrettini, W. H. (2011). The genetics of anorexia nervosa. *Clinical Pharmacology and Therapeutics,* Dec. 21.

Cleckley, H. M. (1976). *The mask of sanity* (5th ed.). St. Louis: Mosby.

Coccaro, E. F. (2010). A family history study of intermittent explosive disorder. *Journal of Psychiatric Research, 44*(15), 1101–1105.

Coccaro, E. F., Lee, R. J., & Kavoussi, R. J. (2009). A double-blind, randomized, placebo-controlled trial of fluoxetine in patients with intermittent explosive disorder. *Journal of Clinical Psychiatry, 70*(5), 653–662.

Coccaro, E. F., Lee, R., & Kavoussi, R. J. (2010). Inverse relationship between numbers of 5-HT transporter binding sites and life history of aggression and intermittent explosive disorder. *Journal of Psychiatric Research, 44*(3), 137–142.

Cocchi, L., Harrison, B. J., Pujol, J., Harding, I. H., Fornito, A., Pantelis, C., et al. (2012). Functional alterations of large-scale brain networks related to cognitive control in obsessive-compulsive disorder. *Human Brain Mapping, 33*(5), 1089–1106.

Coelho, C. M., Goncalves, D. C., Purkis, H., Pocinho, M., Pachana, N. A., & Byrne, G. J. (2010). Specific phobias in older adults: Characteristics and differential diagnosis. *International Psychogeriatrics, 22*(5), 702–711.

Cohen-Kettenis, P. T., & Pfafflin, F. (2010). The *DSM* diagnostic criteria for gender identity disorder in adolescents and adults. *Archives of Sexual Behavior, 39*, 499–513.

Cole, C. S. (2011). Sleep and primary care of adults and older adults. In N. S. Redeker & G. McEnany (Eds.), *Sleep disorders and sleep promotion in nursing practice* (pp. 291–308). New York: Springer Publishing Co.

Collins, F. L., Jr., Leffingwell, T. R., & Belar, C. D. (2007). Teaching evidence-based practice: Implications for psychology. *Journal of Clinical Psychology, 63*(7), 657–670.

Commenges, D., Scotet, V., Renaud, S., Jacqmin-Gadda, H., Barberger-Gateau, P., & Dartigues, J. F. (2000). Intake of flavonoids and risk of dementia. *European Journal of Epidemiology, 16*(4), 357–363.

Committee on Treatment of Posttraumatic Stress Disorder, I. o. M. (2008). *Treatment of posttraumatic stress disorder: An assessment of the evidence.* Washington, DC: National Academies Press.

Consumer Reports. (2009). Evaluating prescription drugs used to treat: Alzheimer's Disease, from http://www .consumerreports.org/health/resources/ pdf/best-buy-drugs/AlzheimersFINAL.pdf

Cook, R., Pan, P., Silverman, R., & Soltys, S. M. (2010). Do-not-resuscitate orders in suicidal patients: Clinical, ethical, and legal dilemmas. *Psychosomatics: Journal of Consultation Liaison Psychiatry, 51*(4), 277–282.

Corneil, T. A., Eisfeld, J. H., & Botzer, M. (2010). Proposed changes to diagnoses related to gender identity in the *DSM*: A World Professional Association for Transgender Health consensus paper regarding the potential impact on access to health care for transgender persons. *International Journal of Transgenderism, 12*, 107–114.

Costa, P. T., Jr., & McCrae, R. R. (1992). *NEO-PI-R manual.* Odessa, FL: Psychological Assessment Resources.

Couineau, A.-L., & Forbes, D. (2011). Using predictive models of behavior change to promote evidence-based treatment for PTSD. *Psychological Trauma: Theory, Research, Practice, and Policy, 3*(3), 266–275.

Cowen, P. J. (2008). Serotonin and depression: Pathophysiological mechanism or marketing myth? *Trends in Pharmacological Science, 29*(9), 433–436.

Cox, B. J., Turnbull, D. L., Robinson, J. A., Grant, B. F., & Stein, M. B. (2011). The effect of avoidant personality disorder on the persistence of generalized social anxiety disorder in the general population: Results from a longitudinal, nationally representative mental health survey. *Depression and Anxiety, 28*, 250–255.

Cox, D. J., Cox, B. S., & Cox, J. C. (2011). Self-reported incidences of moving vehicle collisions and citations among drivers with ADHD: A cross-sectional survey across the lifespan. *The American Journal of Psychiatry, 168*(3), 329–330.

Coyle, J. T., Balu, D., Benneyworth, M., Basu, A., & Roseman, A. (2010). Beyond the dopamine receptor: Novel therapeutic targets for treating schizophrenia. *Dialogues in Clinical Neuroscience, 12*, 359–382.

Craske, M. G., Kircanski, K., Epstein, A., Wittchen, H. U., Pine, D. S., Lewis-Fernandez, R., et al. (2010). Panic disorder: A review of *DSM-IV* panic disorder and proposals for *DSM-V*. *Depression and Anxiety, 27*(2), 93–112.

Crean, R. D., Crane, N. A., & Mason, B. J. (2011). An evidence-based review of acute and long-term effects of cannabis use on executive cognitive functions. *Journal of Addiction Medicine, 5*(1), 1–8.

Crisafulli, C., Fabbri, C., Porcelli, S., Drago, A., Spina, E., De Ronchi, D., & Serretti, A. (2011). Pharmacogenetics of antidepressants. *Frontiers in Pharmacology, 2*(6).

Crowther, J. H., Armey, M., Luce, K. H., Dalton, G. R., & Leahey, T. (2008). The point prevalence of bulimic disorders from 1990 to 2004. *International Journal of Eating Disorders, 41*(6), 491–497.

Cserjési, R., Vermeulen, N., Luminet, O., Marechal, C., Nef, F., Simon, Y., & Lénárd, L. (2010). Explicit vs. implicit body image evaluation in restrictive anorexia nervosa. *Psychiatry Research, 175*(1–2), 148–153.

D

Dahl, M. H., Rønning, O. M., & Thommessen, B. (2010). Delirium in acute stroke— Prevalence and risk factors. *Acta Neurologica Scandinavica, 122*(Suppl 190), 39–43.

Dal Forno, G., Palermo, M. T., Donohue, J. E., Karagiozis, H., Zonderman, A. B., & Kawas, C. H. (2005). Depressive symptoms, sex, and risk for Alzheimer's disease. *Annals of Neurology, 57*(3), 381–387.

Dalton, K. M., Nacewicz, B. M., Johnstone, T., Schaefer, H. S., Gernsbacher, M. A., Goldsmith, H. H., . . . Davidson, R. J. (2005). Gaze fixation and the neural circuitry of face processing in autism. *Nature Neuroscience, 8*(4), 519–526.

Dana, R. H. (2002). Multicultural assessment: Teaching methods and competence evaluations. *Journal of Personality Assessment, 79*(2), 195–199.

Davis, T. E., III, & Ollendick, T. H. (2011). Specific phobias. In D. McKay & E. A. Storch (Eds.), *Handbook of child and adolescent anxiety disorders* (pp. 231–244). New York, NY: Springer Science + Business Media.

Dawson, G., Webb, S. J., Carver, L., Panagiotides, H., & McPartland, J. (2004). Young children with autism show atypical brain responses to fearful versus neutral facial expressions of emotion. *Developmental Science, 7*(3), 340–359.

de Guise, E., Leblanc, J., Gosselin, N., Marcoux, J., Champoux, M. C., Couturier, C., et al. (2010). Neuroanatomical correlates of the clock drawing test in patients with traumatic brain injury. *Brain Injury, 24*(13–14), 1568–1574.

de Jong, P. J., & Merckelbach, H. (2000). Phobia-relevant illusory correlations: The role of phobic responsivity. *Journal of Abnormal Psychology, 109*(4), 597–601.

de Jong, P. J., & Peters, M. L. (2007). Blood-injection-injury fears: Harm- vs. disgust-relevant selective outcome associations. *Journal of Behavior Therapy and Experimental Psychiatry, 38*(3), 263–274.

Delinsky, S. S. (2011). Body image and anorexia nervosa. In T. F. Cash & L. Smolak (Eds.), *Body image: A handbook of science, practice, and prevention* (2nd ed.) (pp. 279–287). New York, NY: Guilford Press.

DeLongis, A., Folkman, S., & Lazarus, R. S. (1988). The impact of daily stress on health and mood: Psychological and social resources as mediators. *Journal of Personality and Social Psychology, 54*, 486–495.

Denollet, J., & Pedersen, S. S. (2011). Type D personality in patients with cardiovascular disorders. In R. Allan & J. Fisher (Eds.), *Heart and mind: The practice of cardiac psychology* (2nd ed.) (pp. 219–247). Washington, DC: American Psychological Association.

Derogatis, L. R. (1994). *Manual for the symptom check list-90 revised (SCL-90-R).* Minneapolis, MN: National Computer Systems.

Deutsch, A. (1949). *The mentally ill in America* (2nd ed.). New York: Columbia University Press.

Dhawan, N., Kunik, M. E., Oldham, J., & Coverdale, J. (2010). Prevalence and treatment of narcissistic personality disorder in the community: A systematic review. *Comprehensive Psychiatry, 51*, 333–339.

Dick, D. M., Aliev, F., Edwards, A., Agrawal, A., Lynskey, M., Lin, P., . . . Bierut, L. (2011). Genome-wide association study of conduct disorder symptomatology. *Molecular Psychiatry, 16*(8), 800–808.

Dickerson, F. B., Tenhula, W. N., & Green-Paden, L. D. (2005). The token economy for schizophrenia: Review of the literature and recommendations for future research. *Schizophrenia Research, 75*, 405–416.

Dimaggio, G., Carcione, A., Salvatore, G., Nicolò, G., Sisto, A., & Semerari, A. (2011). Progressively promoting metacognition in a case of obsessive-compulsive personality disorder treated with metacognitive interpersonal therapy. *Psychology and Psychotherapy: Theory, Research and Practice, 84*, 70–83.

Disney, K. L., Weinstein, Y., & Oltmanns, T. F. (2012). Personality disorder symptoms are differentially related to divorce frequency. *Journal of Family Psychology, 26*, 959–965. doi:10.1037/a0030446

Dodson, W. W. (2005). Pharmacotherapy of adult ADHD. *Journal of Clinical Psychology, 61*(5), 589–606.

Doherty, G. H. (2011). Obesity and the ageing brain: Could leptin play a role in neurodegeneration? *Current Gerontology and Geriatric Research, 2011*, 708154.

Doley, R. (2003). Pyromania: Fact or fiction? *British Journal of Criminology, 43*(4), 797–807.

Driessen, E., & Hollon, S. D. (2010). Cognitive behavioral therapy for mood disorders: Efficacy, moderators and mediators. *Psychiatric Clinics of North America, 33*(3), 537–555.

Dudley, M., Goldney, R., & Hadzi-Pavlovic, D. (2010). Are adolescents dying by suicide taking SSRI antidepressants? A review of observational studies. *Australasian Psychiatry, 18*(3), 242–245.

Duke, D. C., Bodzin, D. K., Tavares, P., Geffken, G. R., & Storch, E. A. (2009). The phenomenology of hairpulling in a community sample. *Journal of Anxiety Disorders, 23*(8), 1118–1125.

Duke, D. C., Keeley, M. L., Geffken, G. R., & Storch, E. A. (2010). Trichotillomania: A current review. *Clinical Psychology Review, 30*(2), 181–193.

E

Edelstein, B., Martin, R. R., & McKee, D. R. (2000). Assessment of older adult psychopathology. In S. K. Whitbourne (Ed.), *Psychopathology in later life* (pp. 61–88). New York: Wiley.

Eley, T. C., Rijsdijk, F. V., Perrin, S., O'Connor, T. G., & Bolton, D. (2008). A multivariate genetic analysis of specific phobia, separation anxiety and social phobia in early childhood. *Journal of Abnormal Child Psychology: An official publication of the International Society for Research in Child and Adolescent Psychopathology, 36*(6), 839–848.

Ellenstein, A., Kranick, S. M., & Hallett, M. (2011). An update on psychogenic movement disorders. *Current Neurology and Neuroscience Reports, 4*(11), 396–403.

Ellis, A. (2005). *The myth of self-esteem.* Buffalo, NY: Prometheus.

Engelhard, I. M., & van den Hout, M. A. (2007). Preexisting neuroticism, subjective stressor severity, and posttraumatic stress in soldiers deployed to Iraq. *Canadian Journal of Psychiatry, 52*(8), 505–509.

Enserink, M. (1998). First Alzheimer's disease confirmed. *Science, 279*, 2037.

F

Fakier, N., & Wild, L. G. (2011). Associations among sleep problems, learning difficulties and substance use in adolescence. *Journal of Adolescence, 34*(4), 717–726.

Falsetti, S. A., & Davis, J. (2001). The nonpharmacologic treatment of generalized anxiety disorder. *Psychiatric Clinics of North America, 24*(1), 99–117.

Fang, A., & Hofmann, S. G. (2010). Relationship between social anxiety disorder and body dysmorphic disorder. *Clinical Psychology Review, 30*(8), 1040–1048.

Faraone, S. V., Perlis, R. H., Doyle, A. E., Smoller, J. W., Goralnick, J. J., Holmgren, M. A., & Sklar, P. (2005). Molecular genetics of attention-deficit/hyperactivity disorder. *Biological Psychiatry, 57*(11), 1313–1323.

Farooqui, A. A., Farooqui, T., Panza, F., & Frisardi, V. (2012). Metabolic syndrome as a risk factor for neurological disorders. *Cellular and Molecular Life Sciences, 69*(5), 741–762.

Farrell, H. M. (2010). Dissociative identity disorder: No excuse for criminal activity. *Current Psychiatry, 10*(6), 33–40.

Farrell, H. M. (2011). Dissociative identity disorder: Medicolegal challenges. *Journal of the American Academy of Psychiatry and the Law, 39*(3), 402–406.

Federal Bureau of Investigation. (2004). Age-specific arrest rates and race-specific arrest rates for selected offenses 1993–2001: Uniform crime reports, from http://www.fbi.gov/about-us/cjis/ucr/additional-ucr-publications/age_race_arrest93-01.pdf

First, M. B., & Gibbon, M. (2004). The structured clinical interview for *DSM-IV* Axis I Disorders (SCID-I) and the structured clinical interview for *DSM-IV* Axis II Disorders (SCID-II). In M. J. Hilsenroth & D. L. Segal (Eds.), *Comprehensive handbook of psychological assessment, Vol. 2: Personality assessment* (pp. 134–143). Hoboken, NJ: John Wiley & Sons, Inc.

Fisher, C. B., & Fried, A. L. (2008). Internet-mediated psychological services and the American Psychological Association Ethics Code. In D. N. Bersoff (Ed.), *Ethical conflicts in psychology* (4th ed.) (pp. 376–383). Washington, DC: American Psychological Association.

Fisher, C. B., & Vacanti-Shova, K. (2012). The responsible conduct of psychological research: An overview of ethical principles, APA Ethics Code standards, and federal regulations. In S. J. Knapp, M. C. Gottlieb,

M. M. Handelsman, & L. D. VandeCreek (Eds.), *APA handbook of ethics in psychology, Vol 2: Practice, teaching, and research* (pp. 335–369). Washington, DC: American Psychological Association.

Fisk, J. E., Murphy, P. N., Montgomery, C., & Hadjiefthyvoulou, F. (2011). Modelling the adverse effects associated with ecstasy use. *Addiction, 106*(4), 798–805.

Flessner, C. A., Woods, D. W., Franklin, M. E., Keuthen, N. J., & Piacentini, J. (2009). Cross-sectional study of women with trichotillomania: A preliminary examination of pulling styles, severity, phenomenology, and functional impact. *Child Psychiatry and Human Development, 40*(1), 153–167.

Foley, D. L., Pickles, A., Maes, H. M., Silberg, J. L., & Eaves, L. J. (2004). Course and short-term outcomes of separation anxiety disorder in a community sample of twins. *Journal of the American Academy of Child and Adolescent Psychiatry, 43*(9), 1107–1114.

Folstein, M. F., Folstein, S. E., & McHugh, P. R. (1975). Mini-Mental State: A practical method for grading the cognitive state of patients for the clinician. *Journal of Psychiatric Research, 12*, 189–198.

Fombonne, E., Wostear, G., Cooper, V., Harrington, R., & Rutter, M. (2001). The Maudsley long-term follow-up of child and adolescent depression: 1. Psychiatric outcomes in adulthood. *British Journal of Psychiatry, 179*(3), 210–217.

Foote, B., Smolin, Y., Kaplan, M., Legatt, M. E., & Lipschitz, D. (2006). Prevalence of dissociative disorders in psychiatric outpatients. *The American Journal of Psychiatry, 163*(4), 623–629.

Forcano, L., Ýlvarez, E., Santamaría, J. J., Jimenez-Murcia, S., Granero, R., Penelo, E., . . . Fernández-Arand, F. (2011). Suicide attempts in anorexia nervosa subtypes. *Comprehensive Psychiatry, 52*(4), 352–358.

Forman, E. M., Herbert, J. D., Moitra, E., Yeomans, P. D., & Geller, P. A. (2007). A randomized controlled effectiveness trial of acceptance and commitment therapy and cognitive therapy for anxiety and depression. *Behavior Modification, 31*(6), 772–799.

Forsyth, K., Maciver, D., Howden, S., Owen, C., & Shepherd, C. (2008). Developmental coordination disorder: A synthesis of evidence to underpin an allied health professions' framework. *International Journal of Disability, Development and Education, 55*(2), 153–172.

Fortune, E. E., & Goodie, A. S. (2011). Cognitive distortions as a component and treatment focus of pathological gambling: A review. *Psychology of Addictive Behaviors.*

Frank, E. (2007). Interpersonal and social rhythm therapy: A means of improving depression and preventing relapse in bipolar disorder. *Journal of Clinical Psychology, 63*(5), 463–473.

Frank, E., Maggi, L., Miniati, M., & Benvenuti, A. (2009). The rationale for combining interpersonal and social rhythm therapy (IPRST) and pharmacotherapy for the treatment of bipolar disorders. *Clinical Neuropsychiatry: Journal of Treatment Evaluation, 6*(2), 63–74.

Frank, J., Cichon, S., Treutlein, J., Ridinger, M., Mattheisen, M., Hoffmann, P., . . . Rietschel, M. (2012). Genome-wide significant association between alcohol dependence and a variant in the ADH gene cluster. *Addiction Biology, 17*(1), 171–180.

Frankl, V. (1963). *Man's search for meaning.* New York: Simon & Schuster.

Franklin, M. E., Zagrabbe, K., & Benavides, K. L. (2011). Trichotillomania and its treatment: A review and recommendations. *Expert Review of Neurotherapeutics, 11*(8), 1165–1174.

Franklin, T. B., & Mansuy, I. M. (2011). The involvement of epigenetic defects in mental retardation. *Neurobiology of Learning and Memory, 96*(1), 61–67.

Frattaroli, J. (2006). Experimental disclosure and its moderators: A meta-analysis. *Psychological Bulletin, 132*(6), 823–865.

Freeman, R. D., Soltanifar, A., & Baer, S. (2010). Stereotypic movement disorder: Easily missed. *Developmental Medicine & Child Neurology, 52*(8), 733–738.

Freud, S. (1911). Formulations of the two principles of mental functioning (J. Strachey, Trans.). In J. Strachey (Ed.), *The standard edition of the complete psychological works of Sigmund Freud* (Vol. 12). London: Hogarth.

Freud, S. (1923). The ego and the id (J. Strachey, Trans.). In J. Strachey (Ed.), *The standard edition of the complete psychological works of Sigmund Freud* (Vol. 19). London: Hogarth.

Freud, S. (1913–14/1963). *Further recommendations in the technique of psychoanalysis.* New York: Collier.

Furness, D. L., Dekker, G. A., & Roberts, C. T. (2011). DNA damage and health in pregnancy. *Journal of Reproductive Immunology, 89*(2), 153–162.

G

Ganguli, M., Dodge, H. H., Shen, C., Pandav, R. S., & DeKosky, S. T. (2005). Alzheimer disease and mortality: A 15-year epidemiological study. *Archives of Neurology, 62*(5), 779–784.

Garbutt, J. C., Kranzler, H. R., O'Malley, S. S., Gastfriend, D. R., Pettinati, H. M., Silverman, B. L., . . . Ehrich, E. W. (2005). Efficacy and tolerability of long-acting injectable naltrexone for alcohol dependence: A randomized controlled trial. *Journal of the American Medical Association, 293*(13), 1617–1625.

Geary, D. C. (2011). Consequences, characteristics, and causes of mathematical learning disabilities and persistent low achievement in mathematics. *Journal of Developmental and Behavioral Pediatrics, 32*(3), 250–263.

Genevsky, A., Garrett, C. T., Alexander, P. P., & Vinogradov, S. (2010). Cognitive training in schizophrenia: A neuroscience-based approach. *Dialogues in Clinical Neuroscience, 12,* 416–421.

Gersten, R., Beckman, S., Clarke, B., Foegen, A., Marsh, L., Star, J. R., & Witzel, B. (2009). Assisting students struggling with mathematics: Response to intervention (TR1) for elementary and middle schools (NCEE 2009-4060). Washington, DC: National Center for Education Evaluation and Regional Assistance, Institute of Education Sciences, U.S. Department of Education.

Gibbons, R. D., Hur, K., Bhaumik, D. K., & Mann, J. J. (2005). The relationship between antidepressant medication use and rate of suicide. *Archives of General Psychiatry, 62*(2), 165–172.

Gillett, G. (2011). The gold-plated leucotomy standard and deep brain stimulation. *Journal of Bioethical Inquiry, 8*(1), 35–44.

Gilman, S., Koeppe, R. A., Little, R., An, H., Junck, L., Giordani, B., . . . Wernette, K. (2005). Differentiation of Alzheimer's disease from dementia with Lewy bodies utilizing positron emission tomography with [18F]fluorodeoxyglucose and neuropsychological testing. *Experimental Neurology, 191 Suppl 1,* S95–S103.

Gisslen, M., Hagberg, L., Brew, B. J., Cinque, P., Price, R. W., & Rosengren, L. (2007). Elevated cerebrospinal fluid neurofilament light protein concentrations predict the development of AIDS dementia complex. *Journal of Infectious Diseases, 195*(12), 1774–1778.

Glass, S. J., & Newman, J. P. (2009). Emotion processing in the criminal psychopath: The role of attention in emotion-facilitated memory. [Article]. *Journal of Abnormal Psychology, 118,* 229–234.

Glaze, L. E. (2011). Correctional population in the United States, 2010, from http://bjs.ojp.usdoj.gov/index.cfm?ty=pbdetail&iid=2237

Gleason, M. M., Fox, N. A., Drury, S., Smyke, A., Egger, H. L., Nelson, C. A., III, . . . Zeanah, C. H. (2011). Validity of evidence-derived criteria for reactive attachment disorder: Indiscriminately social/disinhibited and emotionally withdrawn/inhibited types. *Journal of the American Academy of Child & Adolescent Psychiatry, 50*(3), 216–231.

Goldsmith, S. K., Pellman, R. C., Kleinman, A. M., & Bunney, W. E. (Eds.) (2002). *Reducing suicide: A national imperative.* Washington, DC: The National Academies Press.

Gómez-de-Regil, L., Kwapil, T. R., Blanqué, J. M., Vainer, E., Montoro, M., & Barrantes-Vidal, N. (2010). Predictors of outcome in the early course of first-episode psychosis. *The European Journal of Psychiatry, 24,* 87–97.

Gons, R. A., van Norden, A. G., de Laat, K. F., van Oudheusden, L. J., van Uden, I. W., Zwiers, M. P., . . . de Leeuw, F. E. (2011). Cigarette smoking is associated with reduced microstructural integrity of cerebral white matter. *Brain, 134*(Pt 7), 2116–2124.

Gottesman, I. I., & Gould, T. D. (2003). The endophenotype concept in psychiatry: Etymology and strategic intentions. *American Journal of Psychiatry, 160*(4), 636–645.

Gottesman, I. I., & Shields, J. (1972). *Schizophrenia and genetics: A twin study vantage point.* New York: Academic Press.

Gottesman, I. I., & Shields, J. (1973). Genetic theorizing and schizophrenia. *British Journal of Psychiatry, 122*(566), 15–30.

Govind, V., Gold, S., Kaliannan, K., Saigal, G., Falcone, S., Arheart, K. L., . . . Maudsley, A. A. (2010). Whole-brain proton MR spectroscopic imaging of mild-to-moderate traumatic brain injury and correlation with neuropsychological deficits. *Journal of Neurotrauma, 27*(3), 483–496.

Graham, C. A. (2010). The *DSM* diagnostic criteria for female orgasmic disorder. *Archives of Sexual Behavior, 39,* 256–270.

Grant, J. E. (2005). Clinical characteristics and psychiatric comorbidity in males with exhibitionism. *Journal of Clinical Psychiatry, 66,* 1367–1371.

Grant, J. E. (2006). SPECT imaging and treatment of pyromania. *Journal of Clinical Psychiatry, 67*(6), 998.

Grant, J. E., Chamberlain, S. R., Odlaug, B. L., Potenza, M. N., & Kim, S. W. (2010). Memantine shows promise in reducing gambling severity and cognitive inflexibility in pathological gambling: A pilot study. *Psychopharmacology, 212*(4), 603–612.

Grant, J. E., & Kim, S. W. (2007). Clinical characteristics and psychiatric comorbidity of pyromania. *Journal of Clinical Psychiatry, 68*(11), 1717–1722.

Grant, J. E., Kim, S. W., & Odlaug, B. L. (2009). A double-blind, placebo-controlled study of the opiate antagonist, naltrexone, in the treatment of kleptomania. *Biological Psychiatry, 65*(7), 600–606.

Grant, J. E., Levine, L., Kim, D., & Potenza, M. N. (2005). Impulse control disorders in adult psychiatric inpatients. *American Journal of Psychiatry, 162*(11), 2184–2188.

Grant, J. E., Odlaug, B. L., & Kim, S. W. (2010). Kleptomania: Clinical characteristics and relationship to substance use disorders. *The American Journal of Drug and Alcohol Abuse, 36*(5), 291–295.

Grant, J. E., Odlaug, B. L., Davis, A., & Kim, S. W. (2009). Legal consequences of kleptomania. *Psychiatric Quarterly, 80*(4), 251–259.

Grant, J. E., Odlaug, B. L., Potenza, M. N., Hollander, E., & Kim, S. W. (2010). Nalmefene in the treatment of pathological gambling: Multicentre, double-blind, placebo-controlled study. *British Journal of Psychiatry, 197*(4), 330–331.

Griffin, J. A., Umstattd, M. R., & Usdan, S. L. (2010). Alcohol use and high-risk sexual behavior among collegiate women: A review of research on alcohol myopia theory. *Journal of American College Health, 58*(6), 523–532.

Gross, C. G. (1999). "Psychosurgery"in renaissance art. *Trends in Neurosciences, 22*, 429–431.

Grover, S., Chakrabarti, S., Shah, R., & Kumar, V. (2011). A factor analytic study of the Delirium Rating Scale-Revised-98 in untreated patients with delirium. *Journal of Psychosomatic Research, 70*(5), 473–478.

Gu, Y., Luchsinger, J. A., Stern, Y., & Scarmeas, N. (2010). Mediterranean diet, inflammatory and metabolic biomarkers, and risk of Alzheimer's disease. *Journal of Alzheimer's Disease, 22*(2), 483–492.

Guay, D. R. P. (2009). Drug treatment of paraphilic and nonparaphilic sexual disorders. *Clinical Therapeutics: The International Peer-Reviewed Journal of Drug Therapy, 31*, 1–31.

Gunderson, J. G. (2011). Clinical practice. Borderline personality disorder. *New England Journal of Medicine, 364*, 2037–2042.

Gunderson, J. G., & Links, P. S. (2008). *Borderline personality disorder: A clinical guide* (2nd ed.). Washington, DC: American Psychiatric Press, Inc.

Gunderson, J. G., Stout, R. L., McGlashan, T. H., Shea, M. T., Morey, L. C., Grilo, C. M., . . . Skodol, A. E. (2011). Ten-year course of borderline personality disorder: Psychopathology and function from the Collaborative Longitudinal Personality Disorders study. *Archives of General Psychiatry, 68*, 827–837.

Gunter, T. D., Vaughn, M. G., & Philibert, R. A. (2010). Behavioral genetics in antisocial spectrum disorders and psychopathy: A review of the recent literature. *Behavioral Sciences & the Law, 28*, 148–173.

Gur, R. E., & Gur, R. C. (2010). Functional magnetic resonance imaging in schizophrenia. *Dialogues in Clinical Neuroscience, 12*, 333–343.

H

Haji, I. (2010). Psychopathy, ethical perception, and moral culpability. *Neuroethics, 3*, 135–150.

Hall, B. J., Tolin, D. F., Frost, R. O., & Steketee, G. (2013). An exploration of comorbid symptoms and clinical correlates of clinically significant hoarding symptoms. *Depression and Anxiety, 30*(1), 67–76. doi:10.1002/da.22015

Hall, R. C. (2007). A profile of pedophilia: Definition, characteristics of offenders, recidivism, treatment outcomes, and forensic issues. *Mayo Clinic Proceedings, 82*, 457–471.

Hammen, C. (2005). Stress and depression. *Annual Review in Clinical Psychology, 1*, 293–319.

Hare, R. D. (1997). *Hare psychopathy checklist—Revised (PCL-R)*. Odessa, FL: Personality Assessment Resources.

Hare, R. D., & Neumann, C. S. (2005). Structural models of psychopathy. *Current Psychiatry Reports, 7*, 57–64.

Hare, R. D., & Neumann, C. S. (2009). Psychopathy: Assessment and forensic implications. *Canadian Journal of Psychiatry, 54*, 791–802.

Harpur, T. J., & Hare, R. D. (1994). Assessment of psychopathy as a function of age. *Journal of Abnormal Psychology 103*, 604–609.

Hatch, A., Madden, S., Kohn, M., Clarke, S., Touyz, S., & Williams, L. M. (2010). Anorexia nervosa: Towards an integrative neuroscience model. *European Eating Disorders Review, 18*(3), 165–179.

Hayes, J. P., LaBar, K. S., McCarthy, G., Selgrade, E., Nasser, J., Dolcos, F., et al. (2011). Reduced hippocampal and amygdala activity predicts memory distortions for trauma reminders in combat-related PTSD. *Journal of Psychiatric Research, 45*(5), 660–669.

Heath, A. C., Whitfield, J. B., Martin, N. G., Pergadia, M. L., Goate, A. M., Lind, P. A., . . . Montgomery, G. W. (2011). A quantitative-trait genome-wide association study of alcoholism risk in the community: Findings and implications. *Biological Psychiatry, 70*(6), 513–518.

Helgeson, V. S., Reynolds, K. A., & Tomich, P. L. (2006). A meta-analytic review of benefit finding and growth. *Journal of Consulting and Clinical Psychology, 74*(5), 797–816.

Hempenius, L., van Leeuwen, B. L., van Assert, D. Z. B., Hoekstra, H. J., Wiggers, T., Slaets, J. P. J., & de Bock, G. H. (2011). Structured analyses of interventions to prevent delirium. *International Journal of Geriatric Psychiatry, 26*(5), 441–450.

Herbert, P. B. (2002). The duty to warn: A reconsideration and critique. *Journal of the American Academy of Psychiatry and the Law, 30*(3), 417–424.

Herpertz, S., Hagenah, U., Vocks, S., von Wietersheim, J., Cuntz, U., Zeeck, A., & Wagstaff, K. (2011). The diagnosis and treatment of eating disorders. *Deutsches Ärzteblatt International, 108*(40), 678–685.

Hettema, J. M., Prescott, C. A., & Kendler, K. S. (2004). Genetic and environmental sources of covariation between generalized anxiety disorder and neuroticism. *American Journal of Psychiatry, 161*(9), 1581–1587.

Hillemacher, T., Heberlein, A., Muschler, M. A., Bleich, S., & Frieling, H. (2011). Opioid modulators for alcohol dependence. *Expert Opinion on Investigational Drugs, 20*(8), 1073–1086.

Hinderliter, A. C. (2010). Disregarding science, clinical utility, and the *DSM*'s definition of mental disorder: The case of exhibitionism, voyeurism, and frotteurism. *Archives of Sexual Behavior, 39*, 1235–1237.

Hipwell, A. E., Stepp, S., Feng, X., Burke, J., Battista, D. R., Loeber, R., & Keenan, K. (2011). Impact of oppositional defiant disorder dimensions on the temporal ordering of conduct problems and depression across childhood and adolescence in girls. *Journal of Child Psychology and Psychiatry, 52*(10), 1099–1108. doi: 10.1111/j.1469-7610.2011.02448.x

Hirvonen, J., van Erp, T. G., Huttunen, J., Aalto, S., Nagren, K., Huttunen, M., . . . Cannon, T. D. (2005). Increased caudate dopamine D2 receptor availability as a genetic marker for schizophrenia. *Archives of General Psychiatry, 62*, 371–378.

Hodgins, D. C., & Peden, N. (2008). Cognitive-behavioral treatment for impulse control disorders. *Revista Brasileira de Psiquiatria, 30*(Suppl 1), S31–S40.

Hoffman, E. J., & State, M. W. (2010). Progress in cytogenetics: Implications for child psychopathology. *Journal of the American Academy of Child and Adolescent Psychiatry, 49*, 736–751.

Hofmann, S. G., Rief, W., & Spiegel, D. A. (2010). Psychotherapy for panic disorder. In D. J. Stein, E. Hollander, & B. O. Rothbaum (Eds.), *Textbook of anxiety disorders* (2nd ed.) (pp. 417–433). Arlington, VA: American Psychiatric Publishing, Inc.

Hogan, M. F. (2003). The President's New Freedom Commission: Recommendations to transform mental health care in America. *Psychiatric Services, 54*, 1467–1474.

Hoge, C. W., Castro, C. A., Messer, S. C., McGurk, D., Cotting, D. I., & Koffman, R. L. (2004). Combat duty in Iraq and Afghanistan, mental health problems, and barriers to care. *New England Journal of Medicine, 351*(1), 13–22.

Hoge, C. W., Terhakopian, A., Castro, C. A., Messer, S. C., & Engel, C. C. (2007). Association of posttraumatic stress disorder with somatic symptoms, health care visits, and absenteeism among Iraq war veterans. *Americal Journal of Psychiatry, 164*(1), 150–153.

Hollingshead, A. B., & Redlich, F. C. (1958). *Social class and mental illness: A community study*. New York: Wiley.

Hollon, S. D., & Ponniah, K. (2010). A review of empirically supported psychological therapies for mood disorders in adults. *Depression and Anxiety, 27*(10), 891–932.

Holmes, T. H., & Rahe, R. H. (1967). The social readjustment rating scale. *Journal of Psychosomatic Research, 11*, 213–218.

Holtkamp, K., Konrad, K., Kaiser, N., Ploenes, Y., Heussen, N., Grzella, I., & Herpertz-Dahlmann, B. (2005). A retrospective study of SSRI treatment in adolescent anorexia nervosa: Insufficient evidence for efficacy. *Journal of Psychiatric Research, 39*(3), 303–310.

Hopper, K., Harrison, G., Janca, A., & Sartorius, N. (2007). *Recovery from schizophrenia: An international perspective: A report from the WHO Collaborative Project, the international study of schizophrenia.* New York: Oxford University Press.

Hopwood, C. J., & Thomas, K. M. (2012). Paranoid and schizoid personality disorders. In T. A. Widiger (Ed.), *The Oxford handbook of personality disorders* (pp. 582–602). New York: Oxford University Press. doi:10.1093/oxfordhb/9780199735013.013.0027.

Houben, K., Nederkoorn, C., Wiers, R. W., & Jansen, A. (2011). Resisting temptation: Decreasing alcohol-related affect and drinking behavior by training response inhibition. *Drug and Alcohol Dependence, 116*(1–3), 132–136.

Hoven, C. W., Duarte, C. S., Lucas, C. P., Wu, P., Mandell, D. J., Goodwin, R. D., ... Susser, E. (2005). Psychopathology among New York city public school children 6 months after September 11. *Archives of General Psychiatry, 62*(5), 545–552.

Howe, E. (2008). Ethical considerations when treating patients with schizophrenia. *Psychiatry (Edgmont), 5*, 59–64.

Howland, M., Hunger, J. M., & Mann, T. (2012). Friends don't let friends eat cookies: Effects of restrictive eating norms on consumption among friends. *Appetite, 59*(2), 505–509. doi:10.1016/j.appet.2012.06.020

Hrabosky, J. I. (2011). Body image and binge-eating disorder. In T. F. Cash & L. Smolak (Eds.), *Body image: A handbook of science, practice, and prevention* (2nd ed.) (pp. 296–304). New York: Guilford Press.

Huang, X.-Q., Lui, S., Deng, W., Chan, R. C. K., Wu, Q.-Z., Jiang, L.-J., ... Gong, Q.-Y. (2010). Localization of cerebral functional deficits in treatment-naive, first-episode schizophrenia using resting-state fMRI. *NeuroImage, 49*(4), 2901–2906.

Hudson, J. I., Hiripi, E., Pope, H. G., Jr., & Kessler, R. C. (2007). The prevalence and correlates of eating disorders in the National Comorbidity Survey Replication. *Biological Psychiatry, 61*(3), 348–358.

Hughes, J. R. (2007). Review of medical reports on pedophilia. *Clinical Pediatrics, 46*, 667–682.

Hunsley, J., & Mash, E. J. (2007). Evidence-based assessment. *Annual Review of Clinical Psychology, 3*, 29–51.

Huppert, J. D., Foa, E. B., McNally, R. J., & Cahill, S. P. (2009). Role of cognition in stress-induced and fear circuitry disorders. In G. Andrews, D. S. Charney, P. J. Sirovatka, & D. A. Regier (Eds.), *Stress-induced and fear circuitry disorders: Advancing the research agenda for DSM-V* (pp. 175–193). Arlington, VA: American Psychiatric Publishing, Inc.

Hurwitz, T. A. (2004). Somatization and conversion disorder. *Canadian Journal of Psychiatry, 49*(3), 172–178.

Hyman, S. E. (2011). Diagnosis of mental disorders in light of modern genetics. In D. A. Regier, W. E. Narrow, E. A. Kuhl, & D. J. Kupfer (Eds.), *The conceptual evolution of DSM-5* (pp. 3–17). Washington, DC: American Psychiatric Publishers.

I

Inouye, S. K., Bogardus, S. T., Charpentier, P. A., Leo-Summers, L., Acampora, D., Holford, T. R., & Cooney, L. M., Jr. (1999). A multicomponent intervention to prevent delirium in hospitalized older patients. *The New England Journal of Medicine, 340*(9), 669–676.

Iverson, G. L. (2005). Outcome from mild traumatic brain injury. *Current Opinion in Psychiatry, 18*(3), 301–317.

Iverson, K. M., Follette, V. M., Pistorello, J., & Fruzzetti, A. E. (2011). An investigation of experiential avoidance, emotion dysregulation, and distress tolerance in young adult outpatients with borderline personality disorder symptoms. *Personality Disorders: Theory, Research, and Treatment.*

J

Jablensky, A. (2010). The diagnostic concept of schizophrenia: Its history, evolution, and future prospects. *Dialogues in Clinical Neuroscience, 12*, 271–287.

Jaffee, S. R., Caspi, A., Moffitt, T. E., Dodge, K. A., Rutter, M., Taylor, A., & Tully, L. A. (2005). Nature × nurture: Genetic vulnerabilities interact with physical maltreatment to promote conduct problems. *Development and Psychopathology, 17*(1), 67–84.

Jain, G., Chakrabarti, S., & Kulhara, P. (2011). Symptoms of delirium: An exploratory factor analytic study among referred patients. *General Hospital Psychiatry, 33*(4), 377–385.

Jarry, J. L. (2010). Core conflictual relationship theme-guided psychotherapy: Initial effectiveness study of a 16-session manualized approach in a sample of six patients. *Psychology and Psychotherapy: Theory, Research and Practice, 83*(4), 385–394.

Jellinger, K. A., & Attems, J. (2010). Prevalence and pathology of vascular dementia in the oldest-old. *Journal of Alzheimer's Disease, 21*(4), 1283–1293.

Jobe, T. H., & Harrow, M. (2010). Schizophrenia course, long-term outcome, recovery, and prognosis. *Current Directions in Psychological Science, 19*, 220–225.

Johansson, A., Sundbom, E., Höjerback, T., & Bodlund, O. (2010). A five-year follow-up study of Swedish adults with gender identity disorder. *Archives of Sexual Behavior, 39*, 1429–1437.

Johnson, J., Wood, A. M., Gooding, P., Taylor, P. J., & Tarrier, N. (2011). Resilience to suicidality: The buffering hypothesis. *Clinical Psychology Review, 31*(4), 563–591.

Johnson, J. G., Cohen, P., Kasen, S., Smailes, E., & Brook, J. S. (2001). Association of maladaptive parental behavior with psychiatric disorder among parents and their offspring. *Archives of General Psychiatry, 58*(5), 453–460.

Johnston, L. D., O'Malley, P. M., Bachman, J. G., & Schulenberg, J. E. (2011). Monitoring the future national survey results on drug use, 1975–2010. Volume I: Secondary school students (p. 744). Ann Arbor, MI: Institute for Social Research, The University of Michigan.

Jones, K. M., Whitbourne, S. K., Whitbourne, S. B., & Skultety, K. M. (2009). Identity processes and memory controllability in middle and later adulthood. *Journal of Applied Gerontology, 28*(5), 582–599.

Jones, R. M., Arlidge, J., Gillham, R., Reagu, S., van den Bree, M., & Taylor, P. J. (2011). Efficacy of mood stabilisers in the treatment of impulsive or repetitive aggression: Systematic review and meta-analysis. *British Journal of Psychiatry, 198*(2), 93–98.

Jonsbu, E., Dammen, T., Morken, G., Lied, A., Vik-Mo, H., & Martinsen, E. W. (2009). Cardiac and psychiatric diagnoses among patients referred for chest pain and palpitations. *Scandinavian Cardiovascular Journal, 43*(4), 256–259.

Jonsbu, E., Dammen, T., Morken, G., Moum, T., & Martinsen, E. W. (2011). Short-term cognitive behavioral therapy for non-cardiac chest pain and benign palpitations: A randomized controlled trial. *Journal of Psychosomatic Research, 70*(2), 117–123.

Jonson, R. (2011). *The psychopath test: A journey through the madness industry.* New York: Penguin.

Jorstad-Stein, E. C., & Heimberg, R. G. (2009). Social phobia: An update on treatment. *Psychiatric Clinics of North America, 32*(3), 641–663.

Joseph, J. A., Shukitt-Hale, B., & Casadesus, G. (2005). Reversing the deleterious effects of aging on neuronal communication and behavior: Beneficial properties of fruit polyphenolic compounds. *American Journal of Clinical Nutrition, 81*(1 Suppl), 313S–316S.

Juliano, L. M., & Griffiths, R. R. (2004). A critical review of caffeine withdrawal: Empirical validation of symptoms and signs, incidence, severity, and associated features. *Psychopharmacology (Berlin), 176*(1), 1–29.

Jung, C. G. (1916). General aspects of dream psychology. In H. Read, M. Fordham, & G. Adler (Eds.), *The collected works of C. G. Jung* (Vol. 8, pp. 237–280). Princeton, NJ: Princeton University Press.

Jung, C. G. (1961). *Memories, dreams, reflections*. New York: Pantheon.

Jurbergs, N., & Ledley, D. R. (2005). Separation anxiety disorder. *Pediatric Annals, 34*(2), 108–115.

K

Kalk, N. J., Nutt, D. J., & Lingford-Hughes, A. R. (2011). The role of central noradrenergic dysregulation in anxiety disorders: Evidence from clinical studies. *Journal of Psychopharmacology, 25*(1), 3–16.

Kamali, M., & McInnis, M. G. (2011). Genetics of mood disorders: General principles and potential applications for treatment resistant depression. In J. F. Greden, M. B. Riba, & M. G. McInnis (Eds.), *Treatment resistant depression: A roadmap for effective care* (pp. 293–308). Arlington, VA: American Psychiatric Publishing, Inc.

Kanaan, R. A., & Wessely, S. C. (2010). The origins of factitious disorder. *History of the Human Sciences, 23*(2), 68–85.

Kane, J. M., & Correll, C. U. (2010). Pharmacologic treatment of schizophrenia. *Dialogues in Clinical Neuroscience, 12,* 345–357.

Kawas, C., Gray, S., Brookmeyer, R., Fozard, J., & Zonderman, A. (2000). Age-specific incidence rates of Alzheimer's disease: The Baltimore Longitudinal Study of Aging. *Neurology, 54*(11), 2072–2077.

Kearney, C. A., & Vecchio, J. L. (2007). When a child won't speak. *The Journal of Family Practice, 56*(11), 917–921.

Keel, P. K., Gravener, J. A., Joiner Jr., T. E., & Haedt, A. A. (2010). Twenty-year follow-up of bulimia nervosa and related eating disorders not otherwise specified. *International Journal of Eating Disorders, 43*(6), 492–497.

Kellner, M. (2010). Drug treatment of obsessive-compulsive disorder. *Dialogues in Clinical Neuroscience, 12*(2), 187–197.

Kessing, L. V., Hellmund, G., Geddes, J. R., Goodwin, G. M., & Andersen, P. K. (2011). Valproate v. lithium in the treatment of bipolar disorder in clinical practice: Observational nationwide register-based cohort study. *British Journal of Psychiatry, 199,* 57–63.

Kessler, R. C., Adler, L., Barkley, R., Biederman, J., Conners, C. K., Demler, O., . . . Zaslavsky, A. M. (2006). The prevalence and correlates of adult ADHD in the United States: Results from the National Comorbidity Survey replication. *The American Journal of Psychiatry, 163*(4), 716–723.

Kessler, R. C., Berglund, P., Demler, O., Jin, R., Merikangas, K. R., & Walters, E. E. (2005). Lifetime prevalence and age-of-onset distributions of *DSM-IV* disorders in the National Comorbidity Survey Replication. *Archives of General Psychiatry, 62*(6), 593–602.

Kessler, R. C., Chiu, W. T., Demler, O., Merikangas, K. R., & Walters, E. E. (2005). Prevalence, severity, and comorbidity of 12-month *DSM-IV* disorders in the National Comorbidity Survey Replication. *Archives of General Psychiatry, 62*(6), 617–627.

Kessler, R. C., Coccaro, E. F., Fava, M., Jaeger, S., Jin, R., & Walters, E. (2006). The prevalence and correlates of *DSM-IV* intermittent explosive disorder in the National Comorbidity Survey Replication. *Archives of General Psychiatry, 63*(6), 669–678.

Kessler, R. C., Green, J. G., Adler, L. A., Barkley, R. A., Chatterji, S., Faraone, S. V., . . . Van Brunt, D. L. (2010). Structure and diagnosis of adult attention-deficit/hyperactivity disorder: Analysis of expanded symptom criteria from the Adult ADHD Clinical Diagnostic Scale. *Archives of General Psychiatry, 67*(11), 1168–1178.

Kessler, R. C., Hwang, I., LaBrie, R., Petukhova, M., Sampson, N. A., Winters, K. C., & Schaffer, H. J. (2008). *DSM-IV* pathological gambling in the National Comorbidity Survey Replication. *Psychological Medicine: A Journal of Research in Psychiatry and the Allied Sciences, 38*(9), 1351–1360.

Khodarahimi, S. (2009). Satiation therapy and exposure response prevention in the treatment of obsessive compulsive disorder. *Journal of Contemporary Psychotherapy, 39*(3), 203–207.

Kihlstrom, J. R. (2005). Dissociative disorders. *Annual Review of Clinical Psychology, 1*(1), 227–253.

Killam, C., Cautin, R. L., & Santucci, A. C. (2005). Assessing the enduring residual neuropsychological effects of head trauma in college athletes who participate in contact sports. *Archives of Clinical Neuropsychology, 20*(5), 599–611.

Kimura, M., & Higuchi, S. (2011). Genetics of alcohol dependence. *Psychiatry and Clinical Neurosciences, 65*(3), 213–225.

Kinsey, A. C., Pomeroy, W. B., & Martin, C. E. (1948). *Sexual behavior in the human male.* Philadelphia: Saunders.

Kinsey, A. C., Pomeroy, W. B., Martin, C. E., & Gebhard, P. H. (1953). *Sexual behavior in the human female.* Philadelphia: Saunders.

Kirsch, I., Deacon, B. J., Huedo-Medina, T. B., Scoboria, A., Moore, T. J., & Johnson, B. T. (2008). Initial severity and antidepressant benefits: Ameta-analysis of data submitted to the Food and Drug Administration. *PLoS Medicine, 5*(2), e45.

Knapp, S., & VandeCreek, L. (2001). Ethical issues in personality assessment in forensic psychology. *Journal of Personality Assessment, 77*(2), 242–254.

Knopman, D. S. (2007). Cerebrovascular disease and dementia. *British Journal of Radiology, 80* Spec No 2, S121–127.

Knopman, D. S., & Roberts, R. (2010). Vascular risk factors: Imaging and neuropathologic correlates. *Journal of Alzheimer's Disease, 20*(3), 699–709.

Ko, H.-C., & Kuo, F.-Y. (2009). Can blogging enhance subjective well-being through self-disclosure? *CyberPsychology & Behavior, 12*(1), 75–79.

Kodituwakku, P. W. (2009). Neurocognitive profile in children with fetal alcohol spectrum disorders. *Developmental Disabilities Research Reviews, 15*(3), 218–224.

Kodituwakku, P. W., & Kodituwakku, E. L. (2011). From research to practice: An integrative framework for the development of interventions for children with fetal alcohol spectrum disorders. *Neuropsychology Review, 21*(2), 204–223.

Koegel, R. L., Koegel, L. K., & McNerney, E. K. (2001). Pivotal areas in intervention for autism. *Journal of Clinical Child Psychology, 30*(1), 19–32.

Koeter, M. W. J., van den Brink, W., & Lehert, P. (2010). Effect of early and late compliance on the effectiveness of acamprosate in the treatment of alcohol dependence. *Journal of Substance Abuse Treatment, 39*(3), 218–226.

Kohut, H. (1966). Forms and transformations of narcissism. *Journal of the American Psychoanalytic Association, 14,* 243–272.

Kohut, H. (1971). *The analysis of the self.* New York: International Universities Press.

Krafft-Ebing, R. V. (1886/1950). *Psychopathia sexualis.* New York: Pioneer Publications.

Krystal, J. H., Rosenheck, R. A., Cramer, J. A., Vessicchio, J. C., Jones, K. M., Vertrees, J. E., et al. (2011). Adjunctive risperidone treatment for antidepressant-resistant symptoms of chronic military service–related PTSD: A randomized trial. *JAMA: Journal of the American Medical Association, 306*(5), 493–502.

Kuhl, E. S., Hoodin, F., Rice, J., Felt, B. T., Rausch, J. R., & Patton, S. R. (2010). Increasing daily water intake and fluid adherence in children receiving treatment for retentive encopresis. *Journal of Pediatric Psychology, 35*(10), 1144–1151.

Kurlan, R. (2010). Tourette's syndrome. *The New England Journal of Medicine, 363*(24), 2332–2338.

L

La Fond, J. Q. (1994). Law and the delivery of involuntary mental health services. *American Journal of Orthopsychiatry, 64*(2), 209–222.

Labouvie-Vief, G., & Diehl, M. (2000). Cognitive complexity and cognitive-affective integration: Related or separate domains of adult development? *Psychology and Aging, 15*(3), 490–504.

Laing, R. D. (1959). *The divided self.* New York: Penguin.

Lamb, D. H., Catanzaro, S. J., & Moorman, A. S. (2004). A preliminary look at how psychologists identify, evaluate, and proceed when faced with possible multiple relationship dilemmas. *Professional Psychology: Research and Practice, 35*(3), 248–254.

Lambert, M., Karow, A., Leucht, S., Schimmelmann, B. G., & Naber, D. (2010). Remission in schizophrenia: Validity, frequency, predictors, and patients' perspective 5 years later. *Dialogues in Clinical Neuroscience, 12,* 393–407.

Långström, N. (2010). The DSM diagnostic criteria for exhibitionism, voyeurism, and frotteurism. *Archives of Sexual Behavior, 39,* 317–324.

Långström, N., & Seto, M. C. (2006). Exhibitionistic and voyeuristic behavior in a Swedish national population survey. *Archives of Sexual Behavior, 35,* 427–435.

Lau, J. Y. F., & Eley, T. C. (2010). The genetics of mood disorders. *Annual Review of Clinical Psychology, 6,* 313–337.

Laumann, E. O., & Waite, L. J. (2008). Sexual dysfunction among older adults: Prevalence and risk factors from a nationally representative U.S. probability sample of men and women 57–85 years of age. *Journal of Sexual Medicine, 5,* 2300–2311.

Lazarus, A. A. (1968). Learning theory and the treatment of depression. *Behaviour Research and Therapy, 6,* 83–89.

Lazarus, R. S., & Folkman, S. (1984). *Stress, appraisal, and coping.* New York: Springer.

Le Jeune, F., Vérin, M., N'Diaye, K., Drapier, D., Leray, E., Du Montcel, S. T., et al. (2010). Decrease of prefrontal metabolism after subthalamic stimulation in obsessive-compulsive disorder: A positron emission tomography study. *Biological Psychiatry, 68*(11), 1016–1022.

LeBeau, R. T., Glenn, D., Liao, B., Wittchen, H. U., Beesdo-Baum, K., Ollendick, T., et al. (2010). Specific phobia: A review of *DSM-IV* specific phobia and preliminary recommendations for *DSM-V. Depression and Anxiety, 27*(2), 148–167.

Lebel, C., Roussotte, F., & Sowell, E. R. (2011). Imaging the impact of prenatal alcohol exposure on the structure of the developing human brain. *Neuropsychology Review, 21*(2), 102–118.

Leckman, J. F., Denys, D., Simpson, H. B., Mataix-Cols, D., Hollander, E., Saxena, S., et al. (2010). Obsessive-compulsive disorder: A review of the diagnostic criteria and possible subtypes and dimensional specifiers for *DSM-V. Depression and Anxiety, 27*(6), 507–527.

Leombruni, P., Pierò, A., Lavagnino, L., Brustolin, A., Campisi, S., & Fassino, S. (2008). A randomized, double-blind trial comparing sertraline and fluoxetine 6-month treatment in obese patients with binge eating disorder. *Progress in Neuro-Psychopharmacology & Biological Psychiatry, 32*(6), 1599–1605.

LePage, J. P., DelBen, K., Pollard, S., McGhee, M., VanHorn, L., Murphy, J., . . . Mogge, N. (2003). Reducing assaults on an acute psychiatric unit using a token economy: A 2-year follow-up. *Behavioral Interventions, 18*(3), 179–190.

Levy, K. N., Clarkin, J. F., Yeomans, F. E., Scott, L. N., Wasserman, R. H., & Kernberg, O. F. (2006). The mechanisms of change in the treatment of borderline personality disorder with transference focused psychotherapy. *Journal of Clinical Psychology, 62,* 481–501.

Levy, K. N., Ellison, W. D., Scott, L. N., & Bernecker, S. L. (2011). Attachment style. *Journal of Clinical Psychology, 67*(2), 193–201.

Lewinsohn, P. M. (1974). A behavioral approach to depression. In R. J. Friedman & M. M. Katz (Eds.), *The psychology of depression: Contemporary theory and research.* Oxford, England: John Wiley & Sons.

Lewis, A. J., Dennerstein, M., & Gibbs, P. M. (2008). Short-term psychodynamic psychotherapy: Review of recent process and outcome studies. *Australian and New Zealand Journal of Psychiatry, 42*(6), 445–455.

Lewis, R. W., Fugl-Meyer, K. S., Corona, G., Hayes, R. D., Laumann, E. O., Moreira, E. D., Jr., . . . Segraves, T. (2010). Definitions/epidemiology/risk factors for sexual dysfunction. *Journal of Sexual Medicine, 7,* 1598–1607.

Lichtenstein, P., Yip, B. H., Bjork, C., Pawitan, Y., Cannon, T. D., Sullivan, P. F., & Hultman, C. M. (2009). Common genetic determinants of schizophrenia and bipolar disorder in Swedish families: A population-based study. *Lancet, 373,* 234–239.

Lin, R. Y., Heacock, L. C., & Fogel, J. F. (2010). Drug-induced, dementia-associated and non-dementia, non-drug delirium hospitalizations in the United States, 1998–2005: An analysis of the National Inpatient Sample. *Drugs & Aging, 27*(1), 51–61.

Lindberg, N., Holi, M. M., Tani, P., & Virkkunen, M. (2005). Looking for pyromania: Characteristics of a consecutive sample of Finnish male criminals with histories of recidivist fire-setting between 1973 and 1993. *BMC Psychiatry, 5,* 47.

Linehan, M. M., Cochran, B. N., & Kehrer, C. A. (2001). Dialectical behavior therapy for borderline personality disorder. In D. H. Barlow (Ed.), *Clinical handbook of psychological disorders: A step-by-step treatment manual* (3rd ed.) (pp. 470–522). New York: Guilford Press.

Lisanby, S. H. (2007). Electroconvulsive therapy for depression. *New England Journal of Medicine, 357*(19), 1939–1945.

Liu, J., Raine, A., Venables, P. H., & Mednick, S. A. (2004). Malnutrition at age 3 years and externalizing behavior problems at ages 8, 11, and 17 years. *American Journal of Psychiatry, 161,* 2005–2013.

Livesley, W. J. (2011). An empirically-based classification of personality disorder. *Journal of Personality Disorders, 25,* 397–420.

Lobo, D. S., Souza, R. P., Tong, R. P., Casey, D. M., Hodgins, D. C., Smith, G. J., . . . Kennedy, J. L. (2010). Association of functional variants in the dopamine D2-like receptors with risk for gambling behaviour in healthy Caucasian subjects. *Biological Psychology, 85*(1), 33–37.

Lochner, C., Grant, J. E., Odlaug, B. L., & Stein, D. J. (2012). DSM-5 field survey: Skin picking disorder. *Annals of Clinical Psychiatry, 24*(4), 300–304.

Loeber, R., & Burke, J. D. (2011). Developmental pathways in juvenile externalizing and internalizing problems. *Journal of Research on Adolescence, 21*(1), 34–46.

Lopez, O. L., Schwam, E., Cummings, J., Gauthier, S., Jones, R., Wilkinson, D., . . . Schindler, R. (2010). Predicting cognitive decline in Alzheimer's disease: An integrated analysis. *Alzheimers and Dementia, 6*(6), 431–439.

Lorains, F. K., Cowlishaw, S., & Thomas, S. A. (2011). Prevalence of comorbid disorders in problem and pathological gambling: Systematic review and meta-analysis of population surveys. *Addiction, 106*(3), 490–498.

Lovaas, O. I. (1987). Behavioral treatment and normal educational and intellectual functioning in young autistic children. *Journal of Consulting and Clinical Psychology, 55*(1), 3–9.

Luciana, M. (2003). Practitioner review: Computerized assessment of neuropsychological function in children: Clinical and research applications of the Cambridge Neuropsychological Testing Automated Battery (CANTAB). *Journal of Child Psychology and Psychiatry, 44*(5), 649–663.

Lueken, U., Kruschwitz, J. D., Muehlhan, M., Siegert, J., Hoyer, J., & Wittchen, H.-U. (2011). How specific is specific phobia? Different neural response patterns in two subtypes of specific phobia. *NeuroImage, 56*(1), 363–372.

Lykken, D. I. (1957). A study of anxiety in the sociopathic personality. *Journal of Abnormal and Social Psychology, 55,* 6–10.

Lykken, D. T. (2000). The causes and costs of crime and a controversial cure. *Journal of Personality, 68,* 559–605.

M

Machado, M., & Einarson, T. R. (2010). Comparison of SSRIs and SNRIs in major depressive disorder: A meta-analysis of head-to-head randomized clinical trials. *Journal of Clinical Pharmacy and Therapeutics, 35*(2), 177–188.

Maher, W. B., & Maher, B. A. (1985). Psychopathology: I. From ancient times to the eighteenth century. In G. A. Kimble & K. Schlesinger (Eds.), *Topics in the history of psychology* (Vol. 2, pp. 251–294). Hillsdale, NJ: Lawrence Erlbaum.

Mainous, A. G., 3rd, Everett, C. J., Diaz, V. A., Player, M. S., Gebregziabher, M., & Smith, D. W. (2010). Life stress and atherosclerosis: A pathway through unhealthy lifestyle. *International Journal of Psychiatry in Medicine, 40*(2), 147–161.

Makrygianni, M. K., & Reed, P. (2010). A meta-analytic review of the effectiveness of behavioural early intervention programs for children with Autistic Spectrum Disorders. *Research in Autism Spectrum Disorders, 4*(4), 577–593.

Malinauskas, B. M., Aeby, V. G., Overton, R. F., Carpenter-Aeby, T., & Barber-Heidal, K. (2007). A survey of energy drink consumption patterns among college students. *Nutrition Journal, 6*, 35.

Mannuzza, S., Klein, R. G., & Moulton, J. L., III. (2008). Lifetime criminality among boys with attention deficit hyperactivity disorder: A prospective follow-up study into adulthood using official arrest records. *Psychiatry Research, 160*(3), 237–246.

Mao, A. R., Babcock, T., & Brams, M. (2011). ADHD in adults: Current treatment trends with consideration of abuse potential of medications. *Journal of Psychiatric Practice, 17*(4), 241–250.

Marcantonio, E. R., Kiely, D. K., Simon, S. E., John Orav, E., Jones, R. N., Murphy, K. M., & Bergmann, M. A. (2005). Outcomes of older people admitted to postacute facilities with delirium. *Journal of the American Geriatrics Society, 53*(6), 963–969.

Marco, E. M., Adriani, W., Ruocco, L. A., Canese, R., Sadile, A. G., & Laviola, G. (2011). Neurobehavioral adaptations to methylphenidate: The issue of early adolescent exposure. *Neuroscience and Biobehavioral Reviews, 35*(8), 1722–1739.

Marom, S., Munitz, H., Jones, P. B., Weizman, A., & Hermesh, H. (2005). Expressed emotion: Relevance to rehospitalization in schizophrenia over 7 years. *Schizophrenia Bulletin, 31*, 751–758.

Martel, M. M., Nikolas, M., Jernigan, K., Friderici, K., Waldman, I., & Nigg, J. T. (2011). The dopamine receptor D4 gene (DRD4) moderates family environmental effects on ADHD. *Journal of Abnormal Child Psychology: An official publication of the International Society for Research in Child and Adolescent Psychopathology, 39*(1), 1–10.

Martin, C. A., Drasgow, E., Halle, J. W., & Brucker, J. M. (2005). Teaching a child with autism and severe language delays to reject: Direct and indirect effects of functional communication training. *Educational Psychology, 25*(2–3), 287–304.

Martin, C. S., Steinley, D. L., Vergés, A., & Sher, K. J. (2011). The proposed 2/11 symptom algorithm for *DSM-5* substance-use disorders is too lenient. *Psychological Medicine: A Journal of Research in Psychiatry and the Allied Sciences, 41*(9), 2008–2010.

Maslow, A. H. (1962). *Toward a psychology of being.* Princeton, NJ: Van Nostrand.

Mason, W. A., & Windle, M. (2001). Family, religious, school and peer influences on adolescent alcohol use: A longitudinal study. *Journal of Studies on Alcohol, 62*(1), 44–53.

Masters, W. H., & Johnson, V. E. (1966). *Human sexual response.* Boston: Little Brown.

Masters, W. H., & Johnson, V. E. (1970). *Human sexual inadequacy.* Boston: Little Brown.

Masterson, J. F. (1981). *The narcissistic and borderline disorders: An integrated developmental approach.* New York: Brunner/Mazel.

Mataix-Cols, D., Rosario-Campos, M. C., & Leckman, J. F. (2005). A multidimensional model of obsessive-compulsive disorder. *American Journal of Psychiatry, 162*(2), 228–238.

Matsuishi, T., Yamashita, Y., Takahashi, T., & Nagamitsu, S. (2011). Rett syndrome: The state of clinical and basic research, and future perspectives. *Brain & Development, 33*(8), 627-631.

Maulik, P. K., Mascarenhas, M. N., Mathers, C. D., Dua, T., & Saxena, S. (2011). Prevalence of intellectual disability: A meta-analysis of population-based studies. *Research in Developmental Disabilities, 32*(2), 419–436.

May, R. (1983). *The discovery of being: Writings in existential psychology.* New York: Norton.

McCarthy, M. J., Leckband, S. G., & Kelsoe, J. R. (2010). Pharmacogenetics of lithium response in bipolar disorder. *Pharmacogenomics, 11*(10), 1439–1465.

McCloskey, M. S., Kleabir, K., Berman, M. E., Chen, E. Y., & Coccaro, E. F. (2010). Unhealthy aggression: Intermittent explosive disorder and adverse physical health outcomes. *Health Psychology, 29*(3), 324–332.

McCloskey, M. S., Noblett, K. L., Deffenbacher, J. L., Gollan, J. K., & Coccaro, E. F. (2008). Cognitive-behavioral therapy for intermittent explosive disorder: A pilot randomized clinical trial. *Journal of Consulting and Clinical Psychology, 76*(5), 876–886.

McClung, C. A. (2007). Circadian genes, rhythms and the biology of mood disorders. *Pharmacol Ther, 114*(2), 222–232.

McClure, M. M., Harvey, P. D., Goodman, M., Triebwasser, J., New, A., Koenigsberg, H. W., . . . Siever, L. J. (2010). Pergolide treatment of cognitive deficits associated with schizotypal personality disorder: Continued evidence of the importance of the dopamine system in the schizophrenia spectrum. *Neuropsychopharmacology, 35*, 1356–1362.

McCrae, R. R., & Costa, P. T., Jr. (1987). Validation of the five-factor model of personality across instruments and observers. *Journal of Personality and Social Psychology, 52*(1), 81–90.

McDermott, B. E., Leamon, M. H., Feldman, M. D., & Scott, C. L. (2009). Factitious disorder and malingering. In J. A. Bourgeois, R. E. Hales, J. S. Young, & S. C. Yudofsky (Eds.), *The American Psychiatric Publishing board review guide for psychiatry* (pp. 387–396). Arlington, VA: American Psychiatric Publishing, Inc.

McEvoy, J. P. (2007). The costs of schizophrenia. *Journal of Clinical Psychiatry, 68 Suppl 14*, 4–7.

McEwen, B. S., & Gianaros, P. J. (2010). Central role of the brain in stress and adaptation: Links to socioeconomic status, health, and disease. *Annals of the New York Academy of Science, 1186*, 190–222.

McGrath, J., Saha, S., Chant, D., & Welham, J. (2008). Schizophrenia: A concise overview of incidence, prevalence, and mortality. *Epidemiological Review, 30*, 67–76.

McGrath, J., Welham, J., Scott, J., Varghese, D., Degenhardt, L., Hayatbakhsh, M. R., . . . Najman, J. M. (2010). Association between cannabis use and psychosis-related outcomes using sibling pair analysis in a cohort of young adults. *Archives of General Psychiatry, 67*, 440–447.

McGuffin, P. (2004). Nature and nurture interplay: Schizophrenia. *Psychiatrische Praxis, 31*, S189–S193.

McKeith, I., Mintzer, J., Aarsland, D., Burn, D., Chiu, H., Cohen-Mansfield, J., . . . Reid, W. (2004). Dementia with Lewy bodies. *Lancet Neurology, 3*(1), 19–28.

McKhann, G., Drachman, D., Folstein, M., Katzman, R., Price, D., & Stadlan, E. M. (1984). Clinical diagnosis of Alzheimer's Disease: Report of the NINCDS-ADRDA Work Group under the auspices of Department of Health and Human Services Task Force on Alzheimer's Disease. *Neurology, 34*, 939–944.

McKhann, G. M., Knopman, D. S., Chertkow, H., Hyman, B. T., Jack Jr., C. R., Kawas, C. H., . . . Phelps, C. H. (2011). The diagnosis of dementia due to Alzheimer's disease: Recommendations from the National Institute on Aging-Alzheimer's Association workgroups on diagnostic guidelines for Alzheimer's disease. *Alzheimer's and Dementia, 7*(3), 263–269.

McKnight-Eily, L. R., Presley-Cantwell, L. R., Strine, T. W., Chapman, D. P., Perry, G. S., & Croft, J. B. (2008). Perceived insufficient rest or sleep—Four states, 2006. *Morbidity and Mortality Weekly Report, 57*(8), 200–203.

Meares, S., Shores, E. A., Taylor, A. J., Batchelor, J., Bryant, R. A., Baguley, I. J., . . . Marosszeky, J. E. (2011). The prospective course of postconcussion syndrome: The role of mild traumatic brain injury. *Neuropsychology, 25*(4), 454–465.

Meyers, J. E., & Rohling, M. L. (2009). CT and MRI correlations with neuropsychological tests. *Applied Neuropsychology, 16*(4), 237–253.

Mick, E., Byrne, D., Fried, R., Monuteaux, M., Faraone, S. V., & Biederman, J. (2011). Predictors of ADHD persistence in girls at 5-year follow-up. *Journal of Attention Disorders, 15*(3), 183–192.

Millar, H. R., Wardell, F., Vyvyan, J. P., Naji, S. A., Prescott, G. J., & Eagles, J. M. (2005). Anorexia nervosa mortality in Northeast Scotland, 1965–1999. *Am J Psychiatry, 162*(4), 753–757.

Miller, W. R. (2002). Project COMBINE, Combined Behavioral Intervention Therapist Manual.

Miller, W. R., & Rose, G. S. (2009). Toward a theory of motivational interviewing. *American Psychologist, 64*(6), 527–537.

Millon, T., Davis, R., Millon, C., Escovar, L., & Meagher, S. (2000). *Personality disorders in modern life.* New York: Wiley.

Minden, S. L., Carbone, L. A., Barsky, A., Borus, J. F., Fife, A., Fricchione, G. L., & Orav, E. J. (2005). Predictors and outcomes of delirium. *General Hospital Psychiatry, 27*(3), 209–214.

Minshew, N. J., & Williams, D. L. (2007). The new neurobiology of autism: Cortex, connectivity, and neuronal organization. *Archives of Neurology, 64*(7), 945–950.

Mitchell, K. J., Becker, K. A., & Finkelhor, D. (2005). Inventory of problematic internet experiences encountered in clinical practice. *Professional Psychology: Research and Practice, 36*, 498–509. doi: 10.1037/0735-7028.36.5.498.

Mohr, H. M., Zimmermann, J., Röder, C., Lenz, C., Overbeck, G., & Grabhorn, R. (2010). Separating two components of body image in anorexia nervosa using fMRI. *Psychological Medicine: A Journal of Research in Psychiatry and the Allied Sciences, 40*(9), 1519–1529.

Molina, V., Sanz, J., Sarramea, F., Benito, C., & Palomo, T. (2005). Prefrontal atrophy in first episodes of schizophrenia associated with limbic metabolic hyperactivity. *Journal of Psychiatric Research, 39*, 117–127.

Money, J., & Ehrhardt, A. (1973/1996). *Man and woman, boy and girl.* Northvale, NJ: Jason Aronson.

Moore, A. A., Gould, R., Reuben, D. B., Greendale, G. A., Carter, M. K., Zhou, K., & Karlamangla, A. (2005). Longitudinal patterns and predictors of alcohol consumption in the United States. *American Journal of Public Health, 95*(3), 458–465.

Moran, P. (1999). The epidemiology of antisocial personality disorder. *Social Psychiatry and Psychiatric Epidemiology, 34*, 231–242.

Morasco, B. J., Ledgerwood, D. M., Weinstock, J., & Petry, N. M. (2009). Cognitive-behavioral approaches to pathological gambling. In G. Simos (Ed.), *Cognitive behaviour therapy: A guide for the practising clinician*(Vol. 2) (pp. 112–126). New York: Routledge/Taylor & Francis Group.

Morey, L. C. (1992). *Personality Assessment Inventory professional manual.* Odessa, FL: Psychological Assessment Resources.

Morin, C. M., Savard, J., & Ouellet, M. (2013). Nature and treatment of insomnia. In A. M. Nezu, C. Nezu, P. A. Geller, & I. B. Weiner (Eds.), *Handbook of psychology, Vol. 9: Health psychology* (2nd ed.) (pp. 318–339). Hoboken, NJ: John Wiley & Sons, Inc.

Morin, J. W., & Levenson, J. S. (2008). Exhibitionism: Assessment and treatment. In D. R. Laws & W. T. O'Donohue (Eds.), *Sexual deviance: Theory, assessment, and treatment* (2nd ed.) (pp. 76–107). New York: Guilford Press.

Morizot, J., & Le Blanc, M. (2005). Searching for a developmental typology of personality and its relations to antisocial behavior: A longitudinal study of a representative sample of men. *Journal of Personality, 73*, 139–182.

Mukherjee, N., Kang, C., Wolfe, H. M., Hertzberg, B. S., Smith, J. K., Lin, W., . . . Gilmore, J. H. (2009). Discordance of prenatal and neonatal brain development in twins. *Early Human Development, 85*, 171–175.

Murphy, K. (2005). Psychosocial treatments for ADHD in teens and adults: A practice-friendly review. *Journal of Clinical Psychology, 61*(5), 607–619.

Murphy, W. D., & Page, I. J. (2008). Exhibitionism: Psychopathology and theory. In D. R. Laws & W. T. O'Donohue (Eds.), *Sexual deviance: Theory, assessment, and treatment* (2nd ed.) (pp. 61–75). New York: Guilford Press.

Mychasiuk, R., Ilnytskyy, S., Kovalchuk, O., Kolb, B., & Gibb, R. (2011). Intensity matters: Brain, behaviour and the epigenome of prenatally stressed rats. *Neuroscience, 180*, 105–110.

N

Nagahama, Y., Okina, T., Suzuki, N., Nabatame, H., & Matsuda, M. (2005). The cerebral correlates of different types of perseveration in the Wisconsin Card Sorting Test. *Journal of Neurology, Neurosurgery & Psychiatry, 76*(2), 169–175.

Nagoshi, J. L., & Brzuzy, S. I. (2010). Transgender theory: Embodying research and practice. *Affilia: Journal of Women & Social Work, 25*, 431–443.

Nass, R., & Ross, G. (2008). Developmental disabilities. In W. G. Bradley, R. B. Daroff, G. M. Fenichel, & J. Jankovic (Eds.), *Neurology in clinical practice.* Philadelphia, PA: Butterworth-Heinemann.

National Institute on Alcohol Abuse and Alcoholism. (2007). Helping patients who drink too much: A clinician's guide.

National Institute on Drug Abuse. (2010). Comorbidity: Addiction and other illnesses. Bethesda, MD: National Institute on Drug Abuse.

National Institute on Drug Abuse. (2011a). NIDA InfoFacts: Cigarettes and other tobacco products, from http://www .drugabuse.gov/publications/infofacts/ cigarettes-other-tobacco-products

National Institute on Drug Abuse. (2011b). NIDA InfoFacts: Cocaine, from http:// drugabuse.gov/pdf/infofacts/Cocaine10.pdf

National Institute on Drug Abuse. (2011c). NIDA InfoFacts: Hallucinogens-LSD, Peyote, Psilocybin, and PCP, from http:// www.drugabuse.gov/publications/ infofacts/hallucinogens-lsd-peyote-psilocybin-pcp

National Institute on Drug Abuse. (2011d). NIDA InfoFacts: Heroin, from http://www .drugabuse.gov/publications/infofacts/ heroin

National Institute on Drug Abuse. (2011e). NIDA InfoFacts: Inhalants, from http:// www.drugabuse.gov/publications/infofacts/ inhalants

National Institute on Drug Abuse. (2011f). NIDA InfoFacts: MDMA (Ecstasy), from http://www.drugabuse.gov/publications/ infofacts/mdma-ecstasy

National Institute on Drug Abuse. (2011g). Prescription drugs: Abuse and addiction. *Research report series*, from http://www .drugabuse.gov/publications/research-reports/prescription-drugs

National Institute on Drug Abuse. (2011h). *Research report series*, from http://www .drugabuse.gov/ResearchReports/Cocaine/ Cocaine.html

Navarrete, L. P., Pérez, P., Morales, I., & Maccioni, R. B. (2011). Novel drugs affecting tau behavior in the treatment of Alzheimer's disease and tauopathies. *Current Alzheimer Research, 8*(6), 678–685.

Neumann, N., Dubischar-Krivec, A. M., Braun, C., Löw, A., Poustka, F., Bölte, S., & Birbaumer, N. (2010). The mind of the mnemonists: An MEG and neuropsychological study of autistic memory savants. *Behavioural Brain Research, 215*(1), 114–121.

Nobre, P. J. (2010). Psychological determinants of erectile dysfunction: Testing a cognitive-emotional model. *Journal of Sexual Medicine, 7*, 1429–1437.

Nobre, P. J., & Pinto-Gouveia, J. (2009). Cognitive schemas associated with negative sexual events: A comparison of men and women with and without sexual dysfunction. *Archives of Sexual Behavior, 38*, 842–851.

Nonkes, L. J. P., van Bussel, I. P. G., Verheij, M. M. M., & Homberg, J. R. (2011). The interplay between brain

5-hydroxytryptamine levels and cocaine addiction. *Behavioural Pharmacology, 22*(8), 723–738.

Novak, C. E., Keuthen, N. J., Stewart, S. E., & Pauls, D. L. (2009). A twin concordance study of trichotillomania. *American Journal of Medical Genetics Series B: Neuropsychiatry of Genetics, 150B*(7), 944–949.

Nutt, D. J., & Malizia, A. L. (2001). New insights into the role of the GABA(A)-benzodiazepine receptor in psychiatric disorder. *British Journal of Psychiatry, 179*, 390–396.

O

O'Brian, S., Jones, M., Packman, A., Menzies, R., & Onslow, M. (2011). Stuttering severity and educational attainment. *Journal of Fluency Disorders, 36*(2), 86–92.

O'Connor, M. J., Frankel, F., Paley, B., Schonfeld, A. M., Carpenter, E., Laugeson, E. A., & Marquardt, R. (2006). A controlled social skills training for children with fetal alcohol spectrum disorders. *Journal of Consulting and Clinical Psychology, 74*(4), 639–648.

O'Connor v. Donaldson. (1975). 95 S. Ct. 2486.

Odlaug, B. L., Marsh, P. J., Kim, S. W., & Grant, J. E. (2011). Strategic vs nonstrategic gambling: Characteristics of pathological gamblers based on gambling preference. *Annals of Clinical Psychiatry, 23*(2), 105–112.

Ollikainen, M., Smith, K. R., Joo, E. J., Ng, H. K., Andronikos, R., Novakovic, B., . . . Craig, J. M. (2010). DNA methylation analysis of multiple tissues from newborn twins reveals both genetic and intrauterine components to variation in the human neonatal epigenome. *Human Molecular Genetics, 19*, 4176–4188.

Ornstein, R. M., Rosen, D. S., Mammel, K. A., Callahan, S., Forman, S., Jay, M., & . . . Walsh, B. (2013). Distribution of eating disorders in children and adolescents using the proposed *DSM-5* criteria for feeding and eating disorders. *Journal of Adolescent Health.* doi:10.1016/j.jadohealth.2013.03.025.

Ouyang, L., Grosse, S., Raspa, M., & Bailey, D. (2010). Employment impact and financial burden for families of children with fragile X syndrome: Findings from the National Fragile X Survey. *Journal of Intellectual Disability Research, 54*(10), 918–928.

Oxman, T. E., Barrett, J. E., Sengupta, A., & Williams Jr., J. W. (2000). The relationship of aging and dysthymia in primary care. *The American Journal of Geriatric Psychiatry, 8*(4), 318–326.

P

Pail, G., Huf, W., Pjrek, E., Winkler, D., Willeit, M., Praschak-Rieder, N., & Kasper, S. (2011). Bright-light therapy in the treatment of mood disorders. *Neuropsychobiology, 64*(3), 152–162.

Palmer, A. A., & de Wit, H. (2011). Translational genetic approaches to substance use disorders: Bridging the gap between mice and humans. *Human Genetics.*

Papademetriou, V. (2005). Hypertension and cognitive function. Blood pressure regulation and cognitive function: A review of the literature. *Geriatrics, 60*(1), 20–22, 24.

Papadimitriou, G. N., Calabrese, J. R., Dikeos, D. G., & Christodoulou, G. N. (2005). Rapid cycling bipolar disorder: Biology and pathogenesis. *International Journal of Neuropsychopharmacology, 8*(2), 281–292.

Parsons, T. D., & Rizzo, A. A. (2008). Affective outcomes of virtual reality exposure therapy for anxiety and specific phobias: A meta-analysis. *Journal of Behavior Therapy and Experimental Psychiatry, 39*(3), 250–261.

Pennebaker, J. W. (1997). *Opening up: The healing power of expressing emotions* (rev. ed.). New York: Guilford.

Pennebaker, J. W., Colder, M., & Sharp, L. K. (1990). Accelerating the coping process. *Journal of Personality and Social Psychology, 58*, 528–537.

Pérez Benítez, C. I., Shea, M. T., Raffa, S., Rende, R., Dyck, I. R., Ramsawh, H. J., et al. (2009). Anxiety sensitivity as a predictor of the clinical course of panic disorder: A 1-year follow-up study. *Depression and Anxiety, 26*(4), 335–342.

Perlis, R. H., Ostacher, M. J., Patel, J. K., Marangell, L. B., Zhang, H., Wisniewski, S. R., . . . Thase, M. E. (2006). Predictors of recurrence in bipolar disorder: Primary outcomes from the Systematic Treatment Enhancement Program for Bipolar Disorder (STEP-BD). *American Journal of Psychiatry, 163*(2), 217–224.

Perls, T. (2004). Centenarians who avoid dementia. *Trends in Neuroscience, 27*(10), 633–636.

Petry, N. M. (2003). A comparison of treatment-seeking pathological gamblers based on preferred gambling activity. *Addiction, 98*(5), 645–655.

Petry, N. M. (2011). Discounting of probabilistic rewards is associated with gambling abstinence in treatment-seeking pathological gamblers. *Journal of Abnormal Psychology, 121*(1).

Phillips, K. A., Menard, W., Fay, C., & Pagano, M. E. (2005). Psychosocial functioning and quality of life in body dysmorphic disorder. *Comprehensive Psychiatry, 46*(4), 254–260.

Phillips, K. A., Wilhelm, S., Koran, L. M., Didie, E. R., Fallon, B. A., Feusner, J., & Stein, D. J. (2010). Body dysmorphic disorder: Some key issues for *DSM-V*. *Depression and Anxiety, 27*(6), 573–591.

Pincus, A. L. (2011). Some comments on nomology, diagnostic process, and narcissistic personality disorder in the *DSM-5* proposal for personality and personality disorders. *Personality Disorders: Theory, Research, and Treatment, 2*, 41–53.

Pinninti, N. R., Rissmiller, D. J., & Steer, R. A. (2010). Cognitive-behavioral therapy as an adjunct to second-generation antipsychotics in the treatment of schizophrenia. *Psychiatric Services, 61*, 940–943.

Polanczyk, G., de Lima, M. S., Horta, B. L., Biederman, J., & Rohde, L. A. (2007). The worldwide prevalence of ADHD: A systematic review and metaregression analysis. *The American Journal of Psychiatry, 164*(6), 942–948.

Pollack, M. H., & Simon, N. M. (2009). Pharmacotherapy for panic disorder and agoraphobia. In M. M. Antony & M. B. Stein (Eds.), *Oxford handbook of anxiety and related disorders* (pp. 295–307). New York: Oxford University Press.

Pope, H. G., Jr., & Yurgelun-Todd, D. (2004). Residual cognitive effects of long-term cannabis use. In D. Castle & R. Murray (Eds.), *Marijuana and madness: Psychiatry and neurobiology* (pp. 198–210). New York: Cambridge University Press.

Prescott, D. S., & Levenson, J. S. (2010). Sex offender treatment is not punishment. *Journal of Sexual Aggression, 16*, 275–285.

Pridmore, S., Chambers, A., & McArthur, M. (2005). Neuroimaging in psychopathy. *Australian and New Zealand Journal of Psychiatry, 39*, 856–865.

PubMedHealth. (2011a). Developmental reading disorder.

PubMedHealth. (2011b). Down syndrome: Trisomy 21.

PubMedHealth. (2011c). Fragile X syndrome.

PubMedHealth. (2011d). Phenylketonuria: PKU; Neonatal phenylketonuria.

PubMedHealth. (2011e). Tay-Sachs disease.

Q

Quick, V. M., & Byrd-Bredbenner, C. (2012). Weight regulation practices of young adults. Predictors of restrictive eating. *Appetite, 59*(2), 425–430. doi:10.1016/j.appet.2012.06.004.

Qiu, M.-g., Ye, Z., Li, Q.-y., Liu, G.-j., Xie, B., & Wang, J. (2011). Changes of brain structure and function in ADHD children. *Brain Topography, 24*(3–4), 243–252.

Quinn, P. O. (2005). Treating adolescent girls and women with ADHD: Gender-specific issues. *Journal of Clinical Psychology, 61*(5), 579–587.

R

Rabin, L. A., Barr, W. B., & Burton, L. A. (2005). Assessment practices of clinical neuropsychologists in the United States and Canada: A survey of INS, NAN, and APA Division 40 members. *Archives of Clinical Neuropsychology, 20*(1), 33–65.

Rademaker, A. R., van Zuiden, M., Vermetten, E., & Geuze, E. (2011). Type D personality and the development of PTSD symptoms: A prospective study. *Journal of Abnormal Psychology, 120*(2), 299–307.

Ramchandani, P. (2004). Treatment of major depressive disorder in children and adolescents. *British Medical Journal, 328*(7430), 3–4.

Ravindran, L. N., & Stein, M. B. (2009). Pharmacotherapy of PTSD: Premises, principles, and priorities. *Brain Research, 1293*, 24–39.

Ravindran, L. N., & Stein, M. B. (2011). Pharmacotherapy for social anxiety disorder in adolescents and young adults. In C. A. Alfano & D. C. Beidel (Eds.), *Social anxiety in adolescents and young adults: Translating developmental science into practice* (pp. 265–279). Washington, DC: American Psychological Association.

Reas, D. L., Kjelsas, E., Heggestad, T., Eriksen, L., Nielsen, S., Gjertsen, F., & Gotestam, K. G. (2005). Characteristics of anorexia nervosa-related deaths in Norway (1992–2000): Data from the National Patient Register and the Causes of Death Register. *International Journal of Eating Disorders, 37*(3), 181–187.

Reichenberg, A. (2010). The assessment of neuropsychological functioning in schizophrenia. *Dialogues in Clinical Neuroscience, 12*, 383–392.

Reid, H., & Bahar, R. J. (2006). Treatment of encopresis and chronic constipation in young children: Clinical results from interactive parent-child guidance. *Clinical Pediatrics, 45*(2), 157–164.

Reissig, C. J., Strain, E. C., & Griffiths, R. R. (2009). Caffeinated energy drinks—a growing problem. *Drug and Alcohol Dependence, 99*(1–3), 1–10.

Reme, S. E., Tangen, T., Moe, T., & Eriksen, H. R. (2011). Prevalence of psychiatric disorders in sick listed chronic low back pain patients. *European Journal of Pain, 15*(10), 1075–1080.

Renner, M. J., & Mackin, R. S. (1998). A life stress instrument for classroom use. *Teaching of Psychology, 25*, 46–48.

Resnick, R. J. (2005). Attention deficit hyperactivity disorder in teens and adults: They don't all outgrow it. *Journal of Clinical Psychology, 61*(5), 529–533.

Rettew, D. C. (2000). Avoidant personality disorder, generalized social phobia, and shyness: Putting the personality back into personality disorders. *Harvard Review of Psychiatry, 8*, 283–297.

Richings, C., Cook, R., & Roy, A. (2011). Service evaluation of an integrated assessment and treatment service for people with intellectual disability with behavioural and mental health problems. *Journal of Intellectual Disabilities, 15*(1), 7–19.

Rizvi, S. L., & Nock, M. K. (2008). Single-case experimental designs for the evaluation of treatments for self-injurious and suicidal behaviors. *Suicide and Life-Threatening Behavior, 38*, 498–510.

Robbins, C. A. (2005). ADHD couple and family relationships: Enhancing communication and understanding through Imago Relationship Therapy. *Journal of Clinical Psychology, 61*(5), 565–577.

Roberson-Nay, R., & Brown, R. C. (2011). Neurodevelopmental aspects of social anxiety. In C. A. Alfano & D. C. Beidel (Eds.), *Social anxiety in adolescents and young adults: Translating developmental science into practice* (pp. 53–71). Washington, DC: American Psychological Association.

Roberts, R. E., Alegría, M., Roberts, C. R., & Chen, I. G. (2005). Mental health problems of adolescents as reported by their caregivers: A comparison of European, African, and Latino Americans. *The Journal of Behavioral Health Services & Research, 32*, 1–13.

Robins, L. N. (1966). *Deviant children grow up: A sociological and psychiatric study of sociopathic personality.* Baltimore: Williams & Wilkins.

Roepke, S. K., & Grant, I. (2011). Toward a more complete understanding of the effects of personal mastery on cardiometabolic health. *Health Psychology, 57*(2), 539–548.

Rogers, C. R. (1951). *Client-centered therapy: Its current practice implications, and theory.* Boston: Houghton Mifflin.

Roid, G. H., & Barram, R. A. (2004). *Essentials of Stanford-Binet Intelligence Scales (SB5) assessment.* Hoboken, NJ: Wiley.

Ronningstam, E. (2011). Narcissistic personality disorder: A clinical perspective. *Journal of Psychiatric Practice, 17*, 89–99.

Rosebush, P. I., & Mazurek, M. F. (2011). Treatment of conversion disorder in the 21st century: Have we moved beyond the couch? *Current Treatment Options in Neurology, 13*(3), 255–266.

Rosen, R., Brown, C., Heiman, J., Leiblum, S., Meston, C., Shabsigh, R., . . . D'Agostino, R., Jr. (2000). The Female Sexual Function Index (FSFI): A multidimensional self-report instrument for the assessment of female sexual function. *Journal of Sex & Marital Therapy, 26*, 191–208.

Rosso, I. M., Makris, N., Britton, J. C., Price, L. M., Gold, A. L., Zai, D., et al. (2010). Anxiety sensitivity correlates with two indices of right anterior insula structure in specific animal phobia. *Depression and Anxiety, 27*(12), 1104–1110.

Rush, A. J., Trivedi, M. H., Wisniewski, S. R., Nierenberg, A. A., Stewart, J. W., Warden, D., . . . Fava, M. (2006). Acute and longer-term outcomes in depressed outpatients requiring one or several treatment steps: A STAR*D report. *American Journal of Psychiatry, 163*(11), 1905–1917.

Rylands, A. J., McKie, S., Elliott, R., Deakin, J. F., & Tarrier, N. (2011). A functional magnetic resonance imaging paradigm of expressed emotion in schizophrenia. *Journal of Nervous and Mental Disease, 199*, 25–29.

S

Salekin, R. T. (2008). Psychopathy and recidivism from mid-adolescence to young adulthood: Cumulating legal problems and limiting life opportunities. *Journal of Abnormal Psychology, 117*, 386–395.

Salekin, R. T., Worley, C., & Grimes, R. D. (2010). Treatment of psychopathy: A review and brief introduction to the mental model approach for psychopathy. *Behavioral Sciences & the Law, 28*, 235–266.

Salyers, M. P., McGuire, A. B., Rollins, A. L., Bond, G. R., Mueser, K. T., & Macy, V. R. (2010). Integrating assertive community treatment and illness management and recovery for consumers with severe mental illness. *Community Mental Health Journal, 46*, 319–329.

Samuel, D. B., & Gore, W. L. (2012). Maladaptive variants of Conscientiousness and Agreeableness. *Journal of Personality, 80*, 1669–1696. doi:10.1111/j.1467-6494.2012.00770.x.

Sansone, R. A., Dittoe, N., Hahn, H. S., & Wiederman, M. W. (2011). The prevalence of borderline personality disorder in a consecutive sample of cardiac stress test patients. *Prim Care Companion CNS Disord, 13.*

Santangelo, S. L., & Tsatsanis, K. (2005). What is known about autism: Genes, brain, and behavior. *American Journal of Pharmacogenomics, 5*(2), 71–92.

Santucci, L. C., Ehrenreich, J. T., Trosper, S. E., Bennett, S. M., & Pincus, D. B. (2009). Development and preliminary evaluation of a one-week summer treatment program for separation anxiety disorder. *Cognitive and Behavioral Practice, 16*(3), 317–331.

Sar, V., Akyuz, G., Kundakci, T., Kiziltan, E., & Dogan, O. (2004). Childhood trauma, dissociation, and psychiatric comorbidity in patients with conversion disorder. *American Journal of Psychiatry, 161*(12), 2271–2276.

Savica, R., & Petersen, R. C. (2011). Prevention of dementia. *Psychiatr Clin North Am, 34*(1), 127–145.

Scarpini, E., Bruno, G., Zappalà, G., Adami, M., Richarz, U., Gaudig, M., . . . Schäuble, B. (2011). Cessation versus continuation of galantamine treatment after 12 months of therapy in patients with Alzheimer's disease: A randomized, double blind, placebo controlled withdrawal trial. *Journal of Alzheimer's Disease, 26*(2), 211–220.

Scarr, S., & McCartney, K. (1983). How people make their own environments: A theory of genotype → environment effects. *Child Development, 54*(2), 424–435.

Scherrer, J. F., Slutske, W. S., Xian, H., Waterman, B., Shah, K. R., Volberg, R., & Eisen, S. A. (2007). Factors associated with pathological gambling at 10-year follow-up in a national sample of middle-aged men. *Addiction, 102*(6), 970–978.

Schneck, C. D., Miklowitz, D. J., Miyahara, S., Araga, M., Wisniewski, S., Gyulai, L., . . . Sachs, G. S. (2008). The prospective course of rapid-cycling bipolar disorder: Findings from the STEP-BD. *The American Journal of Psychiatry, 165*(3), 370–377.

Schneiderman, N., Ironson, G., & Siegel, S. D. (2005). Stress and health: Psychological, behavioral, and biological determinants. *Annual Review of Clinical Psychology, 1*(1), 607–628.

Schulza, J. B., Rainer, M., Klünemann, H.-H., Kurz, A., Wolf, S., Sternbergf, K., & Tennigkeit, F. (2011). Sustained effects of once-daily memantine treatment on cognition and functional communication skills in patients with moderate to severe Alzheimer's disease: Results of a 16-week open-label trial. *Journal of Alzheimer's Disease, 25*(3), 463–475.

Schulze, K. K., Walshe, M., Stahl, D., Hall, M. H., Kravariti, E., Morris, R., . . . Bramon, E. (2011). Executive functioning in familial bipolar I disorder patients and their unaffected relatives. *Bipolar Disorders, 13*(2), 208–216.

Scorolli, C., Ghirlanda, S., Enquist, M., Zattoni, S., & Jannini, E. A. (2007). Relative prevalence of different fetishes. *International Journal of Impotence Research, 19*, 432–437.

Segal, D. L., Coolidge, F. L., & Rosowsky, E. (2000). Personality disorders. In S. K. Whitbourne (Ed.), *Psychopathology in later life.* New York: Wiley.

Segal, D. L., Hook, J. N., & Coolidge, F. L. (2001). Personality dysfunction, coping styles, and clinical symptoms in younger and older adults. *Journal of Clinical Geropsychology, 7*(7), 201–212.

Segerstrom, S. C., Roach, A. R., Evans, D. R., Schipper, L. J., & Darville, A. K. (2010). The structure and health correlates of trait repetitive thought in older adults. *Psychology and Aging.*

Segraves, R. T. (2010). Considerations for an evidence-based definition of premature ejaculation in the *DSM-V. Journal of Sexual Medicine, 7*, 672–679.

Seltzer, M. M., Krauss, M. W., Shattuck, P. T., Orsmond, G., Swe, A., & Lord, C. (2003). The symptoms of autism spectrum disorders in adolescence and adulthood. *Journal of Autism and Developmental Disorders, 33*, 565–581.

Serby, M., & Samuels, S. C. (2001). Diagnostic criteria for dementia with Lewy bodies reconsidered. *American Journal of Geriatric Psychiatry, 9*(3), 212–216.

Shah, D. B., Pesiridou, A., Baltuch, G. H., Malone, D. A., & O'Reardon, J. P. (2008). Functional neurosurgery in the treatment of severe obsessive compulsive disorder and major depression: Overview of disease circuits and therapeutic targeting for the clinician. *Psychiatry (Edgmont), 5*(9), 24–33.

Shapiro, D. I., Cubells, J. F., Ousley, O. Y., Rockers, K., & Walker, E. F. (2011). Prodromal symptoms in adolescents with 22q11.2 deletion syndrome and schizotypal personality disorder. *Schizophrenia Research, 129*, 20–28.

Sharma, P., & Sinha, U. K. (2010). Defense mechanisms in mania, bipolar depression and unipolar depression. *Psychological Studies, 55*(3), 239–247.

Sharp, S. I., Aarsland, D., Day, S., Sønnesyn, H., & Ballard, C. (2011). Hypertension is a potential risk factor for vascular dementia: Systematic review. *International Journal of Geriatric Psychiatry, 26*(7), 661–669.

Shastry, B. S. (2005). Bipolar disorder: An update. *Neurochemistry International, 46*(4), 273–279.

Shear, K., Jin, R., Ruscio, A. M., Walters, E. E., & Kessler, R. C. (2006). Prevalence and correlates of estimated *DSM-IV* child and adult separation anxiety disorder in the National Comorbidity Survey Replication. *American Journal of Psychiatry, 163*(6), 1074–1083.

Shedler, J. (2010). The efficacy of psychodynamic psychotherapy. *American Psychologist, 65*(2), 98–109.

Sheldon, A. E., & West, M. (1990). Attachment pathology and low social skills in avoidant personality disorder: An exploratory study. *Canadian Journal of Psychiatry, 35*, 596–599.

Shenton, M. E., Whitford, T. J., & Kubicki, M. (2010). Structural neuroimaging in schizophrenia: From methods to insights to treatments. *Dialogues in Clinical Neuroscience, 12*, 317–332.

Shindel, A. W., & Moser, C. A. (2011). Why are the paraphilias mental disorders? *Journal of Sexual Medicine, 8*, 927–929.

Shriver, M. D., Segool, N., & Gortmaker, V. (2011). Behavior observations for linking assessment to treatment for selective mutism. *Education & Treatment of Children, 34*(3), 389–411.

Shusterman, A., Feld, L., Baer, L., & Keuthen, N. (2009). Affective regulation in trichotillomania: Evidence from a large-scale internet survey. *Behaviour Research and Therapy, 47*(8), 637–644.

Sigman, M., & Ruskin, E. (1999). Continuity and change in the social competence of children with autism, Down syndrome, and developmental delays. *Monographs of the Society for Research in Child Development, 64*(1), v–114.

Simone, M. J., & Tan, Z. S. (2011). The role of inflammation in the pathogenesis of delirium and dementia in older adults: A review. *CNS Neuroscience & Therapeutics, 17*(5), 506–513.

Skinner, B. F. (1953). *Science and human behavior.* New York: Free Press.

Snorrason, I., Belleau, E. L., & Woods, D. W. (2012). How related are hair pulling disorder (trichotillomania) and skin picking disorder? A review of evidence for comorbidity, similarities and shared etiology. *Clinical Psychology Review, 32*(7), 618–629. doi:10.1016/j.cpr.2012.05.008.

Snyder, H. N. (2000). Sexual assault of young children as reported to law enforcement: Victim, incident, and offender characteristics. Washington, DC: U.S. Department of Justice.

Solem, S., Håland, Å. T., Vogel, P. A., Hansen, B., & Wells, A. (2009). Change in metacognitions predicts outcome in obsessive-compulsive disorder patients undergoing treatment with exposure and response prevention. *Behaviour Research and Therapy, 47*(4), 301–307.

Sommer, M., Hajak, G., Dohnel, K., Schwerdtner, J., Meinhardt, J., & Muller, J. L. (2006). Integration of emotion and cognition in patients with psychopathy. *Progress in Brain Research, 156*, 457–466.

Sorensen, P., Birket-Smith, M., Wattar, U., Buemann, I., & Salkovskis, P. (2011). A randomized clinical trial of cognitive behavioural therapy versus short-term psychodynamic psychotherapy versus no intervention for patients with hypochondriasis. *Psychological Medicine, 41*(2), 431–441.

South, S. C., & Krueger, R. F. (2011). Genetic and environmental influences on internalizing psychopathology vary as a function of economic status. *Psychological Medicine: A Journal of Research in Psychiatry and the Allied Sciences, 41*(1), 107–117.

Spetie, L., & Arnold, L. E. (2007). Ethical issues in child psychopharmacology research and practice: Emphasis on preschoolers. *Psychopharmacology, 191*(1), 15–26.

St. George-Hyslop, P. H., & Petit, A. (2005). Molecular biology and genetics of Alzheimer's disease. *Comptes Rendus Biologies, 328*(2), 119–130.

Stade, B. C., Bailey, C., Dzendoletas, D., Sgro, M., Dowswell, T., & Bennett, D. (2009). Psychological and/or educational interventions for reducing alcohol consumption in pregnant women and women planning pregnancy. *Cochrane Database Syst Rev*(2), CD004228.

State v. Darnall. (1980). 161, 614 P. 2d 120 (Or. Ct. App. 1980).

State v. Greene. (1998). 960 P.2d 980 (Wash. Ct. App. 1998).

State v. Jones. (1998). 743 P. 2d 276 P 2d 1183, 1185 (Washington Court Appellate 1987) affiliated 759.

State v. Lockhart. (2000). 542 S.E.2d 443 (W. Va. 2000).

State v. Milligan. (1978). No. 77-CR-11-2908 (Franklin County, Ohio, December 4, 1978).

Stein, D. J., & Vythilingum, B. (2007). Social anxiety disorder: Psychobiological and evolutionary underpinnings. *CNS Spectrum, 12*(11), 806–809.

Steinberg, M. (1994). *Structured clinical interview for DSM-IV dissociative disorders—Revised (SCID-D-R).* Washington, DC: American Psychiatric Association.

Steinbrecher, N., Koerber, S., Frieser, D., & Hiller, W. (2011). The prevalence of medically unexplained symptoms in primary care. *Psychosomatics, 52*(3), 263–271.

Stilo, S. A., & Murray, R. M. (2010). The epidemiology of schizophrenia: Replacing dogma with knowledge. *Dialogues in Clinical Neuroscience, 12*, 305–315.

Striegel-Moore, R. H., Rosselli, F., Perrin, N., DeBar, L., Wilson, G. T., May, A., & Kraemer, H. C. (2009). Gender difference in the prevalence of eating disorder symptoms. *International Journal of Eating Disorders, 42*(5), 471–474.

Stucki, S., & Rihs-Middel, M. (2007). Prevalence of adult problem and pathological gambling between 2000 and 2005: An update. *Journal of Gambling Studies, 23*(3), 245–257.

Sturmey, P. (2009). Behavioral activation is an evidence-based treatment for depression. *Behavior Modification, 33*(6), 818–829.

Substance Abuse and Mental Health Services Administration. (2011). Results from the 2010 National Survey on Drug Use and Health: Summary of National Findings, NSDUH Series H-41, HHS Publication No. (SMA) 11-4658. Rockville, MD: Substance Abuse and Mental Health Services Administration.

Sullivan, P. F., Kendler, K. S., & Neale, M. C. (2003). Schizophrenia as a complex trait: Evidence from a meta-analysis of twin studies. *Archives of Genera; Psychiatry, 60*, 1187–1192.

Sunderland, T., Hill, J. L., Mellow, A. M., Lawlor, B. A., Gundersheimer, J., Newhouse, P. A., & Grafman, J. H. (1989). Clock drawing in Alzheimer's disease: A novel measure of dementia severity. *Journal of the American Geriatrics Society, 37*(8), 725–729.

Sungur, M. B., Soygür, H., Güner, P., Üstün, B., Çetin, İ., & Falloon, I. R. (2011). Identifying an optimal treatment for schizophrenia: A 2-year randomized controlled trial comparing integrated care to a high-quality routine treatment. *International Journal of Psychiatry in Clinical Practice, 15*, 118–127.

Swann, A. C. (2010). The strong relationship between bipolar and substance-use disorder. *Annals of the New York Academy of Sciences, 1187*, 276–293.

Swartz, M. S., Wilder, C. M., Swanson, J. W., Van Dorn, R. A., Robbins, P. C., Steadman, H. J., . . . Monahan, J. (2010). Assessing outcomes for consumers in New York's assisted outpatient treatment program. *Psychiatric Services, 61*(10), 976–981.

T

Tarasoff v. The Regents of the University of California. 551 P 2d334 (California 1976).

Terracciano, A., McCrae, R. R., Brant, L. J., & Costa, P. T. J. (2005). Hierarchical linear modeling analyses of the NEO-PI-R Scales in the Baltimore Longitudinal Study of Aging. *Psychology and Aging, 20*(3), 493–506.

Thibaut, F., De La Barra, F., Gordon, H., Cosyns, P., & Bradford, J. M. (2010). The World Federation of Societies of Biological Psychiatry (WFSBP) guidelines for the biological treatment of paraphilias. *World Journal of Biological Psychiatry, 11*, 604–655.

Thioux, M., Stark, D. E., Klaiman, C., & Schultz, R. T. (2006). The day of the week when you were born in 700 ms: Calendar computation in an autistic savant. *Journal of Experimental Psychology: Human Perception and Performance, 32*(5), 1155–1168.

Thomasius, R., Zapletalova, P., Petersen, K., Buchert, R., Andresen, B., Wartberg, L., . . . Schmoldt, A. (2006). Mood, cognition and serotonin transporter availability in current and former ecstasy (MDMA) users: The longitudinal perspective. *Journal of Psychopharmacology, 20*(2), 211–225.

Tiwari, A. K., Zai, C. C., Muller, D. J., & Kennedy, J. L. (2010). Genetics in schizophrenia: Where are we and what next? *Dialogues in Clinical Neuroscience, 12*, 289–303.

Tolin, D. F. (2011). Understanding and treating hoarding: A biopsychosocial perspective. *Journal of Clinical Psychology, 67*(5), 517–526. doi:10.1002/jclp.20795.

Tolin, D. F., Franklin, M. E., Diefenbach, G. J., Anderson, E., & Meunier, S. A. (2007). Pediatric trichotillomania: Descriptive psychopathology and an open trial of cognitive behavioral therapy. *Cognitive Behaviour Therapy, 36*(3), 129–144.

Tombaugh, T. N., Stormer, P., Rees, L., Irving, S., & Francis, M. (2006). The effects of mild and severe traumatic brain injury on the auditory and visual versions of the Adjusting-Paced Serial Addition Test (Adjusting-PSAT). *Archives of Clinical Neuropsychology, 21*(7), 753–761.

Tomiatti, M., Gore, W. L., Lynam, D. R., Miller, J. D., & Widiger, T. A. (2012). A five-factor measure of histrionic personality traits. In A. M. Columbus (Ed.), *Advances in psychology.*

Traish, A. M., Feeley, R. J., & Guay, A. T. (2009). Testosterone therapy in women with gynecological and sexual disorders: A triumph of clinical endocrinology from 1938 to 2008. *Journal of Sexual Medicine, 6*, 334–351.

Trull, T. J., Jahng, S., Tomko, R. L., Wood, P. K., & Sher, K. J. (2010). Revised NESARC personality disorder diagnoses: Gender, prevalence, and comorbidity with substance dependence disorders. *Journal of Personality Disorders, 24*, 412–426.

Trzepacz, P. T., Mittal, D., Torres, R., Kanary, K., Norton, J., & Jimerson, N. (2001). Validation of the Delirium Rating Scale-Revised-98: Comparison with the Delirium Rating Scale and the Cognitive Test for Delirium. *The Journal of Neuropsychiatry and Clinical Neurosciences, 13*(2), 229–242.

Turner, E. H., Matthews, A. M., Linardatos, E., Tell, R. A., & Rosenthal, R. (2008). Selective publication of antidepressant trials and its influence on apparent efficacy. *The New England Journal of Medicine, 358*(3), 252–260.

U

UK ECT Review Group. (2003). Efficacy and safety of electroconvulsive therapy in depressive disorders: A systematic review and meta-analysis. *The Lancet, 361*(9360), 799–808.

U.S. Department of Health and Human Services, A. o. C., Youth, and Families. (2005). Child maltreatment 2003. Washington, DC: U.S. Government Printing Office.

V

Vaidyanathan, U., Patrick, C. J., & Cuthbert, B. N. (2009). Linking dimensional models of internalizing psychopathology to neurobiological systems: Affect-modulated startle as an indicator of fear and distress disorders and affiliated traits. *Psychological Bulletin, 135*(6), 909–942.

Vaivre-Douret, L., Lalanne, C., Ingster-Moati, I., Boddaert, N., Cabrol, D., Dufier, J.-L., . . . Falissard, B. (2011a). Subtypes of developmental coordination disorder: Research on their nature and etiology. *Developmental Neuropsychology, 36*(5), 614–643.

Vaivre-Douret, L., Lalanne, C., Ingster-Moati, I., Boddaert, N., Cabrol, D., Dufier, J. L., . . . Falissard, B. (2011b). Subtypes of developmental coordination disorder: Research on their nature and etiology. *Developmental Neuropsychology, 36*(5), 614–643.

van Haren, N. E. M., Schnack, H. G., Cahn, W., van den Heuvel, M. P., Lepage, C., Collins, L., . . . Kahn, R. S. (2011). Changes in cortical thickness during the course of schizophrenia. *Archives of General Psychiatry, 68,* 871–880.

van Hoeken, D., Veling, W., Sinke, S., Mitchell, J. E., & Hoek, H. W. (2009). The validity and utility of subtyping bulimia nervosa. *International Journal of Eating Disorders, 42*(7), 595–602.

van Os, J., Linscott, R. J., Myin-Germeys, I., Delespaul, P., & Krabbendam, L. (2009). A systematic review and meta-analysis of the psychosis continuum: Evidence for a psychosis proneness-persistence-impairment model of psychotic disorder. *Psychological Medicine, 39,* 179–195.

van Rijsbergen, M. W. A., Oldenbeuving, A. W., Nieuwenhuis-Mark, R. E., Nys, G. M. S., Las, S. G. M., Roks, G., & de Kort, P. L. M. (2011). Delirium in acute stroke: A predictor of subsequent cognitive impairment?: A two-year follow-up study. *Journal of the Neurological Sciences, 306*(1–2), 138–142.

Veale, D. (2010). Cognitive behavioral therapy for body dysmorphic disorder. *Psychiatric Annals, 40*(7), 333–340.

Vecchio, J., & Kearney, C. A. (2009). Treating youths with selective mutism with an alternating design of exposure-based practice and contingency management. *Behavior Therapy, 40*(4), 380–392.

Veling, W., Selten, J. P., Susser, E., Laan, W., Mackenbach, J. P., & Hoek, H. W. (2007). Discrimination and the incidence of psychotic disorders among ethnic minorities in the Netherlands. *International Journal of Epidemiology, 36,* 761–768.

Vergés, A., Jackson, K. M., Bucholz, K. K., Grant, J. D., Trull, T. J., Wood, P. K., & Sher, K. J. (2011). Deconstructing the age-prevalence curve of alcohol dependence: Why "maturing out" is only a small piece of the puzzle. *Journal of Abnormal Psychology, 121,* 511–523.

Vitale, J. E., MacCoon, D. G., & Newman, J. P. (2011). Emotion facilitation and passive avoidance learning in psychopathic female offenders. *Criminal Justice and Behavior, 38,* 641–658.

Vocks, S., Busch, M., Grönemeyer, D., Schulte, D., Herpertz, S., & Suchan, B. (2010). Neural correlates of viewing photographs of one's own body and another woman's body in anorexia and bulimia nervosa: An fMRI study. *Journal of Psychiatry & Neuroscience, 35*(3), 163–176.

Volkmar, F. R., Klin, A., Schultz, R. T., Rubin, E., & Bronen, R. (2000). Asperger's disorder. *The American Journal of Psychiatry, 157*(2), 262–267.

Volkow, N. D., McLellan, T. A., Cotto, J. H., Karithanom, M., & Weiss, S. R. (2011). Characteristics of opioid prescriptions in 2009. *Journal of the American Medical Association, 305*(13), 1299–1301.

Volkow, N. D., Wang, G.-J., Kollins, S. H., Wigal, T. L., Newcorn, J. H., Telang, F., . . . Swanson, J. M. (2009). Evaluating dopamine reward pathway in ADHD: Clinical implications. *JAMA: Journal of the American Medical Association, 302*(10), 1084–1091.

von Gontard, A. (2011). Elimination disorders: A critical comment on *DSM-5* proposals. *European Child & Adolescent Psychiatry, 20*(2), 83–88.

W

Walker, J. C., Dosen, A., Buitelaar, J. K., & Janzing, J. G. E. (2011). Depression in Down syndrome: A review of the literature. *Research in Developmental Disabilities, 32*(5), 1432–1440.

Wang, K.-S., Liu, X., Zhang, Q., Pan, Y., Aragam, N., & Zeng, M. (2011). A meta-analysis of two genome-wide association studies identifies 3 new loci for alcohol dependence. *Journal of Psychiatric Research, 45*(11), 1419–1425.

Wasserstein, J. (2005). Diagnostic issues for adolescents and adults with ADHD. *Journal of Clinical Psychology, 61*(5), 535–547.

Wattmo, C., Wallin, A. K., Londos, E., & Minthon, L. (2011). Long-term outcome and prediction models of activities of daily living in Alzheimer disease with cholinesterase inhibitor treatment. *Alzheimer Disease and Associated Disorders, 25*(1), 63–72.

Wechsler, D. (2002). *Wechsler Preschool and Primary Scale of Intelligence (WIPPSI-III).* San Antonio, TX: Psychological Corporation.

Wechsler, D. (2003). *Wechsler Intelligence Scale for Children-IV (WISC-IV).* San Antonio, TX: Psychological Corporation.

Wechsler, D. (2008). *Wechsler Adult Intelligence Scale–Fourth Edition.* San Antonio, TX: Psychological Corporation.

Weiner, I. B., & Greene, R. L. (2008). *Handbook of personality assessment.* Hoboken, NJ: John Wiley & Sons, Inc.

Weiss, M., & Murray, C. (2003). Assessment and management of attention-deficit hyperactivity disorder in adults. *Canadian Medical Association Journal, 168*(6), 715–722.

Weissman, M. M. (2007). Recent non-medication trials of interpersonal psychotherapy for depression. *International Journal of Neuropsychopharmacology, 10*(1), 117–122.

Whitbourne, S. K., & Meeks, S. (2011). Psychopathology, bereavement, and aging. In K. W. Schaie & S. L. Willis (Eds.), *Handbook of the psychology of aging* (7th ed.) (pp. 311–324). London: Elsevier.

Whitbourne, S. K., & Whitbourne, S. B. (2011). *Adult development and aging: Biopsychosocial perspectives* (4th ed.). Hoboken, NJ: Wiley.

White, K. S., Brown, T. A., Somers, T. J., & Barlow, D. H. (2006). Avoidance behavior in panic disorder: The moderating influence of perceived control. *Behaviour Research and Therapy, 44*(1), 147–157.

Widiger, T. A., & Trull, T. J. (2007). Plate tectonics in the classification of personality disorder: Shifting to a dimensional model. *American Psychologist, 62,* 71–83.

Wilens, T. E., Faraone, S. V., & Biederman, J. (2004). Attention-deficit/hyperactivity disorder in adults. *JAMA: Journal of the American Medical Association, 292*(5), 619–623.

Wilens, T. E., Martelon, M., Joshi, G., Bateman, C., Fried, R., Petty, C., & Biederman, J. (2011). Does ADHD predict substance-use disorders? A 10-year follow-up study of young adults with ADHD. *Journal of the American Academy of Child & Adolescent Psychiatry, 50*(6), 543–553.

Wilhelm, S., Buhlmann, U., Hayward, L. C., Greenberg, J. L., & Dimaite, R. (2010). A cognitive-behavioral treatment approach for body dysmorphic disorder. *Cognitive and Behavioral Practice, 17*(3), 241–247.

Willhite, R. K., Niendam, T. A., Bearden, C. E., Zinberg, J., O'Brien, M. P., & Cannon, T. D. (2008). Gender differences in symptoms, functioning and social support in patients at ultra-high risk for developing a psychotic disorder. *Schizophrenia Research, 104,* 237–245.

Williams, D. E., Kirkpatrick-Sanchez, S., Enzinna, C., Dunn, J., & Borden-Karasack, D. (2009). The clinical management and prevention of pica: A retrospective follow-up of 41 individuals with intellectual disabilities and pica. *Journal of Applied Research in Intellectual Disabilities, 22*(2), 210–215.

Williams, J., Hadjistavropoulos, T., & Sharpe, D. (2006). A meta-analysis of psychological and pharmacological treatments for body dysmorphic disorder. *Behaviour Research and Therapy, 44*(1), 99–111. doi: 10.1016/j.brat.2004.12.006

Williams, K. E., Riegel, K., & Kerwin, M. L. (2009). Feeding disorder of infancy or early childhood: How often is it seen in feeding programs? *Children's Health Care, 38*(2), 123–136.

Wilson, G. T., & Sysko, R. (2009). Frequency of binge eating episodes in bulimia nervosa and binge eating disorder: Diagnostic considerations. *International Journal of Eating Disorders, 42*(7), 603–610.

Wilson, G. T., Grilo, C. M., & Vitousek, K. M. (2007). Psychological treatment of eating disorders. *American Psychologist, 62*(3), 199–216.

Wilson, R. S., Krueger, K. R., Arnold, S. E., Schneider, J. A., Kelly, J. F., Barnes, L. L., . . . Bennett, D. A. (2007). Loneliness and risk of Alzheimer disease. *Archives of General Psychiatry, 64*(2), 234–240.

Wittchen, H. U., Gloster, A. T., Beesdo-Baum, K., Fava, G. A., & Craske, M. G. (2010). Agoraphobia: A review of the diagnostic classificatory position and criteria. *Depression and Anxiety, 27*(2), 113–133.

Witthoft, M., & Hiller, W. (2010). Psychological approaches to origins and treatments of somatoform disorders. *Annual Review of Clinical Psychology, 6,* 257–283.

Wonderlich, S. A., Gordon, K. H., Mitchell, J. E., Crosby, R. D., & Engel, S. G. (2009). The validity and clinical utility of binge eating disorder. *International Journal of Eating Disorders, 42*(8), 687–705.

World Health Organization. (2010). *International Classification of Diseases* (10th Revision) *(ICD-10).* http://www.who.int/classifications/icd/en/

World Health Organization. (2001). The World Health Report 2001. Mental health: New understanding, new hope, from http://www.who.int/whr2001/2001/main/en/index.htm

World Health Organization. (2011). Suicide rates per 100,000 by country, year and sex, from http://www.who.int/mental_health/prevention/suicide_rates/en/

Wright, S. (2010). Depathologizing consensual sexual sadism, sexual masochism, transvestic fetishism, and fetishism. *Archives of Sexual Behavior, 39,* 1229–1230.

Wu, Y. C., Zhao, Y. B., Tang, M. G., Zhang-Nunes, S. X., & McArthur, J. C. (2007). AIDS dementia complex in China. *Journal of Clinical Neuroscience, 14*(1), 8–11.

Wyatt v. Stickney. 325 F. Supp. 781 (M.D. Ala. 1971); 344 F. Supp. (M.D. Ala. 1972).

Wykes, T., Steel, C., Everitt, B., & Tarrier, N. (2008). Cognitive behavior therapy for schizophrenia: Effect sizes, clinical models, and methodological rigor. *Schizophr Bulletin, 34,* 523–537.

X

Xu, Z., Kochanek, K. D., Murphy, S. L., & Tejeda-Vera, B. (2010). Deaths: Final data for 2007 *National Vital Statistics Reports (Volume 58 No. 19).* Hyattsville, MD: National Center for Health Statistics.

Y

Yalom, I. D. (1995). *The theory and practice of group psychotherapy* (4th ed.). New York: Basic Books.

Young, R. M., Connor, J. P., & Feeney, G. F. X. (2011). Alcohol expectancy changes over a 12-week cognitive–behavioral therapy program are predictive of treatment success. *Journal of Substance Abuse Treatment, 40*(1), 18–25.

Youngberg v. Romeo. 457 U.S. 307 (1982).

Z

Zhang, J., & Wheeler, J. J. (2011). A meta-analysis of peer-mediated interventions for young children with autism spectrum disorders. *Education and Training in Autism and Developmental Disabilities, 46*(1), 62–77.

Zoellner, T., Rabe, S., Karl, A., & Maercker, A. (2008). Posttraumatic growth in accident survivors: Openness and optimism as predictors of its constructive or illusory sides. *Journal of Clinical Psychology, 64*(3), 245–263.

Zubin, J., & Spring, B. (1977). Vulnerability: A new view of schizophrenia. *Journal of Abnormal Psychology, 86*(2), 103–126.

Zuchner, S., Wendland, J. R., Ashley-Koch, A. E., Collins, A. L., Tran-Viet, K. N., Quinn, K., . . . Murphy, D. L. (2009). Multiple rare SAPAP3 missense variants in trichotillomania and OCD. *Molecular Psychiatry, 14*(1), 6–9.

Zucker, R. A., & Gomberg, E. S. (1986). Etiology of alcoholism reconsidered: The case for a biopsychosocial process. *American Psychologist, 41*(7), 783–793.

CREDITS

PHOTOS

BRIEF CONTENTS

Page viii (l): © Krista Bettino, (r): Photodisc/Getty Images RF; p. ix (l): Yagi Studio/Digital Vision/Getty Images RF, (r): Don Farrall/Stone/Getty Images; p. x (l): Steve Cole/Getty Images RF, (r): Alexstar/Veer RF; p. xi (t): Alexstar/Veer RF, (b): Brand X Pictures/PunchStock RF; p. xii (l): Brand X Pictures/PunchStock RF, (r): © Paul Grecaud/Alamy RF; p. xiii: (l) fStop/PunchStock RF, (r): Brand X Pictures/PunchStock RF; p. xiv (l): © Eye-Stock/Alamy, (r): Photodisc/Getty Images RF; p. xv: © Ocean/CORBIS RF.

CHAPTER 1

Opener: © Krista Bettino; p. 4: Yuri Arcurs/Cutcaster RF; p. 5: altrendo images; p. 7: © BananaStock/PunchStock RF; p. 9 (l): © Scala/Art Resource, NY, (r): © The Print Collector/Alamy; p. 10 (top): © Tom Wagner/Alamy, (bottom): Library of Congress Prints & Photographs Division [LC-USZ62-9797] PD; p. 11: McGraw-Hill Companies, Inc./Gary He, photographer; p. 12: NYPL/Science Source/Photo Researchers/Getty Images; p. 13: Chris Ryan/OJO Images/Getty Images RF; p. 18: SuperStock/Getty Images RF; p. 22: © Martin Shields/Alamy.

CHAPTER 2

Opener: © Photodisc/Getty Images RF; Page 27: Tetra Images/Getty Images RF; p. 36: © Alex Mares-Manton/Asia Images/CORBIS; p. 38: © Geri Engberg/The Image Works; p. 39: © James Shaffer/PhotoEdit; p. 40 (t): © Sonda Dawes/The Image Works, (b): John Moore/Getty Images; p. 42: © Brian David Stevens/CORBIS.

CHAPTER 3

Opener: Yagi Studio/Digital Vision/Getty Images RF; Page 48: Will & Deni McIntyre/Photo Researchers, Inc.; p. 60: Spencer Grant/Photo Researchers/Getty Images; p. 61: © Amy Etra/PhotoEdit; p. 62: © Andrea Morini/Getty Images RF; p. 65: Footage supplied by Goodshoot/PunchStock RF; p. 66: Library of Congress Prints and Photographs Division [LC-USZ62-29499] PD; p. 68: © Mark Harmel/Alamy.

CHAPTER 4

Opener: Don Farrall/Stone/Getty Images; Page 82: Vladimir Piskunov/Vetta/Getty Images RF RF; p. 84: © AF archive/Alamy; p. 85 (tl): © Jon Helgason/Alamy RF, (tr): Ted Humble-Smith/Photonica/Getty Images, (b): © Creatas/PunchStock RF; p. 86: Michael Blann/Digital Vision/Getty Images RF; p. 88: © Rainer Jensen/dpa/

CORBIS; p. 91: ASSOCIATED PRESS RF; p. 92: John Lund/Marc Romane/age footstock RF; p. 94: Rubberball/Getty Images RF; p. 96: © Bettmann/CORBIS.

CHAPTER 5

Opener: Steve Cole/Getty Images RF; Page 106: moodboard/Getty Images RF; p. 107: © Bonnie Korman (2010) www.fragilexfiles.com; p. 108: Betty Udesen KRT/Newscom; p. 111: Realistic Reflections RF; p. 112: Joanne Rathe/The Boston Globe via Getty Images; p. 113: Photo courtesy of the Mary Black Foundation and Carroll Foster; p. 115: © Megan Sorel Photography; p. 117: Drew Farrell/Photoshot/Getty Images; p. 125: © Stockbyte/PictureQuest RF; p. 131: NICHOLAS KAMM/AFP/Getty Images/Newscom.

CHAPTER 6

Opener: Alexstar/Veer RF; Page 142: © Roy McMahon/CORBIS RF; p. 146: Rubberball Getty Images RF; p. 149: © Big Cheese Photo/Jupiter Images; p. 151: Courtesy of Vincent Magnotta; p. 152: Courtesy of the John D & Catherine T. MacArthur Foundation; p. 154 (t): ASSOCIATED PRESS RF, (b): JGI/Blend Images/LLC RF; p. 159: © Terry Vine/Blend Images/LLC RF.

CHAPTER 7

Opener: Alexstar/Veer RF; Page 168: FilmMagic/Jason LaVeris/Contributor/Getty Images; p. 172: SW Productions/Getty Images RF; p. 173: Jeffrey Coolidge/Getty Images RF; p. 175: WILL & DENI MCINTYRE/Photo Researchers/Getty Images; p. 178: Geoff Manasse/Getty Images RF; p. 179: © Scientifica/Visuals Unlimited/CORBIS.

CHAPTER 8

Opener: © Brand X Pictures RF/PunchStock RF; Page 188: Design Pics/Kelly Redinger RF; p. 190: Design Pics/Yuri Arcurs RF; p. 193: © Comstock/age footstock RF; p. 195: PhotoAlto/John Dowland/PhotoAlto Agency RF Collections/Getty Images RF; p. 196: Paul Drinkwater/NBC/NBCU Photo Bank; p. 199: © Zigzag Images/Alamy RF; p. 202: ASSOCIATED PRESS RF; p. 204: Herman Agopian/Riser/Getty Images; p. 209: George Skene/Orlando Sentinel/MCT via Getty Images.

CHAPTER 9

Opener: Brand X Pictures RF/PunchStock RF; Page 217: © Steve Atkins Photography/Alamy; p. 218: Tom Lau/Landov; p. 222: © Ariel Skelley/Blend Images LLC RF;

p. 226 (t): © Alistair Heap/Alamy, (b): UpperCut Images/Getty Images RF; p. 229: © Ocean/CORBIS RF; p. 230: Stockbyte/Getty Images RF; p. 231: ASSOCIATED PRESS RF; p. 232: West Rock/Taxi/Getty Images.

CHAPTER 10

Opener: © Paul Grecaud/Alamy RF; Page 240: © AF archive/Alamy; p. 242: © BananaStock/PunchStock RF; p. 243: Jack Star/PhotoLink/Getty Images RF; p. 250: The McGraw-Hill Companies Inc./Ken Karp, photographer; p. 251: Ingram Publishing; p. 252: Redfx/Alamy; p. 254: The McGraw-Hill Companies, Inc./Christopher Kerrigan, photographer.

CHAPTER 11

Opener: fStop/PunchStock RF; Page 261(t): © Bettmann/CORBIS, (b): NBC/NBCU Photo Bank via Getty Images; p. 263: © Bubbles Photolibrary/Alamy; p. 265: © ColorBlind Images/Blend Images LLC RF; p. 266: ASSOCIATED PRESS RF; p. 267: The McGraw-Hill Companies, Inc./Jill Braaten, photographer; p. 270: ASSOCIATED PRESS RF; p. 274: © Stuwdamdorp/Alamy; p. 277: © PhotoAlto/PunchStock RF; p. 279: Courtesy of Sue William Silverman/www.SueWilliamSilverman.com; p. 282: © Clinton Wallace/Globe Photos/ZUMAPRESS.com/Alamy.

CHAPTER 12

Opener: Brand X Pictures RF/PunchStock RF; Page 297: Dr. P. Marazzi/Photo Researchers, Inc.; p. 299: © BananaStock/PunchStock RF; p. 301: © Royalty-Free/CORBIS RF; p. 302: © travelib india/Alamy RF; p. 305: © Scott Houston/Sygma/CORBIS; p. 309: © The McGraw-Hill Companies/Jill Braaten, photographer; p. 310: © Armando Gallo/Retna Ltd./CORBIS; p. 314: © Brand X Pictures RF.

CHAPTER 13

Opener: © Eye-Stock/Alamy; Page 324: ASSOCIATED PRESS RF; p. 331: © BSIP/CORBIS; p. 336: © ColorBlind Images/Blend Images LLC RF; p. 338: Photographs in the Carol M. Highsmith Archive, Library of Congress, Prints and Photographs Division PD; p. 342: © Jens Kalaene/dpa/CORBIS.

CHAPTER 14

Opener: © Photodisc/Getty Images RF; Page 360: ASSOCIATED PRESS RF; p. 362: AP Photo; p. 363: © PhotoAlto/PictureQuest RF; p. 365: © Somos Photography/Veer; p. 370: © Flint/CORBIS RF; p. 372: © Design Pics/Nathan Lau RF; p. 374: ASSOCIATED PRESS RF.

TEXT

CHAPTER 1

p 18 From *Dear Theo: The Autobiography of Vincent van Gogh* edited by Irving Stone. ©1937 by Irving Stone. Table 1.2, p 12 Source: Healthypeople.gov; http://www .healthypeople.gov/2020/topicsobjectives 2020/pdfs/MentalHealth.pdf. Figure 1.1, p 20 Source: Rizvi, S. L., & Nock, M. K. (2008). Single-case experimental designs for the evaluation of treatments for self-injurious and suicidal behaviors. *Suicide and Life-Threatening Behavior, 38*, 498–510. Used by permission of John Wiley & Sons Inc.

CHAPTER 2

Table 2.1, p 29 Reprinted with permission from the Diagnostic and Statistical Manual of Mental Disorders, Fourth Edition, Text Revision. Copyright © 2000 American Psychiatric Association. Table 2.2, p 31 Reprinted with permission from the Diagnostic and Statistical Manual of Mental Disorders, Fourth Edition, Text Revision. Copyright © 2000 American Psychiatric Association. Table 2.3, p 31 Reprinted with permission from the Diagnostic and Statistical Manual of Mental Disorders, Fourth Edition, Text Revision. Copyright © 2000 American Psychiatric Association. Table 2.4, p 32 Reprinted with permission from the Diagnostic and Statistical Manual of Mental Disorders, Fourth Edition, Text Revision. Copyright © 2000 American Psychiatric Association. Ch 2, p 40 From "The Devil and Daniel Johnston" written and directed by Jeff Feuerzeig. ©2005 by Yip! Jump, L.L.C

CHAPTER 3

Table 3.3, p 49 Source: First, M. B., & Gibbon, M. (2004). The Structured Clinical Interview for DSM-IV Axis I Disorders (SCID-I) and the Structured Clinical Interview for DSM-IV Axis II Disorders (SCID-II). In M. J. Hilsenroth & D. L. Segal (Eds.), *Comprehensive handbook of psychological assessment, Vol. 2: Personality assessment.* (pp. 134–143). Used by permission of John Wiley & Sons Inc. Table 3.4, p 53 Roid, G. H., & Barram,

R. A. (2004). *Essentials of Stanford-Binet Intelligence Scales (SB5) assessment.* Used by permission of John Wiley & Sons Inc. Table 3.7, p 57 Clinical and Validity Scales of the MMPI-2, with Adapted Items. Source: MMPI®-2 (Minnesota Multiphasic Personality Inventory®-2) Manual for Administration, Scoring, and Interpretation. Copyright © 2001 by the Regents of the University of Minnesota. All rights reserved. Used by permission of the University of Minnesota Press. Table 3.8, p 57 Source: Ben-Porath, Y. (2010). *An introduction to the MMPI-2-RF (Reconstructed Form).* Used by permission. Figure 3.2, p 58 Ben's MMPI-2 Profile. Source: MMPI®-2 (Minnesota Multiphasic Personality Inventory®-2) Manual for Administration, Scoring, and Interpretation. Copyright © 2001 by the Regents of the University of Minnesota. All rights reserved. Used by permission of the University of Minnesota Press. Figure 3.3, p 62 Source: http://www .granddriver.net/data/media/docs/UIowa_ trailMaking.pdf. Figure 3.4, p 63 Reproduced by special permission of the Publisher, Psychological Assessment Resources, Inc., 16204 North Florida Avenue, Lutz, Florida 33549 from the Wisconsin Card Sorting Test by David A. Grant., PhD and Esta A. Berg, PhD, Copyright 1981, 1993 by Psychological Assessment Resources, Inc. (PAR). Further reproduction is prohibited without permission of PAR. Ch 3 p 64 From *The Key to Genius* by D. Jablow Hersman and Julian Lieb. ©1988 by D. Jablow Hershman and Julian Lieb. Used by permission of Prometheus Books. pp. 96–97 From *Bitter Fame: A Life of Sylvia Plath* by Anne Stevenson. Copyright © 1989 Anne Stevenson. Used by permission of Houghton Mifflin Company.

CHAPTER 4

Figure 4.1, p 74 Source: NHGRI, www.genome .gov Figure 4.2, p 76 Source: National Institute on Aging. (2010). 2009 progress report on Alzheimer's disease: U.S. Department of Health and Human Services. Table 4.2, p 78 Source: http://www.nimh.nih .gov/health/publications/mental-health-medications/complete-index.shtml Figure 4.5, p 80 Source: http://www.dandebat.dk/ eng-person3.htm. Table 4.7, p 90 Source: Adapted from A. T. Beck, A. J. Bush, B. F. Shaw, & G. Emery in *Cognitive Therapy of Depression.* Copyright © 1979 Guilford Publications, Inc. Reprinted by permission.

CHAPTER 5

Table 5.1, p 105 Source: http://www.aamr. org/content_106.cfm?navID=23. Courtesy American Association on Intellectual and Developmental Disabilities. Table 5.2, p 108 Source: Bertrand, J., Floyd, R. L., Weber, M. K., O'Connor, M., E.P., R., Johnson, K. A., & D.E., C. (2004). National Task Force on FAS/FAE. Fetal Alcohol

Syndrome: Guidelines for Referral and Diagnosis. Atlanta, GA. p 116 Reprinted and edited with the permission of Free Press, a Division of Simon & Schuster, Inc. and Andrew Lownie Literary Agency from *Born on a Blue Day: Inside the Mind of an Autistic Savant* by Daniel Tammet. Copyright © 2006 by Daniel Tammet. All rights reserved. Table 5.4, p 123 Source: Barkley, R. A., & Murphy, K. R. (2011). The nature of executive function (EF) deficits in daily life activities in adults with ADHD and their relationship to performance on EF tests. *Journal of Psychopathology and Behavioral Assessment, 33*(2), 137–158. Used by permission of Springer. Figure 5.1, p 124 Source: Polanczyk, G., de Lima, M. S., Horta, B. L., Biederman, J., & Rohde, L. A. (2007). The worldwide prevalence of ADHD: A systematic review and metaregression analysis. *The American Journal of Psychiatry, 164*(6), 942–948. Used by permission of American Psychiatric Publishing. Table 5.5, p 127 Gersten, R., Beckman, S., Clarke, B., Foegen, A., Marsh, L., Star, J. R., & Witzel, B. (2009). Assisting students struggling with mathematics: Response to intervention (TR1) for elementary and middle schools (NCEE 2009–4060). Washington, D.C.: National Center for Education Evaluation and Regional Assistance, Institute of Education Sciences, U.S. Department of Education.

CHAPTER 6

p 152 From *The Center Cannot Hold: My Journey Through Madness* by Elyn Saks. ©2007 by Elyn Saks. Used with permission from Hyperion. All rights reserved. Figure 6.1, p 161 Source: From Technology Review. Used by permission. Figure 6.2, p 166 Source: Reichenberg, A. (2010). The assessment of neuropsychological functioning in schizophrenia. *Dialogues in Clinical Neuroscience, 12*(3), 383–392. Used by permission of the publisher, Les Laboratoires Servier, Neuilly-sur-Seine, France. Figure 6.3, p 167 Source: Genevsky, A., Garrett, C. T., Alexander, P. P., & Vinogradov, S. (2010). Cognitive training in schizophrenia: a Neuroscience-based approach. *Dialogues in Clinical Neuroscience, 12* (3), 416–421. Used by permission of the publisher, Les Laboratoires Servier, Neuilly-sur-Seine, France. Figure 6.4, p 168 Source: Stilo, S. A., & Murray, R. M. (2010). The epidemiology of schizophrenia: replacing dogma with knowledge. *Dialogue in Clinical Neuroscience, 12* (3), 305–315. Used by permission of the publisher, Les Laboratoires Servier, Neuilly-sur-Seine, France.

CHAPTER 7

Figure 7.1, p 166 Source: http://www.nimh .nih.gov/statistics/1MDD_ADULT.shtml p 168 From *Wishful Drinking* by Carrie Fisher. ©2008 by Deliquesce Inc. Used with permission from Simon & Schuster. Figure 7.2, p 170 Source: http://www.nimh.nih.gov/health/publications/bipolar-disorder/complete-index.shtml. Table 7.4, p 177 Adapted from A.T. Beck, A.J. Bush, B.F. Shaw, & G. Emery in Cognitive Therapy of Depression. Copyright© 1979 Guilford Publications, Inc. Reprinted by permission. Figure 7.3, p 181 Source: http://www.who.int/mental_health/prevention/suicide/suicideprevent/en/. Used by permission of WHO.

CHAPTER 8

Figure 8.1, p 187 Source: http://nimh.nih.gov/statistics/1ANYANX_ADULT.shtml p 196 Reprinted and adapted with the permission of Simon & Schuster, Inc., from *Paula Deen It Ain't All About the Cookin'* by Paula Deen with Sherry Suib Cohen. ©2007 by Paula Deen. All rights reserved. Table 8.1, p 189 Source: Santucci, L. C., Ehrenreich, J. T., Trosper, S. E., Bennett, S. M., & Pincus, D. B. (2009). Development and preliminary evaluation of a one-week summer treatment program for separation anxiety disorder. *Cognitive and Behavioral Practice, 16* (3), 317–331. Used by permission of Elsevier. Table 8.2, p 191 Source: From W. K. Goodman, L. H. Price, S. A. Rasmussen, C. Mazure, P. Delgado, G. R. Heninger, and D. S. Charney (1989a), "The Yale-Brown Obsessive-Compulsive Scale II. Validity" in *Archives of General Psychiatry, 46*, pp. 1012–1016. Reprinted with permission of Wayne Goodman. Table 8.4, p 202 Source: http://www.veale.co.uk/wp-content/uploads/2010/11/BDD-YBOCS-Adult.pdf ©1997, Katharine A. Phillips, M.D., Eric Hollander, M.D. Figure 8.2, p 207 Gleason, M. M., Fox, N. A., Drury, S., Smyke, A., Egger, H. L., Nelson, C. A., III, . . . Zeanah, C. H. (2011). Validity of evidence-derived criteria for reactive attachment disorder: Indiscriminately social/disinhibited and emotionally withdrawn/inhibited types. *Journal of the American Academy of Child & Adolescent Psychiatry, 50*(3), 216–231. Used by permission of Elsevier. Figure 8.3, p 208 Source: Boe, H. J., Holgersen, K, & Holen, A. (2011). Mental Health outcomes and predictors of chronic disorders after the North Sea oil rig disaster: 27-year longitudinal follow-up study. *Journal of Nervous and Mental Disease,199* (1), 49–54. Used by permission of Wolters Kluwer.

CHAPTER 9

p 218 From *Breaking Free: My Life with Dissociative Identity Disorder* by Herschel Walker with Gary Brozek and Charlene Maxfield. ©2008 by Herschel Walker. Used with permission by Touchstone and Howard Books, a division of Simon & Schuster, Inc. Table 9.1, p 221 Source: Steinberg, M.

(1994). *Structured clinical interview for DSM-IV dissociative disorders—Revised (SCID-D-R)*.Washington DC: American Psychiatric Association. Table 9.3, p 233 From C.D. Jenkins, S.J. Zyzanski and R. H. Rosenman, The Jenkins Activity Survey. Copyright© 1965, 1966, 1969, 1979 by The Psychological Corporation. Copyright © 2001 by C.D. Jenkins, S.J. Zyzanski and R.H. Rosenman. Reprinted by permission of the author.

CHAPTER 10

Ch 10, p 240 "Unbearable Lightness: A Story of Loss and Gain" by Portia de Rossi Atria Books, a division of Simon & Schuster. Table 10.1, p 248 Source: Fortune, E. E., & Goodie, A. S. (2011). Cognitive distortions as a component and treatment focus of pathological gambling: A review. *Psychology of Addictive Behaviors.* Used by permission of American Psychological Association. Table 10.2, p 257 Shusterman, A., Feld, L., Baer, L., & Keuthen, N. (2009). Affective regulation in trichotillomania: Evidence from a large-scale internet survey. *Behaviour Research and Therapy, 47*(8), 637–644. Used by permission of American Psychological Association.

CHAPTER 11

Figure 11.1, p 261 Source: Mitchell, K. J., Becker-Blease, K. A., & Finkelhor, D. (2005). Inventory of Problematic Internet Experiences Encountered in Clinical Practice. *Professional Psychology: Research and Practice, 36*, 498-509. Used by permission of American Psycological Association. Table 11.2, p 272 Source: Rosen, R., Brown, C., Heiman, J., Leiblum, S., Meston, C., Shabsigh, R., . . . D'Agostino, R., Jr. (2000). The Female Sexual Function Index (FSFI): A multidimensional self-report instrument for the assessment of female sexual function. Journal of Sex & Marital Therapy, 26, 191–208. Used by permission of Taylor & Francis. p 278 From Love Sick: One Woman's Journey through Sexual Addiction by Sue William Silverman. ©2001 by Sue William Silverman. Used with permission from W.W. Norton & Company, Inc. Table 11.3, p 280 Source: Nobre, P. J., & Pinto-Gouveia, J. (2009). Cognitive schemas associated with negative sexual events: A comparison of men and women with and without sexual dysfunction. *Archives of Sexual Behavior, 38*, 842–851. Used by permission of Springer. Table 11.4, p 283 Source: APA Standards of Care for the Treatment of Gender Identity Disorders. Used by permission of American Psychological Association.

CHAPTER 12

Figure 12.1, p 291 Substance Abuse and Mental Health Services Administration. (2011). Results from the 2010 National

Survey on Drug Use and Health: Summary of National Findings, NSDUH Series H–41, HHS Publication No. (SMA) 11–4658. Rockville MD: Substance Abuse and Mental Health Services Administration. Figure 12.2, p 292 Substance Abuse and Mental Health Services Administration. (2011). Results from the 2010 National Survey on Drug Use and Health: Summary of National Findings, NSDUH Series H–41, HHS Publication No. (SMA) 11–4658. Rockville MD: Substance Abuse and Mental Health Services Administration. Figure 12.3, p 292 Source: http://nida.nih.gov/scienceofaddiction/brain.html. Table 12.1, p 296 Source : National Institute on Alcohol Abuse and Alcoholism. (2007). Helping patients who drink too much: A clinician's guide. Table 12.2, p 298 Miller, W. R. (2002). Project COMBINE Combined Behavioral Intervention Therapist Manual. Figure 12.5, p 300 Source: http://amphetamines.com/braindamage.html from *The New York Times* 7/20/04. Figure 12.6, p 301 Source: National Institute on Drug Abuse. (2011h). Research Report Series, from http://www.drugabuse.gov/Research Reports/Cocaine/Cocaine.html. Figure 12.7, p 306 Source: http://www.drugabuse.gov/publications/teaching-packets/neurobiology-ecstasy. Figure 12.8, p 308 National Center for Injury Prevention and Control. Centers for Disease Control and Prevention. (2010). Unintentional drug poisoning in the United States. Figure 13.4, p 335 Source: National Institute on Drug Abuse. (2010). Comorbidity: Addiction and other illnesses. Bethesda MD: National Institute on Drug Abuse.

CHAPTER 13

Table 13.1, p 323 Source: Trzepacz, P. T., Mittal, D., Torres, R., Kanary, K., Norton, J., & Jimerson, N. (2001). Validation of the Delirium Rating Scale-Revised–98: Comparison with the Delirium Rating Scale and the Cognitive Test for Delirium. *The Journal of Neuropsychiatry and Clinical Neurosciences, 13*(2), 229–242. American Psychiatric Publishing. Figure 13.1, p 326 Source: http://www.cdc.gov/traumaticbraininjury/statistics.html Alzheimers/Publications/adfact.htm. Table 13.3, p 328 Source: Consumer Reports. (2009). Evaluating prescription drugs used to treat: Alzheimer's Disease, from http://www.consumerreports.org/health/resources/pdf/best-buy-drugs/Alzheimers FINAL.pdf. Used by permission. Table 13.4, p 329 Source: Reproduced by special permission of the Publisher, Psychological Assessment Resources, Inc., 16204 North Florida Avenue, Lutz, Florida 33549, from the Mini Mental State Examination, by Marshal Folstein and Susan Folstein. Copyright 1975, 1998, 2001 by Mini Mental LLC. Published 2001 by Psychological Assessment Resources, Inc. Further

NAME INDEX

SUBJECT INDEX

Bold locators indicate definitions of terms.